Financial and Managerial Accounting for School Administrators

Superintendents, School Business Administrators, and Principals

R.E. Everett
Raymond L. Lows
Donald R. Johnson

Published in partnership with the
Association of School Business Officials International

ScarecrowEducation
Lanham, Maryland • Toronto • Oxford
1996

Published in partnership with
the Association of School Business Officials International

Published in the United States of America
by ScarecrowEducation
An imprint of The Rowman & Littlefield Publishing Group, Inc
4501 Forbes Boulevard, Suite 200, Lanham, Maryland 20706
www.scaroweducation.com

PO Box 317
Oxford
OX2 9RU, UK

Copyright © 2003, 1996 by ASBO International

All rights reserved. No part of this publication may be reproduced, stored in a retrieval system, or transmitted in any form or by any means, electronic, mechanical, recording, or otherwise, without the prior permission of the publisher.

Library of Congress Cataloging-in-Publication Data Available

**Originally published by the Association of School Business Officials International
ISBN 1-57886-027-X
Reprinted by ScarecrowEducation**

∞™ The paper used in this publication meets the minimum requirements of American National Standard for Information Sciences—Permanence of Paper for Printed Library Materials, ANSI/NISO Z39.48-1992. Manufactured in the United States of America.

Table of Contents

ix   **Preface**

1   **Accounting and School Business Administration**
A Framework • History of School Business Management and School Business Administration in the United States • What is School Business Administration? • How Are/Should School Business Administrators Be Trained? • Other Indicators Of The Importance of Accounting To School Business Administration • The Difference Between Governmental and Public School Accounting From Private Sector Accounting • Basic Public School District Accounting Concepts

2   **What Is Accounting?**
Auditing • Annual Financial Reports • Consolidated Annual Financial Report (CAFR) • Government Funds • Proprietary Funds • Fiduciary Funds • Account Groups • Accounts Within A Fund

3   **Basic Principles of Accounting**
Accounts Within A Fund • Accounting Procedures • Basic Financial Statements • Balance Sheets • Operating Statements

4   **Basic Accounting Techniques**
Debits and Credits Defined • Relationship Between Accounts, Debits and Credits • Equality of Debits and Credits • Trial Balance

5   **The General Ledger**
General Ledger Defined • Asset Classification • Liabilities, Reserves and Fund Balance Classification • Revenue and Other Fund Sources Classification • Expenditure Classification • Expenditure Classification By Program • Expenditure Classification By Function • Expenditure Classification By Object • Expenditure Classification By Project • Analysis of Financial Transactions

iv • TABLE OF CONTENTS

6 Journals
General Journal • Posting to the General Ledger • Cash Receipts Journal • Cash Disbursements Journal

7 Revenue Accounting
Revenue Defined • Taxes Receivable and Estimated Uncollectible Taxes • Recording Estimated Revenue and Actual Revenue • Interim Statement of Revenue

8 Expenditure Accounting
Expenditure Defined • The Encumbrance System • Interim Financial Reports

9 Special Entries
Budget Adoption • Closing Entries • Post Closing Trial Balance

10 Basic Financial Statements
Fund Equity • Financial Statements • Interim Financial Statements • Combined Financial Reports

11 Changes in Financial Position
Financial Resources Concept • Financial Statements • Working Capital Concept • Cash Concept

12 Special Revenue Funds
Special Revenue Fund Defined • Types of Special Revenue Funds • Sources of Special Revenue • Accounts and Transactions • Financial Statements

13 Capital Projects Funds
Types of Bonds • Sources of Capital • Accounts and Transactions • Financial Statements

14 Debt Service Funds
Types of Debt Service Funds • Accounts and Transactions • Financial Statements • Adjusting Entries • Closing Entries

15 General Fixed Asset Account Group
Definition of an Account Group • Definition of Fixed Assets • Uses of Fixed Asset Accounting • Challenges of Fixed Asset Record-Keeping • Ensuring Quality Inventory Records • Ensuring Current Inventory Records • Taking Inventory • Determining Costs • Inventory Control Systems • Accounting for Fixed Assets • Sample Transaction • Financial Statements • Problems with Accounting in the GFAAG • The Future of Fixed Asset Accounting

16 General Long-Term Debt Account Group
Long-Term Debt Accounts • Accounts and Transactions • Long-Term Liability for Compensated Absences • Financial Statements

17 Enterprise Funds
National School Lunch, Breakfast and Special Milk Programs • The Child Nutrition Program • Implementation Procedures • Meal/Milk Income Verification Procedures • Food Distribution • Accounts and Transactions • Depreciation Accounting

18 Internal Service Funds
Creation of an Internal Service Fund • Operation of an Internal Service Fund • Types of Operations Applicable to Internal Service Funds • Closing the Books of an Internal Service Fund

19 Trust Funds
Non-Expendable Trust Funds • Expendable Trusts • Sample Transactions

20 Agency Funds
Fiduciary Funds • The Central Payroll Agency Fund • Sample Transactions in the Central Payroll Agency Fund • Financial Statements

21 Payroll Accounting/Development
Employment and Payroll Activities • Accounts and Transactions • Financial Statements and Reports • Bank Reconciliations

22 Internal Cash Control
Internal Accounting Controls • Sources of Cash Receipts • Cash Disbursements • Vouchers and Warrants • Cash Forecasting • Imprest and Petty Cash Funds

23 Student Accounting
Planning and Student Counts • Enrollment Projections • District Census • Student Attendance

24 Advanced Financial Statements
Financial Statements • The Comprehensive Annual Financial Report (CAFR) • Introductory Section • Financial Section • Combined Statements

25 Auditing
Audit Reports • Request for Proposals • Determination of Need • Request for Proposal (RFP) • Evaluation of Proposals/Selection of the Auditor • Contracting for Audit Services • Engagement Letter • Financial Statements

26 ASBO's Certificate of Excellence: Financial Statements and Reports
What is ASBO International? • The Current Status of COE • The Benefits of COE to School Districts • Program Benefits • COE Requirements • The COE Application/Submission Process

27 Beyond Traditional Measures of Financial Health: What Can School Districts Learn From the Private Sector
Private Sector Financial Statements • Fundamental Analysis In The Private Sector: A Brief Look • Ratios In The Corporate World • Components Of The Balance Sheet • The Income Statement • Analyzing Financial Statements • Liquidity Ratios • Capitalization Ratios • Coverage Ratios • Evaluation Of Earnings

28 Using Accounting Information to Measure Fiscal Health and Manage a School District
Indicators of Financial Difficulty • Financial Ratio Analysis Research and Applications • Other Internal Ratios • Expenditures • Ratio Analysis for Making External Comparisons • Benchmarking: Setting Standards of Fiscal Performance

29 The Future of Financial and Managerial Accounting in the School Setting

APPENDICES

Appendix A	Minimum Classifications (Chart of Accounts) Essential for Federal Reporting
Appendix B	Classifying Balance Sheet Accounts
Appendix C	1993-94 Adopted Budget
Appendix D	Federal Single Program Audit 1993-94
Appendix E	1993-94 Audit
Appendix F	Cash Receipts Journal
Appendix G	Cash Disbursements Journal
Appendix H	Federal Withholding Tax Tables
Appendix I	Annual Financial Report 1993-94
Glossary	Glossary of Financial and Managerial Terms used in this textbook and the profession

*We dedicate this book to our wives June, Suzanne and Karen
and our families for their support of this project and our careers.*

Preface

In 1960, the book *Public School Fund Accounting Principles and Procedures* by Sam B. Tidwell was published by Harper and Brothers Publishers, New York, NY. This first effort was followed by a second edition published in 1974 and a third edition, published by the Research Corporation of the Association of School Business Officials International in 1985. From before 1960 until the present, a continuous stream of publications and circulars on accounting have become available. These publications have come from agencies of the federal government, professional associations that serve accountants and school administrators, nonprofit organizations and university faculty. These publications have satisfied a variety of professional needs such as:

- Better definitions of terms crucial to the accounting process;
- Improved standards of financial and managerial accounting;
- The development and improvement of revenue and expenditure classifications;
- The development and improvement of generally accepted accounting principles and reporting procedures; and
- The creation and expansion of auditing standards.

During this era of significant accounting changes, the school business administration profession was also changing dramatically. Those who administered the public schools began to realize that a knowledge of liabilities, assets, cash and the like was important information if organizational goals were to be met. In today's school financial environment school business administrators are concerned with the total fiscal structure of the district. This includes the financial position and the current status of the various funds and accounting groups used.

Between 1960 and today, publication of *Handbook II – Principles of Public School Accounting* by the United States Office of Education (USOE) was a major step in managerial and financial accounting for governmental and nonprofit accounting. *Handbook II* illustrated and encouraged the use of double-entry bookkeeping as the basis for financial accounting for educational agencies. With this action, the emphasis shifted from the cash basis of recording only selected financial transactions to a basis of financial accounting that is referred to in the literature as generally accepted accounting principles. This new basis of accounting complied with the reporting requirements of federal and state laws.

The Association of School Business Officials in the United States and Canada (now called ASBO International) was very active in accounting developments during this time. During the 1970s, guidelines were established for what is now called the Certificate of Excellence (COE) in Financial Reporting by School Systems Program. This association service encouraged school districts to use generally accepted accounting principles and budgetary and reporting procedures that met high standards.

Other agencies, associations and organizations were also very active in the accounting changes and refinements that were evolving and that would influence governmental accounting and financial accounting for school districts. Some of these, not already referenced were:

- American Association of School Administrators;
- National School Boards Association;
- Council of Chief State School Officers;
- American Institute of Certified Public Accountants;
- Municipal Finance Officers Association of United States and Canada;
- National Committee on Governmental Accounting;
- National Center for Educational Statistics of the United States;
- Office of Education Financial Accounting Standards Board (FASB); and
- Financial Accounting Foundation.

Out of all of these, FASB was established as the organization in the private sector that created the rules and standards governing the preparation of financial statements. In the public sector, the Governmental Accounting Standards Board (GASB) performs a similar function and provides much of the leadership in the continuing study and efforts to improve governmental accounting at all levels, including the public schools.

This book builds on the monumental foundation of Tidwell's three editions. His works have become classics and their contribution to the elevation of accounting knowledge and skills in the school business administration profession are well documented. This work adds to Tidwell, but, with his permission, also draws on his earlier work. The three authors of this text have used Tidwell's earlier editions in graduate level courses over the past three decades. As we began our work, a deeper appreciation of Tidwell's earlier works developed. In some instances minor updating of his work was all that was needed. In other instances major revisions to his work have been made. Several new chapters and original new material have been inserted.

This work is designed to be much more than an introduction. It is designed for all school administrators. It deals with creating and expanding the user's knowledge base concerning school fund accounting. It is designed to expand and enhance understanding of financial and managerial accounting and reporting principles as well as the procedures as applied to fund and account groups.

This book assumes that the user has no or at best an introductory understanding of accounting. It is intended to serve those totally unfamiliar with accounting as well as those who bring some formal accounting training and experience to this stage of their professional development. While it is normal for those who have no formal training or background in accounting to be very anxious as they begin their serious study of the subject, *no* accounting background is necessary to benefit from the use of this book. This book is designed to be used primarily as a textbook at the graduate level with students training to be school administrators, school business administrators or principals. The appropriate audience for this book is anyone who is responsible for creating and/or using accounting-produced information about school districts.

The book consists of 29 chapters, each of which can be covered in one class period. Professors or instructors who select this work for the basic text for their courses are encouraged to enrich the material in each chapter with additional examples and supplemental material specific to a school district in their particular state so the students are exposed to their state's documents, forms and procedures. This book should lend itself to the teaching style of a wide variety of instructors.

Now to the organization of this book. The book has two parts: The first part spans chapters 1 through 12 and part two covers chapters 13 through 29. The first twelve chapters and chapters 26 and 29 comprise the content normally covered in a one-semester course. For those who cover this material more rapidly, one or two chapters from the second part could be added. In those programs that offer or require two semesters of accounting work, chapters 13 through 29 can serve as the content for the second semester. The authors recognize that some chapters address topics that may not be appropriate or even required in some states or provinces.

The chapter organization consists of:

- A brief introduction;
- A short list of learner outcomes;
- Chapter content;
- Summary;
- Activities; and
- References/Selected Readings.

The appendices are a very important part of this book and should be carefully studied when suggested by the text or chapter activities. To the students or readers who use this book for whatever reason, the authors wish to point out that:

- This book will not make you accountants or CPAs;
- Going through the chapters in sequence is important;
- The illustrations and examples should be carefully studied and reviewed;
- Chapter activities have been carefully designed to teach basic ideas, skills and concepts;
- The activities which refer to the glossary are intentionally redundant; and
- The glossary and appendices are very important components of this book.

While there are many different and correct ways to demonstrate accounting principles and concepts, only one method generally is given in this book. The instructors and students are encouraged to develop the additional problems as needed.

The authors acknowledge that many people have contributed to the completion of this work. The first one we wish to acknowledge is Sam Tidwell, who not only pioneered school fund accounting but provided the classic editions that will remain as monumental contributions for years to come.

Second, Dr. Sandra Graczyk, chair and professor of educational administration at SUNY Brockport, who provided great insight and assistance in the initial organization of this book and contributed material to some of the chapters.

The authors appreciate the contribution Bernie Gatti, of ASBO International, made to Chapter 26 on the Certificate of Excellence Program.

We are grateful to the ASBO Accounting, Auditing and Budgeting Committee members who assisted in the review of the manuscript. Also to James Tapscott, partner, McGladrey Pullen, Olympia Fields, IL; Mark Staehlin, controller, Community High School District 99, Downers Grove, IL; Sue Bertram, assistant superintendent for business, West Aurora School District 129, Aurora, IL; and Dr. Joe Saban, superintendent, Community High School District 155, Crystal Lake, IL, who also served as reviewers.

Last but certainly not least, the authors appreciate the secretarial and clerical support provided by the Illinois ASBO staff, specifically Barbara Koca and Julie Warner. The patience, encouragement and cooperation of Don Tharpe, executive director of ASBO International and Peg Kirkpatrick, director of communications and marketing, also of ASBO International, really made this book happen.

R. E. Everett
Raymond L. Lows
Donald R. Johnson
January 1996

1

Accounting and School Business Administration

INTRODUCTION

School business administrators in the United States will receive, expend and account for the use of over a half a *trillion* dollars during 1994-95 to provide the staff, materials, facilities, supplies and services to deliver educational programs. While the tasks and functions performed by school business administrators are extensive and complex, the knowledge and skills of accounting are basic to all of them.

This chapter will explore the importance of accounting in the school environment and demonstrate the overall binding effect it has on all of the tasks and functions performed by the school district business administrator. The point will be made that knowledge about accounting and accounting skills pervades *all* aspects of the day-to-day operation of a school and school district. The proper day-to-day operation of the schools and quality planning and decision-making cannot realistically take place unless administrators and Board members have an understanding of school fund accounting.

OUTCOMES

In this chapter, you will learn:

1. How school districts are organized to manage the resources made available to them.
2. What the tasks, functions, duties and responsibilities of those individuals a school district retains to manage its resources are.
3. How important financial and managerial accounting is to a school district.
4. How accounting spans and impacts on every aspect of the school business administration profession.

(*Note*: Throughout this book the reader will find the expressions school district, school system, educational agency, educational institution, district, and the like. These terms all relate to the term "school district.")

A FRAMEWORK

Data reported in September 1993 by the U.S. Department of Education indicated that overall educational spending in the United States would reach nearly $495 billion in 1993-94. This figure represented 7.9 percent of the gross domestic product—the highest figure ever reported for the United States. This information reflects an increase of 50 percent since 1983 using the annual statistics issued by the U.S. Department of Education. Breaking this data down reveals spending for public elementary and secondary pupils for 1993-94 was projected to approach $5,920 per pupil. This $5,920 per pupil was projected to result in $3,589 or 60.6 percent being spent on instruction (teacher salaries, benefits, teaching supplies and materials). About $626 or 10.6 percent would be used for school building maintenance and operations. Administrative costs would be approximately $513 or 8.6 percent, while student services (libraries, media and computer centers, guidance, health, attendance, security and other services) would consume about $511 or 8.6 percent. Food services, transportation and other miscellaneous costs would make up the balance of $680 or 11.5 percent.

While these figures are interesting and important, the facts reported will change over time. In the context of the material the reader will find in this book, the data given demonstrates two important and related concepts.

First, some form of accounting was necessary to produce these facts and figures. Without some system of organizing, recording, describing, analyzing and reporting, this information could not have been presented. Without a system of accounting, appropriate and useful comparisons and classifications could not exist.

Second, the sheer volume of dollars needed to provide products and services to public school children and the pressures to relate the use of these dollars to some type(s) of outcome measures makes an accounting (accountability) system essential. Society should and does expect excellence in accounting just on the basis of the number of dollars used, if for no other reason.

For the purpose of this book, two accounting distinctions will be made and used. The two distinctions are between *financial accounting* and *managerial accounting*.

In his book, *Finance and Accounting for Nonfinancial Managers*, Finkler (1992) gives the following definitions:

Financial Accounting: a formalized system designed to record the financial history of an organization over time and report that history to interested individuals normally in an annual or some other regular report(s) (pp 3-4).

Managerial Accounting: provides information that can be used for making improved decisions regarding the future. This assumes that virtually any decisions that could be improved by a forecast or an analysis is the responsibility of the managerial accountant (p. 4).

The recognition of these two distinctions does not mean that the two practices are mutually exclusive. Financial and managerial accounting can be provided by a single individual or by different individuals and systems.

This dichotomy is consistent with the living systems theory (LST) of Miller (1978), which separates accounting quantities into:

- Measurement of concrete process; and
- Interpretation of those measurements.

The most fundamental information produced by accounting is the measurement of concrete processes and thereby is information prepared to be disclosed in public reports. The spin off of this publicly reported information, however, is its use in general and specific decision-making settings (pp. 55-73).

There was a time when resources for education were fairly plentiful, and expectations were not as high, delivery of desired services was relatively simple and technology was practically nonexistent as we know it today. At that time, most, if not all accounting was financial in nature, i.e., simple recording sources, timing and amounts of revenue received and reporting on what these revenues purchased in terms of products and services, when, and what each cost. Managerial accounts were created in response to: calls for greater accountability, the growing complexity of society, increased competition for limited resources, expanding technological capabilities and the requirement that resources be more accurately related to outcomes. This also spurred a growth and maturation in accounting that promises a sophistication in the future that is currently beyond our imagination.

The future will see the need for both financial and managerial accounting. One will not overshadow the other. Both will continue to evolve and develop to satisfy the needs of society and the education community. Financial and managerial accounting together can be thought of as the process that gathers, produces, organizes and presents information that can be consumed by a wide variety of users for the purpose of keeping an organization operating, growing, improving and changing.

If financial and managerial accounting are not done well, then the survival of the organization is at risk and difficult times will be created for not only the organization, but for the clientele it serves. This is true for public sector and private sector organizations and especially for public education.

HISTORY OF SCHOOL BUSINESS MANAGEMENT AND SCHOOL BUSINESS ADMINISTRATION IN THE UNITED STATES

Before anyone begins the study of school financial accounting and school managerial accounting, some understanding of the school organization is helpful. Public schools exist in the United States to provide *mass* public education at public expense (and some use of private resources) to all those who present themselves to receive instruction. Many people refer to public education as the most important service government is expected to provide and teaching as the profession that makes all other professions possible. While some may argue the relative importance of education, few will argue that education is not important.

In order to provide educational opportunities to the masses, society must commit a tremendous amount of its resources to this purpose. Society rightfully expects that the resources that are made available be effectively and efficiently managed so that the purposes for which these resources have been committed are maximized (or nearly so).

The basic resource that we are referring to here is money. Dollars are received directly from the taxpayers, students, parents and others and indirectly from taxpayers through state, federal, municipal, or intermediate governmental units that collect and distribute dollars to school districts. These dollars are used to purchase other resources like teachers, administrators, support staff, textbooks, supplies, materials, buildings, busses, electrical power, heat, food, water and on and on.

Those who provide the dollars directly and/or indirectly expect and require that the receipt and use of these resources be described and explained on a regular, complete, accurate, comprehensive, detailed, understandable and useful basis. The public requires accountability. Accountability is the obligation to report, explain and justify. Financial and managerial accounting strive to at least partially satisfy these obligations.

One of the many great experiments that the settling of the western hemisphere by Europeans allowed to take place was the creation and development of public school systems that were locally controlled by school committees, school trustees, school boards and the like. In early colonial times when schools were small and education was fairly simple, the day-to-day operation of the school or schools within a geographic area was provided by one of these groups. These school boards were the educational policy arm of their area and its administration. These committees were also the "chief cooks and bottle washers" of the schools. They had to see to every detail of the local school operation.

For nearly 200 years this approach to operating and managing the public schools in the United States worked reasonably well. Colonial life, however, changed and so did education: School systems grew in size, education became more complex, the expectations for the schools expanded to include more than reading, writing and arithmetic, and the time demands and expertise needed to provide a livelihood for a family increased. Communities began to recognize that the day-to-day operation of the school(s) had become too complex and time consuming to adequately be performed by lay volunteers regardless of their intelligence, willingness, desire, enthusiasm and energy.

Even attempts at compensating one or more board members to perform specific tasks proved only to be an intermediate solution. Whether the manager/clerk was paid or unpaid, it became evident that in terms of both time and expertise, these individuals were overextended. In response to this condition, Hill (1983) reports that in the 1840s the Cleveland, OH, school district became the first to hire a full-time "acting manager" to "keep the books, prepare the payroll and care for the school buildings" (p. 3).

Early school business managers were not considered educators expected (or allowed) to participate in educational decision making. History makes it pretty clear that educators were not to make school business decisions and the business managers were to keep their noses out of the educational domain. The position of school business manager was not viewed as very important at its inception. In fact, it was not until the last quarter of the 19th century and early 20th century that educators started to recognize and stress the importance of the school business administrator role. It was during this same time period that some specific defining of the role began and people started to take an interest in how individuals prepared themselves to perform this role.

It was also in the early 1900s that leading school business administrators realized the importance of their duties, the effects of their services on education and the need for defining specific aspects of their duties and responsibilities. Specific course work at the university level started to pop up and books and journal articles devoted exclusively to school business management started to appear. The multi-dimensional aspects of school business management became apparent from reading the literature, and from the certification and licensing requirements that were developing.

It is clear today that decisions relating to the teaching, learning and curriculum dimension of a school district are interdependent upon decisions that are accepted as being in the school business domain. Understanding and accepting this relationship between curriculum and resource allocation is crucial to understanding a school district and what it can and cannot provide.

School business administrators must be trained and experienced in the field of education with emphasis on school business administration or trained and experienced in various phases of business with a knowledge of educational practices. The school business manager must be viewed as a crucial element in school reform and school improvement if educational opportunities are to be available to all students.

WHAT IS SCHOOL BUSINESS ADMINISTRATION?

A majority of those who use this book will either be preparing themselves to function in one or more of the roles within the profession of school business administration or will be enhancing their knowledge base and accounting skills to more effectively and efficiently perform current duties and responsibilities. Therefore, an understanding of what school business administration is all about as a profession and role, with its accompanying tasks, functions, duties and responsibilities is needed. To facilitate this understanding, ASBO International created a professional registration program to enhance the credentials of those seeking to demonstrate that they possess superior skills and knowledge relevant to school business administration. This program is particularly important in states and provinces where certification is not required.

Within this registration program three distinctions are defined: registered school business administrators (RSBA), registered school business officials (RSBO), and registered school business specialists (RSBS). Those with RSBAs deal with the total area of school business, and with subordinates. Those with RSBOs deal with specific phases of school business administration, but not to the breadth and scope of the RSBA. The RSBS is even more focused, having highly specialized skills in a single area of school business administration. These nomenclatures serve only as a guide and are helpful only to the degree that they expand the understanding of these roles.

Like every other key role involved in the central office administration of the public schools, no two school business administrator positions are exactly alike even though there is a commonality in terms of duties, tasks, functions, knowledge base, skills and attitudes. Often characterized as the "invisible, add-on" profession, the role has been supportive and subordinated to the board and superintendent. The school business administrator's job description, when viewed from an historical perspective, reveals that over the years the list of responsibilities of a school business administrator has become longer as new programs and mandates trickle down to the school business administrator's desk. Over the past 50 years very little has been removed from the school business administrator's duties, but much has been added.

The role of school business administrators has been the subject of researchers for nearly 70 years. The nature of much of these research efforts has focused on attempts to summarize, define, delimit and bring understanding to what the school business administrator does.

Carnahan (1965) categorized major responsibilities of the school business administrator as follows:

- school funds excluding student activity funds;
- school audits and school accounting, except attendance accounting;
- records and supervision of non-instruction personnel;
- school insurance;
- establishment of standards and specifications for supplies; and
- managing rentals.

Many other researchers have arrived at very similar conclusions.

Hill, in his book *The School Business Administrator* (1982), took the earlier works of Linn (1965), Knezevich and Fowlkes (1960), Jordan (1969), Kaiser and Webb (1957), McGuffey (1980) and others to delineate the work areas usually associated with school business administration and generated the following specific task clusters (p. 16).

Capital Fund Management (a)
Cash Management (b)
Classified Personnel Management (c)
Community Relations (d)
Construction Management (e)
Data Processing (f)
Educational Facilities Planning (g)
Educational Resource Management (h)
Financial Planning and Budgeting (i)
Fiscal Accounting and Financial Reporting (j)
Fiscal Audits and Reports (k)
Foodservice (l)
Grantsmanship (m)
Insurance and Risk Management (n)
Legal Control (o)
Office Management (p)
Payroll Management (q)
Plant Management (r)
Plant Operations (s)

Plant Security and Property Protection (t)
Professional Negotiations (u)
Property Management (v)
Purchasing (w)
Staff Development (x)
Student Activity Funds (y)
Transportation Services (z)
Warehousing and Supplies Management (aa)

(The lower case letters following each task cluster relate to Figure 1-1.)

Figure 1-1

	Tasks/Processes							
A	**B**	**C**	**D**	**E**	**F**	**G**	**H**	
								a
								b
								c
								d
								e
								f
								g
								h
								i
								j
								k
								l
								m
								n
								o
								p
								q
								r
								s
								t
								u
								v
								w
								x
								y
								z
								aa

Functions

This list was never intended to be all inclusive of what school business administrators do. Over the past few years many new tasks have been created and assigned to this role, for example, energy management, environmental issues, legal concerns, legislative management, and the like. Hill's categories have been used to organize and assign responsibilities as well as to help give definition to the profession of school business administration.

While these tasks and work areas do help to identify what the school business administrator does, this list and related lists do not set forth the particular functions that are so necessary to insure that efficient and effective business services are delivered at all times. The basic management functions, like the aforementioned tasks, have also undergone the scrutiny of researchers over time. The following eight processes (Hill, 1982) are most commonly suggested:

- Planning (A)
- Organizing (B)
- Staffing (C)
- Influencing or Directing (D)
- Controlling (E)
- Coordinating (F)
- Decision Making (G)
- Evaluating (H)

(The upper case letters following each task/process relate to Figure 1-1.)

To really begin to grasp what school business management and administration is really all about, it must be recognized that each of the above functions can and usually is applied to each of the earlier mentioned tasks. Figure 1-1 suggests a means of visualizing exactly how these tasks and functions work together to define school business management and administration.

While the actual skills and knowledge base necessary to adequately perform in each of the cells created by the above grid vary from school district to school district, the magnitude of what might be expected is clear. It becomes evident that there is a common core of cells that will be done every day, week, month and/or year regardless of the district type, size or location. It should also be evident that some cells are repeated, but in a random chaotic cycle over time. Over time, it may be completely unnecessary to perform certain tasks or function cells at all.

The task and function approach is useful as a means of ordering our thinking about school business administration, but using the "typical duties" approach expands the understanding of the role. Once again, drawing from Hill's work, a broader understanding can be obtained. Such a listing of typical duties can be useful to board members, superintendents, lay citizens and others who have an interest in the role.

The following list taken from Hill (1983), while fairly comprehensive, is not all inclusive:

I. Financial Planning and Budgeting
   A. Budget compilation, in coordination with educational planning
   B. Long-term fiscal planning — operating budget
   C. Estimating
      1. Receipts
      2. Disbursements
   D. Budget Control
   E. Fiscal relationships with other government units
   F. Use of systems analysis and Program Planning Budgeting Evaluation System (PPBES)
   G. Cash flow management

II. Accounting
   A. General fund
   B. Capital reserve funds, trust funds and special purpose grants
   C. Construction funds
   D. Internal accounts
   E. Student activity funds
   F. Voucher and payroll preparation
   G. Inventory
   H. Attendance, census, tax roll accounting
   I. Government tax and pension accounting — categorical aids
   J. Special trust funds
   K. Cost accounting — cost analysis — unit and comparative costs — cost distribution
   L. Student stores, bookstores
   M. Source documentation
   N. PPBES — Evaluation Resource Management (ERM) concepts and procedures

O. Employer benefits accounting — vacations, sick leave, seniority status
P. Petty cash funds

III. Debt Service and Capital Fund Management
A. Long-term and short-term financing
B. Maturities and debt payments
C. Long-range capital programs
D. Investments and cash flow
E. Reporting
F. Bond and note register
G. Debt service payment procedures
H. Short-term debt management
I. Revenue anticipation loans; emergency loans
J. Bond prospectus
K. Credit data — credit ratings

IV. Auditing
A. Pre-audit, or internal procedures
B. Determination that prepared statements present fairly the financial position
C. Propriety, legality and accuracy of financial transactions
D. Proper recording of all financial transactions
E. Post-audit procedures
F. External audits
G. Reconciliation of internal and external audits
H. Legal advertising and reporting

V. Purchasing and Supply Management
A. Ethics in purchasing
B. Official purchasing agent designation
C. Legal aspects of purchasing and contracting
D. Purchase methods — seasonal and off-season buying
E. Stock requisition and buying cycles
F. Standards and specifications
G. Requisition and purchase orders
H. Purchase bids
I. Cooperative purchasing — state contracts, local contracts
J. Testing and value analysis
K. Purchases of supplies and equipment
L. Warehousing and distribution procedures
M. Storage, delivery, trucking services

N. Inventory controls
O. Management of supplies, furniture, equipment
P. Computerized purchasing and supply management

VI. School Plant Planning and Construction
A. Establishment of educational standards for sites, buildings and equipment
B. Plant utilization studies
C. Projections of facility needs
D. Design, construction and equipment of plant
E. Safety standards
F. Contracts management
G. Architect selection

VII. Operation of Plant — Custodial, Gardening, Engineering Services
A. Standards and frequency of work
B. Manpower allocations
C. Scheduling
D. Inspection and evaluation of services
E. Relationship with educational staff
F. Operating of related school-community facilities, such as recreation, park, museum, library programs, etc.
G. Community use of facilities
H. Protection of plant and property
I. Security and police forces
J. Salvage, surplus and waste disposal

VIII. Maintenance of Plant
A. Repair of buildings and equipment
B. Upkeep of grounds
C. Maintenance policies, standards and frequency of maintenance
D. Scheduling and allocation of funds and manpower
E. Modernization and rehabilitation versus replacement

IX. Real Estate Management
A. Site acquisition and sales
B. Rental, leases
C. Rights-of-way and easements
D. Assessments and taxes

E. After school use of buildings
F. Dormitories, student unions, concessions

X. Personnel Management
   A. Records
      1. Probationary and tenure status of employees
      2. Sick leave and leave of absence
      3. Official notices of appointments and salaries
      4. Retirement data and deductions
      5. Salary schedules and payments
      6. Individual earnings records
      7. Withholding, tax and group insurance or fringe benefits
      8. Civil Service and Social Security
      9. Substitute and part-time employees
      10. Dues checkoffs

   B. Supervision of non-instructional staff
      1. Recruitment
      2. Selection
      3. Placement
      4. Training
      5. Advancement
      6. Working conditions
      7. Disciplinary action
      8. Termination of services

   C. Relationship to instructional staff
      1. Good will and service concept
      2. Cooperation in procurement
      3. Cooperation in budget preparation
      4. Information on pay and retirement
      5. Personnel records and reports

XI. Permanent Property Records and Custody of Legal Papers
   A. Security and preservation of records
   B. Maintenance of storage files
   C. Purging of records no longer legally required

XII. Transportation of Pupils
   A. Policies, rules, regulations and procedures
   B. Contract versus district-owned equipment
   C. Routing and scheduling

D. Inspection and maintenance
E. Staff supervision and training
F. Utilization and evaluation of services
G. Standards and specifications

XIII. Foodservice Operations
A. Policies, rules, regulations and procedures
B. Staffing and supervision
C. Menus, prices and portion controls
D. Purchasing, storage and distribution
E. Accounting, reporting and cost analysis
F. In-service training
G. Coordination with educational program
H. Procurement and operation of contract services

XIV. Insurance
A. Insurance policies
B. Insurable values — buildings and contents
C. Coverages to be provided
D. Claims and reporting
E. Insurance and procurement procedures
F. Insurance and claims record
G. Distribution of insurance to companies, agents and brokers

XV. Cost Analysis
A. Unit costs
B. Comparative costs
C. Cost distribution studies

XVI. Reporting
A. Local financial and statistical reports
B. State financial and statistical reports
C. Federal financial and statistical reports
D. Miscellaneous reports
E. Required legal advertising
F. Relationships with public information media

XVII. Collective Negotiations
A. Service on management team when required
B. Preparation of pertinent fiscal data for management team
C. Development of techniques and strategies of collective negotiations
D. Sharing of proper information with employee units

E. Use of outside negotiations, agencies
F. Mediation, arbitration, grievances

XVIII. Data Processing
A. Selection of system
B. Programming
C. Utilization of systems analysis
D. Forms preparation
E. Broad use of equipment for all pertinent applications

XIX. School Board Policies and Administrative Procedures as Related to Fiscal and Non-instructional Matters

XX. Responsibilities for Elections and Bond Referenda

XXI. Responsibilities for School Assessment, Levy and Tax Collection Procedures as May Be Set by Law (pp. 28-32)

Reviewing the definitions of financial accounting and managerial accounting and applying them to the list of duties and/or each of the cells in Figure 1-1, even with a minimal amount of understanding, one thing should become very clear: Accounting spans all tasks, functions and duties of the school business administrator. The more one learns about school business administration and accounting, the more evident this becomes. Accounting is the glue that binds all aspects of school business administration together. The following section will reinforce this concept, but from an entirely different and independent logic.

HOW ARE/SHOULD SCHOOL BUSINESS ADMINISTRATORS BE TRAINED?

A strong case can be made that if a person really wants to find out how important a particular skill and/or knowledge base is to a particular role, it can be obtained by asking those (or at least a sample) who are incumbents in the role of interest. If one wants to know how important knowledge about accounting skills is to the school business administrator, ask practicing school business administrators.

Studies done in the late 1960s and throughout the 1970s pointed to accounting as being one of the top responsibilities (if not the top) of the school business administrator. Whether the researchers were examining perceptions, competency statements, harvesting ideas on pre-service training or just organizing and categorizing statements from job descriptions, the results found accounting at or near the top of all lists.

McGuffey (1980), using survey techniques, rank ordered twenty-eight task duties and established the following "importance scores" (nine being the highest possible). The range of scores for all twenty-eight items was 7.94 to 3.44. The top five items were:

- Financial Planning and Budgeting   7.94
- Fiscal Accounting and Financial Reporting   7.47
- Cash Management   7.34
- Fiscal Audits and Reports   7.28
- General Management   7.18

Clearly, accounting knowledge, understanding and skills are an important area of study for those already in the school business administration profession and for those preparing to enter it.

In 1986, a survey of school business administrators in the United States and Canada was conducted by Everett and Glass (1986, May) to investigate what tasks business administrators performed on a daily basis, the perceived importance of these tasks, and the types of training school business administrators had received prior to employment. The survey also asked school business administrators what types of professional preparation and training they wanted and how they wanted it delivered. In late 1991, Everett and Glass (1991) replicated the 1986 survey. It examined whether a shift in function and opinions of school business administrators had taken place.

The survey produced the following general findings:

- Even though most school districts carry on without professionally prepared school business administrators, the importance of the role is increasing. For example, the annual budgets of school districts climbed during the 1980s and despite the economic recession of the early 1990s, promise to continue rising in future years but at a reduced rate.
- The complexity of school operations has increased in the past due to expanding government regulations, court decisions and statutory requirements.
- In addition to being stewards of public monies, school business administrators are now expected to be responsible for problem solving and planning in important management functions such as

collective bargaining, risk management, investments and contracting. These functions require knowledge and skills that must be current and relevant.

- The contemporary school business administrator is no longer the chief bookkeeper or "bean counter" for the school district, but instead, an important member of the district management team responsible for leading significant numbers of employees in the business office and making competent decisions (Candoli, et al., 1973). While this statement reflects that the role has and is changing, it would be inappropriate to conclude that accounting (chief bookkeeper/bean counter) is becoming less important compared to other functions now expected of the school business administrator (pp. 1-15).

The overall goal of the Everett-Glass study was to form a composite picture of the professional characteristics of today's school business administrator. The findings of this survey along with the 1986 survey, can be used by those individuals responsible for the development of pre-service and in-service training of school business administrators.

So what do school business administrators in the 1990s do?

School business administrators are responsible for a variety of management tasks in school districts. Many of these tasks and functions are not necessarily within the framework of the management of funds. Many have to do with employees (collective bargaining) or with educational programs (special education and compensatory programs).

The respondents were asked to prioritize the relative importance of each function to job success using a Likert type scale (1-5) with the designators being: Absolutely essential = 1; Very important = 2; Medium importance = 3; Not very important = 4; Not appropriate = 5. The respondents rated the top three absolutely essential and the remaining 13 as very important. (The first figure in parenthesis indicates the mean, and the second the standard deviation.)

1. Budget Planning (1.640, 1.248)
2. Accounting (1.751, 1.202)
3. Finance (1.869, 1.202)
4. Cash Management (2.031, 1.191)
5. Purchasing (2.088, 1.064)
6. Data Processing (2.221, .984)

Figure 1-2
Function Areas Supervised by School Business Officials, By Size of District

Enrollment	0 to 999		1,000 to 3,499		3,500 to 9,999		10,000 to 19,999		20,000 and over		Total	
Accounting	34	100%	151	97%	116	92%	33	85%	35	80%	369	93%
Property Management	32	94%	147	94%	106	84%	24	62%	31	70%	340	85%
Risk Management	28	82%	141	90%	108	86%	25	64%	28	64%	330	83%
Purchasing	32	94%	146	94%	112	90%	29	74%	31	70%	350	88%
Strategic Planning	13	38%	76	49%	46	37%	22	56%	16	36%	173	44%
Data Processing	27	79%	131	84%	98	78%	21	54%	23	52%	300	75%
Auditing	33	97%	136	87%	108	86%	30	77%	23	52%	330	83%
Salary Administration	26	77%	126	81%	68	54%	16	41%	17	39%	253	63%
Finance	34	100%	152	97%	118	94%	34	87%	29	66%	367	92%
Federal Programs	26	77%	88	56%	59	47%	17	44%	13	30%	203	51%
Special Education	17	50%	58	37%	29	23%	10	26%	6	14%	120	30%
Cash Management	33	97%	140	90%	109	87%	31	80%	29	66%	342	86%
Budget Planning	34	100%	153	98%	123	98%	33	84%	34	77%	377	95%
Facilities	17	50%	116	74%	86	68%	16	41%	25	57%	260	65%
Auxiliary Services	22	65%	119	76%	86	68%	21	54%	23	52%	271	68%
Collective Bargaining	12	35%	98	63%	53	42%	11	28%	11	25%	185	46%
Total in Category	34		156		126		39		44		399	

7. Risk Management (2.258, .972)
8. Auditing (2.309, .961)
9. Salary Administration (2.390, .995)
10. Strategic Planning (2.431, 1.062)
11. Collective Bargaining (2.460, 1.077)
12. Federal Programs (2.498, .902)
13. Auxiliary Services (2.508, .818)
14. Property Management (2.533, .904)
15. Facilities (2.544, .890)
16. Special Education (2.595, .941)

The first three, budget planning, accounting and finance, are commonly thought to be the heart of the position. However, there was not much common agreement among the respondents in how the three should be ranked. Probably, respondents felt the top three should be of equal importance.

Figure 1-2 breaks down the above function areas by school district enrollment size. To interpret the data in Figure 1-2, first note how many respondents there were in each size category, then how many times the group indicated responsibility for the function. For instance, there are 34 respondents in the size of district category with less than 1,000 students and all 34 of them indicated that they were responsible for accounting, finance and budget planning. Only half indicated that they were responsible for special education programs.

The types of preparation/formal training that school business administrators generally receive follows what they think to be their most important job functions and responsibilities (Figure 1-3).

Accounting and auditing are two of the top five priority functions in which school business administrators generally have received their pre-service training. In budget planning and finance, about half received formal training before employment and half afterwards. Data processing, risk management, purchasing, strategic planning, collective bargaining and facilities are areas that have not been generally addressed in academic preparation programs until recently. Overall, the data seemed to indicate that a majority of school business administrators receive the major part of their job preparation/training on the job during in-service sessions. There are advantages and disadvantages to this. In-service sessions can be more current but can also be superficial with little, if any, follow-up and supervision by trainers.

Figure 1-3
Training and Preparation Received*

	Pre-Service	In-Service
Budget Planning	191	169
Accounting	236	135
Finance	185	181
Cash Management	166	166
Purchasing	137	203
Data Processing	151	191
Risk Management	92	228
Auditing	194	141
Salary Administration	97	218
Strategic Planning	106	205
Collective Bargaining	98	217
Federal Programs	73	244
Auxiliary Services	70	236
Property Management	151	170
Facilities	93	201
Special Education	47	257

**Note:* Order of functions given is the same order used on the survey instrument.

Respondents indicated they desired additional training in the areas they had prioritized as having the highest importance (Figures 1-4 and 1-5). Budget planning was the area in which they most wanted future training.

OTHER INDICATORS OF THE IMPORTANCE OF ACCOUNTING TO SCHOOL BUSINESS ADMINISTRATION

If the reader is still not convinced of the importance of studying school accounting as part of preparing to become a school business administrator, perhaps an examination of the state certification requirements to be a chief school business official (CSBO) will provide some added insight. A survey conducted in 1993 by Everett and Mastro (1994) examined the present status of such certification. Only seventeen states and three provinces in Canada have CSBO certification requirements. The specific requirements vary dramatically from state to state and province to province but most include an accounting component.

Figure 1-4
Priorities of Role Functions in School Business for Future Training, By Size of District

Rank	0 to 999	1,000 to 3,499	3,500 to 9,000	10,000 to 19,999	20,000 and over
1	Accounting	Budget Planning	Budget Planning	Budget Planning	Budget Planning
2	Budget Planning	Accounting	Accounting	Accounting	Accounting
3	Cash Management	Finance	Finance	Finance	Finance
4	Finance	Cash Management	Cash Management	Cash Management	Purchasing
5	Purchasing	Purchasing	Purchasing	Strategic Planning	Cash Management

Figure 1-5
Priorities of Role Functions in School Business for Future Training, By Years of Experience

Rank	0 to 2 years	3 to 5 years	6 to 10 years	11 to 14 years	15+ years
1	Budget Planning	Budget Planning	Budget Planning	Budget Planning	Budget Planning
2	Accounting	Accounting	Accounting	Accounting	Accounting
3	Finance	Finance	Finance	Finance	Finance
4	Cash Management	Cash Management	Cash Management	Cash Management	Purchasing
5	Purchasing	Data Processing	Purchasing	Purchasing	—

In 1990, ASBO International finalized its *Guidelines For The Initial Preparation of Chief School Business Officials* (ASBO International, 1991) and had them approved in 1991 by the National Council for the Accreditation of Teacher Education (NCATE). Since 1992, any NCATE college or university unit that offers a graduate degree in school business administration must comply with these standards. What do these guidelines say about accounting? The major division of the Guideline "Financial Resource Management" is composed of four subsections, one of which is "Accounting, Auditing and Financial Reporting." Ten competency statements relating to this subsection are specified. They are:

- Present fairly and with full disclosure the financial position and results of financial operations of the funds and account groups of the school district in compliance with generally accepted accounting principles.
- Establish and verify compliance with finance-related legal and contractual provisions.
- Develop and maintain all fixed assets in a general fixed asset account group.
- Utilize the appropriate basis of accounting in measuring financial position and operating results: modified accrual basis of accounting; accrual basis of accounting; or cash basis of accounting.
- Prepare appropriate interim and annual financial statements and reports of financial position, and operating results to facilitate management control of all financial operations and funds using appropriate technology.
- Prepare revenue and expenditures by fund (use appropriate state chart of accounts, electronic data processing, etc.)
- Communicate the relationships between the institution program and process to the budget and available resources of the school district.
- Analyze both monthly and annual financial statements and reports.
- Develop specifications for the employment of an independent auditor.
- Understand the use and role of an internal auditor.

State certification requirements and NCATE standards are further indications that the study of school fund accounting is necessary and proper for anyone interested in becoming a school business administrator.

THE DIFFERENCE BETWEEN GOVERNMENTAL AND PUBLIC SCHOOL ACCOUNTING FROM PRIVATE SECTOR ACCOUNTING

Profit-oriented businesses must operate in a free enterprise/market environment. These entities must report to owners who have a vested interest in earning a return on their investments. Accounting reports for these organizations focus on the profitability and resources of the business entity often referred to as "the bottom line." Part of this reporting is to determine whether resources are being managed efficiently and effectively. This can, in part, be assessed by examining the earnings performance of the business.

In a school district, resource allocation is often set by policy rather than by the forces of supply and demand. The revenues resulting from the sale of goods and services by a public school district do not necessarily reveal the demand of consumers for these goods or services, and costs cannot be compared to earned revenues to determine whether the operating costs of the public school district are at an acceptable level. Without the components of a free market economy, public school districts are at a disadvantage relative to businesses in assessing the quantity and quality of goods and services to provide. Many of the unique features of public school district accounting and reporting result from the special needs these organizations have for controlling resources and costs and for providing accountability in the absence of market forces.

Ingram and others (1991) were quick to point out that in addition to the lack of market forces, governmental organizations such as public school districts differ from businesses in that operating procedures and policies are heavily influenced by legal and political constraints and issues. Authority to spend may be conveyed by a legally adopted budget enacted by elected or appointed members of a board of education.

Additionally, external sources of funding may come with legal constraints as to their use. Authority for action is based on laws or rules derived from a political process. Accountability is often a response to political demands rather than a response to the need for financial information that helps determine profitability. Thus, unlike corporate accounting and reporting, demonstration of compliance with laws and regulations and/or political agendas is a major objective of public school district accounting and reporting (Ingram et. al., pp. 1-16).

It is important to understand that public school districts can be thought of as a single entity, but also as an entity made up of a variety of different types of entities sometimes called auxiliary enterprises. Some of these entities operate similarly to business enterprises in that they sell goods and services to customers. For example, bookstores and cafeterias often operate as business enterprises within a public school district. The general operations of public school districts is an example of a nonbusiness type organization. By focusing on examples of business organizations at one end of the spectrum and public school districts as nonbusiness organizations at the other end of the spectrum, the extreme types of differences that may be observed between business and nonprofit educational organizations may be presented.

BASIC PUBLIC SCHOOL DISTRICT ACCOUNTING CONCEPTS

The basic concepts of public school district accounting are examined in this section and are contrasted with profit-oriented accounting concepts. These concepts apply to those activities of public school districts that result in products and services that are not sold to customers as part of a business enterprise.

In accounting for business organizations, revenues are inflows or other enhancements of assets of an entity or settlements of its liabilities from delivering or producing goods, rendering services, or other activities that constitute the entity's ongoing major or primary operations. Therefore, business revenue arises from the sale of products or services. The right to receive cash (accounts receivable) from sales is as legitimate a revenue as a cash receipt. In contrast, public school district revenues arise from taxes, fees or donations. Public school districts currently record the right to receive cash as revenue only when it is reasonably certain that the cash will be available to finance the operations of the current fiscal period.

SUMMARY

This chapter sets the stage for the remainder of this book. It establishes a comprehensive definition of what the role of the school business administrator is. This was done by listing most of the tasks and functions currently assigned to the individuals who perform these important roles. The relative importance of the accounting function and its overlapping nature with the various duties and responsibilities of the school business administrator were presented. Accounting was described as the product/service that ties everything together in a school district.

The accounting process not only satisfies the reporting needs of multiple users of such information but also produces information for decision making. Those who currently provide school business administration services validate the absolutely essential nature of having accounting knowledge and skills. The chapter closed by suggesting that the accounting performed by governmental/school district/nonprofit agencies is significantly different from that used in the business/private sector. While there are many significant similarities in accounting in the public sector versus the private sector there are also significant differences.

ACTIVITIES

1. Read the preface of this book.
2. Carefully review the definition of the following terms as given in the glossary:
   a. Financial accounting
   b. Managerial accounting
   c. School Business Administrator
   d. School Business Official
   e. School Business Specialist
   f. School Business Management

REFERENCES/SPECIAL READINGS

Association of School Business Officials International. (1991). *Model preparation program for school business administrators.* Reston, VA: Author.

Candoli, I. C., et. al. (1973). *School business administration: A compilation of exemplary management techniques.* Park Ridge, IL: Research Corporation of the Association of School Business Officials.

Carnahan, O. (1965). *A study of the duties, responsibilities and training of school business officials in cities of the United States between 25,000 and 50,000 population.* Unpublished doctoral dissertation, University of Idaho, Moscow, ID.

Everett, R. E., & Glass, T. E.(1986, May). Survey defines school business officials responsibilities. *School Business Affairs*, 52 (8), pp. 14-28, 27

Everett, R. E., & Glass, T. E. (1992). School business administrators in the 1990s. *The Journal of Business Management*, 4 (1) pp. 5-18.

Everett, R. E., & Glass, T. E. (1992, July). School business administrators in the 1990s. *School Business Affairs*, 58 (7), pp. 28-36.

Everett, R. E., & Mastro, L. (1994, September). Certification: Little progress for school business administration. *School Business Affairs*, 60 (9) pp. 6-15.

Finkler, S. A. (1992). *Finance and accounting for nonfinancial managers*, Englewood Cliffs, NJ: Prentice Hall.

Hill, F. W. (1982). *The school business administrator*, Park Ridge, IL: Research Corporation of the Association of School Business Officials.

Ingram, R., Peterson, R. J., & Martin, S. W. (1991). *Accounting and financial reporting for governmental and nonprofit organizations: Basic concepts*, New York: McGraw-Hill.

McGuffey, C. W. (1980). *Competencies needed by chief school business administrators*, Park Ridge, IL: Research Corporation of the Association of School Business Officials.

Miller, J. G. and Swanson, G. A. (1989). *Measurement and interpretation in accounting*, New York: Quorum Books.

2

What Is Accounting?

INTRODUCTION

If a person wants to keep track of the financial transactions that occur in a school district during any given period of time, it would soon become apparent that one needs a method to summarize the different categories of transactions and the number of transactions within categories. For the school business official it is essential to be able to plan for financial aspects of school operations, to implement and maintain the financial plan, and to summarize the results of financial transactions associated with school operations.

OUTCOMES

In this chapter, you will learn how to:

1. Define accounting.
2. Define a school budget — plan for financial aspects of school operations for a given period.
3. Recognize the layout of a typical budget document.
4. Define an audit — summary of the financial aspects of school operations for a given period.
5. Recognize the layout for a typical independent audit.
6. Recognize the layout for the Annual Financial Report (AFR).
7. Recognize the layout for the Consolidated Annual Financial Report (CAFR).

ACCOUNTING

The accounting profession has defined accounting as the art of analyzing, recording, summarizing, interpreting and communicating the results of financial transactions. State and local school administrators realize the need to have a well-organized system for managing and reporting comparable financial transactions. The National Center for Education Statistics (NCES) has a responsibility to provide and interpret comprehensive statistics about the condition of education. In order to facilitate the task of obtaining comparable statistics, NCES regularly revises documents designed to promote the collection of comparable information. *Handbook II, (Financial Accounting for Local and State School Systems: 1990)* is the latest document prepared by NCES to facilitate the collection of comparable financial data from school districts across the United States.

Although there is no Federal law mandating the use of the handbook, many state school systems use terms and definitions presented in the handbook. The state school systems may use Handbook II to develop state-specific accounting manuals, e.g., *Illinois Program Accounting Manual for Local Education Agencies: Chart of Accounts*; and *North Carolina Public Schools: Chart of Accounts*.

BUDGETING

Chris A. DeYoung (1946) defined the budget as follows:

> The ideal school budget contains three parts: (1) the *work* plan, which is a definite statement of the educational policies and program; (2) the *spending* plan which is a translation of the accepted policies into proposed expenditures; and (3) the *financing* plan, which proposes means for meeting the cost of the education needs. (p. 7)

The definition of budgeting by DeYoung sets forth an enormous task for NCES to produce comprehensive and compatible sets of standard terminology for use in education management and reporting. Although NCES has developed other handbooks to facilitate the collection of comparable data, the primary concern in this document is with Handbook II, Financial Accounting. Other handbooks developed by NCES include the following:

Handbook I: *The Common Core of State Educational Information –1953*
Handbook III: *Property Accounting for Local and State School Systems –1959*
Handbook IV: *Staff Accounting for Local and State School Systems –1965*
Handbook V: *Pupil Accounting for Local and State School Systems –1964*

Handbook VI: *Standard Terminology for Curriculum and Instruction in Local and State School Systems – 1970*

Handbook II (Fowler 1990) focuses on the spending plan (expenditures) and the financing plan (revenues) as defined by DeYoung. Standard terminology for the work plan is not discussed in Handbook II. For the sake of expediency this text follows the content of Handbook II in discussing the budget and neglects consideration of the work plan (educational program) in the treatment of the budget. The budget for purposes of this text contains:

- A statement of cash on hand at the beginning of the fiscal year
- An estimate of the cash expected to be received during the fiscal year
- An estimate of the expenditures contemplated for the fiscal year
- A statement of the estimated cash expected to be on hand at the end of the fiscal year

Although the above definition seems to reflect the *cash basis* of accounting, the budget may reflect operations which are recorded on the *accrual basis* of accounting. The *cash basis* of accounting implies that transactions are recorded when cash changes hands. (Tax monies are actually distributed to school districts; Equipment is paid from district monies.) On the other hand, the *accrual basis* of accounting implies that transactions are recorded when they are reduced to legal obligations. (Taxes are levied; Purchase orders for equipment are issued.)

Although state legislatures may permit school districts to record transactions on a cash basis, the accounting profession recognizes that the accrual basis of accounting provides a more complete picture of the financial condition of the district.

The simple statement that a school district must provide a statement of cash on hand at the beginning of the fiscal year causes one to ask questions about the comparability of data across school districts. What is cash (assets)? How much is in "cash in the bank?" How much is in investments? How much is on loan?

The NCES has attempted to compile a comprehensive list and description of all items which reflect "cash" or current assets. Handbook II identifies and defines the following current assets: cash, cash with fiscal agents, investments, taxes receivable, interfund receivables, other receivables, bond proceeds receivable, inventories, prepaid expenses, and other current assets. Handbook II provides subclassifications and descriptions to facilitate consistent reporting across districts of assets in each of the categories.

NCES has also attempted to develop a comprehensive list and description of expenditure items. NCES has established several *dimensions* that may be used to describe expenditure transactions. Three basic dimensions are fund, function and object. *Funds* are established to carry on specific activities in accordance with legislation, rules or regulations. *Function* describes the activity for which a service or material object is acquired. *Object* is the service or commodity bought. The use of fund, function and object enables NCES, state and local education agencies to gain a better understanding of the operations of a school district.

AUDITING

At the most general level, an audit is a methodical examination of use of resources and a written report of the findings. The audit may be conducted by independent public accountants, governmental accountants, or by internal auditors. The audit may focus on selected areas — financial and compliance audits, program compliance audits, or performance audits. *Financial and compliance audits* are concerned with fairness of presentation of basic financial statements in conformity with Generally Accepted Accounting Principles (GAAP). *Program Compliance Audits* are concerned with the extent to which the local education agency (LEA) conformed to requirements of the funding agency. *Performance Audits* are concerned with the economy and efficiency of the LEA and the extent to which the program objectives are being attained. As Tidwell notes (1985, p. 13),

> ....for purposes of school fund accounting, the word audit involves examination of the documents, records, reports, system of internal control, accounting procedures, and other evidence for the purpose of determining the propriety, legality, and propriety of proposed or consummated transactions, or for the purpose of ascertaining whether all transactions have been recorded and properly reported.

Generally speaking, the external financial audit is a way for the school district to show stewardship in the use of resources granted by the taxpayers in the school district. Although few persons may actually examine the external audit, it nevertheless compels the school district to greater accountability than would occur without an external audit. [Refer to Appendix E for an example of an external financial audit.]

ANNUAL FINANCIAL REPORTS

Annual financial reports are detailed financial statements that conform to state guidelines for reporting revenues and expenditures and is parallel to information contained in the budget. NCES has developed guidelines for reporting financial information that will facilitate collecting and reporting annual general education statistics at the federal level.

Each state is expected to develop a manual that will outline comparable account classifications across school districts within the respective states. In addition, each state is expected to develop a set of models of the reporting formats used with the account classifications. The account classifications of the annual financial report include revenues, expenditures (fund, function, and object), assets, liabilities, and fund equities. To facilitate analysis, the structure of the budget and annual financial report are similar. The budget sets forth the planned financial transactions for a given period of time and the annual financial report sets forth the actual financial transactions for that period of time. [Refer to Appendix C for a sample of a Budget and to Appendix I for a sample of an Annual Financial Report.]

CONSOLIDATED ANNUAL FINANCIAL REPORT (CAFR)

NCES does not mandate that each state adopt identical accounting manuals as suggested by Handbook II. Each state is encouraged to use the handbook as a guide in developing accounting systems that are uniquely suited to that state. A major difference that arises in reporting summary information is that there is considerable variance in the "funds" used by each state. Therefore, NCES has established general guidelines to walk the various funds used by the states into "broad funds" — General Fund; Special Revenue Funds; Capital Projects Funds; Debt Service Funds; Enterprise Funds; Internal Service Funds; Trust and Agency Funds; General Fixed Assets Account Group; and General Long-Term Debt Account Group.

The only difference between the annual financial report and the CAFR is that state-specific information is presented in the annual financial report and information presented in the CAFR is aggregated by funds defined by NCES. (Compare information and formats of the annual financial report and the CAFR presented in Appendix E.)

In order to carry out its mission, a school district may operate a number of *funds*. For the school business administrator, the term *fund* has come to hold a specific meaning, and the school business official will be quick to point out that a school district may use several funds.

The term *fund*, as it is used in governmental accounting, is defined as a fiscal and accounting entity with a self-balancing set of accounts recording cash and other financial resources, together with all related liabilities and residual equities or balances, and changes therein, which are segregated for the purpose of carrying on specific activities or attaining certain objectives in accordance with special regulations, restrictions or limitations. (MFOA, 1980)

Although the annual financial report of each school district may be organized around the funds authorized in the respective states, the Consolidated Annual Financial Report should reflect data which is comparable across the states. To this end, Handbook II (pp. 77-78) has defined these funds as follows:

Government Funds

General Fund – Accounts for all financial resources of the LEA except those required to be accounted for in another fund.

Special Revenue Funds – Account for the proceeds of specific revenue sources that are legally restricted to expenditures for specified purposes.

Capital Projects Funds – Account for financial resources used to acquire or construct major capital facilities.

Debt Service Funds – Account for the accumulation of resources for, and the payment of, general long-term debt, principal and interest.

Proprietary Funds

Enterprise Funds – Account for operations that are financed and operated in a manner similar to private enterprises where the stated intent is that the costs of providing goods or services to the students or general public on a continuing basis are financed or recovered through user charges.

Internal Service Funds – Account for the operation of LEA functions that provide goods or services to other LEA functions, other LEA's, or to other governmental units, on a cost-reimbursable basis.

Fiduciary Funds
Trust and Agency Funds – Account for assets held by an LEA in a trustee capacity or as an agent for individuals, private organizations, other governmental units, and/or other funds.

Account Groups
General Fixed Assets Account Group – Records the cost of all property, plant and equipment other than those accounted for in the proprietary funds or fiduciary funds.

General Long-Term Debt Account Group – Records the principal amount of all long-term liabilities, excluding those of the proprietary funds or fiduciary funds.

ACCOUNTS WITHIN A FUND

A fund, as an independent accounting entity, uses a self-balancing set of accounts to provide full information about financial transactions pertinent to meeting the objectives for financial transactions pertinent to meeting the objective for which the fund was established. Accounts that record financial transactions of an LEA fund may be classified a follows:

- Asset accounts.
- Liability accounts.
- Fund equity accounts.
- Estimated revenue accounts.
- Revenue accounts.
- Appropriation accounts/estimated expenditure accounts.
- Expenditure accounts.
- Encumbrance accounts.
- Summarizing and closing accounts.

SUMMARY

Accounting, budgeting and auditing were defined. Descriptions of layouts for the budget document, audit, annual financial report, and consolidated annual financial report were presented. Budget and annual financial report documents included in the appendices were referenced.

The term *fund* was defined and several types of funds were described. The accounts necessary for the self-balancing set of accounts for a fund were listed.

ACTIVITIES

1. Carefully examine the sample budget, annual financial report and consolidated annual financial report provided in the appendices.

2. Study the definitions of the following terms as provided in the Glossary:
   a. Budget
   b. Annual Financial Report (AFR)
   c. Consolidated Annual Financial Report (CAFR)
   d. Cash
   e. Asset
   f. Cash Basis
   g. Accrual Basis
   h. Current Asset
   i. Fund
   j. Function
   k. Object
   l. Audit
   m. Financial and Compliance Audit
   n. Program Compliance Audit
   o. Performance Audits
   p. General Fund
   q. Special Revenue Fund
   r. Capital Projects Fund
   s. Debt Service Fund
   t. Enterprise Fund
   u. Internal Service Funds
   v. Trust and Agency Funds

w. General Fixed Assets Account Group
x. General Long-Term Debt Account Group
y. Liabilities
z. Fund Equities

3. Obtain a copy of the accounting manual for your state and examine the dimensions of accounting used in your state. What funds are used? Observe the account subclassifications under assets, revenues, liabilities, fund equities (balances), and expenditures. What dimensions in addition to fund, function, and object are used to identify expenditures?

4. Obtain copies of your school district's budget, audit, and annual financial report. Compare the layout of the documents. Observe the parallel among the three documents. What is the difference between the audit and the consolidated annual financial report?

5. Students who are using this book as a textbook for a course may first find it helpful to collect the following documents so they can refer to specific documents that are relevant to a specific setting.
   - The accounting manual for your state.
   - The accounting manual for your school district (if available).
   - The budget document for your school district.
   - The audit for your school district.
   - The consolidated annual financial report for your school district.

REFERENCES/SELECTED READINGS

Fowler, W. J., Jr. (1990). *Financial accounting for local and state school systems, 1990.* Washington, DC: Superintendent of Documents, Government Printing Office.
The accounting manual for your state.
The accounting manual for your school district (if available).
The budget document for your school district.
The audit for your school district.
The consolidated annual financial report for your school district.

3

Basic Principles of Accounting

INTRODUCTION

The information presented in this chapter is designed to acquaint the superintendent, school business administrator or principal with a rudimentary understanding of accounting processes in order that they may communicate accounting needs to certified public accountants and to enable them to communicate reports of certified public accountants to school personnel and to lay boards of education. The text is not designed to prepare public accountants nor to eliminate the need for persons with advanced accounting training or certified public accountants.

Tidwell (1985, p. 8) states that the objectives of financial accounting for school systems may be summarized as follows:

1. To provide a complete record of all financial transactions of the school system.
2. To summarize, with reasonable promptness, financial transactions of the school system in financial reports required for proper, effective and efficient administration.
3. To provide financial information that would be helpful for budget preparation, adoption and execution.
4. To provide financial controls or safeguards for the school system's money and property.
5. To provide a basis whereby the governing board can place administrative responsibility and minimize the possibility of waste, carelessness, inefficiency and possible fraud.
6. To provide clear and concise financial reports to the public as a basis for judging past, present and future financial operation of the school system.
7. To provide an historical record which, over a period of years, can be studied and analyzed critically and constructively for the purpose of aiding citizens, the governing board and the school system's administrative officers in keeping pace with changing concepts of education.

OUTCOMES

In this chapter, you will learn how to:

1. Perform selected accounting procedures (discover, record, classify and summarize financial transactions).
2. Distinguish between the cash and accrual bases of accounting.
3. Recognize the accounting equation.
4. Operate within the constraints of the accounting equation.
5. Use the accounting equation in the preparation of financial reports.

ACCOUNTS WITHIN A FUND

As noted in the previous chapter, a fund, as an accounting entity, uses a self-balancing set of accounts to provide full information about financial transactions pertinent to meeting the objectives for which the fund was established. Accounts that record financial transactions of an LEA fund may be classified as follows:

1. Asset accounts
2. Liability accounts
3. Fund equity accounts
4. Estimated revenue accounts
5. Revenue accounts
6. Appropriation accounts
7. Expenditure accounts
8. Encumbrance accounts
9. Summarizing and closing accounts

ACCOUNTING PROCEDURES

Accounting procedures discover, record, classify and summarize financial information to produce financial reports and to provide internal control. Procedures used in analyzing and recording transactions are as follows:

1. Determine the specific fund to which the transaction is related. (What fund?)
2. Determine the specific accounts that are affected by the transaction. (What accounts?)

3. Record each transaction in the book of original entry. (Keep a journal.)
4. Post each part of the transaction to the specific account affected. (Post to ledger or journal.)
5. Prepare financial statements from the accounts. (Summarize and report.)

BASIC FINANCIAL STATEMENTS

Basic financial statements present information concerning an LEA's financial position on a specific date, *or* changes in that position and results of operation during a period ending on that date. Financial statements presenting the financial positions as of a certain date are called *balance sheets*, and statements reflecting changes in that position and results of operation during a period ending on that date are called *operating statements*.

BALANCE SHEETS

The financial position information presented on the balance sheet indicates what an LEA owns (assets), what it owes (liabilities), and the excess of assets over liabilities (fund equity). Therefore, the basic accounting equation for a fund is expressed as:

$$\text{Assets} - \text{Liabilities} = \text{Fund Equity}$$
$$\text{or}$$
$$\text{Assets} = \text{Liabilities} + \text{Fund Equity}$$

Assets—Assets may be defined as resources owned or held by an LEA that have monetary value. Current assets are those assets that are available or can be made readily available to finance current operations or to pay current liabilities. General fixed assets are those that the LEA intends to hold or continue in use over a long period of time. A partial list of current assets common to LEAs are listed below.

Cash in bank—All funds on deposit with a bank or savings and loan institution, normally in non-interest bearing accounts. Interest-bearing accounts are recorded in investments.

Investments—Securities and real estate held for producing income in the form of interest, dividends, rentals or lease payments.

Taxes receivable—The uncollected portion of taxes that an LEA or governmental unit has levied and which has become due, including any interest or penalties that may be accrued.

Loans receivable–Amounts that have been loaned to people or organizations, including notes taken as security for such loans, where permitted by statutory authority.

Prepaid expenses–Expenses paid for benefits not yet received.

A listing of current asset account titles with account code numbers, as recommended by the National Center for Education Statistics (NCES), can be found on pages 36-37 of Fowler (1990).

Liabilities – Liabilities may be defined as debt or other legal obligations arising out of transactions in the past that must be liquidated, renewed or refunded at some future date. Current liabilities are those debts the LEA expects to pay within a short period of time, usually a year or less. Long-term liabilities are debts with a maturity of more than one year after date of issuance. A partial list of current liabilities common to an LEA are listed below:

Interfund loans payable – A liability account used to record a debt owed by one fund to another fund in the same governmental unit.

Accounts payable – Liabilities on open account owing to private people, firms or corporations for goods and services received by an LEA (but not including amounts due to other funds of the same LEA or to other governmental units).

Warrants payable – Amounts due to designated payees in the form of a written order drawn by the LEA directing the LEA treasurer to pay a specific amount, i.e., unpaid teacher/employee salaries, unpaid payroll witholdings.

Contracts payable – Amounts due on contracts for assets, goods and services received by an LEA.

Deferred revenues – A liability account that represents revenues collected before they become due.

A listing of current liability account titles, with account code numbers, as recommended by NCES, can be found on pages 38-39 of Fowler (1990).

Fund equity – These are accounts showing the excess in assets of a fund over its liabilities. Portions of that balance may be reserved for future use. A partial list of fund equity accounts commonly used by LEAs is as follows:

Reserve for encumbrances – A reserve representing that portion of a fund balance segregated to provide for unliquidated encumbrances. Separate accounts may be maintained for current encumbrances and prior-year encumbrances.

Reserved-fund balance – A reserve representing that portion of a fund balance segregated to indicate that assets equal to the amount of reserve are restricted and are, therefore, not available for appropriation. A separate reserve should be established for each special purpose. One example of a special purpose would be restricted federal programs.

Unreserved-fund balance – The excess of the assets of a fund over its liabilities and reserves.

A listing of current fund equity account titles with account code numbers, as recommended by NCES, can be found on page 40 of Fowler (1990).

The balance sheet – The balance sheet is a basic financial statement that discloses the assets, liabilities and fund equities of an entity at a specific date in conformity with generally accepted accounting principles (GAAP), (MFOA, 1980). A balance sheet for the general fund of Kimberly Hills School District as of the end of 1995 is shown in Illustration 3-1.

The balance sheet should contain the following information:

- The name of the school district;
- The name of the fund;
- The name of the financial statement (balance sheet);
- The date
- All asset, liability and fund equity accounts which have non-zero balances.

OPERATING STATEMENTS

Results of operation can be measured and reported in several different ways. Increases and decreases in net current assets are called revenues and expenditures. A statement of revenues, expenditures, and fund equity or a statement of changes in financial position summarize the effect revenues and expenditures have had on the fund equity during a specific period of time.

Revenues of a fund recognized in a certain period have a direct positive impact upon the fund equity account. Expenditures refer to

Illustration 3-1

Kimberly Hills School District
General Fund
Balance Sheet
June 30, 1995

Assets

Cash in Bank		$ 20,000
Investments		80,000
Taxes receivable	$300,000	
less: Est. Uncollectible Taxes	15,000	$285,000
Loan receivable		30,000
Total assets		$415,000

Liabilities and Fund Equity

Liabilities:

Accounts Payable	$ 27,000	
Warrants Payable	82,000	
Loan Payable	161,000	$270,000
Fund Equity:		
Reserved for Encumbrances	$115,000	
Unreserved-Fund Balance	30,000	
Total Fund Equity		145,000
Total Liability & Fund Equity		$415,000

the charges incurred, whether paid or unpaid, which are presumed to benefit the current fiscal year. A fund's revenues increases the fund equity balance and expenses decrease the fund equity balance. Given these relationships, the basic accounting equation can be expanded to the following:

$$\text{Assets} = \text{Liabilities} + (\text{Fund Equity} + \text{Revenues} - \text{Expenditures})$$
or
$$\text{Assets} = \text{Liabilities} + \text{Fund Equity} + \text{Revenues} - \text{Expenditures}$$

A statement of revenues, expenditures and fund equity is shown in Illustration 3-2.

Illustration 3-2

Kimberly Hills School District
General Fund
Statement of Revenues,
Expenditures and Fund Equity
For the period ended June 30, 1995

Fund Equity, July 1, 1994 (beginning of period)		$25,000
Add excess of revenues over expenditures		
Revenues	$300,000	
less Expenditures	180,000	120,000
Fund Equity, June 30, 1995 (end of period)		$145,000

The balance sheet provides information regarding the financial condition of a fund as of a specific date and the statement of revenues, expenditures and fund equity provide information regarding the results of operation for a specified period of time.

Examples 1 and 2 illustrate the use of the balance sheet and the statement of revenues, expenditures and fund equity in summarizing transactions in a school district.

Example 1-A

On July 1, 1994, the unreserved fund balance of Cape Jennifer School District was $323,000. During the year, revenues amounting to $420,000 were realized and expenses amounting to $300,000 were paid. Asset and liability account balances in the general fund on June 30, 1995 were as follows:

Cash in Bank	$ 20,000
Investments	370,000
Taxes Receivable	640,000
Prepaid Expense	3,000
Accounts Payable	590,000

Given the above information:
a. Prepare a statement of revenues, expenditures, and fund equity for the general fund for the period ending June 30, 1995.
b. Prepare a balance sheet for the general fund as of June 30, 1995.

Illustration of Example 1-A

Cape Jennifer School District
General Fund
Statement of Revenues,
Expenditures and Fund Equity
For the period ended June 30, 1995

Fund Equity, July 1, 1994		$323,000
Add excess of revenues over expenditures		
Revenues	$420,000	
less: Expenditures	300,000	120,000
Fund Equity, June 30, 1995		$443,000

Cape Jennifer School District
General Fund
Balance Sheet
June 30, 1995

Assets

Cash in Bank	$ 20,000
Investments	370,000
Taxes Receivable	640,000
Prepaid Expense	3,000
Total Assets	$1,033,000

Liabilities and Fund Equity

Liabilities:	
Accounts Payable	$590,000
Fund Equity:	
Unreserved Fund Balance	443,000
Total Liabilities and Fund Equity	$1,033,000

Example 1-B
On July 2, 1994, Cape Jennifer School District (refer to Example 1-A) sold its investments for cash and received cash for the total amount due in taxes receivable. The balance sheet for the general fund for Cape Jennifer School District on July 2, 1994, would be as follows:

Cape Jennifer School District
**General Fund
Balance Sheet**
July 2, 1994

Assets
Cash in Bank	$1,030,000	
Prepaid Expense	3,000	
Total Assets		$1,033,000

Liabilities and Fund Equity
Liabilities:		
Accounts Payable	$ 590,000	
Fund Equity:		
Unreserved Fund Balance	443,000	
Total Liabilities and Fund Equity		$1,033,000

Example 2
Timton School District has the following account balances in the general fund on June 30, 1995:

Unreserved Fund Balance	$353,000
Accounts Payable	35,000
Investments	420,000
Loans Receivable	180,000
Contracts Payable	300,000
Cash in Bank	6,000
Taxes Receivable	560,000
Prepaid Expense	12,000
Warrants Payable	40,000
Accrued Salaries and Benefits	450,000

Hint: Identify and group assets, liabilities and fund equities accounts and list in order of liquidity or by account number.

The balance sheet for the general fund for Timton School District on June 30, 1995, would appear as follows:

Timton School District
**General Fund
Balance Sheet**
June 30, 1995

Assets

Cash in Bank	$ 6,000	
Investments	420,000	
Taxes Receivable	560,000	
Loans Receivable	180,000	
Prepaid Expense	12,000	
Total Assets		$1,178,000

Liabilities and Fund Equity

Liabilities:

Accounts Payable	$ 35,000	
Warrants Payable	40,000	
Contracts Payable	300,000	
Accrued Salaries and Benefits	450,000	$ 825,000
Fund Equity:		
Unreserved Fund Balance		353,000
Total Liabilities and Fund Equity		$1,178,000

SUMMARY

Definitions were given of accounting and descriptions were given of selected account subcategories. Illustrations were provided for selected accounting procedures and examples of balance sheets and statements of revenues, expenditures and fund equity were shown. The accounting equation was introduced and reports were derived through the use of that equation.

ACTIVITIES

1. Define each of the following terms:
   a. Accounting
   b. Fund
   c. Accounting entity
   d. Asset

e. Liability
f. Fund equity
g. Balance sheet accounts

2. Review the definitions of the following terms found in the glossary:
   a. Transaction
   b. Journalize
   c. Post
   d. Post to ledger
   e. Operating statement
   f. Current assets
   g. General fixed assets
   h. Cash in bank
   i. Interfund loans payable
   j. Accounts payable
   k. Warrants payable
   l. Contracts payable
   m. Deferred revenue
   n. Reserve for encumbrances
   o. Reserved-fund balance account
   p. Unreserved-fund balance
   q. Investments
   r. Taxes receivable
   s. Prepaid expenses
   t. Liabilities
   u. Current liabilities
   v. Long-term liabilities
   w. Loans Receivable

3. What types of accounts are included in the school fund accounting equation?

4. What is the purpose of the "Statement of Revenues, Expenditures and Fund Equity Report"?

5. On June 30, 1995, the account balances of the general fund of Christopher Point School District were:
Cash in bank	$ 20,000
Accounts payable	30,000
Investments	25,000
Taxes receivable	200,000

Unreserved fund balance	120,000
Contracts payable	95,000

Instructions:
- Prepare a balance sheet as of June 30, 1995, for Christopher Point School District.

6. On July 1, 1994, the fund equity balance of the general fund of Randyville School System was $75,000. During the year, revenues amounting to $96,000 were realized and expenditures amounting to $474,000 were paid. Prepare a statement of revenues, expenditures and fund equity for the period ending June 30, 1995.

7. On July 1, 1994, the fund equity balance of the general fund of New Douglas School System was $97,455. During the year, revenues amounting to $346,000 were realized and expenditures amounting to $213,613 were incurred. Asset and liability account balances as of June 30, 1995 were as follows:

Taxes receivable	$600,050
Accounts payable	54,965
Cash in bank	29,415
Warrants payable	422,381
Contracts payable	242,227
Investments	317,950
Loans receivable	2,000

Instructions:
- Prepare a statement of revenues, expenditures and fund equity for the year ended June 30, 1995.
- Prepare a balance sheet as of June 30, 1995.

REFERENCES/SELECTED READINGS

Fowler, W. J., Jr. (1990). *Financial accounting for local and state school systems.* Washington, DC: Government Printing Office.

Municipal Finance Officers Association. (1980). *Governmental accounting, auditing, and financial reporting.* Chicago, IL: Author. (See Appendix B).

Robert Davis Associates. (1981). *Principles of public school fund accounting.* Washington, DC: National Technical Information Service.

Tidwell, S. B. (1985). *Financial and managerial accounting for elementary and secondary school systems (3rd ed.)*. Reston, VA: Research Corporation of the Association of School Business Officials.

4

Basic Accounting Techniques

INTRODUCTION

Although most accounting in school systems has been automated, the best way to *learn* accounting is to study and apply paper and pencil techniques. This chapter harks back to the day before modern technology when "real people did real work."

Electronic data processing is fast and efficient. However, if one does not understand what is being done, then one is in the position of placing blind trust in a silicon monster.

What is the accounting mystery? What are debits and credits? How do you know you haven't made mistakes? What do the numbers tell you? Grab a paper and pencil and probe the mysteries of accounting.

OUTCOMES

In this chapter, you will learn how to:

1. Define "debits" and "credits."
2. Debit and credit accounts.
3. Define a "trial balance."
4. Compute a trial balance.

DEBITS AND CREDITS DEFINED

Financial transactions may result in increases or decreases to an account. A convenient method of displaying the increases or decreases is through the use of debits and credits to "T-accounts." A T-account, shown in Figure 4-1, looks like a "T" and the left side of the T-account is called the debit side and the right side is called the credit side.

Figure 4-1
T-Account

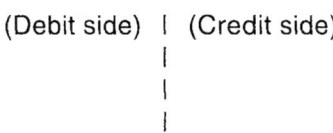

	Name of the Account
(Debit side)	(Credit side)

The terms "debit" and "credit" are of Latin origin and do not carry any increase/decrease meaning in and of themselves. As an *adjective*, debit means "left" and credit means "right"; as a *noun*, debit means "an entry in the debit or left-hand side of an account" and credit means "an entry in the credit or right-hand side of an account"; and as a *verb*, debit means "to enter a sum on the debit or left-hand side of an account" and credit means "to enter a sum on the credit or right-hand side of an account."

The terms debit and credit do carry increase/decrease meaning when used in conjunction with a specific group of accounts. The relationship between accounts, debits and credits, and increases and decreases is shown in the basic accounting equation as follows (dr = debit; cr = credit):

Assets	=	Liabilities	+	Fund Equity	+	Revenues	−	Expenditures
dr | cr	=	dr | cr	+	dr | cr	+	dr | cr	−	dr | cr
+ | −	=	− | +	+	− | +	+	− | +	−	+ | −
|	=	|	+	|	+	|	−	|

RELATIONSHIP BETWEEN ACCOUNTS, DEBITS AND CREDITS

The relationship between accounts, debits and credits, and increases and decreases may be stated as follows:
1. To *increase* an asset account, debit.
    To *decrease* an asset account, credit.
2. To *increase* a liability account, credit.
    To *decrease* a liability account, debit.
3. To *increase* a fund equity account, credit.
    To *decrease* a fund equity account, debit.
4. To *increase* a revenue account, credit.
    To *decrease* a revenue account, debit.

5. To *increase* an expenditure account, debit.
   To *decrease* an expenditure account, credit.

The above relationships may be summarized as follows:
1. To *increase* asset and expenditure accounts, debit.
2. To *decrease* asset and expenditure accounts, credit.
3. To *increase* liability, fund equity and revenue accounts, credit.
4. To *decrease* liability, fund equity and revenue accounts, debit.

EQUALITY OF DEBITS AND CREDITS

In a self-balancing set of accounts, the debit amounts must equal the credit amounts. Therefore, each transaction has at least one debit and at least one credit, and the total amount of debits must equal the total amount of credits. A transaction may have more than one debit and/or more than one credit. Such a transaction is called a *compound entry*. For example, the use of cash (credit: reduction of an asset) to pay principal (debit: reduction of a liability) and interest (debit: increase in expenditures) results in a compound entry.

Illustrations of the use of debits and credits in recording transactions are presented in the following examples.

TRIAL BALANCE

If all transactions have been recorded correctly, then the total of all debits should be equal to the total of all credits. After all transactions have been recorded, a trial balance is prepared to prove the equality of debits and credits.

Example 1
Assume that the Kimberly Hills School District began the year with assets of $30,000, liabilities of $10,000 and a fund equity of $20,000 in the general fund.

Assets	=	Liabilities	+	Fund Equity	+	Revenues	−	Expenditures
dr | cr	=	dr | cr	+	dr | cr	+	dr | cr	−	dr | cr
(1) 30000 |	=	| 10000	+	| 20000	+	|	−	|
(T) 30000 |	=	| 10000	+	| 20000	+	|	−	|

Note: Transaction 1 has equal debits and credits ($30,000) and the totals (T) of debits and credits are equal ($30,000).

Example 2
Assume that property taxes are assessed and levied in the amount of $40,000. What accounts are affected? (Assets are increased/debited and revenues are increased/credited.)

	Assets	=	Liabilities	+	Fund Equity	+	Revenues	−	Expenditures
	dr | cr	=	dr | cr	+	dr | cr	+	dr | cr	−	dr | cr
(1)	30000 |	=	| 10000	+	| 20000	+	|	−	|
(2)	40000 |	=	|	+	|	+	| 40000	−	|
(T)	70000 |	=	| 10000	+	| 20000	+	| 40000	−	|

Note: Transaction (2) has equal debits and credits ($40,000) and the totals (T) of debits and credits are equal ($70,000).

Example 3
Assume supplies in the amount of $8,000 were purchased on account. What accounts are affected? (Expenditures are increased/debited and liabilities are increased/credited.)

	Assets	=	Liabilities	+	Fund Equity	+	Revenues	−	Expenditures
	dr | cr	=	dr | cr	+	dr | cr	+	dr | cr	−	dr | cr
(1)	30000 |	=	| 10000	+	| 20000	+	|	−	|
(2)	40000 |	=	|	+	|	+	| 40000	−	|
(3)	|	=	| 8000	+	|	+	|	−	8000 |
(T)	70000 |	=	| 18000	+	| 20000	+	| 40000	−	8000 |

Note: Transaction (3) has equal debits and credits ($8,000) and the totals (T) of debits and credits are equal ($78,000).

Example 4
Assume the school district borrows $15,000 from the bank. What accounts are affected? (Assets are increased/debited and liabilities are increased/credited.)

	Assets	=	Liabilities	+	Fund Equity	+	Revenues	−	Expenditures
	dr | cr	=	dr | cr	+	dr | cr	+	dr | cr	−	dr | cr
(1)	30000 |	=	| 10000	+	| 20000	+	|	−	|
(2)	40000 |	=	|	+	|	+	| 40000	−	|
(3)	|	=	| 8000	+	|	+	|	−	8000 |
(4)	15000 |	=	| 15000	+	|	+	|	−	|
(T)	85000 |	=	| 33000	+	| 20000	+	| 40000	−	8000 |

Note: Transaction (4) has equal debits and credits ($15,000) and the totals (T) of debits and credits are equal ($93,000).

Ilustration 4-1

Kimberly Hills School District
General Fund
Trial Balance
June 30, 1995

Accounts	Debits	Credits
Assets	$85,000	
Liabilities		$33,000
Fund Equity		20,000
Revenues		40,000
Expenditures	8,000	
Total	$93,000	$93,000

The Municipal Finance Officers Association (1980, p. 76) defines a trial balance as:

> a list of the balances of the accounts in a ledger kept in double entry, with the debit and credit balances shown in separate columns. If the totals of the debit and credit columns are equal or their net balance agrees with a control account, the ledger from which the figures are taken is said to be "in balance."

To prepare a trial balance, the following steps should be followed:

1. *Find* the total debits and total credits of each account. Make sure to include any beginning balance in the appropriate total.
2. *Determine* the account balance by calculating the difference between the debit and credit totals in each account.
3. *List* each account and its balance on paper that has two amount columns. Debit balances will be placed in the left column and credit balances in the right column.
4. *Compare* the sum of the two columns. (The sum of the column of debits should be equal to the sum of the column of credits.)

The trial balance as of June 30, 1995, for the Kimberly Hills School District in Example 4 is shown in Illustration 4-1.

SUMMARY

Debits and credits were defined and their use was illustrated in the accounting equation. Trial balance was defined and an example was given.

ACTIVITIES

1. Define each of the following terms:
   a. Debit (adjective, noun and verb)
   b. Credit (adjective, noun and verb)
   c. Trial balance
   d. T-account
   e. Compound entry
   f. Debit account
   g. Credit account
   h. Transaction

2. Give an example of a compound entry.

3. What is the purpose of preparing a trial balance?

4. Describe which accounts are to be debited and which are to be credited for each of the following transactions:
   a. General state aid is received.
   b. Teachers salaries are paid.
   c. Money is borrowed from the bank.
   d. A utility bill is paid
   e. Investments are purchased.
   f. Custodial salaries are paid.
   g. Investments are sold.
   h. A loan is repaid.
   i. Supplies are purchased for cash.
   j. Equipment is purchased on account.

5. Fort Steven School District began the year with assets of $95,000, no liabilities, and a fund equity of $95,000 in the general fund. During the year which ended June 30, 1995, the following transactions were completed:
   a. Property taxes were assessed and levied in the amount of $85,000.
   b. An amount of $65,000 was borrowed from the Fort Steven National Bank by means of tax anticipation warrants.
   c. Cash was received for the entire amount of the property tax levy as specified in transaction (a).
   d. Teachers salaries of $40,000 were paid.
   e. Supplies and materials in the amount of $35,000 were purchased on account.

f. Paid tax anticipation warrants of $50,000 (See transaction (b)).
g. Received $90,000 in general state aid.

Instructions:
- Record the beginning balances and enter the transactions in T-accounts.
- Prepare a trial balance.

6. The Markham City School System began the year with assets of $125,000, liabilities of $30,000 and a fund equity of $95,000 in the general fund. During the year which ended June 30, 1995, the following transactions were completed:
    a. Property taxes were assessed and levied in the amount of $75,000.
    b. A general state aid payment of $70,000 was received.
    c. A loan was obtained from the Markham City State Bank in the amount of $35,000.
    d. Tuition in the amount of $3,300 was collected.
    e. School property was sold for $5,500.
    f. Teacher salaries of $45,000 were paid.
    g. Equipment in the amount of $123,000 was purchased on account.
    h. Investments of $40,000 were sold for $30,000. (Loss on investments is an expenditure.)
    i. Heating costs of $12,000 were paid.
    j. Auditor's fee of $8,000 was paid.

Instructions:
- Record the beginning balances and enter the transactions in T-accounts.
- Prepare a trial balance.

7. Briancon School District began the year with assets of $220,000, some liabilities, and a fund equity of $85,000 in the general fund. During the year which ended June 30, 1995, the following transactions were completed:
    a. Property taxes were assessed and levied in the amount of the liabilities.
    b. Cash was received for the entire amount of the property tax levy.
    c. Cash was used to pay all liabilities.
    d. A loan was obtained from the Briancon National Bank in the amount of $135,000.

e. Equipment in the amount of $85,000 was purchased for cash from the Randyville Lawn and Garden Center.

Instructions:
- Record the beginning balances and enter the transactions in T-accounts.
- Prepare a trial balance.
- Prepare a statement of revenues, expenditures and fund equity.
- Prepare a balance sheet.

REFERENCES/SELECTED READINGS

Municipal Finance Officers Association. (1980). *Governmental accounting, auditing, and financial reporting.* Chicago, IL: Author.

Robert Davis Associates. (1981). *Principles of public school fund accounting.* Washington, DC: National Technical Information Service.

5

The General Ledger

INTRODUCTION

An organization, such as a school system, may have numerous accounting transactions during a month, week or day. In order to facilitate record keeping, it is necessary to identify all accounts the organization expects to use during the accounting period. The accounts should then be grouped by type of accounts and arranged in such a manner as to be similarly located across accounting periods.

The general ledger is the "book" that accommodates all accounts, grouped by type of account, which are necessary to reflect the financial operations of a school district.

OUTCOMES

In this chapter, you will learn how to:

1. Define general ledger.
2. Recognize accounts, grouped by type of account, within the general ledger.
3. Analyze financial transactions.
4. Debit and credit entries in the general ledger.
5. Obtain an account balance for accounts in the general ledger.

GENERAL LEDGER DEFINED

The National Center for Educational Statistics (Roberts and Lichtenberger, 1973) defines the general ledger as:

> a book, file, or other device in which accounts are kept to the degree of detail necessary, that summarized the financial transactions of the LEA [local education agency]. General

ledger accounts may be kept for any group of items of receipts or expenditures on which an administrative officer wishes to maintain a close check.

NCES (Barn, 1980) recommends the following accounts and account code numbers for asset, liability, fund equity, revenue and expenditure accounts.

ASSET CLASSIFICATION

Assets and other debits include what is owned and what is not owned but is expected to become fully owned at some future date.

- 100 Current Assets
    - 101 Cash in Bank
    - 102 Cash on Hand
    - 103 Petty Cash
    - 104 Change Cash
    - 105 Cash with Fiscal Agents
    - 111 Investments
    - 112 Unamortized Premiums on Investments
    - 113 Unamortized Discounts on Investments (Credit)
    - 114 Interest Receivable on Investments
    - 115 Accrued Interest on Investments Purchased
    - 121 Taxes Receivable
    - 122 Estimated Uncollectible Taxes (Credit)
    - 131 Interfund Loans Receivable
    - 132 Interfund Accounts Receivable
    - 141 Intergovernmental Accounts Receivable
    - 151 Loans Receivable
    - 152 Estimated Uncollectible Loans (Credits)
    - 153 Other Accounts Receivable
    - 154 Estimated Uncollectible Accounts Receivable (Credit)
    - 161 Bond Proceeds Receivable
    - 171 Inventories for Consumption
    - 172 Inventories for Resale
    - 181 Prepaid Expenses
    - 191 Deposits
    - 199 Other Current Assets
- 200 Fixed Assets
    - 211 Sites
    - 221 Site Improvements

      222   Accumulated Depreciation on Site Improvements
      231   Building and Building Improvements
      232   Accumulated Depreciation on Buildings and Building Improvements
      241   Machinery and Equipment
      242   Accumulated Depreciation on Machinery and Equipment
      251   Construction in Progress
300   Budgeting Accounts and Other Debits
      301   Estimated Revenues (Budget Account)
      302   Revenues
      303   Amount Available in Debt Service Funds
      304   Amount to be Provided for Retirement of General Long-Term Debt

LIABILITIES, RESERVES AND FUND BALANCE CLASSIFICATION

Liabilities, reserves and fund balance are LEA debts plus items that are not debts but which may become debts at some future time. Also included are other budgeting accounts that normally appear only on the interim financial statements.

400   Current Liabilities
      401   Interfund Loans Payable
      402   Interfund Accounts Payable
      411   Intergovernmental Accounts Payable
      421   Accounts Payable
      422   Judgments Payable
      423   Warrants Payable
      431   Contracts Payable
      432   Construction Contracts Payable-Retained Percentage
      433   Construction Contracts Payable
      441   Matured Bond Payable
      442   Bonds Payable
      443   Unamortized Premiums on Bonds Sold
      451   Loans Payable
      455   Interest Payable
      461   Accrued Salaries and Benefits
      471   Payroll Deductions and Withholdings
      481   Deferred Revenues
      491   Deposits Payable
      492   Due to Fiscal Agent

              499   Other Current Liabilities
       500   Long-Term Liabilities
              511   Bonds Payable
              521   Loans Payable
              531   Lease Obligations
              541   Unfunded Pension Liabilities
              590   Other Long-Term Liabilities
       600   Budgeting Accounts
              601   Appropriations (Budget Account)
              602   Expenditures/Expenses
              603   Encumbrances
       700   Fund Equity
              711   Investment in General Fixed Assets
              721   Contributed Capital
              730   Reserved-Retained Earnings
              740   Unreserved-Retained Earnings
              751   Reserve for Inventories
              752   Reserve for Prepaid Expenses
              753   Reserve for Encumbrances
              760   Reserved-Fund Balance
              770   Unreserved-Fund Balance

REVENUE AND OTHER FUND SOURCES CLASSIFICATION

Revenues are classified by type and source for the various funds of an LEA. Revenues are defined as additions to assets that do not increase any liability, do not represent the recovery of an expenditure, and do not represent the cancellation of certain liabilities which a corresponding increase in other liabilities or a decrease in assets.

       1000   Revenue from Local Sources
              1100   Taxes levied/assessed by the LEA
                     1110   Ad valorem taxes
                     1120   Sales and use taxes
                     1130   Income taxes
                     1140   Penalties and interest on taxes
                     1190   Other taxes
              1200   Revenue from local governmental units other than LEAs
                     1210   Ad valorem taxes
                     1220   Sales and use taxes
                     1230   Income taxes

1240 Penalties and interest on taxes
1280 Revenue in lieu of taxes
1290 Other taxes
1300 Tuition
    1310 Tuition from individuals
    1320 Tuition from other LEAs within the state
    1330 Tuition from other LEAs outside the state
    1340 Tuition from other sources
1400 Transportation fees
    1410 Transportation fees from individuals
    1420 Transportation fees from other LEAs within the state
    1430 Transportation fees from other LEAs outside the state
    1440 Transportation fees from other sources
1500 Earnings on investments
    1510 Interest on investments
    1520 Dividends on investments
    1530 Gains or losses on sale of investments
    1540 Earnings on investment in real property
1600 Food services
    1610 Daily sales–reimbursable programs
    1611 Daily sales–school lunch program
    1612 Daily sales–school breakfast program
    1613 Daily sales–special milk program
    1620 Daily sales–non-reimbursable programs
    1630 Special functions
1700 Student Activities
    1710 Admissions
    1720 Bookstore sales
    1730 Student organization membership dues and fees
    1740 Fees
    1790 Other student activity income
1800 Community services activities
1900 Other revenue from local sources
    1910 Rentals
    1920 Contributions and donations from private sources
    1930 Gains or losses on sale of fixed assets (proprietary funds only)
    1940 Textbook sales and rentals
    1941 Textbook sales

	1942	Textbook rentals
	1950	Services provided other LEAs
		1951 Services provided other LEAs within the state
		1952 Services provided other LEAs outside the state
	1960	Services provided other local governmental units
	1970	Services provided other funds
	1990	Miscellaneous
2000		Revenue From Intermediate Sources
	2100	Unrestricted grants-in-aid
	2200	Restricted grants-in-aid
	2800	Revenue in lieu of taxes
	2900	Revenue for/on behalf of the LEA
3000		Revenue From State Sources
	3100	Unrestricted grants-in-aid
	3200	Restricted grants-in-aid
	3800	Revenue in lieu of taxes
	3900	Revenue for/on behalf of the LEA
4000		Revenue From Federal Sources
	4100	Unrestricted grants-in-aid direct from the federal government
	4200	Unrestricted grants-in-aid from the federal government through the state
	4300	Restricted grants-in-aid direct from the federal government
	4500	Restricted grants-in-aid from the federal government through the state
	4700	Grants-in-aid from the federal government through other agencies
	4800	Revenue in lieu of taxes
	4900	Revenue for, or on behalf of, the LEA
5000		Other Sources (Governmental Funds Only)
	5100	Sale of bonds
		5110 Bond principal
		5120 Premium
		5130 Accrued interest
	5200	Interfund transfers
	5300	Sale or compensation for loss of fixed assets

EXPENDITURE CLASSIFICATION

Expenditures can be classified along several dimensions. Handbook II specifies the classifications that are essential to meet many of the important federal (and most state) reporting requirements that are found within the following dimensions:

Program
- Function
- Object
- Project/Reporting (formerly called Source of Funds)

EXPENDITURE CLASSIFICATION BY PROGRAM

A program is a plan of activities and procedures designed to accomplish a predetermined objective or set of objectives. This dimension provides LEAs the framework to classify expenditures to determine costs by program.

100 Regular Programs—Elementary/Secondary
200 Special Programs
    210 Mentally retarded
        211 Educable mentally retarded
        212 Trainable mentally retarded
    220 Physically handicapped
        221 Hard of hearing
        222 Deaf
        223 Deaf-blind
        224 Visually handicapped
        225 Speech impaired
        226 Crippled
        227 Other health impaired
    230 Emotionally disturbed
    240 Learning disabled
    250 Culturally deprived
    260 Bilingual
    270 Gifted and talented
300 Vocational Programs
    310 Agriculture
    320 Distributive education
    330 Health occupations
    340 Home economics
        341 Occupational
        342 Consumer and homemaking
    350 Industrial arts
    360 Office occupations
    370 Technical education

             380 Trades and industrial occupations
             390 Other vocational programs
      400 Other Instructional Programs—Elementary/Secondary
             410 School-sponsored co-curricular activities
             420 School-sponsored athletics
             490 Other
      500 Nonpublic school programs
      600 Adult/Continuing education programs
      700 Community/Junior college education programs
      800 Community services programs
             810 Community recreation
             820 Civic services
             830 Public library services
             840 Custody and child care services
             850 Welfare activities
             890 Other community services
      900 Enterprise Programs
             910 Food services
             990 Other enterprise programs
      000 Undistributed Expenditures

EXPENDITURE CLASSIFICATION BY FUNCTION

Handbook II describes the function dimension as follows:

> The function describes the activity being performed for which a service or material object is acquired. The functions of an LEA are classified into five broad areas: Instruction, Support Services, Operation of Non-Instructional Services, Facilities Acquisition and Construction Services, and Other Outlays. Functions and subfunctions consist of activities which have somewhat the same operational objectives. Furthermore, categories of activities comprising each of these divisions and subdivisions are grouped according to the principle that the activities should be combinable, comparable, relatable and mutually exclusive.

      1000 Instruction
      2000 Support Services
             2100 Support services — students
                    2110 Attendance and social work services
                    2120 Guidance services
                    2130 Health services

	2140	Psychological services
	2150	Speech pathology and audiology services
	2190	Other support services — students
2200	Support services — instructional staff	
	2210	Improvement of instruction services
	2220	Educational media services
	2290	Other support services — instructional staff
2300	Support services — general administration	
	2310	Board of education services
	2320	Executive administration services
	2330	Special area administration services
2400	Support services — school administration	
	2410	Office of principal services
2500	Support services — business	
	2510	Fiscal services
	2520	Purchasing services
	2530	Warehousing and distributing services
	2540	Printing, publishing and duplicating services
	2590	Other support services — business
2600	Operation and maintenance of plant services	
	2610	Operation of building services
	2620	Care and upkeep of grounds services
	2630	Care and upkeep of equipment services
	2640	Vehicle operation and maintenance services (Other than student transportation vehicles)
	2650	Security services
	2690	Other operation and maintenance of plant services
2700	Student transportation services	
	2710	Vehicle operation
	2720	Monitoring
	2730	Vehicle servicing and maintenance
	2790	Other student transportation services
2800	Support services — central	
	2810	Planning, research, development and evaluation services
	2820	Information services
	2830	Staff services
	2840	Data processing services
2900	Other support services	
3000	Operation of Non-Instructional Services	
3100	Foodservices operations	
3200	Other enterprise operations	

                3300   Community services operations
        4000   Facilities Acquisition and Construction Services
                4100   Site acquisition services
                4200   Site improvement services
                4300   Architecture and engineering services
                4400   Educational specifications development services
                4500   Building acquisition and construction services
                4600   Building improvements services
                4900   Other facilities acquisition and construction services
        5000   Other Uses (Governmental Funds Only)
                5100   Debt service
                5200   Fund transfers

EXPENDITURE CLASSIFICATION BY OBJECT

Handbook II describes "object" as the service or commodity obtained as a result of a specific expenditure. Major object categories are:

- Personnel Services—Salaries
- Personnel Services—Employee Benefits
- Purchased Professional and Technical Services
- Purchased Property Services
- Other Purchased Services, Supplies
- Property, and Other Objects.

Representative Object categories and corresponding code numbers are listed below.

        100   Personnel Services—Salaries
                110   Of regular employees
                120   Of temporary employees
                130   For overtime
                140   For sabbatical leave
        200   Personnel Services—Employee Benefits
                210   Group insurance
                220   Social security contributions
                230   Retirement contributions
                240   Tuition reimbursement
                250   Unemployment compensation
                260   Workers compensation
                290   Other employee benefits
        300   Purchased Professional and Technical Services
                310   Official/Administrative

	320	Professional/Educational
	330	Other professional
	340	Technical
400		Purchased Property Services
	410	Utility services
	420	Cleaning services
	430	Repair and maintenance services
	440	Rentals
	450	Construction services
	490	Other purchased property services
500		Other Purchased Services
	510	Student transportation services
	520	Insurance, other than employee benefits
	530	Communications
	540	Advertising
	550	Printing and binding
	560	Tuition
	570	Foodservice management
	580	Travel
	590	Miscellaneous purchased services
600		Supplies
	610	General supplies
	620	Energy
	630	Food
	640	Books and periodicals
700		Property
	710	Land and improvements (governmental funds only)
	720	Buildings (governmental funds only)
	730	Equipment (governmental funds only)
	740	Depreciation (proprietary funds only)
800		Other Objects
	810	Dues and fees
	820	Judgments against the LEA
	830	Interest
	840	Contingency (for budgeting purposes only)
	890	Miscellaneous expenditures
900		Other Uses of Funds (Governmental Funds Only)
	910	Redemption of principal
	920	Housing authority obligations
	930	Fund transfers

EXPENDITURE CLASSIFICATION BY PROJECT

Handbook II permits LEAs to account for and report separately, expenditures to meet a variety of specialized reporting requirements at local, state and federal levels. Refer to *Financial Accounting for Local and State School Systems 1990* (Fowler, 1990) for information regarding this classification.

ANALYSIS OF FINANCIAL TRANSACTIONS

According to Lynn and Thompson (1974):

> A *transaction* is an economic event that affects the asset or equities of a fund. The effects of the event must be recorded as changes in the accounting equation; that is, they must be recorded in the proper accounts. The recording of every transaction will be composed of an equal dollar amount of debits and credits.

The analysis of transactions involves the following questions:

1. What type of account(s) is (are) affected (asset, liability, fund equity, revenue, expenditure)?
2. What specific accounts are affected (cash in bank, accounts payable, unreserved—fund balance)?
3. What is the change (increase or decrease) in the account balance?
4. Does the increase or decrease in an account balance require a debit or credit entry?

The general ledger consists of all accounts, grouped by type of accounts, which are necessary to reflect the financial operations of each fund of a school district.

Accounts in the general ledger follow the order in which the accounts appear on the financial statements—assets, liabilities, fund equities, revenues and expenditures. The account form should provide for the following information:

1. The complete title of the account.
2. The code number of the account.
3. A column for the date of the transaction (year/month/day).
4. A column for explanation pertaining to the transaction.
5. A posting reference column (P.R.).

6. A column for the debit amount.
7. A column for the credit amount.

The format for the general ledger accounts that will be used in illustrations and activities is demonstrated in Examples 1 to 5.

		Name of account in full	Account No. XX		
Date	P.R.	Amount	Date	P.R.	Amount
01/01/94	J1	$9,999,999	02/02/94	J2	$8,888,888

Example 1
Assume that Kimberly Hills School District began the fiscal year 1994 with account balances as follows: cash in bank, $10,000; investments, $20,000; contracts payable, $10,000; and unreserved-fund balance, $20,000. Record the balances in the appropriate accounts.

		Cash in Bank	Account No. 101		
Date	P.R.	Amount	Date	P.R.	Amount
T1		$10,000			

		Investments	Account No. 111		
Date	P.R.	Amount	Date	P.R.	Amount
T1		$20,000			

		Contracts Payable	Account No. 431		
Date	P.R.	Amount	Date	P.R.	Amount
			T1		$10,000

		Unreserved Fund Balance	Account No. 770		
Date	P.R.	Amount	Date	P.R.	Amount
			T1		$20,000

Example 2
Assume that local property taxes are assessed and levied in the amount of $40,000.

		Cash in Bank	Account No. 101		
Date	P.R.	Amount	Date	P.R.	Amount
T1		$10,000			

14 • CHAPTER 5

		Investments		Account No. 111		
Date	P.R.	Amount		Date	P.R.	Amount
T1		$20,000				

		Taxes Receivable		Account No. 121		
Date	P.R.	Amount		Date	P.R.	Amount
T2		$40,000				

		Contracts Payable		Account No. 431		
Date	P.R.	Amount		Date	P.R.	Amount
				T1		$10,000

		Unreserved-Fund Balance		Account No. 770		
Date	P.R.	Amount		Date	P.R.	Amount
				T1		$20,000

		Revenue—Local Ad Valorem Taxes		Account No. 1110		
Date	P.R.	Amount		Date	P.R.	Amount
				T2		$40,000

Example 3
Assume general supplies in the amount of $8,000 were purchased on account:

		Cash in Bank		Account No. 101		
Date	P.R.	Amount		Date	P.R.	Amount
T1		$10,000				

		Investments		Account No. 111		
Date	P.R.	Amount		Date	P.R.	Amount
T1		$20,000				

		Taxes Receivable		Account No. 121		
Date	P.R.	Amount		Date	P.R.	Amount
T2		$40,000				

		Accounts Payable		Account No. 421		
Date	P.R.	Amount		Date	P.R.	Amount
				T3		$8,000

		Contracts Payable		Account No. 431		
Date	P.R.	Amount		Date	P.R.	Amount
				T1		$10,000

	Unreserved-Fund Balance		Account No. 770		
Date	P.R. Amount		Date T1	P.R.	Amount $20,000

	Revenue— Local Ad Valorem Taxes		Account No. 1110		
Date	P.R. Amount		Date T2	P.R.	Amount $40,000

	Expenditures—General Supplies		Account No. 610		
Date T3	P.R. Amount $8,000		Date	P.R.	Amount

Example 4
Received $120,000 in unrestricted grants-in-aid from the state:

	Cash in Bank		Account No. 101		
Date T1 T4	P.R. Amount $ 10,000 $120,000		Date	P.R.	Amount

	Investments		Account No. 111		
Date T1	P.R. Amount $20,000		Date	P.R.	Amount

	Taxes Receivable		Account No. 121		
Date T2	P.R. Amount $ 40,000		Date	P.R.	Amount

	Accounts Payable		Account No. 421		
Date	P.R. Amount		Date T3	P.R.	Amount $ 8,000

	Contracts Payable		Account No. 431		
Date	P.R. Amount		Date T1	P.R.	Amount $10,000

	Unreserved-Fund Balance		Account No. 770		
Date	P.R. Amount		Date T1	P.R.	Amount $20,000

	Revenue— Local Ad Valorem Taxes		Account No. 1110		
Date	P.R.	Amount	Date	P.R.	Amount
			T2		$40,000

	Revenue— State-Unrestricted Grant-in-Aid		Account No. 3100		
Date	P.R.	Amount	Date	P.R.	Amount
			T4		$120,000

	Expenditures—General Supplies		Account No. 610		
Date	P.R.	Amount	Date	P.R.	Amount
T3		$8,000			

Example 5
Paid salaries of regular employees in the amount of $30,000.

	Cash in Bank		Account No. 101		
Date	P.R.	Amount	Date	P.R.	Amount
T1		$ 10,000	T5		$30,000
T4		$120,000			

	Investments		Account No. 111		
Date	P.R.	Amount	Date	P.R.	Amount
T1		$20,000			

	Taxes Receivable		Account No. 121		
Date	P.R.	Amount	Date	P.R.	Amount
T2		$40,000			

	Accounts Payable		Account No. 421		
Date	P.R.	Amount	Date	P.R.	Amount
			T3		$ 8,000

	Contracts Payable		Account No. 431		
Date	P.R.	Amount	Date	P.R.	Amount
			T1		$10,000

	Unreserved-Fund Balance		Account No. 770		
Date	P.R.	Amount	Date	P.R.	Amount
			T1		$20,000

	Revenue— Local-Ad Valorem Taxes		Account No. 1110		
Date	P.R.	Amount	Date	P.R.	Amount
			T2		$40,000

	Revenue— State-Unrestricted Grant-in-Aid		Account No. 3100		
Date	P.R.	Amount	Date	P.R.	Amount
			T4		$120,000

	Expenditures— Salaries-Regular Employees		Account No. 110		
Date	P.R.	Amount	Date	P.R.	Amount
T5		$30,000			

	Expenditures—General Supplies		Account No. 610		
Date	P.R	Amount	Date	P.R.	Amount
T3		$ 8,000			

TRIAL BALANCE

The trial balance is prepared by computing the balance of each account or by summing the debits in each account and the credits in each account. If the sum of the debits exceeds the sum of the credits, then the difference is a debit balance. If the sum of the credits exceeds the sum of the debits, then the difference is a credit balance. The debit and credit balances of each account are used to prepare a trial balance. The trial balance for Kimberly Hills School District is shown in Illustration 5-1. Illustrations showing how the general ledger accounts are affected by transactions follow.

SUMMARY

General ledger was defined and accounts in the general ledger recommended by the National Center for Educational Statistics were presented. A methodology for analyzing financial transactions was presented. Debiting and crediting accounts in the general ledger were illustrated. Computational procedures for preparing a trial balance were presented.

Illustration 5-1

Kimberly Hills School District
General Fund
Trial Balance
(Date)

Cash in Bank	$100,000	
Investments	20,000	
Taxes receivable	40,000	
Accounts Payable		$ 8,000
Contracts Payable		10,000
Unreserved-Fund Balance		20,000
Revenue-Local-Ad Valorem Taxes		40,000
Revenue-State-Unrestricted Grants		120,000
Expenses-Salaries-Employees	30,000	
Expenses-General Supplies	8,000	
Total	$198,000	$198,000

ACTIVITIES

1. Study the definitions of the following terms as provided in the Glossary:
   a. General ledger
   b. Asset
   c. Current asset
   d. Fixed asset
   e. Liability
   f. Reserve
   g. Fund balance
   h. Debit balance
   i. Credit balance
   j. Current liability
   k. Long-Term liability
   l. Budgeting accounts
   m. Fund equity account
   n. Revenue type
   o. Revenue source
   p. Expenditures
   q. Program dimension
   r. Function dimension
   s. Object dimension
   t. Project/Reporting dimension

2. The Susanville School System had general ledger account balances in its general fund on July 1, 1994, as follows:

101	Cash in Bank	$30,000
111	Investments	180,000
121	Taxes Receivable	210,000
770	Unreserved-Fund Balance	420,000

The following transactions occurred during the year:
  a. Local property taxes of $250,000 were assessed and levied.
  b. General supplies were purchased on account for $20,000.
  c. General state aid in the amount of $145,000 was received.
  d. Collected $200,000 from taxes receivable.
  e. Paid salaries of regular employees, $215,000.
  f. Paid the full amount of accounts payable.
  g. Sold investments of $180,000 for $180,000.
  h. Paid for electricity in the amount of $8,500.
  i. Paid for natural gas in the amount of $4,800.
  j. Paid salaries of regular employees in the amount of $215,000.

Assume the chart of accounts for the school district consists of the following:
- Assets (code nos. 101,111,121)
- Liabilities (421)
- Fund equity (770)
- Revenue (1110, 3100)
- Expenditure (object codes 110, 610, 620)

Instructions:
- Record the beginning balances to the general ledger accounts.
- Record the transactions to the general ledger accounts.
- Prepare a trial balance for June 30,1995.

3. Janet Ridge School System began the fiscal year July 1, 1994 with the following account balances in the general fund:

101	Cash in Bank	$ 5,000
111	Investments	90,000
770	Unreserved-Fund Balance	95,000

During the year which ended June 30, 1995, the following transactions were completed:
  a. Local property taxes were assessed and levied in the amount of $85,000.

b. Cash was received for the entire amount of the local property tax levy of transaction a.
c. Local property taxes were assessed and levied in the amount of $70,000.
d. An amount of $65,000 was borrowed from the Cape Jennifer National Bank against anticipated tax revenues.
e. Cash was received for the amount of the property tax levy in transaction c.
f. Paid the amount due on the tax anticipation warrants issued in transaction d.
g. Paid regular teachers salaries of $40,000.
h. Purchased general supplies in the amount of $35,000.
i. Paid regular custodial salaries of $20,000.
j. Paid salaries of regular bus drivers in the amount of $15,000.

Assume the chart of accounts for the school district consists of the following:
- Assets (code nos. 101,111,121)
- Liabilities (423)
- Fund equity (770)
- Revenue (1110)
- Expenditure (object codes 110, 610)

Instructions:
- Record the beginning balances to the general ledger accounts.
- Record the transactions to the general ledger accounts.
- Prepare a trial balance for June 30, 1995.

4. Kimberly Hills School System began the fiscal year July 1, 1994, with the following account balances in the general fund:

101	Cash in Bank	$30,000
101	Cash in Bank	5,000
101	Cash in Bank	12,000
111	Investments	45,000
121	Taxes Receivable	33,000
770	Unreserved-Fund Balance	?????*

* To be computed by reader

During the year which ended June 30, 1995, the following transactions were completed:
a. Local property taxes were assessed and levied in the amount of $150,000.
b. Received $200,000 in general state aid.

c. Paid salary of instructional staff of the mentally retarded program in the amount of $58,000.
d. Purchased equipment for the vocational home economics program in the amount of $35,000.
e. Paid salary of the instructional staff of the bilingual program in the amount of $15,000.
f. Collected $120,000 of the taxes that were previously assessed and levied.
g. Purchased general supplies in the amount of $35,000 for the mentally retarded program.
h. Paid salary of $15,000 for custodian for the bilingual program area.
i. General supplies for the bilingual program were purchased on account in the amount of $6,000.
j. An amount of $65,000 was borrowed from the New Douglas State Bank against anticipated tax revenues.

Assume the chart of accounts for the school district consists of the following:
- Assets (101,111,121)
- Liabilities (421,423)
- Fund equity (770)
- Revenue (1110, 3100)
- Expenditures (program codes 210, 260, 340)

Instructions:
- Record the beginning balances to the general ledger accounts.
- Record the transactions to the general ledger accounts.
- Prepare a trial balance for June 30, 1995.
- Prepare a statement of revenues, expenditures and fund equity.
- Prepare a balance sheet.

REFERENCES/SELECTED READINGS

Barr, R.H. (1980). *Financial accounting for local and state school systems.* Washington, DC: Government Printing Office.

Fowler, W. J., Jr. (1990). *Financial accounting for local and state school systems.* Washington, DC: US Government Printing Office.

Lynn, E. S. & Thompson, J. W. (1974). *Introduction to fund accounting.* Reston, VA: Reston Publishing.

Municipal Finance Officers Association. (1980). *Governmental accounting, auditing, and financial reporting.* Chicago, IL: Author.

Robert Davis Associates. (1981). *Principles of public school fund accounting*. Washington, DC: National Technical Information Service.

Roberts, C. T. & Lichtenberger. (1973). *Financial accounting: Classification and standard terminnology for local and state school systems*. Washington, DC: U.S. Government Printing Office.

6

Journals

INTRODUCTION

The recording of debits and credits to separate accounts within the general ledger, as was done in the previous chapter, makes it difficult to reconstruct a given financial transaction after only a limited number of transactions. Obviously, a method is needed to facilitate tracing transactions over time. The journal is designed to fill this need.

OUTCOMES

In this chapter, you will learn how to:

1. Define the general journal.
2. Journalize financial transactions.
3. Post from the general journal to the general ledger.
4. Define special journals.
5. Record transactions in special journals.

GENERAL JOURNAL

The journal is the accounting record in which details of financial transactions are first recorded. Information is transferred from the general journal to the affected accounts in the general ledger.

Journal – A book of original entry. (MFOA, 1980)

The journal entry carries a summary of the transaction – date, the account(s) debited, the amount of the debit(s), the account(s) credited, the amount of the credit(s), and a brief description of the nature of the transaction.

The journal satisfies the need to have a chronological record of transactions. It also is the record from which postings are made to ledgers. The ledger contains all accounts of a particular fund (general ledger) or all detail accounts that support a particular general ledger account.

For purposes of illustration, the following conventions relating to the use of the general journal should be noted:

Date – a column for the date is provided where the year, month and day are to be entered.
Theory of debits and credits – the theory of debits and credits is applied to each transaction.
Debit entry – the debited part (all of the debits if a compound entry) of the entry is always recorded first and indented.
Credit entry – the credited part (all of the credits if a compound entry) of the entry is always recorded next and indented.
Explanation – each entry is supported with a brief explanation of the transaction.
Posting reference – a column for the posting reference in which the account number of the general ledger account is recorded after the transaction has been posted to that account.

The general journal is shown in Illustration 6-1.

POSTING TO THE GENERAL LEDGER

Posting is the process of transferring information from the general journal to the ledger accounts. A systematic process of posting can facilitate the reduction of errors that otherwise might occur. The following steps are recommended in posting from the general journal to the accounts in the general ledger:

1. Record in the proper ledger account
   a. the amount for the account cited in the journal
   b. the date of the transaction cited in the journal
   c. the page number of the general journal on which the transaction is listed. Enter the page number in the posting reference column of the general ledger account.
2. Record the account number of the ledger account in the posting reference column of the general journal.

Illustration 6-1

Kimberly Hills School District
General Fund
General Journal

Date	Account Titles	Post	Debit	Credit
BB	Cash in Bank		$ 10,000	
	Investments		20,000	
	Contracts Payable			$ 10,000
	Fund Balance-Unreserved			20,000
	To record beginning balances			
T1	Taxes Receivable		40,000	
	Revenue-Local-ad valorem tax			40,000
	To record levy of property tax			
T2	Expenditures–General Supplies		8,000	
	Accounts Payable			8,000
	To record purchase of supplies on account			
T3	Cash in Bank		120,000	
	Revenue–State–Unrestricted Grant-in-Aid			120,000
	To record receipt of general state aid.			
T4	Expenditures–Salaries–Regular Employees		40,000	
	Cash in bank			40,000
	To record payment of salaries			
T5	Accounts payable		6,000	
	Cash in bank			6,000
	To record payment on accounts payable			
T6	Cash in bank		35,000	
	Taxes receivable			35,000
	To record collection of taxes previously assessed and levied			
T7	Contracts payable		9,000	
	Cash in bank			9,000
	To record payment on contracts payable			

Illustration 6-2

Kimberly Hills School District
General Fund
General Journal

Date	Account Titles	Post	Debit	Credit
BB	Cash in Bank	101	$ 10,000	
	Investments	111	20,000	
	Contracts Payable	431		$ 10,000
	Fund Balance–Unreserved	770		20,000
	To record beginning balances			
T1	Taxes Receivable	121	40,000	
	Revenue–Local–ad valorem tax	1110		40,000
	To record levy of property tax			
T2	Expenditures–General Supplies	610	8,000	
	Accounts Payable	421		8,000
	To record purchase of supplies on account			
T3	Cash in Bank	101	120,000	
	Revenue–State–Unrestricted Grant-in-Aid	3100		120,000
	To record receipt of general state aid			
T4	Expenditures–Salaries–Regular Employees	110	40,000	
	Cash in bank	101		40,000
	To record payment of salaries			
T5	Accounts payable	421	6,000	
	Cash in bank	101		6,000
	To record payment on accounts payable			
T6	Cash in bank	101	35,000	
	Taxes receivable	121		35,000
	To record collection of taxes previously assessed and levied			
T7	Contracts payable	431	9,000	
	Cash in bank	101		9,000
	To record payment on contracts payable			

Illustration 6-2 shows transactions which have been recorded in the general journal and posted to the general ledger accounts. After posting to the general ledger accounts, account balances are determined as shown in Illustration 6-3. Illustration 6-4 presents a trial balance.

Illustration 6-3

Kimberly Hills School District
General Fund
General Ledger

		Cash in Bank		*Account No. 101*	
Date	P.R.	Amount	Date	P.R.	Amount
BB	1	$10,000	T4	1	$40,000
T3	1	120,000	T5	1	6,000
T6	1	35,000	T7	1	9,000

		Investments		*Account No. 111*	
Date	P.R.	Date	Date	P.R.	Amount
BB	1	$20,000			

		Taxes Receivable		*Account No. 121*	
Date	P.R.	Amount	Date	P.R.	Amount
T1	1	$40,000	T6	1	$35,000

		Accounts Payable		*Account No. 421*	
Date	P.R.	Amount	Date	P.R.	Amount
T5	1	$6,000	T2	1	$8,000

		Contracts Payable		*Account No. 431*	
Date	P.R.	Amount	Date	P.R.	Amount
T7	1	$9,000	BB	1	$10,000

		Unreserved–Fund Balance		*Account No. 770*	
Date	P.R.	Amount	Date	P.R.	Amount
			BB	1	$20,000

		Revenue–Local–Ad Valorem Taxes		*Account No. 1110*	
Date	P.R.	Amount	Date	P.R.	Amount
			T1	1	$40,000

		Revenues–State–Unrestricted Grants-in-Aid		*Account No. 3100*	
Date	P.R.	Amount	Date	P.R.	Amount
			T3	1	$120,000

		Expenditures–Salaries–Regular Employees		*Account No. 110*	
Date	P.R.	Amount	Date	P.R.	Amount
T4	1	$40,000			

		Expenditures-General Supplies		*Account No. 610*	
Date	P.R.	Amount	Date	P.R.	Amount
T2	1	$8,000			

Illustration 6-4

Kimberly Hills School District
General Fund
Trial Balance
(Date)

Cash in Bank	$110,000	
Investments	20,000	
Taxes Receivable	5,000	
Accounts Payable		$ 2,000
Contracts Payable		1,000
Unreserved Fund Balance		20,000
Revenue–Local–Ad Valorem Taxes		40,000
Revenue-State-Unrestricted Grants		120,000
Expenditures-Salaries-Regular Employees	40,000	
Expenditures-General Supplies	8,000	
	$183,000	$183,000

CASH RECEIPTS JOURNAL

In order to improve internal control in the accounting for numerous cash receipts, a cash receipts journal may be used to record these transactions. The cash receipts journal is not used to record all transactions, but is used to record the debit and credit entries associated with the numerous cash receipts transactions that a district frequently encounters during the accounting period. There are a wide variety of practices and procedures for handling cash receipts. One form for managing cash receipts is shown in Illustration 6-5.

CASH DISBURSEMENTS JOURNAL

Similar in nature to the cash receipts journal is the cash disbursements journal. As with the cash receipts journal, there are a variety of practices and procedures for handling cash disbursements. One form to facilitate handling of cash disbursement is shown as Illustration 6-6.

Illustration 6-5

Kimberly Hills School District
Cash Receipts Journal
For the Month of _____

Date	Explanation	P. R.	Revenue From Federal Sources	Revenue From State Sources	Revenue From Local Sources	Revenue From Property Taxes	Accounts Receivable	Taxes Receivable	Account Titles	Amount	Debit Cash

Illustration 6-6

Kimberly Hills School District
General Fund
Cash Disbursements Journal
For the Month of _____

Expenditures (602)		Other General Ledger Debits		Date	Explanation or Payee	Doc. Ref. No.	Other General Ledger Credits		Cash (101)	Encumbrance Liquidation Credit 601 Debit 701
Amount	Account Number	Amount	Acct. No.				Amount	Account No.		

SUMMARY

The purpose of the general journal was presented and data fields commonly occurring in the general journal were listed. Procedures were presented for posting to the general ledger. Examples of special journals, the cash receipts journal and the cash disbursements journal, were illustrated.

ACTIVITIES

1. Carefully review the definition of the following terms given in the glossary:
   a. General journal
   b. Journal
   c. Post
   d. General ledger
   e. Special journal
   f. Journal entry
   g. Debit entry
   h. Credit entry
   i. Cash receipts journal
   j. Posting reference

2. Use the transaction information from Activity 2 of Chapter 5.
   Instructions:
   - Journalize the transactions in the general journal.
   - Post the general journal transactions to the accounts in the general ledger.
   - Determine the account balances and prepare a trial balance.

3. Use the transaction information from Activity 3 of Chapter 5.
   Instructions:
   - Journalize the transactions in the general journal.
   - Post the general journal transactions to the accounts in the general ledger.
   - Determine the account balances and prepare a trial balance.

4. Use the transaction information from Activity 4 of Chapter 5.
   Instructions:
   - Journalize the transactions in the general journal.
   - Post the general journal transactions to the accounts in the general ledger.

- Determine the account balances and prepare a trial balance.

5. Fort Steven School District began the fiscal year July 1, 1995, with the following account balances in the general fund:

101	Cash in Bank	$ 14,750
111	Investments	175,000
121	Taxes Receivable	23,000
770	Unreserved Fund Balance	212,750

   The following transactions occurred during July:
   a. Local property taxes of $350,000 were assessed and levied.
   b. The district borrowed $120,000 from the First National Bank of Fort Steven by means of tax anticipation warrants.
   c. The district received equipment for which it was billed $40,000.
   d. The district paid regular instructional employees $114,500.
   e. The district received $370,000 for payment of property taxes which were previously assessed and levied. (Note: Tax anticipation warrants must be paid as soon as tax monies are received.)
   f. The district paid for equipment received in transaction c.
   g. The district paid regular custodial employees $23,750.
   h. The district purchased equipment on account in the amount of $80,000.
   i. Defective equipment in the amount of $15,000 was returned for credit.
   j. The district paid $45,000 on outstanding accounts.

   Assume the chart of accounts for the school district consists of the following:
   - Assets (code nos. 101, 111, and 121)
   - Liabilities (code nos. 421 and 423)
   - Fund Equity (code no. 770)
   - Revenue (code no. 1110)
   - Expenditures (object code nos. 110 and 730)

   Instructions:
   - Journalize the beginning balances and the transactions for the month of July in the general journal.
   - Post the general journal transactions to the account in the general ledger.

- Determine the account balances and prepare a trial balance as of July 31, 1995.

REFERENCES/SELECTED READINGS

Lynn, E. S. & Thompson, J.W. (1974) . Reston, VA: Reston Publishing.

Robert Davis Associates. (1981). Washington: National Technical Information Service.

Tidwell, S. B. (1974). Chicago, IL: The Research Corporation, Association of School Business Officials.

7

Revenue Accounting

INTRODUCTION

Revenue is an increase in assets or a decrease in liabilities that increases the fund equity. Some revenue results in increases in cash, however the accrual basis of accounting does recognize revenue without the receipt of cash. The budget is a plan of financial operation for a school district. As part of the plan, it is necessary to know the amount of estimated revenue and the amount of actual revenue.

OUTCOMES

In this chapter, you will learn how to:

1. Define revenue.
2. Distinguish between actual revenue and estimated revenue.
3. Identify the different revenue classifications.
4. Make allowances for estimated uncollectible taxes.

REVENUE DEFINED

Revenue is defined as an addition to assets that does not increase any liability, does not represent the recovery of an expenditure, and does not represent the cancellation of certain liabilities without a corresponding increase in other liabilities or a decrease in assets (Fowler, 1990).

Budgetary accounts are those accounts necessary to reflect budget operations and conditions, such as estimated revenues, appropriations and encumbrances, as distinguished from proprietary accounts. Proprietary accounts are those accounts that show actual financial conditions and operations such as actual assets, liabilities, reserves, revenues and expenditures.

In this chapter, the topics of estimated revenue and actual revenue will be discussed. Discussion of appropriations, encumbrances and expenditures will be presented in the next chapter.

Estimated revenue represents the amount of revenue expected to be received or to become receivable during the fiscal period. At the end of the fiscal period, estimated revenue is closed out and does not appear in the balance sheet. *Actual revenue* represents the amount of revenue actually realized during a period and represents the increase in ownership equity during that period. Revenue appears only in balance sheets prepared during the fiscal period (interim balance sheets). At the end of the fiscal period, revenue is closed into the unreserved fund balance and does not appear in the balance sheet prepared at the end of the year.

In order to conveniently display relevant information, the general ledger account form for revenues is altered to permit the recording of estimated revenue, actual revenue and the unrealized balance on the same form. Conceptually, the unrealized revenue balance is the difference between the estimated revenue and actual revenue.

A modified ledger account form for the display of estimated revenue, actual revenue and the unrealized balance of revenue is shown in Illustration 7-1.

Illustration 7-1
Modified Form for Revenue Ledger Account

Revenue Account: Local Ad Valorem Taxes — Account No. 1110

Date	Explanation	P.R.	Estimated Revenue Dr.	Estimated Revenue Cr.	Actual Revenue Dr.	Actual Revenue Cr.	Unrealized Balance
T1	To adopt budget	1	$100,000				$100,000
T2	To record levy	2				$90,000	10,000

TAXES RECEIVABLE AND ESTIMATED UNCOLLECTIBLE TAXES

At the time taxes are assessed and levied, an entry is made in the general journal to indicate a debit to taxes receivable and a credit to revenue from taxes. Only the "eternal optimist" would expect that the entire amount of taxes assessed and levied would be collected. Therefore, experience dictates that one should make allowance for uncollectible taxes. The allowance for the amount of uncollectible taxes should be based upon past experience and knowledge of expected departures from previous collection and distribution practices. A typical entry to show that taxes had been assessed and levied, and that allowance had been made for estimated uncollectible taxes is as follows:

Taxes receivable	$100,000	
Estimated uncollectible taxes		$ 3,000
Revenue from taxes		97,000
To record assessment and levy of taxes		

When taxes receivable are collected, the following entry is noted in the general journal to record collection of taxes receivable:

Cash	$60,000	
Taxes receivable		$60,000
To record collection of taxes receivable		

If an additional $40,000 were collected in taxes receivable, then the following entry would be made in the general journal:

Cash	$40,000	
Estimated uncollectible taxes	3,000	
Taxes receivable		$40,000
Revenue from taxes		3,000
To record collection of taxes receivable and to adjust the amount of the estimate of uncollectible taxes and the amount of revenue from taxes		

If $30,000 in taxes receivable had been collected instead of $40,000, then the entry to the general journal would be as follows:

Cash	$30,000	
Taxes receivable		$30,000
To record collection of taxes receivable		

The balance sheet should reflect the effect of estimated uncollectible taxes on the assets of the LEA. For example, after the collection of $60,000 and $30,000 in taxes receivable of the $100,000 in taxes that were assessed and levied, the balance sheet would show the following:

Taxes receivable	$10,000	
Less estimated uncollectible taxes	3,000	$7,000

If taxes are determined to be uncollectible and it is decided to write off the balance of taxes receivable, then the following entry should be made in the general journal:

Estimated uncollectible taxes	$3,000	
Revenue from taxes	7,000	
Taxes receivable		$10,000
To write off remainder of taxes receivable		

RECORDING ESTIMATED REVENUE AND ACTUAL REVENUE

At the time the budget is adopted, estimated revenue is recorded for each revenue source. As soon as revenue is actually realized, the unrealized balance would be reduced by the amount of actual revenue. For example, if taxes were assessed and levied in the amount of $30,000, then the general journal entry would indicate a debit to taxes receivable and a credit to actual revenue for ad valorem taxes. The modified revenue ledger form would indicate the posted transaction as follows:

Revenue Account: Local Ad Valorem Taxes   Account No. 1110

Date	Explanation	P.R.	Estimated Revenue Dr.	Cr.	Actual Revenue Dr.	Cr.	Unrealized Balance
T1	To adopt budget	1	$45,000				$45,000
T2	To record levy	2				$30,000	15,000

There are many sources of revenue and it is necessary to maintain an account for each revenue source. In order to reduce the "size" of the general ledger, subsidiary control accounts and subsidiary ledgers are used for revenue. The subsidiary control accounts for revenue (budgeting accounts for interim reporting only) are as follows:

- Estimated Revenue   Acct. No. 301
- Revenue   Acct. No. 302

Handbook II defines these budgetary accounts:

Estimated Revenue (Budget Account) (Account No. 301)
The amount of revenue estimated to be received or to become receivable during the fiscal period. At the end of the fiscal period, the amount is closed out and does not appear in the balance sheet. This account would appear in interim financial statements.

Revenue (Account No. 302)
The total of all revenue actually realized during a period. This represents the increase in ownership equity during a designated period of time. The account appears only in a balance sheet prepared during the fiscal period. At the end of the fiscal period, the account is closed out and does not appear in the balance sheet.

The subsidiary control accounts for revenue (301 and 302) are used as summary accounts. That is, the balances in these accounts are summaries of the balances in the detailed revenue accounts maintained in separate subsidiary ledgers. For example, revenue received from the federal government, the state, and from local sources is posted in total to the revenue control account (Account 302). However, it is also necessary to keep a record of revenue from each source—federal, state, and local. Therefore, a subsidiary revenue ledger is maintained that contains an account for each source of revenue in order to provide the detailed record needed. This ledger is called the revenue subsidiary ledger, or simply, the revenue ledger. At all times the total revenue shown in the general ledger revenue control account should equal the total of the revenue amounts posted in the revenue ledger. When posting an item or items for which there is a control account, one would post the total to the control account and then post the individual amount(s) to the proper accounts in the subsidiary ledger.

The use of the revenue control account and the subsidiary revenue is shown in Illustration 7-1.

Illustration 7-1

Kimberly Hills School District adopted the following budget:

Revenue–Local (Acct. No. 1100)	$50,000
Revenue–State (Acct. No. 3100)	50,000
Revenue–Federal (Acct. No. 4800)	100,000

Assume that Kimberly Hills School Disctrict receives revenue from the following sources:

Federal–Revenue in lieu of taxes (Acct. No. 4800)	$20,000
State–Unrestricted grant (Acct. No. 3100)	25,000
Local–Ad valorem tax (Acct. No. 1100)	40,000

Kimberly Hills School District
General Fund
General Journal

Page 1

Date	Account Titles	Post	Debit	Credit
T1	Cash in Bank		$20,000	
	Actual Revenue			$20,000
	To record collection of revenues			
	Federal sources: Revenue in lieu of taxes			
T2	Cash in Bank		25,000	
	Actual Revenues			25,000
	To record collection of revenues			
	State sources: Unrestricted grant-in-aid			
T3	Cash in Bank		40,000	
	Actual Revenue			40,000
	To record collection of revenues			
	Local sources: Ad valorem Taxes			

Illustration 7-2

Kimberly Hills School District
General Fund
General Journal

			Cash in Bank		Account No. 101		
Date	Explanation	P.R.	Amount	Date	Explanation	P.R.	Amount
T1			$20,000				
T2			$25,000				
T3			$40,000				

			Revenue		Account No. 302		
Date	Explanation	P.R.	Amount	Date	Explanation	P.R.	Amount
				T1			$20,000
				T2			$25,000
				T3			$40,000

Illustration 7-3

Revenue (Control)

Estimated Revenue Account No. 301
Revenue Account No. 302

Date	Explanation	P.R.	Estimated Revenue Dr.	Cr.	Actual Revenue Dr.	Cr.	Unrealized Balance
BB			$200,000				$200,000
T1						$20,000	180,000
T2						25,000	155,000
T3						40,000	115,000

Illustration 7-4

Revenue Federal: Revenue in lieu of taxes   Account No. 4800

Date	Explanation	P.R.	Estimated Revenue Dr.	Cr.	Actual Revenue Dr.	Cr.	Unrealized Balance
BB			$100,000				$100,000
T1						$20,000	80,000

Revenue State: Unrestricted grant   Account No. 3100

Date	Explanation	P.R.	Estimated Revenue Dr.	Cr.	Actual Revenue Dr.	Cr.	Unrealized Balance
BB			$50,000				$50,000
T2						$25,000	25,000

Revenue Local: Ad valorem tax   Account No. 1100

Date	Explanation	P.R.	Estimated Revenue Dr.	Cr.	Actual Revenue Dr.	Cr.	Unrealized Balance
BB			$50,000				$50,000
T3						$40,000	10,000

After posting the transactions from the general journal to the appropriate accounts in the general ledger, the general ledger should appear as shown in Illustration 7-2. The revenue control account can also take the modified form of a revenue account to display estimated revenue, actual revenue and the unrealized balance as shown in Illustration 7-3. The revenue (subsidiary) ledger would appear as shown in Illustration 7-4.

Illustration 7-5

Kimberly Hills School District
General Fund
Interim Statement of Revenue
For the period July 1, 1995 through July 31, 1995

Revenue from:		Estimated Revenue	Revenue	Unrealized Revenue
1110	Local–ad valorem tax	$50,000	$40,000	$10,000
3100	State–Unrestricted grant	50,000	25,000	25,000
4800	Federal–Revenue in lieu of taxes	100,000	20,000	80,000
	Total	$200,000	$85,000	$115,000

INTERIM STATEMENT OF REVENUE

Interim financial statements may be prepared during the year to provide information to administrators and board members. The interim statement of revenue is shown in Illustration 7-5 for the month of July 1995 but could be for any interim period.

SUMMARY

Revenue was defined. Procedures were illustrated for recording actual revenue and estimated revenue. The use of revenue subsidiary ledgers and revenue control accounts was presented. Procedures for accounting for uncollectible taxes were shown. The interim statement of revenue was illustrated.

ACTIVITIES

1. Carefully review the definition of the following terms given in the glossary:
   a. Revenue
   b. Estimated revenue
   c. Actual revenue
   d. Proprietary accounts
   e. Subsidiary control account for revenue
   f. Revenue subsidiary ledger

2. Review procedures for handling estimated revenue and actual revenue. Obtain copies of relevant subsidiary ledgers from your school district.

3. The following transactions occurred during the fiscal year in Timton School District:
   T1: Property taxes were levied in the amount of $100,000. It is estimated that 3 percent of these taxes will be uncollectible.
   T2: The district received $44,000 in payment of property taxes previously levied (T1).
   T3: Unrestricted grant-in-aid from the state was received in the amount of $30,000.
   T4: Tuition in the amount of $4,000 was collected.
   T5: Earning on investments in the amount of $3,000 was received.
   T6: Revenue in lieu of taxes from the federal government was received in the amount of $9,000.
   T7: The district received $47,000 in payment of property taxes previously levied (T1).
   T8: Tuition in the amount of $6,000 was collected.
   T9: Unrestricted grant-in-aid from the state was received in the amount of $45,000.
   T10: Revenue in lieu of taxes from the federal government was received in the amount of $15,000.

Instructions:
- Record all transactions in the general journal.
- Post all general journal entries to the general ledger and to the revenue ledger.
- Prepare an interim statement of revenues.

4. During the fiscal year, the following transactions were completed in the general fund in Randyville School District:
   T1: Property taxes were assessed and levied in the amount of $270,000 and past history indicates 10 percent of local property taxes will be uncollectible.
   T2: The district received $125,000 in payment of property taxes previously assessed and levied (T1).
   T3: Unrestricted grant-in-aid from the state was received in the amount of $45,000.
   T4: Received $100,000 in collections from property taxes assessed and levied (T1).
   T5: A general state aid payment of $70,000 was received.

T6: Revenue in lieu of taxes from the federal government was received in the amount of $75,000.
T7: The district received $22,000 in payment of property taxes previously levied (T1).
T8: Tuition in the amount of $6,000 was collected.
T9: Unrestricted grant-in-aid from the state was received in the amount of $65,000.
T10: Revenue in lieu of taxes from the federal government was received in the amount of $65,000.

Instructions:
- Record all transactions in the general journal.
- Post all general journal entries to the general ledger and to the revenue ledger.
- Prepare an interim statement of revenues.

5. From July 1, 1995, to September 30, 1995, the following transactions were completed in the general fund of New Douglas School District:

T1: Property taxes were assessed and levied in the amount of $147,000. It is estimated that 5 percent of local property taxes will be uncollectible.
T2: The district received $145,000 in payment of property taxes previously assessed and levied (T1).
T3: Unrestricted grant-in-aid from the state was received in the amount of $44,000.
T4: State revenue in lieu of taxes in the amount of $15,000 was received.
T5: A general state aid payment of $120,000 was received.
T6: Revenue in lieu of taxes from the federal government was received in the amount of $45,000.
T7: Tuition from students in the amount of $24,000 was received.
T8: State revenue in lieu of taxes in the amount of $12,000 was received.
T9: Unrestricted grant-in-aid from the state was received in the amount of $110,000.
T10: Revenue in lieu of taxes from the federal government was received in the amount of $22,000.

Instructions:
- Record all transactions in the general journal.
- Post all general journal entries to the general ledger and to the revenue ledger.
- Prepare an interim statement of revenues.

REFERENCES/SELECTED READINGS

Fowler, W. J., Jr. (1990). *Financial accounting for local and state school systems.* Washington, DC: U. S. Government Printing Office.

Tidwell, S. B. (1974). *Financial and managerial accounting for elementary and secondary school systems.* Chicago, IL: Research Corporation of the Association of School Business Officials.

8

Expenditure Accounting

INTRODUCTION

Expenditures are charges incurred, whether paid or unpaid, which are presumed to benefit the current fiscal year. Some expenditures are paid with decreases in cash, however, the accrual basis of accounting does recognize expenditures without decreases in cash. Just as revenue is part of the plan of financial operation for a school district, so are expenditures. As part of the budget, or financial plan, it is necessary to know about appropriations, expenditures/expenses, encumbrances and reserve for encumbrances.

OUTCOMES

In this chapter, you will learn how to:

1. Define expenditures.
2. Distinguish between appropriations, expenditures, encumbrances and reserve for encumbrances.
3. Identify the different expenditure dimensions.
4. Make debit and credit entries to the appropriate accounts.

EXPENDITURE DEFINED

Expenditures are decreases of net financial resources (MFOA, 1980). Expenditures include current operating expenses that require the current or future use of net assets.

As stated in the previous chapter, budgetary accounts are those accounts necessary to reflect budget operations and conditions, such as revenue, appropriations and encumbrances, as distinguished from proprietary accounts. Proprietary accounts are those accounts that show actual financial conditions and operations such as actual assets, liabilities, reserves, revenues and expenditures.

In the previous chapter, revenue and estimated revenue were discussed. In this chapter, the discussion continues with appropriations (budget account), expenditures, encumbrances and reserve for encumbrance.

Appropriations (Budget Account) – Account No. 601. This account records authorizations granted by the school board or legislative body to make expenditures for specific purposes. This account appears in a balance sheet prepared *during* the fiscal period. It is closed out and does not appear in the balance sheet prepared at the close of the fiscal period.

Expenditures/Expenses – Account No. 602. This account appears in balance sheets prepared during the fiscal period and designates the total expenditures (or operating expenses in proprietary funds) charged against appropriations during this period. The expenditure account is shown in each governmental fund balance sheet as a deduction from the appropriations account to arrive at the unexpended balance of total appropriations.

Encumbrances – Account No. 603. This account designates obligations in the form of purchase orders, contracts or salary commitments chargeable to an appropriation and for which part of the appropriation is reserved. In an interim balance sheet, encumbrances are deducted, along with the expenditures from the appropriations account, to arrive at the unexpended balance of total appropriations.

Reserve for Encumbrances – Account No. 753. This is a reserve representing that portion of a fund balance segregated to provide for unliquidated encumbrances. Separate accounts may be maintained for current encumbrances and prior year encumbrances.

The expenditure subsidiary control accounts (601, 602, and 603) and the reserve for encumbrance account (753) are normally used as summary or control accounts. This simply means that the balances in these accounts are summaries of the balances of the detailed budget, expenditure or encumbrance accounts maintained in separate subsidiary ledgers. The subsidiary expenditure ledger should be summarized in the expenditure control account of the general ledger.

THE ENCUMBRANCE SYSTEM

In order to keep track of purchase orders and contracts outstanding, it is recommended that the encumbrance control account (603), and the appropriate subsidiary account, be charged, and the reserve for encumbrance account (753) credited, as each purchase order or contract is issued. When goods or services are received, two entries are necessary: (1) reserve for encumbrance (753) is debited, and encumbrances (603) and the proper subsidiary account are credited for the appropriate amount; and (2) expenditure control (602) and the proper subsidiary accounts are debited, and a liability account is credited for the amount to be paid to the creditor.

The following transactions demonstrate the sequence described above:

1. A purchase order is issued for $25,000.
    Encumbrances $25,000
        Reserve for Encumbrance $25,000
    To record issuance of a purchase order

2. The goods are received and the invoice is in the amount of $30,000.
    a. Reserve for Encumbrance $25,000
        Encumbrance $25,000
    To reverse the encumbrance in the amount of the purchase order

    b. Expenditures $30,000
        Accounts Payable $30,000
    To record an expenditure in the amount of the invoice

It is not unusual for the amount of the invoice to be different from the amount of the purchase order. This does not present a problem. Simply reverse the encumbrance account and the reserve for encumbrance account in the amount of the purchase order. After receipt of the invoice and a disbursement is made or a liability is created, the expenditure account is charged and the encumbrance account ceases to be necessary to reserve the appropriation.

INTERIM FINANCIAL REPORTS

Interim financial statements may be prepared during the year to provide information to administrators and board members. The interim statement comparing expenditures and encumbrances with appropriations is shown in Illustration 8-1.

Illustration 8-1

Kimberly Hills School District
**General Fund
Interim Statement Comparing
Expenditures and Encumbrances with Appropriations**
For the Period July 1, 1995 through September 30, 1995

Account Code	Account Title	Appropri- ations	Expendi- tures	Encum- brances	Unencumbered Balance
110	Regular Salaries	$40,000	$20,000	$ 5,000	$15,000
210	Group Insurance	14,000	14,000	-0-	-0-
580	Travel	10,000	2,000	4,000	4,000
610	General Supplies	12,000	8,000	1,000	3,000
620	Energy	9,000	5,000	3,000	1,000
	Total	$85,000	$49,000	$13,000	$23,000

SUMMARY

Expenditures, encumbrances and reserve for encumbrances were defined. Procedures were illustrated for recording encumbrances, reserve for encumbrances and expenditures. The use of expenditure subsidiary ledgers and expenditure control accounts were presented. The interim statement comparing expenditures and encumbrances with appropriations was illustrated.

ACTIVITIES

1. Carefully review the definition of the following terms given in the glossary:
   a. Appropriation
   b. Encumbrances
   c. Expenditures/expenses
   d. Accrual basis
   e. Reserve for encumbrances
   f. Budgetary account

2. The following appropriations were approved in Timton School District at the beginning of the fiscal year:

110	Regular Salaries	$350,000
210	Group Insurance	5,000
610	General Supplies	20,000
620	Energy	10,000
640	Books and Periodicals	20,000

The following transactions occurred during the year:

T1: An order was placed for general supplies estimated to cost $10,000.
T2: The material ordered in T1 was received and the actual cost was $12,000.
T3: Salaries were paid in the amount of $20,000.
T4: Salaries in the amount of $10,000 were paid.
T5: Group insurance in the amount of $3,000 was paid.
T6: Purchased general supplies on account in the amount of $3,000.
T7: Paid regular teacher salaries of $115,000.
T8: Regular teacher salaries were paid in the amount of $90,000.
T9: General supplies in the amount of $1,000 were purchased on account.
T10: Paid regular teacher salaries in the amount of $45,000.

Instructions:
- Record the budget as adopted in the general journal.
- Record all transactions in the general journal.
- Post all general journal entries to the general ledger and to the expenditure ledger.
- Prepare an interim statement comparing expenditures and encumbrances to appropriations.

3. The general ledger account balances in the general fund of the New Douglas School District at the beginning of the fiscal year were:

Cash in Bank	$200,000
Investments	150,000
Accounts Payable	85,000
Contracts Payable	45,000
Unreserved Fund Balance	220,000

The New Douglas School District approved the following appropriation on the first day of the fiscal year:

110	Regular Salaries	$85,000
210	Group Insurance	11,000
610	General Supplies	32,000
620	Energy	44,000
640	Books & Periodicals	45,000

The following transactions occurred during the fiscal year:

- T1: A purchase order, in the amount of $31,000, was issued for general supplies.
- T2: The general supplies ordered in T1 were received and the actual cost was $35,500.
- T3: Salaries were paid in the amount of $3,750.
- T4: Salaries were paid in the amount of $54,000.
- T5: Group insurance in the amount of $12,000 was paid.
- T6: Periodical subscriptions in the amount of $14,000 were issued.
- T7: A purchase order, in the amount of $9,000, was issued for books.
- T8: The books ordered in T7 were received and the actual cost was $8,500.
- T9: Charges for electricity in the amount of $11,000 were paid.
- T10: A purchase order for paper supplies was issued in the amount of $6,000.

Instructions:
- Enter the account balances in the ledger accounts.
- Record the appropriations in the general journal.
- Record all transactions in the general journal.
- Post all general journal entries to the general ledger and to the expenditure ledger.
- Prepare an interim statement of expenditures and encumbrances compared with appropriations.

REFERENCES/SELECTED READINGS

Fowler, W.J., Jr. (1990). *Financial accounting for local and state school systems, 1990.* Washington, DC: U. S. Government Printing Office.

Tidwell, S. B. (1974). *Financial and managerial accounting for elementary and secondary school systems.* Chicago, IL: Research Corporation of the Association of School Business Officials.

9

Special Entries

INTRODUCTION

The budget is a plan of financial operation for a school district. The budget details all sources of revenue and all objects of expenditure. Therefore it is necessary to record the financial detail contained in the budget document in the general journal.

Likewise, closing the books to provide for separation of transactions into fiscal periods requires certain entries to the general journal. In order that results of operation can be determined at the end of the fiscal year, all revenue and expenditure accounts must be summarized. The use of "closing accounts" facilitates this procedure.

OUTCOMES

In this chapter, you will learn how to:

1. Record the budget.
2. Record closing entries.
3. Prepare a post closing trial balance.

BUDGET ADOPTION

When the budget is adopted, the resolution contains a list of sources and amounts of revenue the school district expects to receive during the fiscal year. In addition, the resolution contains a list of appropriations for objects of expenditure to be made during that period.

Budgetary accounts are temporary accounts, since they record estimates of revenues and expenditures for a specified period of time. At the end of the accounting period the temporary accounts are closed.

In simplest terms, the budget could specify estimated revenues (without regard for source) and appropriations (without regard for object).

General journal entries, such as the following, may record the budget in budgetary accounts:

Estimated revenue	$50,000	
Fund equity		$50,000
To record estimated revenues		
Fund equity	45,000	
Appropriations		45,000
To record appropriations		

Unless there are unforeseen changes in estimated revenues and appropriations, these budgetary accounts will remain unchanged until the end of the fiscal year. At the end of the year these budgetary accounts are closed. To illustrate the closing process, the estimated revenue accounts and the appropriations accounts will be taken separately.

At the end of the accounting period, each actual revenue account is closed into its corresponding estimated revenue account (revenue from taxes into estimated revenue from taxes; revenue from tuition into estimated revenue from tuition; and revenue from state sources into estimated revenue from state sources).

For purposes of illustration, assume that the actual revenue received was $40,000 of the estimated $50,000. The closing entries for estimated revenue would be as follows:

Revenue	$40,000	
Estimated revenue		$40,000
To close the revenue account into		
the estimated revenue account		
Fund equity	10,000	
Estimated revenue		10,000
To close the estimated revenue		
account into the fund equity at		
the end of the fiscal period		

CLOSING ENTRIES

During the fiscal year, transactions in the general fund are analyzed, recorded in the general journal, posted to accounts in the general ledger, account balances are determined, and work sheet and financial statements are prepared. What happens at the end of the fiscal year? How does one "end" or "close the books" of one fiscal year and "start" or "open the books" to another fiscal year?

The objective of the closing process is to transfer balances from "temporary accounts" (i.e., revenues and expenditures) into the fund balance account at the end of the fiscal year (or accounting period). Although there are several different ways of making the closing entries, the method to be used in this text is simple and direct. The procedure is a straightforward two-step process:

- Close each revenue account into the unreserved fund balance account.
- Close each expenditure account into the unreserved fund balance account.

A necessary procedure at the end of the fiscal year is to "close the books." This implies recording the necessary entries in the general journal to close out revenue and expenditure accounts that have been active during the year. These temporary accounts are closed into the fund balance account to obtain the actual end-of-the-year fund balance. After the temporary accounts have been closed, the only accounts in the general ledger which will have a non-zero balance are assets, liabilities, and fund balance accounts.

At the end of the fiscal year, a pre-closing trail balance should be prepared to check the equality of debits and credits prior to recording the closing entries. The pre-closing trial balance will probably contain non-zero balances for assets, liabilities, fund balances, revenues and expenditures. If the trial balance indicates equality of debits and credits, then the process of "closing the books" may begin.

Revenue accounts will normally have a credit balance. Therefore, in order to close out a revenue account the account should be debited in the amount of the credit balance and the unreserved fund balance account should be credited for this amount. Since the revenue account has been debited in the amount of the credit balance, the new

Illustration 9-1

Kimberly Hills School District
General Fund
General Ledger

		Cash in Bank		Account No. 101		
Date	P.R.	Amount		Date	P.R.	Amount
BB		$75,000				

		Investments		Account No. 111		
Date	P.R.	Amount		Date	P.R.	Amount
BB		$125,000				

		Unreserved Fund Balance		Account No. 770		
Date	P.R.	Amount		Date	P.R.	Amount
				BB		$180,000

		Revenue-local-ad valorem tax		Account No. 1110		
Date	P.R.	Amount		Date	P.R.	Amount
				BB		$230,000

		Expenditures-salaries-regular		Account No. 110		
Date	P.R.	Amount		Date	P.R.	Amount
BB		$210,000				

balance in the revenue account is <u>zero</u>. If the balance at the end-of-the-year is zero, the account is said to be closed.

Expenditure accounts will normally have a debit balance. Therefore, in order to close out an expenditure account (produce a zero balance) the account should be credited in the amount of the debit balance <u>and</u> the unreserved fund balance should be debited in that amount.

ILLUSTRATION OF CLOSING ENTRIES

Assume the general ledger for Kimberly Hills School District contains the account balances shown in Illustration 9-1.

The pre-closing trial balance for Kimberly Hills School District with the above account balances is shown in Illustration 9-2.

Illustration 9-2

Kimberly Hills School District
General Fund
Pre-Closing Trial Balance
June 30, 1995

Accounts		
Cash in Bank	$ 75,000	
Investments	125,000	
Unreserved Fund Balance		$180,000
Revenue-Local-ad valorem Tax		230,000
Expenditures-Salaries-Regular	210,000	
	$410,000	$410,000

Illustration 9-3

Kimberly Hills School District
General Fund
General Journal

Date	Account Titles	Post	Debit	Credit
C1	Revenue-local-ad valorem tax		$230,000	
	Unreserved Fund Balance			$230,000
	To close revenue from local ad valorem tax			
C2	Unreserved Fund Balance		210,000	
	Expenditures-Salaries-Regular			210,000
	To close expenditure for salaries of regular employees			

Entries in the general journal which are necessary to close the revenue and expenditure accounts (i.e., leave them with a zero balance) are shown in Illustration 9-3.

After the closing entries have been posted to the ledger accounts, then the "temporary accounts" (revenues and expenditures) can be ruled to indicate they are closed at the end of the fiscal year (or accounting period). Double ruling after the closing entry in a revenue or expenditure account indicates that the account has been closed for that fiscal year.

Illustration 9-4

Kimberly Hills School District
General Fund
General Ledger

		Cash in Bank		Account No. 101	
Date	P.R.	Amount	Date	P.R.	Amount
BB		$75,000			

		Investments		Account No. 111	
Date	P.R.	Amount	Date	P.R.	Amount
BB		$125,000			

		Unreserved Fund Balance		Account No. 770	
Date	P.R.	Amount	Date	P.R.	Amount
C2		210,000	BB		$180,000
			C1		230,000

		Revenue-local-ad valorem tax		Account No. 1110	
Date	P.R.	Amount	Date	P.R.	Amount
C1	2	$230,000	BB		$230,000

		Expenditures-salaries-regular		Account No. 110	
Date	P.R.	Amount	Date	P.R.	Amount
BB		$210,000	C2	2	$210,000

After posting the closing entries to the general ledger accounts, the general ledger accounts would appear as shown in Illustration 9-4.

Balance sheet accounts (i.e., assets, liabilities and fund equities) are not "temporary accounts" and are not closed at the end of the fiscal year. However, balance sheet account balances are brought forward to the next fiscal year without general journal entry. Systematic procedures should be followed to ensure that appropriate balance sheet account balances have been brought forward to the next fiscal year.

POST CLOSING TRIAL BALANCE

A post-closing trial balance is prepared after the "temporary" accounts have been closed and after each balance sheet account balance has been brought forward to the new fiscal year. The post-closing

Illustration 9-5

Kimberly Hills School District
General Fund
Post-Closing Trial Balance
June 30, 1995

Accounts

Cash in Bank	$ 75,000	
Investments	125,000	
Unreserved Fund Balance		$200,000
	$200,000	$200,000

trial balance is taken directly from the general ledger to prove that the general ledger is in balance at the beginning of the new fiscal period. The post-closing trial balance is the last step in the accounting cycle.

The post-closing trial balance for the above example is shown in Illustration 9-5.

SUMMARY

Selected special entries were presented in this chapter. Special entries required for opening and closing temporary accounts were discussed. Illustrations were presented to show the closing of revenue accounts and expenditure accounts. Illustrations presented the unreserved fund equity account as an essential account in closing the temporary accounts.

ACTIVITIES

1. Define the following terms:
   a. Closing Accounts
   b. Post Closing Trial Balance

2. The trial balance for Kimberly Hills School District as of June 30, 1995, was as follows:

Kimberly Hills School District
General Fund
Pre-Closing Trial Balance
June 30, 1995

Accounts		
Cash in bank	$200,300	
Investments	70,050	
Interfund loan receivable	7,350	
Unreserved fund balance		$277,700
Revenue-local-ad valorem tax		118,820
Revenue from tuition		44,558
Revenue from earnings on investments		29,705
Revenue from unrestricted state aid		89,115
Revenue from federal-revenue in lieu of taxes		14,852
Expenditures-salaries-regular	257,000	
Expenditures-employee benefits group insurance	38,550	
Expenditures-purchased services-rentals	1,500	
	$574,750	$574,750

Assume the chart of accounts for the school district consists of the following:
- Assets (101, 111, 131)
- Fund equity (770)
- Revenue (1110, 1300, 1500, 3100, 4800)
- Expenditures (object codes 110, 210, 440)

Instructions:
- Record the balances shown in the trial balance as of June 30, 1995, in "T" accounts.
- Record the necessary closing entries in general journal form.
- Post closing entries to the "T" accounts.
- Prepare a post-closing trial balance.

3. The trial balance of Randyville School District as of May 31, 1995, was as follows:

Randyville School District
General Fund
Trial Balance
May 31, 1995

Accounts	Debits	Credits
Cash in Bank	$150,000	
Interfund Loan Receivable	25,000	
Unreserved Fund Balance		$ 40,000
Revenue-Local-ad valorem Tax		125,000
Revenue from unrestricted state aid		195,000
Expenditures-Salaries-Regular	150,000	
Expenditures-general supplies	35,000	
	$360,000	$360,000

During the month of June, the following transactions were completed:

T1: Purchased general supplies in the amount of $25,000.
T2: Received a general state aid payment of $75,000.
T3: Paid employee health insurance of $42,000.
T4: Purchased equipment of $32,000.
T5: Payment of the entire amount due from other funds was received.
T6: Purchased investments for $100,000.

Instructions:
- Use accounts as needed.
- Record the balances shown on the Trial Balance as of May 31, 1995 in "T" accounts.
- Record the transaction for June in a general journal.
- Post transactions from the general journal to the ledger accounts.
- Prepare a pre-closing trial balance.
- Record the necessary closing entries in the general journal.
- Post to the general ledger.
- Prepare a post-closing trial balance.

4. Account balances in the general fund of the New Douglas School System as of June 30, 1995 were as follows:

Cash in bank	$115,000
Taxes receivable	75,000
Expenditures-salaries-regular	200,000
Expenditures-supplies-general	55,000

Expenditures-purchase property services-utility services	23,000
Expenditures-supplies-food	20,000
Revenue from earnings on investments	15,000
Unreserved fund balance	?????*
Revenue from tuition	35,000
Expenditures-employee benefits-retirement contributions	14,000
Revenue from local ad valorem tax	400,000

To be computed by the reader.

Instructions:
- Use accounts as needed.
- Prepare a pre-closing trial balance as of June 30, 1995.
- Record the necessary closing entries in general journal form.
- Post closing entries to the "T" accounts.
- Prepare a post-closing trial balance.

REFERENCES/SELECTED READINGS

Robert Davis Associates. (1981). *Principles of public school fund accounting.* Washington, DC:National Technical Information Service.

Lynn, E. S. & Thompson, J. W. (1974). *Introduction to fund accounting.* Reston, VA: Reston Publishing Company, Inc.

Tidwell, S. B. (1974). *Financial and managerial accounting for elementary and secondary school systems.* Chicago, IL: The Research Corporation, Association of School Business Officials.

10

Basic Financial Statements

INTRODUCTION

Previously, fund balance was defined as the "balancing factor" reflecting the difference between assets and liabilities. In addition, fund balance was identified as one group of the three groups of balance sheet accounts. *Handbook II* expands the concept of fund balance into fund equity. It is appropriate at this time to explore more fully the ramifications of fund equity.

One of the primary purposes of school fund accounting is to facilitate the communication of financial information to interested people. Of particular interest to people, are the balance sheet and the statement revenues, expenditures and changes in fund balance. These reports may be combined reports that reflect financial conditions across all funds or they may be combined reports that compare budgeted and actual amounts.

OUTCOMES

In this chapter, you will learn how to:

1. Define fund equity.
2. Distinguish between reserved fund balance accounts and unreserved fund balance accounts.
3. Prepare a balance sheet.
4. Identify balance sheet accounts.
5. Prepare an interim balance sheet.
6. Prepare a statement of changes in financial position (statement of revenues, expenditures and fund balance).
7. Identify the purposes of combined financial reports.

FUND EQUITY

Handbook II (1990) defines fund equity as the "accounts showing the excess of a fund over its liabilities." It further states that "portions of the balance may be reserved for future use."

Throughout this text, the term "fund balance" has referred to balance sheet account number 770, Unreserved-fund balance. This convention has expedited discussion of accounting procedures, but does not accurately reflect the true meaning of balance sheet account number 770. Unreserved-fund balance refers to the excess of the assets of a fund over its liabilities and *reserves.*

Fund equity consists of the following accounts: Investment in general fixed assets (711); Contributed capital (721); Retained earnings – Reserved-retained earnings (730); Unreserved-retained earnings (740); Fund balance – Reserve for inventories (751); Reserve for prepaid expenses (752); Reserve for encumbrances (753); Reserved-fund balance (760); and Unreserved fund balance (770).

Since the purpose of this text is to introduce individuals to basic concepts of school fund accounting, a discussion of fund equity accounts other than balance sheet account number 770, Unreserved fund balance, will not be presented. Such discussion is left to advanced topics in school fund accounting.

FINANCIAL STATEMENTS

School personnel are frequently asked to relate the financial condition of a school district. One way to respond is to present a balance sheet and/or a statement of changes in financial position. The balance sheet is able to provide information about the financial condition of a school district *as of* a particular point in time. On the other hand, the statement of changes in financial position is used to provide information about the financial condition of a school district *during a* specific period of time. Drawing information from the two different reports an individual may gain a better indication of the financial condition of the district than could be obtained from an analysis of only one of the reports.

The balance sheet contains account balances in balance sheet accounts only. Therefore, prior to preparing a balance sheet, the revenue and expenditure accounts must be closed into the fund balance account. That is, if one wants to prepare both of these financial reports at the end of the fiscal year, then one must first prepare a statement of changes in financial position (statement of revenues, expenditures and fund balance) and then prepare a balance sheet after the new fund balance has been determined.

The following examples demonstrate the procedures for preparing a statement of revenues, expenditures and fund balance, and a balance sheet.

On July 1, 1995, the unreserved fund balance of Cape Jennifer School District was $323,000. During the year, revenue amounting to $420,000 was realized and expenses amounting to $300,000 were paid. Asset and liability account balances in the general fund on June 30, 1996, were as follows:

Cash in bank	$ 20,000
Investments	370,000
Taxes receivable	640,000
Prepaid expense	3,000
Accounts payable	590,000

Example 1
Prepare the statement of revenues, expenditures and fund equity for the period ending June 30, 1996.

Cape Jennifer School District
General Fund
Statement of Revenues, Expenditures and Fund Equity
For the period ending June 30, 1996

Fund equity, July 1, 1995		$323,000
Add excess of revenues over expenditures		
Revenues	$420,000	
less: Expenditures	300,000	120,000
Fund equity, June 30, 1996		$443,000

Example 2
Use the new ending fund equity to prepare a balance sheet as of June 30, 1996.

Cape Jennifer School District
General Fund
Balance Sheet
June 30, 1996

Assets
Cash in bank	$ 20,000
Investments	370,000
Taxes receivable	640,000
Prepaid expense	3,000
Total assets	$1,033,000

Liabilities and Fund Equity
Liabilities:
Accounts payable	$ 590,000

Fund equity:
Unreserved fund balance	443,000
Total liabilities and fund equity	$1,033,000

INTERIM FINANCIAL STATEMENTS

Interim financial statements may be prepared during the year to provide information to administrators and board members. The interim financial statements should contain an interim statement of revenue, an interim statement comparing expenditures and encumbrances with appropriations, and an interim balance sheet. The interim statement of revenue and the interim statement comparing expenditures and encumbrances with appropriations were presented in previous chapters. An interim balance sheet might appear as shown in Illustration 10-1.

COMBINED FINANCIAL REPORTS

Appendix E contains an illustration of combined financial reports. Combined reports reflect totals from a number of funds as well as comparisons of budgeted and actual amounts.

Illustration 10-1

New Douglas School District
Interim Balance Sheet
General Fund
April 30, 1996

Assets and Resources
Current assets:
Cash in bank			$ 20,000
Investments			370,000
Accounts receivable			640,000
Prepaid expense			3,000
Total current assets			$1,033,000
Resources:			
Estimated revenue		$500,000	
less: revenue		420,000	
Balance to be realized			80,000
Total assets and resources			$1,113,000

Liabilities, Appropriations and Fund Balance
Current liabilities:
Accounts payable		$ 590,000	
Total current liabilities			$ 590,000
Appropriations		500,000	
Less: Expenditures	$300,000		
Encumbrances	40,000	340,000	
Balance to be expended			160,000
Fund balance:			
Reserve for encumbrance		40,000	
Unreserved fund balance		323,000	
Total fund balance			363,000
Total liabilities, appropriations and fund equity			$ 1,113,000

SUMMARY

Fund equity includes reserved and unreserved balances. In this introductory discussion, fund equity is limited to the analysis of unreserved fund balances.

This chapter has illustrated procedures used in preparing basic financial statements. A balance sheet and a statement of revenues, expenditures and fund equity was illustrated. Elements of interim financial reports were reviewed and expanded to include the interim balance sheet. The reader was directed to the appendices for examples of consolidated financial reports.

ACTIVITIES

1. Carefully review the definition of the following terms found in the glossary:
   a. Fund balance
   b. Fund equity
   c. Reserved fund balance accounts
   d. Unreserved fund balance accounts
   e. Balance sheet
   f. Statement of changes in financial position
   g. Combined financial report

2. Study Appendix E.

3. The general ledger account balances in the general fund of the Timton School District as of July 1, 1996, were as follows:

Cash in bank	$100,000
Investments	30,000
Accounts payable	70,000
Contracts Payable	10,000
Unreserved fund balance	50,000

   The Timton School District adopted the following budget for the general fund on July 15, 1996:

301	Estimated revenues				
1000	From local sources:				
1110	Ad valorem taxes		$45,000		
1300	Tuition		6,000		
1500	Earnings on investments		5,000	$56,000	
3000	From state sources:				
3100	Unrestricted grants-in-aid		35,000		
3800	Revenue in lieu of taxes		9,000	$44,000	$100,000
601	Estimated Expenditures:				
110	Regular salaries		35,000		
210	Group insurance		4,000		
610	General Supplies		15,000		
620	Energy		11,000		
640	Books and periodicals		20,000		$85,000
770	Unreserved fund balance				$15,000

The following transactions occurred during the year:
T1: Property taxes were levied in the amount of $45,000. It is estimated that 3 percent of these taxes will be uncollectible.
T2: An order was placed for general supplies estimated to cost $10,000.
T3: The materials ordered in T2 were received and the actual cost was $12,000.
T4: Salaries were paid in the amount of $20,000.
T5: The district received $44,000 in payment of property taxes previously levied.
T6: The entire amount of accounts payable was paid.
T7: Unrestricted grants-in-aid from the state was received in the amount of $30,000.
T8: Tuition in the amount of $4,000 was collected.
T9: Earnings on investments in the amount of $3,000 were received.
T10: Revenue in lieu of taxes from the state was received in the amount of $9,000.
T11: Salaries in the amount of $10,000 were paid.
T12: Group insurance in the amount of $3,000 was paid.

Instructions:
- Enter the account balances in the ledger accounts.
- Record the budget as adopted in the general journal.
- Record all transactions in the general journal.
- Post all general journal entries to the general ledger and to the revenue ledger and the expenditure ledger.
- Prepare a trial balance.
- Prepare an interim statement of revenues.
- Prepare an interim statement of appropriations, encumbrances and expenditures.
- Prepare an interim balance sheet.
- Prepare a statement of revenues, expenditures and fund equity for the period.
- Prepare a balance sheet as of the end of the period.

4. The general ledger account balances in the general fund of the Randyville School District as of July 1, 1996, were as follows:
Cash in bank $291,000
Accounts payable   273,000
Unreserved fund balance   18,000

The Randyville School District adopted the following budget for the general fund on July 1, 1996:

301	Estimated revenues			
1000	From local sources:			
1110	Ad valorem taxes	$400,000		
1300	Tuition	20,000		
1500	Earnings on investments	5,000	$425,000	
3000	From state sources:			
3100	Unrestricted grants-in-aid	150,000		
3800	Revenue in lieu of taxes	30,000	$180,000	$605,000
601	Estimated expenditures:			
110	Regular salaries	350,000		
210	Group insurance	35,000		
610	General supplies	150,000		
620	Energy	20,000		$555,000
770	Unreserved fund balance			$ 50,000

The following transactions occurred during the year:

T1: Local property taxes were assessed and levied in the amount of $270,000 and past history indicates 10 percent of these taxes will be uncollectible.

T2: Purchased general supplies of $40,000 on account.

T3: Paid $55,000 on accounts payable.

T4: Paid regular teacher salaries of $115,000.

T5: The district received $45,000 from the state in unrestricted grants.

T6: A general state aid payment of $70,000 was received.

T7: Tuition in the amount of $4,000 was collected.

T8: Regular teacher salaries were paid in the amount of $90,000.

T9: Received $295,000 in collections from property taxes assessed and levied in T1.

T10: A general state aid payment of $70,000 was received.

T11: Salaries in the amount of $90,000 were paid.

T12: General supplies in the amount of $123,000 were purchased on account.

T13: The entire amount due on general supplies purchased in T12 was paid.

T14: Of the general supplies purchased in T12, $45,000 was returned and a cash refund was received.

Instructions:
- Enter the account balances in the ledger accounts.
- Record the budget as adopted in the general journal.
- Record all transactions in the general journal.

- Post all general journal entries to the general ledger and to the revenue ledger and the expenditure ledger
- Prepare a trial balance
- Prepare an interim statement of revenue.
- Prepare an interim statement of appropriations, encumbrances and expenditures.
- Prepare an interim balance sheet.
- Prepare a statement of revenues, expenditures and fund equity for the period.
- Prepare a balance sheet as of the end of the period.

5. The general ledger account balances in the general fund of the New Douglas School District as of July 1, 1996 were as follows:

Cash in bank	$200,000
Investments	150,000
Accounts payable	85,000
Contracts payable	45,000
Unreserved fund balance	220,000

The New Douglas School District adopted the following budget for the general fund on August 1, 1996:

301	Estimated revenues				
1000	From local sources:				
1110	Ad valorem taxes	$45,000			
1300	Tuition	23,000			
1500	Earnings on investments	42,000	$110,000		
3000	From state sources:				
3100	Unrestricted grants-in-aid	68,000			
3800	Revenue in lieu of taxes	27,000	$ 95,000	$205,000	
601	Estimated expenditures:				
110	Regular salaries	85,000			
210	Group insurance	11,000			
610	General Supplies	32,000			
620	Energy	44,000			
640	Books and periodicals	45,000		$217,000	
7701	Unreserved fund balance			($ 12,000)	

The following transactions occurred during the year:

T1: Property taxes were assessed and levied in the amount of $147,000. It is estimated that 5 percent of these taxes will be uncollectible.

T2: A purchase order, in the amount of $31,000, was issued for general supplies.

T3: Contracts for employment of regular faculty and staff in the amount of $75,000 were signed and issued.

T4: Due to an unanticipated enrollment increase, additional contracts for employment of regular faculty and staff in the amount of $15,000 were signed and issued.

T5: The general supplies ordered in T2 were received and the actual cost was $35,500.

T6: Salaries were paid in the amount of $3,750.

T7: The district received $145,000 in payment of property taxes, which were levied in T1.

T8: The district paid $65,000 of the amount in the accounts payable account.

T9: Salaries were paid in the amount of $54,000.

T10: A general state aid payment of $44,000 was received.

T11: State revenue in lieu of taxes in the amount of $15,000 was received.

T12: Tuition from students in the amount of $26,000 was received.

T13: State revenue in lieu of taxes in the amount of $12,000 was received.

T14: Group insurance in the amount of $12,000 was paid.

Instructions:
- Enter the account balances in the ledger accounts.
- Record the budget as adopted in the general journal.
- Record all transactions in the general journal.
- Post all general journal entries to the general ledger, the revenue ledger and the expenditure ledger.
- Prepare a trial balance.
- Prepare an interim statement of revenue.
- Prepare an interim statement of appropriations, encumbrances and expenditures.
- Prepare an interim balance sheet.
- Prepare a statement of revenues, expenditures and fund equity for the period.
- Prepare a balance sheet as of the end of the period.

REFERENCES/SELECTED READINGS

Fowler, W. J., Jr. (1990). *Financial accounting for local and state school systems, 1990.* Washington, DC: U. S. Government Printing Office.

Robert Davis Associates. (1981). *Principles of public school fund accounting.* Washington, DC: National Technical Information Service.

Tidwell, S. B. (1974). *Financial and managerial accounting for elementary and secondary school systems.* Chicago, IL: Research Corporation of the Association of School Business Officials.

11

Changes in Financial Position

INTRODUCTION

The statement of changes in financial position is useful as a communication device between school systems and taxpayers because the statement identifies the amount of financial resources provided from all sources and shows how the amount was used during the fiscal period. The statement shows what money it takes to run the school system.

OUTCOMES

In this chapter, you will learn how to:

1. Identify financial resources.
2. Determine working capital.
3. Prepare a fund's statement of changes in financial position.

FINANCIAL RESOURCES CONCEPT

The statement of changes in financial position for a fund is more than a balance sheet; a statement of revenues and expenditures; a statement of changes in fund equity; an analysis of cash receipts and disbursements; a schedule of working capital; or a schedule of changes in working capital. It presents financial information in a way that no other financial statement does. When using the "all financial resources" concept, it shows what it takes to run a school district. For the individual fund, the statement of changes in financial position shows the total financial resources that were required to operate the fund for a specific fiscal period. When combined with the statement of changes in financial position for each fund, it gives a picture of the economic magnitude of the school district that is not possible otherwise.

When the combined statement is published along with the combined balance sheet, combined statement of revenues, expenditures and changes in fund balance, it is possible for the taxpayer to have full information about the financial operations of the school system. A fully informed public is more likely to be sympathetic to the problems of elementary and secondary education and to be more willing to support its goals, aims and objectives. This is particularly important at the time voters are called upon to make decisions on financial matters of a school system by voting on tax rates and bond issues.

Managerial accounting is concerned with identifying all of the financial resources that are available to the school system and developing ways for a maximum use of each. This is essential if these resources, property and property rights are to be adequately safeguarded and effectively used for desired educational programs and activities. Financial resources are provided from any or all of the following. (Note that all are account credits.) These resources are:

- Converting assets,
- Incurring debt,
- Increasing a fund's fund balance as a result of correcting a prior year's error or by transfers from another fund,
- Recording revenue, or
- Recording an expenditure reimbursement.

Management is also concerned with allocating financial resources to both short-term and long-term educational programs, goals and objectives in order that the highest quality of education can be offered with the financial resources that are available. Therefore, identification and control of the ways by which financial resources may be applied to educational goals and objectives are important. Financial resources may be applied to any or all of the following. (Note that all are account debits.) These are:

- Increasing assets,
- Decreasing debts,
- Decreasing a fund's fund balance as a result of correction of a prior year's error or by a transfer to another fund,
- Recording revenue rebates, or
- Recording expenditures.

The balance sheet is frequently referred to as a statement of financial position. Therefore, the statement of changes in financial position is prepared from a fund's comparative balance sheets – the balance sheet at the beginning of the fiscal period and the balance sheet at the end of the fiscal period – computing the difference between the beginning and ending balances of each account. Its preparation, using the "all financial resources" concept, shows gross revenue and gross expenditures, which are computed from the fund's statement of revenue and expenditures. Other financial resources and uses of financial resources may be found on the fund's statement of changes in fund equity.

Thus, a broader interpretation of the statement of changes in financial position is possible for school systems than is possible by using either the "working capital" concept, which includes only those transactions that affect the current assets or current liabilities, or changes in working capital, cash or changes in cash concepts.

Example 1
Assume that a school system wishes to purchase land for $100,000 and construct a new school building costing $1,400,000. The school district plans to accomplish this by issuing bonds of $1,000,000 at 103 (103 is a method used to express the price as 103 cents for each 100 cents contained in the principal amount stated on the face of the bond). The school system additionally would pay $470,000 from cash. When the transactions are completed, the statement shows the source of $1,000,000 as proceeds from the principal of bonds sold, $30,000 from a premium on bonds issued, and $470,000 from a reduction in the cash balance. It shows a total of $1,500,000 to be applied to the purchase of land and construction of the new school building. This series of transactions results in the following:

Financial resources provided by:	
Decreasing assets	
Cash	$ 470,000
Increasing liabilities:	
Principal of bonds issued	1,000,000
Premium on bonds issued	30,000
Total financial resources provided	$1,500,000
Financial resources applied to:	
Increasing assets:	
Land	$ 100,000
Building	1,400,000
Total financial resources applied	$1,500,000

Example 2

Assume that certain general fixed assets of the school system are sold for $1,000 and the proceeds are deposited in the general fund. No other general fixed assets are purchased. The statement shows a total revenue of $1,000 from the sale of general fixed assets and a corresponding $1,000 applied to increase the cash balance.

This transaction results in the following:
Financial resources provided by:
   Increasing revenue:
      Sale of general fixed assets $1,000

Financial resources applied to:
   Increasing assets:
      Cash $1,000

Illustration 11-1 shows how the statement of changes in financial position is prepared from the statement of revenues, expenditures and fund equity and from the balance sheets at the beginning and end of the fiscal period for each fund used in the operation of the school district.

Part 1. Assume the general fund's statement of revenues, expenditures and fund equity appears as shown in Illustration 11-1, Part 1, 2 and 3.

The debits in the "Net Change in Accounts" column represent resources applied and the credits represent resources provided. From the statement of revenues, expenditures and fund equity, revenues represent resources provided and expenditures represent resources applied.

The $200,000 net change in fund equity is eliminated by a debit because it is a net figure, the nature of which can be found by referring to the statement of changes in fund equity. There, it is found to be the net excess of revenues over expenditures and the net change in fund equity is substituted by a credit identified for what it is: excess of revenues over expenditures. When making this elimination and substitution, note that debits equal credits.

The $200,000 representing net excess of revenue over expenditures is also a net figure, which is eliminated by a debit. In its place is substituted the things that caused this net result. From the statement of revenue and expenditures, it is found to be the excess of revenue of $3,000,000 over expenditures of $2,800,000. When making this

Illustration 11-1, Part 1

New Douglas School District
General Fund
Statement of Revenues, Expenditures and Fund Equity
For the year ended December 31, 1995

Exhibit B

Revenues:

From local sources		$1,400,000
From intermediate sources		200,000
From state sources		1,230,000
From federal sources		120,000
From other school districts:		
In the state	$ 30,000	
In another state	20,000	50,000
Total revenues		$3,000,000

Expenditures:

Administration	$ 200,000	
Instruction	2,000,000	
Attendance and health services	10,000	
Pupil transportation services	400,000	
Operation of plant	40,000	
Maintenance of plant	60,000	
Fixed charges	20,000	
Community services	40,000	
Debt service	30,000	
Total expenditures		$2,800,000
Excess revenues over expenditures		$ 200,000
Fund equity, January 1, 1995		10,000
Fund equity, December 31, 1995		$ 210,000

---

elimination and substitution, note that the debits equal the credits. The column totals for eliminations and substitutions must also be equal. Prior to drafting the formal statement of changes in financial position, the following observations can be made:

- Resources were provided by reduction or conversion of assets identified as temporary investments, due from other funds, and inventory of supplies. The reduction in these assets provided financial resources that are not reported when a school system uses a cash basis of recording financial transactions. Conversion

Illustration 11-1, Part 2
Assume further that comparative balance sheets of the general fund are as follows:

New Douglas School District
General Fund
Comparative Balance Sheet

Exhibit A

Assets	January 1	December 31
Cash	$ 4,000	$ 21,000
Temporary investments	25,000	18,000
Taxes receivable	40,000	242,200
Accounts receivable	10,000	22,300
Due from other funds	20,000	1,000
Inventory of supplies	1,000	500
Total Assets	$100,000	$305,000
Liabilities, Reserves and Fund Equity		
Vouchers payable	$ 40,000	$ 50,000
Due to other funds	10,000	5,000
Taxes collected in advance	20,000	36,000
Total Liabilities	$ 70,000	$ 91,000
Reserve for inventories	$ 1,000	$ 500
Reserve for encumbrances	19,000	3,500
Fund equity	10,000	210,000
Total Liabilities, Reserves and Fund Equity	$100,000	$305,000

of assets should come under the control of the board of education so that property of the school system can be properly safeguarded.

- Financial resources were also provided by increasing the liabilities of the general fund during the year, i.e. vouchers payable and the deferred revenue account, taxes collected in advance. Full disclosure of financial transactions of the school system to the public requires that liability accounts be an integral part of the public school system's accounting structure.
- Financial resources were applied to increase asset account balances during the year. Cash, taxes receivable and accounts receivable were increased. A financial statement that shows how much money was spent for things other than operating expenses of the school system is important to an inquiring public.
- Financial resources were applied to the reduction of the liability

Illustration 11-1, Part 3

From the balance sheets at the beginning and end of the fiscal year, comparisons are made to determine the net changes that have occurred in the balance sheet.

	Jan 1 1995	Dec 31 1995	Debit	Net Change in Accounts Credit
Cash	$ 4,000	$ 21,000	$ 17,000	
Temporary investments	25,000	18,000		$ 7,000
Taxes receivable	40,000	242,200	202,200	
Accounts receivable	10,000	22,300	12,300	
Due from other funds	20,000	1,000		19,000
Inventory	1,000	500		500
Total	$100,000	$305,000		
Vouchers payable	$ 40,000	$ 50,000		10,000
Due to other funds	10,000	5,000	5,000	
Taxes collected in advance	20,000	36,000		16,000
Reserve for encumbrance	20,000	4,000	16,000	
Fund equity	10,000	210,000		200,000
Total	$100,000	$305,000	$252,500	$252,500

due to other funds. Only the statement of changes in financial position has the capacity to show the amount of financial resources used during the year to reduce liabilities of the school system.

- Reserve for encumbrances was reduced during the period by $16,000, and such a reduction represented an application of resources (See Illustration 11-1, Part 4).

FINANCIAL STATEMENTS

A balance sheet for each fund accompanies the fund's statement of changes in financial position. The balance sheet is a statement of financial position that shows each asset, liability, and fund equity account balance at the end of the fiscal period. The balance sheet is not in the statement of changes in financial position nor is that statement a substitute for a balance sheet. Each presents different

8 • CHAPTER 11

Illustration 11-1, Part 4
The formal Statement of Changes in Financial Position is prepared:

New Douglas School District
General Fund
Statement of Changes in Financial Position
For the Year Ended December 31, 1995

Exhibit C

Resources provided:			
From revenues:			
Local sources		$1,400,000	
Intermediate sources		200,000	
State sources		1,230,000	
Federal sources		120,000	
From other school districts:			
In the state	$ 30,000		
In another state	20,000	50,000	$3,000,000
From reduction in assets:			
Sale of temporary investments		$ 7,000	
Collection of account, due from other funds		19,000	
From decrease in inventory of supplies		500	26,500
From increasing liabilities:			
Vouchers payable		$ 10,000	
Taxes collected in advance		16,000	26,000
Total resources provided			$3,052,500
Resources Applied:			
To expenditures of school district:			
Administration		$ 200,000	
Instruction		2,000,000	
Attendance and health services		10,000	
Pupil transportation services		400,000	
Operation of plant		40,000	
Maintenance of plant		60,000	
Fixed charges		20,000	
Community services		40,000	
Debt service		30,000	$2,800,000
To increase assets:			
Increase in cash		$ 17,000	
Taxes receivable		202,200	
Accounts receivable		12,300	231,500
To reduction in liabilities:			
Reduction in amount due to other funds			5,000
To reduction in reserves:			
Reserve for inventories			500
Reserve for encumbrances			15,500
Total resources applied			$3,052,500

financial information. For preparation of the comprehensive annual financial report, NCGA's Statement 1 lists those considered to be general purpose financial statements as:

1. Combined balance sheet-all fund types and account groups.
2. Combined statement of revenues, expenditures and changes in fund balances – all governmental fund types.
3. Combined statement of revenues, expenditures and changes in fund balances – budget and actual – general and special revenue fund types for which annual budgets have been legally adopted.
4. Combined statement of revenues, expenses and changes in retained earnings (or equity) – all proprietary fund types.
5. Combined statements of changes in financial position – all proprietary fund types.
6. Notes to financial statements.

For purposes of the comprehensive annual financial report, GASB's Statement 1 states that the general outline and minimum content of the CAFR of a governmental unit include:

1. Combining statements – by fund type – where a governmental unit has more than one fund of a given fund type.
2. Individual fund and account group statements, where a governmental unit has only one fund of a given type, and for account groups and/or where necessary to present prior year and budgetary comparisons.
3. Schedules.
   a. Schedules necessary to demonstrate compliance with finance-related legal and contractual provisions.
   b. Schedules to present information spread throughout the statements that can be brought together and shown in greater detail (i.e., taxes receivable, including delinquent taxes; long-term debt; investments; and cash receipts, disbursements and balances).
   c. Schedules to present greater detail for information reported in the statements (i.e., additional revenue sources detail and object of expenditure data by departments).

Narrative explanations useful in understanding combining and individual fund and account group statements and schedules that are not included in the notes to financial statements should be presented on divider pages, directly on the statements and schedules, or in a separate section.

These CAFRs will be presented throughout the text by presenting annual financial reports that have earned ASBO's Certificate of Excellence in Financial Reporting. For management purposes, financial statements of individual funds and account groups will be emphasized.

The statement of changes in financial position is prepared primarily for presentation of financial information in a manner meaningful to the public. For that reason, it shows revenues and expenditures by broad classification; to provide detail about revenues and expenditures, the statement of revenues, expenditures and fund equity should accompany the statement of changes in financial position.

The statement of changes in fund equity contains all elements that caused a change from the beginning to the ending balance of fund equity. In addition to showing the excess of revenue over expenditures or the excess of expenditures over revenue, transfers in and/or out may have occurred, and errors of prior years may have been detected and corrected through fund equity. Appropriations of fund equity may have been made or the purposes for which fund equity may have been appropriated in prior periods may have been completed which may have resulted in a return from an appropriated fund equity account to the unappropriated fund equity account.

Each of these transactions, if they occur, have an effect upon changes in financial position. Therefore, the statement of changes in fund equity should accompany the statement of changes in financial position to provide more detailed information than would appear on the statement. Generally, revenue provides the largest amount of financial resources for a school district during a fiscal period. As revenue is shown in detail on the statement of revenue and expenditures, only the total amount of revenue is shown on the statement of changes in financial position when the "all financial resources" concept is used.

Resources are provided if any asset account is reduced at the end of the fiscal period to a figure below its balance at the beginning of the fiscal period. For example, if $100,000 was invested in an asset at the beginning of the year and only $70,000 is reported as the account balance at the end of the period, $30,000 has been provided. The question arises: Where did the $30,000 go? A number of transactions, each having a different effect on an account, may have occurred. To provide complete information about an account balance, it is necessary to analyze all transactions in the account during the accounting period, if that is desired. In some cases, an asset account is reduced because of converting it into cash, exchanging it for another asset or recognizing it as a loss. However, whatever the cause, the amount of the reduction is reported.

Some accountants have prepared statements of changes in financial position that report only the excess of revenue over expenditures for the period as a source of working capital or as a source of cash. But, it must be emphasized that the statement is prepared primarily for public information and that off-setting revenue with expenditures by reporting the difference only, conceals the amount of revenue actually used to operate the school system. Therefore, for the public to understand what amount of financial resources is required for the operation of the school system, revenue should be reported by total amount on the face of the statement of changes in financial position.

A fund's financial resources may come from transfers of fund equity from another fund. This amount would be found on the statement of changes in the recipient fund's equity rather than on its statement of revenue and expenditures, but it does provide financial resources to the recipient fund and, therefore, should be reported in the statement of changes in financial position for the recipient fund.

All expenditures and expenses are applications of financial resources. Generally, operating expenditures, capital outlay and debt service, consume the greatest amount of a school district's financial resources. Although the statement of changes in financial position could be presented in a shorter form by off-setting expenditures against revenue, such an offset would conceal the total amount of expenditures of a school system. Therefore, the full amount of expenditures should be reported on the statement of changes in financial position. The statement can present amounts by broad expenditure classification or in total because the required accompanying statement of revenue and expenditures shows the nature and amount of the expenditures in detail. Such a disclosure shows in large part what happened to the school system's financial resources.

Within a fund, an increase in the balance of any asset account at the end of the fiscal period over the balance at the beginning of the fiscal period represents an application of financial resources. For full information, it is important that the nature and amount of each asset account that is increased be shown in the statement of changes in financial position. Such a disclosure does show in part how the financial resources were used.

Financial resources are applied when any liability account is reduced at the end of the fiscal period to an amount less than at the beginning of the fiscal period. A number of transactions, each having a different effect on a liability account, may have occurred. Full disclosure of how a school system's financial resources were used requires reporting the nature and amount of each liability account that was reduced in the statement of changes in financial position. Reduction in liabilities may be a major cause of change in financial position of a school district.

Reductions in the balances of all fund equity accounts to an amount at the end of the fiscal period less than at the beginning of the fiscal period represents an application of a school system's financial resources. A reduction in the reserve for encumbrances or any other appropriated fund equity account to an amount at the end of the fiscal period less than at the beginning is a change in financial position. A transfer of fund equity unappropriated to another fund is a change in financial position of the fund and its disclosure should be reported. The amounts by which all fund equity accounts have been reduced should be found on the statement of changes in fund equity rather than on the statement of revenue and expenditures.

Some accountants have prepared the statement of changes in financial position by reporting only the excess of expenditures over revenue as an application or use of financial resources, working capital or cash. But it must be emphasized that the statement of changes in financial position is prepared primarily for public information and that offsetting expenditures with revenue by reporting the difference only conceals the amount of expenditures of the school system. Thus, total expenditures should be shown. Detailed information about each expenditure is reported in the accompanying required statement of revenue and expenditures. Therefore, broad classifications of expenditures or the total amount of expenditures may be shown in the statement of changes in financial position.

An individual statement of changes in financial position is prepared for each fund used. When these statements are combined for all funds, full disclosures of the financial size of the school system is made. This is the statement that can be compared meaningfully with the statement of changes in financial position of any other business entity. It will allow a comparison of the economic impact of the school system with the economic impact or size of the business entity in terms of dollars for a fiscal year.

Comparisons of combined balance sheets of the school system with balance sheets of business entities also provide information about comparative sizes, but this comparison is as of one day only because the balance sheet presents financial position on one date only. Comparisons of the combined statement of revenue and expenditures of the school system with income statements of business entities provide comparisons of income or revenue and comparisons of expenses or expenditures for a fiscal period, but these are only parts of the financial structure of both entities. Only the combined statement of changes in financial position of all funds provides the overall financial dimensions of a school system.

Complete financial accounting and reporting serves as one of the strongest ways that school systems can keep the public informed about the financial needs of education. Public support is needed as the school board and its administrators strive to provide the highest quality education possible with the financial resources of the school system. The following chapters discuss the nature and financial operation of each of the funds and account groups used by elementary and secondary school systems.

Illustration 11-2 shows that resources are provided from major sources in addition to revenue. Total resources were $10,081,000, while revenue provided $7,357,000. Where did the remaining $2,724,000 come from? The $1,936,000 came from either voluntary or involuntary conversion of assets, a common business transaction. It is important for the board of education and administrative officers to control amounts realized from disposition of assets.

The illustration also shows that major resources are provided by increasing the school system's liabilities by $788,000. It is important to emphasize that goods and services generally come from increasing liabilities. A major source of cash can come from increasing interest-bearing, short-term or long-term notes payable or bonds payable. Therefore, the amount that is available for the board of education to allocate to educational programs, goals and objectives is not restricted to either budgeted or realized revenue. Purchasing power comes from many other sources that must be controlled.

In addition, the illustration shows that financial resources can be applied to many things other than instructional programs. In this case, a number of asset accounts were increased by a total of $2,452,000 while resources of $860,000 were applied to the reduction of the school system's liabilities, bonds payable. The reserve for

Illustration 11-2

New Douglas School District
Statement of Changes in Financial Position
For the Year Ended June 30, 1995

Exhibit C

Resources provided:

From reduction in assets:			
Taxes receivable, current		$ 1,454,000	
Taxes receivable, delinquent		5,000	
Notes receivable		40,000	
Due from other governmental units		200,000	
Inventories		237,000	$ 1,936,000
From increasing liabilities:			
Vouchers payable		$ 13,000	
Contracts payable		775,000	788,000
From revenues:			
From local sources		$ 5,075,500	
From state sources		1,490,000	
From federal sources		735,500	
From sale of lunches		56,000	7,357,000
Total resources provided			$10,081,000

Resources applied:

To increase assets:			
Cash		$1,800,000	
Accounts receivable		10,000	
Loans receivable		100,000	
Amount available for retirement of			
debt and interest		182,000	
Investments, temporary		360,000	$ 2,452,000
To reduce liabilities:			
Bonds payable			860,000
To reduce reserves:			
Reserve for encumbrance			140,000
To operations:			
Instruction		$2,005,000	
Supporting services:			
Pupil	$ 601,000		
General administration	288,000		
School administration	161,000		
Business administration	2,206,000		
Central administration	1,130,000	4,386,000	
Community services		238,000	6,629,000
Total resources applied			$10,081,000

Illustration 11-3

New Douglas School District
General Fund
Schedule of Working Capital
(Date)

Current Assets:		
Cash		$ 21,000
Temporary investments		18,000
Taxes receivable		242,200
Accounts receivable		22,300
Due from other funds		1,000
Inventory of supplies		500
Total current assets		$ 305,000
Current Liabilities:		
Vouchers payable	$ 50,000	
Due to other funds	5,000	
Taxes collected in advance	36,000	
Total current liabilities	$ 91,000	
Working Capital	$ 214,000	

encumbrances was reduced by $140,000 and the remaining $6,629,000 was applied to operations of the school system. Note that a broad classification was used to show how the financial resources were applied to operations, rather than showing one total amount.

WORKING CAPITAL CONCEPT

In commercial enterprises, working capital is extremely important because it measures the ability of a firm to pay its current debts by computing the excess of current assets over current liabilities. A ratio of better than one dollar of current assets to each dollar of current liabilities is a management objective to be achieved consistently. Theoretically, in governmental accounting and financial accounting for school systems, the general fund is working capital because it should have only current assets and current liabilities, as its long-term fixed assets are carried in the general fixed assets account group and its long-term debts are carried in the general long-term debt account group.

A schedule of working capital for any fund can be prepared for management use at any time or at the end of each month and submit-

Illustration 11-4

New Douglas School District
Statement of Changes in Working Capital
For the year ending December 31, 1995

	Jan 1	Changes Increase Debit	Changes Decrease Credit	Dec 31
Working Capital:				
Current Assets:				
Cash	$ 4,000	$ 17,000		$ 21,000
Temporary investments	25,000		$ 7,000	18,000
Taxes receivable	40,000	202,200		242,200
Accounts receivable	10,000	12,300		22,300
Due from other funds	20,000		19,000	1,000
Inventory of supplies	1,000		500	500
Total current assets	$100,000			$ 305,000
Current Liabilities:				
Vouchers payable	40,000		10,000	50,000
Due to other funds	10,000	5,000		5,000
Taxes collected in advance	20,000		16,000	36,000
Total current liabilities	70,000			91,000
Working Capital	$ 30,000	$ 236,500	$ 52,500	$ 214,000

ted as a supporting schedule to interim and annual financial statements. Illustration 11-3 shows a schedule of working capital. A statement showing changes in working capital is shown in Illustration 11-4.

CASH CONCEPT

Cash presents a serious problem not only to school systems but in commercial enterprises also and that problem is how to have enough cash to pay currently maturing obligations. A schedule of cash receipts and disbursements can be prepared daily or presented as a supporting schedule to interim financial statements. A study of when cash is received from each source during the year, and an analysis of the consistency with which cash is received during certain periods of time during the year from each source is an excellent cash manage-

Illustration 11-5

New Douglas School District
General Fund
Interim Schedule of Cash Receipts and Disbursements
For period ended June 30, 1995

Cash balance, July 1994		$ 288,798
Add:		
Cash receipts to date		<u>3,269,842</u>
Cash available for use		$ 3,558,640
Less:		
Cash disbursements to date		<u>$ 3,300,286</u>
Cash balance, June 30, 1995		$ 258,354

Reconciliation

Balance per bank statement		$ 864,487
Add:		
Deposit in transit		<u>76,842</u>
Total		$ 941,329
Less:		
Outstanding checks:		
1096	$ 25	
1097	234,650	
1099	150,782	
1101	146,812	
1104	<u>150,706</u>	<u>682,975</u>
Cash balance (date)		$ 258,354

ment procedure. The study can be made by use of schedules of cash receipts and disbursements. Illustration 11-5 shows the format of a schedule of cash receipts and disbursements and a bank reconciliation for a fund.

SUMMARY

This chapter described the construction of the Statement of Changes in Financial Position and its uses as a communication vehicle. The statement identifies the amount of financial resources available from all sources and indicates how the amount was used. The Statement of Changes in Financial Position basically shows what amount of money it took to operate the school district over the period reported.

ACTIVITIES

1. Identify the statements used by a school system to prepare a Statement of Changes in Financial Position.

2. Discuss the differences between the all financial resources concept, working capital concept and cash concept for preparing a Statement of Changes in Financial Position for a school system.

3. Determine if financial resources have been provided or applied when:
   a. A liability account is reduced at the end of a fiscal period to an amount less than it was at the beginning of the period.
   b. Expenditures exceed revenue for a fiscal period.
   c. Assets are sold for more money than their original cost.
   d. The fund balance is increased at the end of a fiscal period as a result of finding that an invoice for $1,400 was paid at $1,500.
   e. The fund balance was decreased due to a transfer of accumulated interest to another fund.

4. Comparative balance sheets at the beginning and end of the calendar year for the Ft. Steven School District general fund are:

	January 1	December 31	Application	Source
Cash	$ 22,000	$ 40,000		
Temporary investments	30,000	19,000		
Taxes receivable	35,000	20,000		
Accounts receivable	22,000	19,500		
Due from other funds	12,000	15,000		
Inventory of supplies	800	1,200		
Total	$121,800	$ 114,700		
Vouchers payable	$ 28,000	$ 31,000		
Due to other funds	15,000	20,000		
Taxes collected in advance	45,000	32,000		
Reserve for encumbrances	20,000	15,000		
Matured bonds payable	10,000	8,000		
Fund equity	3,800	8,700		
Total	$ 121,800	$ 114,700		

Instructions:
- Compute the change in account balances and indicate whether the change provided or applied financial resources by recording the change in the appropriate column.

5. Comparative balance sheets for Michago School District are shown below:

	July 1	June 30
Cash	$ 180,000	$2,450,000
Temporary investments	340,000	0
Taxes receivable	900,000	900,000
Accounts receivable	210,000	210,000
Due from other funds	100,000	20,000
Inventory of supplies	35,000	35,000
Total	$1,765,000	$3,615,000
Vouchers payable	$ 265,000	$ 265,000
Due to other funds	100,000	100,000
Taxes collected in advance	150,000	220,000
Reserve for encumbrance	600,000	600,000
General fund equity	650,000	2,430,000
Total	$1,765,000	$3,615,000

The following transactions took place during the school year:

a. Collected additional taxes in advance — $ 70,000
b. Collected revenue from state — $4,400,000
c. Collected state grant-in-aid — $3,200,000
d. Collected taxes from local sources assessed and levied during the year — $2,500,000
e. Collected revenue from federal sources — $ 500,000
f. Sold temporary investments — $ 250,000
g. Collected revenue from intermediate sources — $ 900,000
h. Collected on amount due from other funds — $ 80,000
i. Paid administrative expenses — $ 900,000
j. Paid for pupil transportation — $ 80,000
k. Paid instructional salaries — $6,500,000
l. Paid cost of plant operation — $1,250,000
m. Paid fixed charges — $ 300,000
n. Paid community services costs — $ 350,000
o. Paid debt service items — $ 250,000

Instructions:
- Prepare a Statement of Changes in Financial Position for the general fund of the district for the year ending June 30.

Petersburg School System 10
General Fund
Statement of Revenues, Expenditures and Fund Equity
For the Year Ended December 31, 1996

Revenues:		
From local sources	$ 800,000	
From state sources	750,000	
From federal sources	50,000	
From other school systems in the state	15,000	
Total Revenues		$1,615,000
Expenditures:		
Administration	$ 75,000	
Instruction	1,215,000	
Health services	4,500	
Transportation services	16,000	
Operation of plant	8,000	
Maintenance of plant	9,500	
Food services	18,500	
Fixed charges	7,500	
Community services	10,000	
Debt service	6,800	
Total Expenditures		1,370,800
Excess revenues over expenditures		$ 244,200
Fund equity, January 1, 1996		15,000
Fund equity, December 31, 1996		$ 259,200

---

6. The statement of revenues, expenditures and fund equity for the year ended December 31, 1996, is shown above, and the comparative balance sheets for January 1, 1996, and December 31, 1996, for Petersburg School System 10 is shown on the next page.

Instructions:
- Prepare a Statement of Changes in Financial Position for the general fund of Petersburg School System 10 for the year ended

Petersburg School System 10
General Fund
Comparative Balance Sheets
1996

Assets	January 1	December 31
Cash	$ 3,500	$ 37,600
Temporary investments	22,500	17,000
Long-term investments	50,000	47,500
Taxes receivable	20,000	300,000
Accounts receivable	8,500	12,100
Due from other funds	1,500	6,000
Inventory of supplies	1,500	300
Total Assets	$107,500	$420,500
Liabilities, Reserves and Fund Equity		
Vouchers payable	$ 25,000	$ 70,000
Due to other funds	15,000	4,500
Taxes collected in advance	34,500	83,300
Total Liabilities	$ 74,500	$157,800
Reserve for encumbrances	18,000	3,500
Fund equity	15,000	259,200
Total Liabilities, Reserves and Fund Equity	$107,500	$420,500

December 31, 1996, using:
a. All financial resources concept.
b. Working capital concept.
c. Cash concept.

REFERENCES/SELECTED READINGS

Fowler, W.J., Jr. (1990). *Financial accounting for local and state systems, 1990*. Washington, DC: Superintendent of Documents, U.S. Government Printing Office.

Tidwell, S.B. (1985). *Financial and managerial accounting for elementary and secondary school systems (3rd edition)*. Reston, VA: Research Corporation of the Association of School Business Officials.

12

Special Revenue Funds

INTRODUCTION

Special revenue funds are used to account for revenue received from a source designated to be used for a specific educational purpose to supplement the basic educational or foundation program.

OUTCOMES

In this chapter, you will learn how to:

1. Create a special revenue fund.
2. Determine uses of a special revenue fund.
3. Use budgetary accounts to record special revenue fund transactions.
4. Prepare financial statements for a special revenue fund.

SPECIAL REVENUE FUND DEFINED

A special revenue fund is created when a school district receives revenue from a special source designated to be used for a specific educational purpose, which supplements the basic educational or foundation program. In order to be a special revenue fund, the revenue must be designated for a specific educational program, not a supporting service. Sources of revenue for special revenue funds may be similar to sources of revenue of the general fund, but a separate self-balancing group of accounts gives better financial control and a clearer picture of how the special sources of revenue are being used. This leaves the general fund clearly responsible for the basic educational program or foundation program.

Special revenue funds may be used at the discretion of the board of education to provide a basis for better managerial control and public understanding. These funds have been found to be particularly useful to school districts when new or different sources of revenue for educational programs are of a temporary nature. Use of a special revenue fund for temporary educational programs can prevent such revenue from being placed in the general fund where it could become commingled or could give a distorted impression of the amount of money that is available for the basic educational program.

Special revenue funds require adoption of a budget by the board of education each year. The funds require use of budgetary accounts that serve special revenue funds in the same way that they serve the general fund. Some accountants hold the concept that any fund can be a special revenue fund if it has special sources of revenue to be used for special or restricted purposes, regardless of whether it is an educational program or a supporting service. These advocates say that a fund, such as a school food services fund, can be either a special revenue fund or an enterprise fund. They maintain that the decision or choice should be based upon the sources and amounts of revenue from each source. For example, if the majority of revenue comes from tax sources at the local, state or federal level, it should be classified as a special revenue fund. If however, use of either fund type among districts is widespread, but usually once a district decides to use one type, the district seldom changes. If the majority of revenue comes from charges for services rendered, it should be classified as an enterprise fund.

Such a classification technique defeats good financial reporting. Since the ratio of revenue from service charges to revenue from tax sources can be determined only at the end of the fiscal period, interim financial reports may not be consistent with the annual report. Comparing year-to-year operations of the school district is impossible when decisions are made to report a fund as a special revenue fund one year and as an enterprise fund the next. Statistical comparisons among school districts is impossible when such fund shifts are made.

TYPES OF SPECIAL REVENUE FUNDS

There may be any number of special revenue funds, each having a separate, self-balancing general ledger with subsidiary ledgers. Some may be required by statute or ordinance, and others may be established through policies of governmental agencies at the federal, state or local level. Others may be established by resolutions of the board of education for better administration. No fund or account group should be created unless by minutes of a meeting of the board of education. The Governmental Accounting Standards Board (GASB) Statement 1 recommends that the number of funds should be kept to a minimum consistent with legal and operational requirements. Special revenue funds may account for revenue from sources similar to the general fund's sources but they may also receive revenue from other sources that are restricted by the purposes for which expenditures can be made.

Many advantages may accrue to a school district by creating separate special revenue funds under certain circumstances. Although revenue may be from sources similar to those of the general fund, certain kinds of revenue may not be assured in future years. For instance, through federal grants-in-aid, state aid or aid from sources such as foundations, individuals or corporations, money may be provided on a temporary basis to a school district for experimental educational programs. Whether or not the programs will continue to be financed from these sources in the future may not be known and, as a result, it may not be considered a permanent part of the school district's educational program. In such a case, this temporary kind of program is accounted for separately from the on-going basic foundation program. In the event a temporary program proves to be one that will continue to be financed from sources that are relatively certain in the future, such programs may be transferred from special revenue funds to the school district's general fund where they may be considered part of the on-going educational program. When this occurs, the special revenue fund may cease to be needed.

Governmental agencies, foundations, individuals, corporations and others who contribute to special educational programs generally require periodic audits of accounts of the school district to determine that the financial resources are being used for the purpose for which they were provided. Interim and annual financial statements, which divide the revenues and expenditures for the continuing basic educational program from those that are temporary or experimental in nature, are much easier to understand and to control.

GASB identified some of the serious disadvantages of special revenue funds. It warned that if revenues raised through compulsory tax rates for special revenue funds exceed the normal use requirements, the fund may build up a balance, leading to unnecessary expansion of an activity in an effort to spend all of the available income. On the other hand, a low rate of revenue set by law may lead to a deficit in a special revenue fund, and the general fund may have to use its resources for purposes that are designated to be accomplished by the special revenue fund.

Transactions are recorded in a separate general journal or in a separate set of books of original entry designed specifically for use by each special revenue fund. Recording transactions of each special revenue fund in separate books of original entry assists in dividing the work of employees of the school district and avoiding confusion as to the fund to which a certain revenue or a certain expenditure is applicable.

SOURCES OF SPECIAL REVENUE

Special revenue may be provided from local, intermediate, state or federal sources for special programs. Local or intermediate revenue could be provided from a voted but temporary tax, from tuition charges or fees, from gifts or from other sources. Revenue from these sources may be segregated from the general fund in order to assist administrative officers and the board of education to determine the adequacy of revenue and the limits that must be placed upon expenditures for these programs.

Revenue from state sources may come from direct grants by the state for special programs such as for mentally handicapped, orthopedic, speech correction, visiting teacher, driver education or other categorical aid. The state may also provide revenue to a local school district that represents redistribution of federal grants-in-aid for vocational education, homemaking, trades and industry, cooperative training and many others.

Revenue from federal sources may be provided for special programs, which are of a temporary or experimental nature. The grants may be made for programs such as vocational education in agriculture, distributive education, health occupations, home economics, trades and industrial education, manpower development training, welfare education, public health training, vocational rehabilitation and many others. For example, the Elementary and Secondary Education Act (ESEA) provides programs for the educationally disadvantaged, supplementary education and special education. (In October 1994 President Clinton signed the Improving America's Schools Act, which reauthorized ESEA for 5 years.) Among the many federal acts are adult education for Indian programs, maintenance and operation in federally impacted areas, assistance to public schools affected by major disasters and the Area Redevelopment Act. Federal grants may be made either directly to local school districts or through state departments of education to develop educational programs. Unless the revenues become permanent programs and a part of the foundation program of the school district, it is appropriate to account for these restricted revenues and expenditures through special revenue funds. As emphasis moves to and from areas of special concern, legislation at all levels will be developed to permit focused educational programs. In these cases, particularly if the program is temporary, experimental or uncertain of future financial support, the concept of special revenue funds provides timely and meaningful information for management, boards of education, governmental entities and taxpayer purposes.

Once a special revenue fund is created, it remains in operation until the purpose for which it was created is served or until it is abolished by an act of the board of education.

ACCOUNTS AND TRANSACTIONS

Because revenue of a special revenue fund can arise from public sources, formal budgets are required. When adopted by the board, the budget is recorded in the minutes of the board's meeting. Therefore, budgetary accounts for appropriations, estimated revenues, encumbrances, reserve for encumbrances and budgeted fund balance are as effective for management accounting and financial control in special revenue funds as they are in the general fund.

The budgetary accounts compare estimated revenue with actual revenue and, as a result, assist the school district to realize the maximum revenue during the fiscal period from each source that is available to it. They also assist the board in controlling expenditures and encumbrances by requiring administrative officers to keep them within the limits established. Budgetary accounts record estimated revenue both from public sources and from the special sources. Appropriation accounts also are established to control all expenditures of the fund and not merely that portion of revenue raised through the tax levy. Accounting principles and procedures applicable to special revenue funds are identical to those used in financial and managerial accounting for the general fund.

Transactions that occur in the operation of a special revenue fund are similar to those that occur in the operation of a general fund. Budgetary accounts for estimated revenues, appropriations, encumbrances reserve for encumbrances, and budgeted fund balance are used in connection with proprietary accounts for assets, liabilities, fund equity, revenue and expenditures accounts for each special revenue fund.

FINANCIAL STATEMENTS

Reporting the interim and annual financial position and results of operation of each special revenue fund is important to effective administration of a school district. It is the individual special revenue fund that is most important for financial control and financial management purposes. Interim and annual financial statements for each special revenue fund include the balance sheet, the statement comparing estimated with actual revenue, the statement comparing expenditures and encumbrances with appropriations, the statement of changes in fund equity and the statement of changes in financial position.

The format for each financial statement for a special revenue fund is identical to the format of the financial statements used by the general fund. Interim financial statements, which compare estimated with actual revenues by source and which compare expenditures and encumbrances with appropriations by organizational unit and object are the most effective, efficient and economical ways to classify financial statements. Financial responsibility can be best placed and internal accounting and financial controls can be most effective when expenditures are classified by organizational unit and by object. Expenditures can be classified in many more ways if financial resources are available to permit it. Among additional ways that expenditures can be classified are by location, grade level, subject matter or program.

Illustration 12-1 shows comparative balance sheets for a special revenue fund. Illustration 12-2 shows a statement of revenues, expenditures and fund equity for a special revenue fund. Illustration 12-3 shows a statement of changes in financial position for a special revenue fund.

Illustration 12-1

Kimberly Hills School District
Special Revenue Fund
Comparative Balance Sheets

Assets	July 1, 1995	June 30, 1996
Imprest cash fund	$1,000	$999
Cash in banks:		
First National Bank	167,187	43,034
Superior National Bank	83,130	88,772
Accounts receivable		38,413
Taxes receivable	47,909	42,283
Inventories	17,958	13,440
Prepaid insurance	2,293	1,994
Total Assets	$319,477	$228,935
Liabilities and fund equity		
Current and short-term loans	$210,000	$114,000
Accounts payable	1,556	2,083
Salaries payable	85,761	95,653
Accrued expenses payable		4,650
Total liabilities	$297,317	$216,386
Fund equity	22,160	12,549
Total liabilities and fund equity	$319,477	$228,935

A different kind of problem in financial reporting occurs when "combining" financial statements for all special revenue funds are prepared to present a comprehensive annual financial report for all funds and account groups used in financial administration of the school district. Individual special revenue funds require a separate set of books of original entry, a general ledger, subsidiary ledgers, adequate competent business papers (which provide evidence of financial transactions), interim and annual financial statements for effective financial administration and control. The technique effectively combines financial statements for all of the special revenue funds into one set composed of a combining balance sheet, a combining statement of revenue, expenditures and fund equity and a statement of changes in fund balances. Users of financial statements for individual special revenue funds focus attention on the fact that combined statements without supporting financial statements for each special revenue fund can be misleading and create problems in

Illustration 12-2

Kimberly Hills School District
Special Revenue Fund
Statement of Revenues, Expenditures and Fund Equity
For the Year Ended June 30, 1996

Fund Equity, July 1, 1995		$ 22,160
Revenues:		
From local sources	$ 493,494	
From state sources	776,110	
From federal sources	102,375	
From gifts and bequests	260	
From other school districts in the state	68,754	
Total Revenues		$1,440,993
Expenditures:		
Instruction	$1,077,928	
Administration	49,378	
Attendance and health services	23,443	
Operation of plant	187,094	
Maintenance of plant	82,249	
Fixed charges	20,897	
Capital outlay	8,346	
Student services	1,267	
Total Expenditures		$1,450,602
Excess revenues over expenditures		$ (9,609)
Fund equity, June 30, 1996		$ 12,551

the mind of the board and the general public about the status and management of the special revenue funds. Appendix E illustrates combined financial statements for the consolidated annual financial report.

Illustration 12-4 shows a combining balance sheet for several special revenue funds. Illustration 12-5 shows a combining statement of revenues, expenditures and changes in fund equity.

Illustration 12-3

Special Revenue Fund
Statement of Changes in Financial Position
For the Year Ended June 30, 1996

Resources provided:		
From revenues:		
Local sources	$ 493,494	
State sources	776,110	
Federal sources	102,375	
Gifts and bequests	260	
Other school districts in the state	68,754	$1,440,993
From reduction in assets:		
Cash:		
Imprest cash fund	$ 27	
General Fund	122,153	
Taxes receivable	5,624	
Inventories	4,517	
Prepaid insurance	298	$ 132,619
From increasing liabilities:		
Accounts payable	$ 503	
Salaries payable	9,891	
Accrued expenses	4,650	$ 15,045
Total resources provided		$1,588,657
Resources applied:		
To expenditures of school system:		
Instruction	$1,077,928	
Administration	49,378	
Attendance and health services	23,443	
Operation of plant	187,094	
Maintenance of plant	82,249	
Fixed charges	20,897	
Capital outlay	8,346	
Student services	1,171	
Outgoing transfer	96	$1,450,602
To increase assets:		
Increase in cash	$ 5,641	
Accounts receivable	36,410	42,051
To reduction in liabilities:		
Reduction in amount due on loan		96,004
Total resources applied		$1,588,657

Illustration 12-4

New Douglas School District
Special Revenue Fund
Combining Balance Sheet
September 30, 1995 With Comparative Totals For September 30, 1994

Assets	Title I	Title II	Title VI	Special Education	Vocational Education	Educationally Disadvantaged	Driver Education	Student Teaching	Drug-Free Schools	Bilingual	Gifted and Talented	Refugee Children Assistance Act	Totals September 30 1995	Totals September 30 1994
Cash	$ 184	$4,252	$41,391	$8,694	$ -	$1,471	$ -	$1,381	$731	$355	$4,315	$ -	$62,774	$16,571
Receivables:														
Due From State of Texas					43,900								43,900	6,042
Interfund Loans Receivable-														
Student Activity Fund-														159
Inventories					43,645								43,645	
Prepaid Expenses				7,493	9,062		1,211	369		453			18,588	8,465
Total Assets	$ 184	$4,252	$41,391	$16,187	$96,607	$1,471	$1,211	$1,750	$731	$808	$4,315	$ -	$168,907	$31,237
Liabilities and Fund Balance														
Liabilities:														
Accounts Payable		1,156	2,635	10,412	13,487		1,178	35		447	93		29,443	35,639
Fund Overdraft	1,042				68,064		33					2,904	72,043	37,255
Accrued Liabilities				3,786	10,690								14,476	866
Interfund Loans Payable														
General Fund														5,000
Deferred Income			36,587										36,587	
Total Liabilities	$1,042	$1,156	$39,222	$14,198	$92,241	$ -	$1,211	$35	$ -	$447	$93	$2,904	$152,549	$78,760
Fund Balance (Deficit):														
Reserved:														
ESEA, Title I	(858)												(858)	(4,628)
ESEA, Title II		3,096											3,096	1,421
ESEA, Title VI			2,169										2,169	
Reserved for Encumbrances				74	2,637		123						2,834	30,566
Unreserved:														
Designated for Specific Programs				1,915	1,729	1,471		1,715	731	361	4,222		12,144	2,657
Undesignated							(123)					(2,904)	(3,027)	(77,539)
Total Fund Balance (Deficit)	(858)	3,096	2,169	1,989	4,366	1,471		1,715	731	361	4,222	(2,904)	16,358	(47,523)
Total Liabilities and Fund Balance	$ 184	$4,252	$41,391	$16,187	$96,607	$1,471	$1,211	$1,750	$731	$808	$4,315	$ -	$168,907	$31,237

Illustration 12-5

New Douglas School District
Special Revenue Fund
Combining Balance Sheet
September 30, 1995 With Comparative Totals For September 30, 1994

	Title I	Title II	Title VI	Special Education	Vocational Education	Educationally Disadvantaged	Driver Education	Student Teaching	Drug-Free Schools	Bilingual	Gifted and Talented	Refugee Children Assistance Act	Totals September 30 1995	Totals September 30 1994
Revenue:														
From Local Sources:														
Tuition From Patrons	$ -	$ -	$ -	$ -	$ -	$ -	$67,848	$ -	$ -	$ -	$ -	$ -	$67,848	$42,140
From State Sources:														
Per Capita And Foundation	-	-	-	1,282,201	798,509	46,452	-	-	-	-	-	-	2,127,162	1,902,206
Transportation	-	-	-	88,530	-	-	-	-	-	-	-	-	88,530	66,176
Other Foundation Revenue	-	-	-	-	-	-	14,175	8,950	-	3,076	32,275	-	58,476	27,900
Vocational	-	44,77	-	-	114,557	-	-	-	-	-	-	-	114,557	33,124
E.S.E.A. Revenue	111,105		-	-	-	-	-	-	-	-	-	-	155,881	179,808
Other State Distributed Revenue	-	-	123,298	-	-	-	-	-	-	-	-	9,597	132,895	80,042
Other State Revenue				4,475									4,475	
Total revenues	111,105	44,776	123,298	1,375,206	913,066	46,452	82,023	8,950		3,076	32,275	9,597	2,749,824	2,331,396
Expenditures:														
Instruction:														
Payroll Costs	105,765	-	41,943	1,263,417	861,524	44,904	98,448	7,154	-	172,696	25,550	11,756	2,633,157	2,148,389
Purchased And Contracted Services	-	-	-	13,402	1,966	-	21,983	-	-	-	220	-	37,571	28,910
Supplies and Materials	1,570	7,691	2,765	19,511	92,998	-	3,704	52	1,335	722	1,786	275	132,409	145,690
Other Operating Expenses	-	-	-	3,804	24,817	-	(3,362)	-	-	-	497	470	26,226	36,874
Capital Outlay		35,268	12,758	9,329	101,667	663							159,685	111,171
	107,335	42,959	57,466	1,309,463	1,082,972	45,567	120,773	7,206	1,335	173,418	28,053	12,501	2,989,048	2,471,034
Instructional Administration:														
Payroll Costs	-	-	337	103,140	62,954	-	-	-	-	-	-	-	166,431	151,805
Purchased And Contracted Services	-	-	1,420	385	-	-	-	-	-	-	-	-	1,805	2,491
Supplies And Materials	-	-	17	597	628	-	-	-	-	-	-	-	1,242	1,703
Other Operating Expenses	-	-	1,895	6,662	4,999	-	-	-	-	-	-	-	13,556	7,255
Capital Outlay				233									233	191
			3,669	111,017	68,581								183,267	163,445
Instructional Resources And Media Services:														
Capital Outlay	-	13	-	-	-	-	-	-	-	-	-	-	2,651	2,067
		13											2,651	2,067
School Administration:														
Supplies and Materials	-	-	-	-	-	-	-	-	5	-	-	-	5	-
									5				5	
Curriculum And Personnel Development:														
Purchased and Contracted Services	$ -	$ -	$1,102	$ -	$ -	$ -	$ -	$ -	$ -	2,638	$ -	$ -	$1,102	$2,039
Other Operating Expenses			1,102							2,638			1,102	176
														2,215

Illustration 12-5 (Continued)

New Douglas School District
Special Revenue Fund
Combining Balance Sheet
September 30, 1995 With Comparative Totals For September 30, 1994

	Title I	Title II	Title VI	Special Education	Vocational Education	Educationally Disadvantaged	Driver Education	Student Teaching	Drug-Free Schools	Bilingual	Gifted and Talented	Refugee Children Assistance Act	Totals 1995	Totals September 30 1994
Communication And Dissemination: Supplies And Materials	-	-	-	-	-	-	-	-	-	-	-	-	-	-
Guidance and Counseling Services:														
Payroll Costs	-	-	42,160	201,684	73,564	-	-	-	-	-	-	-	317,408	256,775
Purchased and Contracted Services	-	-	-	-	-	-	-	-	-	-	-	-	-	-
Supplies and Materials	-	-	55	19,098	-	-	-	-	-	-	-	-	19,098	15,849
Other Operating Expenses	-	-	760	8,307	2,199	-	-	-	-	-	-	-	10,561	10,231
Capital Outlay	-	-	-	1,788	1,243	-	-	-	-	-	-	-	3,791	3,441
	-	-	-	4,210	-	-	-	-	-	-	-	-	4,210	1,165
	-	-	42,975	235,087	77,006	-	-	-	-	-	-	-	355,068	287,461
Pupil Transportation- Exceptional Children:														
Payroll Costs	-	-	17,995	86,520	-	-	-	-	-	-	-	-	104,515	59,055
Purchased And Contracted Services	-	-	-	468	-	-	-	-	-	-	-	-	468	-
Supplies And Materials	-	-	-	22,425	-	-	-	-	-	-	-	-	22,425	13,097
Other Operating Expenses	-	-	-	1,321	-	-	-	-	-	-	-	-	1,321	1,272
Capital Outlay	-	-	-	22,916	-	-	-	-	-	-	-	-	22,916	51,239
	-	-	17,995	133,650	-	-	-	-	-	-	-	-	151,645	124,663
Plant Maintenance And Operations: Supplies And Materials														
Total Expenditures	107,335	42,972	123,207	1,789,217	1,228,559	45,567	120,773	7,206	1,340	176,056	28,053	12,501	3,682,786	3,050,885
Excess of Revenues Over (Under) Expenditures	3,770	1,804	91	(414,011)	(315,493)	885	(38,750)	1,744	(1,340)	(172,980)	4,222	(2,904)	(932,962)	(719,489)
Other Financing Sources: Operating Transfer From General Fund	-	-	-	459,536	325,240	-	38,750	-	-	173,317	-	-	996,843	639,690
Excess of Revenue And Other Financing Sources Over (Under) Expenditures	-3,770	1,804	91	45,525	9,747	885	-	1,744	(1,340)	337	4,222	(2,904)	63,881	(79,799)
Fund Balance, September 30, 1994	(4,628)	1,292	-	(41,458)	(5,381)	586	-	(29)	2,071	24	-	-	(47,523)	32,276
Reclassification of Fund Balance	-	-	2,078	(2,078)	-	-	-	-	-	-	-	-	-	-
Fund Balance (Deficit), September 30, 1995	$(858)	$3,096	$2,169	$1,989	$4,366	$1,471	$ -	$1,715	$731	$361	$4,222	$(2,904)	$16,358	$(47,523)

SUMMARY

A special revenue fund is created when a school district receives revenue from a special source designated to be used for a specific educational purpose that supplements the basic educational or foundation program. Special revenue funds may be used at the discretion of the board of education to provide a basis for better managerial control and public understanding. The budgetary accounts compare estimated revenue with actual revenue. Budgetary accounts compare estimated revenue with actual revenue.

ACTIVITIES

1. Review the definition of the following terms found in the glossary:
   a. Special revenue fund
   b. Enterprise fund
   c. Proprietary account
   d. Subsidiary ledger
   e. Budgetary account
   f. Agency fund

2. Carefully study and review Appendix I.

3. Fort Steven School District created a special revenue fund in order to account for revenues and expenditures associated with a vocational education project. The following transactions occurred:

   a. The budget adopted for the 1995-96 school year was as follows:

Estimated revenue - income taxes	$ 600,000
Estimated revenue - tuition	150,000
Estimated revenue - federal sources	1,200,000
Appropriations:	
Salaries	$1,100,000
Employee benefits	200,000
Materials and supplies	500,000

   b. 1994-95 school year encumbrances were closed into the special revenue fund's equity, leaving a reserve for encumbrances in the amount of $10,000. Commitments had been

issued for supplies and materials.
c. The Fort Steven School District used an agency fund for collection of all taxes and an agency fund for central payroll.
d. Employee contracts in the amount of $1,100,000 were signed with a corresponding estimate of employee benefits amounting to $200,000.
e. The Department of Education formally approved the project in the amount of $1,200,000.
f. Student registration and cash tuition for the project realized $140,000.
g. First quarter income tax distribution to the district produced $150,000.
h. Payroll vouchers received from the central payroll fund billed the special revenue fund for $180,000 salaries and $21,000 employee benefits. A check in the amount of $201,000 was issued to the central payroll fund.
i. The tax collection agency fund remitted $150,000 to the special revenue fund (representing collections from (g).
j. Issued purchase orders for materials and supplies in the amount of $480,000.
k. Received the materials and supplies in (j) invoiced at $490,000. Checks were issued in the amount of $225,000 representing partial payment of the invoices for (j).

Instructions:
- Record the transactions in general journal form.

4. Michago School Corporation 2 Special Revenue Fund had the following accounts and balances on July 1, 1995:

2-101	Cash	$24,000
2-111	Investments	18,500
2-402	Accounts payable	2,200
2-770	Special revenue fund balance	43,300

During the year, the following transactions occurred:
a. The board of education adopted the following budget:

2-1100	Revenue from local sources - taxes	$200,000
2-1910	Revenue from local sources - rentals	4,000
2-3000	Revenue from state sources - grants in aid	80,000
2-4000	Revenue from federal sources - grants in aid	60,000
	Appropriations	
2-1200	Special programs	85,000
2-1300	Adult/continuing education programs	26,000

2-2100	Support services: Pupils	15,000
2-2120	Guidance	12,000
2-2200	Instructional staff	2,000
2-2220	Instructional media	30,000
2-2320	General administration	20,000
2-2350	Facilities acquisition	28,000
2-2370	Foodservices	7,500
2-2384	Central support services	13,800
2-2390	Information services	5,000
2-2410	Operation of plant	18,800

b. The board of education authorized the sale of investments, and the investments were sold for $18,500.
c. Teacher's contracts were approved for special programs, $83,000, and for adult/continuing education, $24,000.
d. The special revenue fund received an invoice from operations and maintenance fund for $18,000, representing its share of costs for the year.
e. Received the state grant-in-aid in the amount of $82,000.
f. Cash was collected from rentals in the amount of $4,200.
g. The federal grant-in-aid was received for $43,500.
h. Taxes had been assessed and levied for the school corporation resulting in the special revenue fund's share amounting to $122,000.
i. Prior to the start of the school year, a special programs teacher resigned who previously had signed a contract with the district for $31,500.
j. During the year, vouchers were paid as follows:

	Expenditure	*Encumbered*
Special programs	$ 70,300	$70,000
Adult/continuing education programs	24,000	22,000
Support programs:		
Pupils	13,200	
Guidance	12,000	
Instructional staff	500	
Instructional media	31,200	
General administration	17,400	
Facilities acquisition	20,000	
Food services	4,000	
Central support services	11,000	
Information services	2,400	
Operation of plant	2,200	
	$208,200	$92,000

k. Collected $121,000 from the central tax collection agency fund.
l. Paid $222,000 on accounts payable.

Instructions:
- Record the account balances as of July 1, 1995, in general ledger accounts.
- Record transactions during the year in general journal form using both general ledger and subsidiary ledger accounts.
- Post to the general ledger and subsidiary ledger.
- Prepare a trial balance as of June 30, 1996.
- Prepare a pre-closing balance sheet.
- Prepare supporting schedules of the revenue and expenditures ledgers for the balance sheet prepared in (5).
- Record closing entries in general journal form for both the general and subsidiary ledger accounts.
- Post closing entries to the general and subsidiary ledger accounts.
- Prepare a post-closing trial balance.

REFERENCES/SELECTED READING

Fowler, W.J., Jr. (1990). *Financial Accounting for local and state systems*. Washington, DC: U.S. Government Printing Office.

Tidwell, S.B. (1985). *Financial and managerial accounting for elementary and secondary school systems* (3rd edition). Reston, VA: Research Corporation of the Association of School Business Officials.

13

Capital Projects Funds

INTRODUCTION

Changing demographics mean school districts are faced with the problem of securing the money necessary to acquire sites, construct facilities, equip facilities, repair and/or remodel facilities. Expenditures for these purposes are classified as capital outlay expenditures or capital projects fund expenditures.

If revenue of the general fund is adequate each year to meet the constantly changing needs for fixed assets, accounting for their acquisition could be handled through the capital outlay expenditure accounts in the general fund or in special revenue funds. Frequently this is not possible and other methods of financing have to be found. Capital projects funds are created to account for acquisition, construction or for major remodeling of fixed assets when not provided for in the general fund, special revenue funds, internal services funds or enterprise funds.

Capital projects funds are used to account for revenue from a bond issue or from other sources designated for capital outlay purposes. Capital projects fund revenue is provided by issuing bonds. Bonds may also be issued for other capital project fund purposes such as eliminating a deficit resulting from operation of the general fund, a special revenue fund, an internal services fund, an enterprise fund or refinancing, retiring or refunding maturing bond issues. Grants received from gifts or from other units of government at the local, state, province or federal level also provide major sources of revenue designated for capital projects of school districts.

OUTCOMES

In this chapter, you will learn how to:

1. Determine why school districts may issue bonds.

2. Properly use bond proceeds.
3. Differentiate between bond premium and bond discount.
4. Use budgetary accounts to record capital projects fund transactions.

TYPES OF BONDS

A bond, frequently referred to as a debenture, is a written promise to pay a certain amount of money at a fixed or determinable future date. The bond may be issued by a school district or the governmental unit under which the school district operates as evidence of debt and usually indicates a specific rate of interest payable on certain dates. A note is a form of a bond that is issued for a short period of time; while a bond is issued for a longer period of time. Investors find bonds issued by public school districts to be an attractive investment because income earned from the bonds is usually exempt from federal income tax and may be exempt from local and state income taxes as well.

In the past, bonds may have been issued as coupon bonds, registered bonds or a combination of both. A coupon bond had coupons attached, each indicating the amount of interest and the date on which interest is payable. On or within a reasonable time subsequent to the interest payment date, the bondholder presented the coupons to the school district or to its fiscal agent, and the interest was paid. Federal legislation has now required all "municipal" bonds to be registered. Ownership of every long-term, tax-exempt security issued now must be a matter of record. Today, a bond may be registered as to principal or interest or both. Registered bonds have no coupons attached. Instead, the name of the owner is registered on the books of the school district or its fiscal agent. On interest payment dates, interest checks are issued to the owners of record, and when the bond's maturity date arrives, checks for the maturity value of the bonds are issued to owners of record in exchange for the matured bonds. The problems related to recording the liability as a result of issuing general long-term debt instruments are handled through the general long-term debt account group, while problems related to payment of interest and principal are handled through the debt service fund and/or the general fund.

SOURCES OF CAPITAL

The power to issue bonds may be vested in the school board or in the governmental unit under which the school district operates. If bonds are issued by the governmental entity over the school district, the proceeds of the issue may be transferred to the board of education for proper administration. If the board has the power and authority to issue its own bonds, all procedures necessary for securing proper authorization under the laws as well as those related to selling the bonds are the responsibility of the board of education. Under either procedure, the board of education is charged with the responsibility of accounting for the expenditure of proceeds in accordance with the purpose for which the capital projects fund was created.

Bonding power of the board or the governmental unit through which bonds are issued is restricted by law, and a favorable referendum vote is usually required before bonds can be issued. The purposes for which proceeds of a bond issue are to be used is information voters should have before they vote for or against a bond issue. As a result, the board is under an obligation to use the proceeds of a bond issue only for those purposes specified. There have been instances where money raised through bond issues intended to acquire fixed assets was used to pay current operating expenses. Whether intentional or unintentional on the part of the administrative officers who permitted such expenditures, or whether done with or without the knowledge of the governing board, the fact remains that the money was used for a purpose other than that for which it was raised.

Business operations of a school district that permit such a thing to happen destroy the confidence of the voters and taxpayers in the board and its administrative officers. This can be avoided by full disclosure of financial facts and by use of financial accounting principles and reporting procedures applicable to capital projects funds, segregating them from the general fund.

The Governmental Accounting Standards Board, American Institute of Certified Public Accountants, the National Center for Education Statistics and the Association of School Business Officials International recommend that a separate group of self-balancing accounts be maintained for each capital project. Differences in each bond issue's proceeds, interest rate, interest payment dates, maturity dates and in the purposes for which revenue may be used make it desirable to use separate and independent funds for each major capital project.

ACCOUNTS AND TRANSACTIONS

When a bond issue is authorized to be sold, an account entitled bonds authorized and unissued is debited and appropriations is credited. Both are budgetary accounts. The differences between these amounts is applied to the budgeted fund balance account or to the capital projects unappropriated fund equity account. The bonds authorized and unissued account serves the same purpose for a capital projects fund as the estimated revenue account serves for the general fund. It is debited for the face value of the bonds. Although this is not an asset of the fund, it is a financial resource through which money is obtained. For that reason, the bonds authorized and unissued account is reported on the assets and resources side of interim and annual balance sheets.

Proceeds from a bond issue provide revenue to the capital projects fund because the capital projects fund does not assume the liability for retirement of the bonds or for the payment of interest on bonds outstanding. Once bonds are issued, the long-term liability is recorded in and reported by the general long-term debt account group as long as the bonds are outstanding. The responsibility for bond interest payment and bond principal retirement at maturity is placed upon a debt service fund and/or the general fund.

Authority to expend the proceeds of a bond issue is granted by the board of education when all procedures required by law have been fulfilled. Procedures necessary for issuing bonds and for securing other sources of revenue needed for a capital projects fund are initiated by the school board. If approval of the voters is required, a proposal setting forth the terms of the bond issue and the purposes for which the bond proceeds are to be used is presented to the voters as required by law. If approval of a governmental unit under which the school district operates is required, all procedures prescribed by that governmental unit must be completed. Therefore, budgetary accounts for both revenue and expenditures are as helpful to the board and to management during the life of a capital projects fund as they are to the general fund because large sums of money are required for capital projects and the life of a capital projects fund often extends over a number of years. Controlling accounts in the general ledger and subsidiary ledger accounts for capital projects funds use the same format as previously used.

The amount of revenue that can be raised by a bond issue and from all other sources for specified capital projects is limited. To assist management in realizing all revenue that is available to a capital projects fund, budgetary accounting for revenue is as important as in the general fund. Therefore, estimated revenue and actual revenue accounts are used in each capital projects fund.

Authority granted by the board of education to administrative officers to make expenditures in a capital projects fund is an appropriation, just as it is in the general fund. As a result, budgetary accounts are established in capital projects funds to control expenditures and they serve the same purposes for capital projects funds as they serve for the general fund. Expenditure controls are provided by general ledger and subsidiary ledger accounts for appropriations, encumbrances, and the reserve for encumbrances.

Because of the amount of money involved, the number of contracts issued, the number of revisions made in contracts during the life of a capital projects fund, and the length of time required to complete a capital project, it is as important to a school district that it have as effective control over expenditures for each capital projects fund as it is to have control over expenditures of the general fund. Budgetary control over expenditures is effectively gained in capital projects funds by using the expenditure account format from previous chapters in both the general ledger and subsidiary expenditure ledger.

These expenditure accounts are used as a basis for interim financial reporting during the life of each capital project fund. The budgetary expenditure accounts in the general ledger and/or in the subsidiary expenditures ledger serve effectively to prevent expenditures and encumbrances from being made in excess of the appropriation for each object. The accounts of a capital projects fund operate on a basis similar to accounts in the general fund; however, there are some major differences. In fact, all revenue needed for a capital project is usually authorized before a capital projects fund is created, not on an annual or fiscal year basis as it is in the case of the general fund. Furthermore, appropriations that authorize expenditures in a capital projects fund do not lapse at the end of a year or fiscal period as they do in the case of the general fund.

Although many accountants continue to close all capital projects funds' revenue and expenditure accounts at the end of each year or fiscal period, a need for year-end closing entries in capital projects funds does not exist. All capital projects fund accounts, budgetary and proprietary, are kept open until the purposes for which the capital projects fund was created have been accomplished. The revenue accounts continue accumulating total revenue that is provided for a capital project and expenditure accounts continue to accumulate total costs until the project is completed. After all bonds have been issued and revenue from all other sources has been expended for the purposes authorized, the capital projects fund accounts are closed. The capital projects fund serves no further purpose other than to provide a record of what happened to the money.

The liability created by the bond issue is recorded and reported, as long as the bonds are outstanding, as a part of another group of accounts known as the general long-term debt account group. Because a capital projects fund is not responsible for retirement of the principal of bonds issued for capital projects purposes and for interest on them, a debt service fund is created when the bonds are issued to serve these purposes for the school system. A debt service fund is created for each bond issue.

General fixed assets acquired as a result of expenditures in capital projects funds are recorded and reported as a part of another separate self-balancing group of accounts known as the general fixed assets account group. As construction expenditures and/or other costs are incurred in the long period of time required for completing the capital project, construction-in-progress accounts may be recorded in the general fixed asset account group. If, on the other hand, a capital projects fund is created to acquire fixed assets for an enterprise fund or an internal service fund, the fixed assets become a part of the enterprise fund or the internal service fund where they are recorded as assets of these funds and not as assets in the general fixed assets account group. However, these fixed assets are reported in footnotes to the financial statements of the general fixed assets account group. Because internal services funds and enterprise funds can record long-term liabilities along with fixed assets, it is infrequent that capital projects funds would be used to acquire fixed assets for these special purpose funds.

In the event all assets of a capital projects fund are not used or needed to complete the capital projects, the remaining assets, by direction of the board of education in accordance with the bond indenture, may be transferred either to the general fund or to the debt service fund created to accumulate resources in amounts sufficient to retire the bonds that were issued to finance the capital projects at the maturity date of the bond issue.

The following entries illustrate typical capital projects fund transactions. When all legal procedures have been completed and $50,000 of bonds have been authorized to be issued by the Kimberly Hills School District, the following entry is made in the general journal of the capital projects fund:

Bonds authorized and unissued	$50,000	
Appropriations, capital improvements		$50,000
To record authorization to issue		
capital projects fund bonds		

As bonds are issued by the school system or the governmental unit under which the school district operates, the following entry is made:

Cash or due from other governmental unit	$50,000	
Revenue from bonds issued		$50,000
To record sale of bonds		

When the other governmental unit, if used, deposits the cash in the capital projects fund, the following entry is made:

Cash	$50,000	
Due from other governmental unit		$50,000
To record collection of cash		
from other governmental unit		

The cash now on hand can be used for the purposes designated. At this point, assume that the money is to be used for certain improvements. When part of the improvements are completed and payment amounting to $20,000 is approved, the following entry is made:

Expenditures, capital improvements	$20,000	
Accounts payable		$20,000
To record expenditures for improvements		

When purchase orders or other forms of financial commitment are issued for certain authorized improvements costing $20,000, the following entry is made:

Encumbrances, capital improvements	$20,000	
Reserve for encumbrances		$20,000
To record estimated cost of authorized		
improvements		

When authorized improvements have been completed and a final $21,000 contract price determined, the following two entries are made:

Reserve for encumbrances	$20,000	
Encumbrances, capital improvements		$20,000
To reverse encumbrances entry		
Expenditures, capital improvements	$21,000	
Accounts payable		$21,000
To record expenditures for authorized improvements		

Assume that additional purchase orders and commitments are issued for authorized improvements in the amount of $8,000, the following entry is recorded:

Encumbrances, capital improvements	$8,000	
Reserve for encumbrances		$8,000
To record the estimated cost of authorized improvements		

The entry to record payment on accounts payable is recorded as follows:

Accounts payable	$15,000	
Cash		$15,000
To record payment of account		

A trial balance of the capital projects fund prepared at this point follows:

Kimberly Hills School District
Capital Projects Fund
Trial Balance
(Date)

Cash	$35,000	
Accounts payable		$26,000
Reserve for encumbrances		8,000
Bonds authorized and unissued	50,000	
Appropriations, capital improvements		50,000
Revenue from bonds issued		50,000
Expenditures, capital improvements	41,000	
Encumbrances, capital improvements	8,000	
Total	$134,000	$134,000

Assume that the capital projects fund makes a $7,600 expenditure for improvements, which were originally estimated to cost $8,000. The two following entries are made:

Reserve for encumbrances	$8,000	
Encumbrances, capital improvements		$8,000
To reverse the encumbrances entry		
Expenditures, capital improvements	$7,600	
Accounts payable		$7,600
To record the expenditure for authorized improvements		

When all accounts payable are paid, the following entry is made:

Accounts payable	$33,600	
Cash		$33,600
To record payment of accounts payable		

At this point, assume that all authorized improvements have been completed. A trial balance of the accounts appears as follows:

Kimberly Hills School District
Capital Projects Fund
Trial Balance
(Date)

Cash	$ 1,400	
Expenditures, capital improvements	48,600	
Appropriations, capital improvements		$50,000
Total	$50,000	$50,000

When the purpose for which the capital projects fund was created has been served the accounts of the fund are closed. The following entries close the appropriation and expenditures accounts:

Appropriations, capital improvements	$50,000	
Expenditures, capital improvements		$48,600
Revenue and expenditure summary		1,400
To close the expenditures and appropriation accounts		

Revenue and expenditure summary	$1,400	
Capital projects fund equity		$1,400
To close the revenue and expenditure summary account		

The capital projects fund has a remaining cash balance of $1,400. The amount of cash represents the excess amount of bonds issued over the actual cost of authorized improvements. Reference to the trust agreement may provide a number of ways by which the board may make disposition of the remaining cash balance. Some may advocate transfer of the balance to the general fund. However, the expenditure of the cash by the general fund for purposes other than those authorized when bonds were issued would not be in accordance with the purposes for which the bonds were issued. Therefore, in this case, the board would probably direct that the cash be transferred to the debt service fund created for the purpose of accumulating sufficient cash to retire the bond issue when it matures. The entry to record the transfer of the remaining cash balance to the debt service fund appears as follows:

Capital projects fund equity	$1,400	
Due to debt service fund		$1,400
To record authority to transfer the remaining cash to the debt service fund, leaving an audit trail to in dictate what happened to the remaining cash balance in the fund		
Due to debt service fund	$1,400	
Cash		$1,400
To record transfer of cash to the debt service fund		

When the cash balance is transferred to the debt service fund, the capital projects fund accounts are closed; the fund having served completely the purpose for which it was created.

A separate capital projects fund should be created for each capital project to provide financial management control of each capital project. A capital project may be to achieve one purpose such as acquisition of land or for construction of a building. Or a capital project may include a combination of objectives such as the acquisition of land, the construction of one or more buildings, the purchase of machinery and equipment, the remodeling, expansion or renovation of certain other fixed assets, the absorption of a fund deficit, and/or the retirement of bonds payable. Each capital projects fund should have its own separate, self-balancing set of accounts.

Because sources of revenue of a capital projects fund may be few in number, it may not be necessary for a subsidiary revenue ledger to be maintained that would contain accounts for both estimated and actual revenue from each source but instead revenue accounts for both budgeted revenue and actual revenue from each source would be maintained in the general ledger. In either case, it is necessary that adequate standards of budgetary accounting control for each source of revenue be maintained in each capital projects fund. If authorized expenditures of a capital projects fund are restricted to a few objects, a subsidiary expenditures ledger containing accounts for appropriations, expenditures and encumbrances for each object may not be required but instead appropriation, expenditure, and encumbrance accounts for each object may be maintained in the general ledger. In both cases, the reserve for encumbrances account is maintained in the general ledger. However, in either case, it is essential for each capital projects fund to have adequate standards of budgetary accounting control for each expenditure object.

FINANCIAL STATEMENTS

From the trial balance, all financial statements of capital projects funds can be prepared. As budgetary and actual revenue and expenditure accounts of each capital projects fund are not closed until the capital project is completed, interim financial statements are prepared for each fund. These interim financial statements—prepared for management purposes—are the balance sheet, statement comparing estimated and actual revenue, statement of expenditures and encumbrances compared with appropriations, statement of changes in fund equity, and statement of changes in financial position. Because significant financial resources are provided for school districts through revenue accounts in capital projects funds and because material financial resources are applied through expenditure accounts of capital projects funds, the financial magnitude of a school district is not disclosed fully unless the financial statements for capital projects funds include a statement of changes in financial position. The problem of combining financial statements of all capital projects funds is similar to the problem of combining financial statements for special revenue funds.

If bonds are issued in a capital projects fund to eliminate a deficit of a fund, when money is transferred from the capital projects fund to a fund having a deficit, the following entry is made:

Transfers to _____ fund	XXX	
Due to _____ fund		XXX
To record the expenditure to transfer money to absorb a deficit in the _____ fund		
Due to the _____ fund	XXX	
Cash		XXX
To record transfer of cash to the _____ fund		

When money in a capital projects fund is to be used in a debt service fund for the purpose of retiring matured bonds payable, the following entry is made:

Transfers to debt service fund	XXX	
Due to debt service fund		XXX
To record expenditure to transfer amount to the debt service fund to retire bonds		
Due to debit service fund	XXX	
Cash		XXX
To record transfer of cash to the debt service fund		

Transfer of money generated by revenue of a capital projects fund created for these purposes is recorded through a fund balance account such as "transfer to the general fund" to distinguish it from an expenditure account. When fund equity is no longer needed, a transfer is recorded by a debit to a fund equity account of the transferring fund as no additional expenditures are required for the purpose for which the fund was created. The recipient fund records the transfer by crediting a fund equity account such as "transfer from capital projects fund" to distinguish it from a revenue account as no additional revenue is generated for the school district by the transaction.

A bond premium exists when a bond issue is sold at a price in excess of the principal amount of the bonds. If a bond issue does produce a premium, the question arises as to its proper disposition because the money cannot be used as an additional expenditure in excess of the appropriation for the capital project. In all probability, the board of education would direct that the premium be transferred to the debt service fund charged with the responsibility of paying the principal and/or interest on the bonds issued to finance the capital projects fund.

A bond discount exists when a bond issue is sold at a price less than that of the principal amount of the bonds. In many instances, the sale of bonds at a discount is prohibited. However, in the event a bond issue does produce a discount, the facts of the case should be fully disclosed as shown in the following illustration. Assume that bonds are authorized in the amount of $100,000, and that the entire amount is to be used for the purchase of land. The entries to create the capital projects fund and to record their issue are as follow:

Bonds authorized and unissued	$100,000	
Appropriations, land		$100,000
To record authorization to issue capital projects fund bonds for purchase of land		
Cash	$ 98,800	
Appropriations, land	1,200	
Revenue from bonds issued		$100,000
To record the sale of bonds at a discount		

Illustration 13-1 shows the general ledger after posting these transactions.

Observe that the appropriation is reduced to the amount of cash that is available for use. Not identified as a discount on bonds payable in the capital projects fund, the only accounting disclosure that the discount caused a reduction in the appropriation is the general journal entry. Therefore, for management to be informed through accounting reports and statements what did happen, it would be a sound business practice for the board of education to provide a budgeted fund balance at the time of appropriating money for capital project expenditures. The examples following Illustration 13-1 show how the facts may be fully disclosed.

Observe that $200 remains in the budgeted fund balance account and may be appropriated by action of the board to cover future, but presently unknown and unanticipated costs. This procedure does not authorize expenditures in excess of appropriations for purposes contained in the budget.

Illustration 13-1

	Cash	
8	$98,800	

Revenue From Bonds Issued

			Bonds Authorized & Issued		Revenue from Bonds Issued		Unrealized
Date	Explanation	PR	Debit	Credit	Debit	Credit	Revenue
3			$100,000				$100,000
8						$100,000	0

Expenditures: Land

Date	Explanation	PR	Encumbrances	Expenditures	Appropriation	Balance
3					$100,000	$100,000
				$1,200	98,800	

Example 1
Assume a bond issue is authorized for $100,000 and that the board appropriates $98,800 for capital projects expenditures:

Bonds authorized and unissued	$100,000	
Appropriations, building		$98,800
Budgeted fund balance		1,200
To record capital project budget		

Example 2
Assume that the bonds could be sold at $99,000. Prior to issuing the bonds, the board would authorize an additional appropriation of $1,000 to acknowledge that the discount on bonds issued is a part of the cost of the capital project:

Budgeted fund balance	$1,000	
Appropriation, discount on bonds issued		$1,000
To record approval to issue bonds at a discount		

Example 3
Assume that the bonds did sell for $99,000:

Cash	$99,000	
Expenditures, discount on bonds issued	1,000	
Revenue from bonds issued		$100,000
To record the sale of bonds at a discount		

A most effective management accounting technique can be used which includes accounts to record a provision in all capital projects fund construction contracts to withhold a stated percentage or stated amount of the total contract price for a reasonable period of time at the conclusion of each project to permit the school district to conduct a thorough and complete inspection of the project and to satisfy itself that the provisions of the contract have been satisfactorily completed. Inspection is usually a service of the architect, who notifies the contractors of unacceptable conditions in the project, if any. Upon correction of these conditions, the architect issues a certificate of satisfactory completion to the school district, which it uses as the basis for releasing the retained percentage to the contractors. The amount to be retained should be sufficient to encourage the contractor to correct all items identified by the architect at the earliest possible date. In this way, school systems can expedite early, total completion of capital projects.

An illustration of entries to record use of the contracts payable retained percentage accounting procedure is contained in the entries that follow. Typical of the use of capital projects funds is that of a state that permits a capital projects fund (identified as a building fund), to receive cash from the sale of bonds. In addition, this fund may receive revenue from a county school tax levy, state income tax distributions and revenue from other sources. If there is a balance left in the building fund after the building project has been completed and all claims against the building fund have been paid, the balance may be, according to the state's law, transferred to a fund established for the purpose of paying indebtedness incurred in the building project. If no indebtedness has been incurred, the unused balance in the building fund may be transferred to the general fund. Although the fund may be referred to as a building fund, it is accounted for through the use of principles of accounting applicable to capital projects funds.

In this particular case, expenditures authorized from this fund are land, buildings, new furniture and equipment, other building expenditures and transfers to other funds. Under the heading of new furniture and equipment, provisions are made for library books, office furniture and equipment, instructional furniture and equipment, engineers' and janitors' equipment, cafeteria and lunchroom equipment, and transportation equipment.

Because money for capital outlay also may be raised from sources other than bonds, this case illustrates that expenditures for a capital outlay project are controlled through one fund. The name by which a capital projects fund may be identified may vary but underlying principles of accounting remain the same.

Example 4
Assume that authorization had been granted to issue $500,000 of 12½ percent bonds maturing in five years; a project had been approved by the state government to assist in construction in the amount of $300,000; and the project had been approved for a grant of $1,200,000 from the federal government. The governing board authorized creation of a capital projects fund for this project, designated as project number 93:

Step 1: *A capital project fund for the Kimberly Hills School District is created by the following entry:*

Bonds authorized and unissued	$500,000	
Estimated revenue from state sources	300,000	
Estimated revenue from federal sources	200,000	
Appropriations		$2,000,000
To record creation of capital projects fund		

Budget made appropriations as follows:
Land	$ 50,000
Building	1,650,000
Equipment	300,000
	$2,000,000

Step 2: *Subsidiary appropriation and expenditure ledger accounts would be created to avoid the possibility of over-expenditure of resources available for the project:*

Cash	$500,000	
Revenue from bonds issued		$500,000
To record issuance of 5-year bonds at face value, 12½ percent		

At the time the bonds are issued, the school system becomes liable for both the principal and interest on indebtedness. As a result, a debt service fund is created to accumulate resources sufficient to pay interest throughout the life of the bonds and the principal at the maturity date of the bonds. Corresponding entries are made in the general long-term debt account group to record the long-term bonds payable. These entries will be illustrated in the following chapter and in the chapter on the general long-term debt account group.

Step 3: *When the project is approved and the board authorizes notification of other governmental agencies of its claims, the following entry is made:*

Due from state government	$ 300,000	
Due from federal government	1,200,000	
Revenue from state sources		$ 300,000
Revenue from federal sources		1,200,000
To record notification of state and federal agencies that the project is underway and that a claim is filed for each unit's share of its cost		
Cash	$ 300,000	
Due from state government		$ 300,000
To record collection of claim against the state government		
Cash	$1,200,000	
Due from federal government		$1,200,000
To record collection of claim against the federal government		
Encumbrances	$1,800,000	
Reserve for encumbrances		$1,800,000
To record issuance of purchase orders, signing of contracts for construction and other documents of commitment for:		

Land	$ 50,000	
Buildings	1,450,000	
Equipment	300,000	
	$1,800,000	

Expenditures	$195,000	
Cash		$195,000
To record expenditures for building materials not previously encumbered		
Reserve for encumbrances	$ 50,000	
Encumbrances		$ 50,000
To reverse original encumbrance		
Expenditures	$ 50,000	
Cash		$ 50,000
To record expenditure for project		

18 • CHAPTER 13

Reserve for encumbrances	$300,000	
Encumbrances		$300,000
To record reversal of original encumbrances		
Expenditures	$300,000	
Cash		$300,000
To record expenditure for equipment		
Reserve for encumbrances	$1,450,000	
Encumbrances		$1,450,000
To reverse original encumbrance for building construction		
Expenditures	$1,448,000	
Contracts payable		$1,448,000
To record expenditure for completion of building contract		
Contracts payable	$1,448,000	
Cash		$1,348,000
Contracts payable, retained percentage		100,000
To record payment of contract less amount to be retained until formal acceptance of building		
Contracts payable	$100,000	
Cash		$100,000
To record payment of retained percentage upon completion and acceptance of building		

Step 4: *The general ledger, including all revenue accounts, would appear as follows:*

```
            Cash                              Contracts Payable
2   $  500,000  |  7  $  195,000          11   $1,448,000   | 10  $1,448,000
4      300,000  |  8       50,000                           |
5    1,200,000  |  9      300,000
                | 10    1,348,000          Contracts Payable,
                | 12      100,000          Retained Percentage

Due from State Government                 12   $  100,000   | 10   $  100,000
3   $  300,000  |  4  $  300,000


                |                          Reserve for Encumbrances
Due from Federal Government                8   $   50,000   |  6  $1,800,000
3   $1,200,000  |  4  $1,200,000           9      300,000   |
3    1,200,000  |  4   1,200,000          10    1,450,000   |
```

Revenue From Bonds Issued

Date	Explanation	PR	Bonds Authorized & Unissued Debit	Credit	Revenue from Bonds Issued Debit	Credit	Unrealized Revenue
		1	$500,000				$500,000
		2				$500,000	0

Revenue From State Sources

Date	Explanation	PR	Estimated Revenue Debit	Credit	Actual Revenue Debit	Credit	Unrealized Revenue
		1	$300,000				$300,000
		3				$300,000	0

Revenue From Federal Sources

Date	Explanation	PR	Estimated Revenue Debit	Credit	Actual Revenue Debit	Credit	Unrealized Revenue
		1	$1,200,000				$1,200,000
		3				$1,200,000	0

Expenditure: Control

Date	Explanation	PR	Encumbrances	Expenditures	Appropriation	Unencumbered Balance
		1			$2,000,000	$2,000,000
		6	$1,800,000			200,000
		7	195,000			5,000
		8	50,000	50,000		5,000
		9	300,000	300,000		5,000
		10	1,450,000	1,448,000		7,000

Step 5: *The subsidiary expenditures ledger would appear as follows:*

Expenditure: Land

Date	Explanation	PR	Encumbrances	Expenditures	Appropriation	Unencumbered Balance
		1			$50,000	$50,000
		6	$50,000			0
		8	$50,000	$50,000		0

Expenditure: Building

Date	Explanation	PR	Encumbrances	Expenditures	Appropriation	Unencumbered Balance
		1			$1,650,000	$1,650,000
		6	$1,450,000			200,000
		7		$ 195,000		5,000
		10	1,450,000	1,448,000		7,000

Expenditure: Equipment

Date	Explanation	PR	Encumbrances	Expenditures	Appropriation	Unencumbered Balance
		1			$300,000	$300,000
		6	$300,000			0
		9	300,000	$300,000		0

Step 6: *A trial balance of the capital project fund would appear as follows:*

Kimberly Hills School District
Capital Project Fund
Trial Balance
(Date)

Cash	$ 7,000	
Bonds authorized and unissued	500,000	
Revenue from bonds issued		$500,000
Estimated revenue from state sources	300,000	
Estimated revenue from federal sources	1,200,000	
Revenue from state sources		300,000
Revenue from federal sources		1,200,000
Appropriations		2,000,000
Expenditures	1,993,000	
	$4,000,000	$4,000,000

Step 7: *The closing entries for all revenue and expenditure accounts, both budgetary and actual, are as follows:*

Appropriations	$2,000,000	
Expenditures		$1,993,000
Revenue and expenditure summary		7,000
To close appropriations and expenditure accounts in the general ledger and in the subsidiary ledgers as follows:		

Appropriations for:
Land	$50,000	
Buildings	1,650,000	
Equipment	300,000	
	$2,000,000	

Expenditures for:
Land	$50,000	
Buildings	1,643,000	
Equipment	300,000	
	$1,993,000	

Revenue from bonds issued	$500,000	
Revenue from state sources	300,000	
Revenue from federal sources	1,200,000	
Bonds authorized and unissued		$500,000
Estimated revenue from state sources		300,000
Estimated revenue from federal sources		1,200,000
To close all revenue accounts, budgetary and actual		
Revenue and expenditure summary	$7,000	
Capital project fund equity		$7,000
To close revenue and expenditure summary		

Step 8: *Assume that the governing board authorized transfer of the unencumbered balance of the unappropriated fund equity balance to the debt service fund:*

Capital project fund equity	$7,000	
Due to debt service fund		$7,000
To record authorization by board to transfer		
unencumbered balance of the capital project fund		
to the debt service fund		

Step 9: *The entry to record transfer of cash to the debt service fund would appear as follows:*

Due to debt service fund	$7,000	
Cash		$7,000
To transfer cash to the debt service fund		

As an exercise, using the general ledger and the subsidiary expenditures ledger presented before the preceding trial balance, post all closing entries and entries to record the disposition of the remaining cash balance to these ledgers. When this posting is completed, observe that all accounts of the capital project fund 93 are in balance.

Illustration 13-2

Kimberly Hills School District
Capital Project Funds
Combining Balance Sheet
June 30, 1996
With Comparative Totals for June 30, 1995

	Capital Outlay	Capital Bonding Program	Totals 1996	1995
Assets				
Investments, at cost plus accrued interest	$4,251,334	$2,785,407	$7,036,741	$14,538,824
Delinquent property taxes receivable	353,360	0	353,360	369,601
Prepaid expenditures	3,145	0	3,145	246,750
Contracts receivable plus accrued interest	2,334,922	0	2,334,922	2,452,434
Total Assets	$6,942,761	$2,785,407	$9,728,168	$17,607,609
Liabilities and Fund Balance				
Liabilities:				
Accounts payable	$888,249	$74,638	$962,887	$2,414,549
Due to Operations & Maintenance	99,724	0	99,724	1 3,227
Deferred property tax revenue	460,396	0	460,396	258,207
Deferred revenue on contracts receivable	2,170,039	0	2,170,039	2,295,412
Total Liabilities	$3,618,408	$74,638	$3,693,046	$ 4,981,395
Fund Balance:				
Reserved for encumbrances	$703,665	$493,110	$1,196,775	$6,146,161
Unreserved - unappropriated	2,620,688	2,217,659	4,838,347	6,480,053
Total Fund Balance	3,324,353	2,710,769	6,035,122	12,626,214
Total Liabilities and Fund Balance	$6,942,761	$2,785,407	$9,728,168	$17,607,609

To complete the exercise, balance and rule all accounts in both the general ledger and subsidiary expenditures ledger. The fund has served its purpose. All books of original entry, financial statements, and documents giving evidence of the financial transactions of this fund may be bound together and filed for future use by auditors of the school district.

Illustration 13-3

Kimberly Hills School District
Capital Project Funds
Combining Statement of Revenue, Expenditures and Fund Balance
June 30, 1996
With Comparative Totals for June 30, 1995

	Capital Outlay	Bonding Program	Totals 1996	Totals 1995
Revenues				
Local sources	$3,815,917	$0	$ 3,815,917	$ 6,908,665
Federal sources	4,681	0	4,681	0
Total Revenues	$3,820,598	$0	$ 3,820,598	$ 6,908,665
Other Financial Sources				
Sale of bonds	$ 0	$0	$ 0	$ 7,000,000
Sale of real property	134,823	0	134,823	1 25,112
Total Revenues Other Sources	134,823	0	134,823	7,125,112
Total Revenues	$3,955,421	$0	$ 3,955,421	$14,033,777
Expenditures				
General supervision	$ 75,517	$ 27,081	$ 102,598	$ 108,696
Site acquisition and improvements	495,289	730,016	1,225,305	1,175,289
Construction	6,168,988	1,561,303	7,730,291	14,511,932
Equipment	341,371	982,941	1,324,312	727,448
Other expenditures	164,007	0	164,007	170,388
Total Expenditures	$7,245,172	$3,301,341	$10,546,513	$16,693,753
Excess Revenue over Expenditures	($3,289,751)	($3,301,341)	($6,591,092)	($2,659,976)
Fund Balance – Unappropriated, July 1, 1995	2,250,910	4,229,143	6,480,053	2,632,592
Decrease in reserve for encumbrances	3,659,529	1,289,857	4,949,386	6,507,437
Fund Balance – Unappropriated, June 30, 1996	$2,620,688	$2,217,659	$4,838,347	$6,480,053

Illustration 13-2 shows the reporting format to combine all capital projects funds balance sheets for the year ending June 30, 1996, of the Kimberly Hills School District. Illustration 13-3 shows the format for combining statements of revenues, expenditures and fund balances for capital project funds in Kimberly Hills for the same time period.

SUMMARY

Capital projects funds are used to account for revenue from a bond issue or from other sources designated for capital outlay purposes. Capital projects fund revenue is provided by issuing bonds. Bonds may also be issued for other capital projects fund purposes such as eliminating a deficit resulting from operation of the general fund, a special revenue fund, an internal services fund or an enterprise fund, or refinancing, retiring or refunding maturing bond issues.

Bonding power of the board or the governmental unit through which bonds are issued is restricted by law and a favorable referendum vote is usually required before bonds can be issued.

When a bond issue is authorized to be sold, budgetary accounts entitled bonds authorized and unissued are debited and appropriations are credited. The differences between debits and credits is credited to the budgeted fund balance account or to the capital projects unappropriated fund equity account. The bonds authorized and unissued account serves the same purpose for a capital projects fund as the estimated revenue account serves for the general fund. It is debited for the face value of the bonds.

ACTIVITIES

1. Review the definition of the following terms found in the glossary:
   a. Capital projects fund
   b. Capital outlays
   c. Bond
   d. Bond proceeds
   e. Bond premium
   f. Bond discount
   g. Debt service fund
   h. Bond issue
   i. Maturity date
   j. Unappropriated fund equity account
   k. Face value of bonds
   l. Debenture
   m. Interest payable
   n. Rate

o. Note
p. Coupon bonds
q. Registered bonds
r. Self-balancing
s. General fixed assets account group
t. Internal service fund
u. Retire bonds
v. Indebtedness

2. Why do school districts issue bonds? Can districts issue bonds for the same project at varying times? If so, why would they do that?

3. Differentiate between a bond and a note.

4. Select a local school district and examine the capital needs and funding of bonds for the district. How does the district account for bonds? Does the district account for bonds for new construction differently than for remodeling?

5. Prepare journal entries necessary to record authorization of a $12,000,000 bond issue for a school system and for the cash sale of the entire issue.

6. Prepare the journal entries necessary to close the capital projects fund accounts created in Activity 5 above. Assume total expenditures were $11,500,000, and that they were paid. Also prepare the general journal entry to transfer any cash remaining to the debt service fund for payment of interest.

7. Why are budgetary accounts used in capital projects funds?

8. On June 25, 1995, Fort Steven School System received authorization to issue bonds in the amount of $7,500,000 for improvements on certain buildings. The following transactions occurred after the authorization:
   a. $6,500,000 of bonds were sold on July 1 of that year.
   b. On July 6, 1995, contracts were issued for the improvements estimated to cost $6,750,000.
   c. The remaining bonds were sold on July 8, 1995.
   d. A partial payment invoice for work completed in the amount of $2,000,000 was received on July 25, 1995.

e. On August 1, 1995, materials were purchased on account for $750,000.
f. The improvements were completed on August 15, 1995. An invoice for the total balance due in the amount of $4,400,000 was received that day. Assume there were change orders issued and approved to the original contract price.
g. Accounts payable were paid in full on September 15, 1995.

Instructions:
- Using a capital projects fund general journal, prepare entries to record the authorization of the bonds and the transactions that occurred as indicated above.

9. On September 1, 1995, the New Douglas School System Board of Education appropriated $11,500,000 to erect a new school building, furnish it and to repair the Columbus Manor School driveways and walks. Of this amount, $9,500,000 was appropriated for the new building, $1,800,000 to furnish it, and $200,000 for repairing and replacing the Columbus Manor School driveways and walks. To finance these projects, the board received authorization to issue $11,500,000 in bonds. As of the following January 1, among account balances of the capital projects fund, the following appeared:

Cash	$ 9,700,000
Bonds authorized and unissued	11,500,000
Appropriations	11,500,000
Revenue from bonds issued	9,700,000

The following transactions took place during the calendar year beginning that January:

January 31 – The remaining bonds were sold.
February 1 – A contract for replacing/repairing driveways and sidewalks was signed at an estimated cost of $175,000.
February 15 – A contract for $9,500,000 was signed for the new building.
April 1 – Purchase orders totaling $1,750,000 to furnish the new building were issued.
May 15 – The replacing/repairing driveway project was completed, and an invoice for $175,000 was received.
June 1 – The invoice for the driveway project was paid in full.

Instructions:
- Record account balances in the general and subsidiary ledgers.
- Prepare general journal entries for transactions that occurred during the year and post to the general and subsidiary ledgers.
- Prepare an interim statement of appropriations, encumbrances and expenditures of the capital project fund as of July 1, 1996.
- Prepare a trial balance as of July 1, 1996.

REFERENCES/SELECTED READINGS

Fowler, W. J., Jr. (1990). *Financial accounting for local and state systems, 1990.* Washington, DC: U.S. Government Printing Office.

Tidwell, S. B. (1985). *Financial and managerial accounting for elementary and secondary school systems (3rd edition).* Reston, VA: Research Corporation of the Association of School Business Officials.

14

Debt Service Funds

INTRODUCTION

Once a school district borrows money by issuing bonds, it is faced not only with the problem of paying interest on bonds payable annually but it is also faced with the problem of retiring the bonds when they mature. Debt service funds are created to serve as the accounting device through which long-term debt can be managed effectively as long as bonds payable are outstanding.

Debt service funds are used to pay principal and interest on bonds payable and to accumulate resources over the outstanding life of a bond issue in an amount equal to the maturity value.

OUTCOMES

In this chapter, you will learn how to:

1. Determine why debt service funds are used.
2. Use budgetary accounts to record debt service fund transactions.
3. Prepare financial statements for a debt service fund.

TYPES OF DEBT SERVICE FUNDS

Two methods are frequently used by school districts to retire outstanding bonds and to pay interest on them. The method selected is determined, in part at least, by the type of bonds issued. One type of bonds can be retired and interest on them paid each year from the general fund when revenue of the general fund is adequate. This type is referred to as serial bonds, a part of which is retired annually over the outstanding life of the issue. The second type is referred to as term bonds, the entire principal of which comes due or matures on one date, the type usually retired through use of a debt service fund.

When debt service funds are used, interest can be paid either by the debt service fund or by the general fund. While accumulating resources, cash of the debt service fund is invested in income producing securities. At the maturity date, the securities are converted into cash, which is used to retire the bonds. A set of accounting principles has been developed for debt service funds, which has been found to be effective for accumulating resources over the outstanding life of a long-term bond issue to retire it at maturity.

If the amount of serial bonds maturing at periodic dates is not too great each year, it is possible to pay annual interest and to retire the bonds from the general fund. This method of bond retirement requires general fund revenue annually from a tax levy or from some other source in an amount sufficient to retire the year's maturing bonds. In the general fund, appropriations can be made for debt service expenditures for bond interest and for bond principal. As retirement of serial bonds is ordinarily out of revenue of the year in which the bonds mature, there is no need to accumulate resources over a long period of time. In the general fund an appropriation usually lapses at the end of the budget period. For that reason, it is unusual that an accumulation of revenues from one year to another would be possible in the general fund.

Illustration 14-1 shows how revenue from taxes in the general fund can be authorized for payment of principal and interest.

Serial bonds mature in series during the last few years of long life. For example, if 20 percent of the issue matures each year during the twenty-first, twenty-second, twenty-third, twenty-fourth and twenty-fifth years, debt service funds can also be used to retire what, in effect, are term bonds.

Debt service funds are established to account for the annual accumulation of resources for the retirement of long-term bonds over the outstanding life of term bonds. Annual accumulation spreads the tax burden equally over the life of the bonds. A separate group of accounts effectively provides information from each year's revenue requirements from taxation and interest earnings and provides information clearly throughout the life of the bonds about the adequacy of the fund. Published financial reports prepared by some accountants should contain this vital information for management, the board of education, taxpayers or the bondholder.

Illustration 14-1

Budgeted fund balance	$55,000	
Appropriation, bond principal		$50,000
Appropriation, bond interest		5,000
To record the general fund appropriation for expenditures for bond principal retirement and bond interest expense		
Expenditures, bond interest expense	5,000	
Cash		5,000
To record check issued for payment of bond interest expense		
Expenditures, bond principal	50,000	
Matured bonds payable		50,000
To record liability for currently maturing long-term bonds		
Cash for bond principal	50,000	
Cash		50,000
To record check issued for retirement of bond principal		
Matured bonds payable	50,000	
Cash for bond principal		50,000
To record receipt of cancelled bonds completing the retirement of bonds matured		

Revenue of a debt service fund usually is raised through taxation and earnings on investments. Taxes can be levied for the specific purpose of debt retirement. Accounting for the tax assessment, levy and collection should be the function of the debt service fund. To relieve the debt service fund of the tax assessment, levy and collection function, frequently the levy and collection is made by either the general fund or a central tax collection agency fund, which turns cash collected for it over to the debt service fund. Chapter 20 on Agency Funds illustrates further operation of a tax collection agency fund.

When cash is received by the debt service fund, it can be placed in revenue producing investments. Income earned on investments reduces taxation that otherwise would be required to retire bonds at maturity. Special accounting principles apply to debt service funds. Each year taxes are assessed, levied and collected either by the debt

Example 1

In order to accumulate a reserve for debt retirement of $100,000 by a series of five equal tax levies that earn 10 percent compounded annually, a tax levy of $16,379 is required. From an annuity table, the amount of an annuity of $1 per period at 10 percent for five periods is found to be 6.1051. The required tax levy of $16,379, therefore, is computed by dividing $100,000 by 6.1051. The accumulated total illustrated below is $99,997 due to rounding.

Debt Service Fund
Accumulation Schedule

Year	Required Annual Earnings	Total Additions Taxation	Required Annual Accumulated Each Year	Fund Total
1		$16,379	$16,379	$16,379
2	$1,638	16,379	18,017	34,396
3	3,440	16,379	19,819	54,215
4	5,422	16,379	21,801	76,016
5	7,602	16,379	23,981	$99,997
	$18,102	$81,895	$99,997	

service fund, the general fund or a tax collection agency fund in an amount sufficient that the aggregate amount accumulated over the life of the bonds will be equal to the bonds' maturity value. The tax levy can be a special voted tax or it can be a portion of the general property tax assessment and levy.

ACCOUNTS AND TRANSACTIONS

The page format for budgetary revenue accounts and revenue accounts in the debt service fund is identical to the page format used in the general fund. However, observe that some account titles are different. Because of the limited number of sources of revenue of a debt service fund frequently, a subsidiary revenue ledger is not necessary. However, if needed, a subsidiary revenue ledger can be used. The page format for budgetary expenditure accounts (appropriations, and accounts for expenditures and encumbrances) in debt services funds is identical to the page format of these accounts in the general fund. Because of the limited number of expenditure accounts needed in a debt service fund frequently, a subsidiary expenditure ledger can be used but may not be necessary.

The following paragraphs provide definitions and explanations of selected terms.

Required Taxation – If the general fund collects taxes for debt retirement or if the tax is collected by the debt service fund, budgetary accounts are used. Budgetary accounts in debt service funds take on different titles, however. The title of one account is "required taxation." This account records the amount that had to be raised from taxation or from other revenue sources each year to meet the bonds' accumulation schedule requirements plus the amount required to meet annual interest costs if interest is to be paid from the debt service fund. An accumulation schedule is included in the bond prospectus prepared prior to the issuance of bonds and shows how much taxes and earnings are required each year until the fund accumulates the maturity value of the bonds at the maturity date. In a debt service fund, this account may have another title such as "required contributions," a title frequently used in the debt service fund when taxes are collected by the general fund as revenue of the general fund and transferred to the debt service fund. This account serves debt service funds in the same way that the "estimated revenue" account serves other budgetary funds like the general fund, special revenue funds and capital projects funds.

Required earnings – A second budgetary account is "required earnings." This account records the amount required by the bonds' accumulation schedule to be earned each year from investments. It, too, serves the debt service fund in the same way that the "estimated revenue" account serves other budgetary funds.

Budgeted fund balance – If interest is to be paid from the debt service fund annually, revenue from taxes or other sources must be provided in the budget through the budgetary account "required taxation" which is debited with a corresponding credit to "budgeted fund balance." If interest is to be paid from this fund, an appropriation has to be made by debiting "budgeted fund balance" and crediting "appropriation, bond interest expense." The budgeted fund balance account serves the debt service fund in the same way that it serves the general fund.

Reserve for encumbrances – The reserve for encumbrances account in the debt service fund is identical to the reserve for encumbrances account used in the general fund and it serves an identical purpose in the debt service fund.

Reserve for debt retirement – The reserve for debt service account is not a budgetary account, but rather an appropriation of the debt service fund equity and is introduced as a most effective debt management account. The account title is "reserve for retirement of principal of debt." Instead of crediting either the debt service fund unappropriated equity account or a budgeted fund balance account for the total, the reserve for retirement of principal of debt account is credited each year for the combined amounts of required taxation and required earnings if interest is not to be paid by the debt service fund. If the current year's interest is to be paid by the debt service fund, budgeted fund balance is credited for the amount of revenue required to meet the current year's interest cost.

As a result, the reserve for retirement of principal of debt shows the amount required at the end of each year by the accumulation schedule throughout the life of the bonds outstanding. Annual variances between required taxation and revenue from taxes and between required earnings and revenue from earnings are closed into the revenue and expenditure summary, and the balance is closed into the debt service fund equity account. The debt service fund equity account indicates each year the amount that the fund exceeds or the amount the fund falls short of the requirements of the bonds' accumulation schedule.

When information provided by use of both budgetary and actual revenue and expenditure accounts is shown in interim and annual financial statements of each debt service fund, the board of education can take whatever action is necessary to bring the fund more closely into agreement with the accumulation schedule requirements. This information, not disclosed without use of the reserve for retirement of debt account or other similar account, is important as a way to focus the attention of the board on the amount of the cumulative variances to date. If the variance is an unfavorable variance, appropriate board decision and management actions can be taken each year throughout the outstanding life of each bond issue to meet the requirements rather than to discover at the maturity of the bonds that financial resources are not available to retire the bond issue. If the variance is favorable, decisions of the board may reduce the amount needed from taxation each year.

Appropriation, bond interest expense – If the debt service fund pays interest, the budgetary account, "appropriation, bond interest expense" is credited for the amount for the year and the "budgeted fund balance" account is debited. Because the amount is already committed, a corresponding debit is made to "encumbrances, debt service-interest," and a credit is made to "reserve for encumbrances."

Appropriation, principal of bond debt – The annual budget for each debt service fund must specify the amount to be appropriated for bonds maturing during the year, which are to be paid from the debt service fund. The entry to record the budget debits "budgeted fund balance" and credits "appropriation, principal of bond debt." Because the amount is already committed, a corresponding debit is made to "encumbrances, principal of bond debt" and a credit is made to the "reserve for encumbrances." The amount of cash required to retire a bond issue can be accumulated by a series of tax levies, which are equal in amount when computed on an actuarial basis. As cash is collected from taxes and interest on investments, it is invested in income producing investments. This plan to retire the principal of debt is commonly called an annuity program, a series of equal additions at equal periods of time. Annuity ordinarily refers to one year but the periods may be any length of time. The interest rate is the rate per period.

The bond prospectus contains a debt service fund accumulation schedule that generally provides that annual deposits from taxation be at a fixed amount which, when added to earnings each year, will produce the maturity value of the bonds at the maturity date. The accumulation schedule is based on compound interest and compound interest or annuity tables are used to determine the *equal* annual required taxation. Annuity tables are published that specify the amount of an annuity of $1 per period with interest rates which range from 2 percent up for one or more periods.

Assume that the tax levy resulted in revenue of $16,379 each year, all of which is collected. At the end of the first year, the reserve for debt retirement is $16,379. At the end of the second year, the reserve is increased by revenue from tax of an additional $16,379 plus interest of 10 percent. The total of the reserve for debt retirement is $34,396. Earnings in the following year are based on the total being invested at the beginning of the year. Observe that the accumulated amount equals $99,997 at the end of the fifth year due to rounding.

Various factors such as fluctuations in the rate of interest earned, fluctuations in the amount of revenue from taxation caused by differences between estimated and actual uncollectible taxes receiv-

Example 2

Assume that the general fund or the central tax collection agency fund records all taxes receivable, makes allowances for estimated uncollectible taxes receivable and collects taxes as an agent for the debt service fund. The general fund or the central tax collection agency fund transfers the amount of taxes collected to the debt service fund. The amount is not revenue of the general fund or the central tax collection agency fund but instead is revenue of the debt service fund.

In The Debt Service Fund (First Year)
Required taxation	$16,379	
Reserve for debt retirement		$16,379
To record debt service fund budget for the first year		

In the General Fund
Taxes receivable	$ XXX	
Estimated uncollectible taxes receivable		$ XXX
Revenue from taxes		XXX
Due to debt service fund		16,379
To record the tax assessment and levy, a part of which is revenue of the debt service fund		

In the Debt Service Fund
Due from the general fund	$16,379	
Revenue from taxes		$16,379
To record claim from the general fund for debt service fund taxes collected by it		

In the Tax Collection Agency Fund – If Used
Taxes receivable	$ XXX	
Estimated uncollectible taxes receivable		$ XXX
Due to the general fund		XXX
Due to the special revenue fund		XXX
Due to debt service fund		16,379
To record tax assessment and levy and to distribute liability to each fund		

In the Debt Service Fund if Tax Agency Fund Is Used
Due from tax collection agency fund	$ 16,379	
Revenue from taxes		$16,379
To record claim for tax levy from the tax collection agency fund		

Example 3
After taxes are collected by the general fund, cash is transferred from the general fund to the debt service fund. Assume that $16,379 is collected by the general fund and transferred to the debt service fund.

In the General Fund
Due to debt service fund	$16,379	
Cash		$16,379
To record transfer of cash from tax collections to the debt service fund		

In the Debt Service Fund
Cash	$16,379	
Due from the general fund		$16,379
To record transfer of cash from the general fund for debt service fund revenue collections		
Investments	16,379	
Cash		16,379
To record investment in certificates of deposit		

At the end of the fiscal period, the following closing entries would be made:

Revenue from taxes	$16,379	
Required taxation		$16,379
To close budgetary and actual revenue accounts		

Example 4
Consistency in accounting principles and procedures requires that the accounts be closed through the revenue and expenditure summary. However, as no variances existed, no balance would appear in the account.

(Balance Sheet)
Assets:	
Investments	$16,379
Fund equity:	
Appropriated:	
Reserve for debt retirement	$16,379

Example 5

For the second year in the debt service fund, entries for several situations are in the following steps.

Step 1: Record the budget entry from the accumulation schedule for the debt service fund for the second year as follows:

Required taxation	$16,379	
Required earnings	1,638	
Reserve for debt retirement		$18,017
To record the budget for the		
debt service fund for the second year		

Step 2: When the general fund makes the tax assessment and levy, the following entry is made in the debt service fund:

Due from the general fund	$16,379	
Revenue from taxation		$16,379
To record the claim against the general fund		
at the time of the tax assessment and levy by the general fund		

Step 3: Assuming that the exact amount of taxes was collected by the general fund and was transferred to the debt service fund, the following entry is made in the debt service fund:

Cash	$1,738	
Revenue from interest earned		$1,738
To record collection of interest earned		

Step 4: As soon as cash is received, it should be invested. Therefore, the following entry records investment of total cash:

Investments	$18,117	
Cash		$18,117
To record investment in certificates of deposit		

Step 5: At the end of the fiscal year, the following closing entries are made:

Revenue from taxation	$16,379	
Revenue from interest earned	1,738	
Revenue and expenditure summary		$18,117
To close revenue accounts		
Revenue and expenditure summary	18,017	
Required taxation		16,379
Required earnings		1,638
To close budgetary revenue accounts		
Revenue and expenditure summary	100	
Debt service fund equity		100
To close the revenue and expenditure summary		

Step 6: The debt service fund balance sheet at the end of the second year would contain the following accounts:

Assets:
Investments $ 34,496

Fund Equity:
Unappropriated $ 100
Reserve for debt retirement 34,396
$34,496

Example 6

Assume that an investment in bonds of $10,000 made at a premium of $200 plus accrued interest is purchased in the amount of $100.

Step 1: The entry to record the purchase follows:

Investments	$10,000	
Unamortized premium on investments	200	
Accrued interest receivable	100	
Cash		$10,300
To record purchase of bonds at a premium plus accrued interest		

Step 2: On the interest payment date, the following entry is made to record collection of interest:

Cash	$900	
Revenue from earnings, interest		$800
Accrued interest receivable		100
To record collection of interest on investments		

Step 3: Assume that an investment of $12,000 is made on which a discount of $240 is applicable. The following entry records the investment:

Investments	$12,000	
Unamortized discount on investment		$ 240
Cash		11,760
To record investments purchased at a discount		

Example 7

Assume that the $12,000 investment at a discount of $240 is to be held for four years. Either at each interest collection date or at the end of the fiscal year, the discount should be amortized. Amortization always affects interest earned on investments and is, as a result, amortized through the revenue from interest account. The following entry records amortization of one-fourth of the discount:

Revenue from interest	$60	
Unamortized discount on investments		$60
To amortize one-fourth of the discount on investments		

Example 8

Assume that the investment of $10,000 at a $200 premium is to be held for four years. The entry to amortize the premium at the end of the first year is as follows:

Unamortized premium on investments	$50	
Revenue from interest		$50
To amortize one-fourth of the premium on investments		

able, and gains or losses on sale of investments, frequently cause a variance between required earnings and actual earnings. If the reserve for debt retirement is to be maintained at the amount required by the accumulation schedule, revenue must be adjusted for earnings or for taxes that differ from the required amounts. If actual annual earnings on the investments do not equal the required earnings or if revenue from taxes does not equal required taxation, the amount of the annual tax levy or the amount of revenue required from other sources must be adjusted upward. If the actual earnings on investments exceed the required earnings, or if revenue from taxes exceeds the required taxation, the amount of the annual tax levy can be adjusted downward. The objective of the debt service fund is to accumulate sufficient but not excessive resources to be used to retire the bonds outstanding.

Budgetary accounts for each bond issue facilitate periodic comparisons of actual earnings with required earnings and periodic comparisons of actual revenue from taxation or other sources with required taxation or revenue from other sources. These comparisons throughout the outstanding life of each bond issue serve as effective debt management techniques for adjusting the amount of taxes required to retire each bond issue.

Observe that the reserve for debt retirement balance is in agreement with the debt service fund accumulation schedule at the end of each year throughout the outstanding life of the bonds. In this illustration, a favorable variance of $100 exists at the end of the second year. In future years, revenue from taxation or revenue from earnings may fall short of the requirements of the debt service fund accumulation schedule or losses may occur when converting investments into cash. In the event that the unappropriated debt service fund equity develops a deficit (a debit balance) attention of the board would be focused on the unfavorable variance and corrective action could be taken by the board of education.

The bond prospectus usually restricts the debt service fund to certain kinds of investments—investments that are conservative, yet, able to provide income for the debt service fund. If investments in bonds are authorized, they may be purchased at a price in excess of face value (called a premium) or they may be purchased at a price less than face value (called a discount). An additional characteristic of investment in bonds is that if purchased between interest payment dates, interest accrued since the authorized date of issue or since the last interest payment date is included in the purchase price. The following illustrations will record the purchase at a premium, the purchase at a discount and the purchase including accrued interest to date of purchase.

When long-term investments are made at a discount or a premium, the discount or premium affects the amount of interest that will be earned on the investment. A prorata share of the discount or premium should be amortized or written off each year over the remaining outstanding life of the investment. Amortization of the premium or discount changes the rate of interest from the nominal rate, i. e., the rate stated on the face of the investment, to an effective rate of interest. Amortization of a discount increases the nominal rate of interest to the effective rate of interest while amortization of a premium decreases the nominal rate of interest to the effective rate of interest. In either case, interest earned each interest period on each investment will be the same amount, leaving the investment recorded at its maturity value.

Over the outstanding life of the investment, the discount or the premium will be written off through the revenue from interest earned account.

Illustration 14-2

New Douglas School District
Debt Service Fund
Trial Balance
(Date)

Cash	$ 3,730	
Investments	22,000	
Unamortized premium on investment	180	
Unamortized discount on investment		$ 210
Required taxation	24,600	
Required earnings	1,200	
Revenue from taxation		24,600
Revenue from interest		1,100
Reserve for debt retirement		25,650
Debt service fund equity		150
Totals	$51,710	$51,710

Illustration 14-3

Revenue from taxation	$24,600	
Revenue from interest	1,110	
Revenue and expenditure summary	90	
Required taxation		$24,600
Required earnings		1,200
To close the actual and budgetary account into the revenue and expenditure account		

FINANCIAL STATEMENTS

Illustration 14-2 shows a trial balance of the debt service fund accounts. Procedures are available for closing temporary and budgetary accounts of the debt service fund at the end of each fiscal period and are shown in Illustration 14-3.

In this case, the difference between the actual earnings and the required earnings must be transferred to the debt service fund equity account through the revenue and expenditure summary at the end of the fiscal period by the following entry:

Debt service fund equity	$90	
Revenue and expenditure summary		$90
To close the revenue and expenditure summary account		

Illustration 14-4

New Douglas School District
Debt Service Fund
Trial Balance
(Date)

Cash	$ 3,740	
Investments	22,000	
Unamortized premium on investments	180	
Unamortized discount on investments		$ 210
Reserve for debt retirement		25,650
Debt service fund equity		60
Totals	$25,920	$25,920

Example 9

Assume that at the maturity of a bond issue for which a debt service fund had been used, the amount of cash on hand is $100,000 and the reserve for debt retirement is $100,000. An entry is made to record matured bonds which have been carried in the general long-term debt group of accounts.

Step 1: The entries to record debt retirement in the debt service fund follow.

Reserve for debt retirement	$100,000	
Appropriation, debt service, principal of debt		$100,000
To record the appropriation of the board of education		
to retire the principal of matured bonds		
Expenditures, debt service, principal of debt	100,000	
Matured bonds payable		100,000
To record the expenditure for retirement of principal of debt		

Step 2: The entry to record the transfer of cash to a fiscal agent for payment of the maturity value of the matured bonds is as follows:

Cash with fiscal agent for debt retirement	$100,000	
Cash		$100,000
To record transfer of cash to fiscal agent		
for payment of maturity value of long-term bonds		

Step 3: When the report of the fiscal agent is received along with each canceled, paid or redeemed bond, the following entry is made:

Matured bonds payable	$100,000	
Cash with fiscal agent for debt retirement		$100,000
To record payment of matured bonds payable by		
the fiscal agent and receipt of canceled bonds		

Example 10

Assume that $100,000 of 12 percent serial bonds have been issued, $20,000 maturing at the end of each year for five years, and that the general fund serves as the tax collection agency for the debt service fund. To pay both principal and interest, the following debt service requirements are established prior to issue:

Year	Bonds Outstanding Beginning of Year	Interest	Principal Requirement	Requirement	Bonds Outstanding End of Year
1	$100,000	$12,000	$20,000		$80,000
2	80,000	9,600	20,000		60,000
3	60,000	7,200	20,000		40,000
4	40,000	4,800	20,000		20,000
5	20,000	2,400	20,000		0

Step 1: In the General Fund:

Cash	$32,000	
Due to debt service fund		$32,000
To record collection of tax that is due to debt service fund		

Step 2: In the Debt Service Fund:

Required taxation	$32,000	
Appropriation, principal, bonds		$20,000
Appropriation, interest, bonds		12,000
To record budget for debt service		
Due from general fund	32,000	
Revenue from taxes		32,000
To record assessment and levy of tax by the general fund		
Cash	32,000	
Due from general fund		32,000
To record collection from general fund		
Expenditures, interest, bonds	12,000	
Cash		12,000
To record payment of interest on bonds		
Expenditures, principal, bonds	20,000	
Matured bonds payable		20,000
To record expenditure to assume liability for matured bonds payable		
Matured bonds payable	20,000	
Cash		20,000
To record retirement of serial bonds from debt service fund		

Step 3: *Closing Entries*

Revenue from taxes	$32,000	
Appropriation, principal, bonds	20,000	
Appropriation, interest, bonds	12,000	
Required taxation		$32,000
Expenditures, interest, bonds		12,000
Expenditures, principal, bonds		20,000
To close budgetary and actual revenue and expenditure accounts		

Example 11

Assume that a tax is authorized to be collected directly by the debt service fund in an amount necessary to retire principal and pay interest. In this case, all accounting for debt service, including assessing, levying and collection of taxes, is accomplished in the debt service fund.

Required taxation	$32,000	
Appropriation, principal, bonds		$20,000
Appropriation, interest, bonds		12,000
To record adoption of budget		
Taxes receivable	34,000	
Revenue from taxes		32,000
Estimated uncollectible taxes receivable		2,000
To record assessment and levy of taxes applicable to debt service		
Cash	18,400	
Taxes receivable		18,400
To record collection of taxes receivable		
Cash	14,200	
Taxes receivable		14,200
To record collection of taxes receivable		
Expenditures, interest, bonds	12,000	
Cash		12,000
To record payment of interest on bonds		
Expenditures, principal, bonds	20,000	
Matured bonds payable		20,000
To record expenditure and assume liability for matured bonds payable		
Matured bonds payable	20,000	
Cash		20,000
To record retirement of matured bonds		

The use of budgetary revenue accounts with actual revenue accounts on the same page puts important information together and easily indicates the variance between each source of budgeted revenue and actual revenue for the debt service fund.

In the case of debt service funds, revenue comparisons between required and actual revenue during the accounting period or studies of the income productivity of investments tend to provide a basis whereby the board of education can make investments of cash in the debt service funds for the best advantage of the school district. The greater the earnings on investments in debt service funds, the lesser the amount of taxes that will have to be assessed, levied and collected in order to retire the long-term debt.

Illustration 14-4 shows a balance sheet that can be prepared when the closing entries have been posted to the debt service fund accounts having a balance.

Having closed the accounts at the end of the accounting period, the debt service fund is ready to begin transactions of the next year. Ultimately, sufficient assets will be accumulated in the debt service fund so that by their conversion into cash at the maturity date of the bond issue, the bonds can be retired (Example 9).

At this point, all investments of the debt service fund will have been converted into cash, and the reserve for debt retirement account will have been used for the purpose for which the fund was created. The assets accumulated in the debt service fund will have been used to retire the bonds at maturity. Therefore, all accounts in the debt service fund will be closed and, for that bond issue, no need exists for the debt service fund to continue in operation.

The advantages that result from the use of accounting principles applicable to debt service funds for each long-term debt issue justify analyzing, recording and reporting through the use of a separate group of self-balancing accounts. This management accounting structure can focus the attention of the board and its administrative officers on the financial requirements of each debt issue throughout its outstanding life and, thus, provide the type of information necessary for the school district to get the maximum amount from every tax dollar for public purposes.

In addition to the accounts illustrated, other accounts may be used such as taxes receivable, allowance for estimated uncollectible taxes,

Illustration 14-5

New Douglas School District
Debt Service Fund
Trial Balance
(Date)

Cash	$ 600	
Taxes receivable	1,400	
Estimated uncollectible taxes receivable		$ 2,000
Required taxation	32,000	
Revenue from taxes		32,000
Appropriation, principal, bonds		20,000
Appropriation, interest, bonds		12,000
Expenditures, principal, bonds	20,000	
Expenditures, interest, bonds	12,000	
Totals	$66,000	$66,000

receivable delinquent, allowance for estimated uncollectible taxes delinquent, interest and penalties receivable, allowance for estimated uncollectible interest and penalties, tax liens, and others if the debt service fund assesses, levies and collects its own taxes receivable.

Previous examples have been restricted to long-term bonds, the principal of which matures at one time. Different circumstances surround serial bonds, a portion of which matures during different years.

Illustration 14-5 shows a trial balance of the debt service fund after making the above entries.

ADJUSTING ENTRIES

Obviously, an allowance has been made for estimated uncollectible taxes receivable in the amount of $2,000. Observe that taxes receivable amount to $1,400, and there is no need at the present time to have an allowance for more than $1,400. An error was made when the estimated uncollectible taxes receivable was recorded. This error understated the current year's revenue because the error was detected during the year in which it was made. Therefore, the following adjusting entry is made:

Estimated uncollectible taxes receivable	$600	
Revenue from taxes		$600
To reduce the estimated uncollectible taxes receivable to $1,400		

If an error is discovered, however, in the balance sheet at the beginning of the period, resulting from transactions of prior fiscal periods, the error is not corrected through current revenue and expenditure accounts but is, instead, corrected through the debt service fund equity account. Corrections of errors of prior years should not affect the current year's revenue and expenditure accounts.

CLOSING ENTRIES

Illustration 14-6 shows the closing entries at this time to the general ledger accounts and to the revenue and expenditure summary accounts. Illustration 14-7 shows the balance sheet of the debt service fund after making the closing entries.

Financial statements which are useful to the board of education, administrative officers, investors, financial analysts and taxpayers or each debt service fund are: the balance sheet, the statement comparing required revenue with revenue, the statement comparing expenditures and encumbrances with appropriations, the statement of changes in fund equity, and the statement of changes in financial position. For preparation of the CAFR, refer to Appendix E.

In debt service funds, large amounts of financial resources are provided by taxation and interest earned while large amounts of financial resources are applied to pay interest on bonds outstanding and to retire principal of debt. When the statement of changes in financial position is prepared on the total financial resources concept, it will disclose effectively the financial resources provided by tax revenue and interest earned and financial resources applied for debt service, including both interest cost and retirement of bond principal. The problem of combining financial statements for all debt service funds into one set of financial statements to be included in the comprehensive annual financial report is the same as it is for special revenue funds and capital projects funds. Examples of the reporting format for debt service funds follow.

Illustration 14-6

Revenue from taxes	$32,600	
Appropriation, principal, bonds	20,000	
Appropriation, interest, bonds	12,000	
Required taxation		$32,000
Expenditures, principal, bonds		20,000
Expenditures, interest, bonds		12,000
Revenue and expenditure summary		600
To close revenue and expenditure accounts, both actual and budgeted		
Revenue and expenditure summary	600	
Debt service fund equity		600
To close revenue and expenditure summary account		

Illustration 14-7

New Douglas School District
Debt Service Fund
Trial Balance
(Date)

Assets:			
Cash	$ 600		
Taxes receivable	1,400		
Less estimated uncollectible		$1,400	
Total Assets			$600
Fund balance			
Debt service fund equity			$600

Example 12, Part 1

The two following financial statements taken from New Douglas School District, Comprehensive Annual Financial Report for the Fiscal Year Ended June 30, 1995, illustrate the way by which financial statements of each separate debt service fund can be combined. The first is the combining balance sheet for all debt service funds.

New Douglas School District
Combining Balance Sheet
All Debt Service Funds
June 30, 1995

	Combined Total	Bond & Interest Fund	Rent Fund
Assets:			
Cash	$ 158,500	$158,500	$0
Investments	667,700	667,700	$0
Receivables, net of allowance for uncollectible amounts:			
Property taxes	5,195,900	5,026,000	169,900
Corporate personal property tax	217,200	217,200	
Interest	39,600	39,600	
Due from other funds	80,200	41,100	39,100
Total Assets	$6,359,100	$6,150,100	$ 209,000
Liabilities and Fund Balance:			
Liabilities:			
Interest payable	$8,300	$8,300	$0
Deferred property tax revenue	2,738,200	2,639,000	99,200
Total Liabilities	$2,746,500	$2,647,300	$ 99,200
Fund Balance:	$3,612,600	$3,502,800	$109,800
Total Liabilities and Fund Balance	$6,359,100	$6,150,100	$ 209,000

Example 12, Part 2
The second is the combining statement of fund operations which presents revenue, expenditures and the changes in fund balance for all debt service funds.

New Douglas School District
**Combining Statement of Fund Operations
All Debt Service Funds**
June 30, 1995

	Combined Total	Bond & Interest Fund	Rent Fund
Revenue:			
Local property taxes	$2,697,200	$2,600,100	$ 97,100
Corporate personal property tax	885,000	885,000	0
Earnings on investments	45,500	45,500	0
Total Revenues	$3,627,700	$3,530,600	$ 97,100
Expenditures, debt service:			
Principal repayment	$1,920,000	$1,920,000	$0
Interest payments on bonds	1,107,900	1,107,900	0
Payment on lease/purchase contract	102,000	0	102,000
Service charges	3,500	3,500	0
Interest on tax anticipation warrants and notes	48,300	48,300	0
Total Expenditures	$3,181,700	$3,079,700	$102,000
Excess Revenue Over Expenditures	$446,000	$450,900	($4,900)
Fund Balance, July 1, 1994	$3,166,600	$3,003,600	$163,000
Fund Balance, June 30, 1995	$3,612,600	$3,454,500	$ 158,100

SUMMARY

Debt service funds are used to pay principal and interest on bonds payable and to accumulate resources over the outstanding life of a bond issue in an amount equal to the maturity value. The funds are used to provide an orderly and organized accounting for the accumulation and disbursement of money for the payment of interest and the retirement at maturity of long-term bonds.

Serial bonds can be retired and interest on them paid each year from the general fund when revenue of the general fund is adequate. Term bonds are usually retired through use of a debt service fund. When debt service funds are used, interest can be paid either by the debt service fund or by the general fund. While accumulating resources, cash of the debt service fund should be invested.

24 • CHAPTER 14

Example 13
The following two financial statements are taken from the Kimberly Hills School District Comprehensive Annual Financial Report, Fiscal Year Ended August 31, 1996. The first financial statement illustrates how one combined balance sheet can be presented for all debt service funds in the comprehensive annual financial report.

Illustration of Example 13, Part 1

Kimberly Hills School District
Debt Service Fund
Balance Sheet
August 31, 1996

Assets			
Cash in bank		$ 64,863	
Cash with tax collector in escrow		4,962	
Cash with paying agent		363,594	$443,419
Temporary investment – Certificate of deposit			275,000
Receivables:			
Property taxes – Delinquent:			
1995 tax roll	$17,264		
1994 tax roll	8,117		
1993 tax roll	10,070		
1992 tax roll	31,672		
1991 tax roll	69,018	136,141	
Property taxes – Penalty and interest		25,325	
		161,466	
Allowance for estimated uncollectible taxes		(58,988)	102,478
Accrued interest on investments			2,145
Total Assets			$813,042
Liabilities and Fund Balance			
Liabilities:			
Accounts payable			$4,962
Fund balance:			
Reserved for debt service			808,080
Total Liabilities and Fund Balance			$813,042

Illustration of Example 13, Part 2
The second financial statement illustrates how one combined statement of revenues, expenditures and changes in fund balances can be presented in the comprehensive annual financial report for all debt service funds.

Kimberly Hills School District
Debt Service Fund
Statement of Revenues, Expenditures and Changes in Fund Balance
Budget (GAAP Basis) and Actual
Year Ended August 31, 1996

	Budget	Actual	Variance-Favorable (Unfavorable)
Revenues:			
Property taxes, penalties and interest	$3,591,988	$3,606,866	14,878
Interest on investments	116,000	115,894	(106)
Interest on sale of bonds	20,321	20,321	0
Total Revenues	3,728,309	3,743,081	14,772
Expenditures:			
Retirement of serial bonds	1,599,000	1,599,000	0
Interest on serial bonds	2,035,784	2,035,784	0
Paying agent's fees	28,500	28,382	118
Total Expenditures	3,663,284	3,663,166	118
Excess revenue over expenditures	65,025	79,915	14,890
Fund balance, September 1, 1995	728,165	728,165	0
Fund balance, August 31, 1996	$ 793,190	$ 808,090	$ 14,890

ACTIVITIES

1. Review the definition of the following terms found in the glossary:
    a. Debt service fund
    b. Long-term debt
    c. Serial bond
    d. Term bond
    e. Bonds maturity value
    f. Levy
    g. Subsidiary revenue ledger
    h. Subsidiary expenditure ledger
    i. Required taxation

j. Discount
k. Premium
l. Amortization
m. Nominal rate
n. Effective rate
o. Maturity value
p. Self balancing
q. Account
r. Adjusting entry
s. Required earnings
t. Budgeted fund balance
u. Reserve for encumbrances
v. Reserve for debt retirement
w. Appropriation, bond interest expense
x. Appropriation, principal of bond debt
y. Unappropriated debt service fund equity
z. Debt service fund equity account
aa. Matured bonds
bb. Fiscal agent for payment
cc. Redeemed bond

2. Distinguish between term bonds and serial bonds.

3. Describe the process for establishing and maintaining a debt service fund.

4. Identify the financial statements commonly prepared from debt service fund accounts.

5. Fort Steven School District uses a debt service fund to retire its long-term bonds. The following transactions took place during the period from January 1, 1995, to December 31, 1995.

    January 1 – The budget for the debt service fund required revenue from taxes of $50,000 and required revenue from earnings of $2,400.
    March 15 – Taxes collected by the general fund and transferred to the debt service fund amounted to $30,000.
    April 1 – The district purchased 10-year, 10 percent bonds, face value of $30,000, dated January 1, at a premium of $500 with interest payable semi-annually on June 30 and December 31.
    June 15 – Taxes collected by the general fund and transferred to the debt service fund amounted to $20,000.

July 1 – The district purchased 20-year, 9 percent bonds, face value of $20,000, at a discount of $600, with interest payable semi-annually on June 30 and December 31.

Instructions:
- Prepare journal entries to record all transactions that occurred in the debt service fund during the year.
- Prepare a trial balance of the debt service fund as of December 31, 1995.
- Prepare closing entries in general journal form.

6. Newbridge School Parish maintains a debt service fund which has accounts with balances as is listed in the following:

Reserve for debt retirement	$300,000
Debt service fund equity	3,000
Cash	60,000
Unamortized premium on investments	100
Earnings on investments	32,900
Investments	260,000
Required taxation	287,000
Unamortized discount on investments	200
Required earnings	16,000
Revenue from taxes	287,000

Instructions:
- Prepare a trial balance for the debt service fund as of December 31, 1996, from the above listed account balances.
- Make the necessary journal entries to close the appropriate accounts as of December 31, 1996.

7. Westbury School Corporation issued $2,000,000 par value of serial bonds on July 1, 1996. The bonds will pay 10 percent per year, to be called in blocks of $200,000 every two years, beginning July 31, 1998. On July 31, 2003, the fund had the following account balances:

Cash	$ 40,000
Taxes receivable	64,000
Estimated uncollectible taxes	32,000
Investments at cost	148,000
Bond interest payable	8,000
Debt service fund equity	12,000
Reserve for debt retirement	200,000

The following transactions occurred on July 31, 2003:
a. Taxes receivable of $30,000 were collected.
b. $138,000 of investments were converted into cash.
c. Interest payable of $8,000 was paid.
d. Following the corporation board's directions, the balance in the reserve for debt retirement was transferred to the debt service fund equity account, and an appropriation for debt service, principal, was made in the amount of $200,000.
e. An expenditure, debt service, principal, was recorded for $200,000, and the debt service fund assumed the liability for matured bonds payable.
f. A check for $200,000 was issued to the fiscal agent to retire bonds presented for payment.

Instructions:
- Prepare a schedule beginning with year 1997 showing the bond principal outstanding during each year and the amount of interest required for each year.
- Record and post the transactions of July 31, 2003.
- Record and post closing entries for the year ended July 31, 2003.
- Record and post the budget for the following year.

REFERENCES/SELECTED READINGS

Fowler, W. J., Jr. (1990). *Financial accounting for local and state systems, 1990.* Washington, DC: U. S. Government Printing Office.

Tidwell, S. B. (1985). *Financial and managerial accounting for elementary and secondary school systems (3rd edition).* Reston, VA: Research Corporation of the Association of School Business Officials.

15

General Fixed Asset Account Group

A school district makes many investments--in people, in securities, and in tangible items. Over the years, the accumulated dollar value of school district acquisitions of land, buildings, and equipment can amount to millions of dollars. Because of this sizable investment, it is important for the school business administrator to accurately account for and report on district possessions. While this chapter devotes a fair amount of time and space to establishing inventory "cards" for each district asset, this approach is used to develop understanding. Current practices rely upon computerization of these records, not the "cards" themselves. A variety of software is available to users to create individual "records" for each asset.

OUTCOMES

In this chapter, you will learn how to:

1. How to establish an inventory system for land, buildings, and equipment owned by a school district;
2. How to produce written records for this inventory;
3. To use double entry accounting to record the dollar value of the land, buildings, and equipment owned by a school district;
4. How to produce reports that summarize the dollar value and annual change in dollar value of the land, buildings, and equipment owned by a district.

DEFINITION OF AN ACCOUNT GROUP

An account group, also known as a group of accounts, is composed of selected, self-balancing ledger accounts grouped together for a common purpose. Unlike funds, account groups have no current assets, current liabilities, fund balance, revenues, or expenditures (Tidwell, 1985). There are two account groups: the general long-term debt account group, used to record the principal and interest on long-term obligations (see Chapter 16) and the general fixed assets account group (GFAAG).

DEFINITION OF FIXED ASSETS

Fixed assets are those intended to be used over a period of more than one year. Typically fixed assets are categorized as land, buildings, or equipment (Jensen, 1973):

1. Land includes all real estate owned by the district, including improvements or upgrades, such as playing fields, driveways, and drainage systems;
2. Buildings are district-owned structures, including their electrical, plumbing, and HVAC systems and permanent, non-movable, built-in furnishings such as student lockers, closets, and cabinets. Also included are renovations, improvements, and additions to the original structure;
3. Equipment, which is movable, long-lived furnishings.

USES OF FIXED ASSET ACCOUNTING

An accurate and current record of fixed assets has many uses (Mutter, Nichols, & Honaker, 1985; Office of the State Comptroller, 1990):

1. Inventory records indicate the age and the condition of equipment and buildings. This can aid long-range planning for equipment maintenance and replacement to spread budget expenditures over a period of years while still providing adequate mechanical support for instructional activities;
2. Fixed asset accounting provides records of financing sources which can be used to analyze available revenues for future purchases;
3. Inventory records indicate the location of equipment which can promote equitable distribution of resources among buildings and staff;
4. Comparisons of physical inventories with equipment records can detect theft and unauthorized borrowing of equipment and help discourage such activities in the future;
5. Fixed asset values are necessary for insurance records and claims for replacement of lost, damaged, or stolen property.

CHALLENGES OF FIXED ASSET RECORD-KEEPING

Ensuring Complete Inventory Records

A major question with fixed asset accounting is what to include in the physical inventory. To start, the administration and the board of education should determine which fixed assets are of "significant value." This is a subjective decision, often based on the size of the district and the amount of fixed assets it owns (Office of the State Comptroller, 1990, sec. 3.0202, p. 1).

Other useful criteria, when trying to determine what to include in – and sometimes more importantly what to exclude from – a fixed asset inventory, are definitions of equipment and supplies. Although large, expensive items, like copying machines and trucks, are easily classified as equipment, smaller items, like pencil sharpeners which resemble equipment in appearance, are actually supplies and therefore should not be included in the inventory. Jensen (1973) provides useful distinctions between these two kinds of fixed assets. He defines equipment as:

> ...a movable or fixed unit of furniture or furnishings, an instrument, a machine, or a set of articles meeting all the following conditions:
> 1. It retains its original shape and appearance with use.
> 2. It is nonexpendable; thus, if the article is damaged or some of its parts are lost or worn out, it is usually more feasible to repair it than replace it with an entirely new unit.
> 3. It represents an investment of money which makes it feasible and advisable to capitalize the item.
> 4. It does not lose its identity through incorporation into a different or more complex unit or substance. (Jensen, 1973, pp. 1-2)

When inventorying equipment it is common to group like items of smaller value together. For example, a pick-up truck worth $20,000 would be listed as a separate item on the inventory; however, all cafeteria tables and chairs of the same make and model, purchased at the same time for the high school, would be listed as two groups: 20 student cafeteria tables in the high school, valued at $150 each or $3,000 total and 120 student cafeteria chairs in the high school, valued at $25 each or $3,000 total.

Jensen (1973, p. 2) goes on to differentiate supplies as those items meeting any of these qualifications:

1. It is consumed in use.
2. It loses its original shape or appearance with use.
3. It is expendable; thus, if the article is damaged or some of its parts are lost or worn out, it is usually more feasible to replace it with an entirely new unit rather than repair it.
4. It is an inexpensive item, having characteristics of equipment, whose small unit cost makes it inadvisable to capitalize the item.
5. It loses its identity through incorporation into a different or more complex unit or substance. (Jensen, 1973, p. 2)

ENSURING QUALITY INVENTORY RECORDS

After the district has decided on its capitalization policy, it should determine whether the inventory will be conducted by in-house staff or contracted with a commercial appraisal company. If done in-house, it is incumbent upon the district to train the inventory workers to perform their tasks in the most complete, accurate, and uniform way possible. District-generated forms are useful for this purpose. Most districts use computerized spreadsheet or database software to record this information. The documents discussed below (Jensen, 1973, pp. 19-23, E2-E6; Office of the State Comptroller, 1990, sec. 3.2060, pp. 10-16; Tidwell, 1985, pp. 383-385) are appropriate for either conducting an initial inventory or updating existing records;

- *The Initial Inventory Sheet for Equipment* is used for the first gross recording of equipment and leads to a list of equipment by building or department. The description, age, condition, building and room location, number of units, and original cost should be noted for each piece of equipment (or equipment group as discussed above). The person responsible for the inventory and the date of the count should also be shown for control purposes. Figure 15-1 (Jensen, 1973, p. E-2) shows a sample Initial Inventory Sheets.
- *The Equipment Inventory Card* is completed for each piece of equipment (or equipment group) listed on the Initial Inventory Sheet for Equipment. The card typically provides information on description, location, quantity (for equipment groups like student desks), acquisition (date of purchase, original cost, and funding

Figure 15-1
Initial Inventory Sheet

			AnywhereSchool District **Initial Inventory Sheet**	
Building Name and No.: _____			Inventoried by: _____	___ Page of ___ Pages Date(s) _____
Room No. Locations	Units No.	EGFP	Description – Remarks	Current Unit Price

Figure 15-2
Equipment Inventory Card

Item Description				Chair Student – tub. steel and plastic, 13" K, Acme 304K or equal				
Type & Date of Entry	Quantity Change	Total Quantity	Unit Cost	Remarks	Central School District		Class Group	06 1
PI-5/9A		225	$8.23	Approx 80% are ACME 304 K	Bldg.	01	Card	1
P8/9A	10	235	$8.57	P/0 66-18 (Nat'l	Initial Inventory Data			
D-9/9A	30	205		Scrapped	R/C Total $1,852			
T-4/9B	10	195		To bldg. 04	ACV Total $1,383			
					Condition: E G F P			
					Date of Inventory Check:			
					Mo.			
					Yr.			
					Responsibile Official:			
					U. Jones, Bldg. Principal			
							ITEM CARD	

Explanation of Symbols
PI   = Physical Inventory – This symbol should be used to indicate entries resulting from the initial inventory, and and other future complete physical inventory.
P   = Purchase
D   = Deleted; Lost, traded in, scrapped or otherwise disposed of, but not transferred.
T   = Transferred; Moved to or from another building.
R/C = Replacement Cost
ACV= Actual Cash Value
IC   = Inventory Check.

Note: This document may be reprinted without permission of either the authors or the publisher.

Figure 15-3
Equipment Inventory Card

Anywhere School District
Equipment–Subsidiary Ledger Account
Accumulated Depreciation–Subsidiary Ledger Account

		Subsidiary Ledger	General Ledger
	Account Number: ____		
	Account Number: ____		

Description _____ Classification _____
Location _____ Manufacturer _____
Identification:
  Inventory Number _____ Cost _____ Voucher Number _____ Date _____
  Manufacturer's Number _____ Cost _____ Voucher Number _____ Date _____
  Serial Number _____ Freight _____ Voucher Number _____ Date _____

How Acquired:
  General Fund $_____ Additions _____ Voucher Number _____ Date _____
  Special Revenue Fund $_____ Additions _____ Voucher Number _____ Date _____
  Enterprise Fund $_____ **Disposition:** How Disposed of: _____
  Internal Services Fund $_____ Date of Disposition: _____ Proceeds $_____
  Trust Fund Authority to dispose recorded in
   Cost of Disposition: $_____
   Proceed records in what fund? _____

Date		Explanation	P.R.	Asset			P.R.	Accumulated Depreciation			Book Value
Mo.	Day Year			Debit	Credit	Balance		Debit	Credit	Balance	

Figure 15-4
Building Inventory Card

Description and Location						Bldg. No.	
						Site No.	

Col. No.		199A	199B	199C	199D	199E	Col. No.
1	Basic Structure Incl. Perm. Fix., Arch. Fees & Legal						1
2	-Subtract- Uninsured Items & Legal Fees						2
3	Sub-Total						3
4	-Add- Value of Contents Insurable W/Bldg.						4
5	Insurable Total						5
	Annual Value Modif.: % Factor | Date						
	Source of Values						

- Original Cost Data-		Col. 1 for K102 Account Col. 5 for Insurance Valuation	Date of Disposition:	
Basic Structure:	$	Building Valuation Data - See Over for Additional Information	Type of Disposition:	
Permanent Fixtures:	$	Sq. Feet of Area:		
Architect Fees:	$	Cubic Feet:		
Legal Fees:	$	Front - REPLACEMENT COST	Card No.	
Total Orig. Cost:	$	**BUILDING CARD**	Responsible Official	
Date of Construction: Date of Acquisition:			CENTRAL SCHOOL DISTRICT	

source), and other cost measures (optional). Changes in the equipment, such as movement to a new location, disposal, or accumulated depreciation (optional) should also be recorded on the card. Combined together, these cards form a master equipment inventory list. Figure 15-2 (Jensen, 1973, p. E-4) and Figure 15-3 (Tidwell, 1985, p. 385) display various kinds of Equipment Inventory Cards.

- The *Building Inventory Card*, similar in purpose to the Equipment Item Card, provides description, cost, and location data as well as an acquisition and disposition history for each district-owned building. Figure 15-4 (Jensen, 1973, p. E-7) and Figure

Figure 15-4
Building Inventory Card (continued)

Col. No.		199A	199B	199C	199D	199E	Col. No.
1	Basic Structure Incl. Perm. Fix., Arch. Fees & Legal						1
2	-Subtract- Uninsured Items & Legal Fees						2
3	Sub-Total						3
4	-Add- Value of Contents Insurance W/Bldg.						4
5	Insurable Total						5
	Depreciation Factor						

Record of Repairs or Additions to Bldg. Use Separate Card for Additions that are Separately Rated for Fire Insurance Purposes.			Col. 1 for K102 Account Col. 5 for Insurance Valuation		Additional Bldg. Valuation Data:	
Date	Cost	Description				
						Back - Actual Cash Value	
						BUILDING CARD	

15-5 (Tidwell, 1985, p. 384) are examples of Building Inventory Cards.

- The *Land Inventory Card* documents each parcel of land owned by the district. Information included on the card is similar to that for buildings. Figure 15-6 (Jensen, 1973, p. E-6) and Figure 15-7 (Tidwell, 1985, p. 383) can be used for site inventories.

From the inventory cards for equipment, buildings, and land, a master district inventory list can be compiled.

Figure 15-5
Building Inventory Card

Anywhere School District
Building–Subsidiary Ledger Account
Accumulated Depreciation, Building–Subsidiary Ledger Account

		Subsidiary Ledger	General Ledger
	Account Number:		
	Account Number:		

Description _____
Proposed Use _____ Location _____
Estimated Useful Life _____ Present Use _____
Additions Authorized by Resolution # _____
  Resolution # _____ Acquired Board of Resolution # _____
  Resolution # _____ Date of Resolution _____ Date Added _____
Disposition Authorized by Resolution # _____ Date of Resolution _____ Date Added _____
How Acquired: Construction Work Order # _____ Date of Resolution _____ Date Added _____
  Contact Number _____ Date of Resolution _____ Date Added _____
  Date Completed _____ Cost of Construction _____
  Purchase Order # _____ Cost _____
Fund Source: General Fund _____ Posting Reference _____
  Special Revenue Fund _____ Cost _____ : Date Purchased _____
  Capital Project Fund _____ Appraisal Value on Date Received _____
How disposed of: _____ Enterprise Fund _____
Cost to dismantle: _____ Internal Service Fund _____
  Trust Fund _____
  Proceeds from disposition _____

Date			Explanation	P.R.	Asset			P.R.	Accumulated Depreciation		Book Value
Mo.	Day	Year			Debit	Credit	Balance		Debit	Credit	Balance	

Figure 15-6
Land Inventory Card

Description and Location						SITE NO.	
- ORIGINAL COST DATA -		Year	R/C of Land	R/C of Land Improvements	R/C Mod Factor Land Imp	ACV of Land Improvements	Deprec Factor Land Imp
Purchase Price	$	199A					
Acquisition Expense - (Legal Fees, Searches)	$	199B					
Cost to Demolish Structure	$	199C					
Other Costs (Improvements)	$	199D					
Total Orig Cost of Site	$	199E					
SITE ADDITIONS OR DELETIONS		199F					
Date	indicate "A" or "D"	VALUE Explain Transaction On Other Side	199G				
		$	199H				
		$	199I				
		$	199J				
		$	SCHOOL DISTRICT				
		$	Date Site Acquired	Building Numbers			Card No
		$	SITE CARD		Source of Values:		
		$			Responsible Officials		

ENSURING CURRENT INVENTORY RECORDS

Most school districts have, at one time or another, undertaken an initial comprehensive inventory of their fixed assets. However, many districts fail to keep their inventories current, resulting in poor accounting in the GFAAG and inaccurate insurance records. Inventory records and the GFAAG are affected by both acquisitions and disposals of equipment, buildings, and land.

Acquisition. Whenever the district acquires new fixed assets, proper purchasing procedures should be used to minimize fraud and to provide an audit trail for accounting in the fund of origin and the GFAAG. Expenditure figures in the fund of origin should coincide with historical costs on the inventory records and in the GFAAG.

New fixed assets should be recorded on a master Acquisition Report; source data for the Acquisition List can include purchase orders,

Figure 15-7
Land Inventory Card

```
                    ANYWHERE SCHOOL DISTRICT
                         Subsidiary Ledger
                              Land
General Description _____
Location _____
Size _____
Proposed Use _____
Present Use _____
Legal Information _____
Legal Description _____
_____
_____
_____

Plat Book Page Number _____   Property Number _____
Type of Deed _____   Date of Deed _____
Deed Recorded _____   Volume _____ Date _____
Copy of Deed Filed in _____

Accounting Information
Date Purchased _____   Amount _____
Voucher Number _____   Posting Reference _____

Additional Costs:
Nature of Additional Costs _____   Amount _____

Posting Reference _____   Amount _____

If acquired by a way other than purchased, Explain:
_____
Valuation Basis _____   Amount _____

How Acquired              Amount        Disposition
  General Fund            _____       How Disposed of _____
  Special Revenue Fund    _____       Date of Disposition _____
  Capital Projects Fund   _____       Proceeds _____
  Gifts, Bequests         _____       Proceeds Recorded in _____
```

original invoices, and fund expenditure reports. The information on the master list should then be used to update the inventory cards, the master inventory list, and the GFAAG.

Disposals. Typically, the board of education declares a fixed asset obsolete or of no further use to the district prior to its disposal. Riddance of the fixed asset can then occur in a number ways:

- *Obsolete equipment bid* – Open to the community and other interested buyers, this is a formal procedure which follows local competitive bidding laws. It is often used for higher-priced items like school buses;
- *Obsolete equipment auction* – This provides an opportunity for community members to bid orally for items of their choice. Many school districts turn this into a festive event by combining it with a social activity sponsored by a parent group. The auction is often used for lower-price items, like typewriters and student desks;
- *Destruction of equipment* – By burning or trash collection.

As with acquisitions, a master Property Disposition List can record the above transactions; the data on the list can then be transferred to the inventory cards, the master inventory list, and the GFAAG. Source data for disposition records include revenue receipts from obsolete equipment bids and auctions, board minutes for donated items, and physical inventories for lost or stolen equipment.

Rather than using separate reports for property acquisition and disposal, some districts use a master Inventory Change Report showing additions, deletions, location changes, and other corrections to the fixed asset inventory. This report can then be used to update the individual cards and the GFAAG. Figure 15-8 from the Campbell-Savona Central School District, Campbell, New York, shows a master Inventory Change Report, using a form provided by the Industrial Appraisal Company.

TAKING INVENTORY

Counting fixed assets, whether for a comprehensive inventory or to update existing records, should be a planned, organized, and thorough project. A number of steps are involved (Jensen, 1973, pp. 7-8):

- *Appointment of a property control manager* – This individual, usually recommended by the school business administrator, oversees all aspects of fixed asset control, from initial inventory procedures to updates of the GFAAG;

- *Determination of inventory practices* – To ensure uniformity, decisions must be made regarding level of detail (recording each

Figure 15-8
Inventory Change Report

INVENTORY CHANGE REPORT

(1) ACCOUNT NAME _____Central School_____

(2) TYPE TRANSACTION: ADDITION (✓) DELETION ( ) TRANSFER ( ) CORRECTION ( )

D-T-C	A-D-T-C	A-D-T-C	A-D-T-C	T	T	T	A-C	A-D-T-C	A-D-T-C	A-C	A-D-T-C	A-C	A-C	A-C	A-C	A-C	A-C
LINE NO. (3)	CURRENT LOCATION			FORMER LOCATION			Prop. Class or Equip. Code (10)	Identification No. (11)	QTY. (12)	DESCRIPTION (13) Item Name, Brand Name, Model #, Serial #, Dimensions	Acquisition Cost (Dollars Only) (14)	DATE ACQUIRED		LIFE (17)	FUND CODE (18)	PURCHASE ORDER (19)	INS. ONLY (20)
	Bldg (4)	Area (5)	Dept. (6)	Bldg (7)	Area (8)	Dept. (9)						Mo. (15)	Yr. (16)				
	1B	B	E49				21	3501	1	Bronx Booster Pump (1022B) (HVABEV)	207.00	8	88		A	12713	
	1B	B	B63				31	3502	1	Steel Service Chart (# 43955)	151.00	9	88		A	12713	
	1B	1	A20				31	3504	1	Wooden Desk Maj - 10671 - HH	397.00	12	88		A	12128	
		1	A21				31	3505	1	Desk Chair HN 5504 - HMJJ21	251.00	12	88		A	12125	
		1	A24				31	3506 -3517	1	2 drawer filing cabinet NN-212 N-R	200.00	8	88		A	12562	
	1B	2	B51				31	3518 3519	12	14" Stack Chairs - Blue 1101 Series	374.00	10	88		A	12540	
	2B	2	C63				31	3520	2	Sun Gro Lamp (SG2020)	262.00	9	88		A	12692	
	2B	2	C61				31	3521	1	Sunyo Transcriber TRC 8010A (735079921)	238.00	8	88		A	12692	
	2B	2	C				31	3522	1	Sunyo Transcriber TRC8010A (48505154)	238.00	8	88		A	12692	
	2B	1	C				31	3523	1	New Home Sewing Machine #552015 (7401487711)	299.00	9	88		A	12668	

student desk vs. grouping and recording student desks by buildings, etc.) and valuation (replacement cost vs. sound value vs. historical cost);

- *Assignment of duties* – Every person involved in the inventory should have a global understanding of the entire inventory process, their role in it, and specific directions for their tasks. The importance of accuracy, completeness, and uniformity in counting fixed assets and recording data should be stressed at this time;

- *Preparation of forms* – Based on the inventory practices previously determined, forms should be prepared to aid inventory workers (see section on Determining How to Count);

- *Undertaking the inventory* – Each individual involved in the process then counts and values the equipment in their assigned area; Initial Inventory Sheets for Equipment can be used for this task, with the data subsequently being transferred to the Inventory Cards for Equipment. Those responsible for the inventory of real property can record their information on Inventory Cards for Land and Inventory Cards for Buildings. Full descriptions should be recorded for each fixed asset, along with their cost value(s);

- *Preparation of master inventory lists* – District-wide inventory lists should then be developed. As a minimum, these should include a master list for all fixed assets in the district. Subsidiary lists by location can also be developed; computerization of the master data base can simplify this task. The GFAAG should then be updated to reflect the current inventory;

- *Establishment of change procedures* – Written procedures to record acquisition of new assets, disposal of old assets, and changes in locations and values of existing assets should be established and disseminated to those having responsibility over the assets, such as central office administrators, directors of support services, building principals, and department heads. Inventory cards and the GFAAG books should then be updated annually.

DETERMINING COSTS

There are a number of ways that the dollar value of a fixed asset can be determined. School districts use different cost measures for different purposes.

- *Historical cost* is the original price paid for the item. The physical inventory must include historical costs for all items; NCGA Statement 1, paragraph 47 Paragraph 48 requires that fixed assets be accounted for in the GFAAG at their original cost. Included in this is the price of the item and any additional charges to render the item usable at the site, such as delivery fees and setup charges. Historical costs can be determined by original source documents, such as purchase orders and invoices for equipment and deeds, maps, assessor's records, and tax rolls for real property. If the original cost data are not available, estimated costs can be used using one of two methods recommended (Government Finance Officers Association [GFOA], 1988, p. 54):

- *Similar purchase estimation*, in which the school district estimates through written documentation or discussion with knowledgeable individuals the cost of a like item during the time period of its purchase;

- *Normal costing* or back trending, in which the current cost of the item is divided by a price index figure. The index figure, available from appraisal companies, is equal to 1 plus the percentage the item has risen in value from its data of purchase to the present.

- *Replacement cost* is the value of the fixed asset in today's dollars. Replacement costs are found on inventories prepared by commercial appraisal companies and are also used for insurance purposes. Replacement costs are not recorded in the GFAAG; however, they should be listed on the inventory cards to aid future purchasing decisions and insurance loss claims. Current catalogs and vendors' sales literature can be used to determine replacement costs. Replacement costs for real property include the current market value of the land and the cost of replacing the entire building at its present location, including renovations and improvements. Replacement costs should be updated annually on the inventory cards and master inventory list to provide accurate values for adequate insurance coverage (Jensen, 1973).

- *Actual Cash Value*, also known as sound value, is the replacement cost of an item less accumulated depreciation (Jensen, 1973, p. 3; Tidwell, 1985, p. 624). Sound insurable value is similar to sound value, except that it does not include uninsurable building structures, such as foundations, excavations, and wiring and plumbing below the surface of the lowest floor of the structure (Jensen, 1973, p. 5). Sound values are often found on inventories prepared by commercial appraisal companies and are used for insurance purposes; these cost figures are not recorded in the GFAAG.

- *Depreciation* – GFOA defines depreciation as "expiration in the service life of fixed assets, other than wasting assets, attributable to wear and tear, deterioration, action of the physical elements, inadequacy, and obsolescence" (1988, p. 161). There are many methods that can be used to calculate depreciation: straight-line method, useful hours method, units of output method, accelerated depreciation, declining balance method, sum of the years digit method, blanket rates, and reducing charge. The straight-line method is the simplest and most often used. In this method, the life of the item is estimated in years and then divided into the cost of the item, resulting in an annual amount of depreciation (Tidwell, 1985, pp. 422-423). If sound values and depreciation are used, they should be recorded along with other cost figures on the inventory cards and the master inventory list. Although it is prudent to adjust these values annually, most school districts only update them when complete inventories are taken.

INVENTORY CONTROL SYSTEMS

Although required by GAAP, the main purpose of general fixed asset inventories and accounting is to prevent loss of district property, particularly movable equipment. However, counting fixed assets is only the start; tagging equipment with identification numbers provides further loss control. An ID number displayed in a prominent place on each item not only makes equipment tracking and inventory updates easier but can also make equipment less desirable to steal. Equipment ID numbers should be recorded on the inventory cards, the master inventory list, and on a master list of inventory numbers.

Sometimes it is impractical to affix an identification tag on each piece of equipment, such as student desks or chairs. In this case, the school district name and/or log can be painted on each item to discourage theft (Jensen, 1973, p. 10).

Computer technology is offering new ways of equipment identification and tracking. Tags containing scannable bar codes can be affixed to each piece of equipment. The information contained on the individual inventory cards matching each tag code can ten be input into a computer, resulting in a data base that makes it easy to obtain accurate and current information on any piece of equipment.

ACCOUNTING FOR FIXED ASSETS

Chart of Accounts. The GFAAG contains only two kinds of general ledger accounts: classifications of fixed assets and types of funding sources (investment accounts). The following are typical fixed asset accounts; these normally have debit balances (Bailey, 1993, p. 68.04; Office of the State Comptroller, 1987, pp. K-3-K-4):

K 101 *Land* – To record the value of district-owned land.
K 102 *Buildings* – To record the value of district-owned buildings and structures.
K 103 *Improvements Other Than Buildings* – To record other assets that cannot be easily classified as land or buildings, such as sidewalks and parking lots. This is an optional account; these items can instead be included in the Land account.
K 104 *Equipment* – To record the value of district-owned equipment.
K 105 *Construction Work-in-Progress* – To record the amount spent to date on a capital construction or renovation project. This is an optional account; the school district can instead wait until the project is completed and then record the total amount in the GFAAG.

The following are typical funding source accounts; these normally have credit balances (Office of the State Comptroller, 1987, p. K-5):
K 151 *Investments in General Fixed Assets, Bonds and Notes* – To record the value of an asset financed through borrowing; this is usually used for large capital projects, such as new building construction or major renovations, whose fund on origin is the capital projects fund.

K 152 *Investment in General Fixed Assets, Current Appropriations* – To record the value of an asset financed with general fund monies.

K 153 *Investment in General Fixed Assets, Gifts* – To record the value of donated assets.

K 156 *Investment in General Fixed Assets, State Aid* – To record the value of assets purchased with state aid

K 157 *Investment in General Fixed Assets, Federal Aid* – To record the value of assets purchased with federal grants.

There also exist optional accounts to record accumulated depreciation; these normally have credit balances (Office of the State Comptroller, 1987, p. K-5):

K 112 *Accumulated Depreciation, Buildings* – To record accumulated depreciation on district-owned buildings.

K 114 *Accumulate Depreciation, Equipment* – To record accumulated depreciation on district-owned equipment.

SAMPLE TRANSACTION

Fixed assets used in the activities of a proprietary fund or an internal service fund are accounted for in those funds and not in those assets must also be recorded as an expense in those funds.

Likewise, fixed assets acquired through trusts and depreciation expense for assets are accounted for in the nonexpendable trust fund. This is in line with the purpose of a trust fund and aids stewardship of trust assets. Also, non-expendable trust funds follow the same accounting practices used in proprietary funds.

All other fixed assets are accounted for in the GFAAG. Because no cash transactions occur in the GFAAG, only a general journal and a general ledger is maintained. Because original source documentation is kept in the fund which purchased the asset, it is important to include in each GFAAG journal entry detailed information identifying the fixed asset. This is illustrated in Examples 15-1 to 15-6.

Illustration 15-1

Recording the purchase of a fixed asset. To record the acquisition of a new fixed asset, the appropriate fixed asset account is debited, and the appropriate investment source account is credited. For example, to record the acquisition of a new school bus costing $50,000 purchased from the current year general fund budget:

(General Fund)		
Expenditures	$50,000	
Purchase of Buses		
Cash		$50,000
(GFAAG)		
Equipment	50,000	
Current Appropriations		50,000
To record the purchase of Bus #107, a 66-passenger GMC bus, model #978534)		
Land $ 35,000		
Buildings	140,000	
Bonds and notes		$175,000
To record the purchase, financed through bonds, of a building to be used to house central office administration (lot price: $35,000; structure price: $140,000) (Office of the State Comptroller, 1987, p. K-7)		

Illustration 15-2

Recording the sale of a fixed asset without depreciation. To record the sale of an old fixed asset for which depreciation has not been recorded, the appropriate investment account is debited by the original amount of the asset (historical cost), and the appropriate fixed asset account is credited. For example, five years after Bus #107 was purchased (see example above), it was declared obsolete and sold to the highest bidder for $7,500; to record this transaction:

(General Fund)		
Cash	$7,500	
Revenues		$7,500
Sale of transportation equipment		
(GFAAG)		
Current Appropriations	50,000	
Equipment		50,000
To record the sale of Bus #107, a 66-passenger GMC bus, model #978534		

Illustration 15-3

Recording the replacement of a fixed asset without depreciation. When an old fixed asset is replaced with a new one, two steps are involved in recording the transaction: (1) recording the disposition of the old fixed asset (similar to the sales transaction above) and (2) acquisition of the new fixed assets (similar to the purchase transaction above). For example, a 1990 red Ford pick-up truck, originally purchased at $20,000 with a bond anticipation note, was traded in for a new 1995 green Chevrolet pick-up truck, whose sticker price was $24,000. The dealer allowed a trade-in value of $9,000 on the 1990 truck; thus, the cost of to the district for the 1995 truck was $15,000 which was paid for from the general fund budget. To record this transaction (Office of the State Comptroller, 1987, p. K-6; Tidwell, 1985, p. K-6, Tidwell, 1985, p. 379):

General Fund		
Expenditures	$15,000	
Cash		$15,000
Maintenance equipment		
GFAAG		
K 151 Bonds and notes	20,000	
K 104 Equipment		20,000
To record the trade-in of the 1990 red Ford		
pick-up truck, serial #653403894090.		
K 104 Equipment	24,000	
K 152 Current appropriations		24,000
To record the purchase of the 1995 green		
Chrevolet pick-up truck, serial #234978905324		

Illustration 15-4

Recording the retirement of a fixed asset without depreciation. To record the donation or trashing of an old fixed asset for which depreciation has not been recorded, the appropriate investment is debited, and the appropriate fixed asset account is credited. No entry is made in the general fund unless there is a cost associated with the retirement of the asset, such as its dismantling. For example, to record the donation to the local parochial school of 100 old student desks, with an original value of $2,500 purchased through the general fund budge (Tidwell, 1985, pp. 379-380):

K 152 Current appropriations	$2,500	
K 104 Equipment		$2,500

Illustration 15-5
Recording a partially completed capital construction project. To record the progress at the end of the fiscal year on an on-going capital project, the fixed asset account, Construction Work in Progress, is debited and the appropriate investment account is credited. For example, the district is undertaking a $10,000,000 capital project, financed with bonds, to construct a new high school. The project is to be completed over the course of two years. By the end of the first year, $6,000,000 worth of work is completed. To record this transaction (Office of the State Comptroller, 1987, p. K-8):

K 105 Construction work in progress	$6,000,000	
K 151 Bonds and notes		$6,000,000

Expenditures for this capital project would be recorded in the capital fund

The project is completed on schedule during the second year. The amount charged to the account, Construction Work in Progress, must be reversed to show that the project is now completed. To record this transaction (GFOA, 1988, p. 55; Office of the State Comptroller, 1987, p. K-5):

K 102 Buildings	$10,000,000	
K 105 Construction Work in Progress		$6,000,000
K 151 Bonds and notes		4,000,000

The above transactions are optional. The district can wait until the entire project is completed to record the additions to fixed assets, as follows:

K 102 Buildings	$10,000,000	
K 151 Bonds and Notes		$10,000,000

Illlustration 15-6
Recording accumulated depreciation of fixed assets
Depreciation of buildings and equipment may be recorded in the GFAAG, but it is not required (GASB Cod. Sec. 1400.118 [NCGA Statement 1, paragraph 56];GASB, 1992, p. 56 [NCGA Statement 1, paragraph 51]). Because it is time-consuming to calculate on a regular basis depreciation of all of the district's fixed assets and then to record the amount of depreciation accumulated to date, districts tend not to record depreciation in the GFAAG.

If depreciation is accounted for in the GFAAG, accumulated depreciation--the total amount of depreciation to date--is recorded in a contra-asset account (GFOA), 1988; Tidwell, 1985). However, depreciation expense– the amount of depreciation for a particular fiscal period recorded as an expense--must be recorded for fixed assets in proprietary and non-expendable trust funds (GASB, 1992, p. 56 [NCGA Statement 1, paragraph 51]); GFOA, 1988). Note that accumulated depreciation simply reflects the decrease in the service life of the fixed asset. However, depreciation expense has an entirely different purpose, which is to show the use of an asset in producing goods or services (GFOA, 1988).

To record accumulated depreciation, the appropriate investment source account is debited, and the appropriate depreciation account is credited. For example, to record accumulated depreciation of $3,000 on a piece of equipment worth $30,000 purchased through the general fund budget (Office of the State Comptroller, 1987, p. K-8):

K 104 Equipment	$30,000	
K 152 Current appropriations		$30,000
To record the original purchase of the equipment.		

K 152 Current appropriation	$ 3,000	
K 114 Accumulated depreciation - equipment		$ 3,000
To record accumulated depreciation at the end of the next fiscal year.		

The accumulated depreciation must be removed when the fixed asset is disposed. Therefore, if accumulated depreciation is calculated and recorded in the GFAAG, it is important that it also be noted on the asset's inventory card. Because accumulated depreciation is recorded in the GFAAG in three broad categories (buildings, improvements, and equipment), it would be laborious to trace prior years' records to determine the amount to be removed for an individual item at disposal time; documentation of the amount of accumulated depreciation on each Inventory Card for Equipment or Buildings facilities that task. For example, to record the sale of the equipment in the above example (Office of the State Comptroller, 1987, p. K-9):

K 114 Accumulated depreciation equipment	$ 3,000	
K 152 Current appropriations	27,000	
K 104 Equipment		$30,000
To record the sale of equipment in the above example.		

FINANCIAL STATEMENTS

There are two basic fixed asset financial statements that should be prepared at year's end:

- *Statement of General Fixed Assets* – Similar to a fund balance sheet, this statement shows the balance in each of the GFAAG ledger accounts at the end of the year. Typically, this statement is not presented alone but as a GFAAG column in the Combined Balance Sheet – All Fund Types and Account Groups (Bailey, 1993, p. 68.12).

Notes to the financial statements should include information on how the value of the fixed assets was determined, the extent to which estimation was used as opposed to actual cost data, the district's capitalization policy (criteria for including an item in the GFAAG), any acquisitions or disposals of large value, special circumstances like installment purchases, and non-monetary transactions involving fixed assets (Bailey, 1993, pp. 68); Below is the text of the notes to financial statements for the GFAAG from the independent auditor's report as of June 30, 1992, for the Holley Central School District, Holley, New York:

> Acquisitions of equipment and capital facilities are treated as expenditures in the various funds of the school district, and are also reflected in the general fixed assets account group. As required by New York State, assets are recorded at historical cost. Any capital improvements which are in process are not reflected in the group until completed. No depreciation has been provided on general fixed assets.

- Other financial statements that can be prepared for the GFAAG include a Statement of General Fixed Assets by Function or source and a Statement of Changes in General Fixed Assets by Function or source. Instead of categorizing fixed assets by type (land, building, equipment) as in the required financial statements, the function statements classify the assets by department or purpose (Bailey, 1993, p. 68-12).

PROBLEMS WITH ACCOUNTING IN THE GFAAG

Although often ignored by school districts until just before the annual external audit, GFAAG accounting is taking on increasing importance in this era of fiscal restraint. Taxpayers are demanding prudent fiscal management, and loss or misplacement of equipment, inaccurate and incomplete inventory records, and confusion in the GFAAG books can be interpreted as poor financial stewardship by the community.

Below are some common non-compliances for the GFAAG found in a sample of independent auditor's reports and management studies of New York State School districts. Each may seem trivial; however, the appearance of one or more on the auditor's report can create a public relations problem for the school district.

Equipment not properly inventoried – This includes new equipment omitted from the inventory or the GFAAG accounts, equipment not being correctly documented, or equipment not marked or tagged. Any of these non-compliances can lead to unauthorized use or theft of equipment.

Inventoried and recorded equipment not able to be located – This may result simply from untimely recording of asset disposal. At worst, this can lead to undetected theft; at best, it can raise community concerns regarding the use of taxpayers dollars;

Equipment not at its assigned location – This can encourage inequitable distribution of equipment among staff and also increase the likelihood of equipment misuse and theft;

Overvalued equipment – This can cause higher insurance premiums for unnecessary coverage;

Poor follow-up on insurance claims for lost or stolen equipment – Poorly kept records make it difficult for the district to know what equipment is missing, leading to under-use of insurance protection;

Poor procedures for equipment lending – Many school districts have equipment loan programs for staff, especially for teachers who wish to take computers home. However, board policies and administrative regulations should be in place to prevent abuses of this privilege;

No property control manager – When the responsibility for fixed asset inventory and accounting is as signed to a single, competent individual, the likelihood of mismanagement and non-compliances is greatly reduced.

THE FUTURE OF FIXED ASSET ACCOUNTING

GASB Statement No. 11, Measurement Focus and Basis of Accounting – Governmental Fund Operating Statements, issued May 1990 (GASB, Appendix A), will change what, how, and when selected transactions are recorded and appear on school district financial statements. Among other changes, Statement 11 requires the inclusion of GFAAG accounts in the financial statements of the general fund. Implementation of this requirement is anticipated to take place during the latter half of the 1990s. Future GASB pronouncements will provide guidelines.

SUMMARY

Proper stewardship of district assets is the main job of the school business administrator. While these duties usually concern monetary issues, fiduciary responsibility also extends to land, buildings, and equipment. Therefore, the proactive business official will institute a system to maintain accurate, complete, and current inventory records and to provide for audit trails and proper accounting procedures in the fund of origin and the GFAAG for the acquisition and disposition of fixed assets.

ACTIVITIES

1. Carefully review the definition of the following terms given in the glossary:
   a. Fixed Asset
   b. Depreciation
   c. Replacement Cost
   d. Actual Cash Value
   e. Historical Cost

2. Record the following opening balances and transactions in the General Fixed Assets Account Group of the Genesee Central School District for the 1995-96 fiscal year. Use general journal and general ledger paper. Then prepare a Statement of General Fixed Assets as of June 30, 1996. Do not record the effect of these transactions in any other fund. (Problems #2 and 3 provided by Kathleen Schaefer, School Business Administrator, Alexander Central School District, Alexander, New York.) Assume all capital fund expenditures are financed through bonds.
   a. *July 1, 1995* – Opening balances in these accounts: K101 Land $1,000,000; K102 Buildings $10,000,000; K104 Equipment $2,500,000; K151 Bonds and notes $10,000,000; K152 Current Appropriations $1,000,000; K153 Gifts $200,000; K156 State Aid $1,800,000; K157 Federal Aid $500,000;
   b. *August 5, 1995* – Improvements to land in the form of landscaping completed at a cost of $1,500; this is part of a larger capital project paid from the capital projects fund;
   c. *November 20, 1995* – New library facilities completed at a cost of $1,250,000; this is part of a larger capital project paid

from the capital projects fund;
d. *January 21, 1996* – Equipment costing $35,000 was purchased from the general fund;
e. *March 10, 1996* – The state government gave 10 acres of land to the district to build a new sports complex; estimated value of the land is $14,000;
f. *May 23, 1996* – A new heating unit was installed in the high school at a cost of $15,000; this is part of a larger capital project paid from the capital project fund.

3. Record the following transactions in the General Fixed Assets Account Group of the Genesee Central School District for the 1996-97 fiscal year. Use general journal and general ledger paper. Assume account balances for July 1, 1996, are those reported on the Statement of General Fixed Assets as of June 30, 1996 (see #2). Prepare a Statement of General Fixed Assets as of June 30, 1997 and a Statement of Changes in General Fixed Assets as of June 30, 1997 comparing account balances of June 30, 1996 and June 30, 1997 (see #2). Assume all capital fund expenditures are financed through bonds. Do not record the effect of these transactions in any other fund;
   a. *July 24, 1996* – A school bus, number 96, purchased five years ago by the general fund at a cost of $16,000, was sold for $2,500; proceeds from the sale were directed to be deposited in the general fund.
   b. *August 5, 1996* – Classroom desks recorded at as cost of $500 are considered to be useless, and authorization was received to discard them. The desks were originally purchased by the general fund.
   c. *November 16, 1996* – Office equipment acquired originally by a capital projects fund was replaced at a cost of $1,000. The old equipment was recorded at an original cost of $750 and was discarded. The new equipment was purchased from proceeds of a bond issue in a capital projects fund.
   d. *February 23, 1997* – Special computer equipment for handicapped students costing $7,500 was purchased with Chapter I funds.
   e. *May 6, 1997* – A local business gave the school district a microwave oven valued at $400 to be used in the Home and Career classes.

REFERENCES/SELECTED READINGS

Bailey, L. P. (1993). *Governmental GAAP Guide 1993*. New York: HBJ Miller Accounting Publications.

Glick, P. E. (Ed.) (1987). *Government Fixed Asset Inventory Systems: Establishing, Maintaining and Accounting*. Chicago: Government Finance Officers Association.

Government Finance Officers Association, (1988). *Governmental Accounting, Auditing and Financial Reporting*. Chicago: GFOA.

Governmental Accounting Standards Board (GASB). (1992, June 30). *Codification of Governmental Accounting and Financial Reporting Standards*. Norwalk, CT.

Industrial Appraisal Company 222 Boulevard of the Allies, Pittsburgh, PA, 15222, phone: 412-471-2566. ????

Jensen, P. E. (1973). *Inventory Control of Fixed Assets by School District Personnel*. Albany, NY: The University of the State of New York, the State Education Department, Division of Educational Management Services.

Mutter, D. W., Nichols, W. R., & Honaker, K. W. (1985). *To Count or not to Count: All Items are not Equal When Developing a Fixed Asset System. School Business Affairs*, *51*(10), 42-43, 64-65, 75.

Office of the State Comptroller. (1985-1990). *Financial Management Guide for Local Governments*. Albany, NY: Division of Municipal Affairs, Municipal Accounting Systems.

Tidwell, S. B. (1985). *Financial and Managerial Accounting for Elementary and Secondary School Systems* (3rd ed.). Reston, VA: Association of School Business Officials International.

16

General Long-Term Debt Account Group

INTRODUCTION

Long-term debt is composed of outstanding bonds, long-term notes payable, long-term leases payable, accumulated liabilities for compensated absence, and prior to 1979 and Statement 1 of the Governmental Accounting Standards Board (GASB), the interest remaining to be incurred over the outstanding life of the bonds and notes. The amount of the outstanding debt must be paid from revenue of the school district. It is important that revenue be provided each year in an amount sufficient to retire the bonds and long-term notes payable when they mature and to pay the interest on them as it becomes due. The general long-term debt account group provides the accounting basis for financial statements, which show the amount of outstanding long-term debt of the school district.

OUTCOMES

In this chapter, you will learn how to:

1. Determine why long-term debt accounts are used.
2. Use transactions with long-term debt accounts.

LONG-TERM DEBT ACCOUNTS

GASB, the American Institute of Certified Public Accountants, the National Center for Education Statistics, and the Association of School Business Officials International recommend that a separate self-balancing account group be carried independently of any other fund or account group to account for general long-term debt. Financial statements prepared from a general long-term debt group of accounts disclose fully the present long-term obligations of the school district, including the accumulated long-term liability for compensated employee absences for future vacation, sick leave and other leave benefits. The proper use of this group of accounts requires that the entire cost of each bond issue be computed and recorded when the bonds are issued and become an obligation of the school district. Annual tax requirements are determined for retirement of bonded debt for each bond issue so long as the school district's bonds remain outstanding. When these requirements are known and presented as a part of the financial reporting procedure of the school district, the board of education is in a position to compare annual tax requirements with the amount authorized by law. Therefore, problems related to financing capital outlay for school districts can be minimized and the board of education can make maximum use of its bonding power.

The general long-term debt group of accounts shows the amount that has been provided in debt service funds for the retirement of long-term bonds as well as the amount that will be needed for their retirement in the future. Long-term debt instruments may be issued in internal services funds and enterprise funds. The instruments are obligations to be paid from those funds and as a result, that kind of long-term debt is not recorded in the general long-term debt account group. The amount of long-term bonds issued by these proprietary type funds are reported in footnotes to the financial statements of the general long-term debt account group. All bonds are recorded in this account group.

In the case of long-term capital leases payable where title to property transfers to the school district at the end of the lease, the long-term liability is recorded in the general long-term debt account group. The amount is recorded at the inception of the lease in the amount of the present value of total future lease payments. As lease payments are made, both the amount to be provided account and the long-term leases payable account are reduced. The current liability and its related expenditure are recorded in the fund that is designated to make the payment.

As bonds are retired and interest on general long-term bonded debt is paid from the general fund or from debt service funds, transactions between the general fund and the general long-term debt group of accounts have to be coordinated. In some cases special revenue funds may be authorized to collect certain revenues for the specific purpose of retiring bonds. In such an event transactions are coordinated between the special revenue fund and the general long-term debt group of accounts.

Capital projects funds are usually established to account for the proceeds from the sale of bonds. When general obligation bonds are sold, the transaction is recorded in a capital projects fund and in the general long-term debt account group. In addition to identifying specific capital projects, the title of a capital projects fund may be referred to by a wide variety of names. Regardless of the name, if general obligation, long-term bonds are issued other than by proprietary funds, they are recorded in and reported by the general long-term debt account group.

ACCOUNTS AND TRANSACTIONS

Business papers which provide adequate, competent evidence that general obligation bonds of the school district have been issued are prepared and submitted to the accounting office. The general journal of the general long-term debt group of accounts used to record the fact that serial bonds and long-term bonds have been issued would be:

Kimberly Hills School District
General Long-Term Debt Group of Accounts
General Journal
(Date)

Amount to be provided for bond retirement	$300,000	
Serial bonds payable		$200,000
Long-term bonds payable		100,000
To record sale of bonds		

LONG-TERM LIABILITY FOR COMPENSATED ABSENCES

The long-term liability for compensated absences should be inventoried and the accounts should be adjusted to increase the amount to be provided for long-term compensated absences and to increase the long-term liability for that purpose. An adjusting entry is made in the general long-term debt group of accounts:

Amount to be provided for long-term compensated absences	XXX	
Long-term compensated absences payable		XXX
To adjust the accounts to show the estimated long-term liability for compensated absences		

If the annual inventory shows a reduction in the amount of the long-term liability for compensated absences, the following adjusting entry would be made:

Long-term compensated absences payable	XXX	
Amount to be provided for long-term compensated absences		XXX
To reduce the long-term liability for compensated absences		

Each year the general fund makes provision in its budget for the amount required to retire bonds maturing during the budget period, and it may also make provisions to pay interest on general obligation bonds. The general fund's appropriations accounts record authorization to make such expenditures during the fiscal year. Later during the year the general fund will actually disburse money in payment of bond principal, and interest on bonded indebtedness. When this occurs, business papers that give evidence that the transactions have occurred are prepared and support the following entry in the general journal of the general long-term debt group of accounts:

Serial bonds payable	$20,000	
Amount to be provided for bond retirement		$20,000
To record general fund's payment for retirement of matured serial bonds		

Each year the preceding entry is made. Ultimately, the bonds payable account is eliminated as a result of annual retirement of the bonds. Each year the balance of the account entitled amount to be provided for bond retirement is reduced by the corresponding amount, ultimately eliminating it.

In the case of long-term bonds being retired by use of a debt service fund, it is possible that the general fund or a tax collection agency fund may serve as the agent to collect taxes for the debt service fund. In other cases, the debt service fund may collect its own taxes. In either case, however, taxes must be levied in an amount that sufficient assets can be accumulated over the life of long-term bonds in debt service funds to retire them at maturity.

At the end of the fiscal period the debt service fund's accounts are closed and the amount actually accumulated during the year for retirement of the long-term bonds is reflected in the accounts. To record the amount accumulated each year in the debt service fund, the following entry is made in the accounts of the general long-term debt group of accounts:

Amount provided in debt service fund for bond retirement	$29,865	
Amount to be provided for bond retirement		$29,865
To record the amount provided by taxes and earnings in the debt service fund for retirement of long-term bonds		

Because interest is paid annually by the general fund or debt service fund on both serial and long-term bonds, entries that reflect the transactions involving interest on general long-term debt are not, necessarily, made a formal part of this group of accounts. However, accounts that reflect the interest status may be effective management instruments.

Each year as payments are made by the general fund or the tax collection agency fund to the debt service fund or as the debt service fund assesses, levies and collects its own taxes and earns interest on its investments, the account entitled amount provided in debt service fund for bond retirement is increased. At the maturity date of the long-term bonds, the amount provided in the debt service fund for bond retirement should equal the maturity value of the long-term bonds. Illustration 16-1 shows how the accounts relative to the bond issue appear in the general long-term debt group of accounts at the maturity date of the long-term bonds.

The entry in the debt service fund to retire bonds is to debit the account entitled matured long-term bonds payable and credit the account entitled cash for $100,000. A corresponding entry is required

Illustration 16-1

Kimberly Hills School District
Statement of General Long-Term Debt
(Date)

Amount provided in debt service fund or bond retirement	$100,000	
Long-term bonds payable		$100,000
Total	$100,000	$100,000

to be made in the general long-term debt group of accounts as follows:

Long-term bonds payable	$100,000	
Amount provided in debt service fund for bond retirement		$100,000
To record use of debt service fund assets to retire long-term bonds		

At this point the purpose for which the general long-term debt group of accounts was created has been served. All of the school district's serial bonds and long-term bonds have matured and have been retired. This being the case, there is no longer any need for the group of accounts to continue operating. Notice that all accounts have been closed in this group.

By formal action of the board of education, the general long-term debt group of accounts for these bond issues would be closed by authority granted in minutes of the meeting of the board. All books of original entry, ledgers, copies of financial statements and business documents affecting the account group should be assembled and stored until examinations by auditors have been completed and formal action of the board authorizes disposition in minutes of the board's meeting.

In the past, many school districts have not used the principles of accounting applicable to general long-term debt account group effectively. Advantages of using this group of accounts may be summarized as follows:

1. The general long-term debt group of accounts records and reports, so long as bonds are outstanding, the amount required to be raised through taxation and other sources of revenue for the purpose of retiring all outstanding bonds at maturity.

Illustration 16-2

Kimberly Hills School District
**General Long-Term Debt
Subsidiary Ledger**

Registered Bonds

Description of Bonds _____ Maturity Date _____

Rate of Interest _____ Interest Payment Dates _____

Name and Address of Interest and Principal Payee:

_____

_____

_____

Date of Bond Issue _____ Purpose of Issue _____

_____

Denomination of Bonds _____ Sale Price _____ Premium _____

Date of Sale _____ Accrued Interest Sold _____ Discount _____

Authorization Information:

Issue authorized by Board recorded in minutes of board meeting date ____

Resolution Number _____ Page Number _____ Book Number _____

Principal

Date of Required
Contribution
Debt Service   Bond Number   Annual Requirement

_____   _____   _____
_____   _____   _____
_____   _____   _____
_____   _____   _____

Interest

Interest Payment Dates   Interest Requirement

_____   _____
_____   _____
_____   _____
_____   _____

Example 1
Assume that a bond issue of $1,000,000 is sold bearing interest at a rate of 10 percent for 10 years.

Amount to be provided for interest	$500,000	
Interest payable in future years		$500,000
To record the liability for interest on bonds payable at the time of issuing bonds		

Each year as interest is paid either by the general fund or by a debt service fund, the following entry is made in the general long-term debt group of accounts:

Interest payable in future years	$ 50,000	
Amount to be provided for interest		$ 50,000
To record payment of annual interest by debt service fund		

---

2. The amounts required to retire all bonds outstanding can be divided into the obligations that must be paid each year through taxation and the school district's other sources of revenue.
3. Through this accounting procedure, the general fund or debt service fund must include a provision for debt service in its budget in an amount sufficient to pay the obligations for debt retirement and bond interest expense for each fiscal year.

Cases are on record where failure to provide adequately for interest obligations on bonds outstanding have caused deficits to be created in the general fund. A school district that requires an annual computation of interest and bond redemption requirements would prevent a deficit due to a mere oversight.

In the case of capital projects funds, other than those in proprietary type funds, a separate group of accounts was created to account for the issue and expenditure of proceeds for each bond issue. In the case of debt service funds, a separate group of accounts was created to account for the accumulation of sufficient financial resources to retire each bond issue at its maturity. However, in the case of the general long-term debt account group, general purpose, general obligation bonds outstanding are recorded in this group. Subsidiary ledger accounts may assist in computing and controlling the amount to be provided for each bond issue.

Example 2
Assume that bonds are sold at a premium of $1,250 and that the governing board directs that the premium be transferred to the debt service fund for interest payments.

Amount provided for interest	$1,250	
Amount to be provided for interest		$1,250
To record amount provided in		
debt service fund for payment of interest		

Registered bond interest is paid only to the holder whose name and address are registered with the school district or its fiscal agent. Subsidiary ledger accounts are designed for the general long-term debt group of accounts to assist in accounting for these kinds of bonds. Illustration 16-2 shows a subsidiary ledger account for a registered bond and details how information about coupon bonds can be recorded as a part of the subsidiary ledger for the general long-term debt group of accounts.

Because of the magnitude of interest that is payable in future years on outstanding, long-term debt, interest payable in future years is fully disclosed from the time the bonds are issued until they are retired. Many advantages accrue to a school district when it formally recognizes interest as an obligation of the school district at the time the bonds or long-term notes are issued (See Example 1).

Amounts are provided in debt service funds specifically designated for payment of interest. If bonds are sold at a premium, the governing board may direct that the premium be transferred to the debt service fund for interest payments (See Example 2).

Advantages of recording interest in the general long-term debt group of accounts include a formal reporting throughout the outstanding life of the debt and tend to avoid repeating cases of administrative oversight of budgetary requirements necessary for annual payment of interest. Interest expense is a material cost to the taxpayer and accounting for school districts is capable of disclosing fully what it costs to use borrowed money.

Illustration 16-3

New Douglas School District
Statement of General Long-Term Debt
June 30, 1995

Amount Provided and to be Provided for the Payment of General Long-Term Debt:	
Amount available in Debt Service Fund	$ 1,084,264
Amount to be provided in Debt Service Funds	16,114,736
Total Available and to be Provided	$17,199,000
General Long-Term Debt:	
General obligation bonds:	
Current	$ 833,000
Long-term	16,366,000
Total General Long-Term Debt Payable	$17,199,000

New Douglas School District
Statement of Changes in General Long-Term Debt
For the Year Ended June 30, 1995

	Balance July 1, 1994	Additions	Balance June 30, 1995
Amount Available and to be Provided for the Payment of General Long-Term Debt:			
Amount available in debt service fund	$ 852,762	$ 231,502	$ 1,084,264
Amount to be provided	14,759,238	1,355,498	16,114,736
Total available and to be provided	$15,612,000	$1,587,000	$17,199,000
General Long-Term Debt Payable:			
General obligation bonds			
Current	$ 764,000	$ 69,000	$ 833,000
Long-term	14,848,000	1,518,000	16,366,000
Total general long-term debt payable	$15,612,000	$1,587,000	$17,199,000

FINANCIAL STATEMENTS

Two financial statements disclose the financial position of the general long-term debt account group and the changes that occur during the fiscal period in this account group. One statement is identified as a statement of long-term debt and the other is the statement of changes in long-term debt. Illustration 16-3 shows the reporting format for the general long-term debt group of accounts.

Illustration 16-4 shows how a district may present important information about the total financial impact of bonded debt principal and interest payments.

SUMMARY

The general long-term debt account group provides the accounting basis for financial statements that show the amount of outstanding long-term debt of the school district. Long-term debt is composed of outstanding bonds, long-term notes payable, long-term leases payable and accumulated liabilities for compensated absence. The amount of outstanding debt must be paid from the revenue of the school district. Sufficient revenue must be provided each year to retire the bonds and long-term notes payable when they mature and to pay interest on them as it becomes due. The general long-term debt group of accounts shows the amount that has been provided in debt service funds for the retirement of long-term bonds and interest payable as well as the amount that will be needed for their retirement in the future. As bonds are retired and interest on general long-term bonded debt is paid from the general fund or from debt service funds, transactions are coordinated between the special revenue fund and the general long-term debt group of accounts.

ACTIVITIES

1. Review the definition for the following terms found in the glossary:
   a. Outstanding bonds
   b. Long-term notes payable
   c. Bonded debt

Ilustration 16-4

Kimberly Hills School District
Schedule of Long-Term Debt
August 31, 1996

Due Fiscal Year Ending 8/31	Principal	Interest	Total
1997	$ 6,109,000	$ 6,102,002	$ 12,211,002
1998	6,572,000	5,556,479	12,128,479
1999	6,998,000	5,196,155	12,194,155
2000	7,343,000	4,824,235	12,167,235
2001	7,678,000	4,451,157	12,129,157
2002	8,061,000	4,062,593	12,123,593
2003	8,464,000	3,651,511	12,115,511
2004	8,864,000	3,217,783	12,081,783
2005	9,102,000	2,763,020	11,865,020
2006	8,745,000	2,348,077	11,093,077
2007	8,885,000	1,923,553	10,808,553
2008	9,122,000	1,472,264	10,594,264
2009	9,177,000	1,018,649	10,195,649
2010	4,665,000	630,125	5,295,125
2011	2,900,000	380,150	3,280,150
2012	2,975,000	213,000	3,188,000
2013	1,125,000	72,000	1,197,000
	$116,785,000	$ 47,882,753	$164,667,753

2. Assume a school system issued 9 percent, 20-year bonds having a face value of $1,000,000. What entry would be made in the general long-term debt group of accounts to record the school district's bond liability?

3. Describe the information that is shown in the general long-term debt group of accounts.

4. Prepare an entry in the general long-term debt group of accounts to record the amount provided by contributions and earnings for the retirement of long-term bonds in the debt service fund.

5. The Bureau County School System issued 9 percent, 10-year bonds in the amount of $1,750,000, and serial bonds in the amount of $1,000,000 bearing interest at the rate of 10 percent,

of which $200,000 will become due at the end of the sixth, seventh, eigthth, ninth and tenth year.

Instructions:
- Compute the amount of interest payable in future years.
- Record the liability in the general long-term debt group of accounts.

6. Notice was given to the general long-term debt group of accounts that the general fund had paid $120,000 in interest due on $800,000 of 8 percent, 10-year bonds and on $500,000 of 9 percent serial bonds. In addition, the general fund deposited $250,000 in a debt service fund for retirement of general bonded debt.

Instructions:
- Record entries made in the general fund to pay interest and to make annual payments to the debt service fund.
- Record entries made in the debt service fund to show receipt from the general fund.
- Record the effect of interest payment and the principal of debt payment to the debt service fund upon the general long-term debt group of accounts.

7. At the end of the sixth year, Cuyahoga Schools retired $150,000 of serial bonds from the debt service fund. What entry is made on the books of the general long-term debt group of accounts to show retirement of these bonds?

8. Fort Steven School District was authorized to issue bonds of $7,500,000 for providing additional school equipment. The authorization provided for issuance of long-term bonds maturing in ten years with interest at 6 percent payable semi-annually. The school district was authorized the use of the debt service fund accounting to accumulate resources to retire the bonds at maturity from taxes collected by the general fund. At the end of the year, $960,000 has been provided for retirement of debt in the debt service fund.

Instructions:
- Prepare the necessary journal entry to record the sale of the bonds in the general long-term debt group of accounts.
- Record the amount provided in the debt service fund as a result of contributions from the general fund and earnings on investments, totaling $960,000.

9. Mesa City Schools issued bonds to finance new equipment for some classrooms. The issue consisted of serial bonds with face value of $800,000. $100,000 is to be retired annually from current revenue. Interest of 6 percent is payable annually.

Instructions:
- Prepare all journal entries necessary to record the issue of the bonds in the general long-term debt group of accounts.
- Prepare the general journal entries necessary to record the retirement of the final installment of bonds in the general long-term debt group of accounts.

REFERENCES/SELECTED READINGS

Fowler, W. J., Jr. (1990). *Financial accounting for local and state systems, 1990.* Washington, DC: U.S. Government Printing Office.

Tidwell, S. B. (1985). *Financial and managerial accounting for elementary and secondary school systems (3rd edition).* Reston, VA: Research Corporation of the Association of School Business Officials.

17

Enterprise Funds

INTRODUCTION

Although school districts are not-for-profit organizations, some of their divisions or departments operate as if they were small businesses concerned with profit and loss. To account for the financial transactions of these special departments, enterprise funds are used.

OUTCOMES

In this chapter, you will learn how to:

1. Understand the history and purpose of enterprise funds.
2. Comply with regulations of various food programs.
3. Account for the financial transactions of enterprise funds.
4. Prepare financial statements for enterprise funds.

DEFINITIONS

Proprietary funds—These funds, also known as income determination funds, non-expendable funds or commercial-type funds, are used for school district operations that provide a product or a service for a fee, similar to a profit-making business in the private sector. There are two kinds of proprietary funds: enterprise and internal service. Enterprise funds account for school district operations that furnish goods or services to the public. The school lunch fund and the school store fund are two examples of enterprise funds used in school districts. Internal service funds account for goods or services rendered to one school district division or department to another. For example, an internal service fund can be established for the district's central data processing department or the central printing and duplicating department.

School lunch fund—The school lunch fund records the financial transactions resulting from school cafeteria operations that serve meals to students and staff. The fund has three purposes:

1. To avoid co-mingling cafeteria money with revenues and expenditures used for other purposes.
2. To more easily monitor the profit and loss resulting from cafeteria operations.
3. To more easily record the state and federal support (cash and food commodities) given to school districts participating in various meal/milk programs.

NATIONAL SCHOOL LUNCH, BREAKFAST AND SPECIAL MILK PROGRAMS

The beginning of federal support of school cafeteria operations began in the 1930s when the government aided the nation's farmers by purchasing their surpluses and donating them to schools. This practice continued on an uneven basis until it was formalized in 1946 by the National School Lunch Act, which, by providing nominal funds to school districts to defray the cost of school lunches, became the basis of the modern federal assistance program. The original act had several purposes:

1. To improve nutrition for the nation's children.
2. To bolster the farming economy through the purchase and subsequent redistribution of surplus food to schools.
3. To improve the physical condition of new soldiers. Many World War II recruits were found to be undernourished, and providing an adequate diet during school years was thought to help mitigate this problem.

When the Child Nutrition Act of 1986 became law, the federal government added monetary incentives for free and reduced price meals, promulgated guidelines for menu offerings and started the Breakfast Program. This act improved the nutrition and health of the nation's youth, especially for those from economically disadvantaged areas. The increased federal support also helped schools establish self-supporting lunch programs, which in turn provided more time for actual instruction by virtually eliminating the home lunch option and concentrating student lunches into shorter, well-defined lunch periods (Colucci, 1988; Goodling, 1990; Van Egmond-Pannell, 1986).

The Child Nutrition Program

School districts have a variety of choices of federally subsidized meal programs for children:

1. Subsidized lunch programs are the most common. They allow schools to offer lunches at reduced prices or at no cost to students whose family incomes fall below designated levels and full price lunches to all other students. The districts receive cash and food commodity subsidies from the federal government and cash subsidies from state governments participating in this program.
2. Breakfast programs are not chosen by as many districts as lunch programs. As federal incentives push to institute breakfast programs in schools, there may be more school district participation in the future. Districts receive cash subsidies from the federal government for participation in this program.
3. Special milk programs allow school districts to offer free milk to pre-kindergarten and half-day kindergarten students who meet economic guidelines. Students who are not present during the school's regular lunch periods are eligible for this program. Districts receive cash subsidies from the federal government for participation in this program.
4. Full price and free milk programs offer options for school districts to charge full price for their served meals, as opposed to the free and reduced meal programs cited above. This option allows school districts to sell milk to all students at a cheaper cost due to the federal subsidies received by the district to offset the purchase price of the milk.
5. Full price milk only programs are available to school districts and allow them to offer milk to all students at reduced prices because the district receives federal cash subsidies to offset the purchase price of the milk.

Implementation Procedures

School districts participating in any of the above child nutrition programs must make the program's benefits available to eligible students each year. To help school districts comply with federal guidelines and to ensure smooth implementation of the program's benefits to school children, the state annually distributes to school districts a free and reduced price policy booklet that summarizes federal guidelines and implementation procedures.

MEAL/MILK INCOME VERIFICATION PROCEDURES

The Child Nutrition Program requires that participating school districts verify the eligibility of selected families receiving meal or milk benefits by December 15 of each year. The school district must send a summary of the verification process results to their local or regional office by January 15 of each year. Shearing (1991) identified the steps in the verification process:

1. The school district determines the sample. The most common method used is a random sample of the lesser of 3 percent or 3,000 approved applications for free or reduced price meals and/or milk. Focused samples are also used by some districts.
2. The school district contacts the families in the sample and requests proof of income.
3. The sample families provide proof of income. A family must list the name and social security number of each household member under the age of 21 and provide written documentation of household income. Acceptable documentation includes paycheck stubs, letters from employers, pension award notices, notification from the state employment security office of unemployment compensation or workers compensation, court decrees or cancelled checks for child support or alimony.
4. The school district then determines the family's eligibility for benefits based upon the income documentation provided by the household.
5. The district then notifies the family in writing of continuation of benefits or ineligibility.

Applications from families who receive food stamps or Aid to Dependent Children (ADC), need not be verified because they are directly certified by the Department of Social Services to receive free meals or milk.

Illustration 17-1 lists income levels according to household size and income levels received either yearly, monthly or weekly. If an applicant's total household income is the same or less than the amounts on the illustration, the applicant's children may be eligible for free or reduced meals or free milk.

The federal and state governments financially assist school districts participating in any of the child nutrition programs by providing cash and commodity support to school districts. Both the state and federal

Illustration 17-1

Income Guidelines – Free Meals/Milk
Effective from July 1, 1994 to June 30, 1995

Household size	Annual	Month	Week
1	$ 9,568	$ 798	$184
2	12,792	1,066	246
3	16,016	1,335	308
4	19,240	1,604	370
5	22,464	1,872	432
6	25,688	2,141	494
7	28,912	2,410	556
8	32,136	2,678	618
For each additional family member add	+3,224	+269	+62

Income Guidelines – Reduced Price Meals
Effective from July 1, 1994 to June 30, 1995

Household size	Annual	Month	Week
1	$13,616	$1,135	$262
2	18,204	1,517	351
3	22,792	1,900	439
4	27,380	2,282	527
5	31,968	2,664	615
6	36,556	3,047	703
7	41,144	3,429	792
8	45,732	3,811	880
For each additional family member add	+4,588	+383	+89

governments pay school districts cash for participation in the programs. The 1994-95 federal cash reimbursement rates per meal are shown in Illustration 17-2.

FOOD DISTRIBUTION

The United States Department of Agriculture (USDA) has also indicated the value of entitlement commodities per lunch is $ .1450. The state also provides cash support to school districts in amounts that vary from state to state. Illustration 17-3 shows the State of Illinois cash support rates per meal for 1994-95.

Illustration 17-2

National School Lunch

	Less than 60%	More Than 60%
Free and Reduced Price Meals		
Paid	$ .1700	$ .1900
Reduced price	1.3575	1.3775
Free	1.7575	1.7775

The maximum a student may be charged for a reduced price lunch is $ .40.

School Breakfast

	Non-severe Need	Severe Need
Paid	$ .1925	$ .1925
Reduced price	.6750	.8600
Free	.9750	1.1600

The maximum a student may be charged for a reduced price breakfast is $ .30.

Special Milk

Paid	$ .1100
Free	Average dairy charge of milk

Illustration 17-3

The reimbursement rate for Illinois Free Breakfast and Lunch Program is $.1220 effective July 1, 1994, through June 30, 1995, a final proration to be made in September 1995.

To ensure adherence to the spirit of the child nutrition programs, the federal government also sets maximum selling prices for meals and milk.

ACCOUNTS AND TRANSACTIONS

Budgetary accounts are generally not used in the operation of enterprise funds. Enterprise funds focus on net income as private sector accounting does. An enterprise fund may be created by capital being transferred from the general fund, a special revenue fund, a capital projects fund or from contributions from a local, state or federal unit of government. The amount of capital originally invested to create the enterprise fund is intended to remain intact. Accounts in the fund equity section of the balance sheet which record the amount of original investment may have titles such as "federal government contribution," "state government contribution" or "contribution from general fund" (See Examples 1 and 2).

Structures, machinery, equipment and other assets such as tools and parts may be acquired through routine purchasing procedures. Sources of revenue may be from sales of finished products, finished jobs, sale of repair parts and supplies or from services provided. Accounting procedures have to be tailored to meet the individual needs of the particular enterprise fund.

Unlike the formal budgetary or governmental type funds, fixed assets used in the operation of an enterprise fund are carried in the fixed assets section of the balance sheet of the enterprise fund. These fixed assets are subject to depreciation. Depreciation is an expense that must be included when setting prices for services rendered or goods produced. By recovering the cost of depreciation in the price for sales or services rendered, it is possible to accumulate an amount equal to the cost of the asset over the useful life of the asset, thereby permitting its replacement without depleting the original fund balance of the enterprise fund.

DEPRECIATION ACCOUNTING

Many different methods may be used to compute the portion of an asset's cost to be properly allocated as an expense during a fiscal period.

Straight-line method—The estimated useful life of each asset is used as the basis for spreading the asset's cost equally to each fiscal period. For example, if an asset cost $50,000 and has an estimated useful life of 10 years, the depreciation is estimated to be $5,000 per year.

Useful hours method—This method estimates depreciation costs using the estimated number of useful hours as the basis for distributing costs to a fiscal period. The total to be depreciated is the difference between the cost of the asset and its estimated scrap value. This total is divided by the estimated useful hours to produce the amount of estimated depreciation per hour. To use this method, records of hours used are required for each fiscal period. The amount is computed by multiplying the number of hours of actual use during the

Example 1

Assume that a school system creates an enterprise fund through which it plans to operate a vocational education project, an automotive repair shop. Capital of $50,000 is to be raised by a contribution from federal sources of $30,000, from state sources of $10,000 and from a long-term advance from the general fund of $10,000.

Due from federal government	$30,000	
Due from state government	10,000	
Due from the general fund	10,000	
Federal government contribution		$30,000
State government contribution		10,000
Advance from general fund		10,000
To record creation of an enterprise fund to operate a vocational education project, an automotive repair shop		

The process of conversion of claims into cash may be lengthy. However, assume that all assets are converted into cash:

Cash	$50,000	
Due from federal government		$30,000
Due from state government		10,000
Due from general fund		10,000
To record receipt of cash from each indicated source		

Example 2

Assume that land of $20,000 is acquired, including all costs of acquisition. A contract is let for construction of a building for servicing the project in an amount not to exceed $25,000. The contract contains a 10 percent retained percentage clause and that $22,500 is paid, withholding $2,500 until final inspection is made.

Land	$20,000	
Cash		$20,000
To record purchase of land		
Building	25,000	
Contracts payable		25,000
To record completion of construction of building		
Contracts payable	25,000	
Cash		22,500
Contracts Payable, retained percentage		2,500
To record payment of contract, withholding 10 percent		

fiscal period by the amount of depreciation per hour.

Units of output method—When an asset is acquired, the number of units to be produced over the useful life of the asset is estimated. That number is divided into the total amount to be depreciated (difference between the asset's cost and its scrap value) over the useful life. To use this method of depreciation, a record of units produced each period must be kept. The number of units produced each fiscal period multiplied by the rate per unit produces the estimated depreciation.

Other methods—Other methods of estimating depreciation can be used including: useful hours method, units of output method, accelerated depreciation, declining balance, sum of the year's digits, average depreciation rates, composite depreciation rates, blanket rates and reducing charge. Each different method is designed to match the cost of an asset to the accounting period in which the benefits of using that asset are derived. Students may consult additional references for a more in-depth discussion and examples of calculating depreciation.

Enterprise funds keep accounts for fixed assets. The accounts are debited for all costs properly chargeable to the asset account. Such charges are frequently referred to as capital charges. The cost of fixed assets is reported in the balance sheet of the fund. A depreciation expense account is debited at the end of the fiscal period to record the estimated depreciation on each of the fixed assets. The corresponding credit is to a balance sheet account, and the amount contained in the account is subtracted on the balance sheet from the corresponding asset's cost. The difference between the cost of the asset as shown in the fixed asset account and the accumulated depreciation reported in the allowance for depreciation account is referred to as the book value of the asset. The allowance for depreciation account is a balance sheet account and remains on the books as long as the fixed asset does. Fixed assets of an enterprise fund are disposed of by sale, exchange, loss or transfer to the general fixed assets group of accounts, to other enterprise funds or to internal services funds.

An enterprise fund is designed to serve a self-supporting activity or operate to provide services. A credit balance in the retained earnings account indicates that, to date, revenue has exceeded expenses. A debit balance in the retained earnings account indicates that expenses have exceeded revenue.

Example 3
Assume that a physical inventory taken at July 1, 1995, amounted to $2,000. During the year, total purchases amounted to $45,500. Purchases of goods for resale are charged to the purchases account and may be made either by cash or on account. Assume purchased goods in the amount of $400 do not meet the purchaser's specifications because of damage, deterioration or not conforming to the specifications. The goods are returned to the vendor for an allowance:

Purchases	$30,000	
Cash		$30,000
To record purchase of merchandise for cash		
Purchases	15,000	
Accounts payable		15,000
To record purchase of merchandise on account		
Accounts payable	400	
Purchase returns and allowances		400
To record return of purchases found to be unacceptable		

Example 4
Commodities valued at $7,600 are received from the USDA. The commodities should be recorded as having been received and at the fair market value on the date received. Assuming that the cost of transporting those goods was $500, the cost of transportation on all goods purchased for the purpose of resale should be recorded as part of the goods sold.

USDA commodities	$7,600	
Revenue from federal government		$7,600
To record receipt of surplus food from USDA at fair market value on date received		
Freight in	500	
Cash		500
To record payment of freight on goods purchased from USDA		

Example 5
Assume than an inventory on June 30, 1996, the end of the fiscal period, amounted to $2,600. On July 1, 1995, the inventory of goods on hand was valued at $2,300.

Revenue and expense summary	$2,300	
Food inventory		$2,300
To remove the beginning inventory from the accounts and to charge the July 1 inventory to the revenue and expense summary account		

Food inventory	2,600	
Revenue and expense summary		2,600
To record the ending inventory as of June 30, 1996		

Example 6

Assume the New Douglas School District operates a vocational education automotive repair shop and that the accounts of the auto repair shop's enterprise fund as of January 1, 1995, had balances as follows:

Cash	$ 250	
Accounts receivable	690	
Allowance for uncollectible accounts		$ 20
Land	3,000	
Building	7,000	
Allowance for depreciation – buildings		700
Equipment	3,500	
Allowance for depreciation – equipment		500
Vouchers payable		680
Advance from the general fund		10,000
Governmental unit's contribution		2,000
Auto repair shop retained earnings		540
	$14,440	$14,440

The following transactions are reported and recorded in summary for the year:

T1	Cash sales for auto services, repairs		$4,700
T2	Repair parts and supplies purchased on account for which a voucher was prepared		2,000
T3	Invoices were received:		
	Electricity	$300	
	Equipment repairs	220	
	Gasoline and oil	750	
	Insurance premiums	830	
	Partially paid $1,780 of the total and vouchered the rest		
T4	Salaries were paid		2,000
T5	Vouchers payable as of January 1 were paid		
T6	Accounts receivable as of January 1 were collected		
T7	Total auto repair services (includes $4,700 from No. 1)		7,000
T8	Interest expense was accrued at 3% on the advance from the general fund		
T9	Estimated depreciation:		
	Buildings	160	
	Equipment	200	
T10	Allowance for uncollectibles was increased		40

Illustration of Example 6 – General Journal Entries

T1	Cash		$4,700	
	Revenue from auto repair services			$4,700
	To record cash sales of services, repairs and/or parts			
T2	Parts and supplies used	2,000		
	Vouchers payable			2,000
	To record repair parts and supplies purchased on account			
T3	Electricity		300	
	Equipment repairs		220	
	Gasoline and oil expense		750	
	Insurance expense		830	
	Cash			1,780
	Vouchers payable			320
	To record invoices paid and vouchered			
T4	Salaries expense		2,000	
	Cash			2,000
	To record payment of salaries			
T5	Vouchers payable		680	
	Cash			680
	To record payment of vouchers payable			
T6	Cash		690	
	Accounts receivable			690
	To record collection of accounts receivable as of January 1			
T7	Accounts receivable		2,300	
	Revenue from auto repair services			2,300
	To record sales on account			
T8	Interest expense		300	
	Interest payable			300
	To record accrued interest for one year at 3 percent on $10,000 advance from the general fund			
T9	Depreciation expense – building		160	
	Depreciation expense – equipment		200	
	Allowance for depreciation – buildings			160
	Allowance for depreciation – equipment			200
	To record depreciation for year			
T10	Loss on uncollectible accounts		40	
	Allowance for uncollectible accounts			40
	To record additional allowance for estimated uncollectible taxes			

Illustration of Example 6 – *Balance Sheet*

New Douglas School District
**Auto Repair Shop - An Enterprise Fund
Balance Sheet**
December 31, 1995

Assets

Current assets:			
Cash		$1,180	
Accounts receivable	$2,300		
Less: Allowance for uncollectible			
accounts	60	2,240	
Total current assets			$ 3,420
Fixed assets:			
Land		3,000	
Buildings	7,000		
Less: Allowance for			
depreciation – buildings	860	6,140	
Equipment	3,500		
Less: Allowance			
for depreciation – equipment	700	2,800	
Total fixed assets			11,940
Total assets			$15,360

Liabilities, Contributions and Fund Balances

Current liabilities:			
Vouchers payable		$2,320	
Interest payable		300	$2,620
Long-term liabilities:			
Advance from general fund			10,000
Total liabilities			12,620
Contributions:			
Governmental unit's contribution			2,000
Unappropriated fund balance:			
Retained earnings, January 1, 1995		540	
Add: net income, interest and expense statement		200	
Retained earnings, December 31, 1995			740
Total liabilities, contributions and fund balance			$15,360

Illustration of Example 6 - Income and Expense Statement

New Douglas School District
Auto Repair Shop – An Enterprise Fund
Income and Expense Statement
For the Year Ended December 31, 1995

Revenue:		
Revenue from auto repair sales and services		$7,000
Expenses:		
Parts and supplies used	$2,000	
Electricity	300	
Equipment repairs	220	
Gasoline and oil expenses	750	
Insurance expense	830	
Interest expense	300	
Depreciation expense – building	160	
Depreciation expense – equipment	200	
Salaries expense	2,000	
Bad debt expense	40	
Total expenses		6,800
Excess Revenue Over Expenditures		$ 200

Illustration of Example 6 – Closing Entries

Revenue from auto repair sales and services	$7,000	
Revenue and expense summary		$7,000
To close the revenue account		
Revenue and expense summary	$6,800	
Parts and supplies used		$2,000
Electricity		300
Equipment repairs		220
Gasoline and oil expense		750
Insurance expense		830
Interest expense		300
Depreciation expense – building		160
Depreciation – equipment		200
Salaries expense		2,000
Bad debt expense		40
To close expense accounts		
Revenue and expense summary	200	
Retained earnings		200
To close the revenue and expense summary		

Cost of goods sold is a major element of cost in the operation of an enterprise fund. Two methods are used to account for cost of goods sold: physical inventory or perpetual inventory. A physical inventory entails physically counting the goods on hand annually or periodically. A perpetual inventory requires an inventory account in which all units purchased are entered at cost, and all units sold or issued are recorded at cost (See Examples 3, 4, 5 and 6).

SUMMARY

School districts provide many supporting services for educational programs such as school food services, athletic programs, school newspapers, yearbooks and vocational education projects such as farms, automotive repair shops, woodworking shops and homebuilding projects. Services rendered by enterprise funds can be available to the public as well as to students, faculty and staff of the school district. Each activity is intended to be partially, if not fully, self-supporting.

The nature of principal revenue source(s) determine whether the activity involved is to be accounted for as a special revenue fund or an enterprise fund. If a substantial portion of the revenue used to finance an activity within a fund is derived from user charges, the fund should be classified as an enterprise fund. In contrast, if only a small portion of the revenue is realized from user charges, the fund should be properly accounted for as a special revenue fund.

The major objective of an enterprise fund is to determine costs of rendering services. These costs serve as a basis for setting fees to be charged for services or goods consumed.

ACTIVITIES

1. Carefully review the definition of the following terms given in the glossary:
   a. Proprietary funds
   b. Income determination funds
   c. Non-expendable funds
   d. Commercial-type funds
   e. Enterprise funds

f. Internal service funds
g. Depreciation accounting
h. Straight-line depreciation
i. Useful hours depreciation
j. Units of output depreciation
k. Book value of an asset
l. Retained earnings

2. Determine the annual, monthly and weekly income eligibility for a single parent family with two school-age children living at home.

3. Assume the remodeling of a cafeteria is begun by a contractor during the current year and that upon completion, 15 percent of total project costs is to be retained until the contractor's work has been inspected and accepted. Prepare the journal entries for the following events:
   a. The contractor submits a bill amounting to the full contract price of $100,000; final inspection and acceptance has not been completed.
   b. Payment is made to the contractor less 15 percent retainage.
   c. Final inspection is satisfactorily completed and the board of education accepts the remodeling project; payment is made.

4. The balance sheet of an enterprise fund for the past year included the following items in the fixed assets section:

   Fixed assets:
Building	$ 80,000	
Less: Allowance for depreciation – building	32,000	$ 48,000
Equipment	70,000	
Less: Allowance for depreciation – equipment	7,000	63,000
Total fixed assets		$111,000

   If the rate of depreciation is 5 percent per year, prepare the entries that would be required at the end of the current year.

5. Show the fixed assets section of the balance sheet after recording the entries in No. 4 above.

6. The Newaygo High School Food Service Fund from Newaygo School District 5 has the following trial balance at the beginning of the school year.

Newaygo School District 5
Newaygo High School Food Service Fund
An Enterprise Fund
Trial Balance
September 1, 1996

	Debit	Credit
Cash	$25,000	
Investments	33,000	
Due from general fund	11,200	
Due from state government	3,500	
Due from federal government	8,900	
Inventories	15,000	
Equipment	75,000	
Accumulated depreciation – equipment		$ 19,000
Accounts payable		27,000
Due to general fund		1,200
Retained earnings		124,400
Total	$171,600	$171,600

The following transactions took place during the fiscal year ended August 31, 1997:

T1: Issued purchased orders for food amounting to $114,500.
T2: Computed the amount due from federal government under the National Child Nutrition Program to be $13,000.
T3: Invoices for the food in T1 amounted to $120,000.
T4: Cash sales to students amounted to $151,000.
T5: Purchase orders for a walk-in cooler and other kitchen equipment were issued inthe amount of $7,500.
T6: Cash sales to faculty amounted to $18,000.
T7: Received earnings on investments of $2,000.
T8: Salaries amounting to $28,000 for the year were paid.
T9: Cash contributions from local sources for the breakfast program amounted to $1,500.
T10: Supplies expense for the year of $3,400 was paid in cash.
T11: Received amount due from the state government.
T12: Paid utility bills amounting to $2,800.
T13: Paid $110,000 on account.
T14: Paid the amount due to the general fund.
T15: Received items ordered in T5 above, invoices were for $8,800.

T16: Administrative expenses for the year were paid amounting to $3,000.

T17: Sold equipment costing $4,000 with accumulated depreciation of $3,200 for $900.

T18: Miscellaneous expenses of $3,100 were paid.

Additional information:
a. Ending inventories were determined to be $17,500.
b. Depreciation on equipment for the year was determined to be $4,000.

Instructions:
- Record account balances as of September 1, 1995, in ledger accounts.
- Journalize transaction data, adjusting and closing entries for the year.
- Post to ledger accounts.
- Prepare a post-closing trial balance.
- Prepare a statement of income and expense.
- Prepare a balance sheet.
- Prepare a statement of changes in retained earnings.

REFERENCES/SELECTED READINGS

Colluci, M.A. (1988, November). *Program considerations for shool lunch services*, School Business Affairs, 55 (11).

Federal Register, Volume 53, No. 148, (August 2, 1988). Washington, DC: Department of Agriculture, Food and Nutrition Service.

Fowler, W. J., Jr. (1990). *Financial accounting for local and state systems, 1990.* Washington, DC: U. S. Government Printing Office.

Goodling, W. F. (1990, November). "The Future of Federal Funding for Child Nutrition Programs", School Business Affairs, 56 (11).

Hess, J.P. & Van Egnond-Pannell, D. (1977, November). *Budeting for food service operations,* School Business Affairs, 53 (11).

Shearing, F. N. (1991, August). Memorandum to superintendents of public schools, Albany, NY: Bureau of School Food Management and Nutrition.

Tidwell, S. B. (1985). *Financial and managerial accounting for elementary and secondary school systems (3rd ed.).* Reston, VA: Research Corporation of the Association of School Business Officials.

18

Internal Service Funds

INTRODUCTION

Internal service funds, classified as proprietary funds, are used to "account for the operation of LEA [local education agency] functions that provide goods and services to other LEA functions, other LEAs or to other governmental units, on a cost-reimbursable basis" (Fowler, 1990). Internal service funds are established to centralize operations to promote economic benefits that may result from more efficient and effective operations. For example, a fund may be established to realize economic advantages that may result from centralized purchasing and warehousing. Funds may also be established to obtain economic returns, which may result in the centralization of services such as central data processing, and central printing and duplicating. The objective of an internal service fund is to cover direct and indirect costs of goods and services by assessing appropriate user charges, which produce no significant profit nor result in any significant loss.

OUTCOMES

In this chapter, you will learn how to:

1. Define and identify an internal service fund.
2. Create an internal service fund.
3. Operate an internal service fund.
4. Close the books on an internal service fund.

CREATION OF AN INTERNAL SERVICE FUND

Ordinarily, internal service funds are established in one of three ways:

1. Contributions of cash or other assets from another fund, such as

the general fund, an enterprise fund, the capital projects fund, or general fixed assets group of accounts.
2. Sale of general obligation bonds.
3. Long-term advances from other funds.

The amount from contributions, sale of bonds or long-term advances becomes the *capital* of the internal service fund. Since the goal of the fund is to provide goods and services with the LEA on a cost-reimbursable basis without significant profit or loss in the long run, the fund is said to be a *non-expendable fund*.

The general journal entry should be as follows to record a contribution from the general fund to the internal service fund:

General Journal
Internal Service Fund

Page XXX

Date	Account Title	Debits	Credits
1995			
12/01	Cash	$15,000.00	
	Contributed capital from general fund		$15,000.00
	To record receipt of contribution from the general fund		

OPERATION OF AN INTERNAL SERVICE FUND

Revenue – The internal service fund should record revenue on the full accrual basis of accounting. Interfund transfers from the user department are considered revenues in the internal service fund (and expenditures in the user department). It is necessary to record interfund transfers as revenue in order to obtain proper determination of the fund's operating results.

As monies are transferred from the user department to the internal service fund, the general journal entry should be as follows:

General Journal
Internal Service Fund

Date	Account Title	Debits	Page XXX Credits
1995			
12/15	Cash	$2,000	
	Due from other funds		$2,000
	To record collection of accounts receivable from the general fund		

Expenses – In the internal service fund, expenses and not expenditures are recorded. The following transactions represent sample general journal entries for expenses and capitalized items:

1. Gasoline, oil, tires and tubes are requisitioned for maintenance and operating purposes. The cost of materials and supplies issued is recorded as follows:

General Journal
Internal Service Fund

Date	Account Title	Debits	Page XXX Credits
1995			
12/16	Maintenance and operating supplies used	$4,000	
	Inventory of maintenance and operating supplies		$4,000
	To record cost of supplies issued		

2. Assume that a bill was received for a building addition in the amount of $20,000. The journal entry is recorded as follows:

General Journal
Internal Service Fund

Date	Account Title	Debits	Page XXX Credits
1995			
12/11	Buildings and building improvements	$20,000	
	Accounts payable		$20,000
	To record receipt of invoice for building addition		

Fixed assets – The internal service fund is "a fiscal and accounting entity with a self-balancing set of accounts recording cash and other financial resources. Therefore, fixed assets acquired for use by the internal service fund to provide the goods or services for which the fund was created are carried in the accounts of the internal service fund, not in the general fixed assets group of accounts. When materials are purchased or other assets are acquired for use by the internal service fund, asset accounts are created in the internal service fund for them.

TYPES OF OPERATIONS APPLICABLE TO INTERNAL SERVICE FUNDS

Two types of operations are handled through the use of internal service funds. The first is a stores department type such as would be used by a school district in operating a central supply department. The second may be described as that of a service department. In operating this type of internal service fund, materials, labor and other production costs may be incurred in converting certain materials into goods or commodities that can be used by the school district or that can be used to render a service to a unit of the school system. The operation of a central printing office, a central computer service department and a maintenance department are examples of services that may be provided by an internal service fund.

Costs of goods sold – Two methods are used in accounting for cost of goods sold – physical inventory (or periodic inventory) and perpetual inventory. The physical inventory (or periodic inventory) involves a physical count of goods on hand once each year. The perpetual inventory does not require a physical count of goods on hand, but a record of inventory is maintained to identify the inventory by account. When goods are purchased, the account is debited for the cost of the goods. As goods are consumed, the account is credited for the cost. The balance in the account should reflect the amount on hand.

The two bases most commonly used to determine the value of inventory are cost, and lower of cost or market. Tidwell states:

> In determining cost of inventory on hand, a number of methods have been developed: specific identification; moving-average; weighted average; last-in, first-out; and

first-in, first-out. When using perpetual inventory cards, cost can be easily computed, based upon the method of determining cost selected. When using a periodic inventory method, the most economical method of pricing on a cost basis is first-in, first-out. In this case, all units remaining in inventory can be traced to the most recent purchase invoices and to cost identified by item, unit price and quantity. (Tidwell, 1985)

Job order cost accounting – Tidwell (1985) summarizes the essentials of job order cost accounting as follows:

Asset accounts consist of cash, due from other funds, materials inventory, work-in-process inventory, machinery and equipment, allowance for depreciation of machinery and equipment, and others.

Liability accounts consist of vouchers payable, salaries payable and others....The fund equity account is the original capital invested in the internal service fund which is to be retained intact and theoretically is not to be increased or depleted. Net income or net loss for each period is closed into the retained earnings account.

Basically, expense accounts are debited when an expense creates a liability account or when cash is paid.... Expense accounts are closed by debiting to a work-in-process account. Work-in-process is an asset account. When a job is completed it is billed to the organization unit ordering and receiving the service and the cost of the job is recorded. Cost of jobs completed is an expense account, which is closed to the revenue and expense summary account at the end of the fiscal period. (pp. 462-463)

CLOSING THE BOOKS OF AN INTERNAL SERVICE FUND

Although the objective of internal service funds is to cover direct and indirect costs of the goods/services by assessing appropriate user charges that produce no significant profit nor result in any significant loss, rarely will revenues match expenses for the year.

The excess of revenues over expenses (or expenses over revenues) may be handled in two ways. One method of handling an excess of revenues over expenses would be to debit revenues and adjust the user departments' accounts. A more practical method of closing the books would be to credit retained earnings for the excess of revenues over expenses and adjust future user charges (Robert Davis Associates, 1981, pp. 367-368).

SUMMARY

Definitions of internal service funds were provided and selected internal service funds were identified. Procedures for creating and operating an internal service fund were discussed. Two methods of closing the books on an internal service fund were given. Robert Davis Associates (1981, pp. 371-372) summarize the essentials of internal service funds as follows:

1. The internal service fund is used to account for services provided by one department exclusively to other departments within the LEA or to other governmental units.
2. A less restrictive budget is needed because the budgets of the user departments act as constraints on the expenses of the fund.
3. The full accrual basis of accounting is recommended for the internal service fund.
4. Transfers to the internal service fund for services provided to user departments are revenue to the fund.
5. Depreciation must be recorded on fixed assets so the full cost of providing services can be billed to user departments.
6. Annual statements required for the internal service fund include:
   a. Balance sheet
   b. Statement of revenues, expenses and changes in retained earnings
   c. Statement of changes in financial position

ACTIVITIES

1. Review the definition for the following terms found in the glossary:
   a. Accrual basis
   b. Captial
   c. Cost of goods sold

    d. Cost basis
    e. Work-in-process
    f. Cost accounting

2. A school bus is purchased for $35,000 and has an estimated useful life of 8 years at which time it is estimated that the bus will have a scrap value of $3,000. What is the amount of annual depreciation computed on the straight line basis?

3. What are two major advantages of operating a central maintenance department of a school system rather than a decentralized department?

4. On July 1, 1996, the board of education of the Kimberly Hills School District created an internal service fund to provide pupil transportation services. To establish this fund, the following were transferred to the school district's Pupil Transportation Service Department:

Cash	$200,000
Transportation vehicles	240,000
Maintenance equipment	60,000
Maintenance and operating supplies	50,000
Prepaid rent, garage (July 1-Dec. 31)	3,000

   During the month of July, the following transactions occurred:

   July 2   Purchased repair parts on account, $10,000.
   July 4   Maintenance and operating supplies requisitioned by mechanics, $1,000.
   July 5   Repair parts requisitioned by mechanics, $8,000.
   July 10 Purchased additional repair parts on account, $25,000.
   July 12 Payment of transportation insurance premium for year beginning July 1, $6,000.
   July 12 Payment on account for repair parts purchased July 2.
   July 15 Purchased maintenance and operating supplies on account, $10,000.
   July 20 Payment on account for repair parts purchased July 10.

   July 30 Paid drivers salaries, $5,000.
            Paid maintenance salaries, $2,000.
            Paid heat, light and power bills, $1,500.

Depreciation on transportation vehicles and maintenance equipment is calculated on a straight-line method. These assets have an estimated life of ten years.

Instructions:
- Prepare the opening entry on the books of the internal service fund and record the transaction for July in general journal form.
- Prepare a trial balance as of July 31, 1996.

REFERENCES/SELECTED READINGS

Fowler, W. J., Jr. (1990). *Financial accounting for local and state school systems*. Washington, DC: U.S. Government Printing Office.

Robert Davis Associates. (1981). *Principles of public school fund accounting*. Washington, DC: National Technical Information Service.

Tidwell, S. B. (1985). *Financial and managerial accounting for elementary and secondary school systems (3rd edition)*. Reston, VA: Research Corporation of the Association of School Business Officials.

19

Trust Funds

INTRODUCTION

The LEA may receive money which is to be used for special purposes by the school district. Donors may specify the restrictions on the use of the money in the trust agreement. Due to the nature of trust agreements, accounting principles have been developed to enable an LEA to act in the capacity of a trustee or fiduciary.

Trust funds entail the management of money or other assets to produce certain results usually specified in the trust agreement. In non-expendable trusts the original amount, or the trust fund principal, is to be retained intact in order to produce an income that may be used to benefit the school system. In expendable trusts, the LEA is to use the principal amount and any income produced in accordance with the terms of the trust agreement.

OUTCOMES

In this chapter, you will learn how to:

1. Understand the accounting principles to be applied in non-expendable trust funds
2. Understand the accounting principles to be applied in expendable trust funds

NON-EXPENDABLE TRUST FUNDS

Non-expendable trust funds are used to account for trusts in which the principal must remain intact. The accounting principles to be applied in non-expendable trust funds are similar to those that applied to proprietary funds. Therefore, the financial statements applicable to non-expendable trust funds are the balance sheet, the statement of revenue and expense, the statement of changes in fund principal, and the statement of change in financial position.

Non-expendable trust funds may be established for a variety of purposes, such as, to purchase books for the library, to promote athletic activities, or to provide loans to teachers to continue educational pursuits. In the case of loans to teachers to continue educational pursuits, the trust agreement may stipulate that the principal is not to be expended and that the interest charged to teachers on the loan is to be added to the trust fund principal.

Complications may arise in non-expendable trust funds when administrative cost are recovered. If income from the trust fund exceeds the amount of the administrative cost, then no problems exist. If, however, administrative costs exceed the amount of income produced, then payment of the administrative cost would result in a violation of the non-expendable trust agreement transforming the non-expendable trust into an expendable trust. In this event, the financial statements to be prepared would follow those of expendable trusts with a notation that the conditions of a non-expendable trust had been violated.

EXPENDABLE TRUSTS

An expendable trust is created to record transactions that arise from a trust agreement that stipulates the trust fund principal is to be used in accordance with the trust fund agreement. In this case, all assets, principal and any resulting income, may be used to carry out the trust fund agreement and there is no stipulation that the trust fund principal is to be retained intact.

The financial statements applicable to expendable trust funds are the balance sheet, the statement of revenue, expenses and fund equity, and the statement of change in financial position.

SAMPLE TRANSACTIONS

Non-expendable trust fund
1. Assume that Randy Holden donates $10,000 to the Kimberly Hills School District to be used as a non-expendable trust fund principal with income from investments to be used to purchase scientific books for the library.
2. Investments were purchased in the amount of $8,000.
3. Income in the amount of $40 was received from interest on the investment.
4. A scientific book in the amount of $35 was purchased.

Example 1

General Journal
Randy Holden Scientific Book Trust Fund

T1	Cash in bank	101	$10,000	
	Contributed capital	721		$10,000
	To record receipt of principal from book fund			
T2	Investments	111	8,000	
	Cash in bank	101		8,000
	To record purchase of investments			
T3	Cash in bank	101	40	
	Earning on investment	1500		40
	To record earning on investment			
T4	Supplies-books	640	35	
	Cash in bank			35
	To record cash balance			

Example 2 – Expendable Trust Fund

Assume that Christopher Simpson donates $50,000 to promote swimming activities at Kimberly Hills High School. Any earnings on the principal amount are to accumulate in the fund, however, when the balance (principal and earnings drops below $100 the fund is to be closed and the balance transferred to the General Fund. Investments of $40,000 were purchased. A timing system was purchased for $15,000. Earnings of $75 were realized on the investments:

General Journal
Christopher Simpson Swimming Trust Fund

T1	Cash in bank	101	$50,000	
	Unreserved fund Balance	770		$50,000
	To record receipt of $50,000 from Christopher Simpson to be used to promote swimming			
T2	Investments	111	40,000	
	Cash in bank	101		40,000
	To record purchase of investments			
T3	Expenditures	602	15,000	
	Cash in bank	101		15,000
	To record purchase of timing system			
T4	Cash in bank	101	75	
	Earning on investment	1500		75
	To record earnings on investments			

Transaction in the general journal for the above transactions would be as shown in Examples 1 and 2.

SUMMARY

The purposes of trust funds were presented and the differences between non-expendable and expendable trust funds were clarified. Accounting principles appropriate to trust funds were noted. Sample transactions affecting non-expendable and expendable trust funds were shown.

ACTIVITIES

1. Why are trust funds created?

2. What happens to the principal in a non-expendable trust fund?

3. What happens to the principal in an expendable trust fund?

4. The Fort Steven School District has an non-expendable trust fund which was established by the donation of $500,000 from John and Freda Hummel. Income, to be deposited in an expendable trust fund, is to be used to promote baseball in the school district.
   a. Assume that the principal amount was invested (7/1/94) to yield an annual rate of 6%.
   b. In addition, assume that on 7/1/95 $2,000 was used to purchase equipment for the baseball team.

Instructions:
- Record the receipt of the principal amount of the non-expendable trust fund,
- Record the collection of interest for the first year in the expendable trust fund.
- Prepare end of the year reports in non-expendable and expendable trust funds at the end of the second year (6/30/96).

REFERENCES/SELECTED READINGS

Fowler, W. J., Jr. (1990). *Financial accounting for local and state school systems, 1990*. Washington, DC: Superintendent of

Documents, U. S. Government Printing Office.

Robert Davis Associates (1981). *Principles of public school fund accounting.* Washington, DC: National Technical Information Service.

Tidwell, S. B. (1985). *Financial and managerial accounting for elementary and secondary school systems, 3rd edition.* Reston, VA: The Research Corporation, Association of School Business Officials.

20

Agency Funds

INTRODUCTION

The local education agency (LEA) retains custody of and fiduciary responsibility for some money, but exercises no independent control over the use of it. For example, deductions are made biweekly from employees' paychecks for taxes and benefits. Some of these amounts are remitted to the appropriate agency every pay period, but other organizations require monthly, quarterly or annual payments. In other words, the school district, acting in a fiduciary capacity as temporary custodian of these dollars, is not permitted to use the money to finance operations. Therefore, in order to prevent unauthorized use of these assets and to account for their accumulation and disbursement, the school district uses agency funds. In agency funds, assets of the agency should equal the liabilities at all times. Therefore, agency funds have no fund equity.

OUTCOMES

In this chapter, you will learn how to:

1. Understand the purposes of agency funds.
2. Account for transactions in an agency fund.
3. Produce periodic and annual financial statements for an agency fund.

FIDUCIARY FUNDS

Fiduciary funds are used to account for assets held by an LEA as trustee or agent. Trust funds were discussed in chapter 19. Agency funds are purely custodial (assets equal liabilities) and do not involve measurements of results of operations.

Agency funds provide a method of accounting for and safekeeping of assets that will be sent to, given to, or used by individuals or organizations at some future time. The funds are custodial in nature with assets remaining in the funds for short periods of time. Typically, agency funds are used to account for the financial transactions of a central treasury, tax collection department, payroll department, or student clubs (Tidwell, 1985). Separate agency funds are kept for each function. Two types of agency funds will be discussed in this chapter—a central payroll agency fund and the student activity fund.

THE CENTRAL PAYROLL AGENCY FUND

The central payroll agency fund (sometimes simply called agency fund) is an important part of the payroll process, because it acts as a temporary repository for salaries as the money moves from the fund of origin (e.g., the general fund) to the employees' paychecks or personal bank accounts. The purpose of this agency fund is to hold employee deductions and school district contributions to external agencies for individual retirement accounts, state retirement plans, disability insurance, group health or life insurance, deferred compensation plans, state and federal income taxes, union or professional association dues, social security taxes, wage garnishments and similar purposes from the various funds financing the payroll. A single payment may then be made to each "vendor" for the amount held in custody.

The central payroll agency fund, as do all agency funds, uses the modified accrual system of accounting. This fund contains only asset and liability accounts with no revenue, expenditure, budgetary or fund equity accounts. (Fowler, 1990).

SAMPLE TRANSACTIONS IN THE CENTRAL PAYROLL AGENCY FUND

Payroll deductions and withholdings forwarded by other funds to the central payroll agency fund would be recorded in that fund's general journal as shown in Illustration 20-1.

In the sample transaction in Illustration 20-1, separate liability accounts could have been established for each benefit, i.e., Social Security (471), Retirement (472), Health Insurance (473), etc.

Illustration 20-1

General Journal
Agency Fund

Page XXX

Date	Account Title	Acct. No.	Debits	Credits
1995				
11/01	Cash in bank	101	$15,000	
	Payroll Deductions and withholdings	471		$15,000
	To record receipt of payroll deductions and withholdings from the general fund			

Illustration 20-2

General Journal
Agency Fund

Page XXX

Date	Account Title	Acct. No.	Debits	Credits
1995				
11/01	Social Security taxes	471	$5,000	
	Cash in bank	101		$5,000
	To record payment of social security taxes			

(Robert Davis Associates, 1985). Similarly, when the liabilities are paid to the appropriate agencies, the general journal entry would be as shown in Illustration 20-2.

FINANCIAL STATEMENTS

An agency fund is used to account for assets held by an LEA acting as an agent for individuals, organizations or other governmental units or other funds. As such, the financial statement for the agency fund would be as shown in Illustration 20-3.

Robert Davis Associates (1985) maintains that "agency funds should be used when the volume of transactions, the amount of money

Illustration 20-3

Kimberly Hills School District
Statement of Changes in Assets and Liabilities
Agency Fund–Social Security Taxes
June 30, 1996

Assets	Balance July 1, 1995	Additions	Deductions	Balance June 30, 1996
Cash	$22,000	$25,000	$28,000	$19,000
Liabilities:				
Social Security Taxes	$22,000	$25,000	$28,000	$19,000

involved or the management and accounting capabilities of the LEA's personnel make it cumbersome or unwise to account for the money in funds of more general use". Agency funds have been used to handle transactions for student activity funds, central payroll, central treasury and central tax collections. The procedures and detail vary with each agency fund, but basic accounting procedures are similar.

The central payroll agency fund involves greater detail than other agency funds. Procedures need to be established for temporary investment of idle cash, individual earnings records need to be established and maintained and procedures for computing gross earnings, payroll taxes and other deductions need to be in conformity with pertinent guidelines.

SUMMARY

The purposes of agency funds were presented and several uses of the agency fund were identified. Procedures were developed for recording financial transactions involving the agency fund and sample transaction were illustrated. An annual financial statement, statement of changes in assets and liabilities, was shown for an agency fund.

ACTIVITIES

1. Review the definition for the following terms found in the glossary:

a. Fiduciary fund type
b. Agency fund
c. Modified accrual basis
d. Statement of changes in assets and liabilities.

2. Why are agency funds created?

3. How are agency funds different from trust funds?

4. Responsibility for payroll administration of the Kimberly Hills School District rests with the central payroll fund. The following account balances were taken from the central payroll fund's trial balance on September 30, 1995:

Due from general fund	$8,688
Due from cafeteria fund	1,532
FICA taxes payable	1,080
Federal income tax withheld and payable	9,140

During the month of October, the following transactions occurred:

a. On October 1, the employer's OASDI tax liability for September was computed. A liability of $918 was applicable to the general fund and $162 was applicable to the cafeteria fund.
b. On October 2, cash was received from the general fund in the amount of $9,606 and from the cafeteria fund in the amount of $1,694.
c. The required monthly deposit of cash for income taxes withheld for both employee and employer's OASDI taxes was made on October 2.
d. The semi-monthly payroll voucher was prepared on October 15 as follows: OASDI taxes withheld, $540; federal income taxes withheld, $1,250; employee retirement contributions withheld, $1,500; teacher retirement contributions withheld, $1,000; savings bond deductions, $300; net payroll, $29,280. Billings against the general fund were computed to be $32,674 and from the cafeteria fund $5,766.
e. On October 15, cash was received from the general fund in the amount of $24,888 and from the cafeteria fund in the amount of $4,392.
f. Salaries were paid on October 15.
g. The semi-monthly payroll voucher was prepared on October 31 identical in amount to the voucher computed in D above.

h. On October 31, the employer's OASDI tax liability for October was computed. A liability of $918 was applicable to the general fund and $162 was applicable to the cafeteria fund.
i. Cash was received on October 31 as follows: $41,378 from the general fund and $7,302 from the cafeteria fund.
j. Salaries were paid on October 31.
k. The required monthly deposit of cash for income taxes withheld and for both the employees' and employers' OASDI taxes was made on November 5.

Instructions:
- Record the foregoing balances and record the transactions in general journal form on the books of the central payroll fund.

REFERENCES/SELECTED READINGS

Fowler, W. J., Jr. (1990). *Financial accounting for local and state school systems.* Washington, DC: U. S. Government Printing Office.

Robert Davis Associates. (1981). *Principles of public school fund accounting.* Washington, DC: National Technical Information Service.

Tidwell, S. B. (1985). *Financial and managerial accounting for elementary and secondary school systems, 3rd edition.* Reston, VA: The Research Corporation, Association of School Business Officials.

21

Payroll Accounting/Development

INTRODUCTION

By using a payroll accounting concept for the entire school district, financial accounting and reporting for each fund that employs people can be greatly simplified. These accounting principles apply to assets held by the school district for its employees and for local, state or federal governments in the case of withholding and social security taxes. The school district deducts federal income tax, social security taxes, local and state income taxes from the salaries of employees and remits the amount withheld to the respective governmental entities within a specified timeframe. The school district acts as an agent for its employees when it makes other authorized deductions from payrolls for retirement, hospitalization insurance, savings bonds and many other purposes. In these cases, the board does not determine the purpose for which the assets are to be used, but instead the board acts or makes disbursements or distributions when proper authority is granted to it by the employee, by law or by contract. The board has the responsibility for establishing adequate internal accounting and management controls needed to safeguard such assets and provide assurance that the assets are being used for the purposes for which they were provided. Increasing demands are being made upon school districts to render services as custodian of assets for others. Therefore, it is necessary that internal controls, accounting procedures and financial responsibility be clearly established by the board of education for the efficient and effective use of these assets.

OUTCOMES

In this chapter, you will learn how to:

1. Determine payroll obligations of the school district for its employees.
2. Record transactions used for payroll activities.

3. Determine withholdings and deductions.
4. Identify payroll reports required to be filed with governmental agencies.

EMPLOYMENT AND PAYROLL ACTIVITIES

Expenditures are made from the general fund and other operating funds for the total employment costs and cash is transferred from each fund by check to the central payroll agency fund. From this one agency fund, all payroll checks are issued, remittances are made to the District Director, Internal Revenue Service, for federal income tax and social security tax withheld, and remittances are made to all other agencies for which money has been withheld from employees and for employer expenses that have been incurred for employee benefits. From this one agency fund, all interim and annual employment tax and withholding reporting forms are prepared and submitted according to requirements of each. Administrative decisions needed to determine academic and staff qualifications and salary are made by the fund employing personnel, not the payroll department. The amounts of money transferred to the payroll fund are held by the payroll fund as an agent for the employees and other agencies related to employment.

The payroll department computes the pay of each employee of the school district. It then computes the cost distribution applicable to each fund for the total cost of employment for that fund. This is made up of its employees gross pay plus the employer's related expenses for employee fringe benefits, including compensated absences.

One check is written each pay period, payable to the central payroll agency fund, by each fund using the services of the central payroll department. The general fund would record its employment costs, including compensated absences as:

Salaries, instruction	XXX
Employee benefits, instruction	XXX
Salaries, special programs	XXX
Employee benefits, special programs	XXX
Salaries, guidance services	XXX
Employee benefits, guidance services	XXX
Salaries, board of education	XXX

Employee benefits, board of education	XXX
Salaries, general administration	XXX
Employee benefits, general administration	XXX
Salaries, school administration	XXX
Employee benefits, school administration	XXX
Salaries, internal services	XXX
Employee benefits, internal services	XXX
Salaries, operation and maintenance of plant	XXX
Employee benefits, operation & maintenance of plant	XXX
Salaries, pupil transportation services	XXX
Employee benefits, pupil transportation services	XXX
Salaries, statistical services	XXX
Employee benefits, statistical services	XXX
Cash	YYY

To record issuance of check of the general fund payable to the central payroll agencyfund for all employment costs for the payroll period

At the end of the accounting period, each fund using services of the central payroll department should inventory its liabilities for compensated absences and make an adjusting entry to current salary costs accounts and to the current liability account for the accrued compensated absences expense payable. The current portion is the amount left unpaid at the end of the reporting period that normally would be liquidated with expendable available financial resources. The remainder of the liability should be reported in the general long-term debt group of accounts.

Only the minimum number of accounts needs to be maintained in the books of each individual fund using the services of the central payroll agency fund. The fund using the central payroll services would be required to provide adequate appropriations to cover total employment cost through budgetary action. Therefore, the payroll fund would not use budgetary accounts.

ACCOUNTS AND TRANSACTIONS

Individual Earnings Records – For each individual employee, a record of earnings should be kept. Information about pay for each individual employee may be recorded on an individual earnings record. This record is important because questions may arise in later

4 • CHAPTER 21

Example 1
Assume that the total payroll shows gross earnings of employees to be paid from the general fund in the amount of $35,000; income tax withheld, $6,820; social security tax withheld, $710; group insurance, $1,240; and savings bond deductions of $1,230.

Due from General Fund	$35,000	
Income tax withheld and payable		$ 6,820
OASDI tax payable		710
Group insurance deductions payable		1,240
Savings bond deductions payable		1,230
Vouchers payable		25,000
To record payroll voucher		

The central payroll fund records the school district's liability for employer's social security tax in an amount equal to that deducted from the employees' salaries. The entry is as follows:

Due from General Fund	$710	
Social security tax payable		$710
To record the employer's contribution for social security taxes		

---

periods about earnings, social security taxes withheld, income taxes withheld, or eligibility for retirement. It also serves the school system as a basis for filing informational returns for state and federal income tax and for federal social security tax purposes.

Payroll Voucher – The payroll voucher usually lists the names of each employee, regular earnings, additional earnings, gross earnings, income tax withheld, social security tax withheld, group insurance, other deductions, net paid and check number. It serves as the basis for the journal entry necessary to record the payroll (See Example 1).

Employees of the school district are usually employed under the provisions of a salary schedule adopted by the board of education for each classification of employee. Salary schedules are adopted based upon consideration of the employee's qualifications, years of service and related matters. Once adopted by the board, the salary schedules, sick leave policies, insurance program, provisions for employment of substitutes and methods of computing salaries become the basis for payroll computation.

As a matter of clerical efficiency, many documents necessary for the payroll department are secured by the personnel office at the time of employment. These documents include a statement from a designated administrative officer notifying the payroll department that an employee has been added to the staff or faculty. It gives authority to the payroll department to prepare a payroll file for the employee and to place the employee's name on the payroll.

Any pay deduction other than federal income tax withholding, mandatory retirement or social security tax deduction should be authorized in writing by the employee at the time of employment, and a copy of the pay deduction authorization should be filed with the payroll department. The employing officer should have each employee file Internal Revenue Service's Form W-4, the Employee's Withholding Exemption Certificate, on which the employee states the number of exemptions claimed, the employee's social security number, name and address. In some cases, the social security number is a prerequisite to entering the name of the employee on the payroll. If the employee does not have a social security number, an application for one should be made on Form SS-5. This form may be secured from the nearest office of the Internal Revenue Service or from the Social Security Administration Office. If no certificate is filed, the employer is not permitted to allow any withholding exemption in the computation of pay and the maximum deduction for federal income tax purposes is necessary. The amount to be withheld from each pay period's gross earnings is computed by reference to the pay period covered, the gross pay for the period, and the number of exemptions claimed on the employee's Form W-4.

Notice of any further change authorized in pay status or deductions should also be furnished to the payroll department. Changes in pay status include authorizations for increases in pay resulting from promotion or additional duties; deductions for absences without accumulated leave; deductions for absences without sick leave; pay adjustments required in the case of substitutes and similar items.

Once an employee has been entered on the payroll, procedures should be developed whereby reports are submitted to the payroll office indicating the continued employment of the individual. Time cards, in the case of hourly employees, or weekly attendance reports should be filed by the administrative department head with the payroll department as a basis for pay computation of each employee. Written notice of separation is required for the name of an employee

Example 2

Assume that John Jones is employed at the rate of $6.00 per hour for the first 40 hours per week and $9.00 per hour for all hours worked in excess of 40 per week. He works as follows: Monday, 8 hours; Tuesday, 8 hours; Wednesday, 9 hours; Thursday, 9 hours; Friday, 8 hours; and Saturday, 8 hours.

	Total Hours Worked	Regular Time	Overtime Hours
Monday	8	8	0
Tuesday	8	8	0
Wednesday	9	8	1
Thursday	9	8	1
Friday	8	0	0
Saturday	8	0	8
Total	50	40	10

Regular time:	40 hours @ $6.00 =	$240.00
Overtime hours:	10 hours @ $9.00 =	90.00
Gross earnings	50	$330.00

---

to be deleted from the payroll and for the employee's payroll file to be closed.

Numerous methods of reporting employment have been developed. It is important under any set of circumstances, however, that responsibility be placed in an administrative officer other than an employee of the payroll or accounting department for initiating all documents that serve as a basis for pay authorization.

The number of days recognized as constituting the pay period is important in computing salary. If it is the policy of the board to deduct an amount from a salary for absences in excess of authorized leave or sick leave, it is obvious that the daily wage rate is necessary for computing the salary. Gross earnings for each employee are calculated for the pay period according to the terms of the individual employee's contract of employment. Under the provisions of the Federal Fair Labor Standards Act, commonly known as the Wage and Hour Law, employers are required to pay 150 percent (time and a half of the regular rate for all hours worked in excess of 40 hours per week). Executives, administrators and certain supervisory persons are not covered by the provisions of this law (See Example 2).

Payroll taxes (federal, state and local) – The school district is required to withhold, deposit, report and pay federal, state and city income taxes withheld from salaries and wages of employees. It is required to withhold, deposit, report and pay social security taxes withheld from employee salaries and wages and also to pay the employer's social security taxes of an amount equal to that withheld from employees. It also must withhold various other kinds of deductions requested by the employee.

Withholding taxes – An employer-employee relationship must exist between the school system and the person being paid if federal income taxes are to be withheld from salary payments. For instance, an individual such as an architect, bond attorney, medical doctor, engineer or outside independent accountant, may be performing services under a contract as a professional consultant. In such a capacity, the person would not be an employee of the school system. Therefore, the school system would not withhold taxes. The general rule in determining whether or not an individual is an employee of the school system, and therefore subject to withholding tax procedures, is that if a person is an employee, the school system has a right to direct and control his/her activities and the manner of accomplishing his/her job.

The school system is required by law to withhold federal income tax from salary and wage payments to the individual employee. The amount to be withheld is computed by reference to government wage-bracket withholding tables or by the use of a percentage method. Each year the Internal Revenue Service, U.S. Department of Treasury, publishes *Circular E, Employer's Tax Guide.* This is available from the local office of the Internal Revenue Service. When the government wage-bracket withholding tables are used, the amount of federal income tax withheld is found by referring to the appropriate table, the wage-bracket in which the gross earnings of the individual falls, and the column of the table which indicates the number of withholding exemptions claimed by the individual employee. Therefore, each employee's case is treated separately. The government wage bracket withholding tax table for married persons based on a biweekly payroll period for wages paid after June 1992 and before July 1993 is subject to change periodically and is presented in Appendix H, Employer's Tax Guide, Circular E (See Example 3).

Similar withholding tax tables have been prepared for both single and married persons for weekly, biweekly, semi-monthly, monthly and daily or miscellaneous pay periods.

Example 3
Assume that a married employee earns $536.80 during that period and that the employee is entitled to three exemptions. The federal income tax to be withheld is $5.00. (Refer to Appendix H.)

For those school systems that prefer not to use the wage bracket withholding tax tables, the percentage method of income tax withholding may be used (See Appendix H).

Wages subject to withholding include compensation for personal services rendered by an employee, whether referred to as salary, wages, vacation pay, sick-leave pay, substitute pay or other similar title. Generally, all wages and salaries paid are subject to withholding taxes.

Programs have been worked out where social security coverage may be in addition to other retirement plans that may be operated by the school system. Unless exempted by state retirement system plans, both the employee and the school system, under provisions of the Old Age Security Disability Income (OASDI) and Medicare Acts, must pay taxes based upon the amount of gross earnings of the employee.

Withholding deductions – The term "tax-sheltered" describes any program eligible for tax-deferred treatment and in the United States, a special type of plan is available to employees of school systems. Under Section 501(c)(3) of the Internal Revenue Code, a school employee may arrange with the school system to divert a portion of salary before taxes to purchase retirement annuity benefits in accordance with tax-deferral provisions in Sections 403(b) and 415 of the Code and related Treasury Regulations. The principal tax benefit of a tax-sheltered annuity is that the employee is allowed to exclude from gross income the employer's contributions toward the annuity and to postpone the payment of income tax on those contributions until after retirement or a specified age, usually 59 $^1/_2$. To invest in a tax-sheltered or tax-deferred annuity, the employee and employer enter into a written agreement under which the employee authorizes a reduction in salary in order to release money for the employer to pay as premiums on an annuity contract that is fully vested in the employee.

The Internal Revenue Service ruled that amounts paid into non-profit organization's Section 403(b) Tax Sheltered Annuity Plan through salary reduction agreements were "wages" for purposes of OASDI and Medicare, even though such amounts were not taxable as wages for income tax purposes. Congress passed legislation requiring this change to be effective only for amounts paid after December 31, 1983.

In addition to federal and state income tax requirements upon employees and the school system, city income taxes may also be required to be withheld. Of course, additional reports would be required. School systems either voluntarily or as a result of contractual agreements may be required to provide other kinds of fringe benefits such as life insurance, disability insurance and hospitalization. Other plans may require joint contributions by the employee and the school system. Authorization to add additional payroll deduction plans should be granted by the school board only because cost of administering each program increases the cost of operating the school system.

The school system may serve its employees by withholding from salaries amounts authorized by the employee for certain purposes such as hospitalization and medical insurance plans, or savings bonds. In these cases, it is essential that the employee furnish the payroll department with a written authorization specifying the amount of the periodic deduction and its disposition.

FINANCIAL STATEMENTS AND REPORTS

Interim – Circular E sets forth dates by which withheld income and other federal taxes are to be deposited. The amount of taxes determines the frequency of deposits. If less than $540 at the end of the calendar quarter, the school district does not have to deposit the taxes immediately. It may pay the taxes to IRS with Form 941 or it may deposit the taxes by the end of the next month. If at the end of any month the total undeposited taxes are $540 or more but less than $3,000, the school district must deposit the taxes within 15 days after the end of the month. If at the end of any eighth-month period, accumulated total undeposited taxes are $3,000 or more, the school district must deposit the taxes within 3 banking days after the end of the eighth-month period. Eighth-month periods end on the third, seventh, eleventh, fifteenth, ninteenth, twenty-second, twenty-fifth and last day of each month.

Quarterly – All employers subject to income tax withholding, OASDI or Medicare taxes, or both must file form 941 quarterly. At the close of the calendar quarter, the school system must remit the amount withheld from the employee's salaries for federal income tax and for OASDI or Medicare taxes, plus the school district's employee benefits expense for OASDI or Medicare tax, to the Internal Revenue Service Center for the region in which the school is located. When remittances are made, the following entry is made in the books of the central payroll fund.

Federal income taxes withheld and payable	XXX	
Old Age Security Disability Income Taxes payable (OASDI)	XXX	
Medicare Taxes payable.	XXX	
Cash		YYY
To record quarterly payment of federal income taxes withheld and payment of employee's and employer's OASDI and Medicare taxes on Form 941		

Annual – Each year the school system is required to notify each employee individually how much salary has been paid to the employee during the preceding calendar year, what amount was subject to OASDI and Medicare taxes, the amount withheld from the employee's salary for OASDI and Medicare taxes, and the amount withheld for federal income tax, if any. This information is provided in Form W-2. Other information contained on Form W-2 includes the name, address, and identification number of the school system as well as the name, address, and account number of the employee. Form W-2 is prepared in quadruplicate, two copies of which are submitted to the employee for his use, one copy forwarded to the Internal Revenue Service Center, and one copy retained. Additional copies may be required if state income tax or city income tax is applicable. With the Internal Revenue Service Center's copy of each W-2, the school system is required to file a form W-3, Transmittal of Wages and Tax Statements, with the Internal Revenue Service Center.

General Accounting Standards Board (GASB), Statement 4, "Accounting and Financial Reporting Principles for Claims and Judgments and Compensated Absences" was issued to provide guidance in application of the requirements of GASB Statement 1 and Statements of Financial Accounting Standards (SFAS), No. 5 and 43 issued by the Financial Accounting Standards Board. GASB Statement 4 adopted the criteria of SFAS 43 for recognizing a liability for compensated absences. SFAS 43 requires employers to accrue a liability for employees' compensation for future absences if all of the following conditions are met:

- The employer's obligation relating to employees' rights to receive compensation for future absences is attributable to employees' services already rendered,
- The obligation relates to rights that accumulate or vest, i.e., those for which the employer has an obligation to make payment even if an employee terminates; thus they are not contingent on the employee's future service,
- Payment of the compensation is probable, and
- The amount can be reasonably estimated.

Because the central payroll department is in the best position to compute the amount that accrues each year to employees for vested interests for compensated absences and thus the liability of the school system for compensated absences as each payroll period occurs, the responsibility for computation should be placed in the payroll department. Upon computation of the amount that is required to meet vested interest claims for compensated absences, the long-term debt account group would record the amount by which the account, amount to be provided for compensated absences, and the liability account, long-term compensated absences payable is increased or decreased. This assessment should be made at least once each year and the accounts of the general long-term debt account group adjusted accordingly.

Also, the central payroll department is in the best position to inform each fund of the school system using personal services of employees of the amount that should be included in each fund's budget to pay currently maturing liabilities for compensated absences. In each of these funds using personnel services, expenditure or expense accounts are debited and the current liability is credited to record current costs for compensated absences.

If, in the future, money is provided by each fund using personnel services on a pay-as-you-go basis to a trust fund, that trust fund, in addition to the general long-term debt account group, should record the effect of administering the accumulating compensated absences program upon the financial position and the results of operation of the school system.

Direct deposits or automated payroll deposits is a method of payment of wages that can reduce the number of payroll checks the central payroll department issues. If the school system's computer system is compatible with a local bank, the school system can issue one check to that bank with all employee bank accounts to be credited being designated electronically. At the same time, the computer can be programmed to produce a separate notice of deposit addressed for mailing to the employee.

Changes frequently occur in payroll taxes to be withheld by the school district. In the case of school employees electing to spread a nine-month salary over a twelve-month period, the payroll usually is prepared in June for the months of June, July and August ending the contract. Wages are considered to be paid when they are constructively received by the employee, when they are credited to the account of the employee or when they are available to the employee to be drawn upon by him/her at any time. Employment taxes must be withheld on wages by the employer when the wages are paid. Therefore, it is appropriate to use the June tax tables to compute the amount to be withheld for federal income tax purposes.

BANK RECONCILIATIONS

Three variations in the process of issuing checks on school district bank accounts are common. One of the following variations should apply to a school district:

1. Warrants are drawn by the board upon the treasurer of the governmental unit under which the school system operates. The treasurer of the governmental unit, in turn, draws a check in payment of warrants issued by the school board.
2. A member of the school board, or administrative officer or an individual independent of the school district may be appointed treasurer of the board. In such a case, all deposits and checks are cleared through the treasurer. Vouchers may be drawn by properly appointed administrative officers of an organizational division of the school system upon the treasurer of the school system. The treasurer of the board, in turn, issues a check on the bank for payment of the voucher.
3. The business manager or an individual independent of the school district may be authorized to deposit all money and have authority to draw checks on bank accounts in the name of the board.

When warrants are drawn by the school board on the governmental unit under which the board of education operates, each fund of the school system uses a "warrants payable" account instead of an "account payable" or a "vouchers payable" account. Instead of the use of a "cash" account, each fund may establish an account of the same nature entitled "due from the treasury."

When a warrant is issued by the administrative officer of a fund, an expenditure account or other appropriately titled account is debited and warrants payable is credited. When the warrant is signed by the school board treasurer, another entry is made debiting the warrants payable account and crediting the due from the treasury account. At the end of each month, the due from the treasury account in each fund should be reconciled with the school district treasurer's account, and any differences should be settled between the fund and the school district treasurer.

When vouchers are drawn on board's treasurer, the treasurer operates as a separate and independent unit in the organizational structure of the school system. It does not work as a unit under the control of the business office. The treasurer is required to maintain accounts which show collections of cash for or from each of the school system's funds and payments made for vouchers drawn upon the treasury by various funds used in operation of the school system. Typical transactions of such a unit are illustrated as follows:

When the treasurer receives cash from the general fund, the treasurer records the following entry:

Cash	$1,000	
Due to general fund		$1,000
To record general fund's deposit		

When the treasurer makes a deposit in banks authorized as depositories of the governmental unit by the board, the following entry is made:

Central Bank	$1,000	
First National Bank	2,000	
National Bank of Commerce	3,000	
Cash		$6,000
To record treasurer's daily deposits		

When the treasurer receives a voucher from the general fund, the following entry is made:

Due to general fund	$500	
Vouchers payable		$500
To record vouchers received from the general fund		

When the voucher is paid by issuance of a check on the bank, the following entry is made:

Vouchers payable	$500	
Central Bank		$500
To record payment of a voucher		

Illustration 21-1 shows a balance prepared for an agency fund.

At the end of each month a reconciliation should be prepared wherein it is possible to prove that the amount shown by the treasury balance is in agreement with the balance shown in each fund's cash account. Through the preparation of this reconciliation, any errors that might have occurred during the period by the depositor or by the central treasury can be detected and any needed corrections can be made.

The business manager may serve as the treasurer. The business manager may be authorized to deposit all money collected to the appropriate fund's bank account and, at the same time, have the authority to sign checks, supported by appropriate documents evidencing each transaction, drawn against the bank accounts of each fund. Internal accounting control requires, however, that there be a separation of duties to prevent one person from having total control over a cash transaction.

Each month the school system's central treasurer should receive a bank statement with canceled checks for each of its bank accounts. In the event the unit operates through a treasurer of a governmental unit, each month's statement should be prepared and submitted to the school system showing all transactions completed by the treasurer in the account of the school system. In either case, it is important that a reconciliation be prepared to correct any errors that may have occurred and in order that entries that should be made will be brought to the attention of the governmental unit and the school system for recording.

Illustration 21-1

Kimberly Hills School District
Central Treasury - An Agency Fund
Balance Sheet
(Date)

Assets
Cash on hand and undeposited		$ 400
Deposits:		
Central Bank	$10,650	
First National Bank	3,620	
National Bank of Commerce	10,330	
Total cash on hand and deposited		$25,000

Liabilities
Due to the general fund	$ 2,200
Due to special revenue fund	1,000
Due to internal service fund	500
Due capital projects fund	21,300
Total liabilities	$25,000

SUMMARY

Payroll accounting provides the method to account for assets which are to be held for others by the school district with the board of education acting as agent.

ACTIVITIES

1. For internal control purposes, identify where the documents that serve as a basis for computation should originate.

2. Give an example of the entries necessary to record social security (OASDI) and Medicare taxes.

3. The following account balances were taken from the Fort Steven School District central payroll fund on September 30, 1995:

Due from general fund	$88,000
Due from cafeteria fund	15,000
Social security (OASDI) taxes payable	10,000
Federal income taxes withheld and payable	91,000

During the month of October, the following transactions occurred:

Oct. 1　The employee's OASDI tax liability from September was computed. For the general fund, $9,500 was applicable and $2,000 was applicable to the cafeteria fund.

Oct. 2　Cash was received from the general fund in the amount of $96,000 and from the cafeteria fund in the amount of $16,500.

Oct. 2　The required monthly cash deposit for income taxes withheld and for both the employee and employer OASDI taxes was made.

Oct. 15　The semimonthly payroll voucher was prepared as follows:

OASDI taxes withheld	$ 5,400
Federal income taxes withheld	45,700
Group insurance premiums withheld	12,500
Retirement contributions withheld	15,000
Credit union deductions	3,000
Net payroll	$292,800

Billings against the general fund were computed to be $326,700 and against the cafeteria fund to be $57,600.

Oct. 15　Cash was received from the general fund in the amount of $248,800 and from the cafeteria fund in the amount of $43,900.

Oct. 15　Salaries were paid.

Oct. 31　The semimonthly payroll voucher was prepared as in (d).

Oct. 31　The employer tax liability for Oct. was computed, and $91,800 was applicable to the general fund and $16,200 to the cafeteria fund.

Oct. 31　Cash was received in the amount of $413,700 from the general fund and $73,000 from the cafeteria fund.

Oct. 31　Salaries were paid.

Nov. 5　The required monthly deposit of cash for income taxes withheld and for both the employee and employer OASDI taxes was made.

Instructions:
- Record the above balances and transactions in general journal form on the books of the central payroll fund.
- Post to the central payroll fund general ledger accounts.
- Prepare a trial balance as of November 5, 1995.
- Record the general journal entries to the general fund.

4. The annual United Way campaign is taking place in the Michago School System. Students at the system's schools are collecting for the drive, and weekly collections are turned over to the business office. The money is remitted to the United Way, and remitted amounts for the first three weeks follow:

	Friday September 7	*Friday September 14*	*Friday September 21*
Westridge High School	$2,000	$2,000	$2,200
Eastside High School	1,800	1,900	1,900
Bayshore Middle School	900	950	950
Woods Middle School	750	750	750
Area 2 Elementary School	1,250	1,200	1,200
South Main Elementary School	1,400	1,400	1,500
Center Elementary School	800	800	800
Total	$8,900	$9,000	$9,300

Instructions:
- Record the receipt of cash by the United Way in general journal form.
- Prepare a trial balance as of January 21, 1995.
- Record the entry by the business office to remit the proceeds of the campaign to the United Way.

REFERENCES/SELECTED READINGS

Fowler, W. J., Jr. (1990). *Financial accounting for local and state systems.* Washington, DC: U. S. Government Printing Office.

Tidwell, S. B. (1985). *Financial and managerial accounting for elementary and secondary school systems (3rd edition).* Reston, VA: Research Corporation of the Association of School Business Officials.

22

Internal Cash Control

INTRODUCTION

Internal accounting controls provide a school district with procedures that produce accurate and reliable financial statements that safeguard assets, financial resources and integrity of every employee charged with the responsibility of handling money or property.

OUTCOMES

In this chapter, you will learn how to:

1. Identify sources of cash receipts.
2. Determine internal controls for cash receipts accounting.
3. Account for cash disbursements.
4. Use vouchers.
5. Use imprest and petty cash accounts.
6. Prepare reports needed to account for cash.

INTERNAL ACCOUNTING CONTROLS

A well-planned internal accounting controls system provides a school district with procedures that produce accurate and reliable financial statements and, at the same time, safeguards the assets, financial resources and the integrity of every employee charged with the responsibility of handling money or property. This latter part of the accounting function is known as internal accounting control. Byproducts of effective internal accounting control are operational efficiency, adherence to established policies and confidence in the financial administration. Responsibility for its operation extends to every level of authority.

To provide adequate internal accounting control, it is necessary for certain procedures to be developed at the operating level to prevent errors from occurring. A most important internal accounting control procedure is double-entry bookkeeping, the generally accepted procedure that provides the basis for analyzing, recording and summarizing financial transactions. The double-entry bookkeeping concept makes it possible to analyze and record the effect of all financial transactions on each element of each fund and account group used in the operation of the school district.

In an ideal situation, the work of one employee is verified by the work of another, each working separately and independently. One employee should not have control of a complete financial transaction that includes authorizing the transaction, receiving, disbursing, recording and/or posting the transaction to the accounts. Instead, different employees should participate at various stages in the transaction so that each would arrive at the same results independently and, without unnecessary duplication of work, verify the accuracy of the work of the other. Such a division of duties provides a procedure whereby errors of omission or commission, whether intentional or unintentional, can be minimized.

There are numerous ways of establishing effective and efficient internal accounting controls for a school district. The chart of accounts for each of the funds and account groups indicates the nature of the assets, liabilities and fund equity accounts, the sources of revenue and reasons for expenditures. This in itself is a control. Combining financial statements, which requires presentation of the financial position of each of the funds as well as presentation of the results of each fund's operation, provides a form of internal control. Comparisons that take into consideration changes that have occurred between one year's financial statements and those of prior years indicate trends. In this way, some control is provided. In the formal budgetary funds, the use of budgetary accounts that provide for comparisons between estimated revenue and actual revenue and comparisons between appropriations and expenditures plus encumbrances serves as an effective and efficient tool of management control.

The use of an internal auditing department reduces the occurrence of costly, material and time-consuming errors. When an invoice's prices, extensions and footings can be verified and compared with the transaction's authorization, purchase order, receiving reports and voucher prior to recording the transaction, significant losses can be avoided. Such a phase of work frequently is referred to as a pre-audit to contrast this internal control procedure with the post-audit conducted by the outside independent accountants.

The extent to which internal control procedures are to be developed depends upon the circumstances surrounding the individual school district. However, use of those procedures (which provide a district of checks and balances to safeguard the interests of the taxpayer and the financial integrity of the board, its administrative officers, and employees of the school district) is important to the effective operation of the school district and to the accomplishment of its educational goals and objectives.

SOURCES OF CASH RECEIPTS

There is no financial need greater than that of adequate internal control for cash receipts and disbursements. Cash receipts include all money coming into the possession of each organizational unit of the school district. It is within the function of accounting to establish internal control procedures to safeguard, to record and to report all cash collected by all organizational units. Methods of verification should be provided whereby it is possible to reconcile the amount of cash that should have been collected with the amount actually collected. Once money is collected, evidential materials should be provided to show that it was deposited intact in an authorized depository.

Cash receipts should be deposited intact daily. Regardless of the method of verifying cash receipts, if cash collected is used temporarily or permanently without first being deposited, the purpose of the internal control and the effectiveness of its operation are destroyed.

All disbursements, whatever the urgency or nature, should be made only when authorized through the official processes that have been established by the board. Proper authorization may be given by preparation of a pre-numbered voucher. To each voucher is attached supporting documentation with authorized signatures that indicate the need, itemize the goods or services and that specify the amount involved in the request for payment. A system of internal control, which produces a way by which cash receipts can be verified and traced to the depository in addition to requiring properly executed business documents to support each disbursement, provides the basis for safeguarding the integrity of all persons associated with financial transactions of the school district.

To speed the processes related to disbursements of small amounts, a petty cash system may be used. A small amount of money may be entrusted to a custodian of petty cash who is authorized by the board and is given the responsibility to pay small bills upon receipt of a properly authorized petty cash voucher. When a petty cash account operates on an imprest system, internal control continues to be effective. A separation of duties between the person who is authorized to approve payments from the petty cash and the person who is custodian of the money provides a basis for adequate internal control.

Some of the sources of cash receipts of a school district are from:

Collection of taxes receivable – Taxes receivable was debited and a revenue account was credited at the time of the tax levy. It is important to know what taxes have been assessed and levied if the school district is to know how much cash it should receive. Cash collected from taxes receivable is an example of converting an asset into cash.

Collection of a revenue directly without being first recorded in an asset account – For example, when a tuition fee is collected the revenue is realized at the time the cash is collected. If however, collection is postponed until a later date, a receivable should be set up on the books at the time of the enrollment so that a record is made of the amount that should be collected. In the latter case, the collection of a receivable would be another example of converting an asset into cash, similar to the illustration in item 1 above.

Collection of cash from sources other than revenues – Items 1 and 2 gave rise to cash resulting from revenue sources. But all cash received does not result in a revenue to the school district. For example, cash may be received from any of the following sources, which do not provide revenue from:

Sale of a fund's assets – Any asset carried in a fund may be sold. Therefore, it is important that the accounting structure include and record all of its assets as an integral part of the accounting structure, particularly if all assets and resources are to be safeguarded. Any change in the balance of an asset account may indicate that cash should have been received and, if that is the case, it is important to determine that the cash actually was received by the school district.

Expenditure refunds or rebates – This source of cash receipts arises after a cash payment has been made and a portion of the payment is returned to the school district. It is a difficult source of cash to trace because it arises after all documents indicating a completed transaction have been processed. However, it may arise as a result of a purchase return or allowance. Close coordination of inventory items with receiving reports and shipping orders provides a basis whereby claims can be established for goods damaged or goods returned. If expenditure refunds or rebates (frequently referred to as an abatement of expenditure) occur, the nature of the transaction should be recorded by adjusting the original expenditure charge or by creating accounts that will indicate that an adjustment has been made as a result of a purchase return or allowance.

Creation of liabilities – Cash may be received from any source that creates a liability of the school district. For example, one fund may borrow money from another fund, the school district may borrow money from another organizational unit, or promissory notes, tax anticipation notes, or bonds may be issued. In order to provide adequate debt control, each should be authorized and recorded in the minutes of the meetings of the board. This does not include those purchases authorized by the purchasing agent.

Collection of accounts or sales of assets previously written off the books – This can occur in the case of a school district's having written off taxes receivable or when an asset has been retired but is kept in storage. These sources of cash receipts are difficult to trace and, here again, the way by which the board can best safeguard the assets of the school district is by requiring all tax account writeoffs or asset disposal or retirement transactions to be authorized and recorded in the minutes of the meetings of the board.

Transfers between funds – A transfer from one fund to another implies that no liability to return the amount is involved on the part of the fund receiving the money. A transfer from one fund to another does not give rise to revenue of the school district, but instead, is a transfer of fund equity.

Trust or agency fund receipts – Examples include the collection of cash for purposes such as the Red Cross, the United Fund, the Community Chest and for other similar purposes.

In order that the system of internal control for cash receipts operates effectively, the following records or their equivalent should be used:

Bill forms – When a bill is prepared, in the case of a student's tuition for example, it should be prepared in sufficient copies so that the department charged with cash collection and the accounting department will have knowledge of and a control over the amount of cash that is to be collected. Pre-numbered tickets provide a basis for computing the amount of cash that should be collected in the case of admission tickets, food service tickets and similar activities.

Receipt forms – A written receipt shows the collection of money and provides information as to the source from which the money was collected. A receipt should be issued for each collection. All receipts should be pre-numbered, transferred from person to person in writing and accounted for by number. The auditors – whether internal, state, federal or independent – will be concerned over duplicate receipt numbers or missing receipts and will investigate the circumstances surrounding the case. By use of receipt forms, each day the amount of cash that should have been received should be compared with the amount actually received. If differences occur, the cause should be determined and action, if required, should be taken to prevent losses.

Deposit tickets – Cash should be deposited intact daily. When cash receipts are deposited in the bank, a duplicate deposit ticket should be secured from the bank and an entry should be made in the depositor's passbook. Duplicate deposit tickets should be filed for the auditor's use in tracing deposits from the cash receipts book to the bank statement. If the school district operates with a treasury established in the governmental unit under which the board operates, a deposit ticket should be issued by the treasury indicating that the deposit was made, and monthly statements similar to those issued by the bank should be prepared by the treasury and submitted to the school district for reconciliation. Reconciliations of the check stub balance and the cash account balance with the bank statement or with the treasury should be made regularly, and they should be brought into agreement.

Special journals – In any organization, financial transactions of a similar kind tend to repeat themselves. When transactions of a similar nature occur, the same accounts are debited or the same accounts are credited. The only difference in repetitious types of transactions may be the amount involved. Therefore, special journals may be designed to record transactions of a similar nature. By recording the transactions in columns specially designed for the transaction, work can be saved by permitting columnar totals to be posted to the general ledger accounts instead of requiring individual amounts to be posted. Even though columnar totals can be posted to the general ledger of a fund, individual amounts have to be posted to subsidiary ledger accounts.

The cash receipts journal is a form of special journal. It does not record all transactions but it records a special type of transaction which tends to be repeated frequently during the accounting period. A cash receipts journal provides for a recording of total debits to the cash account and credits to the accounts determined appropriate by analysis of the transaction. An illustration of a cash receipts journal can be found in Appendix F.

There are any number of other transactions that tend to recur in the operation of a school district and special journals can be designed specifically to meet the needs of the individual district. In some cases, forms may be available through a state or provincial governmental department, but in most cases the forms are merely suggested and are not required. Governmental agencies frequently approve revisions in forms to meet individual needs.

When a form is used merely because it is a form, or because it has been used in the past or because it is a form provided by a governmental agency, accounting can become a matter of rote. Under such circumstances, analysis, recording and reporting become meaningless and useless as a means of management control. Rigid state and federal requirements that a certain form be used lead often to using such a requirement as a basis for justifying a departure from acceptable accounting procedures and practices that adequately safeguard the school district's property. To serve a school district adequately, the purpose of each form should be reviewed periodically and revisions in forms should be encouraged when the revision meets specific management needs.

Fidelity Bonds compensate the school district for known fraud resulting in losses that occur through intentional or unintentional errors of omission or commission of employees in positions of trust. Not only does a fidelity bond on an employee permit recovery in the case of loss but it also tends to prevent losses. Bonding companies are more likely to prosecute when a person is charged with such a loss than the school district would be. In executing a fidelity bond, past employment records of persons covered by the bond are reviewed by the insurer, and the employer is notified by the bonding company if the conduct of any of its employees covered has been in question previously. In this way, employment of persons of doubtful integrity is reduced. Four types of fidelity bonds are available to school districts:

- *Blanket bonds* – A blanket bond can be secured to cover all employees who actually handle money or property and it can be extended to cover those who have access to money or property.
- *Position schedule bond* – A position schedule bond can be secured to cover a particular position regardless of who the employee may be who serves the school district in that position.
- *Name shedule bond* – A name schedule bond covers losses that may occur in the case of any employee whose name is listed on the schedule.
- *Individual bond* – An individual bond may be secured to cover losses in the case of a particular or specified person.

CASH DISBURSEMENTS

A large part of the job of safeguarding public money centers around an orderly process by which cash disbursements are made. One thing to be avoided is rushed, unplanned disbursements for goods or services to meet whims and fancies on the spur of the moment. Such action indicates a lack of advance planning, destroys efficient operation of the business office and creates unnecessary peak work loads, which usually result in unnecessary administrative costs. There should be an efficient and organized process, understood by all employees, by which cash disbursements are made. Through advance planning, the objectives of the school district can be achieved in an orderly, well-planned manner. Such an orderly process begins at the time the budget is prepared and continues until payment is made for the goods and services received. It is true that emergency situations occasionally arise, but administrative controls are destroyed when inadequate planning is disguised as an emergency.

One of two procedures is used in the operation of school districts for safekeeping cash disbursements. The governmental unit under which the board of education operates may act as custodian of cash and have a treasury established to account for all cash of the governmental unit, including the school district. However, more frequently the school district has the authority to deposit and withdraw cash from bank accounts in the name of the school district. In the latter case, one member of the board may serve as treasurer of the board. In either case, protective measures make it possible to withdraw cash only when properly prepared vouchers are submitted for payment.

A system of internal control operates best when the treasurer is not in an administrative position with power to authorize expenditure of money or to make entries in the accounts of the various funds of the school district. The treasurer's position should be one that has the authority to draw a check on the bank accounts of the school district when properly authorized and when prepared vouchers are submitted for payment.

The duties and responsibilities of a treasurer may vary greatly. In some school districts, the treasurer's office is a fully organized unit that receives cash from all sources and draws checks on the bank accounts. In other cases, the office of treasurer is little more than a depository. This is one point at which emphasis must be placed upon the fact that a "standardized" accounting system cannot be established for all school districts. However, whatever the organizational structure may be, accounting principles and procedures are adaptable to the conditions of the individual case. The size of a school district or the amount of money used in the operation of it does not alter accounting principles. An illustration of a cash disbursements journal can be found in Appendix G.

VOUCHERS AND WARRANTS

A voucher or warrant is a business paper prepared by a staff member of the school district and signed by a person authorized by the board to approve the expenditure of money for the purpose stated in the voucher. When a voucher or warrant is properly prepared and issued, an accounting entry is made in the fund affected. Depending upon the nature of the transaction, an asset, liability, fund equity, revenue or expenditure account is debited and an account entitled either accounts payable, vouchers payable or warrants payable is credited. The voucher is submitted to the treasurer of the school district. When a check is drawn in payment of the voucher, a notation is made on the voucher indicating the date paid and the check number used to make payment. A copy marked "paid" is returned to the accounting office. All documents supporting the voucher or warrant should be marked or perforated in such a way as to prevent the possibility of their being used a second time to support a fictitious voucher or warrant. A voucher or warrant marked "paid" gives authority for an accounting entry, which debits either accounts payable, vouchers payable or warrants payable and credits the cash account of the fund affected.

The difference between a voucher and a warrant is that a warrant is the fund's order drawn upon the treasurer of the governmental unit under which the school district operates and a voucher is an order drawn within the school district upon the school district's treasurer. In either case, the voucher or warrant gives the treasurer authority to draw a check on a bank account.

Each voucher or warrant must be properly prepared, supported by business papers that give evidence of a completed transaction and signed by the person designated by the board to approve such payment. Each voucher should be pre-numbered, and each should be accounted for through the system of internal control, whether used, voided or unused.

The voucher or warrant is used to consolidate information about attached invoices. The invoices specify what goods or services have been billed to the school district. A receiving report should be attached to indicate that the goods or services have been received. When the voucher or warrant is signed, it indicates that goods or services covered by the invoice were for items properly contained in the budget, that proper internal control procedures were used to order the goods or services, that the goods or services have been received and that the debt is justly due. The person signing the voucher is responsible for verification of the facts of the transaction and accuracy of extensions and footings. The voucher serves as a basis for an accounting entry in the voucher register. The voucher register is a form of special journal from which certain information about a transaction can be posted to the accounts in the general ledger of the fund affected in total instead of in individual amounts.

When the voucher register is used, the only way by which payment can be made is through the issuance of a check in payment of a voucher. Therefore, a check register should be used. A check register is a special journal in which all checks issued are recorded. All checks should be pre-numbered, and each should be accounted for either as having been used, voided or unused.

CASH FORECASTING

A summary schedule is frequently used that shows each fund's cash balance and the total cash of the school district at a certain date. Such a schedule shows what the cash balance of each fund was at the

Illustration 22-1

Schedule of Cash Position
(Date)

	General Fund	Special Revenue Fund	Internal Service Fund	Debt Service Fund	Capital Projects Fund	Total
Beginning Balance	$160,000	$30,000	$40,000	$25,000	$0	$255,000
Add: Cash receipts, per schedule	40,000	40,000	20,000	25,000	500,000	625,000
Total cash available for use	$200,000	$70,000	$60,000	$50,000	$500,000	$880,000
Less: Cash disbursements, per schedule	75,000	50,000	30,000	0	100,000	255,000
Ending Balance	$125,000	$20,000	$30,000	$50,000	$400,000	$625,000

beginning of a period, what cash has been received by the fund during the period, what cash disbursements have been made by the fund during the period and the balance of each fund's cash account at the end of the period. Transfers of cash from one fund to another can also be shown on the schedule. Such a schedule is referred to as a schedule of cash position and is attached to the interim financial statements of the school district. Illustration 22-1 shows a summary schedule of cash position.

The schedule of cash position can be used to meet the need of the school district for a systematic, predictable cash forecasting strategy. The forecast may use historical data that is adjusted by variable factors such as estimates for inflation, anticipated salary increases and decreases, changing economic conditions affecting the local, state and federal governments, anticipated major changes in programs, facilities, personnel, equipment, materials and supplies.

IMPREST AND PETTY CASH FUNDS

In the operation of a school district, frequently there is need for a small amount of cash to be on hand in order to pay small bills, the amount of which would not justify the expense involved in preparing a regular voucher or warrant and issuing the check. To meet this need through a system of accounting that does provide adequate internal control, accounting procedures applicable to the imprest and petty cash account have been developed.

By resolution of the board, a petty cash account can be established. The resolution should state the amount of the petty cash account. A person is designated as custodian of the petty cash and, based upon resolution of the board, a check in the amount authorized can be drawn and made payable to the petty cash custodian. An entry in the general fund to establish a $100 petty cash account is:

Petty cash	$100	
Vouchers payable		$100
To record creation of a petty cash account to be operated under principles applicable to the district		

When the voucher is paid and a copy of the voucher indicating the check number used to make the payment and the date on which the check was issued is received by the accounting department, the following entry is made:

Vouchers payable	$100	
Cash		$100
To record payment of voucher		

At all times, the custodian of the petty cash should have either $100 in cash or $100 composed partly of cash and partly of properly prepared and receipted petty cash vouchers.

The petty cash voucher is not as complex as a regular voucher or warrant but it does require that a person other than the custodian of the petty cash approve a disbursement from the petty cash by signature. The petty cash voucher also provides for the signature of the person to whom cash is paid. This signature serves as evidence that payment was received by that person. Each petty cash voucher should be pre-numbered and each should be accounted for as either having been used, void or unused.

When the larger part of cash on hand has been disbursed, the custodian may take the paid petty cash vouchers to the person authorized to prepare and issue warrants or vouchers. At that time, a warrant or voucher will be issued in an amount equal to the total of all properly authorized, paid and receipted petty cash vouchers presented. This warrant or voucher gives authority to make the following entry in the general fund:

Expenditures	$76	
Vouchers payable		$76
To record expenditure to reimburse petty cash		

The preceding entry would be based upon an analysis of the purposes for which each petty cash voucher was paid and appropriate expenditure accounts would be debited according to the classification of accounts maintained by the school district.

When notice is received by the accounting department that the voucher has been paid, a general journal entry to record the payment by the general fund is:

Vouchers payable	$76	
Cash		$76
To record payment of voucher		

To avoid a possible loss, even though the amount is small, the custodian of petty cash is in a trusted position and should be covered by a fidelity bond.

In order to avoid the possibility of over-expending an appropriation, an entry should be made in the general fund to appropriate part of the general fund equity in an amount equal to the total of the petty cash account. Note that the nature of the petty cash account has changed to being an account that will remain the same until it is either increased, decreased or eliminated by action of the board of education.

SUMMARY

This chapter has pointed out the necessity for:

- Providing a proof of the amount of cash that should have been received.
- Determining the amount of cash actually received.

- Accounting for any differences and taking what action is appropriate under the circumstances of the case in order to safeguard the resources of the school district.
- Depositing all cash receipts as soon as practical and intact.
- Disbursing cash only by check drawn upon a properly prepared voucher or warrant.

ACTIVITIES

1. Review the definition of the following terms found in the glossary:
    a. Separation of duties
    b. Imprest system
    c. Fidelity bond
    d. Voucher
    e. Warrant

2. Describe internal accounting control.

3. Describe the difference between a voucher and a warrant.

4. If a school district central treasury operates as a separate unit, give the journal entries to record:
    a. Receipt of cash by the treasurer from the general fund.
    b. Deposit of cash in the bank by the treasurer.
    c. The receipt of a voucher.
    d. The payment of a voucher.

5. Fort Steven School District's general fund bank statement for March 1996, indicates a $22,300 balance. The check stub balance and the account balance show $19,800. A comparison of cancelled checks and memoranda accompanying the bank statement with check stubs reveals the following:
    a. Outstanding checks:
No. 2121 for	$1,760
No. 2122 for	$1,240
No. 2135 for	$ 630
No. 2140 for	$1,190
    b. The March 31 deposit of $4,400 is recorded on the books but not on the bank statement.
    c. A $300 bank service charge.
    d. The bank statement shows a credit on the district's account

for collection of a $3,500 note receivable left at the bank for collection. No entry is made on the school district's books.
   e. A $1,400 deposit has been erroneously recorded a second time on the check stubs and in the account.

Instructions:
- Prepare a bank reconciliation as of March 31, 1996.

6. A November 1 internal audit of the Lebanon School Corporation accounts at the close of business on October 31 produced the following information:
   a. Cash balance in bank account $ 52,000
   b. Bank statement account balance   37,000
   c. Outstanding checks:
      No. 401 $170
      No. 410   50
      No. 413   210
      No. 421   675
      No. 438   300
      No. 450   1,050
      No. 456   1,205
   d. October 31 cash receipts were deposited November 1.
   e. The following charges appeared on the bank statement: $25 service charge $120 check payable to the district was returned for non sufficient funds. The check was originally received on October 12 and deposited on October 13. It was charged to the district's account by the bank on October 14.
   f. Check No. 412 for $650 was improperly recorded as $250 on both check stud and in the cash payments journal. The check was issued to pay for teaching supplies.
   g. An October 28 credit memorandum for $1,100, representing proceeds of a note receivable left at the bank for collection, had not been recorded in the checkbook or cash receipts journal.

Instructions:
- Prepare a bank reconciliation for the Lebanon School Corporation as of the end of October.
- Record the journal entries necessary to bring the general fund accounts into agreement with the correct bank balance.

REFERENCES/SELECTED READINGS

Fowler, W. J., Jr. (1990). *Financial accounting for local and state systems*. Washington, DC: U.S. Government Printing Office.

Tidwell, S. B. (1985). *Financial and managerial accounting for elementary and secondary school systems (3rd edition)*. Reston, VA: Research Corporation of the Association of School Business Officials.

23

Student Accounting

INTRODUCTION

There are many items that school districts need to count and record, such as dollars, equipment, supplies, staff and students. Although this book concentrates on financial record keeping, counting pupils is just as important. Not only are students the reason for a school's existence, but the numbers and kinds of students determine the district's programs and finances.

OUTCOMES

In this chapter, you will learn how to:

1. Project future student enrollments.
2. Determine the uses of a student census.
3. Identify applications of student attendance.
4. Use present and future data on student counts to aid school district planning.

PLANNING AND STUDENT COUNTS

If it weren't for students, the school district would not exist. The numbers, types and locations of students provide basic planning data for the school business administrator. If student numbers are growing or declining, the school business administrator is faced with a variety of challenges to meet the students' needs. Even if enrollments are stable, the school business administrator needs to be concerned with the types of students in the district and whether student demographics are changing and the subsequent impact on the district's programs and finances.

It is imperative that the district be able to accurately determine the number of students presently in the district, and depending upon the funding systems, the attendance and types of students in the district. Certainly technology has aided the school business administrator in these tasks. Commercial student accounting packages that run on mainframe or desktop computers are available for any size school district. Larger school districts that have appropriate staff are able to write their own student accounting programs or customize vendor software to their needs. As school administrators become more computer literate, individual applications are shared through networks, professional journals and magazines. Many state systems now accept electronic transmission of data, and that mode of delivery will continue to increase.

ENROLLMENT PROJECTIONS

The school business administrator needs to assess the impact of changing student demographics on the school district operations. The most common measure used is enrollment. Forecasting enrollment involves predicting future numbers and grades of students, and in some cases locations of students. Enrollment forecasts can also be used to determine future class sizes and building populations, future staff numbers and types of personnel, future building renovation, construction, closing and future financial requirements.

One of the most common methods used to predict enrollments is the cohort-survival method. This uses historical trend data to predict future enrollments at various grade levels. Lewis (1983) identifies the following steps to compute a projection using the cohort-survival method:

Step 1 – Determine the number of live births in the school district for each year for the past ten years.
Step 2 – Using that birth information, indicate actual first-grade enrollment for the first five years.
Step 3 – Using the post-enrollment figures for the first five years, calculate the cohort survival ratio by dividing actual enrollments by resident live births.
Step 4 – Complete the table of projected enrollment for all grades.

Lewis cites the following advantages of using the cohort-survival method:

- The method is easy to calculate.
- It can be easily accommodated by the computer.

- Information is easily accessible.

He also cites the following disadvantages:

- Because kindergarten enrollment fluctuates in most school districts, the first grade enrollment should be used as a base to calculate future enrollment.
- Forecasts may be more accurate if first-grade estimates are based on the number of four-year-olds counted in the school district census.
- A "pure" situation hardly ever exists; therefore, many variables may influence future enrollments.
- The method tends to be subjective (See Example 1).

In like fashion, the school business administrator can use each grade's prior ten year's data to determine a cohort-survival ratio for that grade to project future enrollments for that grade. By multiplying that grade's cohort survival ratio by each years' enrollment will produce a projected enrollment for the next five years. The school business administrator should realize that the data projections for the first five years will be relatively accurate since the projections are based on actual live births. Since the second five years combine the survival ratio with trend analysis, the school business administrator should use reasonable care in determining the accuracy of those projections. Ideally, as each new year occurs, actual live birth data can be input to the spreadsheet bringing more reliability to the projections.

In addition to determining actual student enrollment projections, the school business administrator needs to consider additional factors that may affect the enrollment projections including:

- Comparisons with prior enrollment projections noting discrepancies.
- Amount of time lapse between the projection and the present time.
- Economic conditions.
- Special needs of low or high incidence disadvantaged or gifted students.
- Building, development and housing trends including impact of major new highways, roads or other transportation.
- Impact of non-public schools in the area or home schooling efforts.
- Ethnic background.

Example 1
The New Douglas School District determined that the number of live births in the district for the past ten years and the fall first grade enrollments for the first five years of that period were:

Births		First Grade Enrollment	
Calendar Year	Number of Resident Live Births	School Year	Fall Enrollment
(1)	(2)	(3)	(4)
1985	205	1991-92	180
1986	210	1992-93	182
1987	226	1993-94	191
1988	208	1994-95	179
1989	205	1995-96	175
1990	210	1996-97	?
1991	218	1997-98	?
1992	205	1998-99	?
1993	234	1999-2000	?
1994	240	2000-01	?

Illustration of Example 1, Part 1
Dividing the fall enrollment (Column 4) by the number of resident live births (Column 1) produces the survival ratio (Column 5).

Births		First Grade Enrollment	
Calendar Year	Number of Resident Live Births	School Year	Fall Enrollment
(1)	(2)	(3)	(4)
1985	205	1991-92	180 .878
1986	210	1992-93	182 .867
1987	226	1993-94	191 .845
1988	208	1994-95	179 .861
1989	205	1995-96	175 .854
1990	210	1996-97	?
1991	218	1997-98	?
1992	205	1998-99	?
1993	234	1999-2000	?
1994	240	2000-01	?

Illustration of Example 1, Part 2

Calculate the average survival ratio for those five years, by dividing the sum of the ratios for five years by five ((.878+.867+.845+.861+.854)/5=.861). Multiplying the average survival ratio for the five years by the number of resident live births (Column 1) produces the projected fall enrollment (Column 4) for the next five years.

Births		First Grade Enrollment	
Calendar Year (1)	Number of Resident Live Births (2)	School Year (3)	Fall Enrollment (4)
1985	205	1991-92	180 .878
1986	210	1992-93	182 .867
1987	226	1993-94	191 .845
1988	208	1994-95	179 .861
1989	205	1995-96	175 .854
1990	210	1996-97	181 .861
1991	218	1997-98	188 .861
1992	205	1998-99	177 .861
1993	234	1999-2000	202 .861
1994	240	2000-01	207 .861

- Fertility rates.
- Mortality rates.

DISTRICT CENSUS

School districts may conduct a census to determine the actual number of children residing in the district. Much like the federal government, school boards may decide to conduct a census once every decade, or establish some periodic pattern that would provide the needed information for their school district. Generally, school districts in older, stable communities without changing demographics would not need a census since very little changes from year to year. However, in growing communities or communities undergoing changing demographics, a census could be conducted to provide reliable and accurate data that can be used to:

- Update enrollment projections;
- Determine district demographics to help achieve racial balance in each school;
- Help ensure a staff profile that reflects the ethnic composition of the community;
- Determine the need for special programs.;

- Help develop strategies for budget building and support;
- Determine class size;
- Determine staffing needs;
- Determine future building needs including renovation, construction, closing or equity;
- Determine state aid projections when the funding system is pupil-based.
- Complete local, state and federal reports.
- Survey community attitudes and needs to: develop special programs; develop strategies for budget building and support.

STUDENT ATTENDANCE

School districts need to monitor student attendance to provide the district with valuable information or to comply with state requirements. Some common uses of student data include:

- Alerting school administrators to: problem grade levels or buildings; and/or problem seasons, weeks or days of the week.
- Prompting school administrators to take districtwide proaction.
- Demonstrating school and/or district improvement.
- Determining state aid allocations when the funding is pupil-based.

As previously noted, school districts are increasingly using computer programs to assist them in determining student attendance. Even though smaller districts may be able to determine student attendance manually, reporting requirements from the intermediate, state and federal agencies are necessitating the use of computers to assimilate and report the data.

SUMMARY

This chapter has discussed:

- Planning and student counts.
- Procedures for using the cohort survival method for enrollment projections.
- Information and benefits that could be obtained by enrollment projections and a school district census.
- Uses of student attendance data.

ACTIVITIES

1. Interview a school business official to identify measures used to determine student census, enrollments and attendance.

2. Obtain at least two commercially prepared student accounting programs and compare them for ease of understanding, input of data, reports produced and costs associated with using each program.

3. Develop a spreadsheet that employs the cohort survival method of enrollment projection for a school district having grades kindergarten through twelve.

4. Research at least one additional method of forecasting enrollment and compare it to the cohort survival method citing advantages and disadvantages.

5. Identify the planning process and procedures to be followed for a school district to conduct a districtwide census. Identify potential problems and pitfalls.

6. Fort Steven School District's live births for the last ten years and actual student enrollments for the first five years are:

Births		First Grade Enrollment	
Calendar Year	Number of Resident Live Births	School Year	Fall Enrollment
(1)	(2)	(3)	(4)
1985	3,568	1991-92	2,766
1986	3,487	1992-93	2,632
1987	3,502	1993-94	2,687
1988	3,622	1994-95	2,714
1989	3,653	1995-96	2,729
1990	3,598	1996-97	?
1991	3,614	1997-98	?
1992	3,597	1998-99	?
1993	3,612	1999-2000	?
1994	3,651	2000-01	?

Instructions:
- Determine the average cohort survival ratio for the first five years of enrollment data.
- Project the first grade student enrollments for the next five years.

7. Using the information from problem 4, and knowing the average cohort survival ratios for the following grades and enrollments are:

Grade Level	Enrollment	Percent Change
2	2,841	97.2
3	2,754	102.7
4	2,633	99.5
5	2,644	104.5
6	2,685	100.0
7	2,712	99.3
8	2,683	98.8
9	2,598	98.5
10	3,118	97.2
11	3,425	92.9
12	3,567	94.6

Instructions:
- Prepare a spreadsheet for Fort Steven School District which projects the district's student enrollment for the next five years.
- Identify major factors that could influence the accuracy of your enrollment projections.

REFERENCES/SELECTED READINGS

Lewis, J. Jr. (1983). *Long-range and short-range planning for educational administrators.* Boston: Allyn & Bacon.

Tidwell, S. B. (1985). *Financial and managerial accounting for elementary and secondary school systems (3rd edition).* Reston, VA: Research Corporation of the Association of School Business Officials.

Wood, R.C. (1986). *Principles of school business management.* Reston, VA: Association of School Business Officials International.

24

Advanced Financial Statements

INTRODUCTION

One of the primary objectives of managerial and financial management accounting for school districts is the preparation of financial statements and reports which present reliable and timely information completely and clearly. Regardless of how clearly information may be presented, if it is not presented in time to serve those who need it, accounting serves only a historical purpose.

A highly desirable goal of accounting for elementary and secondary school districts is the design of financial reports that may be readily understood by reasonably intelligent people to facilitate better communication between schools and the public. Accounting is essentially a communication process. Three types or levels of accounting reports are used.

- The accounting forms required by governmental units.
- The accounting reports prepared by the staff of the business office of the school district for school administrators who must learn what they contain and how to use them.
- The accounting reports presented to the school board and public.

OUTCOMES

In this chapter, you will learn how to:

1. Review responsibility for preparation of interim financial statements.
2. Identify requirements for the Comprehensive Annual Financial Report.

FINANCIAL STATEMENTS

Both interim and annual financial statements of the school district are the financial statements of the school district. The audited annual financial statements also are the responsibility and formal representations of the district and its' management. The outside, independent auditor, after completing an examination of the financial statements only expresses an opinion on them. The opinion can be an unqualified opinion, a qualified opinion, an adverse opinion, or it can be a disclaimer of opinion. The type of opinion that a school district should strive to obtain is an unqualified opinion indicating that the financial statements present fairly the financial position of each fund and account group on the balance sheet date and the results of operation, the changes in fund equity, and the changes in financial position.

The staff of the business office should prepare interim financial statements throughout the fiscal year for use by operating personnel, administrators, and the board of education. These statements assist the board in making policy decisions and assist administrators in carrying out the financial responsibilities of the board.

The level of reporting focused on in this book has been to provide the managerial accounting structure needed throughout the fiscal period to produce meaningful and timely interim financial statements for all funds and account groups used by a school district. The level of reporting with which ASBO is primarily concerned in its "Certificate of Excellence in Financial Reporting by School Systems" is the comprehensive annual financial report because it is the one which has award potential. ASBO feels strongly, however, that interim financial statements, properly and timely presented, are an integral part of the management-stewardship function. Accordingly, copies of interim financial statements are required to be submitted to ASBO by participants in its certificate of excellence in financial reporting program.

Interim financial statements for each fund and account group should be submitted to every member of the board of education and to administrative officers designated by the board prior to the board's regularly scheduled business meetings. To provide a basis for comparability, the format of statements should be consistent with the format of the financial statements of each fund and account group in the comprehensive annual financial statements of the school district.

In this way, board members can have an opportunity to compare financial statements and study the financial position and results of operation of each fund and account group as at the end of the preceding period. The board and its administrative officers can be in a position to make more reasonable decisions during meeting s of the board of education than if complete financial data were not available.

For management purposes, it is the financial statements of the individual funds and account groups that are essential for financial control. Illustrations of interim financial statements have been presented in the preceding chapters to show how financial statements can be prepared for each fund and account group each month during the fiscal period. Based upon financial statements prepared in accordance with generally accepted accounting principles, the content of interim financial reports should be:

1. A cover sheet naming the entity, its address, the period covered by the report and the date of the report.
2. A table of contents.
3. Combining financial statements of fund types or individual funds and account groups including:
   - Format budgetary funds (government funds): General Fund; Special Revenue Funds; Capital Projects Funds; Debt Service Funds
   - The account groups: The General Fixed Assets Group of Accounts; The General Long-Term Debt Group of Accounts
   - Proprietary Funds; Enterprise Funds; Internal Service Funds
   - Fiduciary Funds; Trust Funds; Agency Funds
4. Schedules necessary to demonstrate compliance with legal or other contractual obligations and/or other schedules deemed necessary to lend cohesion and clarity to data presented in the body of the financial statements.
5. Statistics and other pertinent information useful to management.

THE COMPREHENSIVE ANNUAL FINANCIAL REPORT (CAFR)

The Governmental Accounting Standards Board, GASB, has published the document *Governmental Accounting and Financial Reporting Principles (Statement 1)*. The American Institute of Certified Public Accountants, AICPA, extended its recognition to also include Statement 1 as an authoritative modification of Governmental Accounting, Auditing, and Financial Reporting, GAAFR. The AICPA stated, "...financial statements presented in accordance with Statement 1 are in conformity with generally accepted accounting principles." In Statement 1, GASB states that every governmental unit should prepare and publish, as a matter of public record, a comprehensive annual financial report, CAFR. ASBO has published the following guidelines to school districts for preparing the CAFR for participating in ASBO's Certificate of Excellence (COE) in Financial Reporting by School Systems program:

The CAFR of a school district should be composed of:

Cover – Including this information:
- Title of "Comprehensive Annual Financial Report.
- Name and location of school system.
- Fiscal period covered by report.

The report should be organized into three major sections: introductory, financial and statistical.

Introductory Section
Which should include a title page, table of contents, transmittal letter, organization chart and COE if previously earned.

The following information should be shown on the title page:
- Identification as CAFR.
- Legal name of school system
- Address (City and State/Province).
- Fiscal period covered.
- Principal Officials including: Officers and members of the board of education; Superintendent of schools or chief school administrator; Major administrative officials by name and title showing areas of responsibility.
- Name of official and department issuing report.

The table of contents should include:
- Identification of three major sections of the report.
- Identification of each basic financial statement and each supplemental statement.
- Sufficient detail so a reader can locate any statement or exhibit.

The transmittal letter should contain pertinent information such as:
- Management's representations as to the adequacy of internal accounting controls and the fairness of financial statement presentation, supplemental and statistical schedules.

- Comments concerning the financial condition of the school system at the end of the fiscal period.
- Significant changes in financial condition during the fiscal period.
- Details of significant financial problems or events.
- Forecast of financial prospects.
- Details of any reporting terminology used in a particular locality or state.
- Conflicts between legal requirements and generally accepted accounting principles should be explained.

The transmittal letter should be dated and signed by both the chief financial officer and the chief executive officer.

Financial Section

The Financial Section should include an independent auditor's report, combined statements - overview, combining and individual fund, account group statements and schedules.

The independent auditor's report must clearly specify:
- Financial statements and fund types or account groups included,
- Statements that the auditor has examined "financial statements" rather than "books and records" or "cash transactions" or similar vague references.
- Indication that the examination was performed in accordance with generally accepted auditing standards and whether or not the auditor has performed all audit procedures considered necessary in the circumstances. Details should be given of any procedures which have not been performed and rationale for why not. Examples of such cases might include procedures to test the general fixed assets account group or one in which the school system imposed limitations on or prohibits the application of certain auditing procedures. The auditor must indicate in the opinion whether or not the financial statements are presented in conformity with generally accepted accounting principles (GAAP) and must refer to the consistency of application of accounting principles relative to the prior year.
- Indication of the extent of the responsibility taken for any supplementary data included in the financial section of the comprehensive annual financial report. GASB recommends that the scope of the annual audit include the combining and individual fund and account group financial statements. If the com-

bining and individual fund statements have been subjected to full audit, it should be indicated. Although presentation of combining and individual fund data is not necessary for fair presentation of the "basic general purpose statements," GASB indicates that this data should be subjected to audit tests and other audit procedures. As a minimum, the auditor should state whether such information is "fairly stated" in all material respects in relation to the audited "basic financial statements" taken as a whole.
- Indication of which financial statements and fund types and/or account groups are covered by the opinion.
- Name of the reporting entity and the last day and length of the period covered by the aduitor's examination must be clearly identified in both the scope and opinion paragraphs. The opinion should be dated and addressed to the governing board of the school district.

Combined Statements

Combined Statements should include:
- Combined balance sheet – all find types and account groups
- Combined statement of revenue, expenditure and changes in fund balances for all governmental funds
- Combined statement of revenue, expenditures and changes in fund balances – budget and actual-general special revenue types (and similar governmental fund types for which annual budgets have been legally adopted)
- Combined statement of revenue, expenses and changes in retained earnings (or equity) – all proprietary fund types
- Combined statement of changes in financial position--all proprietary fund types
- Notes to the financial statements
- Trust fund operations may be reported in 2, 4 or 5 above as appropriate or separately
- Agency funds would not have operating statements.

For an illustration of the combined statements, refer to Appendix I. To earn ASBO's Certificate of Excellence in Financial Reporting by School Systems requires the following combining and individual fund and account group statements and schedules to be a part of the comprehensive annual financial report:

Government Fund Types (formal budgetary funds)
General fund [discussed in Chapter 2]

- Balance Sheet
- Statement of revenues, expenditures and changes in fund balances-budget and actual
- Supplementary schedules to give more details and/or to demonstrate legal compliance.

Special revenue funds [discussed in Chapter 12]
- Combining balance sheet – all special revenue funds
- Combining statement of revenues, expenditures and changes in fund balances-budget and actual
- Supplemental individual funds as needed

Debt service funds [discussed in Chapter 14]
- Combining balance sheet
- Combining statement of revenues, expenditures and changes in fund balances
- Supplemental individual funds as needed

Capital projects funds [discussed in Chapter 13]
- Combining balance sheet
- Combining statements of revenues, expenditures and changes in fund balances
- Supplemental individual funds as needed

Proprietary fund types
- Enterprise funds [discussed in Chapter 17]
  Combining balance sheet-all enterprise funds
  Combining statement of revenues, expenses and changes in retained earnings (equity)-all enterprise funds
  Combining statement of charges in financial position-all enterprise funds
  Supplemental statements (for individual funds as needed, to demonstrate legal compliance, etc.)
- Internal service funds [discussed in Chapter 18]
  (Combining) balance sheet
  (Combining) statement of revenues, expenses and changes in retained earnings (equity)
  (Combining) statement of changes in financial position

Fiduciary fund types
- Trust and agency funds [discussed in Chapters 19 and 20]
  Combining balance sheet-all trust and agency funds
- Trust funds [discussed in Chapter 19]

Combining statement of revenue, expenditures and changes in fund balance-expendable trust funds
Combining statement of revenue, expenses and changes in equity-nonexpendable trust funds
Agency Funds [discussed in Chapter 20]
Combining statement of changes in assets and liabilities-all agency funds

Account groups
- General fixed assets account group [discussed in Chapter 15]
Statement of general fixed assets
Statement of changes in general fixed assets
- General long-term debt account group [discussed in Chapter 16]
Statement of general long-term debt
- General supplemental schedules
Schedules giving combined or more than one fund type information

Statistical Section
Statistics on the following for the last ten fiscal years (five years required, ten years recommended):
- General school system expenditures by function
- Revenues by major funding source
- Property tax levies and collections
- Assessed and estimated actual value of taxable property
- Property tax rates (all overlapping governments)
- Ratio of net general bonded debt to assessed value and net bonded debt per capita
- Ratio of annual debt service for general bonded debt to total general expenditures
- Revenue bond coverage
- Property value, construction and bank deposits

Statistics on the following for the current year (or first prior year available):
- Computation of legal debt margin
- Computation of overlapping debt
- Demographic statistics
- Principal taxpayers
- Miscellaneous statistics

If the above financial statements and statistical information is presented in the combined overview or general purpose financial statements portion of the financial section, it does not have to be repeated in the statistical section.

For additional information about ASBO's Certificate of Excellence in Financial Reporting by School System, refer to Chapter 26.

SUMMARY

Accounting information serves only an historical purpose, if it is not presented in timely basis. It must also be presented in clear form so that it may be readily understood by reasonably intelligent people to facilitate communication and the management of the school district.

ACTIVITIES

1. Identify the primary objectives of financial and managerial accounting for school districts.

2. Interview a school board member to determine:
   a. The financial reports used by the school district.
   b. The procedures for preparation of those reports.
   c. A comparison of the district's reports with the comprehensive annual financial report.

3. Discuss the items frequently included in the financial and statistical sections of the comprehensive annual financial report and the rationale for including those items.

4. Accounts in various funds of the Fort Steven School District on December 31, 1995, appear with balances as indicated on the following:

	General Fixed Assets	Special Revenue Fund	Trust Fund	General Fund	Internal Service Fund
Accounts payable		$ 35,000	$ 2,000	$ 21,000	$ 40,000
Reserve for encumbrances		17,000		9,000	
Inventories		55,000		12,000	42,000
Contracts payable		12,000		52,000	
Appropriations		34,000			
Interest receivable			8,000		
Due from other units of government		152,000	21,000	65,000	12,000
Investments in general fixed assets:					
From capital projects	$245,000				
Due to other units of government		22,000	400	2,700	6,000
Principal, capital or fund equity		200,000	136,200	169,300	76,500
Loans receivable			44,000		
Notes receivable			23,600		
Matured bonds and interest payable					96,000
Cash		72,000	42,000	177,000	2,000
Accounts receivable		41,000	32,000		
Land	50,000				10,000
Buildings	160,000				15,000
Improvements other than bldgs	35,000				500
Investments					105,000

Instructions:
- Prepare a balance sheet for each fund as of December 31, 1995.
- Prepare a combined balance sheet for all funds as of December 31, 1995.

REFERENCES/SELECTED READINGS

Fowler, W.J., Jr. (1990). *Financial accounting for local and state systems, 1990.* Washington, DC: Superintendent of Documents, U.S. Government Printing Office.

Tidwell, S.B. (1985). *Financial and managerial accounting for elementary and secondary school systems (3rd edition).* Reston VA: Research Corporation of the Association of School Business Officials.

25

Auditing

INTRODUCTION

School district audits report independently and objectively on the financial position and the results of operation of each fund and account group used in the financial administration of the district. The major purpose of such an examination is to investigate and determine if the financial statements submitted for audit have been prepared in accordance with generally accepted accounting principles and is accomplished by the outside, independent auditor through use of generally accepted auditing standards. Emphasis is placed upon the school district's system of internal control, which should be designed to serve several functions. These are to establish and maintain safeguards for conserving and preserving the school district's financial resources and property, to detect intentional or unintentional errors of omission or commission, and to detect fraud.

OUTCOMES

In this chapter, you will learn how to:

1. Fairly report the financial condition of the school district.
2. Identify advantages of using independent audits.
3. Prepare specifications, recommendations and presentions of the audit report.

AUDIT REPORTS

Financial accounting for elementary and secondary school districts is technical. Limited sources of revenue and restrictions placed upon the purposes for which money may be used make it as complicated as any area of financial and managerial accounting. The accountants for the school district, the internal auditors and independent auditor have to be well trained. Financial accounting, reporting and auditing for elementary and secondary school systems are fields of specialization. Time and study is required in order to acquire the knowledge and the ability to apply principles, procedures and standards effectively in practice.

The independent audit's objective is an attestation of the auditor regarding the fairness and reliability of the financial statements. In the form of a written audit report, which accompanies the financial statements, the opinion of the auditor is addressed to the board of education. In a sense, the audit report accompanying the school district's financial statements may be viewed as the report card for the board of education and the public relating to the propriety and objectivity of the information presented in the statement. To expect management to prepare its own report card without bias is unreasonable.

So far as the taxpayers and the citizens are concerned, the only tangible evidence of an audit is presented in the auditor's report, which accompanies the financial statements and the notes related to them. The auditor's report sets forth the nature or the scope of the examination and contains an expression of an independent, unqualified or qualified opinion a disclaimer of opinion, or an adverse opinion of the auditor on the school system's accompanying financial statements. The Accounting Standards Division of the American Institute of Certified Public Accountants report titled *Accounting and Financial Reporting by Governmental Units* presents six appendices containing possible opinions that may be rendered by accountants in the United States in the following circumstances:

- Unqualified opinion on combined financial statements
- Unqualified opinion on combined financial statements presented with combining, individual fund and account group financial statements and supporting schedules.
- Unqualified opinion on combined financial statements and combining, individual fund and account group financial statements presented with supporting schedules.
- Qualified opinion on combined financial statements (one or more fund types, funds or account group financial statements omitted).
- Adverse opinion (omission of combined financial statements) with and unqualified opinion on the individual fund and account group financial statements.
- Unqualified opinion on an enterprise fund's financial statements.

The short form audit report is referred to as an unqualified opinion report. It is used by the auditor when there are no exceptions to generally accepted accounting principles of the school district and when no restrictions have been placed by the school district upon the scope of the auditor's examination and the application of generally accepted auditing standards.

The auditor may qualify the opinion if restrictions have been placed by the school district upon the scope of the examination or if the auditor is unable to or makes a decision not to follow usual examination practices, procedures and techniques required by generally accepted auditing standards; if the school system has failed to comply with generally accepted accounting principles, if the school system fails to apply generally accepted accounting principles consistently or if there is uncertainty about one or more material items in the financial statements.

The auditor is required to disclaim an opinion and to set forth the reasons for disclaimer when exceptions or the qualifications are judged sufficiently material to disclaim an opinion.

Some of the advantages of audits are as follows:

- An outside, independent audit adds credibility to the financial statements.
- The audit tends to discourage fraud and embezzlement on the part of the school district's financial managers and employees.
- Audited financial statements are required by outside creditors, potential bond holders and governmental agencies at the state and federal levels. They provide potential creditors a more confident basis for decisions about extending credit. They play an important part in state and federal securities laws.
- Independent audits frequently include recommendations for improving internal accounting and management controls and tend to minimize errors and irregularities in the accounting records.
- Audited financial statements provide insurance companies a more confident basis for settling claims for insured losses.
- Audited financial statements provide unions and the board of education an objective basis for contractual agreements.

Through the use of audited financial statements by outside and independent accountants, the board can make complete and timely financial information about the financial affairs of the school system available to the public. In this way, the board can create and maintain public confidence in the financial administration of the school system. Examinations made only once every two, three or four years do not provide the value of timeliness of financial information.

REQUEST FOR PROPOSALS

While there is no specific legal requirement to change auditors annually, many boards of education review auditors annually, even if they choose not to change firms. The task of selecting the independent auditors and defining the scope of the engagement should be reserved for the board or for the audit committee composed of board members. Some boards will find, upon examination, that many shortcomings exist in present accounting and reporting practices and procedures and that adequate financial statements and reports are not being submitted to the board or to the public.

Therefore, the question of how to go about getting improved accounting and reporting practices and procedures arises. The board should ask itself whether professional advice and assistance has been sought for the school system. If so, have recommendations for improving accounting and reporting practices and procedures been secured, adopted and put into operation? It is an obligation of the board either to:

- Staff the business office with people qualified by education, training and experience in accounting;
- Provide in-service training programs for staff members;

Provide adequate technical and professional advice and assistance to the administrative officers of the school system in order to establish effective and meaningful standards of financial accounting and reporting. In many cases, it will be found that the accounting and reporting system has "just grown" and that the only justification for doing a particular task is that "we've always done it like this."

After the board has provided either adequately trained personnel or adequate training opportunities for present personnel, annual examinations should be made to determine that generally accepted accounting principles, practices and procedures are being applied.

In those cases where an adequate system of accounting is in operation and the system of internal control is working effectively, the annual cost of audits by outside independent accountants can be agreed upon by using one of three common methods: the per diem basis, flat fee basis or maximum fee basis. In either the flat fee or maximum fee type of engagement, a provision generally is included whereby an adjustment can be made in the contract in the event the scope of the engagement has to be extended to cover unforeseen circumstances which might develop.

In those cases where special services have to be rendered in establishing an adequate system of accounting, or where work that should have been done by the staff of the business office has to be done by the staff of the accounting firm, the cost is greater. Once a system of accounting is in operation and an effective system of internal control is established, the work required to be performed by the staff of the accounting firm can be reduced and costs can also be reduced accordingly.

It should be noted that neither an audit nor ASBO's Certificate of Excellence Program establish that a school system is fiscally strong. An unqualified audit opinion on each fund and account group used by a school system states that the financial statements present fairly the financial position, the results of operation, the changes in fund equities and the changes in financial position. ASBO's Certificate of Excellence Program recognizes that the comprehensive annual financial report is prepared in keeping with generally accepted accounting principles and generally accepted auditing standards. Whether or not a school district is financially strong is an interpretation that must be made by the reader of the financial statements.

The Illinois State Board of Education's publication *Preparing for Your Local Education Agency Audits*, provides the following general contents of a request for proposal (RFP) and the audit selection process. The RFP process usually entails the following steps:

- Determination of need by the board of education.
- Preparation of a request for proposal including: an introduction to and description of the school district; scope of examination; required reports; timing requirements; proposal content.
- Evaluation of proposals/selection of the auditor.
- Contract for audit services.

DETERMINATION OF NEED

Depending upon the state or province, there may be a legal requirement for the school district to have an annual or some other periodic audit. Barring a legal requirement, the board of education should have a policy stating the need and timing of an independent audit.

REQUEST FOR PROPOSAL (RFP)

The district should provide certain information to prospective auditing firms to enable the firms to have a clear understanding of the school district's needs. By using a standardized format, the RFP provides the district a better understanding and comparison of services that proposed auditors will provide.

Introduction
The RFP should identify the following:
- Name of the entity requesting the proposal.
- LEA contact person, including the title and address, to whom the public accounting firm should address the proposal, and to whom inquiries should be made regarding the proposed request.
- Fiscal year(s) to be audited.
- Date and time all proposals need to be submitted.
- Number of copies of proposal needed.
- Any special instructions as to how the proposal should be delivered or addressed to indicate the contents.

Background
The background information disclosed in the RFP should include:
- Number of students currently enrolled.
- Number of school buildings presently occupied by the district.
- Current-year budgeted revenues and expenditures.
- Current-year budgeted revenue from federally assisted programs, listed by individual programs.
- Brief description of the accounting system, including data processing capabilities used by the LEA.
- Number of personnel: certificated staff, noncertificated staff, and the number of personnel within the business office.
- Any other characteristic unique to the LEA that the evaluator feels is important for the auditing firm to know in order to gain a basic understanding of the LEA.
- Relationship with the school treasurer.

Scope of Examination
This section of the RFP should identify the type of audit required and any special scope requirements, including the type of funds maintained by the LEA, so that the auditing firm will know what is to be expected if awarded the contract. Specifically, this section of the RFP should indicate the examination to be conducted by the firm
- Generally accepted auditing standards promulgated by the American Institute of Certified Public Accountants.
- The requirements under the Single Audit Act, other federal regulations and state regulations.

The LEA should also disclose whether the audit and reports are to be based upon a cash or modified accrual basis, whether the CPA should express an opinion on the combining and individual fund and account group financial statements or provide limited "in relationship" coverage for these statements, and whether any additional services beyond the normal audit scope are required.

Reports Required
This section should specifically identify the type and the number of reports that are to be prepared in connection with the audit examination, such as:
- Financial statements and supplementary information to be included in the annual report of the district.
- Preparation of any annual financial report needed to be filed with the appropriate state and/or federal office.
- Management letter to the board of education, including comments on internal control.
- Any other reports requested by the board.

Timing Requirements
The following information should be included to inform the auditor of expected dates, so that they may be able to determine the timing of the audit work:
- The date the accounting records for the year-end audit will be available and when the accounting firm can begin work.
- The date and final audit report should be submitted to the board of education and whether the LEA desires to have a representative of the firm available for the presentation to the Board of Education.

Proposal Content

In order to alleviate any confusion as to what the audit examination encompasses and who will be performing the audit work, the following requests should be considered for inclusion:

- A statement from the firm regarding the understanding of the work as explained above and a brief description of the audit approach to be used to achieve this objective.
- Qualifications of the public accounting firm, including but not limited to: experience in the school district industry; training programs designed to keep their staff current in the industry; involvement in governmental organizations; and the size and location of the firm.
- The approximate timing of completion of the audit to meet the required deadlines stated above.
- Fee information as to the general audit, as well as any additional costs related to federal programs. This section of the proposal should indicate the extent to which the firm expects assistance from the LEA personnel.
- Resumes of the individuals that will be assigned to the engagement, including school district experience.
- Names, titles, addresses and telephone numbers of at least three school district clients who may be contacted for references.
- An example school district report.
- Indication of whether any individuals will be available for oral interviews.

EVALUATION OF PROPOSALS/ SELECTION OF THE AUDITOR

Prior to reviewing the responses from the RFPs, the board should designate a committee to review the proposals received and submitted to the board:

- A summary of the proposals received.
- A recommendation of the firm to be awarded the audit.

The committee selected may include board members, if desired, as well as a member of management from the business office who will have direct contact with the audit firm selected. This recommendation should include a summary of the basis for their decision as compared to the other firms responding.

The committee designated should establish their priorities for selection prior to commencing a review of the proposals. After these priorities are established, each committee member should review the proposals received, summarize the main points and provide any additional comments regarding the proposals. The individual comments and recommendations should be compared to those of the other committee members. Based upon these comments and the priorities established, the committee should be able to submit to the board an appropriate recommendation. If there appears to be more than one qualified firm, the committee should consider interviewing the firms in order to make the appropriate recommendation and obtain any necessary clarifications.

When reviewing the proposals, special attention should be devoted to the following items:
- References indicated in the proposal should be checked. Inquiries should be made regarding the following: quality of the audits received; service during the audit, as well as throughout the year; timeliness of the audit reports; and integrity and experience of the audit staff assigned.
- Reference checks should include not only the firm, but the individuals.
- Qualifications of the firms should be reviewed to determine: the technical competence of the individuals; experience in the school district industry; adequate manpower to complete the audit in a timely fashion; involvement of the firm with school district organizations; resumes of the individuals should be reviewed to determine if the individuals assigned will have the necessary expertise; the audit approaches indicated should be reviewed as the basis for determining the quality of the audit expected to be conducted; and the costs should be reviewed for reasonableness in conjunction with the services that the district will obtain from the firm awarded the audit.

While costs should be a factor, the decision should not be based solely on fees. Proposals that indicate a greater level of service, including meetings with the board and a continuing contract throughout the year, may be justification for higher fees. However, the above items should be ranked from each proposal received. After discussion among members of the committee, the appropriate recommendation should be reached.

CONTRACTING FOR AUDIT SERVICES

The U.S. Department of Education regulation 34 CFR Part 74, Subpart P (Audit Requirements for State and Local Governments) requires certain standards be followed when arranging for audit services:

- LEAs maintain a code or standards of conduct governing persons awarding and administering contracts using federal funds.
- Officers, employees or agents of the LEA be prohibited from solicitation or acceptance of anything of monetary value, including gratuities and favors from current or potential CPAs.
- The competition for the CPA services be open and free.
- Contracts be made only with responsible CPAs who possess the potential ability to perform the required audit successfully. Consideration should be given to such matters as the CPA's integrity, compliance with public policy, record of past performances, and financial and technical resources.

Subpart P also requires that small audit firms and audit firms owned and controlled by socially and economically disadvantaged individuals (target firms) shall be given the maximum practicable opportunity to participate in contracts awarded to fulfill the Single Audit Act requirements. The following steps should be taken to further that goal:

- Assure that target firms are used to the fullest extent possible.
- Make information on forthcoming opportunities available and arrange time frames for the audit so as to encourage and facilitate participation by target firms.
- Consider in the contract process whether firms competing for larger audits intend to contract with target firms.
- Encourage contracting with target firms which have traditionally audited LEAs and, in such cases where this is not possible, assure that these firms are given consideration for audit subcontracting opportunities.
- Encourage contracting with a consortium of target firms when a contract is too large for an individual target firm.
- Use the services and assistance, as appropriate, of such organizations as the Small Business Administration in the solicitation and utilization of target firms.

ENGAGEMENT LETTER

An engagement letter is a formal contract between the LEA and its CPA. The engagement letter confirms the acceptance of the appointment and documents the agreed upon terms. The engagement letter should establish a mutual understanding between the LEA and CPA of the terms, nature and limitations of the engagement. The auditor should clearly communicate his/her understanding of the LEA's audit and reporting objectives and requirements. This often includes the scope of the audit, the form of reports and any additional responsibilities assumed. This can usually be accomplished by referring to appropriate audit guides, standards, laws or regulations.

Likewise, the engagement letter should stipulate the responsibilities accepted by the LEA. Generally, government audit agreements are formal written contracts that are legally enforceable and difficult to change once executed. Thus, the exact contents of the letter should be carefully determined by the parties involved. Informal understandings or arrangements are not desirable and should be avoided if possible. Any future modifications to the original agreement should also be in writing.

FINANCIAL STATEMENTS

The objective of financial accounting and reporting is to analyze and record financial transactions in a meaningful way. So many limitations are placed upon the way by which money for school systems can be raised and so many strings are attached to the way it can be used for school purposes that simplicity and meaningfulness are difficult to achieve.

It is true that all of the assets and financial resources of a school system could be combined into one fund if all sources of revenue are to be used for general operation and if no strings are attached to any of the money. When these circumstances do not exist, however, the separation of financial transactions into self-balancing groups of accounts, which compose the various funds and account groups, has been found to be the best way of providing meaningful financial statements and effective financial administration.

SUMMARY

In preparing financial statements for the school system, the accountant must keep in mind that not only are the technical objectives of analyzing and recording financial transactions to be achieved, but most important is that meaningful statements and reports are to be prepared for use by the administrators, the board and the public. When statements are presented to the public that convey a full disclosure of financial facts, it is possible to secure the support of the public for achieving desirable educational goals and objectives within limits of financial resources available.

ACTIVITIES

1. Discuss some advantages to having outside and independent examinations of the school district's financial records.

2. Discuss advantages and disadvantages of maintaining continuing contractual relationships with outside auditing firms for more than one year.

3. Identify the purpose of the opinion section of the audit report.

4. Interview a school business official to determine for that district:
   a. Procedures used to secure an outside, independent audit.
   b. District procedure for duration of agreement and changing independent auditors.
   c. Process used to compare costs when selecting an independent auditor.
   d. Explanation of any notes to the last fiscal year audit.
   e. Satisfaction of the school board with information provided by the audit.
   f. Community opinion or reaction to the independent audit.
   g. Copies of an engagement letter for auditing services.

5. Prepare a draft Request for Proposal (RFP) for an independent audit and identify a process that could be used to select an auditor.

REFERENCES/SELECTED READINGS

Fowler, W.J., Jr. (1990). *Financial accounting for local and state systems.* Washington, DC: U.S. Government Printing Office.

Illinois State Board of Education Department of School Finance (1993). *Preparing for local education agency audits.* Springfield, IL: Author.

Tidwell, S.B. (1985). *Financial and managerial accounting for elementary and secondary school systems (3rd edition).* Reston, VA: Research Corporation of the Association of School Business Officials.

26

ASBO's Certificate of Excellence: Financial Statements and Reports

INTRODUCTION

The school business administrator and his/her staff will spend hundreds of hours every year collecting and preparing information that will go on to a myriad of forms and reports. Some of these forms and reports are mandated by federal, state and local governments, while many others are requested by the board of education, administrators, teachers and other groups. Many of these requests are internal to the school district, while others are from and for those outside of the school district. At times the number of forms and reports seem infinite. Regardless of whether the reports and forms are for financial or managerial purposes, there are several basic goals that should govern their preparation. These basic goals are that reports and financial statements must be accurate, timely and clearly present the information it is intended to communicate.

OUTCOMES

In this chapter, you will learn:

1. What the Certificate of Excellence is.
2. What benefits can accrue to school districts that earn the Certificate of Excellence.
3. What steps are involved in making application for the Certificate of Excellence recognition.
4. Tips to follow when making a submission for the Certificate of Excellence.

In 1972, the Association of School Business Officials in the United States and Canada (ASBO), unveiled a voluntary program that was designed to encourage and recognize school districts whose administrators prepared outstanding financial reports. This was called the "Certificate of Excellence in Financial Reporting by School Systems Program," more commonly referred to as simply the Certificate of Excellence (COE). The COE focused on excellence in the preparation, presentation and issuance of a school district's comprehensive annual financial report (CAFR).

WHAT IS ASBO INTERNATIONAL?

At the turn of the twentieth century, the United States Office of Education recognized a federal, state and local need to create a means for developing and delivering continuing professional educational programs to those interested and/or involved in the business services side of school districts. An organization was created in 1910 with this goal in mind but it soon expanded its purposes to include other professional school business management related activities. The organization that developed became known as the Association of School Business Officials in the United States and Canada, ASBO for short. In the mid 1980s, the name of the Association was officially changed to more accurately reflect the changing makeup of its nearly 6,000 members. Thus it became know as the Association of School Business Officials International or ASBO International. Throughout its 85-year history, ASBO International members and staff have been actively involved in providing a wide variety of professional development opportunities for school business administrators that would help develop their knowledge and improve their skills relating to their ever-growing responsibilities and complex roles.

The COE was one of the programs that ASBO International developed for its members. It is not a contest, but rather a recognition program wherein every school district that applies *and* meets the requirements can receive the certificate.

ASBO International is involved in not only providing professional development opportunities and the COE but in developing other national standards such as its Meritorious Budget Award (MBA) recognition program. Another is a model preparation program for the initial training of school business administrators that has become the national program standard used by the National Council for the Accreditation of Teacher Education (NCATE) to accredit master's degree-level programs in school business administration in the United States.

Figure 26-1

Certificate of Excellence Statistics

Program Year	1993	1992	1991
Submissions	297	270	230
Certificates awarded	288	250	215
Certificates denied	9	20	15
First-time awards	49	47	40
First-time denials	6	17	11
Repeat awards	239	203	175
Repeat denials	3	3	4

Figure 26-2

Review Panels

Panels of Review Program Year	1993	1992	1991
Review panels*	96	86	78
Panel members**	160	179	161
Profile of Panel Members			
Independent public accountants from national firms	52	61	62
Independent public accountants from regional/local firms	57	55	42
School district officials/academia/ consultants	51	63	57

*   indicates 50 pooled single-member panels (41 in 1992 and 30 in 1991).
** Includes 15 arbitration review panel members in 1993 and 1992 (12 in 1991).

THE CURRENT STATUS OF COE

In the October 1994, issue of ASBO International's monthly journal, *School Business Affairs*, Bernard Gatti, a retired CPA who coordinates the COE for the Association on a consultant basis, provided a status report for the program year ended 1994 (which covers the fiscal year that ended June 30, 1993 to December 31, 1993). The program continues to grow. Program submissions for the most recent period exceeded 300 and were reviewed by approximately 180 professionals that were organized into COE reviewer panels. Gatti (1994) reports that these reviewers provided well in excess of 5,000 review hours. These reviewers are outstanding governmental accounting and auditing professionals. The following two Figures 26-1 and 26-2 respectively show COE statistics and panels of review information.

THE BENEFITS OF COE TO SCHOOL DISTRICTS

In anticipation of preparing the material in this chapter, a survey was sent in 1993 to every school business administrator who worked in a school district that held the COE for that year (a one-year recognition). The purpose of the survey was to identify why a school business administrator would subject their school district to the expense and their staffs and auditors to the extra work the COE process requires. The open-ended survey simply asks what the school business administrator perceived as being the benefits of receiving the certificate and what local efforts they made to maximize those benefits. The following list reflects a summary of the various statements that the 34 school business administrators who responded to the survey provided. The number in parentheses after each benefit indicates how many of the school business administrators suggested the same benefit.

- Enhances the bond rating of the school district, thereby reducing interest costs when borrowing (17).
- Provides a means to maintain or improve public confidence in the school district/public relations (17).
- Provides an assurance that the finance department/business office is providing high-quality service (14).
- Adds credibility to other reports/budget/business office performance (10).
- Earns the recognition of their professional colleagues (8).
- Helps to improve managing and accounting processes (8).
- Validates data/reports (6).
- Provides an evaluation tool/self-evaluation against national standards (4).
- Indicates a level of staff professionalism (4).
- Provides assurance that taxes are needed/being used wisely (3).
- Creates an expectation to improve/repeat (3).
- Creates a report that boards can use that is better than the audit (3).

- Helps pass a referendum (2).
- Creates pride in the school district (2).
- Creates a goal for the business office (2).
- Enhances the resume of the SBA (1).
- Helps to obtain a line of credit with a financial institution (1).
- Can be used to establish a common starting point for collective bargaining parties (1).
- Provides comparability with other COE awardees (1).

PROGRAM BENEFITS

The COE Program also offers the school business administrator and school district a number of benefits.

Prestigious National Award

Since its inception, the program has gained the distinction of being a prestigious national award recognized by:
- Accounting professionals
- Underwriters
- Securities analysts
- Bond rating agencies
- Educational, teacher and citizen groups
- Federal and state agencies

Fiscal Credibility Validation

Receipt of a Certificate of Excellence validates a school system's fiscal and financial management credibility with its various reporting constituencies, including:
- School board members
- School system management
- State and local government offices
- Federal and state granting agencies
- Educational, taxpayer and teacher organizations

Report Presentations Enhancement

Inclusion of a Certificate of Excellence enhances a school district's financial presentations in:
- Annual reports
- Bond issuance official statements
- Presentations to the media
- Budget presentations and hearings

Uniformity Measure

Adherence to the formatting and terminology as promulgated by the appropriate standard setting bodies (GASB, AICPA, etc.) allows for comparisons between:
- Comparable school systems
- School system reports from year to year
- Trend analyses

Individual Recognition and Development

Receipt of a Certificate of Excellence provides a school system's board and superintendent with a measure of the integrity and technical competence of the system's fiscal administration.

The program stimulates personal technical development through:
- Use of technical materials and attendance at professional seminars.
- Completion of ASBO's self-evaluation worksheet
- Networking between peers, consultants and CPAs
- Implementing constructive comments from the Panel of Review

The program promotes personnel development by documenting technical proficiency. The recognition afforded by receipt of the certificate is personally stimulating and satisfying.

COE REQUIREMENTS

In order to begin the submission process, a school district must publish a Comprehensive Annual Financial Report (CAFR) or in some cases a Component Unit Financial Report (CUFR). Without one of these reports, the school district cannot qualify for the recognition afforded by this program. Whichever report is submitted, it must contain the opinion of the independent CPA that the scope of the audit has not been limited and the opinion is unqualified.

The second component of the survey, "How did the SBA use the receipt of the COE to maximize benefits?," revealed only three activities/methods were common. First, a special ceremony/presentation was arranged at a school board meeting. Second, a press release was prepared and appeared in the local newspaper(s); and third, if the school district was involved in long-term or short-term borrowing the official financial statement prepared in connection with each borrowing included the fact that the school district had received the COE. It seems clear that the recipients of the COE could do much more to enhance and realize greater benefits of this recognition. It appears that the award has more intrinsic than extrinsic value. This could be changed.

THE COE APPLICATION/SUBMISSION PROCESS

Either the CAFR or CUFR must be completed in a timely manner and submitted to ASBO no later than six months after the end of the school districts fiscal year.

A second "program requirement" is the completion of a "Self-Evaluation Worksheet" that can be obtained from ASBO International. The worksheet is a comprehensive technical document in a question and answer format that requires a specific response to each question with either a "yes" or "no" or "not applicable." A comments section is provided to explain "no" and "not applicable" answers. For example, a question might ask: Are columns captioned with fund type titles? If the answer is "no" or "not applicable," an explanation is required.

The worksheet provides a school system with a valuable tool in the preparation of the financial report and acts as a checklist in the review process.

SUMMARY

The COE program is a voluntary program that encourages and recognizes school districts and their administrators that prepare outstanding financial reports. The program focuses on the comprehensive annual financial report in terms of preparation, presentation and distribution. In addition to the positive recognition the COE award brings to the school district, there are many other potential benefits that can accrue.

ACTIVITIES

1. What is the Certificate of Excellence (COE) program?

2. List the benefits that can accrue to school districts that receive the COE recognition.

3. Contact ASBO International and arrange to receive the "Self-Evaluation Worksheet" used in preparing the COE submission.

4. Review the CAFR or CUFR of a school district and compare it against the items listed in the "Self-Evaluation Worksheet."

5. Review ASBO guidelines for preparing the CAFR for participating in ASBO's COE program in Chapter 24.

REFERENCES

Gatti, Bernard. Year in Review—ASBO's Certificate of Excellence in Financial Reporting, *School Business Affairs*, October, 1995, Vol. 61, No. 10.

27

Beyond Traditional Measures of Financial Health: What Can School Districts Learn From the Private Sector

INTRODUCTION

For many years, securities analysts have attempted to predict the future performance of marketable securities. Fundamental analysts, likewise, have focused on the analysis of individual companies and their industry groups. Their analysis tends to be long-term in nature. Both the securities analyst and fundamental analyst depend on ratios and other measures to complete their work.

The history and application of fiscal analysis in the public sector and specifically school districts is relatively short compared to the history of the measures used in the private sector. In the school setting, ratios are not as well understood, developed and used as in business, but it is becoming an important area of school business management research.

This chapter will explore what ratio analysis is, uses in the private sector, the tie of ratio analysis to accounting and benchmarking. The following chapter (Chapter 28) will focus on uses of ratio analysis in the public sector – more specifically the schools and school districts.

OUTCOMES

In this chapter, you will learn how to:

1. Define a ratio and know how it is created.
2. Use ratios in the private sector.
3. Use ratio analysis and how it can benefit an organization.

This chapter begins with a discussion of balance sheets and income statements for private sector companies and then proceeds to discuss ratios that can be calculated from the balance sheet or income statements that have been developed to guide corporate decision makers. Samples of benchmarks are given for some ratios that are discussed.

PRIVATE SECTOR FINANCIAL STATEMENTS

In the private sector, items important to a fundamental analyst include a company's financial statements (such as the balance sheet and income statement), details regarding the company's product line, the experience and expertise of the company's management and the outlook for the company's industry. While the bottom line approach in the private sector drives the decision making process, especially the decision of whether a company will stay in business, ratio analysis for public schools— while having some similarities—does not carry the same bottom line mentality, i.e., public school districts do not (yet) go bankrupt and close the doors. Creating a knowledge base from which the reader may come to understand ratio analysis and its potential for school districts is useful.

FUNDAMENTAL ANALYSIS IN THE PRIVATE SECTOR: A BRIEF LOOK

One of the most widely used, misused and abused forms of financial analysis is the use of ratios. When used properly, ratios can provide a wide variety of information that can be used in all aspects of an organization's management and operation. Ratios can help internal managers gain an awareness of their organization's strengths and weaknesses. If ratios help find weaknesses, these ratios can also suggest the move or moves needed to adjust the ratio before irreparable damage is done to the organization thereby removing the weakness.

If a ratio describes a strength, then understanding the components that make up and cause the strength can be useful to managers in keeping an organization strong.

For a starting point, a ratio in its simplest form is nothing more than a comparison of any two numbers. The number on top, called a numerator, can be a single number or a number that is the result of using several other numbers that relate to one another after some computations. The denominator, or bottom number, can also be the result of a series of computations using a variety of other numbers that have relevance to one another. If we compare one number (numerator) to another (denominator) a ratio has been created. However, for a ratio to have some degree of utility, a relationship between the two numbers must be established. Once a ratio is created, a standard or benchmark must also be established so the user of the ratio information can answer some basic questions:

- Does the ratio describe a favorable condition?
- Does the ratio describe an unfavorable condition?

If managers can act to change the ratio, should the ratio be adjusted by trying to control the denominator (the bottom number in the ratio) or the numerator (the top number in the ratio) or both?

Does the manager want to get from point A to point B with one set of adjustments or many adjustments spread over time?

Administrators and other consumers of ratio information can only assess the appropriateness of the ratios on the basis of some benchmark or standard for comparison.

According to Finkler (1992), there are three principal benchmarks.

> The first benchmark is the organization's history. This is the result of reviewing the same comparisons or ratios from one time period to the next or even over several time periods. Making these comparisons over time enables one to discover favorable or unfavorable trends that are developing gradually over time, as well as pointing out which numbers have changed dramatically in the long term or short term.

> The second benchmark is used to compare the appropriate ratios of one organization with similar ratios of competing organizations. This is accomplished by obtaining the corresponding annual reports and creating and comparing similar ratios. This approach to ratio analysis is valuable in helping to pinpoint why an organization that should be very similar to your own is doing better or worse than your own. By knowing where the ratios differ, one finds what one is doing better or worse than the competition (if a corporation) or neighbor (if a

school district).

A third benchmark is industrywide (or statewide in the case of school districts) comparison. Collecting financial data and computing industrywide ratios allows the determination of relatively how far away from the norms an organization is. (Finkler, 1992)

Benchmarks can be established vertically or horizontally, from data in a single report, or by using data from a combination of reports. For example, comparing one category within a section of the balance sheet against the total in that category or the grand total. This will be demonstrated in the next chapter.

Ratios do have their limitations. They don't give a precise picture of the organization. Ratios are meant to serve as *general* conveyors of information from a broader base. It is inappropriate to attempt to interpret minor changes using ratios. The major interest in the ratio develops if a number is particularly out of line with the benchmark selected (i.e., too low or too high). Clearly, ratios should not be interpreted in isolation. Ratios *help* develop a total fiscal profile for an organization. They merely point out what needs to be examined more closely. The ratios do not provide answers in and of themselves. In the near future, a wider variety of new ratios will be developed, tested and interpreted. Benchmarks will be established that will help managers do a better job of managing, both in the private and public sector. Accounting is and will be the basis of these new ratios not only because accounting produces the numbers but the numbers are the result of clearer standardized definitions and better procedures.

The remainder of this chapter illustrates in a cursory or introductory way how ratios have been developed and used in the private sector and summarizes a more detailed and comprehensive discussion and treatment of these concepts. For a more detailed look at this subject, see *Securities Training Corporation Series 2 and Series 6 Study Guides 1985 through 1994.*

RATIOS IN THE CORPORATE WORLD

One of the key sources of information used by corporations is the balance sheet. The balance sheet represents the financial picture of a company on a specific date. It is divided into three major sections: assets, liabilities and stockholders' equity.

It is called a balance sheet because the total assets will always equal (balance) the sum of the total liabilities and stockholders' equity. (Securities Training Corporation, 1985)

Total Assets = Total Liabilities ÷ Stockholder's Equity

Assets	Liabilities
_____	_____
_____	_____
_____	_____
_____	
_____	Stockholder's Equity
_____	_____
_____	_____
_____	_____

Assets represent everything that is owned by the corporation. The liabilities section indicates all items owed by the corporation. The difference between the total assets and total liabilities is the stockholders' equity (also called the company's net worth).

COMPONENTS OF THE BALANCE SHEET

The Assets section of the balance sheet indicates the items owned by the corporation. There are three basic subsections to this category: current assets, fixed assets and intangible assets.

Current assets consist of those items that could be converted into cash within a short period of time (usually within one year). These include:

- *Cash* – Currency, checking accounts and other bank deposits.
- *Marketable Securities* – Securities owned (such as Treasury bills, stocks and bonds) that are readily convertible into cash. They are normally carried on the balance sheet at the lower of cost or market value.
- *Accounts Receivable* – Money owed to the company by customers who purchased goods and have not yet paid. The company would expect to receive these funds within one to three months.
- *Inventories* – The value of raw material, work in progress and the

company's finished products that are ready for sale to customers (as applicable).

Fixed Assets are items needed by the company in its day-to-day operations to create its products or services. These assets are not intended to be sold or converted into cash. This section of the balance sheet will list the company's physical property such as land, buildings, equipment and furniture. Fixed assets, with the exception of land, lose some of their value each year due to normal use. A company can claim this wear and tear on assets as a deduction against income. Known as depreciation, this deduction may be calculated by either the straight-line or accelerated method. On the balance sheet, fixed assets are shown at a value of their original cost less accumulated depreciation (the amount of depreciation claimed on the asset to date).

Intangible Assets do not have any physical value but may add substantial value to a company. Some intangible assets differentiate the company from competitors and are proprietary such as patents, trademarks, franchises and copyrights.

Another intangible asset – goodwill – represents the amount that would be paid above the value of the assets to acquire the company. Factors contributing to goodwill would be a company's potential earning power due to its reputation in the marketplace, customer relations, skilled staff and existing customers.

The liabilities section of the balance sheet indicates the company's debts. Some of these debts must be paid in a short period of time (current liabilities) while other loans do not have to be repaid for many years (long-term liabilities).

Current liabilities are those debts that will become due in less than one year. They are easily identified by the word "payable." Included in this section are:

- *Accounts Payable* – The amount a company owes for goods and services purchased on credit.
- *Notes Payable* – Short-term loans from banks and other financial institutions.
- *Dividends Payable* – Cash dividends that have been declared but have not been paid.
- *Taxes Payable* – The amount of tax that is owed to the government.

- *Interest Payable* – The amount of interest the company owes on its long-term debt.

Long-term Liabilities are debts that a corporation has incurred that become payable in one year or more. Examples include bonds and long-term bank loans.

The stockholders' equity section represents the company's net worth. It indicates the shareholders' ownership interest in terms of the different classes of stock, retained earnings and capital surplus.

- *Preferred stock* is listed in the balance sheet based upon the par value of the outstanding shares.
- *Common stock* is listed in the balance sheet based upon the par value of the company's outstanding common stock. The par value of a stock is only used for bookkeeping purposes.
- *Capital Surplus* is the amount of premium paid by shareholders above par value for shares sold to the public by the corporation. It is also referred to as "paid-in capital" or "paid-in surplus." This does not include funds the company derives from business profits.
- *Retained Earnings* (also called earned surplus) represents net profits that have been retained for future use by the corporation. Dividends are normally paid from retained earnings.

How these elements are put together to build a balance sheet is illustrated in Illustration 27-1.

THE INCOME STATEMENT

An income statement (often referred to as a profit and loss statement) will indicate a corporation's performance during a specified period of time. The purpose of this statement is to detail the company's net income (or net loss). This is accomplished by offsetting the revenues by expenses.

A sample income statement is illustrated in Illustration 27-2. An explanation of each component immediately follows.

Sales are reduced by day-to-day operating expenses to arrive at operating income.

Illustration 27-1

Corporation
Balance Sheet
December 31, 199X

Assets		Liabilities	
Current Assets		**Current Liabilities**	
Cash	$ 43,000	Accounts Payable	$ 188,000
Marketable Securities	62,000	Interest Payable	27,000
Accounts Receivable	270,000	Notes Payable	40,000
Inventories	330,000	Taxes Payable	72,000
Total Current Assets	$705,000	Total Current Liabilities	$327,000
Fixed Assets		**Long-Term Liabilities**	
Land	$ 54,000	9% Debentures due 2015	300,000
Plant and Equipment	630,000		
Furniture and Fixtures	280,000	Total Liabilities	$627,000
Less: Accumulated Depreciation	(220,000)		
Total Fixed Assets	$754,000		
Intangible Assets		**Stockholders' Equity**	
Goodwill	40,000	6% Preferred Stock par value $100; 500 outstanding shares	50,000
		Common Stock par value $3.00, 300,000 outstanding shares	600,000
		Capital Surplus	52,000
		Retained Earnings	160,000
		Total stockholders' equity	$862,000
Total Assets	$1,489,000	**Total Liabilities and Stockholders' Equity**	$1,489,000

Securities Training Corporation, 1988.

Illustration 27-2

Corporation Income Statement
For period ending December 31, 199X

Sales	$660,000
Less:	
Operating Expenses:	
Cost of goods sold	240,000
Selling and administrative expenses	120,000
Depreciation expense	80,000
Operating Income	220,000
Plus:	
Other income	30,000
Earnings Before Interest and Taxes	250,000
Less:	
Bond Interest Expense	27,000
Earnings Before Tax	223,000
Less:	
Taxes (34% Rate)	75,820
Net Income (or loss)	$147,180

Securities Training Corporation, 1988.

Sales represent the total money received from the company's primary source of business.

Operating expenses reflect the daily costs of doing business. Included here is the amount claimed for the depreciation of fixed assets.

Operating income is adjusted for other income (or expense) not generated by normal operations leaving earnings before interest and taxes.

Other income usually represents income generated by investments (dividends and interest), however, this may also reflect extraordinary items such as earnings from the sale of assets or losses incurred by discontinuing a part of the business.

Earnings before interest and taxes is reduced by bond interest and taxes to arrive at net income (or net loss).

Bond interest must be paid regardless of the company's profitability. If it cannot be paid, the company is in default. The amount of interest paid is found by multiplying the total par value of the bonds by the coupon rate. Interest is paid prior to taxes.

ANALYZING FINANCIAL STATEMENTS

A fundamental analyst uses the information from a company's financial statements, the balance sheet and income statement, to determine the financial strengths and weaknesses of a corporation. These statements are the product of the accounting process. This analysis seeks to compare the company's performance to other companies within the same industry.

To conduct fundamental analysis, the analyst will use various calculations and ratios. The accounting produced numbers will be processed through formulas and reveal information regarding the company's liquidity, capitalization, ability to meet fixed costs, profitability and much more.

The following sections provide only a very few samples of what some of the basic ratios and calculations are and what they help the analyst to do. The discussion is not all inclusive. No in-depth explanation is given since these are shown to illustrate that similar ratios and their uses could and should be developed for public institutions. While the final purpose of their use will differ from that in the private sector, there still is a use. Only a few of the many possible ratios are shown. Once again, the reader is reminded that the accounting process and product creates the numbers that are used to create both the ratios and the benchmarks. The ratios are only as good (or useful) as the accounting system that created the numbers being compared. Garbage in/garbage out applies. The ratios and some of the definitions presented in the next section of this chapter come from Securities Training Corporation, *Investment Company Products/Variable Contracts Representative* (Series 6)(1988).

LIQUIDITY RATIOS

In the private sector, liquidity ratios are used to indicate a company's ability to meet its short-term debts as well as convert current assets into cash. Liquidity is normally analyzed by calculating the company's net working capital, current ratio, quick asset ratio, cash asset ratio, and cash flow.

A company needs working capital to finance its daily operations. This money bridges the gap between production and sales. Maintaining a comfortable yet appropriate level of working capital is important. Doing so will enhance the company's ability to meet its current obligations, expand its production and take advantage of opportunities.

- $\text{Net Working Capital} = \text{Total Current Assets (CA)} - \text{Total Current Liabilities (CL)}$

Net working capital is the difference between the current assets and current liabilities. The current ratio indicates the company's ability to pay its current liabilities by using current assets. A low current ratio may indicate a working capital problem.

- $\text{Current Ratio} = \dfrac{\text{Total Current Assets}}{\text{Total Current Liabilities}}$

This calculation compares current assets to current liabilities.

- $\text{Quick Asset Ratio} = \dfrac{\text{Total Current Assets - Inventory}}{\text{Total Current Liabilities}}$

Quick assets are total current assets reduced by inventories. Quick assets are then divided by current liabilities to find the quick asset ratio.

- $\text{Cash Asset Ratio} = \dfrac{\text{Cash + Marketable Securities}}{\text{Total Current Liabilities}}$

The most stringent test of a company's ability to meet its current obligations is the cash asset ratio. Cash and marketable securities are divided by current liabilities to assess the company's emergency cash position.

- $\text{Cash Flow} = \text{Net Income (or Loss)} + \text{Annual Depreciation}$

Cash flow reflects the amount of money generated by a company's operations. Fundamental analysts tend to look at this figure to assess the company's ability to meet current expenses as well as to pay dividends. To find cash flow, the annual depreciation expense is added back to net income (or net loss). These figures are taken from the income statement.

Each business will establish ratio standards, targets or benchmarks for each of the five liquidity ratios and periodically compare current/interim ratio calculations against these benchmarks. The results from these comparisons will result in a judgment being rendered concerning the current financial health of the business. As a result, decisions will be made that will change the way the company does business and thereby change the ratios in the desired direction and/or amount over the next reporting period.

CAPITALIZATION RATIOS

In addition to liquidity ratios, many analysts use capitalization ratios to assess the company's risk of bankruptcy. Formulas included in this category are the common stock ratio, preferred stock ratio, bond ratio, and debt-to-equity ratio.

All of the capitalization ratios analyze the components of a company's long-term capital. Long-term capital is found on the balance sheet. It consists of the entire stockholders' equity section plus long-term liabilities.

- Common Stock Ratio $= \dfrac{\text{Common Stock at Par } + \text{ Capital Surplus } + \text{ Retained Earnings}}{\text{Total Long-Term Capital}}$

The *common stock ratio* shows the percentage of long-term capital attributable to the common stock.

- Preferred Stock Ratio $= \dfrac{\text{Par Value of Preferred Stock}}{\text{Total Long-Term Capital}}$

The *preferred stock ratio* shows the portion of long-term capital that comes from preferred stock.

- Bond Ratio $= \dfrac{\text{Par Value of Bonds}}{\text{Total Long-Term Capital}}$

The *bond ratio* indicates the percentage of long-term capital that is attributable to bonds. A company with a high percentage of bonds (debt) outstanding is considered to be highly leveraged. This type of company's earnings or profitability is greatly affected by changes in interest rates.

- $\text{Debt-to-Equity Ratio} = \dfrac{\text{Bonds + Preferred Stock}}{\text{Common Stock at Par + Capital Surplus + Retained Earnings}}$

The *debt-to-equity ratio* compares securities with fixed charges (bonds and preferred stock) to those securities without fixed charges (common stock). It is used to evaluate the credit strength of the corporation.

As with liquidity ratios, a business will create benchmarks for capitalization ratios that will in turn be used to measure certain aspects of the company's fiscal health.

COVERAGE RATIOS

In addition to liquidity and capitalization, coverage ratios may also be calculated. Coverage ratios measure a company's ability to meet interest payments to its bondholders and dividend payments to preferred stockholders.

Failing to meet interest payments to bondholders would place a company in default on its debt. By comparing the money available to make interest payments to the amount of interest payments, an analyst can assess a bondholder's degree of safety.

- $\text{Bond Interest Coverage} = \dfrac{\text{Earnings Before Interest \& Taxes}}{\text{Annual Bond Interest Expense}}$

Bond interest coverage is found by dividing earnings before interest and taxes by the annual bond interest expense.

- $\text{Preferred Dividend Coverage} = \dfrac{\text{Net Income Preferred Dividends}}{\text{Profitability And Use Of Assets}}$

While omitting a preferred dividend payment will not place a company in default, it may affect the market value of the preferred stock. Thus, analysts look to determine the safety of the dividend payment.

- *Operating Profit Margin* $= \dfrac{\textit{Operating Income}}{\textit{Net Sales}}$

Profitability calculations show the amount of profit that a company earns from each sales dollar. Analysts often look at both operating profits and net profits to assess profitability. To determine operating profit margin, operating income is divided by net sales. The complement of the operating profit margin is known as the operating expense ratio. If the operating profit margin is 33 percent, then the operating expense ratio is 100 percent – 33 percent or 67 percent. This would mean that the company is spending 67 cents to produce one dollar of net sales.

- *Net Profit Margin* $= \dfrac{\textit{Net Income}}{\textit{Net Sales}}$

To calculate the amount of net profit earned from each sales dollar, net income is divided by net sales.

- *Return on Common Equity* $= \dfrac{\textit{Net Income} - \textit{Preferred Dividends}}{\textit{Common Stock at Par} + \textit{Capital Surplus} + \textit{Retained Earnings}}$

Return on common equity is one of the most important measurements of a company's profitability on a year-to-year basis. This formula compares the amount of income available to the common shareholders each year to the value of the company's common stock.

- *Inventory Turnover Rate* $= \dfrac{\textit{Cost of Goods Sold}}{\textit{Inventory}}$

The inventory turnover rate is calculated by dividing the cost of goods sold by the year-end inventory.

The inventory turnover rate indicates the company's efficiency in managing its inventory level.

A low turnover may indicate that the company's inventory is too large, representing an inefficient use of the company's assets. A high turnover normally shows that products sell quickly and cost of storing the inventory is low.

- *Book Value per Common Share* $= \dfrac{\textit{Total Assets} - \textit{Intangibles} - \textit{Total Liabilities} - \textit{Preferred Stock}}{\textit{Number of Outstanding Common Shares}}$

An analyst would look to the balance sheet to determine the amount of assets that back the securities issued by a company. This figure is called the book value per common share. Also called net tangible asset value.

EVALUATION OF EARNINGS

A major factor that contributes to the market price of a stock is the company's earnings per share (EPS).

- $Earnings\ per\ Share = \dfrac{Net\ Income - Preferred\ Dividends}{Number\ of\ Outstanding\ Shares}$

This calculation indicates the amount of earnings available to the common stockholder. First, any preferred dividends are subtracted from net income. This shows the earnings available to the common stockholders. To find EPS, the income available to the common shareholders is divided by the number of outstanding common shares.

SUMMARY

This chapter is a very brief presentation and discussion of the calculations and uses of ratios and other fiscal health measures used in the private sector. The information provided builds a beginning knowledge base and demonstrates that a wide variety of ratios, measures and uses are well established in the private sector. Much has been written about private sector ratios and their application that go far beyond what is presented here. The next chapter will focus more on ratios, their uses, and benchmarking in school settings.

ACTIVITIES

1. Review the definition of the following terms found in the glossary:

    a. Ratio
    b. Ratio analysis
    c. Benchmarking
    d. Corporate income statement

e. Corporate balance sheet

2. What are the three principal benchmarks Finkler describes?

3. Using the corporate balance sheet in Illustration 27-1 and income statement in Illustration 27-2 calculate the following ratios:
   a. Current ratio
   b. Cash asset ratio
   c. Net profit ratio
   d. Quick asset ratio

REFERENCES/SELECTED READINGS

Finkler, Steven A. (, 1992). *Finance and accounting for nonfinancial managers*, Englewood Cliffs, NJ: Prentice Hall.

Securities Training Corporation. (1995). *General securities registered representative, Series 2 Study Program*. New York, NY: Author.

Securities Training Corporation. (1988). *Investment company products/variable contracts representative, Series 6*. New York, NY: Author.

Securities Training Corporation. (1994). *Investment company products/variable contracts representative, Series 6*. New York, NY: Author.

28

Using Accounting Information to Measure Fiscal Health and Manage a School District

INTRODUCTION

The previous chapter illustrated that the private sector has a highly developed set of ratios that are the product of an accounting system that produces balance sheets and income statements. While the accounting system in the public sector produces audits, annual financial reports and other types of reports, a comparable set of ratios and meaningful benchmarks are not as highly developed. This chapter will explore common ratios that are used by school administrators, newly developed ratios that are being discussed and benchmarking strategies that are unique to education.

OUTCOMES

In this chapter, you will learn how to:

1. Compute horizontal and vertical ratios using a school district budget, audit or other financial reports.
2. Create and interpret benchmark data that is meaningful and unique to your school district.

In today's school business administration climate the proper fiscal management of a school district cannot really take place without the creation and use of meaningful ratios. The growth of the interest in and use of ratios in school business administration is founded in applications that have been successfully used in the business and privates sector for many years. The business ratios discussed in the previous chapter do not generally cross directly over to school business administration and provide an exact application, but they do suggest that ratios specific to school districts can and will be developed that will facilitate the creation of sophisticated financial management models. In the future these models will have the potential to improve the efficiency and effectiveness of all aspects of school district management.

Indicators of financial health and strength of school districts are very important. Indications of fiscal stress and weakness are at least of equal importance if not more important. The importance of ratios is that they can generate the internal information needed by policymakers and administrators of a school district to gain awareness of the school district's strengths and weaknesses. The implication is more than just generating interesting data, but to find strengths in order to become stronger and to find weaknesses so that appropriate action can be taken to correct them before long-term damage occurs.

The following illustrate some of the questions that can be partially resolved using ratios:

- Can you describe your school district's relative financial condition in terms of comparing it to itself, a neighboring school district, "look alike" school districts and districts statewide of the same type?
- Is your description based on intuition, a hunch, a feeling or can you quantify your description?
- Do you really know how well (or poorly) your school district is performing financially?
- Do you know the cost effectiveness of the school district's educational programs?

Monitoring a school district's financial history and comparing that history to the school district's current condition and performance remains the source of the most relevant comparative information for a school district *because every school district is truly unique*. Other comparisons can be helpful in planning, evaluating and in the decision-making process, but no comparisons are as useful as looking at whether its own performance is changing in the correct direction and in increments that are satisfactory based on existing conditions.

In a National School Boards Association (NSBA) publication titled "Budgeting School Dollars," a list of "indicators of financial difficulty" is generated. The authors, Wagner and Sniderman, share the following 30 questions, many of which require ratios being calculated. (Wagner, 1987)

INDICATORS OF FINANCIAL DIFFICULTY

As your board reviews fiscal reports it will be apparent that school officials must be alert to indicators of financial difficulty. Obviously, the degree of difficulty may vary. Whenever financial difficulty looms, however, the board's role is to ask administrators to submit plans for alleviating the difficulty, and for preventing similar problems in the future.

"Yes" answers to the following questions may be indicative of financial difficulty: (* involve ratios)

1. Has your system continually engaged in short-term borrowing?
2. Will "second year" tax anticipation warrants be issued?
3. Has your system recently issued working cash bonds?
4. Does your system close out the working cash fund each year?
5. Have the banks notified your system of a limit on its borrowing?*
6. Have loans from restricted funds been made for other purposes?
7. Have all tax referenda attempts in the last five years been defeated?
8. Are present tax rates at non-referendum limits?
9. Has there been a general decrease in the year-end fund balances over the past three years?*
10. Have budgeted expenditures exceeded budgeted revenues for two consecutive years?*
11. Has the system been delinquent in paying on/for any debt instruments, tuition to other school systems or other obligations based on joint agreements, employee's salaries, or payroll tax/pension liabilities?
12. Is the system involved in pending litigation that could adversely affect the system's financial position?
13. Has enrollment declined more than 15 percent since its peak year?*
14. Has the number of attendance centers remained the same although enrollment has declined?
15. Have cash balances decreased each year for the past three years?*
16. Has the student/staff ratio decreased as enrollment declined?*
17. Have interest monies been dedicated for long-term projects or commitments?

18. Has facility utilization dropped below 70 percent at any school site?*
19. Has state ranking of cost-per-student increased?*
20. Did the rate of inflation outpace the school system's prior year's actual revenue increase?
21. Is the property tax collection rate 95 percent or less?*
22. Have payments to vendors been delayed to solve cash flow shortages and minimize borrowing?
23. Has the percent of budget dedicated for maintenance and repair steadily increased at any one school site?*
24. Has the number of building permits issued within your system's boundaries declined?
25. Has there been an increase in the number of accumulated vacation and sick leave days per employee?*
26. Has there been an increase in the number of unpaid invoices at year end?
27. Has there been an increase in the ratio of bonded indebtedness to total assessed value of property?*
28. Has there been a decrease in the rate of growth in revenues from local sources?*
29. Has there been an increase in mandated expenditures as a percentage of total expenditures?*
30. Has there been an increase in fringe benefits as a percentage of total salary costs?*

There are many sources of data that the school district produces from the accounting process that contain information that can be compared. A few of these sources are:

- District budget
- Audit financial statements
- Comprehensive annual financial report
- Monthly treasurer's report
- Cash flow analysis
- General state aid claim forms
- Transportation reimbursement claim forms

Each state will have its own set of reports and working papers that a school district uses to report and manage the school district. Each document will also contain its unique name and format. These forms generally are very consistent, over time only changing slightly. These forms permit vertical comparisons and horizontal comparisons at a single point in time, comparisons over one time period – the short run, or comparisons over the long run – usually multiple years.

To illustrate how this might be applied, one must become familiar with and knowledgeable about ratios.

As mentioned in the previous chapter simple definition of ratio is a comparison of any two numbers. Anytime one compares two numbers, a ratio has been created. Some ratios are useful, and some ratios have absolutely no value or use. (Finkler, 1992).

In the financial analysis of a school district, many numbers can be taken from a variety of school district documents and reports and compared some of which were noted above. The creation of meaningful financial ratios and their appropriate use and interpretations relative to school districts is just beginning to expand and be perfected. While several ratios currently used in education will be presented, the presentation in this chapter is not intended to be all inclusive. Education must generate ratios that are specifically meaningful to education, just as the private sector developed meaningful ratios.

Once again, any two numbers can be compared thereby creating a new ratio – but that comparison is useless if no relationship between the two numbers can be established. The role of research and best practice in establishing meaningful relationships of a wide variety of educational finance variables available is just dawning.

FINANCIAL RATIO ANALYSIS RESEARCH AND APPLICATIONS

Understanding the financial condition of public educational organizations is an important part of deciding how to respond to internal and external pressures and changes.

To start to develop a knowledge of how this works, examine the school district budget that is Appendix C. Part I is information about the revenue projections for the year of interest. The budget is organized into lines and columns. Each of the nine columns (Funds) can be thought of as nine separate "mini-budgets" that when thought of in total is commonly called the district budget. One of the columns contains "revenue account numbers" that would correspond to a state's chart of accounts. For the example given, revenue account numbers 1110 to 1999 represent Local Revenue. Flow through receipts represent account numbers 2100 to 2200. Revenue account

6 • CHAPTER 28

Illustration 28-1

Total Local Revenue (line 51)	$20,326,880
Total Flow Through Receipts (line 54)	$175,000
State Revenue (line 91)	$9,208,813
Total Federal Revenue (line 142)	$1,924,676
Total Other Revenue (line 155)	$0
Grand Total (line 156)	$31,635,369

Each of these totals can be compared to the Grand Total:

$$\frac{\text{Total Local Revenue}}{\text{Grand Total}} = \frac{\$20{,}326{,}880}{\$31{,}635{,}369} = \frac{6{,}425}{10{,}000} = .6425 = 64.25\%$$

$$\frac{\text{Total Flow Through Revenue}}{\text{Grand Total}} = \frac{\$175{,}000}{\$31{,}635{,}369} = \frac{55}{10{,}000} = .0055 = 0.55\%$$

$$\frac{\text{Total State Revenue}}{\text{Grand Total}} = \frac{\$9{,}208{,}813}{\$31{,}635{,}369} = \frac{2{,}911}{10{,}000} = .2911 = 29.11\%$$

$$\frac{\text{Total Federal Revenue}}{\text{Grand Total}} = \frac{\$1{,}924{,}676}{\$31{,}635{,}369} = \frac{609}{10{,}000} = .0609 = 6.09\%$$

$$\frac{\text{Total Other Financing}}{\text{Grand Total}} = \frac{\$0}{\$31{,}635{,}369} = \frac{0}{10{,}000} = .0000 = 0.00\%$$

numbers 3110 to 3340 are State Revenue sources. Numbers 4110 to 4590 are Federal Revenue sources while numbers 7110 to 7400 represent all Other Financing Sources.

Examine this information (Appendix C) in terms of the education fund only (column 1). Illustration 28-1 shows a correct examination.

These five ratios give a view of the school district in terms of its revenue plan. Since all of the numbers used to calculated the ratios come from the same column these ratios are all vertical ratios. These same ratios should be calculated for the prior year, the year before that, and so on and so on. Now that the ratios are calculated and some histories created, one should look for trends of consistency and change.

Illustration 28-2

Sub-Revenue to Grand Total Revenue Ratios
Seven-Year History

	1993-4	1992-3	1991-2	1990-1	1989-90	1988-9	1987-8
Total Local	64.25	63.25	61.40	60.05	58.70	57.92	54.05
Total	.55						
Flow Thru	.06	1.10	1.11	1.06	1.05	1.11	1.21
Total State	29.10	29.53	30.69	31.69	30.20	34.07	37.86
Total Federal	6.08	6.12	6.80	7.20	7.05	6.90	6.88
Total Other	0.00	0.00	0.00	0.00	0.00	0.00	0.00

*Total percentages in a given year may not equal 100.00% due to rounding.

What observations can be made? Over the past seven years, the revenue mix has shifted in two categories. Total local revenue has become a larger part of the total revenue picture, while total state revenue has declined. Making the observation is one thing, interpreting the observation is another. The interpretation is assisted by responding to a set of questions similar to the following:

- What is causing the shift?
- Does the school district control any of the variables?
- What are the variables of the ratio that cause the shift?
- Which variables are controllable?
- Of the variables that the district controls, which values are in the denominator and which values are in the numerator?
- Should all controllable variables be adjusted, only one or a few?
- How much adjustment should be made and in which direction? Is the shift a threat to the educational programs of the district?
- If nothing is done, what might be the consequences?

These ratios and the brief discussion concern comparing financial data in one fund or budget over time can be thought of as vertical ratio analysis.

For example, there is a set of revenue ratios that can be calculated. This set compares all of the separate Local Revenue pieces to the Total Local Revenue. Using the Education Fund in Appendix C the ratios shown in Illustration 28-2 can be calculated.

Although histories of each of these ratios could be built and an

Illustration 28-3

$$\frac{\text{General Levy}}{\text{Total Local Rev}} = \frac{\$17{,}752{,}847}{\$20{,}326{,}880} = \frac{8734}{10{,}000} = .8734 = 87.34\%$$

$$\frac{\text{Special Ed. Levy}}{\text{Total Local Rev}} = \frac{\$240{,}553}{\$20{,}326{,}880} = \frac{118}{10{,}000} = .0118 = 1.18\%$$

$$\frac{\text{Corporate Personal Property Replacement Taxes}}{\text{Total Local Rev}} = \frac{\$600{,}000}{\$20{,}326{,}880} = \frac{295}{10{,}000} = .0295 = 2.95\%$$

$$\frac{\text{Special Ed. Tuition}}{\text{Total Local Revenue}} = \frac{\$100{,}000}{\$20{,}326{,}880} = \frac{49}{10{,}000} = .0049 = 0.49\%$$

$$\frac{\text{Earnings on Investments}}{\text{Total Local Revenue}} = \frac{\$395{,}000}{\$20{,}326{,}880} = \frac{194}{10{,}000} = .0194 = 1.94\%$$

$$\frac{\text{Food Service}}{\text{Total Local Revenue}} = \frac{\$777{,}800}{\$20{,}326{,}880} = \frac{383}{10{,}000} = .0383 = 3.87\%$$

$$\frac{\text{Pupil Activities}}{\text{Total Local Revenue}} = \frac{\$105{,}180}{\$20{,}326{,}880} = \frac{52}{10{,}000} = .0052 = 0.52\%$$

$$\frac{\text{Textbooks}}{\text{Total Local Revenue}} = \frac{\$259{,}000}{\$20{,}326{,}880} = \frac{127}{10{,}000} = .0127 = 1.27\%$$

$$\frac{\text{Refund of Prior Year Exp}}{\text{Total Local Revenue}} = \frac{\$20{,}500}{\$20{,}326{,}880} = \frac{27}{10{,}000} = .0010 = 0.10\%$$

$$\frac{\text{Sale of Voc. Ed. Proj.}}{\text{Total Local Revenue}} = \frac{\$55{,}000}{\$20{,}326{,}880} = \frac{27}{10{,}000} = .0027 = 0.27\%$$

$$\frac{\text{Local Fees}}{\text{Total Local Revenue}} = \frac{\$21{,}000}{\$20{,}326{,}880} = \frac{10}{10{,}000} = .0010 = 0.10\%$$

$$\frac{\text{Total Other Rev}}{\text{Total Local Rev}} = \frac{\$76{,}000}{\$20{,}326{,}880} = \frac{37}{10{,}000} = .0037 = 0.37\%$$

examination undertaken to discover any trends or consistencies, no history will be shown here. Such an exercise is similar to the analysis demonstrated earlier in this chapter and should be completed by the reader.

Both of the ratio analyses just illustrated above involve a vertical companion at one point in time. Horizontal comparisons can also be

Illustration 28-4

$$\frac{\text{Ed CPPRT}}{\text{Total CPPRT}} = \frac{\$\ 600{,}000}{\$\ 910{,}507^*} = \frac{6{,}589}{10{,}000} = .6590 = 65.89\%$$

$$\frac{\text{O-M CPPRT}}{\text{Total CPPRT}} = \frac{\$\ 75{,}000}{\$\ 910{,}507} = \frac{823}{10{,}000} = .0828 = 8.28\%$$

$$\frac{\text{Bond-int CPPRT}}{\text{Total CPPRT}} = \frac{\$\ 127{,}607}{\$\ 910{,}507} = \frac{1{,}401}{10{,}000} = .1401 = 14.01\%$$

$$\frac{\text{Trans-CPPRT}}{\text{Total CPPRT}} = \frac{\$\ 35{,}000}{\$\ 910{,}507} = \frac{384}{10{,}000} = .0384 = 3.84\%$$

$$\frac{\text{Muni-Retire/SS}}{\text{Total CPPRT}} = \frac{\$\ 72{,}900}{\$\ 910{,}507} = \frac{801}{10{,}000} = .0801 = 8.01\%$$

* Total dollars on line 12 of Appendix C.

created and used. Returning to Appendix C and looking at line 12 whose revenue description is Corporate Personal Property Replacement Taxes (CPPRT), it should be observed that this *one* revenue source has been spread across five funds: 1) Education; 2) Operations and Maintenance; 3) Bond and Interest; 4) Transportation; and 5) Municipal Retirement/Social Security. CPPRT are "unrestricted" dollars, which means that the administrator/board of education has the discretion to put the dollars in any amount into any fund that needs the revenue. (Although these dollars are called "unrestricted," they may still have some conditions as to how the money may be budgeted/used). The ratios of interest dealing with CPPRT compare the amount budgeted in each fund with the total CPPRT projected to be received. From Appendix C, it can be determined what the total CPPRT revenue is projected to be. This means that the five ratios would be as shown in Illustration 28-4. (Total percentage will not equal 100.00% due to rounding.)

These ratios are for one point in time. Have these ratios changed over time? To answer this question, the same ratios would need to be calculated from past years. The amount and direction of any significant changes would need to be assessed. Since the revenue sources in this example are discretionary, they are usually allocated last in the budgeting process to make up revenue short falls/declining revenues in other funds or to cover extraordinary expenditures. In any case, a fund that over time requires more and more discretionary funds to balance its revenue plan against its expenditure plan is headed toward difficulty. Efforts should be made to bring program expenditures into line with revenues. Appropriate early actions on the part of administrators and boards of education can help provide program integrity and can help avoid education program stress or distress.

OTHER INTERNAL RATIOS

In this context, "other internal ratios", means internal to the school district – simply comparing the school district to itself. In some cases this will involve comparing the information within one report. In other cases it may involve comparing data from one report or document with numbers from another report or document.

From a management perspective, the rationale for using other internal financial ratios is that by expressing several figures as ratios, information will be revealed that is missed when the individual numbers are observed. The theory is that managers can then use this information to improve the efficiency and profitability of their operation. By calculating a wide variety of ratios, a profile can be built for the school district or a single program. If a positive profile can be built then a certain measure of success is indicated. This can be done by identifying the presence of factors that measure successor determining that the factors that would signify failure are absent, or some combination of both.

While extensive research has been completed in the private sector on predictors of business failure, similar developments in the public sector are just beginning. The following is a simple list (without standards, benchmarks or discussion) of a few of the ratios currently used by educators. As the reader examines them, it should be noted that some of the numbers to construct the ratio come from *different* reports and documents. In some instances, a series of calculations is required to produce the numbers that will be compared:

- Total expenditures per pupil
- Operating expenditures per pupil
- Pupils per teacher
- Pupils per administrator
- Total revenue per pupil
- Operating revenues per pupil
- Equalized assessed value per pupil

- Instructional expenditures per total expenditure
- Administrative expenditures per total expenditure
- Local revenue per total revenue
- Local revenue per pupil
- State revenue per total revenue
- State revenue per pupil
- General state aid per total revenue
- General state aid per pupil
- Outstanding debt per equalized assessed value
- Total fringe benefit expenditures per total personnel salary

Expenditures

- Transportation operating expenditures per total transportation
- Personnel expenditure
- Total expenditures per total revenues
- Building square footage per custodian
- Number of lunches served per lunch worker

In its report "ASAE Operating Ratio Report" (Lang, 1994), 26 ratios are listed. Each ratio is supported by a brief statement that explains how the ratio is calculated and the potential uses of the ratio information. In some cases, a benchmark is suggested or given. These ratios, referred to as "Key Ratios," are for not-for-profit associations. Although some of these ratios do not apply to not-for-profit school districts they are shown in Illustration 28-5 (on the following pagse) to expose the reader further to possible applications.

The above list is an important beginning in creating financial models to help administrators manage a school district. While it is simple to create a ratio, it must be clearly understood that not every possible ratio will have meaning or utility. It must also be clearly understood that quality accounting that reflects consistent application of generally accepted accounting standards is essential in order for ratios to have any value to managers.

RATIO ANALYSIS FOR MAKING EXTERNAL COMPARISONS

The best financial comparisons that can be made (as mentioned earlier) are against oneself, but it is human nature to also compare

Illustration 28-5
Key Ratios

KEY RATIOS BASED ON BALANCE SHEET ITEMS

Operating Efficiency Ratio (Total Income ÷ Total Assets)	Total Revenue (67) expressed as a percent of Total Assets (222)	Indicates how well an organization is using its total assets to generate income. Generally, the higher the number, the more efficient the company.
Total Liabilities ÷ Fund Balance	Total Liabilities (229) expressed as a percent of Total Fund Balances (248)	Indicates how many times over an organization can meet its obligations with net assets. A ratio of greater than 1:1 (such as 2:1) means that an organization cannot meet its obligations with net assets.[3]
Ratio of Expendable Assets to Total Liabilities	Total Assets (222) - Net Fixed Assets (218 + 219 + 220 + 221) ÷ Total Liabilities (229)	Implies the organization's relative liquidity by showing how many times an organization can meet its obligations from cash and other expendable assets. Any ratio of less that 1:1 indicates that the organization could not meet its debts using cash and other expendable assets.[2]
Net Investment in Fixed Assets to Related Debt	Investment in Land, Buildings & Equipment (218) + Other Investments (219) + Land, Buildings & Equipment (220) + Other Assets (221) ÷ Mortgages and Other Notes Payable	Shows potential for increasing long-term borrowing. Generally, the closer the ratio is to 1:1, the more availability there is to borrow with the fixed asset as collateral.[2]

[2] Derived from *Ratio Analysis in Trade and Professional Associations*, by Peat Marwick Mitchell & Co., 1986. Now out of print.

INTERPRETING THE NUMBERS

(Most ratios are essentially self explanatory, involving the expression of either income or expense items as a percentage of total income or total expenses. Below are ratios from the report that may require additional explanation. Numbers in the calculation refer to the number given to each line on the survey form. The questionnaire is provided in the Appendix.) "Key Ratios" selections in the report that may require addi-

RATIO	CALCULATION	USES
Expendable Fund Balances to Total Expenses	Total Fund Balances (248) - Net Investment in Fixed Assets (218 + 219 + 220 + 221) ÷ Total Expenses (469)	Indicates whether the association could cover expenses if operating income remained stationary. A ratio of .3:1 means that the organization could cover a third of its expenses with expendable fund balances.[2]
Non-Expendable Fund Balances to Total Expenses	Endowment Fund (243) ÷ Total Expenses (469)	Shows the size of the endowment principal relative to the association's operating size. Can serve as a source of financing since, income and capital gains are often used for operating expenses.[2]
Quick Ratio—Cash + Marketable Securities + Accounts Receivable ÷ Current	Cash (208) + Savings 9209) + Accounts Receivable (210) + Pledges Receivable (211) + Grants Receivable (212) + Receivables from Officers and Directors (213) + Other Notes and Loans Receivable (214) + Investments - Securities (217) ÷ Accounts Payable (223) + Grants Payable (224)	Measures liquidity by showing how well an organization can meet its immediate obligations, that is, within days.[3]
Current Ratio (Current Assets ÷ Current Liabilities)	(208 + 209 + 210 + 211 + 212 + 213 + 214) + Inventories for Sale or Use (215) ÷ (223+224) + Loans from Officers and Directors (226)	Indicates how many times over current assets can pay off current liabilities. Generally, a 2:1 ratio is considered healthy.[3]
Cash + Investments ÷ Deferred Revenues	(208 + 209 + 217) + Investment in Land, Buildings and Equipment (218) + Other Investments (219) ÷ Support and Revenue Designated for Future Periods (225)	Another measure of liquidity, it indicates how many times over the organization's cash covers future earnings (e.g., pledges). A ratio of less than 1:1 (such as 3:1) may indicate a weak financial condition because the organization must depend on money it has not yet earned.
Accounts Receivable Turnover	Annual Fees and Sales on Account (410 minus 400 minus 403 minus 404 minus 405) ÷ Total Accounts Receivable (210 + 211)	Indicates the proportion of outstanding receivables to total product sales and the effectiveness of collection procedures. Can help in setting collection policies.
Average Collection Period	365 Days ÷ Accounts Receivable Turnover as defined above	Indicates the effectiveness of collection policies by the speed in which receivables are collected.

[3] See *The Vest Pocket Guide to Business Ratios*, by Michael R. Tyran, Prentice Hall, Englewood Cliffs, New Jersey, 1992.

INTERPRETING THE NUMBERS

(Most ratios are essentially self explanatory, involving the expression of either income or expense items as a percentage of total income or total expenses. Below are ratios from the "Key Ratios" selections in the report that may require additional explanation. Numbers in the calculation specification refer to the number given to each line on the survey form. The questionnaire is provided in the Appendix.)

RATIO	CALCULATION	USES
KEY RATIOS BASED ON INCOME & EXPENSE TABLES		
Net Profitability Ratio (Net Income ÷ Total Income)	Excess or deficit for the year (73) expressed as a percent of Total Revenue (67)	Overall financial performance. Any positive number will show the amount of surplus, while a negative number will show a deficit for the year's operations.
Membership Dues ÷ Total Expenses	Total Dues Revenues (371) expressed as a percent of Total Expenses (469)	Reflects the extent to which income from this area potentially offsets overall organizational expense. NOTE: Income in each ratio reflects gross income, not net income.
Unrelated Business Income ÷ Total Income	Total Unrelated Business Income (295) expressed as a percent of Total Revenue (67)	Shows how much of the organization's available funds are generated by unrelated business income.
Conference and Meetings Income ÷ Total Expense	Total Meetings Revenues (377) expressed as a percent of Total Expenses (469)	Reflects the extent to which income from this area potentially offsets overall organizational expense. NOTE: Income in each ratio reflects gross income, not net income.
Publication Sales ÷ Total Expenses	Periodical Subscription Revenues (379) + Periodical Article Reprint and Other Revenues (380) + Non-Periodical Sales (383) + Royalties from Publication Sales (384) expressed as a percent of Total Expenses (469)	Reflects the extent to which income from this area potentially offsets overall organizational expense. NOTE: Income in each ratio reflects gross income, not net income.
Advertising ÷ Total Expenses	Periodical Advertising Revenues (381) expressed as a percent of Total Expenses (469)	Reflects the extent to which income from this area potentially offsets overall organization expense. NOTE: Income in each ratio reflects gross income, not net income.
Investment Income ÷ Total Expenses	Total Investment Income (403) expressed as a percent of Total Expenses (469)	Reflects the extent to which income from this area potentially offsets overall organizational expense. NOTE: Income in each ratio reflects gross income, not net income.

CHAPTER 28 • 15

Occupancy Expense ÷ Total Expenses	Total Occupancy Expenses (437) expressed as a percent of Total Expenses (469)	Indicates the proportion of building expenses compared to the organization's total expenses. Can be used to help set policy about future occupancy plans.

Personnel Ratios

Occupancy Expense ÷ Total Expenses	Full-time Exempt Staff (7 + 1) ÷ Total Staff (7 + 1 + 8 + 12 + 9 + 13)	Reflects proportion of the organizations' staffs that are exempt from overtime pay according to the Fair Labor Standards Act (FLSA).

[1]FTE: Each part-time position calculated as .5 of a full time position.

INTERPRETING THE NUMBERS

(Most ratios are essentially self explanatory, involving the expression of either income or expense items as a percentage of total income or total expenses. Below are ratios from the "Key Ratios" selections in the report that may require additional explanation. Numbers in the calculation specification refer to the number given to each line on the survey form. The questionnaire is provided in the Appendix.)

RATIO	CALCULATION	USES
Salary Costs ÷ Total Association Expenses	Total Personnel Salary Costs (416) expressed as a percentage of Total Association Expense (469)	Indicates the proportion of association expense that is used for salary costs.
Benefits Costs ÷ Salary Costs	Personnel Benefits (417) expressed as a percent of Total Salary Costs (416)	Reflects the proportion of total salary costs used for benefits.
Salary Costs ÷ Total Staff Members (FTEs)[1]	Salary Costs (416) ÷ Total Staff (as defined above) (7 + 8 + 9 + 11 + 12 + 13)	Indicates how much is spent per staff member. There are many mitigating factors for variations from these norms.
Benefits Costs ÷ Total Staff Members (FTEs)[1]	Total Benefits Costs (417) ÷ Total Number of Staff Members as Defined Above	Reflects how much is spent per staff member on discretionary benefits (excludes mandatory, state and federal taxes).
Total Income ÷ Total Staff Members (FTEs)[1]	Total Income (67) ÷ Total Number of Staff Members as defined above	A type of productivity measure. This ratio shows how much of the organization's income is generated per staff member.
Total Expenses ÷ Total Staff Members (FTEs)[1]	Total Expenses (469) ÷ Total Number of Staff Members as defined above	Average expenditure per full-time employee.[1]

one's performance with others. To this point in the chapter, the ratios that have been suggested are primarily for comparing a school district's performance against itself. There are other comparisons that can be performed.

In order to provide quality educational programs and services, effective financial management tools that address the important relevant indicators are needed. The legislature, the public other audiences should know whether or not the major financial management tools of a school district are effective and relevant, if the tools expose signs of financial distress are effective and relevant, the public needs to know what corrective actions are available.

An effective means of improving school district financial management will use ratio analysis of variables commonly associated with measuring internally, school district's financial conditions on a longitudinal basis.

Experience has demonstrted that no two school districts are alike. The school district can compare itself with a variety of external entities. For example, the school district can compare itself with 1) a single neighbor school district, 2) several neighboring school districts, 3) school districts within the region or the state that are "close look alikes" on relevant school finance or educational program variables, and 4) school districts from throughout the nation. The basis for all of these comparisons are ratios, the same ratios as used earlier in this chapter but calculated over time for all school districts to be used in the comparison grouping or for the selected individual school district. They may be similar in some of the important financial and program variables but significantly different on other variables. This makes direct comparisons range from difficult to meaningless so not only must care be exercised, but sound judgement as well when conclusions, analysis and interpretation of ratio calculations are made.

BENCHMARKING: SETTING STANDARDS OF FISCAL PERFORMANCE

As you were studying the material presented earlier in this chapter it may have crossed your mind that calculating ratios is a simple mathematical process but once the ratio has been determined how does one know what to do with the information. Put more simply-- when is a number too high, too low or about right? The answer to these questions is obtained through the process of benchmarking. According to Finkler (1992) there are three principal benchmarks. The first is the organization's history, the second is to compare the organization to specific look-alikes, and the third (in a school setting) would be statewide.

Benchmarking is the establishment of a standard, a target, or in some cases, a range of values that a school district could use to measure its performance. In the past, these were referred to as "rules of thumb". In today's more sophisticated school business environment these "rules of thumb" are being replaced by measures that are the result of:

- School district experience/past practice
- Research
- Legislation
- State educational agency rules and regulations
- School board policy

In many cases these standards have been little more than arbitrary and capricious.

For example, it is not an uncommon situation during the presentation of the annual audit or during the budget process to get involved in a discussion about "beginning balances" or "unrestricted reserves" or "undistributed reserves". The question often asked is "How big should our reserves be?" It is not uncommon to have someone respond "5 percent of anticipated expenditures or 5 percent of projected revenues". When the 5 percent figure is challenged, the defense or justification of the number is seldom satisfactory. In some cases legislatures and state agencies have fallen into the trap of establishing a random number for a rule or regulation that will be applied to all school districts. The 5 percent number in the above discussion is a benchmark. A number less than 5 percent signifies difficulty, the further below 5 percent the more serious the problem. Anything at or above 5 percent is considered to be okay — a degree of fiscal health.

Recent research reported by Everett (Everett, 1992) and more recently by Vidlicka and Hartman (Vidlicka and Hartman, 1994) has started to provide a more rational approach, not only to a more definitive answer to the unreserved balance question, but in a broader sense, point future research in a new direction. That new direction is this: what educational agencies need is not a benchmark for each ratio that can be formed but rather to define a uniform process that will define a standard that is unique to each and every school district. Everett's (1992) and Vidlicka and Hartman's (1994) work are examples of this approach. What their work suggests is that 5 percent might be the "right number" for one school district but a higher or lower number might be more realistic for another district. This is not to say that benchmarks will not be found for a school district or school districts but that a specific approach to finding a meaningful benchmark will be the goal. The results will be a "range" of numbers that provide guidance to school district managers. In some instances this range may be very tight, to suggest an absolute value. In other instances, the range may be fairly broad.

It is important to remember that for a single school district the benchmark for each ratio will be different. When a set of ratios are examined together, they create a model that can help manage the fiscal affairs of the district. For these models to be of any use, the accounting information used to create the ratios must be accurate and consistent over time.

One final comment – ratio analysis is not an exact science. The ratios help point out trends and conditions that would otherwise be missed. Much research and reporting and sharing of information in the future will be needed.

SUMMARY

It is not only useful to look at ratio analysis as a tool to help assess overall financial performance, but also as a way to assess the value that certain income and expense categories add to the organization's financial well-being.

Ratio analysis is an important financial tool at any given point in time, but its real usefulness comes from comparing benchmarks over time to gain a sense of perspective on the trends of various fiscal indicators. For this reason, it is recommended that organizations calculate their ratios for the past two or three fiscal years and compare them to the sample norms and noting any significant fluctuations and deviations that could signal the need for analysis. Each organization will have its own particular set of circumstances which explain such variations, but being aware of their existence is valuable financial information to have.

CHAPTER 28 • 19

ACTIVITIES

1. Review the definitions found in the glossary.
   a. ratio
   b. benchmark
   c. horizontal ratio
   d. vertical ratio

2. This chapter lists 30 questions that, when answered, can be indicators of fiscal distress for a school district. Review this list and indicate which could use ratio analysis to resolve the question(s).

3. Using Appendix C, calculate the following ratios.
   a. Education Fund Salary Expenses per Total Education Fund Expenses
   b. Local Revenue to Total Revenues
   c. State Revenue to Total Revenues
   d. Total General State Aid to Total State Revenues
   e. Total General State Aid to Total Revenues
   f. Total Expenditures to Total Revenues

4. Assume that benchmarks for the following ratios have been established as shown below. Use the budget information in Appendix C to calculate each ratio and compare your results with the benchmarks. Discuss whether the difference is significant and what actions might be taken to move the calculated ratio(s) closer to the appropriate benchmark.
   a. Education Fund General Levy to Total Receipts/Revenues in the Education Fund from all Sources (50.0%)
   b. Total Receipts/Revenue from State Sources to Total Receipts/Revenues in the Education Fund from all Sources (40.0%)
   c. Total Receipts/Revenue and Other Financing Sources in the Education Fund to all Total Receipts/Revenue and Other Financing Sources in all Funds (80.0%)
   d. Total Regular Program Salaries in the Education Fund to Total Instructional Salaries in the Education Fund (80.0%)
   e. Estimated Fund Balance July 1, 1993 in the Education Fund to 1993-4 Total Receipts/Revenue in the Education Fund (18.0%)

REFERENCES/SELECTED READINGS

Everett, R.E. (1992, July). Using cash flow analysis as part of a process to define an adequate beginning fund balance. *The Journal of School Business Management*, 4 (2).

Finkler, S.A. (1992). *Financial Accounting for Nonfinancial Managers*, New York: Prentice Hall.

Lang, A. and Edans, P.L. (1994). *ASAE operating ratio report, 9th edition*, Washington, DC: American Society of Association Executives.

Lang, A. and Edans, P.L. (1994, June). Benchmarks, performance measurement: Operating ratios as benchmarks. *Association Management*, 46 (6).

Vadlicka, S.R. and Hartman, W.T. (1994, February). How much is enough? Sizing a district's fund balance. *School Business Affairs*, 60 (2).

Wagner, I.D. and Sniderman, S.M. (1987). *Budgeting school dollars: A guide to spending and saving*. Alexandria, VA: National School Board Association.

29

The Future of Financial and Managerial Accounting in the School Setting

It seems somehow fitting that a few ideas and thoughts about the future of the accounting tasks in a school district setting be made at the conclusion of this work. While tracking the history of the school business administrator role since its inception over 150 years ago, it can be documented that the financial accounting or reporting aspect of accounting has been with the role from the very beginning and the managerial aspects of accounting in the school environment are expanding in terms of options and sophistication. As was demonstrated in the first chapter, accounting is the common thread that crosses all topics, duties and responsibilities, and ties the entire profession together.

The almost universal availability of accounting software and the required hardware to run the software has made the financial and managerial aspects of accounting on a timely basis almost a given in school district operations. Detailed reports that were once impossible are now expected and demanded almost instantaneously. The degree of detail that can be obtained will be a simple answer to the question "How much detail do you want and/or need?"

Financial accounting and reporting that were restricted to the district level will become available at the building level, program level, classroom level and even individual student level. Some school districts have already made significant strides in this direction. In terms of timing, many annual reports will become monthly, weekly and daily in their production and use. This will allow for electronic transfer of information (some of which is already in place) and eventually make paperless reporting a reality on a universal basis. The technology already exists, but getting school district personnel trained to use the technology and having the school district develop the funding to acquire the technology at the local level is all that keeps this from happening today. Improved accounting will facilitate the proper implementation of site-based management.

Better accounting will drive school finance reform in the future. Accounting reforms will make the student the unit of school finance, define that student unit in terms of program inputs and performance outputs, and determine what the state and local financial partnership mix will be for each student based on new measures of local ability. Only a few years ago these measures were unheard of, partially because the accounting definitions and processes could not produce the required information.

The breadth and scope of educational research that depends on accurate, consistent, valid and reliable financial data will be expanded in the future. This improved and expanded information base will allow questions to be asked and hypotheses to be tested that will not only improve accountability and the daily operation of a school district but also will suggest new approaches to solve more and more complex educational problems.

Accounting for managerial purposes will expand and be perfected. Models and procedures will be developed so that each school district will be able to create meaningful standards and benchmarks that will describe each district's unique fiscal health/fiscal stress and educational health/educational stress. Accounting produced models will allow for more than a simple description of what is happening; they will actually suggest a set of solutions and prioritize those solutions. The increase in accounting sophistication will allow the linking together of various managerial models that presently stand alone.

The accounting preparation of school business administrators and superintendents will improve. This will also be true for the Certified Public Accountants that will serve school districts.

Accounting standards, definitions, principles and procedures will become even more uniform in their application. This will facilitate more consistent internal reporting over time and between school districts. All of this will let ratio analysis evolve as a tool. The data that comprise the ratio will be more clearly related and the benchmarks that are established will improve.

Audit documents will improve in presentation and content. Part of this will depend on the preparation and experience of the auditors but also the improved accounting skills and accounting knowledge base of school business administrators and external accountants. School business administrators will become better consumers of accounting information. This will put pressure on those who produce the accounting information, whether internally or externally, to step up a notch in their performance.

Internal auditing will improve. The basic "bookkeeping" of the past will soon be unacceptable even in very small school districts. This idea carries some major implications for those employed to develop professionally. They will need to imporve their personal computing skills and their knowledge of accounting.

One final observation: Any individual who is preparing to be a school district superintendent, school business administrator, school principal or any other central office position must make sure that their pre-service and in-service professional development activities possess significant components of accounting. Because of time constraints and other limitations, the accounting knowledge and skills needed by school administrators and school business administrators will continue to be different from that needed by Certified Public Accountants. However, the pursuit of improved accounting should always be an objective.

APPENDICES

About The Appendices

Appendix A	Minimum Classifications (Chart of Accounts) Essential for Federal Reporting
Appendix B	Classifying Balance Sheet Accounts
Appendix C	1993-94 Adopted Budget
Appendix D	Federal Single Program Audit 1993-94
Appendix E	1993-94 Audit
Appendix F	Cash Receipts Journal
Appendix G	Cash Disbursements Journal
Appendix H	Federal Withholding Tax Tables
Appendix I	Annual Financial Report 1993-94
Glossary	Glossary of terms used in this textbook

APPENDIX A

Minimum Classifications (Chart of Accounts) Essential For Federal Reporting

MINIMUM CLASSIFICATIONS ESSENTIAL FOR FEDERAL REPORTING

The information provided in this appendix comes directly from Financial Accounting for Local and State School Systems 1990, William J. Fowler, Jr., Ed.D., Revisions Project Manager. U.S. Department of Education, Office of Educational Research and Improvement (pp. 133-140).

This appendix lists dimensions and categories that are essential to an LEA in meeting most of the major Federal reporting requirements as of 1990. Included are codes needed to prepare the Federal reports. The codes will change as new reporting requirements are developed, issued and implemented.

This minimum lists of accounts includes only a few of the dimensions available to describe expenditures, and also only a limited number of the categories provided within those dimensions. Other categories and dimensions are available for the optional use of SEAs and LEAs. The dimensions are listed in the following order:

	Fund
Expenditures	Program
	Function
	Object
Revenues	Revenue Source
Balance Sheet	Balance Sheet Accounts

The minimum classifications the LEA bookkeeping system must use to comply with current Federal reporting requirements are:

EXPENDITURE

Program Dimension

Code Account Title
- 100 Regular Programs
- 200 Special Programs
  - 211 Educable Mentally Retarded
  - 212 Trainable Mentally Retarded
  - 221 Hard of Hearing
  - 222 Deaf
  - 223 Deaf-Blind
  - 224 Visually Handicapped
  - 225 Speech Impaired
  - 226 Crippled
  - 227 Other Health Impaired
  - 230 Emotionally Disturbed
  - 240 Learning Disabled
- 300 Vocational Progams
  - 310 Agriculture
  - 320 Distributive Education
  - 330 Health Occupation
  - 340 Home Economics
  - 341 Occupational
  - 342 Consumer and Homemaking
  - 350 Industrial Arts
  - 360 Office Occupations
  - 370 Technical Education
  - 380 Trades and Industrial Occupations
  - 390 Other Vocational Programs
- 400 Other Instructioal Programs -Elementary/Secondary
- 500 Nonpublic School Programs
- 600 Adult/Continuing Education Programs
- 700 Community/Junior College Education Programs
- 800 Community Services Programs
- 900 Enterprise Programs
- 910 Food Services

APPENDIX A • 3

FUNCTION DIMENSION
Program Dimension

Code Account Title
1000 Instruction
2000 Support Services
    2100 Support Services-Students
    2110 Attendance and Social Work Services
    2120 Guidance Services
    2123 Appraisal Services
    2130 Health Services
    2200 Support Services-Instructional Staff
    2213 Instructional Staff Training Services
    2220 Educational Media Services
    2222 School Library Services
    2300 Support Services-General Administration
    2400 Support Services-School AdministratioN
    2500 Support Services-Business
    2600 Operation and Maintenance of Plant Services
    2700 Student Transportation Services
    2800 Support Services-Central
    2900 Other Support Services

4000 Facilities Acquisition and Construction Services
    4100 Site Acquisition and Development Services
    4300 Architecture and Engineering Services
    4400 Educational Specifications Development Services
    4500 Building Acquisition and Construction Services
    4600 Building Improvements Services
    4900 Other Facilities Acquisition and Construction Services
    5100 Debt Service

OBJECT DIMENSION
Program Dimension

Code Account Title
100 Personal Services-Salaries
200 Personal Services-Employee Benefits
    220 Social Security Contributions
    230 Retirement Contributions
    440 Rentals
        511 Student Transportation from Other LEAs Witin the State

512 Student Transportation from Other LEAs Outside the State
520 Insurance, Other than Employee Benefits
 561 Tuition to Other LEA's Within the State
 562 Tuition to Other LEA's Outside the State
 592 Services Purchased from Another LEA Within the State
 593 Services Purchased from Another LEA Outside the State

610 General Supplies
 621 Natural Gas
 622 Electricity
 623 Bottled Gas
 624 Oil
 625 Coal
 626 Gasoline
630 Food
640 Books and Periodicals
710 Land and Improvements,
730 Equipment
 732 Vehicles
 733 Furniture and Fixtures
740 Depreciation
830 Interest
910 Redemption of Principa
920 Housing Authority Obligations
930 Fund Transfers

PROJECT/REPORTING DIMENSION
Revenue Account Dimension

Code Account Title

1000 Revenue from Local Sources
 1100 Taxes Levied/Assessed by the LEA
 1110 Ad Valorem Taxes
 1200 Revenue from Local Governmental Units Other than LEAs
 1210 Ad Valorem Taxes
 1300 Tuition
 1310 Tuition from Individuals
 1320 Tuition from Other LEAs Within the State
 1330 Tuition from Other LEA's Outside the State

1400 Transportation Fees
1410 Transportation Fees from Individuals
1420 Transportation Fees from Other LEAs Within the State
1430 Transportation Fees from Other LEAs Outside the State
1500 Earnings on Investments
1600 Food Services
1610 Daily Sales-Reimbursable Program
    1611 Daily Sales –School Lunch Program
    1612 Daily Sales – School Breakfast Program
    1613 Daily Sales – Special Milk Program
1620 Daily Sales – Non-Reimbursable Progams
1700 Student Activities
1800 Community Services Activities
1900 Other Revenue from Local Sources
1920 Contributions and Donations from Private Sources
1940 Textbook Sales and Rentals
    1951 Services Provided Other LEAs Within the State
1952 Services Provided Other LEAs Outside the State
1960 Service Provided Other Local Governmental Units Curr. Exp.
1970 Services Provided Other Funds, Curr. Exp.
2000 Revenue from Intermediate Sources

3000 Revenue from State Sources
    3100 Unrestricted Grants-in-Aid
    3200 Restricted Grants-in-Aid
    – State Aid to Child Nutrition Program
    – State Vocational Aid
    3900 Revenue for/on behalf of the LEA

4000 Revenue from Federal Sources
    4100 Unrestricted Grants-in-Aid Received Directly from the Federal Government
    4200 Unrestricted Grants-in-Aid Received from the Federal Government Through the State
    4300 Restricted Grants-in-Aid Received Directly from the Federal Government
    4330 Vocational Progams
    4370 Desegregation Programs
    4390 Impact Aid, Disaster Assistance Impact Aid, Construction
    4500 Restricted Grants-in-Aid Received from the Federal Government Through the State
        4511-4515 ESEA, Title I
        4516-4519 ESEA, Other Titles

  4530 Vocational Education Act
  4550 Child Nutrition Program
    School Lunch-Regular
    School Lunch-Reduced
    School Lunch-Free
    School Breakfast
    Special Milk
    Non-Food Assistance
    Payments in Lieu of Commodities
    Donated Commodities
  4900 Revenue for/on Behalf of the LEA
5000 Other Sources of Funds

BALANCE SHEET

Code	Account Title
101-104	Cash
111-115	Investments
141	Intergovernmental Accounts Receivable
153	Other Accounts Receivable
171	Inventories for Consumption
181	Prepaid Expenses
241-242	Machinery and Equipment, with Accummulated Depreciation
421	Accounts Payable
431-433	Contracts Payable
441	Matured Bonds Payable
442	Bonds Payable (current)
451	Loans Payable (current)
455	Interest Payable
461	Accrued Salaries and Benefits
471	Payroll Deductions and Withholdings
481	Deferred Revenues
511	Bonds Payable (Long-Term)
521	Loans Payable (Long-Term)

APPENDIX B

Classifying Balance Sheet Accounts

The information provided in this appendix comes directly from Financial Accounting for Local and State School Systems 1990, William J. Fowler, Jr., Ed.D., Revision Project Manager, U.S. Department of Education, Office of Education Research and Improvement.

A summary of the balance sheet accounts and the funds in which they are frequently found is illustrated below. Account numbers are included as an indication of how these accounts may be coded. The description without account numbers are summary accounts that would normally appear on the balance sheet for reporting purposes. X's in brackets [ ] indicate asset accounts normally recorded as debits.

Appendix B-1
Classifying Balance Sheet Accounts

A summary of the balance sheet accounts and the funds in which they are frequently found is illustrated in Table 2. Account numbers are included as an indication of how these accounts may be coded. The descriptions without account numbers are summary accounts that would normally appear on the balance sheet for reporting purposes. X's in brackets ( ) indicate asset accounts normally recorded as debits.

Table B-1. Balance sheet accounts and funds in which these accounts are frequently found

	Balance sheet accounts	Def. page no.	General fund	Special revenue funds	Capital projects funds	Debt service funds	Enterprise funds	Internal service funds	Trust and agency funds	General fixed assets account group	General long-term debt account group
	Assets and Other Debits										
	Current assets										
	Cash										
101	Cash in bank		X	X	X	X	X	X	X		
102	Cash on hand		X	X	X	X	X	X	X		
103	Petty cash		X				X	X			
104	Change cash						X				
105	Cash with fiscal agents					X					
	Cash with fiscal agents										
	Investments										
111	Investments		X	X	X	X	X	X	X		
112	Unamortized premiums on investments				X	X	X	X	X		
113	Unamortized discounts on investments				(X)	(X)	(X)	(X)	(X)		
114	Interest receivable on investments		X	X	X	X	X	X	X		
115	Accrued interest on investments purchased		X	X	X	X	X	X	X		
	Taxes receivable										
121	Taxes receivable		X	X		X					
122	Estimated uncollectible taxes		(X)	(X)		(X)					
	Interfund receivables										
131	Interfund loans receivable		X	X	X	X	X	X			
132	Interfund accounts receivable							X			
	Intergovernmental receivables										
141	Intergovernmental accounts receivable		X	X	X	X	X	X			
	Other receivables										
151	Loans receivable		X						X		
152	Estimated uncollectible loans		(X)						(X)		
153	Other accounts receivable		X	X	X	X	X	X	X		

APPENDIX B • 3

Balance sheet accounts and funds in which these accounts are frequently found—Continued

Def. page no.	Balance sheet accounts	General fund	Special revenue funds	Capital projects funds	Debt service funds	Enterprise funds	Internal service funds	Trust and agency funds	General fixed assets account group	General long-term debt account group
154	Estimated uncollectible accounts receivable	(X)	(X)	(X)	(X)	(X)	(X)	(X)		
161	Bond proceeds receivable Bond proceeds receivable			X						
171 172	Inventories Inventories for consumption Inventories for resale	X	X	X		X X	X X	X		
181	Prepaid expenses Prepaid expenses	X	X	X		X	X	X		
191 199	Other current assets Deposits Other current assets	X X	X	X X	X	X X	X X	X X		
	Fixed assets									
211	Sites Sites								X	
221 222	Site improvements Site improvements Accumulated depreciation on site improvements								X (X)	
231 232	Buildings Buildings and building improvements Accumulated depreciation buildings and building improvements					X (X)	X (X)		X (X)	

4 • APPENDIX B

Balance sheet accounts and funds in which these accounts are frequently found—Continued

Def. page no.	Balance sheet accounts	General fund	Special revenue funds	Capital projects funds	Debt service funds	Enterprise funds	Internal service funds	Trust and agency funds	General fixed assets account group	General long-term debt account group
241	Machinery and equipment									
242	Machinery and equipment					x	x		x	
	Accumulated depreciation on machinery and equipment					(x)	(x)		(x)	
251	Construction in progress									
	Construction in progress								x	
	Budgeting accounts and other debits									
301	Estimated revenues (budget account, interim statements only)	x	x	x						
		(x)	(x)	(x)						
302	Revenues (interim statements only)			x	x					
				(x)	(x)					
303	Amount available in debt service funds									x
304	Amount to be provided for retirement of general long-term debt									x
	Current liabilities									
	Interfund payables									
401	Interfund loans payable	x	x	x	x	x	x	(x)		
402	Interfund accounts payable	x	x	x		x				
	Intergovernmental payables									
411	Intergovernmental accounts payable	x	x	x	x	x	x			
	Other payable									
421	Accounts payable	x	x	x	x	x	x	x		
422	Judgments payable	x	x	x	x	x	x	x		
423	Warrants payable	x	x	x	x					
	Contracts payable									
431	Contracts payable	x	x	x		x	x	x		
432	Construction contracts payable—retained percentage			x						
				x						
433	Construction contracts payable			x						

APPENDIX B • 5

Balance sheet accounts and funds in which these accounts are frequently found—Continued

	Balance sheet accounts	Def. page no.	General fund	Special revenue funds	Capital projects funds	Debt service funds	Enterprise funds	Internal service funds	Trust and agency funds	General fixed assets account group	General long-term debt account group
	Bonds payable										
441	Matured bonds payable					X					
442	Bonds payable					X					
443	Unamortized premiums on bonds sold					X					
	Loans payable										
451	Loans payable		X	X	X		X	X	X		
	Interest payable										
455	Interest payable		X	X	X	X	X	X	X		
	Accrued expenses										
461	Accrued salaries and benefits		X	X	X		X	X	X		
	Payroll deductions and withholdings										
471	Payroll deductions and withholdings		X	X	X		X	X	X		
	Deferred revenues										
481	Deferred revenues		X	X	X	X	X	X	X		
	Other current liabilities										
491	Deposits payable		X	X			X	X	X		
492	Due to fiscal agent					X					
499	Other current liabilities		X	X	X	X	X	X	X		
	Long-term liabilities										
	Bonds payable										
511	Bonds payable										X
	Loans payable										
521	Loans payable										X

APPENDIX C

1993-94 Adopted Budget

The following is a sample of an adopted budget for a school district in Illinois for 1993-94. The budget form is prescribed by the Illinois State Board of Education. This example of a budget is provided for readers who may not have access to such a document. Program and function codes may differ slightly from those found in Handbook II. This example is also provided to facilitate instruction in that all students and instructors can work from a uniform set of documents and financial data. This budget relates directly to Appendix D, E and I.

2 • APPENDIX C

[X] CASH BASIS
[ ] MODIFIED ACCRUAL

SCHOOL DISTRICT BUDGET FORM*
July 1, 1993 - June 30, 1994

Budget of _____NAME_____ School District No. _NUMBER_, County of ___COUNTY___, State of Illinois, for the Fiscal Year beginning _July 1, 1993_ and ending _June 30, 1994_.

WHEREAS the Board of Education of ____SCHOOL DISTRICT____ School District No. _NUMBER_, County of _____COUNTY_____, State of Illinois, caused to be prepared in tentative form a budget, and the Secretary of this Board has made the same conveniently available to public inspection for at least thirty days prior to final action thereon;

AND WHEREAS a public hearing was held as to such budget on the _20th_ day of _SEPTEMBER_ 19_93_, notice of said hearing was given at least thirty days prior thereto as required by law, and all other legal requirements have been complied with;

NOW, THEREFORE, Be it resolved by the Board of Education of said district as follows:

Section 1: That the fiscal year of this School District be and the same hereby is fixed and declared to be beginning _____JULY 1_____, 19 _93_, and ending _____JUNE 30_____, 19 _94_.

Section 2: That the following budget containing an estimate of amounts available in each Fund, separately, and of expenditures from each be and the same is hereby adopted as the budget of this school district for the said fiscal year.

ADOPTION OF BUDGET

The Budget shall be approved and signed below by Members of the School Board.

Adopted this: ____ day of _____ 19 ____, by a roll call vote of _7_ Yeas, and _0_ Nays, to-wit:

MEMBERS VOTING YEA:	MEMBERS VOTING NAY:
Signatures of the Members of the Board of Education	

* Based on the *Illinois Program Accounting Manual for Local Education Agencies (LEAs)* as required by Section 17-1 of the School Code. A copy of this document must be filed with the county clerk within 30 days of adoption as required by Chapter 120, Par. 643, *Illinois Revised Statutes*.

APPENDIX C • 3

Page 2

PART I
ESTIMATED RECEIPTS/REVENUE

DESCRIPTION	ACCT. NO.	(1) EDUCATIONAL	(2) OPERATIONS AND MAINTENANCE	(3) BOND AND INTEREST	(4) TRANSPORTATION	(5) MUNICIPAL RETIREMENT/ SOCIAL SECURITY	(6) SITE AND CON- STRUCTION/CAPITAL IMPROVEMENT	(7) WORKING CASH	(8) RENT	(9) FIRE PREVENTION AND SAFETY
RECEIPTS/REVENUE FROM LOCAL SOURCES	1000									
AD VALOREM TAXES LEVIED BY LOCAL EDUCATION AGENCY	1100									
1. General Levy*	1110	17,752,847.	2,791,000.	3,052,206.	899,300.	917,100.				
2. Tort Immunity Levy	1120		100,000.							
3. Facility Leasing	1130									
4. Special Education Levy	1140	240,553.								
5. Social Security/Medicare Only Levy	1150									
6. Area Vocational Construction Levy	1160									
7. Summer School Levy	1170									
8. Other Tax Levies (Attach Itemization)	1190									
9. TOTAL AD VALOREM TAXES LEVIED BY LOCAL EDUCA- TION AGENCY		17,993,400.	2,891,000.	3,052,206.	899,300.	917,100.				
PAYMENTS IN LIEU OF TAXES	1200									
10. Mobile Home Privilege Tax	1210									
11. Payments from Local Housing Authority	1220									
12. Corporate Personal Property Replacement Taxes**	1230	600,000.	75,000.	127,607.	35,000.	72,900.				
13. Other Payments in Lieu of Taxes	1290									
14. TOTAL PAYMENTS IN LIEU OF TAXES		600,000.	75,000.	127,607.	35,000.	72,900.				

Include taxes for bonds sold that are in addition to those identified separately.

* Corporate personal property replacement tax revenue must be first applied to the Bond and Interest Fund (Bonds issued prior to Jan. 1, 1979), and then the Municipal Retirement/Social Security Fund to replace tax revenue lost due to the abolition of the corporate personal property tax (Chapter 85, Section 616 of the Illinois Revised Statutes). This provision does not apply to taxes levied for medicare only purposes.

4 • APPENDIX C

ESTIMATED RECEIPTS/REVENUE

	ACCT NO	DESCRIPTION	(1) EDUCATIONAL	(2) OPERATIONS AND MAINTENANCE	(3) BOND AND INTEREST	(4) TRANSPORTATION	(5) MUNICIPAL RETIREMENT/ SOCIAL SECURITY	(6) SITE AND CONSTRUCTION/CAPITAL IMPROVEMENT	(7) WORKING CASH	(8) RENT	(9) FIRE PREVENTION AND SAFETY
	1300	TUITION									
15.	1310	Regular Day School Tuition									
16.	1320	Summer School Tuition									
17.	1330	Vocational Education Tuition									
18.	1340	Special Education Tuition	100,000.								
9.	1350	Adult/Continuing Education Tuition									
20.		TOTAL TUITION	100,000.								
	1400	TRANSPORTATION FEES									
	1410	Regular Day School Transportation Fees									
21.	1411	Regular Transportation Fees from Pupils or Parents									
22.	1412	Regular Transportation Fees from Other LEAs									
23.	1413	Regular Transportation Fees from Private Sources									
24.	1415	Regular Transportation Fees from Pupils-Cocurricular Activities									
5.		Total Regular Day School Transportation Fees				60,000.					
26.	1420	Summer School Transportation Fees									
	1430	Vocational Education Transportation Fees									
27.	1431	Vocational Transportation Fees from Pupils or Parents									
28.	1432	Vocational Transportation Fees from Other LEAs									
29.	1433	Vocational Transportation Fees from Other Sources									
30.		Total Vocational Education Transportation Fees				60,000.					

ESTIMATED RECEIPTS/REVENUE

Page 4

	ACCT NO.	DESCRIPTION	(1) EDUCATIONAL	(2) OPERATIONS AND MAINTENANCE	(3) BOND AND INTEREST	(4) TRANSPORTATION	(5) MUNICIPAL RETIREMENT/ SOCIAL SECURITY	(6) SITE AND CON- STRUCTION/CAPITAL IMPROVEMENT	(7) WORKING CASH	(8) RENT	(9) FIRE PREVENTION AND SAFETY
	1440	Special Education Transportation Fees									
31.	1441	Special Education Transportation Fees from Pupils or Parents									
32.	1442	Special Education Transportation Fees from Other LEAs									
33.	1443	Special Education Transportation Fees from Other Sources									
34.		Total Special Education Transportation Fees									
35.	1450	Adult/Continuing Education Transportation Fees									
36.		TOTAL TRANSPORTATION FEES				60,000.					5,000.
37.	1500	EARNINGS ON INVESTMENTS	395,000.		30,000.		10,000.				
38.	1600	FOOD SERVICES	777,800.								
39.	1700	PUPIL ACTIVITIES	105,180.								
40.	1800	TEXTBOOKS	259,000.								
	1900	OTHER RECEIPTS/REVENUE FROM LOCAL SOURCES									
41.	1910	Rentals		30,000.							
42.	1920	Contributions and Donations from Private Sources									
43.	1940	Services Provided Other LEAs									
44.	1950	Refund of Prior Years' Disbursements/Expenditures	20,500.			2,000.					
45.	1990	Other									
46.	1991	Payment from Other LEAs									
47.	1992	Sale of Vocational Projects	55,000.								
	1993	Local Fees	21,000.								

APPENDIX C • 5

6 • APPENDIX C

ESTIMATED RECEIPTS/REVENUE

Page 5

DESCRIPTION	ACCT NO	(1) EDUCATIONAL	(2) OPERATIONS AND MAINTENANCE	(3) BOND AND INTEREST	(4) TRANSPORTATION	(5) MUNICIPAL RETIREMENT/ SOCIAL SECURITY	(6) SITE AND CONSTRUCTION/CAPITAL IMPROVEMENT	(7) WORKING CASH	(8) RENT	(9) FIRE PREVENTION AND SAFETY
48. Other (Attach Itemization)	1999		25,000.							
49. Total Other		76,000.	25,000.		2,000.					5,000.
50. TOTAL OTHER RECEIPTS/REVENUE FROM LOCAL SOURCES*		96,500.	55,000.							
51. TOTAL RECEIPTS/REVENUE FROM LOCAL SOURCES**		20,326,880.	3,021,000.	3,209,813.	996,300.	1,000,000.				
52. FLOW-THROUGH RECEIPTS/REVENUE FROM ONE LEA TO ANOTHER LEA	2000									
52. FLOW-THROUGH RECEIPTS/REVENUE FROM STATE SOURCES	2100	140,000.								
53. FLOW-THROUGH RECEIPTS/REVENUE FROM FEDERAL SOURCES	2200	35,000.								
54. TOTAL FLOW-THROUGH RECEIPTS/REVENUE FROM ONE LEA TO ANOTHER LEA		175,000.								
RECEIPTS/REVENUE FROM STATE SOURCES	3000									
UNRESTRICTED GRANTS-IN-AID	3100									
55. General State Aid	3110	7,172,776.	670,000.							
56. Supplementary State Aid	3120									
57. TOTAL UNRESTRICTED GRANTS-IN-AID		7,172,776.	670,000.							
RESTRICTED GRANTS-IN-AID	3200									
Transportation Aid	3210									
58. Regular	3211				140,000.					
59. Special Education	3212				468,000.					
60. Vocational Education	3213									
61. Total Transportation Aid					608,000.					
Instructional Program Aid	3220-3249									

* Total of Lines 41, 42, 43, 44, 49
** Total of Lines 9, 14, 20, 35, 37, 38, 39, 40, 50

Line 48 Land/Cash Contrib. 25,000.

APPENDIX C • 7

Page 6

ESTIMATED RECEIPTS/REVENUE

DESCRIPTION	ACCT NO	(1) EDUCATIONAL	(2) OPERATIONS AND MAINTENANCE	(3) BOND AND INTEREST	(4) TRANSPORTATION	(5) MUNICIPAL RETIREMENT/ SOCIAL SECURITY	(6) SITE AND CONSTRUCTION/CAPITAL IMPROVEMENT	(7) WORKING CASH	(8) RENT	(9) FIRE PREVENTION AND SAFETY
62. Driver Education	3221	52,268.								
63. Technical Preparation Education	3222									
64. Summer School	3223	186,133.								
65. Bilingual Education	3224									
66. Vocational Education - Regular Part B (Formula Reimbursement)	3225									
67. Vocational Education - Grants and Contracts	3226	20,000.								
68. Gifted Education	3227	53,984.								
69. Adult Education - General	3228									
70. Adult Education - Sec. 10-22.20	3229									
71. Special Education Personnel	3231	749,155.								
72. Special Education Private Facility	3232	132,650.								
73. Special Education Extraordinary	3233	171,933.								
74. Special Education Orphanage	3234	85,000.								
75. Reading Improvement Program	3240	162,260.								
76. Prekindergarten Program for at Risk Students	3245	323,868.								
77. Total Instructional Program Aid*		1,937,251.								
School Lunch Aid	3250	25,350.								
78. Lunch - Free	3251									
79. Breakfast - Free	3252									
80. Total School Lunch Aid		25,350.								

* Total of Lines 62 thru 76

8 • APPENDIX C

ESTIMATED RECEIPTS/REVENUE

	ACCT. NO.	(1) EDUCATIONAL	(2) OPERATIONS AND MAINTENANCE	(3) BOND AND INTEREST	(4) TRANSPORTATION	(5) MUNICIPAL RETIREMENT/ SOCIAL SECURITY	(6) SITE AND CON- STRUCTION/CAPITAL IMPROVEMENT	(7) WORKING CASH	(8) RENT	(9) FIRE PREVENTION AND SAFETY
Capital Development Board	3280									
81. Bond Principal	3281									
82. Bond Interest	3282									
83. Total Capital Development Board										
84. Other Grants-In-Aid (Attach Itemization)	3290	73,436.								
85. TOTAL RESTRICTED GRANTS-IN-AID*		2,036,037.			608,000.					
PAYMENTS RECEIVED IN LIEU OF TAXES	3300									
86. Orphans Tuition	3310									
87. State Owned Housing	3320									
88. Tax Equivalent Grants	3330									
89. State Impaction Aid	3340									
90. TOTAL PAYMENTS RECEIVED IN LIEU OF TAXES										
91. TOTAL RECEIPTS/REVENUE FROM STATE SOURCES**		9,208,813.	670,000.		608,000.					
RECEIPTS/REVENUE FROM FEDERAL SOURCES	4000									
UNRESTRICTED GRANTS-IN-AID RECEIVED DIRECTLY FROM FEDERAL GOVERNMENT	4100									
92. Public Law 81-874	4110	7,000.								
RESTRICTED GRANTS-IN-AID RECEIVED DIRECTLY FROM FEDERAL GOVERNMENT	4300									
93. Emergency School Assistance Act	4320									
94. Elementary and Secondary Education Act (ESEA) Title VII Bilingual	4325	75,400.								
95. Education Act (ESEA) Title VI, P.L. 96-377 Excellence in Education	4330									

* Total of Lines 81, 77, 80, 83, 84
** Total of Lines 57, 85, 90

Line 84 Staff Devev.   13,774.   Drug Alcohol Init.   45,000.
         Learner Outcome   8,662. $73,436.
         Report Card   6,000.

APPENDIX C • 9

Page 8

ESTIMATED RECEIPTS/REVENUE

ACCT NO	DESCRIPTION	(1) EDUCATIONAL	(2) OPERATIONS AND MAINTENANCE	(3) BOND AND INTEREST	(4) TRANSPORTATION	(5) MUNICIPAL RETIREMENT/ SOCIAL SECURITY	(6) SITE AND CON- STRUCTION/CAPITAL IMPROVEMENT	(7) WORKING CASH	(8) RENT	(9) FIRE PREVENTION AND SAFETY
96.	Community Action Program - O.E.O.	4340								
97.	Head Start	4350								
98.	Public Law 81-815 - Construction	4360								
99.	Other (Attach Itemization)	4390								
100.	TOTAL RESTRICTED GRANTS-IN-AID RECEIVED DIRECTLY FROM FEDERAL GOVERNMENT*		75,400.							
	RESTRICTED GRANTS-IN-AID RECEIVED FROM FEDERAL GOVT. THROUGH THE STATE	4400								
101.	Title III Adult Basic Education -P.L. 102-73	4410								
	Carl D. Perkins Vocational and Applied Technology Education Act of 1990, P.L. 101-392	4420								
102.	Vocational Act 1990, P.L. 101-392, Title II Part A - State Leadership	4421								
103.	Vocational Act 1990, P.L. 101-392, Title II Part B - Single Parents	4422								
104.	Vocational Act 1990, P.L. 101-392, Title II Part B - Sex Equity	4423								
105.	Vocational Act 1990, P.L. 101-392, Title II Part C - Secondary Voc. Educ. Prog.	4424								
106.	Vocational Act 1990, P.L. 101-392, Title III Part B Consumer Homemaking	4425								
107.	Vocational Act 1990, P.L. 101-392, Title III Part E - Tech. Prep.	4426								
108.	Vocational Act 1990, P.L. 101-392, Title III Part F Facilities and Equipment	4427								
109.	Vocational Act 1990, P.L.101-392 Other (Attach Itemization)	4429								
110.	Total Carl D. Perkins Vocational and Applied Technology Education Act 1990, P.L. 101-392									
111.	Transition Program for Refugee Children	4430								
112.	Emergency Immigrant Education Assistance	4435								

* Total of Lines 93 thru 99

10 • APPENDIX C

ESTIMATED RECEIPTS/REVENUE

DESCRIPTION	ACCT. NO	(1) EDUCATIONAL	(2) OPERATIONS AND MAINTENANCE	(3) BOND AND INTEREST	(4) TRANSPORTATION	(5) MUNICIPAL RETIREMENT/ SOCIAL SECURITY	(6) SITE AND CON- STRUCTION/CAPITAL IMPROVEMENT	(7) WORKING CASH	(8) RENT	(9) FIRE PREVENTION AND SAFETY
Elementary and Secondary Education Act (ESEA) Chapter 1	4440									
113. ESEA - Chapter 1 Education of Deprived	4441	682,700.								
114. ESEA - Chapter 1 Handicapped (P.L. 89-313)	4442	43,744.								
115. ESEA - Chapter 1 Migrant	4443									
116. ESEA - Chapter 1 Neglected and Delinquent	4444									
7. ESEA - Chapter 1 Engl Prof	4445									
118. Total Elementary and Secondary Education Act (ESEA) Chapter 1		725,450.								
Individuals with Disabilities Education Act (IDEA)	4450									
119. IDEA - Preschool	4451									
120. IDEA - Room and Board Reimbursement	4452									
121. IDEA - Discretionary Programs	4453									
122. IDEA - Flow-Through	4454	237,841.								
123. IDEA - Pass Thru	4455									
4. IDEA - Infant/Toddler	4456									
125. Total Individuals with Disabilities Education Act (IDEA)		237,841.								
School Lunch Program	4460									
126. School Lunch - Regular Lunches	4461	104,000.								
127. School Lunch-Free and Reduced	4462	88,513.								
128. Special Milk	4463	32,000.								

Page 10

APPENDIX C • 11

ESTIMATED RECEIPTS/REVENUE

	DESCRIPTION	ACCT. NO.	(1) EDUCATIONAL	(2) OPERATIONS AND MAINTENANCE	(3) BOND AND INTEREST	(4) TRANSPORTATION	(5) MUNICIPAL RETIREMENT/ SOCIAL SECURITY	(6) SITE AND CON- STRUCTION/CAPITAL IMPROVEMENT	(7) WORKING CASH	(8) RENT	(9) FIRE PREVENTION AND SAFETY
129.	Breakfast	4464	5,500.								
130.	Non-Food Assistance	4465									
131.	Payments in Lieu of Commodities	4466									
132.	Nutrition Education and Training Act	4467									
133.	Total School Lunch Program		550,013.								
134.	ESEA, Chapter 2 - Block Grant	4470	71,100.								
135.	ESEA, Title II - Dwight D. Eisenhower Mathematics and Science Education Act	4475	30,477.								
136.	Department of Rehabilitation Services	4480	23,840.								
137.	Other (Attach Itemization)	4490	202,555.								
138.	TOTAL RESTRICTED GRANTS-IN-AID RECEIVED FROM FEDERAL GOVERN- MENT THROUGH THE STATE*		1,842,276.								
139.	RESTRICTED GRANTS-IN-AID RECEIVED FROM FEDERAL GOVERNMENT THROUGH INTERMEDIATE SOURCES Job Training Partnership Reform Act (J.T.P.R.A.)	4500 4530									
140.	Other (Attach Itemization)	4590									
141.	TOTAL RESTRICTED GRANTS-IN-AID RECEIVED FROM FEDERAL GOVT. THROUGH INTERMEDIATE SOURCES		1,924,676.								
142.	TOTAL RECEIPTS/REVENUE FROM FEDERAL SOURCES**										
143.	TOTAL RECEIPTS/REVENUE (Total of Lines 51, 54, 91, 142)		31,635,369.	3,691,000.	3,209,813.	1,504,300.	1,000,000.				5,000.

* Total of Lines 101, 110, 111, 112, 118, 125, 133 134, 135, 136, 137

** Total of Lines 92, 100, 138, 141

Line 137 Drug Free 67,549.
          EvenStart 135,006.
                   $202,555.

12 • APPENDIX C

ESTIMATED RECEIPTS/REVENUE

DESCRIPTION	ACCT. NO.	(1) EDUCATIONAL	(2) OPERATIONS AND MAINTENANCE	(3) BOND AND INTEREST	(4) TRANSPORTATION	(5) MUNICIPAL RETIREMENT/ SOCIAL SECURITY	(6) SITE AND CONSTRUCTION/CAPITAL IMPROVEMENT	(7) WORKING CASH	(8) RENT	(9) FIRE PREVENTION AND SAFETY
OTHER FINANCING SOURCES	7000									
Transfer from Other Funds	7100									
144. Permanent Transfer from Working Cash Fund Abolishment (Section 20-8)	7110									
145. Permanent Transfer from Working Cash Fund - Interest (Section 20-5)	7120									
146. Permanent Transfer from Educational Fund (Section 17-2A)	7130									
7. Permanent Transfer of Interest (Section 10-22.44)	7140						300,000.			
148. Permanent Transfer from Site and Construction/Capital Improvement Fund (Section 10-22.14)	7150									
149. Permanent Tsf of Excess Accumulated Fire Prevention & Safety Tax Proceeds and Interest Earnings (Sec. 17-2.11)*	7160									
150. Permanent Transfer of Excess Accumulated Fire Prevention & Safety Bond Proceeds and Interest Earnings (Sec. 10-22.14)*	7170									
Sale of Bonds	7200	(1)	(1)	(2)	(1)		(3)			(4)
151. Principal on Bonds Sold	7210									
152. Premium on Bonds Sold	7220									
153. Accrued Interest on Bonds Sold	7230									
4. Sale or Compensation for Fixed Assets**	7300									
155. Other Sources (Attach Itemization)	7400									
TOTAL RECEIPTS/REVENUE AND OTHER FINANCING SOURCES*		31,635,369.	3,691,000.	3,209,813.	1,604,300.	1,000,000.	300,000.			5,000.

* Requires the secretary of the school board to notify the county clerk (within 30 days of the transfer approval) to abate an equal amount of taxes to be next determined.
*** Total of Lines 143, 144-155

** The proceeds from the sale of school sites, buildings, or other real estate shall be used first to pay the principal and interest on any outstanding bonds on the property being sold, and after all such bonds have been retired, the remaining proceeds from the sale next shall be used by the school board to meet any urgent district needs as determined under Sections 2-3.12 and 17-2.11 of the School Code. Once these issues have been addressed, any remaining proceeds may be used for any other authorized purpose and for deposit into any district fund.

NOTE: (1) Funding Bonds or Tort Immunity Bonds
(2) Refunding Bonds Only
(3) Building Bonds
(4) Fire Prevention and Safety

APPENDIX C • 13

Page 12

PART II
ESTIMATED DISBURSEMENTS/EXPENDITURES

DESCRIPTION	FUCT. NO.	(1) SALARIES	(2) EMPLOYEE BENEFITS	(3) PURCHASED SERVICES	(4) SUPPLIES AND MATERIALS	(5) CAPITAL OUTLAY	(6) OTHER OBJECTS	(7) TRANSFERS	(8) TUITION	(9) TOTAL
EDUCATIONAL FUND (1)	1000									
INSTRUCTION	1000									
1. REGULAR PROGRAMS	1100	16,784,747.	1,673,700.	98,587.	544,982.	68,545.			5,600.	19,176,161.
2. SPECIAL EDUCATION PROGRAMS (Total of Funct. No. 1200-1220)	1200	2,486,302.	23,219.	137,632.	52,913.				748,359.	3,448,425.
3. EDUCATIONALLY DEPRIVED/ REMEDIAL PROGRAMS	1250	455,000.	59,000.	500.	5,050.	20,000.				539,550.
4. ADULT/CONTINUING EDUCATION PROGRAMS	1300									
5. VOCATIONAL PROGRAMS	1400	360,568.		8,500.	20,525.	17,900.	2,500.		20,000.	429,993.
6. INTERSCHOLASTIC PROGRAMS	1500	1,925.		76,204.	63,335.	5,200.				146,664.
7. SUMMER SCHOOL PROGRAMS	1600	59,366.		15,000.	5,000.					79,366.
8. GIFTED PROGRAMS	1650	2,810.		550.	12,670.					16,030.
9. BILINGUAL PROGRAMS	1800	480,577.	11,214.	5,755.	24,036.					521,582.
10. TRUANTS' ALTERNATIVE AND OPTIONAL PROGRAMS	1900									
11. TOTAL INSTRUCTION		20,631,295.	1,767,133.	342,728.	728,511.	111,645.	2,500.		773,959.	24,357,771.
SUPPORT SERVICES	2000									
SUPPORT SERVICES - PUPILS	2100									

NOTE: (1) Only for tuition payments made to private facilities. See Function 4100 for estimated public facility disbursements/expenditures

ESTIMATED DISBURSEMENTS/EXPENDITURES

	DESCRIPTION (Fund 1 Continued)	FUCT. NO.	(1) SALARIES	(2) EMPLOYEE BENEFITS	(3) PURCHASED SERVICES	(4) SUPPLIES AND MATERIALS	(5) CAPITAL OUTLAY	(6) OTHER OBJECTS	(7) TRANSFERS	(8) TUITION	(9) TOTAL
12.	Attendance and Social Work Services	2110	258,591.	4,512.		600.					263,703.
13.	Guidance Services	2120	614,716.		6,800.	11,010.					632,526.
14.	Health Services	2130	190,113.		412.	7,500.					198,025.
15.	Psychological Services	2140	187,501.			800.					188,301.
16.	Speech Pathology and Audiology Services	2150	800.								800.
17.	Other Support Services - Pupils (Attach Itemization)	2190									
18.	TOTAL SUPPORT SERVICES - PUPILS		1,251,721.	4,512.	7,212.	19,910.					1,283,355.
	SUPPORT SERVICES - INSTRUCTIONAL STAFF	2200									
19.	Improvement of Instruction Services	2210	312,928.	2,500.	78,182.	103,900.					497,510.
20.	Educational Media Services	2220			6,000.	26,541.					32,541.
21.	Assessment and Testing	2230									
22.	TOTAL SUPPORT SERVICES - INSTRUCTIONAL STAFF		312,928.	2,500.	84,182.	130,441.					530,051.
	SUPPORT SERVICES - GENERAL ADMINISTRATION	2300									
23.	Board of Education Services	2310	78,354.		103,000.	29,386.					210,740.
24.	Executive Administration Services	2320	669,600.	303,780.	62,000.	24,000.					1,059,380.
25.	Special Area Administrative Services	2330	20,799.		1,000.	500.	2,000.				24,299.
26.	TOTAL SUPPORT SERVICES - GENERAL ADMINISTRATION		768,753.	303,730.	166,000.	53,886.	2,000.				1,294,419.
	SUPPORT SERVICES - SCHOOL ADMINISTRATION	2400									
27.	Office of the Principal Services	2410	1,631,925.		29,500.	73,299.					1,734,724.
28.	Other Support Services - School Administration (Attach Itemization)	2490									
29.	TOTAL SUPPORT SERVICES - SCHOOL ADMINISTRATION		1,631,925.		29,500.	73,299.					1,734,724.

Page 13

APPENDIX C • 15

Page 14
(Fund 1 Continued)

ESTIMATED DISBURSEMENTS/EXPENDITURES

	FUCT. NO.	(1) SALARIES	(2) EMPLOYEE BENEFITS	(3) PURCHASED SERVICES	(4) SUPPLIES AND MATERIALS	(5) CAPITAL OUTLAY	(6) OTHER OBJECTS	(7) TRANSFERS	(8) TUITION	(9) TOTAL
		SUPPORT SERVICES - BUSINESS	2500								
30. Direction of Business Support Services	2510				20,000.					20,000.
31. Fiscal Services	2520	169,025.								169,025.
32. Operation and Maintenance of Plant Services	2540	182,857.		311,256.	1,300.	3,000.				498,413.
33. Pupil Transportation Services	2550			64,318.						64,318.
34. Food Services	2560	154,000.		1,251,500.						1,406,800.
35. Internal Services	2570			31,045.	66,500.	196,692.				294,237.
36. TOTAL SUPPORT SERVICES - BUSINESS		505,882.		1,658,119.	89,100.	199,692.				2,452,793.
	SUPPORT SERVICES - CENTRAL	2600									
37. Direction of Central Support Services	2610			9,000.						9,000.
38. Planning, Research, Development and Evaluation Services	2620				10,000.					10,000.
39. Information Services	2630			5,000.						5,000.
40. Staff Services	2640				26,500.	16,000.				42,500.
41. Data Processing Services	2660			14,000.	36,500.	16,000.				66,500.
42. TOTAL SUPPORT SERVICES - CENTRAL		17,779.								17,779.
43. OTHER SUPPORT SERVICES (Attach Itemization)	2900									
44. TOTAL SUPPORT SERVICES		4,488,988.	310,792.	1,959,013.	403,136.	217,692.				7,379,621.
45. COMMUNITY SERVICES	3000	93,760.		4,000.	5,800.					103,560.
46. NONPROGRAMMED CHARGES	4000									
	PAYMENTS TO OTHER GOVT. UNITS (IN-STATE)	4100									
	Payments for Regular Programs	4110									

Line 43 Support Service - Substance Abuse

APPENDIX C

ESTIMATED DISBURSEMENTS/EXPENDITURES

Page 15

	FUCT. NO.	DESCRIPTION (Fund 1 Continued)	(1) SALARIES	(2) EMPLOYEE BENEFITS	(3) PURCHASED SERVICES	(4) SUPPLIES AND MATERIALS	(5) CAPITAL OUTLAY	(6) OTHER OBJECTS	(7) TRANSFERS	(8) TUITION	(9) TOTAL
47.	4120	Payments for Special Education Programs								400,000.	400,000.
48.	4130	Payments for Adult/Continuing Education Programs									
49.	4140	Payments for Voc. Ed. Programs									
50.	4170	Payments for Community College Programs									
51.	4190	Other Payments to In-State Govt. Units (Attach Itemization)								400,000.	400,000.
52.		TOTAL PAYMENTS TO OTHER GOVT. UNITS (IN-STATE)									
53.	4200	PAYMENTS TO OTHER GOVT. UNITS (OUT-OF-STATE)								400,000.	400,000.
54.		TOTAL NONPROGRAMMED CHARGES									
	5000	DEBT SERVICES									
55.	5100	DEBT SERVICES-INTEREST									
	5110	Tax Anticipation Warrants						77,500.			77,500.
56.	5120	Tax Anticipation Notes									
57.	5130	Teachers' Orders									
	5150	Corporate Personal Property Replacement Tax Anticipation Notes									
58.	5160	State Aid Anticipation Certificates									
59.	5190	Other (Attach Itemization)									
60.		TOTAL DEBT SERVICES - INTEREST						77,500.			77,500.
61.	5300	DEBT SERVICES - LEASE/PURCHASE PRINCIPAL RETIRED									
62.								77,500.			77,500.
63.		TOTAL DEBT SERVICES						1,000,000.			1,000,000.
64.	6000	PROVISION FOR CONTINGENCIES									
65.		TOTAL ESTIMATED DISBURSEMENTS/EXPENDITURES*	25,214,043.	2,077,925.	2,305,741.	1,137,447.	329,337.	1,080,000.		1,173,959.	33,318,452.

* Total of Lines 11, 44, 45, 54, 63, 64

Page 16 (Fund 1 Continued)

ESTIMATED DISBURSEMENTS/EXPENDITURES

DESCRIPTION	FUCT NO.	(1) SALARIES	(2) EMPLOYEE BENEFITS	(3) PURCHASED SERVICES	(4) SUPPLIES AND MATERIALS	(5) CAPITAL OUTLAY	(6) OTHER OBJECTS	(7) TRANSFERS	(8) TUITION	(9) TOTAL
OTHER FINANCING USES	8000									
66. Permanent Transfer of Educational Fund (Sec. 17-2A)	8130							300,000.		300,000.
67. Permanent Transfer of Interest (Section 10-22.44)	8140									
68. Other Uses (Attach Itemization)	8190									
69. TOTAL DISBURSEMENTS/ EXPENDITURES AND OTHER FINANCING USES		25,214,043.	2,077,925.	2,305,741.	1,137,447.	329,337.	1,080,000.	300,000.	1,173,959.	33,618,452.

* Total of Lines 65, 66, 67, 68

DESCRIPTION	FUCT NO.	(1) SALARIES	(2) EMPLOYEE BENEFITS	(3) PURCHASED SERVICES	(4) SUPPLIES AND MATERIALS	(5) CAPITAL OUTLAY	(6) OTHER OBJECTS	(7) TRANSFERS	(8) TUITION	(9) TOTAL
OPERATIONS AND MAINTENANCE FUND (2)										
SUPPORT SERVICES	2000									
SUPPORT SERVICES - PUPILS	2100									
OTHER SUPPORT SERVICES - PUPILS (Attach Itemization)	2190									
SUPPORT SERVICES - BUSINESS	2500									
2. Direction of Business Support Services	2510			7,000.			5,600.			12,600.
3. Facilities Acquisition and Construction Services	2530									
4. Operation and Maintenance of Plant Services	2540	1,525,365.	122,600.	388,039.	1,179,395.	17,900.				3,233,299.
5. Public Transportation Services	2550									
6. Food Services	2560									
7. TOTAL SUPPORT SERVICES - BUSINESS		1,525,365.	122,600.	395,039.	1,179,395.	17,900.	5,600.			3,245,899.
8. OTHER SUPPORT SERVICES (Attach Itemization)	2900									
9. TOTAL SUPPORT SERVICES*		1,525,365.	122,600.	395,039.	1,179,395.	17,900.	5,600.			3,245,899.
10. COMMUNITY SERVICES	3000									
NONPROGRAMMED CHARGES	4000									

* Total of Lines 1, 7, 8

APPENDIX C • 17

18 • APPENDIX C

ESTIMATED DISBURSEMENTS/EXPENDITURES

Page 17

DESCRIPTION (Fund 2 Continued)	FUCT. NO.	(1) SALARIES	(2) EMPLOYEE BENEFITS	(3) PURCHASED SERVICES	(4) SUPPLIES AND MATERIALS	(5) CAPITAL OUTLAY	(6) OTHER OBJECTS	(7) TRANSFERS	(8) TUITION	(9) TOTAL
PAYMENTS TO OTHER GOVT. UNITS (IN-STATE)	4100						42,870.			42,870.
11. Payments for Special Education Programs	4120									
12. Payments for Voc. Ed. Programs	4140									
13. Other Payments to In-State Govt. Units (Attach Itemization)	4190						42,870.			42,870.
14. TOTAL PAYMENTS TO OTHER GOVT. UNITS (IN-STATE)										
15. PAYMENTS TO OTHER GOVT. UNITS (OUT-OF-STATE)	4200						42,870.			42,870.
16. TOTAL NONPROGRAMMED CHARGES										
DEBT SERVICES	5000									
DEBT SERVICES - INTEREST	5100									
17. Tax Anticipation Warrants	5110									
18. Tax Anticipation Notes	5120									
19. Corporate Personal Property Replacement Tax Anticipation Notes	5150									
20. State Aid Anticipation Certificates	5160									
21. Other (Attach Itemization)	5190									
22. TOTAL DEBT SERVICES - INTEREST										
23. DEBT SERVICES - LEASE/PURCHASE PRINCIPAL RETIRED	5300									
24. TOTAL DEBT SERVICES										
25. PROVISION FOR CONTINGENCIES	6000						200,000.			200,000.
26. TOTAL ESTIMATED DISBURSEMENTS/EXPENDITURES*		1,525,365.	122,600.	395,039.	1,179,395.	17,900.	248,470.			3,488,769.
OTHER FINANCING USES	8000									
27. Permanent Transfer of Interest (Section 10-22.44)	8140									

* Total of lines 9, 10, 16, 24, 25

APPENDIX C • 19

Page 1B
(Fund 2 Continued)

ESTIMATED DISBURSEMENTS/EXPENDITURES

	FUCT NO	DESCRIPTION	(1) SALARIES	(2) EMPLOYEE BENEFITS	(3) PURCHASED SERVICES	(4) SUPPLIES AND MATERIALS	(5) CAPITAL OUTLAY	(6) OTHER OBJECTS	(7) TRANSFERS	(8) TUITION	(9) TOTAL
28.	8190	Other Uses (Attach Itemization)									
29.		TOTAL DISBURSEMENTS/ EXPENDITURES AND OTHER FINANCING USES*	1,525,365.	122,600.	395,039.	1,179,395.	17,900.	248,470.			3,488,769.

BOND AND INTEREST FUND (3)

	FUCT NO	DESCRIPTION	(1) SALARIES	(2) EMPLOYEE BENEFITS	(3) PURCHASED SERVICES	(4) SUPPLIES AND MATERIALS	(5) CAPITAL OUTLAY	(6) OTHER OBJECTS	(7) TRANSFERS	(8) TUITION	(9) TOTAL
	4000	NONPROGRAMMED CHARGES									
1.	4100	PAYMENTS TO OTHER GOVT. UNITS (IN-STATE)									
2.		TOTAL NONPROGRAMMED CHARGES									
	5000	DEBT SERVICES									
	5100	DEBT SERVICES - INTEREST									
3.	5110	Tax Anticipation Warrants									
4.	5120	Tax Anticipation Notes						659,812.			659,812.
5.	5140	Bonds									
6.	5150	Corporate Personal Property Replacement Tax Anticipation Notes									
7.	5160	State Aid Anticipation Certificates									
8.	5190	Other (Attach Itemization)									
9.		TOTAL DEBT SERVICES - INTEREST						659,812.			659,812.
10.	5200	DEBT SERVICES - BOND PRINCIPAL RETIRED						2,500,000.			2,500,000.
11.	5600	DEBT SERVICES - OTHER (Attach Itemization)									
12.		TOTAL DEBT SERVICES (Total of Lines 9, 10, 11)						3,159,812.			3,159,812.
13.	6000	PROVISION FOR CONTINGENCIES						50,000.			50,000.
14.		TOTAL ESTIMATED DISBURSEMENTS/EXPENDITURES**						3,209,812.			3,209,812.

* Total of Lines 26, 27, 28 ** Total of Lines 2, 12, 13

20 • APPENDIX C

ESTIMATED DISBURSEMENTS/EXPENDITURES

DESCRIPTION (Fund 3 Continued)	FUCT. NO	(1) SALARIES	(2) EMPLOYEE BENEFITS	(3) PURCHASED SERVICES	(4) SUPPLIES AND MATERIALS	(5) CAPITAL OUTLAY	(6) OTHER OBJECTS	(7) TRANSFERS	(8) TUITION	(9) TOTAL
OTHER FINANCING USES	8000									
15. Permanent Transfer of Interest (Section 10-22.44)	8140									
16. Other Uses (Attach Itemization)	8190						3,209,812.			3,209,812.
17. TOTAL DISBURSEMENTS/ EXPENDITURES AND OTHER FINANCING USES*										
TRANSPORTATION FUND (4)										
SUPPORT SERVICES	2000									
SUPPORT SERVICES - PUPILS	2100									
1. OTHER SUPPORT SERVICES - PUPILS (Attach Itemization)	2190									
SUPPORT SERVICES - BUSINESS	2500									
2. Pupil Transportation Services	2550	586,420.	61,250.	905,408.	177,300.	171,800.				1,902,178.
3. OTHER SUPPORT SERVICES (Attach Itemization)	2900									
4. TOTAL SUPPORT SERVICES		586,420.	61,250.	905,408.	177,300.	171,800.				1,902,178.
5. COMMUNITY SERVICES	3000									
NONPROGRAMMED CHARGES	4000									
PAYMENTS TO OTHER GOVT. UNITS (IN-STATE)	4100									
6. Payments for Regular Programs	4110									
7. Payments for Special Education Programs	4120									
8. Payments for Adult/Continuing Education Programs	4130									
9. Payments for Voc. Education Programs	4140									

* Total of Lines 14, 15, 16

Page 20

ESTIMATED DISBURSEMENTS/EXPENDITURES

DESCRIPTION (Fund 4 Continued)	FUCT. NO.	(1) SALARIES	(2) EMPLOYEE BENEFITS	(3) PURCHASED SERVICES	(4) SUPPLIES AND MATERIALS	(5) CAPITAL OUTLAY	(6) OTHER OBJECTS	(7) TRANSFERS	(8) TUITION	(9) TOTAL
10. Payments for Community College Programs	4170									
11. Other Payments to In-State Govt. Units (Attach Itemization)	4190									
12. TOTAL PAYMENTS TO OTHER GOVT. UNITS (IN-STATE)										
13. PAYMENTS TO OTHER GOVT. UNITS (OUT-OF-STATE)	4200									
14. TOTAL NONPROGRAMMED CHARGES										
DEBT SERVICES	5000									
DEBT SERVICES - INTEREST	5100									
15. Tax Anticipation Warrants	5110									
16. Tax Anticipation Notes	5120									
17. Corporate Personal Property Replacement Tax Anticipation Notes	5150									
18. State Aid Anticipation Certificates	5160									
19. Other (Attach Itemization)	5180									
20. TOTAL DEBT SERVICES - INTEREST										
21. DEBT SERVICES - LEASE/PURCHASE PRINCIPAL RETIRED	5300									
22. TOTAL DEBT SERVICES										
23. PROVISION FOR CONTINGENCIES	6000	586,420.	61,250.	905,408.	177,300.	171,800.	55,000.			1,957,178.
24. TOTAL ESTIMATED DISBURSEMENTS/EXPENDITURES*										
OTHER FINANCING USES	8000									
25. Permanent Transfer of Interest (Section 10-22.44)	8140									
26. Other Uses (Attach Itemization)	8190									
27. TOTAL DISBURSEMENTS/EXPENDITURES AND OTHER FINANCING USES**		586,420.	61,250.	905,408.	177,300.	171,800.	55,000.			1,957,178.

* Total of Lines 4, 5, 14, 22, 23   ** Total of Lines 24, 25, 26

APPENDIX C

ESTIMATED DISBURSEMENTS/EXPENDITURES

DESCRIPTION	FUCT. NO.	(1) SALARIES	(2) EMPLOYEE BENEFITS	(3) PURCHASED SERVICES	(4) SUPPLIES AND MATERIALS	(5) CAPITAL OUTLAY	(6) OTHER OBJECTS	(7) TRANSFERS	(8) TUITION	(9) TOTAL
MUNICIPAL RETIREMENT/ SOCIAL SECURITY FUND (5)										
INSTRUCTION	1000									
1. REGULAR PROGRAM	1100		94,744.							94,744.
2. SPECIAL EDUCATION PROGRAMS (Total of Funct. No. 1200-1220)	1200		87,601.							87,601.
3. EDUCATIONALLY DEPRIVED/ REMEDIAL PROGRAMS	1250		8,098.							8,098.
4. ADULT/CONTINUING EDUCATION PROGRAMS	1300		343.							343.
5. VOCATIONAL PROGRAMS	1400		1,140.							1,140.
6. INTERSCHOLASTIC PROGRAMS	1500		5,658.							5,658.
7. SUMMER SCHOOL PROGRAMS	1600		18.							18.
8. GIFTED PROGRAMS	1650		22,827.							22,827.
9. BILINGUAL PROGRAMS	1800									
10. TRUANTS ALTERNATIVE AND OPTIONAL PROGRAMS	1900									
11. TOTAL INSTRUCTION			220,429.							220,429.
SUPPORT SERVICES	2000									

APPENDIX C • 23

Page 22

ESTIMATED DISBURSEMENTS/EXPENDITURES

	FUCT. NO.	DESCRIPTION (Fund 6 Continued)	(1) SALARIES	(2) EMPLOYEE BENEFITS	(3) PURCHASED SERVICES	(4) SUPPLIES AND MATERIALS	(5) CAPITAL OUTLAY	(6) OTHER OBJECTS	(7) TRANSFERS	(8) TUITION	(9) TOTAL
	2100	SUPPORT SERVICES - PUPILS									
12.	2110	Attendance and Social Work Services		2,584.							2,584.
13.	2120	Guidance Services		4,180.							4,180.
14.	2130	Health Services		24,262.							24,262.
15.	2140	Psychological Services		1,516.							1,516.
16.	2150	Speech Pathology and Audiology Services									
17.	2190	Other Support Services - Pupil (Attach itemization)									
18.		TOTAL SUPPORT SERVICES - PUPILS		32,542.							32,542.
	2200	SUPPORT SERVICES - INSTRUCTIONAL STAFF									
19.	2210	Improvement of Instruction Services		3,673.							3,673.
20.	2220	Educational Media Services									
21.	2230	Assessment and Testing									
22.		TOTAL SUPPORT SERVICES - INSTRUCTIONAL STAFF		3,673.							3,673.
	2300	SUPPORT SERVICES - GENERAL ADMINISTRATION									
23.	2310	Board of Education Services		1,848.							1,848.
24.	2320	Executive Administration Services		60,108.							60,108.
25.	2330	Special Area Administrative Services		6,329.							6,329.
26.		TOTAL SUPPORT SERVICES - GENERAL ADMINISTRATION		68,285.							68,285.
	2400	SUPPORT SERVICES - SCHOOL ADMINISTRATION									
27.	2410	Office of the Principal Services		125,690.							125,690.
28.	2490	Other Support Services - School Administration (Attach itemization)									

24 • APPENDIX C

	FUCT. NO.	(1) SALARIES	(2) EMPLOYEE BENEFITS	(3) PURCHASED SERVICES	(4) SUPPLIES AND MATERIALS	(5) CAPITAL OUTLAY	(6) OTHER OBJECTS	(7) TRANSFERS	(8) TUITION	(9) TOTAL
29. TOTAL SUPPORT SERVICES - SCHOOL ADMINISTRATION			125,690.							125,690.
SUPPORT SERVICES - BUSINESS	2500									
30. Direction of Business Support Services	2510									
31. Fiscal Services	2520		36,828.							36,828.
32. Facilities Acquisition and Construction Services	2530									
33. Operation and Maintenance of Plant Services	2540		323,545.							323,545.
34. Pupil Transportation Services	2550		122,782.							122,782.
35. Food Services	2560									
36. Internal Services	2570		12,178.							12,178.
37. TOTAL SUPPORT SERVICES - BUSINESS			495,333.							495,333.
SUPPORT SERVICES - CENTRAL	2600									
38. Direction of Central Support Services	2610									
39. Planning, Research, Development and Evaluation Services	2620									
2. Information Services	2630									
41. Staff Services	2640									
42. Data Processing Services	2660									
43. TOTAL SUPPORT SERVICES - CENTRAL										
44. OTHER SUPPORT SERVICES (Attach Itemization)	2900		1,844.							1,844.
45. TOTAL SUPPORT SERVICES			727,367.							727,367.

Line 44 - Support Service - Substance Abuse

APPENDIX C • 25

Page 24

ESTIMATED DISBURSEMENTS/EXPENDITURES

FUNCT. NO.	DESCRIPTION (Fund 8 Continued)	(1) SALARIES	(2) EMPLOYEE BENEFITS	(3) PURCHASED SERVICES	(4) SUPPLIES AND MATERIALS	(5) CAPITAL OUTLAY	(6) OTHER OBJECTS	(7) TRANSFERS	(8) TUITION	(9) TOTAL
3000	46. COMMUNITY SERVICES		2,204.							2,204.
5000	DEBT SERVICES									
5100	DEBT SERVICES - INTEREST									
5110	47. Tax Anticipation Warrants									
5120	48. Tax Anticipation Notes									
5150	49. Corporate Personal Property Replacement Tax Anticipation Notes									
5160	50. State Aid Anticipation Certificates									
5190	51. Other (Attach Itemization)									
	52. TOTAL DEBT SERVICES - INTEREST									
6000	53. PROVISION FOR CONTINGENCIES						50,000.			50,000.
	54. TOTAL ESTIMATED DISBURSEMENTS/EXPENDITURES*		950,000.				50,000.			1,000,000.
8000	OTHER FINANCING USES									
8140	55. Permanent Transfer of Interest (Section 10-22.44)**									
	56. TOTAL DISBURSEMENTS/ EXPENDITURES AND OTHER FINANCING USES***		950,000.				50,000.			1,000,000.

* Total of Lines 11, 45, 46 52, 53

** The School Code, Section 10-22.44 continues in force and prohibits the transfer of interest earned on the investment of "any funds for purposes of Illinois Municipal Retirement under the Pension Code". This prohibition does not include funds for social security and medicare only purposes

*** Total of Lines 54, 55

26 • APPENDIX C

SITE AND CONSTRUCTION/CAPITAL IMPROVEMENT FUND ($)

ESTIMATED DISBURSEMENTS/EXPENDITURES

DESCRIPTION	FUCT. NO.	(1) SALARIES	(2) EMPLOYEE BENEFITS	(3) PURCHASED SERVICES	(4) SUPPLIES AND MATERIALS	(5) CAPITAL OUTLAY	(6) OTHER OBJECTS	(7) TRANSFERS	(8) TUITION	(9) TOTAL
SUPPORT SERVICES	2000									
SUPPORT SERVICES-BUSINESS	2500									
1. Facilities Acquisition and Construction Services	2530				285,170.					285,170.
2. BUSINESS SUPPORT SERVICES-BUSINESS					285,170.					285,170.
3. OTHER SUPPORT SERVICES (ATTACH ITEMIZATION)	2900									
4. TOTAL SUPPORT SERVICES					285,170.					285,170.
NONPROGRAMMED CHARGES	4000									
PAYMENTS TO OTHER GOVT. UNITS (IN-STATE)	4100									
5. Payment for Special Education Programs	4120									
6. Payment for Vocational Education Programs	4140									
7. Other Payments to In-State Govt. Units (Attach Itemization)	4190									
8. TOTAL PAYMENTS TO OTHER GOVT. UNITS (IN-STATE)										
9. PAYMENTS TO OTHER GOVT. UNITS (OUT-OF-STATE)	4200									
10. TOTAL NONPROGRAMMED CHARGES										
11. PROVISION FOR CONTINGENCIES	6000						10,000.			10,000.
12. TOTAL ESTIMATED DISBURSEMENTS/EXPENDITURES*					285,170.		10,000.			295,170.
OTHER FINANCING USES	8000									
13. Permanent Transfer of Interest (Section 10-22.44)	8140									
14. Permanent Transfer from Site and Construction/Capital Improvement Fund (Section 10-22.14)	8150									
15. Other Uses (Attach Itemization)	8190									
16. TOTAL DISBURSEMENTS/EXPENDITURES AND OTHER FINANCING USES**					285,170.		10,000.			295,170.

* Total of Lines 4, 10, 11
** Total of Lines 12, 13, 14, 15

Page 25

APPENDIX C • 27

ESTIMATED DISBURSEMENTS/EXPENDITURES

Page #6

DESCRIPTION	FUCT. NO	(1) SALARIES	(2) EMPLOYEE BENEFITS	(3) PURCHASED SERVICES	(4) SUPPLIES AND MATERIALS	(5) CAPITAL OUTLAY	(6) OTHER OBJECTS	(7) TRANSFERS	(8) TUITION	(9) TOTAL
WORKING CASH FUND (7)										
OTHER FINANCING USES	8000									
1. Permanent Transfer of Working Cash Fund - Abolishment (Section 20-8)	8110									
2. Permanent Transfer of Working Cash Fund - Interest (Sec. 20-5)	8120									
3. TOTAL OTHER FINANCING USES										
RENT FUND (8)										
DEBT SERVICES	5000									
1. Corporate Personal Property Replacement Tax Anticipation Notes	5150									
2. State Aid Anticipation Certificates	5160									
3. DEBT SERVICE - OTHER (ATTACH ITEMIZATION)	5900									
4. TOTAL DEBT SERVICES										
5. TOTAL ESTIMATED DISBURSEMENTS/EXPENDITURES										
OTHER FINANCING USES	8000									
6. Permanent Transfer of Interest (Section 10-20.44)	8140									
7. Other Uses (Attach Itemization)	8190									
8. TOTAL DISBURSEMENTS/EXPENDITURES AND OTHER FINANCING USES										

28 • APPENDIX C

ESTIMATED DISBURSEMENTS/EXPENDITURES

DESCRIPTION	FUNCT. NO.	(1) SALARIES	(2) EMPLOYEE BENEFITS	(3) PURCHASED SERVICES	(4) SUPPLIES AND MATERIALS	(5) CAPITAL OUTLAY	(6) OTHER OBJECTS	(7) TRANSFERS	(8) NON-CAPITALIZED EQUIPMENT	TOTAL
FIRE PREVENTION AND SAFETY FUND (9)										
SUPPORT SERVICES	2000									
SUPPORT SERVICES - BUSINESS	2500				1,145,000.					1,145,000.
1. Facilities Acquisition and Construction Services	2530									
2. TOTAL SUPPORT SERVICES - BUSINESS					1,145,000.					1,145,000.
3. OTHER SUPPORT SERVICES (ATTACH ITEMIZATION)	2900									
4. TOTAL SUPPORT SERVICES					1,145,000.					1,145,000.
NONPROGRAMMED CHARGES	4000									
5. Other Payments to In-State Govt. Units (Attach Itemization)	4190									
6. TOTAL PAYMENTS TO OTHER GOVT. UNITS (IN-STATE)										
DEBT SERVICES	5000									
7. DEBT SERVICES - INTEREST	5100									
7. Tax Anticipation Warrants	5110									
8. TOTAL DEBT SERVICES - INTEREST										
9. PROVISION FOR CONTINGENCIES	6000									
10. TOTAL ESTIMATED DISBURSEMENTS/EXPENDITURES*					1,145,000.					1,145,000.
OTHER FINANCING USES	8000									
11. Permanent Transfer of Excess Accumulated Fire Prevention & Safety Tax Proceeds and Interest Earnings (Sec. 17-2.11)**	8160									
12. Permanent Transfer of Excess Accumulated Fire Prevention & Safety Bond Proceeds and Interest Earnings (Sec. 10-22.14)**	8170									
13. TOTAL DISBURSEMENTS/EXPENDITURES AND OTHER FINANCING USES***					1,145,000.					1,145,000.

* Total of Lines 4, 6, 8, 9

** Requires the secretary of the school board to notify the county clerk (within 30 days of the transfer approval) to abate an equal amount of taxes to be next extended.

*** Total of Lines 10, 11, 12

Page 26

☒ CASH BASIS   ☐ MODIFIED ACCRUAL

NOTE: A copy of Part III - Budget Summary and Part IV - Summary of Cash Transactions (pages 28-30 as adopted) must be forwarded to your Regional Superintendent by October 15, 1993. Regional Superintendents must forward the Budget Summaries for all the districts in their region to the Illinois State Board of Education, Finance Section, N-335, by November 1, 1993. (The School Code, Section 1A-8)

CODE _____
DISTRICT NAME: WEST AURORA SCHOOL DISTRICT 129
STREET: 80 S. River Street, P.O. Box 4430
CITY: Aurora   ZIP CODE: 60507
COUNTY: KANE   NO. 129

PART III - BUDGET SUMMARY

	Acct No.	(1) EDUCATIONAL	(2) OPERATIONS AND MAINTENANCE	(3) BOND AND INTEREST	(4) TRANSPORTATION	(5) MUNICIPAL RETIREMENT/ SOCIAL SECURITY	(6) SITE AND CONSTRUCTION/CAPITAL IMPROVEMENT	(7) WORKING CASH	(8) RENT	(9) FIRE PREVENTION AND SAFETY
1. ESTIMATED FUND BALANCES, July 1, 1993		(1) 7,100,993.	(47) 70,613.	(80) 1,645,080.	(125) 665,569.	(168) 735,549.	(205) -0-	(233) 3,680,630.	(256)	(284) 1,145,253.
RECEIPTS/REVENUE										
2. Local Sources	1000	(2) 20,326,880.	(48) 3,021,000.	(81) 3,209,813.	(126) 996,300.	(169) 1,000,000.	(206)	(234)	(257)	(285) 5,000.
3. Flow-through Receipts/Revenue from one LEA to another LEA	2000	(3) 175,000.	(49)	(82)	(127)	(170)	(207)			(286)
4. State Sources	3000	(4) 9,208,813.	(50) 670,000.	(83)	(128) 608,000.	(171)	(208)		(258)	(287)
5. Federal Sources	4000	(5) 1,924,676.	(51)	(84)	(129)	(172)	(209)		(259)	(288) 5,000.
6. TOTAL RECEIPTS/REVENUE		(6) 31,635,369.	(52) 3,691,000.	(85) 3,209,813.	(130) 1,604,300.	(173) 1,000,000.		(235)	(259)	
DISBURSEMENTS/EXPENDITURES	Func. No.									
7. Instruction	1000	(7) 24,357,771.	(53)		(131)	(174) 220,429.	(210)		(260)	(289)
8. Support Services	2000	(8) 7,379,621.	(54) 3,245,899.		(132) 1,902,178.	(175) 727,367.				(290) 1,145,000.
9. Community Services	3000	(9) 103,560.	(55)		(133)	(176) 2,204.	(211)			
10. Nonprogrammed Charges	4000	(10) 400,000.	(56) 42,870.		(134)	(177)			(260)	
11. Debt Services	5000	(11) 77,500.	(57)	(95) 3,159,812.	(135) 55,000.	(178) 50,000.	(212) 10,000.			
12. Provision for Contingencies	6000	(12) 1,000,000.	(58) 200,000.	(96) 50,000.	(136)	(179)	(213)		(261)	(291) 1,145,000.
13. TOTAL DISBURSEMENTS/ EXPENDITURES		(13) 33,318,452.	(59) 3,488,769.	(97) 3,209,812.	(137) 1,957,178.	(180) 1,000,000.	(214) 295,170.	(236)	(262)	
14. Excess of Receipts/Revenue Over (Under) Disbursements/Expenditures		(14) (1,683,083.)	(60) 202,231.	(98) 1.	(138) (352,878.)	(181) -0-	(215) (295,170.)	(237)	(263)	(292) (1,140,000.)
OTHER FINANCING SOURCES AND (USES)										
OTHER FINANCING SOURCES	7000	(15)								
15. Transfers From Other Funds	7100									

A Each fund balance should correspond to the fund balance reflected on the books as of June 30th - Balance Sheet Accounts # 703 and # 704 (audit figures, if available)

B Line 6 less Line 13

30 • APPENDIX C

PART III - BUDGET SUMMARY (Continued)

	ACCT NO	(1) EDUCATIONAL	(2) OPERATIONS AND MAINTENANCE	(3) BOND AND INTEREST	(4) TRANSPORTATION	(5) MUNICIPAL RETIREMENT/ SOCIAL SECURITY	(6) SITE AND CON- STRUCTION/CAPITAL IMPROVEMENT	(7) WORKING CASH	(8) RENT	(9) FIRE PREVENTION AND SAFETY
16. Sale of Bonds	7200									
17. Sale or Compensation for Loss of Fixed Assets	7300									
18. Other Sources	7400									
OTHER FINANCING (USES)	8000									
19. Transfers to Other Funds	6110	(300,000.)								
20. Other Uses	8190									
21. TOTAL OTHER FINANCING SOURCES AND (USES) c		(300,000.)					300,000.			
22. ESTIMATED FUND BALANCE, June 30, 1994 D		5,117,910.	272,844.	1,645,081.	312,691.	735,549.	4,830.	3,680,630.		5,253.

c Total of Lines 15-18 minus Lines 19 and 20   D Total of Lines 1, 14, 21

PART IV - SUMMARY OF CASH TRANSACTIONS

	Balance Sheet No.	(1) EDUCATIONAL	(2) OPERATIONS AND MAINTENANCE	(3) BOND AND INTEREST	(4) TRANSPORTATION	(5) MUNICIPAL RETIREMENT/ SOCIAL SECURITY	(6) SITE AND CON- STRUCTION/CAPITAL IMPROVEMENT	(7) WORKING CASH	(8) RENT	(9) FIRE PREVENTION AND SAFETY
1. ESTIMATED BALANCE ON HAND July 1, 1993 (Cash plus investments at cost) E	101-5 180	7,100,993.	70,613.	1,645,080.	665,569.	735,549.	-0-	10,630.		1,145,253.
2. TOTAL RECEIPTS AND OTHER FINANCING SOURCES		31,635,369.	3,691,000.	3,209,813.	1,604,300.	1,000,000.	300,000.			5,000.
3. Add Other Receipts:										
Loans from other Funds	430	3,670,000.						3,670,000.		
4. Loan Repayments from other Funds	150									
5. Corporate Personal Property Tax Replacement Tax Anticipation Notes	408									
6. Tax Anticipation Warrants Issued	407	4,500,000.								
7. Tax Anticipation Notes Issued	408									
8. Teachers' Orders Issued	409									
9. State Aid Anticipation Certificates Issued	410									

E Cash plus investments must be greater than or equal to zero.
F For cash basis budgets, this total will equal the Budget Summary - Part III - Total Receipts/Revenue (Line 6) and Other Financing Sources (Lines 15, 16, 17, 18)

APPENDIX C • 31

Page 30

PART IV - SUMMARY OF CASH TRANSACTIONS (Continued)

	Balance Sheet No.	(1) EDUCATIONAL	(2) OPERATIONS AND MAINTENANCE	(3) BOND AND INTEREST	(4) TRANSPORTATION	(5) MUNICIPAL RETIREMENT/ SOCIAL SECURITY	SITE AND CON- STRUCTION/CAPITAL IMPROVEMENT	(7) WORKING CASH	(8) RENT	(9) FIRE PREVENTION AND SAFETY
10. Other (Attach Itemization)		(31)	(76)	(112)	(153)	(183)	(224)	(246)	(273)	(305)
		(32)	(77)	(113)	(154)	(184)	(225)	(247)	(274)	(306)
		8,170,000.								5,000.
11. Total Other Receipts (Total of Lines 3-10)		(33)	(78)	(114)	(155)	(185)	(226)	(248)	(275)	(307)
		39,805,369.	3,691,000.	3,209,813.	1,604,300.	1,000,000.	300,000.	3,670,000.		
12. TOTAL RECEIPTS, OTHER FINANCING SOURCES, AND OTHER RECEIPTS (Total of Lines 2 and 11)		(34)	(79)	(115)	(156)	(186)	(227)	(249)	(276)	(308)
		46,905,362.	3,761,613.	4,854,893.	2,269,869.	1,735,549.	300,00.	3,680,630.		1,150,253.
13. TOTAL AMOUNT AVAILABLE (Total of Lines 1 and 12)		(35)	(80)	(116)	(157)	(187)	(228)	(250)	(277)	(309)
		33,618,452.	3,488,769.	3,209,812.	1,957,178.	1,000,000.	264,795.			1,145,000.
14. TOTAL DISBURSEMENTS AND OTHER FINANCING USES G	150	(36)								
15. Add Other Disbursements: Loans to Other Funds H		(37)	(81)		(158)			(251)		(310)
								3,670,000.		
16. Loan Repayments to other Funds	430	(38)	(82)	(322)	(159)	(326)	(330)		(278)	(311)
		3,670,000.								
17. Corporate Personal Property Replacement Tax Anticipation Notes Redeemed	505	(39)	(83)	(117)	(160)	(197)				(312)
18. Tax Anticipation Warrants Redeemed	407	(40)	(84)	(118)	(161)	(198)				(313)
		4,500,000.								
19. Tax Anticipation Notes Redeemed	408	(41)		(119)	(162)	(199)				
20. Teacher/ Orders Redeemed	409	(42)	(85)	(120)	(163)	(200)	(331)		(279)	(314)
21. State Aid Anticipation Certificates Redeemed	410	(43)	(86)	(121)	(164)	(201)	(229)	(252)	(280)	(315)
22. Other (Attach Itemization)		(44)	(87)	(122)	(165)	(202)	(230)	(253)	(281)	(316)
		8,170,000.								
23. Total Other Disbursements (Total of Lines 15-22)		(45)	(88)	(123)	(166)	(203)	(231)	(254)	(282)	
		41,788,452.	3,488,769.	3,209,812.	1,957,178.	1,000,000.	264,795.	3,670,000.		1,145,000.
24. TOTAL DISBURSEMENTS, OTHER FINANCING USES, AND OTHER DISBURSEMENTS (Total of Lines 14 and 23)		(46)	(89)	(124)	(167)	(204)	(232)	(255)	(283)	(317)
25. ESTIMATED BALANCE ON HAND 6-30-94 Cash plus Investments at cost (Total of Line 13 minus 24)	101-5 180	5,117,910.	272,844.	1,645,081.	312,691.	735,549.	4,830.	10,630.		5,253.

G For cash basis budgets, this total will equal the Budget Summary - Part III Total Disbursements/Expenditures (Line 13) and Other Financing Uses (Lines 19, 20).
H Working Cash Fund loans may be made to any district fund for which taxes are levied (Section 20-5 of the School Code).
I Cash plus investments must be greater than or equal to zero.

APPENDIX D

Federal Single Program Audit 1993-94

The following is a sample of a Federal Single Program Audit for 1993-94 for a school district in Illinois and relates to the budget found in Appendix C. The Federal Single Program Audit Format is suggested by Handbook II. Each school district's auditor will prepare this audit and the format may vary from auditor to auditor. This example is provided for readers who may not have access to such a document. This example is also provided to facilitate instruction in that all students and instructors can work from a uniform set of documents and financial data. This appendix relates directly to Appendix C, E and I.

2 • APPENDIX D

ILLINOIS STATE BOARD OF EDUCATION
100 North First Street
Springfield, Illinois 62777-0001

ANNUAL FEDERAL FINANCIAL - COMPLIANCE SECTION
District/Joint Agreement
June 30, 1994

[ ]Cash Basis [X]Modified Accrual Basis

SCHOOL DISTRICT		-Received by ISBE-
Administrative Agent if Joint Agreement		
Street Address ADDRESS		
City CITY	Zip Code ZIP	
Please Print District Superintendent or Joint Agreement Administrator Name: BUSINESS MANAGER		Audit Firm I.D. Code: NUMBER
		Name of Audit Firm: AUDIT FIRM
Title of Individual Above if NOT a District Superintendent		Address of Audit Firm: ADDRESS
		CITY, STATE
		Name of Audit Supervisor: AUDITOR
Telephone Number: NUMBER		CPA Firm Registration #: I.D. NUMBER
Date and Signature:		CPA Firm Telephone #: NUMBER

PLEASE MAKE SURE THE FOLLOWING ITEMS ATTACHED TO THIS FORM:

1. Schedule of Federal Financial Assistance (6/30/94)
2. Auditors' Report on Number 1 Above
3. Internal Control Structure Report on Federal Programs
4. Report on Compliance with General Requirements of Federal Programs
5. Report on Compliance with Specific Requirements of Major Federal Programs.
6. Report on Compliance with Program Requirements of Nonmajor Program Transactions
7. Schedule of Findings and Questioned Costs/Corrective Action Plan (ISBE 62-23) - this must include ALL repeated Prior year's Findings

ISBE 62-18 (3/94)

Smith, Jones & Co., Ltd.
Certified Public Accountants
1 Main Street • Anytown, IL 66321
Telephone: 312/555-0000 • Fax: 312/555-9999

September 12, 1994

Board of Education
School District
111 Main Street
Anytown, IL 66321

We have audited the combined financial statements of   SCHOOL DISTRICT   as of and for the year ended June 30, 1994, and have issued our report thereon dated September 12, 1994. These combined financial statements are the responsibility of   SCHOOL DISTRICT   management. Our responsibility is to express an opinion on these combined financial statements based on our audit. In our report, our opinion was qualified because   SCHOOL DISTRICT   does not maintain a detailed record of the historical cost of its fixed assets.

We conducted our audit in accordance with generally accepted auditing standards; *Government Auditing Standards*, issued by the Comptroller General of the United States; and the provisions of Office of Management and Budget (OMB) Circular A-128, "Audits of State and Local Governments." Those standards and OMB Circular A-128 require that we plan and perform the audit to obtain reasonable assurance about whether the combined financial statements are free of material misstatement. An audit includes examining, on a test basis, evidence supporting the amounts and disclosures in the combined financial statements. An audit also includes assessing the accounting principles used and significant estimates made by management, as well as evaluating the overall financial statement presentation. We believe that our audit provides a reasonable basis for our opinion.

Our audit was conducted for the purpose of forming an opinion on the combined financial statements of   SCHOOL DISTRICT , taken as a whole. The accompanying schedule of federal financial assistance is presented for purposes of additional analysis and is not a required part of the combined financial statements. The information in that schedule has been subjected to the auditing procedures applied in the audit of the combined financial statements and, in our opinion, is fairly presented in all material respects in relation to the combined financial statements taken as a whole.

/Signed/
Smith, Jones & Co., Ltd.

4 • APPENDIX D

ILLINOIS STATE BOARD OF EDUCATION
100 North First Street
Springfield, Illinois 62777-0001

LEA SCHEDULE OF FEDERAL FINANCIAL ASSISTANCE
Year Ended June 30, 1994

Original Grantor, Pass-Through Grantor and Program Name	Fund and Account Number (A)	CFDA Number (B)	ISBE Project Number (C)	Receipts/Revenues 7-1-92 to 6-30-93 (D)	Receipts/Revenues 7-1-93 to 6-30-94 (E)	Expend./Disbmt. 7-1-92 to 6-30-93 (F)	Expend./Disbmt. 7-1-93 to 6-30-94 (G)	Oblig./ Encumb. (H)	Final Status (I)	Budget (J)
Illinois State Board of Education:										
(M) Federal National School Lunch - FY '93	1-4460	10.555	IDD5510	370,129	65,277	500,357	2,203	-	502,560	N/A
(M) Federal National School Lunch - FY '94	1-4460	10.555	IED5510	-	442,684	-	381,517	-	381,517	N/A
(M) Fed National School Breakfast - FY '93	1-4464	10.553	WDD5510	17,941	1,947	23,155	-	-	23,155	N/A
(M) Fed National School Breakfast - FY '94	1-4464	10.553	WED5510	-	19,259	-	16,674	-	16,674	N/A
(M) Drug-Free Schools - FY '93	1-4490	84.186	3N88578	68,578	-	66,848	1,287	-	68,135	82,890
(M) Drug-Free Schools - FY '94	1-4490	84.186	3088578	-	49,474	-	60,901	-	60,901	82,304
(M) Title 2 - Math & Science - FY '93	1-4475	84.164	F305810	24,379	5,612	26,284	606	-	26,890	35,601
(M) Title 2 - Math & Science - FY '94	1-4475	84.164	F405810	-	25,471	-	23,298	-	23,298	30,477
(M) Chapter 1 - Low Income - FY '93	1-4441	84.010	R305930	521,287	167,811	470,358	202,738	-	673,096	700,025
(M) Chapter 1 - Low Income - FY '94	1-4441	84.010	R405930	-	629,680	-	521,805	-	521,805	679,732
(M) Chapter 2 - ESEA - FY '93	1-4470	84.151	B32825A	57,018	8,349	62,768	6,395	-	69,163	73,715
(M) Chapter 2 - ESEA - FY '94	1-4470	84.151	B42825A	-	48,574	-	59,044	989	60,033	63,071
Chapter 2 - Discretionary - FY '93	1-4470	84.151	C3UE061	16,248	-	8,347	2,891	-	11,238	16,248
Chapter 2 - Discretionary - FY '94	1-4470	84.151	C4UE061	-	9,191	-	16,087	-	16,087	20,095

(M) Indicated major federal financial assistance program.
NOTE: This Schedule of Federal Financial Assistance is prepared in the modified accrual basis of accounting. The 6/30/93 Schedule of Federal Financial Assistance was prepared on the cash basis. This may cause some differences in project year FY '93.

ILLINOIS STATE BOARD OF EDUCATION
100 North First Street
Springfield, Illinois 62777-0001

LEA SCHEDULE OF FEDERAL FINANCIAL ASSISTANCE
Year Ended June 30, 1994

Original Grantor, Pass-Through Grantor and Program Name	Fund and Account Number (A)	CFDA Number (B)	ISBE Project Number (C)	Receipts/Revenues 7-1-92 to 6-30-93 (D)	Receipts/Revenues 7-1-93 to 6-30-94 (E)	Expend./Disbmt. 7-1-92 to 6-30-93 (F)	Expend./Disbmt. 7-1-93 to 6-30-94 (G)	Oblig./ Encumb. (H)	Final Status (I)	Budget (J)
Illinois State Board of Education:										
Job Training Partnership Reform Act	1-4530	17.250	DE8320R		7,692		6,998		6,998	7,308
(M) IDEA Flow-Through - FY '93	1-4454	84.027	N325930	234,626	-	217,311	2,898	-	220,209	222,160
(M) IDEA Flow-Through - FY '94	1-4454	84.027	N425930	-	251,424	-	187,145	-	187,145	283,686
(M) Chapter 1 - Even Start - FY '94	1-4445	84.213	I405930	-	123,411	-	105,660	-	105,660	128,894
Chapter 1 - Program Improvement - FY '94	1-4490	84.218	042825A	-	2,000	-	1,931	-	1,931	2,000
TOTAL ISBE				1,310,206	1,857,856	1,375,428	1,600,078	989	2,976,495	N/A
Northwestern Illinois Association:										
(M) Chapter 1 - Handicapped - FY '93	1-4442	84.009	S320300	55,367	3,603	67,977	-	-	67,977	67,977
(M) Chapter 1 - Handicapped - FY '94	1-4442	84.009	S420300	-	33,459	-	33,459	-	33,459	56,637
TOTAL NIA				55,367	37,062	67,977	33,459	-	101,436	N/A

(M) Indicated major federal financial assistance program.
NOTE: This Schedule of Federal Financial Assistance is prepared in the modified accrual basis of accounting.
The 6/30/93 Schedule of Federal Financial Assistance was prepared on the cash basis. This may cause some differences in project year FY '93.

6 • APPENDIX D

ILLINOIS STATE BOARD OF EDUCATION
100 North First Street
Springfield, Illinois 62777-0001

LEA SCHEDULE OF FEDERAL FINANCIAL ASSISTANCE
Year Ended June 30, 1994

Original Grantor, Pass-Through Grantor and Program Name	Fund and Account Number (A)	CFDA Number (B)	ISBE Project Number (C)	Receipts/Revenues 7-1-92 to 6-30-93 (D)	Receipts/Revenues 7-1-93 to 6-30-94 (E)	Expend./Disbmt. 7-1-92 to 6-30-93 (F)	Expend./Disbmt. 7-1-93 to 6-30-94 (G)	Oblig./ Encumb. (H)	Final Status (I)	Budget (J)
Vocational Education for Employment System:										
V.E. Occ. Homemaking FY '93	1-2200	84.049	43C130G	-	1,272	1,561	-	-	1,561	1,561
V.E. Occ. Homemaking FY '94	1-2200	84.049	44C130G	-	1,449	-	1,449	-	1,449	1,449
(M) V.E. Secondary FY '93	1-2200	84.048	INC1300	36,017	1,328	48,807	-	-	48,807	42,572
(M) V.E. Secondary FY '94	1-2200	84.048	IOC1300	-	50,901	-	47,845	-	47,845	50,745
(M) VE. Sex Equity FY '93	1-2200	84.048	NND1300	-	2,855	-	2,855	-	2,855	2,855
(M) VE. Sex Equity FY '94	1-2200	84.048	NOD1300	-	16,366	-	5,457	-	5,457	5,457
TOTAL VEES				36,017	74,171	50,368	57,606	-	107,974	N/A
Illinois Department of Rehabilitation Services:										
STEP - FY '93	1-4480	84.126	930 121326	14,521	3,004	22,882	-	-	22,882	23,840
STEP - FY '94	1-4480	84.126	940 121326	-	41,217	-	18,292	-	18,292	18,292
TOTAL DORS				14,521	44,221	22,882	18,292	-	41,174	N/A

(M) Indicated major federal financial assistance program.
NOTE: This Schedule of Federal Financial Assistance is prepared in the modified accrual basis of accounting. The 6/30/93 Schedule of Federal Financial Assistance was prepared on the cash basis. This may cause some differences in project year FY '93.

APPENDIX D • 7

ILLINOIS STATE BOARD OF EDUCATION
100 North First Street
Springfield, Illinois 62777-0001

LEA SCHEDULE OF FEDERAL FINANCIAL ASSISTANCE
Year Ended June 30, 1994

Original Grantor, Pass-Through Grantor and Program Name	Fund and Account Number (A)	CFDA Number (B)	ISBE Project Number (C)	Receipts/Revenues 7-1-92 to 6-30-93 (D)	Receipts/Revenues 7-1-93 to 6-30-94 (E)	Expend./Disbmt. 7-1-92 to 6-30-93 (F)	Expend./Disbmt. 7-1-93 to 6-30-94 (G)	Oblig./ Encumb. (H)	Final Status (I)	Budget (J)
U.S. Department of Education:										
Impact Aid - FY '94	1-4110	84.041	23-IL-94-1828	-	13,070	-	13,070	-	13,070	N/A
ESEA - Title VII Bilingual - FY '94	1-4325	84.003	T-003A-90082-94	-	28,563	-	75,985	-	75,985	75,985
TOTAL USDE				-	41,633	-	89,055	-	89,055	N/A
TOTAL FEDERAL FINANCIAL ASSISTANCE				1,416,111	2,054,943	1,516,655	1,798,490	989	3,316,134	N/A

(M) Indicated major federal financial assistance program.
NOTE: This Schedule of Federal Financial Assistance is prepared in the modified accrual basis of accounting. The 6/30/93 Schedule of Federal Financial Assistance was prepared on the cash basis. This may cause some differences in project year FY '93.

Smith, Jones & Co., Ltd.
Certified Public Accountants
1 Main Street • Anytown, IL 66321
Telephone: 312/555-0000 • Fax: 312/555-9999

September 12, 1994

Board of Education
School District
111 Main Street
Anytown, IL 66321

We have audited the combined financial statements of   SCHOOL DISTRICT   for the year ended June 30, 1994, and have issued our report thereon dated September 12, 1994. We have also audited the compliance of   SCHOOL DISTRICT   with requirements applicable to major federal financial assistance programs and have issued our report thereon dated September 12, 1994. In our report, our opinion was qualified because SCHOOL DISTRICT does not maintain a detailed record of the historical cost of its fixed assets. Therefore, we were unable to obtain sufficient evidence to form an opinion regarding the basis on which the general fixed assets are stated.

We conducted our audits in accordance with generally accepted auditing standards; *Government Auditing Standards*, issued by the Comptroller General of the United States; and Office of Management and Budget (OMB) Circular A-128, "Audits of State and Local Governments." Those standards and OMB Circular A-128 require that we plan and perform the audit to obtain reasonable assurance about whether the combined financial statements are free of material misstatement and whether Aurora Schools District 129, complied with laws and regulations, noncompliance with which would be material to a major federal financial assistance program.

In planning and performing our audits for the year ended June 30, 1994, we considered the internal control structure of   SCHOOL DISTRICT   , in order to determine our auditing procedures for the purpose of expressing our opinions on the combined financial statements of   SCHOOL DISTRICT   , and on the compliance of   SCHOOL DISTRICT   , with requirements applicable to major programs and to report on the internal control structure in accordance with OMB Circular A-128. This report addresses our consideration of internal control structure policies and procedures relevant to compliance with requirements applicable to federal financial assistance programs. We have addressed internal control structure policies and procedures relevant to our audit of the combined financial statements in a separate report dated September 12, 1994.

APPENDIX D • 9

_____ Page two

The management of   SCHOOL DISTRICT   is responsible for establishing and maintaining an internal control structure. In fulfilling this responsibility, estimates and judgements by management are required to assess the expected benefits and relevant costs of internal control structure policies and procedures. The objectives of an internal control structure are to provide management with reasonable, but not absolute, assurance that assets are safeguarded against loss from unauthorized use or disposition, that transactions are executed in accordance with management's authorization and recorded properly to permit the preparation of combined financial statements in accordance with generally accepted accounting principles, and that federal financial assistance programs are managed in compliance with applicable laws and regulations. Because of inherent limitations in any internal control structure, errors, irregularities, or instances of noncompliance may nevertheless occur and not be detected. Also, projection of any evaluation of the structure to future periods is subject to the risk that procedures may become inadequate because of changes in conditions or that the effectiveness of the design and operation of policies and procedures may deteriorate.

For the purpose of this report, we have classified the significant internal control structure policies and procedures used in administering federal financial assistance programs in the following categories:

      Cash Disbursements
      Payroll Expenditures
      General Requirements
        Political activity
        Civil rights
        Allowable costs/cost principles
        Cash management
        Drug-Free Workplace Act
        Specific requirements
      Specific Requirements
        Types of services allowed or unallowed
        Eligibility
        Matching, level of effort, or earmarking
        Reporting

For all of the internal control structure categories listed above, we obtained an understanding of the design of relevant policies and procedures and determined whether they have been placed in operation, and we assessed control risk.

During the year ended June 30, 1994,   SCHOOL DISTRICT   expended 94% of its total federal financial assistance under major federal financial assistance programs.

_____Page three

We performed tests of controls, as required by OMB Circular A-128, to evaluate the effectiveness of the design and operation of internal control structure policies and procedures that we considered relevant to preventing or detecting material noncompliance with specific requirements, general requirements, and requirements governing claims for advances and reimbursements and amounts claimed or used for matching that are applicable to each of  major federal financial assistance programs, which are identified in the accompanying Schedule of Federal Financial Assistance. Our procedures were less in scope than would be necessary to render an opinion on these internal control structure policies and procedures. Accordingly, we do not express such an opinion.

Our consideration of the internal control structure would not necessarily disclose all matters in the internal control structure that might be material weaknesses under standards established by the American Institute of Certified Public Accountants. A material weakness is a reportable condition in which the design or operation of one or more of the internal control structure elements does not reduce to a relatively low level the risk that would be material to a federal financial assistance program, noncompliance with laws and regulations may occur and not be detected within a timely period by employees in the normal course of performing their assigned functions. We noted no matters involving the internal control structure and its operation that we consider to be material weaknesses as defined above.

However, we noted certain matters involving the internal control structure and its operations that we have reported to the management of Aurora Schools District 129, in a separate letter dated September 12, 1994.

This report is intended for the information of the Board of Education, the Illinois State Board of Education and federal granting agencies. However, this report is a matter of public record, and its distribution is not limited.

/Signed/
Smith, Jones & Co., Ltd.

APPENDIX D • 11

Smith, Jones & Co., Ltd.
Certified Public Accountants
1 Main Street • Anytown, IL 66321
Telephone: 312/555-0000 • Fax: 312/555-9999

September 12, 1994

Board of Education
School District
111 Main Street
Anytown, IL 66321

We have audited the financial statements of SCHOOL DISTRICT , as of and for the year ended June 30, 1994, and have issued our report thereon dated September 12, 1994. In our report, our opinion was qualified because SCHOOL DISTRICT does not maintain a detailed record of the historical cost of its fixed assets. Therefore, we were unable to obtain sufficient evidence to form an opinion regarding the basis on which the general fixed assets are stated.

We have also audited SCHOOL DISTRICT compliance with the requirements governing types of services allowed or unallowed; eligibility; matching, level of effort, or earmarking; reporting; special tests and provisions; claims for advances and reimbursements; and amounts claimed or used for matching that are applicable to each of its major federal financial assistance programs, which are identified in the accompanying Schedule of Federal Financial Assistance, for the year ended June 30, 1994. The management of SCHOOL DISTRICT , is responsible for SCHOOL DISTRICT compliance with those requirements. Our responsibility is to express an opinion on compliance with those requirements based on our audit.

We conducted our audit of compliance with those requirements in accordance with generally accepted auditing standards; *Government Auditing Standards*, issued by the Comptroller General of the United States; and Office of Management and Budget Circular A-128, "Audits of State and Local Governments." Those standards and OMB Circular A-128 require that we plan and perform the audit to obtain reasonable assurance about whether material noncompliance with the requirements referred to above occurred. An audit includes examining, on a test basis, evidence about SCHOOL DISTRICT compliance with those requirements. We believe that our audit provides a reasonable basis for our opinion.

The results of our audit procedures did not disclose any immaterial instances of noncompliance with the requirements referred to above.

Page two

In our opinion, SCHOOL DISTRICT complied, in all material respects, with the requirements governing types of services allowed or unallowed; eligibility; matching, level of effort, or earmarking; reporting; special tests and provisions; claims for advances and reimbursements; and amounts claimed or used for matching that are applicable to each of its major federal financial assistance programs for the year ended June 30, 1994.

This report is intended for the information of the Board of Education, the Illinois State Board of Education, management and federal granting agencies. However, this report is a matter of public record, and its distribution is not limited.

/Signed/
Smith, Jones & Co., Ltd.

APPENDIX D • 13

Smith, Jones & Co., Ltd.
Certified Public Accountants
1 Main Street • Anytown, IL 66321
Telephone: 312/555-0000 • Fax: 312/555-9999

September 12, 1994

Board of Education
School District
111 Main Street
Anytown, IL 66321

We have audited the combined financial statements of SCHOOL DISTRICT, as of and for the year ended June 30, 1994, and have issued our report thereon dated September 12, 1994. In our report, our opinion was qualified because SCHOOL DISTRICT does not maintain a detailed record of the historical cost of its fixed assets. In our report, our opinion was qualified because SCHOOL DISTRICT does not maintain a detailed record of the historical cost of its fixed assets. Therefore, we were unable to obtain sufficient evidence to form an opinion regarding the basis on which the general fixed assets are stated.

We have applied procedures to test SCHOOL DISTRICT compliance with the following requirements applicable to its federal financial assistance programs, which are identified in the Schedule of Federal Financial Assistance, for the year ended June 30, 1994:

> Political activity
> Civil rights
> Allowable costs/cost principles
> Drug-Free Workplace Act
> Cash management

Our procedures were limited to the applicable procedures described in the Office of Management and Budget's "Compliance Supplement for Single Audits of State and Local Governments." Our procedures were substantially less in scope than an audit, the objective of which is the expression of an opinion on SCHOOL DISTRICT compliance with the requirements listed in the preceding paragraph. Accordingly, we do not express such an opinion.

Page two

With respect to the items tested, the results of those procedures disclosed no material instances of noncompliance with the requirements listed in the second paragraph of this report. With respect to items not tested, nothing came to our attention that caused us to believe that   SCHOOL DISTRICT   had not complied, in all material respects, with those requirements. Also, the results of our procedures did not disclose any immaterial instances of noncompliance with those requirements.

This report is intended for the information of the Board of Education, the Illinois State Board of Education, management and federal granting agencies. However, this report is a matter of public record, and its distribution is not limited.

/Signed/
Smith, Jones & Co., Ltd.

APPENDIX E

1993-94 Audit

The following is a sample audit for 1993-94 for a school district in Illinois and relates to the budget found in Appendix C. The audit format shown is suggested by the Illinois State Board of Education. Each school district's auditor will prepare this audit, with the format used varying slightly from auditor to auditor. This example of an audit is provided for readers who may not have access to such a document. This example is also provided to facilitate instruction in that all students and instructors can work from a uniform set of documents and financial data. This Appendix relates directly to Appendix C, D and I.

SCHOOL DISTRICT

FINANCIAL STATEMENTS

FOR THE YEAR ENDED JUNE 30, 1994
AND
INDEPENDENT AUDITORS' REPORT

TABLE OF CONTENTS

JUNE 30, 1994

EXHIBIT		*PAGE*
	Independent Auditors' Report	1

COMBINED FINANCIAL STATEMENTS

A	Combined Balance Sheet	3
B	Combined Statement of Revenues, Expenditures and Changes in Fund Balances	5
C	Combined Statement of Revenues, Expenditures and Changes in Fund Balances - Budget and Actual	7
	Notes to Financial Statements	9

COMBINING AND INDIVIDUAL FUND FINANCIAL STATEMENTS

General Funds

D-1	Combining Balance Sheet	27
D-2	Combining Statements of Revenues, Expenditures and Changes in Fund Balances	28
D-3	**Educational Accounts** - Statement of Revenues, Expenditures and Changes in Fund Balances - Budget and Actual	29
D-4	**Operations and Maintenance Accounts** - Statement of Revenues, Expenditures and Changes in Fund Balances - Budget and Actual	39

4 • APPENDIX E

TABLE OF CONTENTS

JUNE 30, 1994

EXHIBIT **PAGE**

COMBINING AND INDIVIDUAL FUND FINANCIAL STATEMENTS (CONTINUED)

Special Revenue Funds

E-1	Combining Balance Sheet	41
E-2	Combining Statement of Revenues, Expenditures and Changes in Fund Balances	42
E-3	**Transportation Fund** - Statement of Revenues, Expenditures and Changes in Fund Balances - Budget and Actual	43
E-4	**Illinois Municipal Retirement Fund** - Statement of Cash Receipts, Expenditures and Changes in Fund Balances - Budget and Actual	44
E-5	**Hope Wall Special Education Joint Agreement** - Statement of Cash Receipts, Expenditures and Changes in Fund Balances - Budget and Actual	46

Debt Service Fund

F-1	Balance Sheet	50
F-2	**Bond and Interest Fund** - Combining Statement of Revenues, Expenditures and Changes in Fund Balance	51

Capital Projects Funds

G-1	Balance Sheet	52
G-2	Combining Statement of Revenues, Expenditures and Changes in Fund Balance - Budget and Actual	53
G-3	**Site and Construction Fund** - Statement of Revenues, Expenditures and Changes in Fund Balance - Budget and Actual	54
G-4	**Fire Prevention and Life Safety Fund** - Statement of Revenues, Expenditures and Changes in Fund Balance - Budget and Actual	55

TABLE OF CONTENTS

JUNE 30, 1994

EXHIBIT **PAGE**

COMBINING AND INDIVIDUAL FUND FINANCIAL STATEMENTS (CONCLUDED)

Fiduciary Funds

H-1 Combining Balance Sheet 56

H-2 **Working Cash Fund** - Statement of Revenues,
Expenditures and Changes in Fund Balance - Budget and Actual 57

6 • APPENDIX E

TABLE OF CONTENTS
JUNE 30, 1994

SCHEDULE   **PAGE**

SUPPLEMENTARY SCHEDULES

1	Three Year Summary of Assessed Valuations, Tax Rates, Extensions and Collections	58
2	Operating Cost and Tuition Charge	59
3	Schedule of Bonds Outstanding - Fire Prevention and Safety Bonds Issued July 1, 1984	60
4	Schedule of Bonds Outstanding - Fire Prevention and Safety Bonds Issued June 30, 1987	61
5	Schedule of Bonds Outstanding - Fire Prevention and Safety Bonds Issued June 1, 1991	62
6	Schedule of Bonds Outstanding - Fire Prevention and Safety Bonds Issued September 1, 1991	63
7	Illinois Municipal Retirement Fund - Analysis of Funding Progress	64

FEDERAL COMPLIANCE REPORTS

Independent Auditors' Report on Compliance
Based on an Audit of Combined Financial Statements
Performed in Accordance with Government Auditing Standards 65

Independent Auditors' Report on the Internal Control
Structure Based on an Audit of Combined Financial Statements
Performed in Accordance with Government Auditing Standards 66

APPENDIX E • 7

Smith, Jones & Co., Ltd.
Certified Public Accountants
1 Main Street • Anytown, IL 66321
Telephone: 312/555-0000 • Fax: 312/555-9999

INDEPENDENT AUDITORS' REPORT

September 12, 1994

Board of Education
School District
111 Main Street
Anytown, IL 66321

We have audited the accompanying combined financial statements of SCHOOL DISTRICT as of and for the year ended June 30, 1994, as listed in the table of contents. These combined financial statements are the responsibility of SCHOOL DISTRICT management. Our responsibility is to express an opinion on these combined financial statements based on our audit.

Except as discussed in the following paragraph, we conducted our audit in accordance with generally accepted auditing standards; <u>Government Auditing Standards</u>, issued by the Comptroller General of the United States; and the provisions of Office of Management and Budget Circular A-128, "Audits of State and Local Governments." Those standards, and OMB Circular A-128, require that we plan and perform the audit to obtain reasonable assurance about whether the combined financial statements are free of material misstatement. An audit includes examining, on a test basis, evidence supporting the amounts and disclosures in the combined financial statements. An audit also includes assessing the accounting principles used and significant estimates made by management, as well as evaluating the overall combined financial statement presentation. We believe that our audit provides a reasonable basis for our opinion.

Because the District does not maintain a detailed record of the historical cost of its fixed assets, we were unable to obtain sufficient evidence to form an opinion regarding the basis on which the general fixed assets are stated.

In our opinion, except for the effect of such adjustments, if any, as might have been disclosed with respect to the General Fixed Assets had historical records been available, the combined financial statements referred to above present fairly, in all material respects, the financial position of SCHOOL DISTRICT as of June 30, 1994, and the results of its operations for the year then ended in conformity with generally accepted accounting principles.

Our audit was made for the purpose of forming an opinion on the combined financial statements taken as a whole. The combining and individual fund financial statements for the year ended June 30, 1994, the individual fund statement of revenues, expenditures and changes in fund balance - budget and actual for the year ended June 30, 1993, and the schedules listed in the accompanying table of contents are presented for purposes of additional analysis and are not a required part of the combined financial statements of _____SCHOOL DISTRICT_____ Such information, except for the individual fund statements of revenues, expenditures and changes in fund balance for the year ended June 30, 1993, which were subjected to the auditing procedures applied in the audit of the combined financial statements for the year ended June 30, 1993, performed by other auditors, has been subjected to the auditing procedures applied in the audit of the combined financial statements for the year ended June 30, 1994 and, in our opinion is fairly presented in all material respects in relation to the combined financial statements taken as a whole.

/Signed/
Smith, Jones & Co., Ltd.

APPENDIX E • 9

ALL FUND TYPES AND ACCOUNT GROUPS
COMBINED BALANCE SHEET
JUNE 30, 1994
WITH COMPARATIVE TOTALS FOR JUNE 30, 1993

	GOVERNMENTAL FUND TYPES			
	GENERAL	SPECIAL REVENUE	DEBT SERVICE	CAPITAL PROJECTS
ASSETS AND OTHER DEBITS				
Cash	$ 541,302	$ 1,015,175	$ 736,823	$ 1,074,904
Investments	15,743,000	950,000	925,000	-
Receivables (net of allowance for uncollectibles):				
Property taxes	10,876,113	987,657	1,601,847	-
Intergovernmental	808,144	179,591	-	-
Due from other funds	-	-	-	-
Inventory	315,456	38,878	-	-
Other current assets	-	-	-	-
Fixed assets	-	-	-	-
Amount available for retirement of general long-term debt	-	-	-	-
Amount to be provided from future receipts	-	-	-	-
Total assets and other debits	$28,284,015	$ 3,171,301	$ 3,263,670	$ 1,074,904
LIABILITIES, FUND EQUITY, AND OTHER CREDITS				
LIABILITIES				
Cash deficit	$ 2,028,808	$ -	$ -	$ -
Accounts payable	227,685	87,935	-	-
Wages payable	3,852,811	75,060	-	-
Due to activity fund Organizations	-	-	-	-
Anticipation warrants payable	3,000,000	-	-	-
Due to other funds	3,670,000	-	-	-
Deferred revenue	10,592,747	961,925	1,560,112	-
Other current liabilities	819,230	491,783	-	-
Bonds payable	-	-	-	-
Early retirement agreements payable	-	-	-	-
Total liabilities	24,191,281	1,616,703	1,560,112	-
FUND EQUITY AND OTHER CREDITS				
Invested in general fixed assets	-	-	-	-
FUND BALANCES				
Reserved:				
Reserved for inventory	315,456	38,878	-	-
Unreserved:				
Undesignated	3,777,278	1,515,720	1,703,558	1,074,904
Total fund equity and other credits	4,092,734	1,554,598	1,703,558	1,074,904
Total liabilities, fund equity, and other credits	$28,284,015	$ 3,171,301	$ 3,263,670	$ 1,074,904

See Accompanying Notes to Combined Financial Statements

Exhibit A

FIDUCIARY FUND TYPES TRUST AND AGENCY	ACCOUNT GROUPS GENERAL FIXED ASSETS	GENERAL LONG-TERM DEBT	TOTAL (MEMORANDUM ONLY) 1994	1993
366,704	$ -	$ -	$ 3,734,908	$ 4,443,357
-	-	-	17,618,000	5,000,000
-	-	-	13,465,617	23,502,100
-	-	-	987,735	1,471,327
3,670,000	-	-	3,670,000	5,086,340
-	-	-	354,334	342,231
-	-	-	-	131,519
-	36,360,813	-	36,360,813	35,711,884
-	-	1,703,558	1,703,558	1,765,497
-	-	9,055,960	9,055,960	9,256,636
$ 4,036,704	$36,360,813	$10,759,518	$86,950,925	$86,710,891
$ -	$ -	$ -	$ 2,028,808	$ -
-	-	-	315,620	329,393
-	-	-	3,927,871	3,758,935
356,074	-	-	356,074	364,725
-	-	-	3,000,000	4,500,000
-	-	-	3,670,000	5,086,340
-	-	-	13,114,784	11,733,808
-	-	-	1,311,013	1,538,783
-	-	7,345,000	7,345,000	9,845,000
-	-	3,414,518	3,414,518	1,177,133
356,074	-	10,759,518	38,483,688	38,334,117
-	36,360,813	-	36,360,813	35,711,884
-	-	-	354,334	342,231
3,680,630	-	-	11,752,090	12,322,659
3,680,630	36,360,813	-	48,467,237	48,376,774
$ 4,036,704	$36,360,813	$10,759,518	$86,950,925	$86,710,891

APPENDIX E • 11

ALL FUND TYPES
COMBINED STATEMENT OF REVENUES, EXPENDITURES AND CHANGES IN FUND BALANCES
FOR THE YEAR ENDED JUNE 30, 1994
WITH COMPARATIVE TOTALS FOR THE YEAR ENDED JUNE 30, 1993

	GOVERNMENTAL FUND TYPES			
	GENERAL	SPECIAL REVENUE	DEBT SERVICE	CAPITAL PROJECTS
REVENUES				
Local Sources:				
Property taxes................$	20,663,135 $	1,948,856 $	3,042,639 $	-
Replacement taxes.............	981,513	116,176	-	-
Tuition.......................	12,755	1,639,062	-	-
Transportation fees...........	-	118,092	-	-
Earnings on investments.......	288,378	16,405	31,756	12,103
Food services.................	873,212	-	-	-
Pupil activities..............	93,121	-	-	-
Textbooks.....................	286,451	-	-	-
Rentals.......................	38,717	-	-	-
Contributions and donations from private sources........	7,667	-	-	-
Refund of prior year's expenditures/disbursements..	4,275	-	-	-
Other local sources...........	455,803	4,486	-	-
Total Local Sources........	23,705,027	3,843,077	3,074,395	12,103
Flow-Through....................	264,650	-	-	-
State Sources...................	10,112,485	1,074,933	-	156,320
Federal Sources.................	1,980,772	129,080	-	-
Total revenues.............	36,062,934	5,047,090	3,074,395	168,423
EXPENDITURES				
Current:				
Instruction..................	24,259,749	2,168,532	-	-
Support Services.............	10,729,343	2,562,270	-	364,915
Community Services...........	100,109	1,920	-	-
Nonprogrammed Charges........	863,296	-	-	-
Debt Service.................	77,994	-	3,136,334	-
Capital Outlay...............	380,221	178,221	-	88,404
Total expenditures.........	36,410,712	4,910,943	3,136,334	453,319
EXCESS (DEFICIENCY) OF REVENUES OVER EXPENDITURES................	(347,778)	136,147	(61,939)	(284,896)
OTHER FINANCING SOURCES (USES)				
Transfers......................	(300,000)	-	-	300,000
Other..........................	-	-	-	-
Total Other Financing Sources (Uses).........................	(300,000)	-	-	300,000
EXCESS (DEFICIENCY) OF REVENUES AND OTHER FINANCING SOURCES OVER EXPENDITURES AND OTHER (USES)...	(647,778)	136,147	(61,939)	15,104
FUND BALANCE, BEGINNING OF YEAR.	4,740,512	1,418,451	1,765,497	1,059,800
FUND BALANCE, END OF YEAR.......$	4,092,734 $	1,554,598 $	1,703,558 $	1,074,904

See Accompanying Notes to Combined Financial Satatements

Exhibit B

FIDUCIARY FUND TYPE EXPENDABLE TRUST	TOTAL (MEMORANDUM ONLY) 1994	1993
$ −	$ 25,654,630	$ 25,312,724
−	1,097,689	977,663
−	1,651,817	1,659,751
−	118,092	88,868
−	348,642	465,602
−	873,212	702,367
−	93,121	98,907
−	286,451	225,988
−	38,717	43,801
−	7,667	28,123
−	4,275	4,275
−	460,289	20,177
−	30,634,602	29,628,246
−	264,650	172,591
−	11,343,738	11,489,056
−	2,109,852	2,087,347
−	44,352,842	43,377,240
−	26,428,281	24,618,893
−	13,656,528	14,156,941
−	102,029	89,080
−	863,296	347,812
−	3,214,328	3,282,622
−	646,846	1,754,511
−	44,911,308	44,249,859
−	(558,466)	(872,619)
−	−	−
−	−	1,677
−	−	1,677
−	(558,466)	(870,942)
3,680,630	12,664,890	13,535,832
$ 3,680,630	$ 12,106,424	$ 12,664,890

APPENDIX E • 13

ALL FUND TYPES
COMBINED STATEMENT OF REVENUES, EXPENDITURES AND CHANGES IN FUND BALANCES – BUDGET AND ACTUAL
FOR THE YEAR ENDED JUNE 30, 1994

	GOVERNMENTAL FUND TYPES					
	GENERAL		SPECIAL REVENUE		DEBT SERVICE	
	BUDGET	ACTUAL	BUDGET	ACTUAL	BUDGET	ACTUAL
REVENUES						
Local Sources:						
Property taxes	$ 20,884,400	$ 20,663,135	$ 1,816,400	$ 1,948,856	$ 3,052,206	$ 3,042,639
Replacement taxes	675,000	981,513	107,900	116,176	127,607	-
Other taxes	-	-	-	-	-	-
Other payments in lieu of taxes	-	-	-	-	-	-
Tuition	100,000	12,755	1,813,483	1,639,062	-	-
Transportation fees	-	-	60,000	118,092	-	-
Earnings on investments	395,000	288,378	22,000	16,405	30,000	31,756
Food services	777,800	873,212	-	-	-	-
Pupil activities	105,180	93,121	-	-	-	-
Textbooks	259,000	286,451	-	-	-	-
Rentals	30,000	38,717	-	-	-	-
Contributions and donations from private sources	-	7,667	-	-	-	-
Services provided other LEA's	-	-	-	-	-	-
Refund of prior year's expenditures/disbursements	20,500	4,275	-	-	-	-
Other local sources	101,000	455,803	4,500	4,486	-	-
Total Local Sources	23,347,880	23,705,027	3,824,283	3,843,077	3,209,813	3,074,395
Flow-Through	175,000	264,650	-	-	-	-
State Sources	9,878,813	10,112,485	1,094,000	1,074,933	-	-
Federal Sources	1,924,676	1,980,772	140,310	129,080	-	-
Total revenues	35,326,369	36,062,934	5,058,593	5,047,090	3,209,813	3,074,395
EXPENDITURES						
Current:						
Instruction	24,357,771	24,259,749	2,268,489	2,168,532	-	-
Support Services	10,625,520	10,729,343	2,851,498	2,562,270	-	-
Community Services	103,560	100,109	2,204	1,920	-	-
Nonprogrammed Charges	442,870	863,296	-	-	-	-
Debt Service	77,500	77,994	-	-	3,159,812	3,136,334
Capital Outlay	-	380,221	-	178,221	-	-
Provision for Contingencies	1,200,000	-	120,875	-	50,000	-
Total expenditures	36,807,221	36,410,712	5,243,066	4,910,943	3,209,812	3,136,334
EXCESS (DEFICIENCY) OF REVENUES OVER EXPENDITURES	(1,480,852)	(347,778)	(184,473)	136,147	1	(61,939)
OTHER FINANCING SOURCES (USES)						
Transfers	(300,000)	(300,000)	-	-	-	-
Bond Proceeds	-	-	-	-	-	-
Other	-	-	-	-	-	-
Total other financing sources (uses)	(300,000)	(300,000)	-	-	-	-
EXCESS (DEFICIENCY) OF REVENUES AND OTHER FINANCING SOURCES OVER EXPENDITURES AND OTHER (USES)	$ (1,780,852)	(647,778)	$ (184,473)	136,147	$ 1	(61,939)
FUND BALANCE, BEGINNING OF YEAR		4,740,512		1,418,451		1,765,497
FUND BALANCE, END OF YEAR		$ 4,092,734		$ 1,554,598		$ 1,703,558

See Notes to Combined Financial Statements

14 • APPENDIX E

Exhibit C

CAPITAL PROJECTS		FIDUCIARY FUND TYPE EXPENDABLE TRUST		TOTAL (MEMORANDUM ONLY)	
BUDGET	ACTUAL	BUDGET	ACTUAL	BUDGET	ACTUAL
$ -	$ -	$ -	$ -	$ 25,753,006	$ 25,654,630
-	-	-	-	910,507	1,097,689
-	-	-	-	-	-
-	-	-	-	-	-
-	-	-	-	1,913,483	1,651,817
-	-	-	-	60,000	118,092
5,000	12,103	-	-	452,000	348,642
-	-	-	-	777,800	873,212
-	-	-	-	105,180	93,121
-	-	-	-	259,000	286,451
-	-	-	-	30,000	38,717
-	-	-	-	-	7,667
-	-	-	-	-	-
-	-	-	-	20,500	4,275
-	-	-	-	105,500	460,289
5,000	12,103	-	-	30,386,976	30,634,602
-	-	-	-	175,000	264,650
-	156,320	-	-	10,972,813	11,343,738
-	-	-	-	2,064,986	2,109,852
5,000	168,423	-	-	43,599,775	44,352,842
-	-	-	-	26,626,260	26,428,281
1,430,170	364,915	-	-	14,907,188	13,656,528
-	-	-	-	105,764	102,029
-	-	-	-	442,870	863,296
-	-	-	-	3,237,312	3,214,328
-	88,404	-	-	-	646,846
10,000	-	-	-	1,380,875	-
1,440,170	453,319	-	-	46,700,269	44,911,308
(1,435,170)	(284,896)	-	-	(3,100,494)	(558,466)
300,000	300,000	-	-	-	-
-	-	-	-	-	-
-	-	-	-	-	-
300,000	300,000	-	-	-	-
$ (1,135,170)	15,104	$ -	-	$ (3,100,494)	(558,466)
	1,059,800		3,680,630		12,664,890
	$ 1,074,904		$ 3,680,630		$ 12,106,424

NOTES TO FINANCIAL STATEMENTS

JUNE 30, 1994

1. SUMMARY OF SIGNIFICANT ACCOUNTING POLICIES

The District's accounting policies conform to generally accepted accounting principles which are appropriate to local governmental units of this type. The accompanying summary of the District's more significant accounting policies is presented to assist the reader in interpreting the financial statements and other data in this report. These polices, as presented, should be viewed as an integral part of the accompanying combined financial statements.

A. *Reporting Entity*

In evaluating how to define the District for financial reporting purposes, management has considered all potential component units. The decision to include a potential component unit in the reporting entity was made by applying the criteria set forth in Generally Accepted Accounting Principles. The definition of a component unit is an organization for which the District is financially accountable and other organizations for which the nature and significance of their relationship with the District are such that exclusion would cause the reporting entity's financial statements to be misleading or incomplete. The District is financially accountable if it appoints a voting majority of the organization's governing body and (1) it is able to impose its will on that organization or (2) there is a potential for the organization to provide specific financial benefits to, or impose specific financial burdens on, the District. The District also may be financially accountable if an organization is fiscally dependent on the District regardless of whether the organization has (1) a separately elected governing board, (2) a governing board appointed by a higher level of government or (3) a jointly appointed board. Even though there are local government agencies within the geographic area served by the District, such as the City of Aurora, library, and park districts, the agencies have been excluded from the report because they are legally separate and the District is not financially accountable for them.

However, the District includes the Hope Wall Joint Agreement for Trainable Mentally Handicapped Program as a blended component unit due to the fact that the District is financially accountable for all of their activity. Separate financial statements can be obtained from the District's administration.

B. *Basis of Presentation - Fund Accounting*

The accounts of the District are organized on the basis of funds and account groups, each of which is considered a separate accounting entity. The operations of each fund are accounted for with a separate set of self-balancing accounts that comprise its assets, liabilities, fund balance, revenues, and expenditures or expenses. District resources are allocated to and accounted for in individual funds as required by the State of Illinois based upon the purposes for which they are to be spent and the means by which spending activities are controlled. The various funds are summarized by type in the combined financial statements. The following summarizes the fund types and account groups used by the District:

(Continued)

NOTES TO FINANCIAL STATEMENTS

JUNE 30, 1994

Governmental Fund Types

Governmental Funds are those through which most governmental functions of the District are financed. The acquisition, use, and balances of the District's expendable financial resources and the related liabilities are accounted for through governmental funds. The measurement focus is upon determination of changes in financial position, rather than upon net income determination. The following are the District's governmental funds.

General Fund - The General Fund is the general operating fund of the District. It is used to account for all financial resources except those required to be accounted for in another fund. The General Fund consists of the following:

Educational Fund - This fund is used for most of the instructional and administrative aspects of the District's operations. The revenue consists primarily of state government aid and local property taxes.

Operations and Maintenance Fund - This fund is used for expenditures made for repair and maintenance of District property. Revenue consists primarily of local property taxes, corporate personal property replacement taxes and general state aid.

Special Revenue Funds - Special Revenue Funds are used to account for the proceeds of specific revenue sources (other than those accounted for in the Debt Service Fund, Capital Projects Fund, or Fiduciary Funds) that are legally restricted to expenditures for specified purposes.

Each of the District's Special Revenue Funds has been established as a separate fund in accordance with the fund structure required by the State of Illinois for local educational agencies. These funds account for local property taxes restricted for specific purposes and for the General Fund of the Hope Wall Joint Agreement, a component unit. A brief description of the District's Special Revenue Funds follows:

Transportation Fund - This fund accounts for all revenue and expenditures made for student transportation. Revenue is derived primarily from local property taxes and state reimbursement grants.

Municipal Retirement/Social Security Fund - This fund accounts for the District's portion of pension contributions to the Illinois Municipal Retirement Fund, payments to Medicare for certified employees and payments to the Social Security System for noncertified employees. Revenue to finance the contributions is derived primarily from local property taxes.

(Continued)

NOTES TO FINANCIAL STATEMENTS
JUNE 30, 1994

Hope Wall Joint Agreement General Fund - This fund accounts for all revenue received and expenditures made for the trainable mentally handicapped program. Revenue consists primarily of tuition payments from District 129, District 131, other Districts, and State reimbursement grants.

Debt Service Fund - The Debt Service Fund accounts for the accumulation of resources for, and the payment of general long-term debt principal, interest and related costs. A brief description of the District's Debt Service Fund is as follows:

Bond and Interest Fund - This fund accounts for the periodic principal and interest payments on the bond issues of the District. The primary revenue source is local property taxes levied specifically for debt service.

Capital Projects Fund - The Capital Projects Fund accounts for the financial resources to be used for the acquisition, construction and/or additions to major capital facilities.

Site and Construction Fund - This fund is used to account for construction projects and renovations financed through serial bond issues.

Fire Prevention and Life Safety Fund - This fund is used to account for State approved life safety projects financed through serial bond issues.

Fiduciary Fund Types (Trust and Agency Funds) - Fiduciary Funds (Trust and Agency Funds) are used to account for assets held by the District in a trustee capacity or as an agent for individuals, private organizations, other governments or other funds.

Expendable Trust Fund - The Expendable Trust Fund (Working Cash Fund) accounts for financial resources held by the District to be used as temporary interfund loans for working capital requirements to the General Fund and the Special Revenue Fund's Transportation Fund. Money loaned by the Working Cash Fund to other funds must be repaid within one year. Also allowed by the School Code of Illinois, this fund may be permanently abolished to the Educational Fund within the General Fund.

(Continued)

NOTES TO FINANCIAL STATEMENTS

JUNE 30, 1994

Agency Funds - The Agency Funds include Student Activity Funds, Convenience Accounts and Other Agency Funds. These funds are custodial in nature and do not involve the measurement of the results of operations. Although the Board of Education has the ultimate responsibility for Activity Funds, they are not local education agency funds. Student Activity Funds account for assets held by the District which are owned, operated and managed generally by the student body under the guidance and direction of adults or a staff member for educational, recreational and cultural purposes. Convenience Accounts account for assets that are normally maintained by a local education agency as a convenience for its faculty, staff, etc. The District maintains no pension trust funds or nonexpendable trust funds.

General Fixed Assets and General Long-Term Debt Account Groups

Account groups are used to establish accounting control and accountability for the District's general fixed assets and general long-term debt. The accounting and reporting treatment applied to the fixed assets and long-term liabilities associated with a fund are determined by its measurement focus.

All governmental funds and Expendable Trust Funds are accounted for on a spending or "financial flow" measurement focus. This means that only current assets and current liabilities are generally included on their balance sheets. Their reported fund balance (net current assets) is considered a measure of "available spendable resources." Governmental Fund operating statements present increases (revenues and other financing sources) and decreases (expenditures and other financing uses) in net current assets. Accordingly, they are said to present a summary of sources and uses of "available spendable resources" during a period.

Fixed Assets - General fixed assets have been acquired for general governmental purposes. At the time of purchase, assets are recorded as expenditures paid in the Governmental Funds and capitalized at cost in the General Fixed Assets Account Group. Donated general fixed assets are listed at estimated fair market value as of the date of acquisition. Depreciation accounting is not applicable, except to determine the per capita tuition charge. Interest costs are not capitalized as part of fixed assets.

Long-Term Liabilities - Long-term liabilities expected to be financed from governmental funds are accounted for in the General Long-Term Debt Account Group, not in the governmental funds. The debt recorded in the District's General Long-Term Debt Account Group consists of serial bond issues and long-term retirements payable.

The two account groups are not "funds." They are concerned only with the measurement of financial position. They are not involved with measurement of results of operations.

(Continued)

NOTES TO FINANCIAL STATEMENTS

JUNE 30, 1994

C. Basis of Accounting

The accounting and financial reporting treatment applied to a fund is determined by its measurement focus. All governmental funds and expendable trust funds are accounted for using a current financial resources measurement focus. With this measurement focus, only current assets and current liabilities generally are included on the balance sheet. Operating statements of these funds present increases (i.e., revenues and other financing sources) and decreases (i.e., expenditures and other financing uses) in net current assets.

The modified accrual basis of accounting is followed by the Governmental Fund Types, Expendable Trust Fund and Agency Funds, in conformity with the Illinois Program Accounting Manual for Local Education Agencies. Under the modified accrual basis of accounting, revenues are recorded when susceptible to accrual, i.e., both measurable and available. Available means collectible within the current period or soon enough thereafter to be used to pay liabilities of the current period. Revenues accrued include local property taxes and restricted state and federal aid.

Expenditures are recognized when the related liability is incurred, if measurable, except for unmatured interest on general long-term debt which is recognized when due, and accumulated sick pay which is recognized when paid. Accumulated vacation pay which is used within sixty days of year end is recognized as an expenditure in the current period. Purchases of general fixed assets are recorded as expenditures in the Governmental Funds and capitalized in the General Fixed Assets Account Group at the time of purchase.

Property tax revenues are recognized when they become due and are available to pay liabilities of the current period. Therefore, property tax revenue reflected in the combined statement of revenues, expenditures and changes in fund balances includes that portion (approximately 50%) of the 1993 property tax levy due and received by, or expected to be received within 60 days after, June 30, 1994. Based on past experience, an allowance for estimated collection losses of 1.0% of the 1993 levy has been recorded to reduce the property taxes receivable to the estimated amounts collectible. The portion of the 1993 tax levy not currently available is reported as deferred in the combined balance sheet.

The District reports deferred revenues on its combined balance sheet. Deferred revenues arise when a potential revenue does not meet both the "measurable" and "available" criteria for recognition in the current period. Deferred revenues also arise when resources are received by the District before it has a legal claim to them, as when grant monies are received prior to the incurrence of qualifying expenditures. In subsequent periods, when both revenue recognition criteria are met, or when the District has a legal claim to the resources, the liability for deferred revenue is removed from the combined balance sheet and revenue is recognized.

(Continued)

NOTES TO FINANCIAL STATEMENTS

JUNE 30, 1994

D. *Budgets and Budgetary Accounting*

The budget for all governmental fund types and for the expendable trust fund is prepared on the cash basis of accounting, which differs from the basis that is used in financial reporting. This is an acceptable method in accordance with Chapter 122, Paragraph 17.1 of the Illinois Compiled Statutes. The budget, which was not amended, was passed on September 20, 1993.

The Board of Education follows these procedures in establishing the budgetary data reflected in the combined financial statements:

1. The Administration submits to the Board of Education a proposed operating budget for the fiscal year commencing July 1. The operating budget includes proposed expenditures and the means of financing them.

2. Public hearings are conducted and the proposed budget is available for inspection to obtain taxpayer comments.

3. Prior to September 30, the budget is legally adopted through passage of an ordinance. By the last Tuesday in December, a tax levy ordinance is filed with the county clerk to obtain tax revenues.

4. The Board of Education is authorized to transfer up to 10% of the total budget between departments within any fund; however, the total budgeted expenditures of any fund may not legally be exceeded unless the budget is revised. Any revisions that alter the total expenditure of any fund must be approved by the Board of Education after following the public hearing procedure mandated by law.

5. Appropriations lapse at the end of the fiscal year.

6. Formal budgetary integration is employed as a management control device during the year for the General Fund, Special Revenue Funds and Debt Service Fund. Encumbrances are integrated into the formal budgetary process during the year. However, at year end, encumbrances are cancelled.

7. Modified accrual basis budgeted amounts are as originally adopted by the Board of Education.

(Continued)

NOTES TO FINANCIAL STATEMENTS

JUNE 30, 1994

E. *Investments*

Investments, which consist of commercial paper and repurchase agreements are carried at the lower of cost or market.

F. *Inventory*

Inventory is valued at cost. Inventory in the General Fund consists of textbooks and supplies held for sale to students. The cost is recorded as an expenditure at the time individual inventory items are purchased. Inventory in the Special Revenue funds consists of transportation supplies.

G. *Property Taxes*

The District must file its tax levy ordinance by the last Tuesday in December of each year. The District's property tax is levied each year on all taxable real property located in the District. The owner of real property on January 1 in any year is liable for taxes of that year. The District has a statutory tax rate limit in various operating funds subject to change only by approval of the voters of the District.

Property taxes are collected by the Kane County Collector/Treasurer who remits to the District its share of collections. Taxes levied in one year become due and payable in two installments in June and September.

The 1993 property tax levy is recorded as a receivable, net of estimated uncollectibles approximating 1%. The net receivable collected within the current year or expected to be collected soon enough thereafter to be used to pay liabilities of the current period less the taxes collected soon enough after the end of the previous fiscal year are recognized as revenue in the Governmental Fund types. Such time thereafter does not exceed 60 days. Net taxes receivable less the amount expected to be within 60 days is reflected as deferred revenue.

(Continued)

NOTES TO FINANCIAL STATEMENTS
JUNE 30, 1994

The tax extension of $27,127,589 for the tax levy year 1993 is based upon an assessed valuation of $665,234,284, which increased by $46,203,044 from 1992. The following are the tax rate limits permitted by the School Code and by local referendum and the actual rates levied per $100.00 of assessed valuation:

	Limit	Actual Levy 1993	1992
Educational	2.8750	2.7751	2.8285
Tort Immunity	NONE	.0150	.0162
Special Education	.0400	.0400	.0383
Operations and Maintenance	.4650	.4636	.4448
Transportation	.2000	.1608	.1433
Illinois Municipal Retirement	NONE	.0707	.0969
Social Security	NONE	.0676	.0872
Bond and Interest	NONE	.4851	.4899
Total		4.0779	4.1451

H. *Special Tax Levies and Restricted Equity*

Tort Immunity - Revenue and the related expenditures of this restricted tax levy are accounted for in the Education Fund. As of June 30, 1994, revenues were fully expended in accordance with Chapter 75, paragraphs 10/9-101 to 10/9-107 of the Illinois Compiled Statutes.

Special Education - Revenue and the related expenditures of this restricted tax levy are also accounted for in the Education Fund. As of June 30, 1994, revenues were fully expended in accordance with Chapter 122, Paragraph 17-2.2A of the Illinois Compiled Statutes.

I. *General Fixed Assets*

General fixed assets have been acquired for general governmental purposes. Assets purchased are recorded as expenditures in the governmental funds and capitalized at cost in the General Fixed Assets Account Group. Contributed fixed assets are recorded in the General Fixed Assets Account Group at estimated fair market value at the time received. No depreciation has been provided on general fixed assets.

(Continued)

NOTES TO FINANCIAL STATEMENTS

JUNE 30, 1994

J. *Comparative Total Data*

Comparative total data for the prior year have been presented in the accompanying financial statements in order to provide an understanding of changes in the District's financial position and operations. However, comparative data (i.e., presentation of prior year totals by fund type) have not been presented in each of the statements, since their inclusion would make the statements unduly complex and difficult to read.

K. *Total Columns on Combined Statements*

Total columns on the combined statements are captioned "Memorandum Only" to indicate that they are presented only to facilitate financial analysis. Data in these columns do not present financial position, results of operations, or changes in financial position in conformity with generally accepted accounting principles. Neither is such data comparable to a consolidation. Interfund eliminations have not been made in the aggregation of this data.

2. CASH AND INVESTMENTS

The District maintains a cash and investment pool that is available for use by all funds. Each fund type's portion of this pool is displayed on the combined balance sheet as "Cash and investments." In addition, investments may be separately held by some of the District's funds.

Illinois State Statutes authorize the District to make deposits/invest in interest-bearing accounts of financial institutions insured by the Federal Deposit Insurance Corporation, obligations of the U.S. Treasury and U.S. Agencies, obligations of states and their political subdivisions, savings accounts, credit union shares, repurchase agreements, commercial paper rated within the three highest classifications by at least two standard rating services, and public treasurers' investment pools.

At June 30, 1994, the District had total cash and investments of $19,324,100 which consisted of the following: cash on hand of $1,047, deposits with financial institutions, of $1,627,188, deposits with the Illinois School District Liquid Assets Fund of $77,865, and investments of $17,618,000.

A. *Deposits*

At June 30, 1994, the carrying amount of the District's deposits was $1,627,188. The bank balance was $2,280,841 and consisted of the following: deposits covered by depository insurance, $181,660; and uninsured, uncollateralized deposits of $2,099,181.

(Continued)

NOTES TO FINANCIAL STATEMENTS
JUNE 30, 1994

B. *Investments*

The following table includes investments that are insured or registered or for which securities are held by the District or its agent in the District's name.

	Carrying Amount
Commercial Paper	$ 13,118,000
Repurchase Agreements	4,500,000
Total Investments	$ 17,618,000

Note: Carrying amount is stated at lower of cost or market.

3. RETIREMENT PLANS

The school district participates in two retirement systems: The Teacher's Retirement System of the State of Illinois (TRS) and the Illinois Municipal Retirement Fund (IMRF). Members of TRS consist of all active nonannuitants who are employed by a TRS-covered employer to provide services for which teacher certification is required. Employees, other than teachers, who meet prescribed annual hourly standards are members of IMRF. The District's total payroll for the year ended June 30, 1994 was $27,618,482; of this amount, $19,602,276 was reported to TRS and $3,969,052 was reported to IMRF.

A. *Teachers' Retirement System*

TRS is a cost-sharing, multiple-employer public members retirement system. Employer contributions to TRS are paid by State of Illinois on behalf of District employees. For the year ended June 30, 1994, contributions made by the State were at the rate of 6.00% of covered salaries, or $1,176,136. When members are paid from federal and trust funds administered by the District, there is a statutory requirement for the District to pay an employer contribution of 10.5% of these salaries. For the year ended June 30, 1994, salaries totalling $702,497 were paid from federal and trust funds which required employer contributions of $73,762.

(Continued)

NOTES TO FINANCIAL STATEMENTS
JUNE 30, 1994

Public Act 87-1265 provides an early retirement benefit known as 5 & 5. The retirement windows are June 1 through September 1 in 1993 and 1994. Retirements may be delayed until 1995 is more than 30 percent of those eligible retire in 1994. Employees may purchase up to five years of additional service and receive an equal number of years of age. Employees contribute 4 percent of the highest salary used in the calculation of final average salary for each year purchased, and employers contribute 20 percent for each year purchased. Employer contributions can be made in either a lump sum, over five years in quarterly installments, or under a different schedule approved by the TRS Board of Trustees. For the year ended June 30, 1994, the District paid $135,725 for employer contributions under the early retirement incentive.

The District is also required to make one-time employer contributions for teachers retiring under the early retirement option if any teachers select that option instead of the early retirement incentive. These payments vary depending on the age and salary of the teacher. The maximum payment of 100 percent of the teacher's highest salary used in the calculation of final average salary is required if the teacher is 55 years old. There were no retirements under the early retirement option during the year ending June 30, 1994.

The System provides retirement benefits, health insurance and death and disability benefits. A single-sum benefit is payable at age 65 to a member with fewer than five years of service. A member qualifies for a retirement annuity after attaining one of the following: age 62 with five years of service credit; age 60 with ten years; age 55 with 20 years. If retirement occurs between ages 55 and 60 with fewer than 35 years of service, the annuity will be reduced at the rate of 1/2 percent for each month the member is under age 60. A member age 55 with fewer than 35 years of service credit may use the early retirement option to avoid a discount for early retirement if retirement occurs before July 1, 1995, application for retirement occurs within six months of the last day of service for which contributions are required, and if the member and employer both make a one-time contribution to TRS.

The retirement benefit is determined by the average of the four highest consecutive salary rates within the last ten years of creditable service and the percentage of average salary to which the member is entitled. This percentage is determined by the following formula: 1.67 percent for each of the first ten years, plus 1.9 percent for each of the next ten years, plus 2.1 percent for each of the next ten years, plus 2.3 percent for each year over 30. The maximum retirement benefit, 75 percent of average salary, is achieved with 38 years of service. Each annuitant receives an annual 3 percent increase beginning January 1 following attainment of age 61 or following the first anniversary in retirement, whichever is later.

Member contributions, established by statute, are 8 percent of earnings. Employer contributions made by the State of Illinois are based on annual appropriations which are less than statutory actuarial funding requirements.

(Continued)

NOTES TO FINANCIAL STATEMENTS
JUNE 30, 1994

B. *Illinois Municipal Retirement Fund*

Plan Description

The District contributes to the Illinois Municipal Retirement Fund ("IMRF"), an agent-multiple-employer public employee retirement system that acts as a common investment and administrative agent for 2,605 local governments and school districts in Illinois. The District's total payroll for the year ended December 31, 1993 was $27,193,572. Of this amount, $4,239,738 in payroll earnings were reported to and covered by the IMRF system.

All employees hired in positions that do not require teacher certification, and that meet or exceed the prescribed annual hourly standard must be enrolled in IMRF as participating members. Pension benefits vest after eight years of service. Participating members who retire at or after age 60 with 8 years of credited service are entitled to an annual retirement benefit, payable monthly for life, in an amount equal to 1 2/3 percent of their final rate of earnings, for each year of credited service up to 15 years, and 2 percent for each year thereafter. IMRF also provides death and disability benefits. These benefit provisions and all other requirements are established by state statute.

Participating members are required to contribute 4.5 percent of their annual salary to IMRF. The District is required to contribute the remaining amounts necessary to fund the System, using the actuarial funding method specified by statute.

Related Party Transactions

There were no securities of the District or related parties included in the System's assets.

Funding Status and Progress

The amount shown below as the "Pension Benefit Obligation" is a standardized disclosure measure of the present value of pension benefits, estimated to be payable in the future as a result of employee service to date. The measure is intended to help users assess the funding status of IMRF on a going-concern basis, assess progress made in accumulating sufficient assets to pay benefits when due, and make comparisons among employers. The measure is the actuarial present value of credited projected benefits prorated on service and is independent of the funding method used to determine contributions to IMRF.

(Continued)

NOTES TO FINANCIAL STATEMENTS

JUNE 30, 1994

The pension benefit obligation was computed as part of an actuarial valuation performed as of December 31, 1993. Significant actuarial assumptions used in the valuation include (a) a rate of return on the investment of present and future assets of 7.5% a year compounded annually, (b) projected salary increases of 4.25% a year compounded annually, attributable to inflation, (c) additional projected salary increases ranging from 0.6% to 6.8% per year, depending on age and service, attributable to seniority/merit, and (d) postretirement benefit increases of 3% annually.

Total unfunded pension benefit obligation applicable to the District's employees was $2,878,446 at December 31, 1993, determined as follows:

Pension benefit obligation:	
Terminated employees not yet receiving benefits	$ 634,580
Current employees-	
Accumulated employee contributions including allocated investment earnings	1,962,435
Employer-financed vested	4,087,167
Employer-financed nonvested	476,120
Total pension benefit obligation	7,160,302
Net assets available for benefits, at cost (market value is $4,785,958)	4,281,856
Unfunded pension benefit obligation	$ 2,878,446

The pension benefit obligation applicable to retirees and beneficiaries currently receiving benefits is not included in the above schedule due to the fact that this obligation was transferred from the District to IMRF as a whole when the annuity became payable.

Actuarially Determined Contribution Requirements and Contributions Made

The IMRF funding policy provides for actuarially determined monthly contributions at rates that will accumulate sufficient assets to pay benefits when due without having to be increased for future generations of taxpayers. The contribution rate for normal cost is determined using the entry age normal actuarial funding method. IMRF used the level percentage of payroll method to amortize the unfunded liability over a 39 year period.

(Continued)

NOTES TO FINANCIAL STATEMENTS
JUNE 30, 1994

The contributions by the District to IMRF for 1993 of $675,390 was made in accordance with actuarially determined requirements computed through an actuarial valuation performed as of December 31, 1991. The contribution consisted of (a) $489,266 normal cost (11.54 percent of 1993 covered payroll), (b) $141,607 amortization of the unfunded actuarial accrued liability (3.4 percent of 1993 covered payroll), (c) $18,231 death and disability cost (.43 percent of 1993 covered payroll), and (d) $26,286 cost of supplemental retirement benefit (.62 percent of 1993 covered payroll). The District contributed $484,602 (11.43 percent of 1993 covered payroll); employees contributed $190,788 (4.5 percent of 1993 covered payroll).

The new actuarial assumptions based on the 1990-1992 experience study were adopted in 1993. The changes will be incorporated into the 1995 contribution rates. The net effect of changes adopted in 1993 is estimated to decrease the obligation by $40,338.

Trend Information

Trend information gives an indication of the progress made in accumulating sufficient assets to pay benefits when due. Seven year trend information may be found in Schedule 7 of this report. For the three years ended 1991, 1992, and 1993, respectively, available assets were sufficient to fund 59.03, 60.00, and 59.80 percent of the pension benefit obligation. Unfunded pension benefit obligation represents 67.62, 65.38, and 67.89 percent of the annual payroll for the participating members covered by IMRF for 1991, 1992, and 1993, respectively.

Showing unfunded pension benefit obligation as a percentage of annual covered payroll approximately adjusts for the effects of inflation for analysis purposes. In addition, for the three years ended 1991, 1992, and 1993, the District's contribution to IMRF, all made in accordance with actuarially determined requirements, were 12.66, 12.71 and 11.43 percent respectively of annual covered payroll.

C. *Social Security*

Employees not qualifying for coverage under the Illinois Teachers' Retirement System or the Illinois Municipal Retirement Fund are considered "nonparticipating employees." These employees and those qualifying for coverage under the Illinois Municipal Retirement Fund are covered under Social Security.

(Continued)

APPENDIX E • 29

NOTES TO FINANCIAL STATEMENTS

JUNE 30, 1994

4. GENERAL FIXED ASSETS

A summary of changes in general fixed assets follows:

District 129	Balance June 30, 1993	Additions	Deletions	Balance June 30, 1994
Land	$ 1,627,157	$ -	$ -	$ 1,627,157
Land Improvements	466,798	-	-	466,798
Buildings	22,813,485	9,000	-	22,822,485
Transportation Equipment	1,898,843	167,413	(97,400)	1,968,856
Other Equipment	7,642,924	559,108	-	8,202,032
District 129 Fixed Assets	34,449,207	735,521	(97,400)	35,087,328

Hope Wall

Land	$ 35,300	$ -	$ -	$ 35,300
Land Improvements	53,416	-	-	53,416
Building	757,778	-	-	757,778
Equipment	416,183	10,808	-	426,991
Hope Wall Fixed Assets	1,262,677	10,808	-	1,273,485
Total Fixed Assets	$35,711,884	$ 746,329	$ (97,400)	$36,360,813

The general fixed assets were appraised at estimated historical cost as of June 30, 1984 with subsequent years additions recorded at cost. Donated assets are recorded at their estimated fair value at the time received. There were no significant amounts of donated assets received during the year.

(Continued)

30 • APPENDIX E

NOTES TO FINANCIAL STATEMENTS
JUNE 30, 1994

5. GENERAL LONG-TERM DEBT

The following is a summary of the components of long-term debt and related transactions of the District for the year ended June 30, 1994:

	Balance June 30, 1993	Issued	Retired	Balance June 30, 1994
General Obligation Bonds	$ 9,845,000	$ -	$ 2,500,000	$ 7,345,000
Long-Term Retirements Payable	1,177,133	2,373,110	135,725	3,414,518
Total	$11,022,133	$ 2,373,110	$ 2,635,725	$10,759,518

At June 30, 1994, the annual cash flow requirements of general obligation bond principal and interest are as follows:

Year Ending June 30,	Principal	Interest	Total Bonds	Long-Term Retirements Payable	Total
1995	$ 2,745,000	$ 450,025	$ 3,195,025	$ 490,749	$ 3,685,774
1996	3,000,000	266,975	3,266,975	710,049	3,977,024
1997	1,600,000	89,600	1,689,600	710,049	2,399,649
1998	-	-	-	710,049	710,049
1999	-	-	-	574,323	574,323
2000-2009	-	-	-	219,299	219,299
Total	$ 7,345,000	$ 806,600	$ 8,151,600	$ 3,414,518	$11,566,118

These payments will be made from amounts budgeted from the debt service tax levies in future periods. There is $1,703,558 of fund equity available in the Debt Service Fund to service outstanding bonds payable. As of June 30, 1994, the District was in compliance with all significant bond covenants.

(Continued)

NOTES TO FINANCIAL STATEMENTS

JUNE 30, 1994

The District is subject to the Illinois School Code which limits the amount of bond indebtedness to 13.8% of the most recent available equalized assessed valuation of the District. As of June 30, 1994, the statutory debt limit for the District was $91,802,331 providing a debt margin of $84,457,331.

6. **INTERFUND LOANS**

    Interfund accounts at June 30, 1994 consisted of a $3,670,000 loan from the Working Cash Fund to the Educational Fund.

7. **GENERAL OBLIGATION TAX ANTICIPATION WARRANTS**

    During the year ended June 30, 1994, the District issued $4,500,000 in general obligation tax anticipation warrants resulting in a balance of $3,000,000 in the General Fund at June 30, 1994, with interest at 2.85%. On June 28, 1994, the District redeemed $1,500,000 of these warrants.

8. **COMMITMENTS AND CONTINGENCIES**

    General:

    The District participates in numerous state and federal grant programs, which are governed by various rules and regulations of the grantor agencies. Costs charged to the respective grant programs are subject to audit and adjustment by the grantor agencies; therefore, to the extent that the District has not complied with the rules and regulations governing the grants, refunds of any money received may be required and the collectibility of any related receivable at June 30, 1994 may be impaired. In the opinion of the District, there are no significant contingent liabilities relating to compliance with the rules and significant contingent liabilities relating to compliance with the rules and regulations governing the respective grants; therefore, no provision has been recorded in the accompanying combined financial statements for such contingencies.

9. **EXPENDITURES IN EXCESS OF BUDGET**

    During the year ended June 30, 1994, expenditures exceeded budget in the following individual fund:

    Site and Construction .... $ 69,434

(Continued)

NOTES TO FINANCIAL STATEMENTS
JUNE 30, 1994

10. RESTATEMENT OF BEGINNING FUND BALANCE

During the year, the District changed its method of recognizing governmental claims to more closely reflect the modified accrual basis of accounting. Previously, revenue was recognized as the claims were made without regard to the timing of their receipt. Currently, revenue is recognized on claims only to the extent that they are available to pay current operating expenditures. Also, the Hope Wall Special Education Joint Agreement, a component unit, General Fund, which is presented as a Special Revenue Fund in the combined financial statements, change its basis of accounting from the cash basis to the modified accrual basis. As a result of these changes, adjustments have been made to the June 30, 1992 fund balances as follows:

	Fund Balance June 30, 1992 as Previously Reported	Adjustment to Claims/ Tuition Receivable	Fund Balance June 30, 1992 as Restated
Educational Fund	$ 6,392,141	$ (1,828,390)	$ 4,563,751
Transportation Fund	$ 1,219,585	$ (608,765)	$ 610,820
Hope Wall-General Fund	$ 390,455	$ (390,455)	$ -0-

The resulting changes to the revenue have been reflected in the 1993 financial data as presented.

(Concluded)

APPENDIX E • 33

Exhibit D-1

GENERAL FUNDS
COMBINING BALANCE SHEET
JUNE 30, 1994
WITH COMPARATIVE TOTALS FOR JUNE 30, 1993

	EDUCATIONAL	OPERATIONS & MAINTENANCE	TOTAL 1994	TOTAL 1993
ASSETS				
Cash	$ -	$ 541,302	$ 541,302	$ 1,270,628
Investments	15,606,000	137,000	15,743,000	5,000,000
Receivables (net of allowance for uncollectibles):				
Property taxes	9,295,730	1,580,383	10,876,113	18,868,130
Intergovernmental	752,311	55,833	808,144	1,245,712
Due from other funds	-	-	-	1,416,340
Inventory	315,456	-	315,456	277,527
Other current assets	-	-	-	121,125
Total Assets	$25,969,497	$ 2,314,518	$28,284,015	$28,199,462
LIABILITIES AND FUND BALANCE				
Liabilities				
Cash deficit	$ 2,028,808	$ -	$ 2,028,808	$ -
Accounts payable	151,512	76,173	227,685	235,299
Wages payable	3,781,942	70,869	3,852,811	3,653,209
Anticipation warrants payable	3,000,000	-	3,000,000	4,500,000
Due to other funds	3,670,000	-	3,670,000	4,846,340
Deferred revenue	9,053,540	1,539,207	10,592,747	9,420,216
Other current liabilities	819,230	-	819,230	803,886
Total Liabilities	22,505,032	1,686,249	24,191,281	23,458,950
Fund Balance				
Reserved:				
Reserved for inventory	315,456	-	315,456	277,527
Unreserved:				
Undesignated	3,149,009	628,269	3,777,278	4,462,985
Total Fund Balance	3,464,465	628,269	4,092,734	4,740,512
Total Liabilities And Fund Balance	$25,969,497	$ 2,314,518	$28,284,015	$28,199,462

Exhibit D-2

GENERAL FUNDS
COMBINING STATEMENT OF REVENUES, EXPENDITURES AND CHANGES IN FUND BALANCES
FOR THE YEAR ENDED JUNE 30, 1994
WITH COMPARATIVE TOTALS FOR THE YEAR ENDED JUNE 30, 1993

	EDUCATIONAL	OPERATIONS & MAINTENANCE	TOTAL 1994	TOTAL 1993
REVENUES				
Local Sources:				
Property taxes	$17,725,457	$ 2,937,678	$20,663,135	$20,143,856
Replacement taxes	845,897	135,616	981,513	727,535
Tuition	12,755	-	12,755	132,852
Earnings on investments	288,378	-	288,378	382,652
Food services	873,212	-	873,212	702,367
Pupil activities	93,121	-	93,121	98,907
Textbooks	286,451	-	286,451	225,988
Rentals	420	38,297	38,717	43,801
Contributions and donations from private sources	2,801	4,866	7,667	28,123
Refund of prior year's disbursements/expenditures	4,275	-	4,275	4,275
Other local sources	372,229	83,574	455,803	13,185
Total Local Sources	20,504,996	3,200,031	23,705,027	22,503,541
Flow-Through	264,650	-	264,650	172,591
State Sources	9,442,485	670,000	10,112,485	10,335,086
Federal Sources	1,980,772	-	1,980,772	1,967,606
Total Revenues	32,192,903	3,870,031	36,062,934	34,978,824
EXPENDITURES				
Current:				
Instruction	24,259,749	-	24,259,749	22,826,161
Support Services	7,437,208	3,292,135	10,729,343	10,759,017
Community Services	100,109	-	100,109	402,984
Nonprogrammed Charges	862,661	635	863,296	33,908
Debt Service	77,994	-	77,994	57,509
Capital Outlay	357,619	22,602	380,221	-
Total Expenditures	33,095,340	3,315,372	36,410,712	34,079,579
EXCESS (DEFICIENCY) OF REVENUES OVER EXPENDITURES	(902,437)	554,659	(347,778)	899,245
OTHER FINANCING SOURCES (USES)				
Transfers	(300,000)	-	(300,000)	(180,079)
Other	-	-	-	1,677
Total Other Financing Sources (Uses)	(300,000)	-	(300,000)	(178,402)
EXCESS (DEFICIENCY) OF REVENUES AND OTHER FINANCING SOURCES OVER EXPENDITURES AND OTHER (USES)	(1,202,437)	554,659	(647,778)	720,843
FUND BALANCE, BEGINNING OF YEAR	4,666,902	73,610	4,740,512	4,019,669
FUND BALANCE, END OF YEAR	$ 3,464,465	$ 628,269	$ 4,092,734	$ 4,740,512

APPENDIX E • 35

Exhibit D-3

GENERAL FUND - EDUCATIONAL ACCOUNTS
STATEMENT OF REVENUES, EXPENDITURES AND CHANGES IN FUND BALANCE - BUDGET AND ACTUAL
FOR THE YEAR ENDED JUNE 30, 1994
WITH COMPARATIVE ACTUAL AMOUNTS FOR THE YEAR ENDED JUNE 30, 1993

	1994 BUDGET	1994 ACTUAL	VARIANCE FAVORABLE (UNFAVORABLE)	1993 ACTUAL
REVENUES				
LOCAL SOURCES				
General tax levy	$17,752,847	$17,480,589	$ (272,258)	$17,143,316
Special education tax levy	240,553	244,868	4,315	232,602
Corporate personal property replacement taxes	600,000	845,897	245,897	632,568
Regular day school tuition	100,000	3,050	(96,950)	132,852
Summer school tuition	-	9,705	9,705	-
Earnings on investments	395,000	288,378	(106,622)	382,652
Food services	777,800	873,212	95,412	702,367
Pupil activities	105,180	93,121	(12,059)	98,907
Textbooks	259,000	286,451	27,451	225,988
Rentals	-	420	420	1,380
Contributions and donations from private sources	-	2,801	2,801	-
Refund of prior years' disbursements/expenditures	20,500	4,275	(16,225)	4,275
Sale of vocational projects	55,000	62,445	7,445	-
Local fees	21,000	12,129	(8,871)	-
Other	-	297,655	297,655	11,257
Total Local Sources	20,326,880	20,504,996	178,116	19,568,164
Flow-Through Revenue From One LEA to Another LEA				
Flow-through from State sources	140,000	190,479	50,479	134,309
Flow-through from Federal sources	35,000	74,171	39,171	38,283
Total Flow-Through	175,000	264,650	89,650	172,592
State Sources				
General state aid	7,172,776	7,191,262	18,486	7,520,874
Supplementary state aid	-	-	-	3,604
Driver education	52,268	53,788	1,520	50,376
Summer school	-	8,897	8,897	8,583
Bilingual education	186,133	201,854	15,721	171,807

Exhibit D-3

GENERAL FUND - EDUCATIONAL ACCOUNTS
STATEMENT OF REVENUES, EXPENDITURES AND CHANGES IN FUND BALANCE - BUDGET AND ACTUAL
FOR THE YEAR ENDED JUNE 30, 1994
WITH COMPARATIVE ACTUAL AMOUNTS FOR THE YEAR ENDED JUNE 30, 1993

	1994 BUDGET	1994 ACTUAL	VARIANCE FAVORABLE (UNFAVORABLE)	1993 ACTUAL
Vocational education - grants and contracts	$ 20,000	$ 53,372	$ 33,372	$ 37,211
Gifted education	53,984	88,430	34,446	54,966
Special education personnel	749,155	674,220	(74,935)	1,168,513
Special education private facility	132,650	186,624	53,974	-
Special education extraordinary	171,933	308,159	136,226	-
Special education orphanage	85,000	3,375	(81,625)	-
Reading improvement program	162,260	169,568	7,308	228,672
Prekindergarten program for at-risk students	323,868	349,026	25,158	285,722
Lunch - free	25,350	28,204	2,854	36,754
Breakfast - free	-	2,535	2,535	1,593
Other Grants-in-Aid	73,436	107,389	33,953	96,426
Orphans tuition	-	15,782	15,782	-
Total State Sources	9,208,813	9,442,485	233,672	9,665,101
Federal Sources				
Public Law 81-874	7,000	13,070	6,070	9,829
Elementary and Secondary Education Act Title VII - Bilingual	75,400	28,563	(46,837)	140,448
Chapter 1 educationally deprived	682,706	797,491	114,785	579,153
Chapter 1 handicapped	43,744	37,062	(6,682)	72,300
Chapter 1 even start	135,006	123,411	(11,595)	182,384
IDEA room and board reimbursement	-	-	-	7,322
IDEA flow-through	237,841	251,424	13,583	239,789
School lunch regular	544,513	507,961	(36,552)	507,903
Breakfast	5,500	21,206	15,706	26,209
ESEA Chapter 2, Block Grant	71,100	66,114	(4,986)	77,977
ESEA Title II Teacher Skills Improvement	30,477	31,083	606	20,673
Department of Rehabilitation Services	23,840	44,221	20,381	23,835
Other	67,549	51,474	(16,075)	79,784
Job Training Partnership Reform Act	-	7,692	7,692	-
Total Federal Sources	1,924,676	1,980,772	56,096	1,967,606
Total Revenues	31,635,369	32,192,903	557,534	31,373,463

APPENDIX E • 37

ibit D-3

GENERAL FUND - EDUCATIONAL ACCOUNTS
STATEMENT OF REVENUES, EXPENDITURES AND CHANGES IN FUND BALANCE - BUDGET AND ACTUAL
FOR THE YEAR ENDED JUNE 30, 1994
WITH COMPARATIVE ACTUAL AMOUNTS FOR THE YEAR ENDED JUNE 30, 1993

	1994 BUDGET	1994 ACTUAL	VARIANCE FAVORABLE (UNFAVORABLE)	1993 ACTUAL
EXPENDITURES				
Instruction				
Regular Programs				
Salaries	$16,784,747	$17,129,590	$ (344,843)	$15,964,167
Employee benefits	1,673,700	874,780	798,920	1,011,446
Purchased Services	98,587	133,650	(35,063)	113,691
Supplies and materials	544,982	319,915	225,067	327,680
Capital outlay	68,545	161,867	(93,322)	119,879
Tuition	5,600	10,882	(5,282)	6,068
Total	19,176,161	18,630,684	545,477	17,542,931
Special Education Programs				
Salaries	2,486,302	2,495,774	(9,472)	2,523,832
Employee benefits	23,219	168,576	(145,357)	164,823
Purchased Services	137,632	160,879	(23,247)	132,628
Supplies and materials	52,913	44,245	8,668	55,065
Capital outlay	-	2,289	(2,289)	-
Tuition	748,359	1,161,100	(412,741)	646,637
Total	3,448,425	4,032,863	(584,438)	3,522,985
Educationally Deprived / Remedial Programs				
Salaries	455,000	487,334	(32,334)	478,910
Employee benefits	59,000	86,871	(27,871)	71,534
Purchased Services	500	-	500	-
Supplies and materials	5,050	16,716	(11,666)	6,767
Capital outlay	20,000	21,888	(1,888)	9,579
Total	539,550	612,809	(73,259)	566,790
Vocational Programs				
Salaries	360,568	380,950	(20,382)	353,179
Employee benefits	-	10,630	(10,630)	12,526
Purchased Services	8,500	1,639	6,861	4,134
Supplies and materials	20,525	18,035	2,490	11,859
Capital outlay	17,900	9,040	8,860	17,962
Other objects	2,500	527	1,973	617
Tuition	20,000	12,307	7,693	32,948
Total	429,993	433,128	(3,135)	433,225

38 • APPENDIX E

Exhibit D-3

GENERAL FUND - EDUCATIONAL ACCOUNTS
STATEMENT OF REVENUES, EXPENDITURES AND CHANGES IN FUND BALANCE - BUDGET AND ACTUAL
FOR THE YEAR ENDED JUNE 30, 1994
WITH COMPARATIVE ACTUAL AMOUNTS FOR THE YEAR ENDED JUNE 30, 1993

	1994 BUDGET	1994 ACTUAL	VARIANCE FAVORABLE (UNFAVORABLE)	1993 ACTUAL
Interscholastic Programs				
Salaries	$ 1,925	$ 907	$ 1,018	$ 1,103
Employee benefits	-	58	(58)	97
Purchased Services	76,204	56,580	19,624	54,550
Supplies and materials	63,335	72,493	(9,158)	70,515
Capital outlay	5,200	8,120	(2,920)	10,849
Total	146,664	138,158	8,506	137,114
Summer School Programs				
Salaries	59,366	48,208	11,158	61,958
Employee benefits	-	358	(358)	443
Purchased Services	15,000	14,582	418	21,420
Supplies and materials	5,000	2,643	2,357	1,514
Total	79,366	65,791	13,575	85,335
Gifted Programs				
Salaries	2,810	5,410	(2,600)	1,074
Employee benefits	-	1,699	(1,699)	-
Purchased Services	550	-	550	225
Supplies and materials	12,670	19,943	(7,273)	12,102
Total	16,030	27,052	(11,022)	13,401
Bilingual Programs				
Salaries	480,577	458,905	21,672	467,037
Employee benefits	11,214	37,798	(26,584)	30,665
Purchased Services	5,755	5,150	605	7,065
Supplies and materials	24,036	20,615	3,421	19,613
Total	521,582	522,468	(886)	524,380
Total Instruction	24,357,771	24,462,953	(105,182)	22,826,161

Support Services

Pupils

Attendance and Social Work Services				
Salaries	258,591	280,565	(21,974)	249,523
Employee benefits	4,512	16,810	(12,298)	19,568
Supplies and materials	600	3,635	(3,035)	525
Total	263,703	301,010	(37,307)	269,616

Exhibit D-3

GENERAL FUND - EDUCATIONAL ACCOUNTS
STATEMENT OF REVENUES, EXPENDITURES AND CHANGES IN FUND BALANCE - BUDGET AND ACTUAL
FOR THE YEAR ENDED JUNE 30, 1994
WITH COMPARATIVE ACTUAL AMOUNTS FOR THE YEAR ENDED JUNE 30, 1993

	1994 BUDGET	1994 ACTUAL	VARIANCE FAVORABLE (UNFAVORABLE)	1993 ACTUAL
Guidance & Social Work Services				
Salaries........................$	614,716 $	535,873 $	78,843 $	671,084
Employee benefits...............	-	37,609	(37,609)	45,243
Purchased Services..............	6,800	8,300	(1,500)	117,795
Supplies and materials..........	11,010	10,394	616	9,662
Total......................	632,526	592,176	40,350	843,784
Health Services				
Salaries........................	190,113	179,071	11,042	137,534
Employee benefits...............	-	(5,621)	5,621	12,271
Purchased Services..............	412	303	109	327
Supplies and materials..........	7,500	6,319	1,181	7,309
Total......................	198,025	180,072	17,953	157,441
Psychological Services				
Salaries........................	187,501	192,032	(4,531)	182,105
Employee benefits...............	-	10,558	(10,558)	8,644
Supplies and materials..........	800	801	(1)	865
Total......................	188,301	203,391	(15,090)	191,614
Speech Pathology and Audiology Services				
Supplies and materials..........	800	302	498	702
Total......................	800	302	498	702
Other Support Services - Pupils				
Purchased Services..............	-	-	-	8,481
Total......................	-	-	-	8,481
Total Pupils.............	1,283,355	1,276,951	6,404	1,471,638
Instructional Staff				
Improvement of Instruction Services				
Salaries........................	312,928	233,077	79,851	257,375
Employee benefits...............	2,500	20,437	(17,937)	22,182
Purchased Services..............	78,182	163,544	(85,362)	131,639
Supplies and materials..........	103,900	107,419	(3,519)	125,402
Total......................	497,510	524,477	(26,967)	536,598

Exhibit D-3

GENERAL FUND - EDUCATIONAL ACCOUNTS
STATEMENT OF REVENUES, EXPENDITURES AND CHANGES IN FUND BALANCE - BUDGET AND ACTUAL
FOR THE YEAR ENDED JUNE 30, 1994
WITH COMPARATIVE ACTUAL AMOUNTS FOR THE YEAR ENDED JUNE 30, 1993

	1994 BUDGET	1994 ACTUAL	VARIANCE FAVORABLE (UNFAVORABLE)	1993 ACTUAL
Educational Media Services				
Purchased Services	$ 6,000	$ 3,777	$ 2,223	$ 3,692
Supplies and materials	26,541	41,612	(15,071)	40,082
Capital outlay	-	-	-	19,132
Total	32,541	45,389	(12,848)	62,906
Total Instructional Staff	530,051	569,866	(39,815)	599,504
General Administration				
Board of Education Services				
Salaries	78,354	84,734	(6,380)	58,793
Employee benefits	-	1,499	(1,499)	3,184
Purchased Services	103,000	33,981	69,019	100,247
Supplies and materials	29,386	94,423	(65,037)	34,427
Total	210,740	214,637	(3,897)	196,651
Executive Administration Services				
Salaries	669,600	702,878	(33,278)	664,763
Employee benefits	303,780	365,108	(61,328)	192,118
Purchased Services	62,000	68,251	(6,251)	62,041
Supplies and materials	24,000	18,947	5,053	17,263
Total	1,059,380	1,155,184	(95,804)	936,185
Special Area Administrative Services				
Salaries	20,799	39,124	(18,325)	39,478
Employee benefits	-	2,093	(2,093)	1,214
Purchased Services	1,000	1,084	(84)	-
Supplies and materials	500	-	500	1,364
Capital outlay	2,000	-	2,000	-
Total	24,299	42,301	(18,002)	42,056
Total General Admin	1,294,419	1,412,122	(117,703)	1,174,892

APPENDIX E • 41

Exhibit D-3

GENERAL FUND - EDUCATIONAL ACCOUNTS
STATEMENT OF REVENUES, EXPENDITURES AND CHANGES IN FUND BALANCE - BUDGET AND ACTUAL
FOR THE YEAR ENDED JUNE 30, 1994
WITH COMPARATIVE ACTUAL AMOUNTS FOR THE YEAR ENDED JUNE 30, 1993

	1994 BUDGET	1994 ACTUAL	VARIANCE FAVORABLE (UNFAVORABLE)	1993 ACTUAL
School Administration				
Office of the Principal Services				
Salaries	$ 1,631,925	$ 1,652,216	$ (20,291)	$ 1,589,255
Employee benefits	-	137,461	(137,461)	117,020
Purchased Services	29,500	39,315	(9,815)	33,757
Supplies and materials	73,299	65,499	7,800	75,070
Total	1,734,724	1,894,491	(159,767)	1,815,102
Total School Admin	1,734,724	1,894,491	(159,767)	1,815,102
Business				
Direction of Business Support Services				
Supplies and materials	20,000	3	19,997	1,332
Total	20,000	3	19,997	1,332
Fiscal Services				
Salaries	169,025	153,204	15,821	176,005
Employee benefits	-	10,215	(10,215)	8,456
Total	169,025	163,419	5,606	184,461
Operation and Maintenance of Plant Services				
Salaries	182,857	175,677	7,180	178,725
Employee benefits	-	6,746	(6,746)	3,080
Purchased Services	311,256	236,450	74,806	296,133
Supplies and materials	1,300	2,306	(1,006)	998
Capital outlay	3,000	518	2,482	721
Total	498,413	421,697	76,716	479,657
Pupil Transportation Services				
Purchased Services	64,318	88,336	(24,018)	53,422
Total	64,318	88,336	(24,018)	53,422

Exhibit D-3

GENERAL FUND - EDUCATIONAL ACCOUNTS
STATEMENT OF REVENUES, EXPENDITURES AND CHANGES IN FUND BALANCE - BUDGET AND ACTUAL
FOR THE YEAR ENDED JUNE 30, 1994
WITH COMPARATIVE ACTUAL AMOUNTS FOR THE YEAR ENDED JUNE 30, 1993

	1994			1993
	BUDGET	ACTUAL	VARIANCE FAVORABLE (UNFAVORABLE)	ACTUAL
Food Services				
Salaries	$ 154,000	$ 116,705	$ 37,295	$ 162,616
Employee benefits	-	3,514	(3,514)	3,094
Purchased Services	1,251,500	1,404,732	(153,232)	1,209,639
Supplies and materials	1,300	1,340	(40)	1,259
Total	1,406,800	1,526,291	(119,491)	1,376,608
Internal Services				
Salaries	-	-	-	-
Employee benefits	-	1	(1)	10
Purchased Services	31,045	32,208	(1,163)	28,523
Supplies and materials	66,500	(17,570)	84,070	247,023
Capital outlay	196,692	127,079	69,613	137,685
Total	294,237	141,718	152,519	413,241
Total Business	2,452,793	2,341,464	111,329	2,508,721
Central				
Planning, Research, Development and Evaluation Services				
Purchased Services	9,000	6,454	2,546	-
Total	9,000	6,454	2,546	-
Information Services				
Supplies and materials	10,000	1,266	8,734	1,081
Total	10,000	1,266	8,734	1,081
Staff Services				
Purchased Services	5,000	3,221	1,779	5,533
Total	5,000	3,221	1,779	5,533
Data Processing Services				
Supplies and materials	26,500	39,986	(13,486)	19,361
Capital outlay	16,000	26,818	(10,818)	26,806
Total	42,500	66,804	(24,304)	46,167
Total Central	66,500	77,745	(11,245)	52,781

APPENDIX E • 43

Exhibit D-3

GENERAL FUND - EDUCATIONAL ACCOUNTS
STATEMENT OF REVENUES, EXPENDITURES AND CHANGES IN FUND BALANCE - BUDGET AND ACTUAL
FOR THE YEAR ENDED JUNE 30, 1994
WITH COMPARATIVE ACTUAL AMOUNTS FOR THE YEAR ENDED JUNE 30, 1993

	1994 BUDGET	1994 ACTUAL	VARIANCE FAVORABLE (UNFAVORABLE)	1993 ACTUAL
Other Support Services				
Salaries.........................$	17,779 $	13,385 $	4,394 $	16,208
Employee benefits...............	-	352	(352)	516
Supplies and materials..........	-	5,247	(5,247)	3,935
Total.....................	17,779	18,984	(1,205)	20,659
Total Support Services	7,379,621	7,591,623	(212,002)	7,643,297
Community Services				
Salaries........................	93,760	84,854	8,906	78,773
Employee benefits...............	-	35	(35)	64
Purchased Services..............	4,000	1,539	2,461	200
Supplies and materials..........	5,800	13,681	(7,881)	10,043
Total.....................	103,560	100,109	3,451	89,080
Nonprogrammed Charges Payments to other Governmental Units (in-State)				
Payments for Special Education Programs				
Tuition........................	400,000	862,661	(462,661)	313,904
Total.....................	400,000	862,661	(462,661)	313,904
Total Payments to Other Governmental Units.....	400,000	862,661	(462,661)	313,904
Total Nonprogrammed Charges..............	400,000	862,661	(462,661)	313,904
Debt Service:				
Interest				
Tax Anticipation Warrants..........	77,500	77,994	(494)	57,509
Total Debt Service Interest..	77,500	77,994	(494)	57,509

Exhibit D-3

GENERAL FUND – EDUCATIONAL ACCOUNTS
STATEMENT OF REVENUES, EXPENDITURES AND CHANGES IN FUND BALANCE – BUDGET AND ACTUAL
FOR THE YEAR ENDED JUNE 30, 1994
WITH COMPARATIVE ACTUAL AMOUNTS FOR THE YEAR ENDED JUNE 30, 1993

	1994 BUDGET	1994 ACTUAL	VARIANCE FAVORABLE (UNFAVORABLE)	1993 ACTUAL
Provision for Contingencies	$ 1,000,000	$ –	$ 1,000,000	$ –
Total Expenditures	33,318,452	33,095,340	223,112	30,929,951
EXCESS (DEFICIENCY) OF REVENUES OVER EXPENDITURES	(1,683,083)	(902,437)	780,646	443,512
OTHER FINANCING SOURCES (USES) –				
Sale or Compensation for Fixed Assets	–	–	–	1,557
Permanent Transfer of Interest	(300,000)	(300,000)	–	(341,918)
Total Other Financing Sources (Uses)	(300,000)	(300,000)	–	(340,361)
EXCESS (DEFICIENCY) OF REVENUES AND OTHER FINANCING SOURCES OVER EXPENDITURES AND OTHER (USES)	$(1,983,083)	(1,202,437)	$ 780,646	103,151
FUND BALANCE, BEGINNING OF YEAR		4,666,902		4,563,751
FUND BALANCE, END OF YEAR		$ 3,464,465		$ 4,666,902

Exhibit D-4

GENERAL FUND - OPERATIONS AND MAINTENANCE ACCOUNTS
STATEMENT OF REVENUES, EXPENDITURES AND CHANGES IN FUND BALANCE - BUDGET AND ACTUAL
FOR THE YEAR ENDED JUNE 30, 1994
WITH COMPARATIVE ACTUAL AMOUNTS FOR THE YEAR ENDED JUNE 30, 1993

	1994 BUDGET	1994 ACTUAL	VARIANCE FAVORABLE (UNFAVORABLE)	1993 ACTUAL
REVENUES				
Local Sources				
General levy	$ 2,791,000	$ 2,840,579	$ 49,579	$ 2,620,456
Tort immunity levy	100,000	97,099	(2,901)	147,482
Corporate personal property replacement taxes	75,000	135,616	60,616	94,967
Rentals	30,000	38,297	8,297	42,421
Contributions and donations from private sources	-	4,866	4,866	28,123
Other	25,000	83,574	58,574	1,928
Total Local Sources	3,021,000	3,200,031	179,031	2,935,377
State Sources				
General state aid	670,000	670,000	-	669,984
Total State Sources	670,000	670,000	-	669,984
Total Revenues	3,691,000	3,870,031	179,031	3,605,361
EXPENDITURES				
Supporting Services				
Business				
Facilities Acquisition and Construction Services				
Purchased services	7,000	7,416	(416)	22,711
Capital outlay	-	4,114	(4,114)	51,272
Other objects	5,600	-	5,600	5,797
Total	12,600	11,530	1,070	79,780
Operation and Maintenance of Plant Services				
Salaries	1,525,365	1,525,074	291	1,439,173
Employee benefits	122,600	115,248	7,352	98,339
Purchased services	388,039	354,975	33,064	331,236
Supplies and materials	1,179,395	1,289,060	(109,665)	1,162,134
Capital outlay	17,900	18,488	(588)	3,030
Total	3,233,299	3,302,845	(69,546)	3,033,912
Total Business	3,245,899	3,314,375	(68,476)	3,113,692

Exhibit D-4

GENERAL FUND - OPERATIONS AND MAINTENANCE ACCOUNTS
STATEMENT OF REVENUES, EXPENDITURES AND CHANGES IN FUND BALANCE - BUDGET AND ACTUAL
FOR THE YEAR ENDED JUNE 30, 1994
WITH COMPARATIVE ACTUAL AMOUNTS FOR THE YEAR ENDED JUNE 30, 1993

	1994 BUDGET	1994 ACTUAL	VARIANCE FAVORABLE (UNFAVORABLE)	1993 ACTUAL
Other Supporting Services				
Purchased services	$ -	$ 469	$ (469)	$ 949
Supplies and materials	-	(107)	107	1,079
Total	-	362	(362)	2,028
Total Support Services	3,245,899	3,314,737	(68,838)	3,115,720
Nonprogrammed Charges				
Payments to other Governmental Units (In-State)				
Payments for Special Education Programs				
Other objects	42,870	635	42,235	33,908
Total	42,870	635	42,235	33,908
Total Payments to Other Governmental Units (in state)	42,870	635	42,235	33,908
Total Nonprogrammed Charges	42,870	635	42,235	33,908
Provision for Contingencies	200,000	-	200,000	-
Total Expenditures	3,488,769	3,315,372	173,397	3,149,628
EXCESS (DEFICIENCY) OF REVENUES OVER EXPENDITURES	202,231	554,659	352,428	455,733
OTHER FINANCING SOURCES (USES)				
Permanent Transfer from Educational Fund	-	-	-	161,839
Sale or Compensation For Fixed Assets	-	-	-	120
Total Other Financing Sources (Uses)	-	-	-	161,959
EXCESS (DEFICIENCY) OF REVENUES AND OTHER FINANCING SOURCES OVER EXPENDITURES AND OTHER (USES)	$ 202,231	554,659	$ 352,428	617,692
FUND BALANCE, BEGINNING OF YEAR		73,610		(544,082)
FUND BALANCE, END OF YEAR		$ 628,269		$ 73,610

Exhibit E-1

SPECIAL REVENUE FUNDS
COMBINING BALANCE SHEET
JUNE 30, 1994
WITH COMPARATIVE TOTALS FOR JUNE 30, 1993

	TRANS-PORTATION	MUNICIPAL RETIREMENT	HOPE WALL GENERAL	TOTAL 1994	TOTAL 1993
ASSETS					
Cash	$ 281,194	$ 242,198	$ 491,783	$1,015,175	$1,037,483
Investments	250,000	700,000	-	950,000	-
Receivables (net of allowance for uncollectibles):					
Property taxes	530,977	456,680	-	987,657	1,856,309
Intergovernmental	179,591	-	-	179,591	225,615
Other current assets	-	-	-	-	10,394
Inventory	38,878	-	-	38,878	64,704
Total Assets	$1,280,640	$1,398,878	$ 491,783	$3,171,301	$3,194,505
LIABILITIES AND FUND BALANCE					
Liabilities					
Accounts payable	$ 11,773	$ 76,162	$ -	$ 87,935	$ 8,641
Wages payable	75,060	-	-	75,060	105,726
Deferred revenue	517,143	444,782	-	961,925	926,790
Other current liabilities	-	-	491,783	491,783	734,897
Total Liabilities	603,976	520,944	491,783	1,616,703	1,776,054
Fund Balance					
Reserved:					
Reserved fund balance	38,878	-	-	38,878	64,704
Unreserved:					
Unrestricted	637,786	877,934	-	1,515,720	1,353,747
Total Fund Balance	676,664	877,934	-	1,554,598	1,418,451
Total Liabilities And Fund Balance	$1,280,640	$1,398,878	$ 491,783	$3,171,301	$3,194,505

Exhibit E-2

SPECIAL REVENUE FUNDS
COMBINING STATEMENT OF REVENUES, EXPENDITURES AND CHANGES IN FUND BALANCES
FOR THE YEAR ENDED JUNE 30, 1994
WITH COMPARATIVE TOTALS FOR THE YEAR ENDED JUNE 30, 1993

	TRANS-PORTATION	MUNICIPAL RETIREMENT	HOPE WALL GENERAL	TOTAL 1994	TOTAL 1993
REVENUES					
Local Sources:					
Property taxes	$ 953,704	$ 995,152	$ -	$1,948,856	$2,060,371
Replacement taxes	44,242	71,934	-	116,176	116,320
Other taxes	-	-	-	-	22,640
Tuition	-	-	1,639,062	1,639,062	1,526,899
Transportation fees	118,092	-	-	118,092	66,228
Earnings on investments	2,082	7,446	6,877	16,405	15,374
Other local sources	-	-	4,486	4,486	6,992
Total Local Sources	1,118,120	1,074,532	1,650,425	3,843,077	3,814,824
State Sources	716,620	-	358,313	1,074,933	1,153,970
Federal Sources	-	-	129,080	129,080	119,741
Total Revenues	1,834,740	1,074,532	2,137,818	5,047,090	5,088,535
EXPENDITURES					
Current:					
Instruction	-	213,832	1,954,700	2,168,532	1,951,001
Support Services	1,730,412	659,548	172,310	2,562,270	2,536,719
Community Services	-	1,920	-	1,920	-
Capital Outlay	167,413	-	10,808	178,221	201,633
Total Expenditures	1,897,825	875,300	2,137,818	4,910,943	4,689,353
EXCESS (DEFICIENCY) OF REVENUES OVER EXPENDITURES	(63,085)	199,232	-	136,147	399,182
FUND BALANCE, BEGINNING OF YEAR	739,749	678,702	-	1,418,451	1,019,269
FUND BALANCE, END OF YEAR	$ 676,664	$ 877,934	$ -	$1,554,598	$1,418,451

Exhibit E-3

TRANSPORTATION FUND
STATEMENT OF REVENUES, EXPENDITURES AND CHANGES IN FUND BALANCE - BUDGET AND ACTUAL
FOR THE YEAR ENDED JUNE 30, 1994
WITH COMPARATIVE ACTUAL AMOUNTS FOR THE YEAR ENDED JUNE 30, 1993

	1994 BUDGET	1994 ACTUAL	VARIANCE FAVORABLE (UNFAVORABLE)	1993 ACTUAL
REVENUES				
Local Sources				
General Levy	$ 899,300	$ 953,704	$ 54,404	$ 954,819
Corporate Personal Property Replacement Taxes	35,000	44,242	9,242	40,600
Transportation Fees from Private Sources	60,000	99,786	39,786	58,467
Transportation Fees from Pupils - Cocurricular Activities	-	3,724	3,724	7,761
Summer School Transportation Fees	-	14,582	14,582	22,640
Earnings on Investments	-	2,082	2,082	830
Other	2,000	-	(2,000)	2,145
Total Local Sources	996,300	1,118,120	121,820	1,087,262
State Sources				
Regular Trans. Aid	140,000	287,559	147,559	351,796
Special Ed. Trans. Aid	468,000	429,061	(38,939)	551,547
Total State Sources	608,000	716,620	108,620	903,343
Total Revenues	1,604,300	1,834,740	230,440	1,990,605
EXPENDITURES				
Support Services				
Business				
Pupil Transportation Services				
Salaries	586,420	600,905	(14,485)	630,088
Employee benefits	61,250	69,687	(8,437)	58,514
Purchased Services	905,408	851,994	53,414	813,051
Supplies and materials	177,300	207,826	(30,526)	168,360
Capital Outlay	171,800	167,413	4,387	191,663
Total	1,902,178	1,897,825	4,353	1,861,676
Total Support Services	1,902,178	1,897,825	4,353	1,861,676
Provision for Contingencies	55,000	-	55,000	-
Total Expenditures	1,957,178	1,897,825	59,353	1,861,676
EXCESS (DEFICIENCY) OF REVENUES OVER EXPENDITURES	$ (352,878)	(63,085)	$ 289,793	128,929
FUND BALANCE, BEGINNING OF YEAR		739,749		610,820
FUND BALANCE, END OF YEAR		$ 676,664		$ 739,749

Exhibit E-4

MUNICIPAL RETIREMENT FUND
STATEMENT OF REVENUES, EXPENDITURES AND CHANGES IN FUND BALANCE - BUDGET AND ACTUAL
FOR THE YEAR ENDED JUNE 30, 1994
WITH COMPARATIVE ACTUAL AMOUNTS FOR THE YEAR ENDED JUNE 30, 1993

	1994 BUDGET	1994 ACTUAL	VARIANCE FAVORABLE (UNFAVORABLE)	1993 ACTUAL
REVENUES				
LOCAL SOURCES				
General Levy	$ 917,100	$ 995,152	$ 78,052	$ 1,105,552
Corporate Personal Property Replacement Taxes	72,900	71,934	(966)	75,720
Earnings on Investments	10,000	7,446	(2,554)	1,634
Total Local Sources	1,000,000	1,074,532	74,532	1,182,906
Total Revenues	1,000,000	1,074,532	74,532	1,182,906
EXPENDITURES				
Instruction				
Regular Programs	94,744	101,238	(6,494)	94,247
Special Education Programs	87,601	76,375	11,226	74,515
Educationally Deprived / Remedial Programs	8,098	7,505	593	7,158
Vocational Educational Programs	343	1,233	(890)	303
Interscholastic Programs	1,140	1,219	(79)	1,007
Summer School Programs	5,658	5,559	99	5,001
Gifted Programs	18	14	4	16
Bilingual Programs	22,827	20,689	2,138	20,177
Total Instruction	220,429	213,832	6,597	202,424
Support Services				
Pupils				
Attendance and Social Work Services	2,584	2,432	152	2,284
Guidance Services	4,180	4,239	(59)	3,694
Health Services	24,262	23,106	1,156	21,445
Psychological Services	1,516	1,445	71	1,340
Total Pupils	32,542	31,222	1,320	28,763
Instructional Staff				
Improvement of Instruction Services	3,673	4,316	(643)	3,247
Total Instructional Staff	3,673	4,316	(643)	3,247

Exhibit E-4

MUNICIPAL RETIREMENT FUND
STATEMENT OF REVENUES, EXPENDITURES AND CHANGES IN FUND BALANCE - BUDGET AND ACTUAL
FOR THE YEAR ENDED JUNE 30, 1994
WITH COMPARATIVE ACTUAL AMOUNTS FOR THE YEAR ENDED JUNE 30, 1993

	1994 BUDGET	1994 ACTUAL	VARIANCE FAVORABLE (UNFAVORABLE)	1993 ACTUAL
General Administration				
Board of Education Services.........$	1,848	$ 92	$ 1,756	$ 144
Executive Administration Services...	60,108	60,654	(546)	63,340
Special Area Administrative Services	6,329	6,115	214	7,084
Total General Administration.....	68,285	66,861	1,424	70,568
School Administration				
Office of the Principal Services....	125,690	114,258	11,432	124,376
Total School Administration......	125,690	114,258	11,432	124,376
Business				
Fiscal Services....................	36,828	34,160	2,668	32,552
Operation and Maintenance of Plant Services.....................	323,545	272,760	50,785	318,661
Pupil Transportation Services.......	122,782	124,748	(1,966)	117,720
Food Services.......................	12,178	9,483	2,695	10,763
Internal Services..................	-	3	(3)	-
Total Business...................	495,333	441,154	54,179	479,696
Central				
Planning, Research, Development and Evaluation Services............	-	29	(29)	3,579
Total Central...................	-	29	(29)	3,579
Other Support Services..............	1,844	1,708	136	-
Total Support Services..........	727,367	659,548	67,819	710,229
Community Services...................	2,204	1,920	284	-
Total Expenditures.....	950,000	875,300	74,700	912,653
EXCESS (DEFICIENCY) OF REVENUES OVER EXPENDITURES........................$	50,000	199,232	$ 149,232	270,253
FUND BALANCE, BEGINNING OF YEAR.......		678,702		408,449
FUND BALANCE, END OF YEAR............		$ 877,934		$ 678,702

Exhibit E-5

GENERAL FUND - HOPE WALL SPECIAL EDUCATION JOINT AGREEMENT
STATEMENT OF REVENUES, EXPENDITURES AND CHANGES IN FUND BALANCE - BUDGET AND ACTUAL
FOR THE YEAR ENDED JUNE 30, 1994
WITH COMPARATIVE ACTUAL AMOUNTS FOR THE YEAR ENDED JUNE 30, 1993

	1994 BUDGET	1994 ACTUAL	VARIANCE FAVORABLE (UNFAVORABLE)	1993 ACTUAL
REVENUES				
Local Sources				
Tuition:				
School District No. 129	$ 718,178	$ 862,661	$ 144,483	$ 580,996
School District No. 131	718,179	635,041	(83,138)	712,667
Other districts	377,126	141,360	(235,766)	233,236
Total Tuition	1,813,483	1,639,062	(174,421)	1,526,899
Earnings on investments	12,000	6,877	(5,123)	12,910
Other	2,500	4,486	1,986	4,847
Total Local Sources	1,827,983	1,650,425	(177,558)	1,544,656
State Sources				
Grant for special education:				
Personnel	306,000	360,629	54,629	209,804
Extraordinary	180,000	(2,316)	(182,316)	40,823
Total State Sources	486,000	358,313	(127,687)	250,627
Federal Sources				
ESEA, Chapter 1	12,893	15,993	3,100	31,116
EHA - Preschool incentive grant	127,417	113,087	(14,330)	88,625
Total Federal Sources	140,310	129,080	(11,230)	119,741
Total Revenues	2,454,293	2,137,818	(316,475)	1,915,024
EXPENDITURES				
INSTRUCTION				
Mental Impairment - Regular Term:				
Salaries	1,517,008	1,438,723	78,285	1,314,991
Employee benefits	164,000	164,783	(783)	149,986
Purchased services	187,091	181,013	6,078	147,071
Supplies and materials	80,281	104,578	(24,297)	87,353
Capital outlay	10,070	10,808	(738)	9,970
Total Mental Impairment Regular Term	1,958,450	1,899,905	58,545	1,709,371

APPENDIX E • 53

Exhibit E-5

GENERAL FUND – HOPE WALL SPECIAL EDUCATION JOINT AGREEMENT
STATEMENT OF REVENUES, EXPENDITURES AND CHANGES IN FUND BALANCE – BUDGET AND ACTUAL
FOR THE YEAR ENDED JUNE 30, 1994
WITH COMPARATIVE ACTUAL AMOUNTS FOR THE YEAR ENDED JUNE 30, 1993

	1994 BUDGET	1994 ACTUAL	VARIANCE FAVORABLE (UNFAVORABLE)	1993 ACTUAL
Mental Impairment – Summer Term:				
Salaries	$ 39,600	$ 24,980	$ 14,620	$ 13,460
Employee benefits	1,750	3,383	(1,633)	1,473
Supplies and materials	700	1,295	(595)	600
Total Mental Impairment Summer Term	42,050	29,658	12,392	15,533
Multi-Handicapped:				
Salaries	41,560	29,401	12,159	29,324
Employee benefits	2,000	2,562	(562)	2,425
Total Multi-Handicapped	43,560	31,963	11,597	31,749
Other Vocational Programs:				
Salaries	4,000	3,982	18	1,894
Total Other Vocational	4,000	3,982	18	1,894
Total Instruction	2,048,060	1,965,508	82,552	1,758,547
SUPPORT SERVICES				
Pupils:				
Social Work:				
Salaries	18,664	–	18,664	–
Total Social Work	18,664	–	18,664	–
Health:				
Salaries	11,054	8,825	2,229	6,892
Employee benefits	1,950	1,386	564	–
Total Health	13,004	10,211	2,793	6,892
Psychological Testing:				
Salaries	67,335	63,830	3,505	58,960
Employee benefits	3,200	4,043	(843)	2,527
Total Psychological testing	70,535	67,873	2,662	61,487
Speech and Audio Services:				
Supplies and materials	–	–	–	215
Total Speech and Audio Services	–	–	–	215
Total Pupils	102,203	78,084	24,119	68,594

Exhibit E-5

GENERAL FUND - HOPE WALL SPECIAL EDUCATION JOINT AGREEMENT
STATEMENT OF REVENUES, EXPENDITURES AND CHANGES IN FUND BALANCE - BUDGET AND ACTUAL
FOR THE YEAR ENDED JUNE 30, 1994
WITH COMPARATIVE ACTUAL AMOUNTS FOR THE YEAR ENDED JUNE 30, 1993

	1994 BUDGET	1994 ACTUAL	VARIANCE FAVORABLE (UNFAVORABLE)	1993 ACTUAL
Instructional Staff				
Improvement of Instruction Service:				
Supplies and materials...........	$ —	$ —	$ —	$ 300
Total Improvement of Instruction Services.......	—	—	—	300
Total Instructional Staff.	—	—	—	300
General Administration				
Board of Education Service:				
Purchased services...............	2,000	2,000	—	2,000
Total Board of Education Services.........	2,000	2,000	—	2,000
Executive Administration Service:				
Employee benefits................	4,500	4,281	219	3,858
Total Executive Administration Services....	4,500	4,281	219	3,858
Total General Administration....	6,500	6,281	219	5,858
School Administration				
Office of the Principal Services:				
Supplies and materials...........	500	409	91	420
Total Office of the Principal Services.........	500	409	91	420
Total School Administration.....	500	409	91	420

Exhibit E-5

GENERAL FUND – HOPE WALL SPECIAL EDUCATION JOINT AGREEMENT
STATEMENT OF REVENUES, EXPENDITURES AND CHANGES IN FUND BALANCE – BUDGET AND ACTUAL
FOR THE YEAR ENDED JUNE 30, 1994
WITH COMPARATIVE ACTUAL AMOUNTS FOR THE YEAR ENDED JUNE 30, 1993

	1994 BUDGET	1994 ACTUAL	VARIANCE FAVORABLE (UNFAVORABLE)	1993 ACTUAL
Business				
Operation and Maintenance of Plant Services:				
Purchased services	$ 39,150	$ 27,546	$ 11,604	$ 28,234
Supplies and materials	68,600	54,990	13,610	52,906
Total Operation and Maintenance of Plant Services	107,750	82,536	25,214	81,140
Other Pupil Transportation Services:				
Purchased services	5,000	5,000	–	165
Total Other Pupil Transportation Services	5,000	5,000	–	165
Total Business	112,750	87,536	25,214	81,305
Total Support Services	221,953	172,310	49,643	156,477
Provision for contingencies	65,875	–	65,875	–
Total Expenditures	2,335,888	2,137,818	198,070	1,915,024
EXCESS OF REVENUES OVER EXPENDIUTRES	$ 118,405	–	$ (514,545)	–
FUND BALANCE, BEGINNING OF YEAR		–		–
FUND BALANCE, END OF YEAR		$ –		$ –

Exhibit F-1

BOND AND INTEREST FUND
BALANCE SHEET
JUNE 30, 1994
WITH COMPARATIVE TOTALS FOR JUNE 30, 1993

	1994	1993
ASSETS		
Cash	$ 736,823	$ 614,638
Investments	925,000	–
Receivables (net of allowance for uncollectibles):		
Property taxes	1,601,847	2,777,661
Total Assets	$ 3,263,670	$ 3,392,299
LIABILITIES AND FUND BALANCE		
Liabilities		
Due to other funds	$ –	$ 240,000
Deferred revenue	1,560,112	1,386,802
Total Liabilities	1,560,112	1,626,802
Fund Balance		
Unreserved:		
Undesignated	1,703,558	1,765,497
Total Fund Balance	1,703,558	1,765,497
Total Liabilities And Fund Balance	$ 3,263,670	$ 3,392,299

Exhibit F-2

BOND AND INTEREST FUND
STATEMENT OF REVENUES, EXPENDITURES AND CHANGES IN FUND BALANCE - BUDGET AND ACTUAL
FOR THE YEAR ENDED JUNE 30, 1994
WITH COMPARATIVE ACTUAL AMOUNTS FOR THE YEAR ENDED JUNE 30, 1993

	1994 BUDGET	1994 ACTUAL	VARIANCE FAVORABLE (UNFAVORABLE)	1993 ACTUAL
REVENUES				
Local Sources				
General Levy	$ 3,052,206	$ 3,042,639	$ (9,567)	$ 3,108,497
Corporate Personal Property Replacement Taxes	127,607	-	(127,607)	127,607
Earnings on Investments	30,000	31,756	1,756	31,881
Total Local Sources	3,209,813	3,074,395	(135,418)	3,267,985
Total Revenues	3,209,813	3,074,395	(135,418)	3,267,985
EXPENDITURES				
Debt service				
Interest:				
Bonds	659,812	629,813	29,999	925,113
Total Debt Service Interest	659,812	629,813	29,999	925,113
Bond Principal Retired	2,500,000	2,500,000	-	2,300,000
Other Debt Service				
Other objects	-	6,521	(6,521)	-
Total	-	6,521	(6,521)	-
Total Debt Service	3,159,812	3,136,334	23,478	3,225,113
Provision for Contingencies	50,000	-	50,000	-
Total Expenditures	3,209,812	3,136,334	73,478	3,225,113
EXCESS (DEFICIENCY) OF REVENUES OVER EXPENDITURES	1	(61,939)	(61,940)	42,872
OTHER FINANCING SOURCES (USES)				
Permanent Transfer of Interest	-	-	-	(240,000)
Total Other Financing Sources (Uses)	-	-	-	(240,000)
EXCESS (DEFICIENCY) OF REVENUES AND OTHER FINANCING SOURCES OVER EXPENDITURES AND OTHER (USES)	$ 1	(61,939)	$ (61,940)	(197,128)
FUND BALANCE, BEGINNING OF YEAR		1,765,497		1,962,625
FUND BALANCE, END OF YEAR		$ 1,703,558		$ 1,765,497

Exhibit G-1

CAPITAL PROJECTS FUNDS
COMBINING BALANCE SHEET
JUNE 30, 1994
WITH COMPARATIVE TOTALS FOR JUNE 30, 1993

	SITE AND CONSTRUCTION	FIRE PREVENTION & LIFE SAFETY	TOTAL 1994	1993
ASSETS				
Cash	$ 91,716	$ 983,188	$ 1,074,904	$ 1,145,253
Total Assets	$ 91,716	$ 983,188	$ 1,074,904	$ 1,145,253
LIABILITIES AND FUND BALANCES				
Liabilities				
Accounts payable	$ -	$ -	$ -	$ 85,453
Total Liabilities	-	-	-	85,453
Fund Balance				
Reserved:				
Reserved fund balance	-	-	-	1,059,800
Unreserved:				
Undesignated	91,716	983,188	1,074,904	-
Total Fund Balance	91,716	983,188	1,074,904	1,059,800
Total Liabilities And Fund Balance	$ 91,716	$ 983,188	$ 1,074,904	$ 1,145,253

Exhibit G-2

CAPITAL PROJECTS FUNDS
COMBINING STATEMENT OF REVENUES, EXPENDITURES AND CHANGES IN FUND BALANCES
FOR THE YEAR ENDED JUNE 30, 1994
WITH COMPARATIVE TOTALS FOR THE YEAR ENDED JUNE 30, 1993

	SITE & CONSTRUCTION	FIRE PREVENTION & LIFE SAFETY	TOTAL 1994	TOTAL 1993
REVENUES				
Local Sources:				
Earnings on investments	$ -	$ 12,103	$ 12,103	$ 34,335
Total Local Sources	-	12,103	12,103	34,335
State Sources	156,320	-	156,320	-
Total revenues	156,320	12,103	168,423	34,335
EXPENDITURES				
Support Services	355,604	9,311	364,915	917,210
Capital Outlay	9,000	79,404	88,404	1,338,604
Total expenditures	364,604	88,715	453,319	2,255,814
EXCESS (DEFICIENCY) OF REVENUES OVER EXPENDITURES	(208,284)	(76,612)	(284,896)	(2,221,479)
OTHER FINANCING SOURCES (USES)				
Transfers	300,000	-	300,000	420,079
Total Other Financing Sources (Uses)	300,000	-	300,000	420,079
EXCESS (DEFICIENCY) OF REVENUES AND OTHER FINANCING SOURCES OVER EXPENDITURES AND OTHER (USES)	91,716	(76,612)	15,104	(1,801,400)
FUND BALANCE, BEGINNING OF YEAR	1,059,800	-	1,059,800	2,861,200
RESIDUAL EQUITY TRANSFER	(1,059,800)	1,059,800	-	-
FUND BALANCE, END OF YEAR	$ 91,716	$ 983,188	$ 1,074,904	$ 1,059,800

Exhibit G-3

SITE AND CONSTRUCTION FUND
STATEMENT OF REVENUES, EXPENDITURES AND CHANGES IN FUND BALANCE - BUDGET AND ACTUAL
FOR THE YEAR ENDED JUNE 30, 1994
WITH COMPARATIVE ACTUAL AMOUNTS FOR THE YEAR ENDED JUNE 30, 1993

	1994 BUDGET	1994 ACTUAL	VARIANCE FAVORABLE (UNFAVORABLE)	1993 ACTUAL
REVENUES				
LOCAL SOURCES				
Earnings on Investments	$ -	$ -	$ -	$ 34,335
Total Local Sources	-	-	-	34,335
State Sources				
Other Grants-in-Aid	-	156,320	156,320	-
Total State Sources	-	156,320	156,320	-
Total Revenues	-	156,320	156,320	34,335
EXPENDITURES				
Support Services				
Facilities Acquisition and Construction Services				
Purchased Services	-	-	-	730,638
Supplies and Materials	285,170	355,604	(70,434)	186,572
Capital Outlay	-	9,000	(9,000)	1,338,604
Total	285,170	364,604	(79,434)	2,255,814
Total Support Services	285,170	364,604	(79,434)	2,255,814
Provision for contingencies	10,000	-	10,000	-
Total Expenditures	295,170	364,604	(69,434)	2,255,814
EXCESS (DEFICIENCY) OF REVENUES OVER EXPENDITURES	(295,170)	(208,284)	86,886	(2,221,479)
OTHER FINANCING SOURCES (USES)				
Permanent Transfer of Interest	300,000	300,000	-	420,079
Total Other Financing Sources (Uses)	300,000	300,000	-	420,079
EXCESS (DEFICIENCY) OF REVENUES AND OTHER FINANCING SOURCES OVER EXPENDITURES AND OTHER (USES)	$ 4,830	91,716	$ 86,886	(1,801,400)
FUND BALANCE, BEGINNING OF YEAR		1,059,800		2,861,200
RESIDUAL EQUITY TRANSFER		(1,059,800)		-
FUND BALANCE, END OF YEAR		$ 91,716		$ 1,059,800

Exhibit G-4

FIRE PREVENTION AND LIFE SAFETY FUND
STATEMENT OF REVENUES, EXPENDITURES AND CHANGES IN FUND BALANCE - BUDGET AND ACTUAL
FOR THE YEAR ENDED JUNE 30, 1994
WITH COMPARATIVE ACTUAL AMOUNTS FOR THE YEAR ENDED JUNE 30, 1993

	1994 BUDGET	1994 ACTUAL	VARIANCE FAVORABLE (UNFAVORABLE)	1993 ACTUAL
REVENUES				
LOCAL SOURCES				
Earnings on Investments	$ 5,000	$ 12,103	$ 7,103	$ -
Total Local Sources	5,000	12,103	7,103	-
Total Revenues	5,000	12,103	7,103	-
EXPENDITURES				
Support Services				
Facilities Acquisition and Construction Services				
Purchased Services	1,145,000	(5,208)	1,150,208	-
Supplies and Materials	-	14,519	(14,519)	-
Capital Outlay	-	79,404	(79,404)	-
Total	1,145,000	88,715	1,056,285	-
Total Support Services	1,145,000	88,715	1,056,285	-
Total Expenditures	1,145,000	88,715	1,056,285	-
EXCESS (DEFICIENCY) OF REVENUES OVER EXPENDITURES	$(1,140,000)	(76,612)	$ 1,063,388	-
FUND BALANCE, BEGINNING OF YEAR		-		-
RESIDUAL EQUITY TRANSFER		1,059,800		
FUND BALANCE, END OF YEAR		$ 983,188		$ -

Exhibit H-1

TRUST AND AGENCY FUNDS
COMBINING BALANCE SHEET
JUNE 30, 1994
WITH COMPARATIVE TOTALS FOR JUNE 30, 1993

	EXPENDABLE TRUST WORKING CASH	DISTRICT AGENCY STUDENT ACTIVITY	HOPE WALL AGENCY STUDENT ACTIVITY	TOTAL 1994	1993
ASSETS					
Cash	$ 10,630	$ 351,842	$ 4,232	$ 366,704	$ 375,355
Due from other funds	3,670,000	–	–	3,670,000	3,670,000
Total Assets	$3,680,630	$ 351,842	$ 4,232	$4,036,704	$4,045,355
LIABILITIES AND FUND BALANCES					
Liabilities					
Due to Activity Fund Organizations	$ –	$ 351,842	$ 4,232	$ 356,074	$ 364,725
Total Liabilities	–	351,842	4,232	356,074	364,725
FUND BALANCE					
Unreserved:					
Undesignated	3,680,630	–	–	3,680,630	3,680,630
Total Fund Balance	3,680,630	–	–	3,680,630	3,680,630
Total Liabilities And Fund Balance	$3,680,630	$ 351,842	$ 4,232	$4,036,704	$4,045,355

Exhibit H-2

FIDUCIARY (EXPENDABLE TRUST) FUND – WORKING CASH FUND
STATEMENT OF REVENUES, EXPENDITURES AND CHANGES IN FUND BALANCE – BUDGET AND ACTUAL
FOR THE YEAR ENDED JUNE 30, 1994
WITH COMPARATIVE ACTUAL AMOUNTS FOR THE YEAR ENDED JUNE 30, 1993

	1994 BUDGET	1994 ACTUAL	VARIANCE FAVORABLE (UNFAVORABLE)	1993 ACTUAL
REVENUES				
LOCAL SOURCES				
Corporate Personal Property Replacement Taxes	$ –	$ –	$ –	$ 6,201
Earnings on Investments	–	–	–	1,360
Total Local Sources	–	–	–	7,561
Total Revenues	–	–	–	7,561
EXPENDITURES				
Total Expenditures	–	–	–	–
EXCESS OF REVENUES OVER EXPENDITURES	$ –	–	$ –	7,561
FUND BALANCE, BEGINNING OF YEAR		3,680,630		3,673,069
FUND BALANCE, END OF YEAR		$ 3,680,630		$ 3,680,630

64 • APPENDIX E

Schedule 1

THREE YEAR SUMMARY OF ASSESSED VALUATIONS, TAX RATES, EXTENSIONS AND COLLECTIONS
JUNE 30, 1994

	1993	1992	1991
ASSESSED VALUATION	$ 665,234,284	$ 619,031,240	$ 557,895,463
TAX RATE (1)			
Education	2.7751	2.8285	2.9260
Tort Immunity	0.0150	0.0162	0.0353
Special Education	0.0400	0.0383	0.0398
Operations and Maintenance	0.4636	0.4448	0.4318
Transportation	0.1608	0.1433	0.1807
Illinois Municipal Retirement/			
Social Security	0.1383	0.1841	0.1866
Bond and Interest	0.4851	0.4899	0.5592
Total Rates Extended	4.0779	4.1451	4.3594
TAX EXTENSION			
Education	$ 18,460,917	$ 17,509,299	$ 16,319,836
Tort Immunity	99,785	100,283	196,887
Special Education	266,094	237,089	221,985
Operations and Maintenance	3,084,026	2,753,451	2,408,375
Transportation	1,069,697	887,072	1,007,859
Illinois Municipal Retirement/			
Social Security	920,019	1,139,636	1,040,768
Bond and Interest	3,227,052	3,032,634	3,118,952
Total Levies Extended	$ 27,127,590	$ 25,659,464	$ 24,314,662
PROPERTY TAX COLLECTIONS			
Education	$ 9,112,661	$ 17,491,568	$ 16,193,602
Tort Immunity	49,256	100,181	195,348
Special Education	131,349	236,849	220,246
Operations and Maintenance	1,522,334	2,750,662	2,389,558
Transportation	528,023	886,173	999,998
Illinois Municipal Retirement/			
Social Security	454,139	1,138,483	1,032,640
Bond and Interest	1,592,934	3,029,562	3,094,592
Total Tax Collections to Date	$ 13,390,696	$ 25,633,478	$ 24,125,984
Percent of Extension	49.36%	99.90%	99.22%

(1) Tax rates are expressed per $100 of assessed valuation.

APPENDIX E • 65

Schedule 2

OPERATING COST AND TUITION CHARGE

JUNE 30, 1994

	1993	1994
OPERATING COST PER PUPIL		
Average daily attendance (ADA)	7,712	7,578
Operating Costs:		
Educational	$ 30,540,908	$ 33,095,340
Operations and Maintenance	3,082,291	3,315,372
Bond and Interest	3,225,113	3,136,334
Transportation	1,793,664	1,897,825
Municipal Retirement	839,709	875,300
Sub-total	39,481,685	42,320,171
Less Expenditures of Nonregular Programs:		
Summer school	90,128	85,932
Tuition	1,175,526	2,046,950
Pre-School (At-Risk Programs)	221,825	349,026
Capital outlay	528,579	547,634
Bond Principal Retired	2,300,000	2,500,000
Community Service	87,701	102,029
Nonprogrammed charges	33,908	635
Sub-total	4,437,667	5,632,206
Operating costs	$ 35,044,018	$ 36,687,965
Operating Cost Per Pupil – based on ADA	$ 4,544	$ 4,841
TUITION CHARGE PER PUPIL		
Operating Costs	$ 35,044,018	$ 36,687,965
Less – revenues from specific programs, such as special education or lunch programs	5,667,265	6,233,630
Net operating cost	29,376,753	30,454,335
Depreciation allowance	944,952	1,693,760
Allowable Tuition Costs	$ 30,321,705	$ 32,148,095
TUITION CHARGE PER PUPIL		
Net operating cost per pupil – based on ADA	$ 3,809	$ 4,019
Tution charge per pupil – based on ADA	$ 3,932	$ 4,242

Schedule 3

SCHEDULE OF BONDS OUTSTANDING

JUNE 30, 1994

FIRE PREVENTION AND SAFETY BONDS ISSUED JULY 1, 1984

YEAR ENDED JUNE 30,	BONDS ISSUED	BONDS PAID	BONDS OUTSTANDING	INTEREST PAYABLE	TOTAL DEBT SERVICE
1984	$ —	$ —	$ —	$ —	$ —
1985	—	—	—	—	—
1986	—	—	—	—	—
1987	175,000	175,000	—	—	—
1988	200,000	200,000	—	—	—
1989	225,000	225,000	—	—	—
1990	250,000	250,000	—	—	—
1991	275,000	275,000	—	—	—
1992	300,000	300,000	—	—	—
1993	325,000	325,000	—	—	—
1994	350,000	350,000	—	—	—
1995	220,000	—	220,000	21,450	241,450
Total	$ 2,320,000	$ 2,100,000	$ 220,000	$ 21,450	$ 241,450

Paying Agent: LaSalle National Bank

Principal payment date: June 1

Interest payment dates: June 1 and December 1

Schedule 4

SCHEDULE OF BONDS OUTSTANDING

JUNE 30, 1994

FIRE PREVENTION AND SAFETY BONDS ISSUED JUNE 30, 1987

YEAR ENDED JUNE 30,	BONDS ISSUED	BONDS PAID	BONDS OUTSTANDING	INTEREST PAYABLE	TOTAL DEBT SERVICE
1989	$ 150,000	$ 150,000	$ —	$ —	$ —
1990	375,000	375,000	—	—	—
1991	400,000	400,000	—	—	—
1992	450,000	450,000	—	—	—
1993	525,000	525,000	—	—	—
1994	575,000	575,000	—	—	—
1995	2,525,000	—	2,525,000	161,600	2,686,600
Total	$ 5,000,000	$ 2,475,000	$ 2,525,000	$ 161,600	$ 2,686,600

Paying Agent: LaSalle National Bank

Principal payment date: January 1

Interest payment dates: July 1 and January 1

Schedule 5

SCHEDULE OF BONDS OUTSTANDING

JUNE 30, 1994

FIRE PREVENTION AND SAFETY BONDS ISSUED JUNE 1, 1991

YEAR ENDED JUNE 30,	BONDS ISSUED	BONDS PAID	BONDS OUTSTANDING	INTEREST PAYABLE	TOTAL DEBT SERVICE
1992	$ —	$ —	$ —	$ —	$ —
1993	—	—	—	—	—
1994	—	—	—	—	—
1995	—	—	—	146,875	146,875
1996	2,500,000	—	2,500,000	146,875	2,646,875
Total	$ 2,500,000	$ —	$ 2,500,000	$ 293,750	$ 2,793,750

Paying Agent: Amalgamated Trust and Savings Bank

Principal payment date: January 1

Interest payment dates: July 1 and January 1

APPENDIX E • 69

Schedule 6

SCHEDULE OF BONDS OUTSTANDING

JUNE 30, 1994

FIRE PREVENTION AND SAFETY BONDS ISSUED SEPTEMBER 1, 1991

YEAR ENDED JUNE 30,	BONDS ISSUED	BONDS PAID	BONDS OUTSTANDING	INTEREST PAYABLE	TOTAL DEBT SERVICE
1992	$ —	$ —	$ —	$ —	$ —
1993	—	—	—	—	—
1994	—	—	—	—	—
1995	—	—	—	120,100	120,100
1996	500,000	—	500,000	120,100	620,100
1997	1,600,000	—	1,600,000	89,600	1,689,600
Total	$ 2,100,000	$ —	$ 2,100,000	$ 329,800	$ 2,429,800

Paying Agent: Amalgamated Trust and Savings Bank

Principal payment date: January 1

Interest payment dates: January 1 and July 1

Schedule 7

ILLINOIS MUNICIPAL RETIREMENT FUND
ANALYSIS OF FUNDING PROGRESS
JUNE 30, 1994

Year	Pension Benefit Obligation	Assets at Cost	Percent Funded	Unfunded Pension Obligation	Annual Covered Payroll	Unfunded as a Percentage of Payroll
1993	$ 7,160,302	$ 4,281,856	59.80%	$ 2,878,446	$ 4,239,738	67.89%
1992	6,601,318	3,960,597	60.00%	2,640,721	4,038,787	65.38%
1991	6,407,545	3,782,322	59.03%	2,625,223	3,882,477	67.62%
1990	6,634,577	3,622,263	54.60%	3,012,314	3,664,850	82.19%
1989	5,529,394	3,066,776	55.46%	2,462,618	3,285,925	74.94%
1988	5,024,550	2,635,519	52.45%	2,389,031	3,056,139	78.17%
1987	4,491,825	2,441,012	54.34%	2,050,813	2,864,916	71.58%

The trend information shown above is provided starting in 1987, which was the first year this information was available.

Smith, Jones & Co., Ltd.
Certified Public Accountants
1 Main Street • Anytown, IL 66321
Telephone: 312/555-0000 • Fax: 312/555-9999

INDEPENDENT AUDITORS' REPORT ON INTERNAL CONTROL STRUCTURE
BASED ON AN AUDIT OF COMBINED FINANCIAL STATEMENTS
PERFORMED IN ACCORDANCE WITH *GOVERNMENT AUDITING STANDARDS*

September 12, 1994

Board of Education
School District
111 Main Street
Anytown, IL 66321

Dear Board Members:

We have audited the combined financial statements of _____SCHOOL DISTRICT_____ as of and for the year ended June 30, 1994, and have issued our report thereon dated September 12, 1994. In our report, our opinion was qualified because the District does not maintain historical cost fixed asset records.

We conducted our audit in accordance with generally accepted auditing standards; Government Auditing Standards, issued by the Comptroller General of the United States; and the provisions of Office of Management and Budget Circular A-128, "Audits of State and Local Governments." Those standards and OMB Circular A-128 require that we plan and perform the audit to obtain reasonable assurance about whether the combined financial statements are free of material misstatement.

In planning and performing our audit of the combined financial statements of ___SCHOOL DISTRICT___ for the year ended June 30, 1994, we considered its internal control structure in order to determine our auditing procedures for the purpose of expressing our opinion on the combined financial statements and not to provide assurance on the internal control structure.

The management of ___SCHOOL DISTRICT___ is responsible for establishing and maintaining an internal control structure. In fulfilling this responsibility, estimates and judgements by management are required to assess the expected benefits and related costs of internal control structure policies and procedures. The objectives of an internal control structure are to provide management with reasonable, but not absolute, assurance that assets are safeguarded against loss from unauthorized use or disposition, and that transactions are executed in accordance with management's authorization and recorded properly to permit the preparation of combined financial statements in accordance with generally accepted accounting principles. Because of inherent limitations in any internal control structure, errors or irregularities may nevertheless occur and not be detected. Also, projection of any evaluation of the structure to future periods is subject to the risk that procedures may become inadequate because of changes in conditions or that the effectiveness of the design and operation of policies and procedures may deteriorate.

For the purpose of this report, we have classified the significant internal control structure policies and procedures in the following categories:

> Cash disbursements
> Payroll expenditures
> ***General Requirements***
>   Political activity
>   Civil rights
>   Allowable costs/cost principles
>   Drug-Free Workplace Act
> ***Specific Requirements***
>   Types of services allowed or not allowed
>   Eligibility
>   Matching, level of effort, or earmarking
>   Reporting

For all internal control structure categories listed above, we obtained an understanding of the design of relevant policies and procedures and whether they have been placed in operation, and we assessed control risk.

Our consideration of the internal control structure would not necessarily disclose all matters in the internal control structure that might be material weaknesses under standards established by the American Institute of Certified Public Accountants. A material weakness is a reportable condition in which the design or operation of one or more of the internal control structure elements does not reduce to a relatively low level the risk that errors or irregularities in amounts that would be material in relation to the combined financial statements being audited may occur and not be detected within a timely period by employees in the normal course of performing their assigned functions. We noted no matters involving the internal control structure and its operation that we consider to be material weaknesses as defined above.

However, we noted other matters involving the internal control structure and its operation that we have reported to the management of   SCHOOL DISTRICT   in a separate letter dated September 12, 1994.

This report is intended for the information of the Board of Education, the Illinois State Board of Education and federal granting agencies. However, this report is a matter of public record and its distribution is not limited.

/Signed/
Smith, Jones & Co., Ltd.

APPENDIX E • 73

Smith, Jones & Co., Ltd.
Certified Public Accountants
1 Main Street • Anytown, IL 66321
Telephone: 312/555-0000 • Fax: 312/555-9999

<u>INDEPENDENT AUDITORS' REPORT</u>

September 12, 1994

Board of Education
School District
111 Main Street
Anytown, IL 66321

Dear Board Members:

We have audited the combined financial statements of the   SCHOOL DISTRICT as of and for the year ended June 30, 1994, and have issued our report thereon dated September 12, 1994. In our report, our opinion was qualified because the District does not maintain historical cost fixed asset records.

We conducted our audit in accordance with generally accepted auditing standards; <u>Government Auditing Standards</u>, issued by the Comptroller General of the United States; and the provisions of Office of Management and Budget Circular A-128, "Audits of State and Local Governments." Those standards and OMB Circular A-128 require that we plan and perform the audit to obtain reasonable assurance about whether the combined financial statements are free of material misstatement.

Compliance with laws, regulations, contracts, and grants applicable to   SCHOOL DISTRICT , is the responsibility of West Aurora Schools District 129's management. As part of obtaining reasonable assurance about whether the combined financial statements are free of material misstatement, we performed tests of the District's compliance with certain provisions of laws, regulations, contracts, and grants. However, the objective of our audit of the combined financial statements was not to provide an opinion on overall compliance with such provisions. Accordingly, we do not express such an opinion.

APPENDIX E

The results of our tests indicate that, with respect to the items tested, _____ SCHOOL DISTRICT _____, complied, in all material respects, with the provisions referred to in the preceding paragraph. With respect to items not tested, nothing came to our attention that caused us to believe that the district had not complied, in all material respects, with those provisions.

This report is intended for the information of the Board of Education, the Illinois State Board of Education and federal granting agencies. However, this report is a matter of public record and its distribution is not limited.

/Signed/
Smith, Jones & Co., Ltd.

APPENDIX F

Cash Receipts Journal

This is an example of a cash receipts journal that is provided for those readers who may be unfamiliar with such a form.

FUND: General

Expenditure and Disbursement Journal

Figure & Page _____

Debits						Credits				Encumbrance Liquidation
Expenditures (602)	Other General Ledger Debits					Other General Ledger Credits				
Amount	Account Number	Amount	Acct. No.	Date	Explanation or Payee	Doc. Ref. No.	Amt.	Accnt. No.	Cash (101)	Credit - 601 Debit - 701
				1980						
44 00	000-2410-530			7/1	Jones Typewriter Co.	17692	44 00	421		44 00
		44 00	421	7/3	Jones Typewriter Co.	C021		421	44 00	
		24005 00	171	7/5	ABC Supply	PO17	2400 00	421		
4,400 00	100-1000-610			7/6	Supply Requisition	R2017	400 00	171		
		2400 00	421	7/7	ABC Supply	C002			2400 00	
		1800 00	181	7/8	Wine Insurance Co	C003			1,300 00	
600 00	000-2030-530			7/8	Expense Current Portion of Insurance		600 00	181		

APPENDIX G

Cash Disbursements Journal

This is an example of a cash disbursements journal that is provided for those readers who may be unfamiliar with such a form. This example is provided by Robert Davis Associates. (1981). Principles of Public School Fund Accounting. Washington, DC: National Technical Information Service, p. 89.

Kimberly Hills School District
Cash Receipts Journal

For the Month of _____

Date 1995	Explanation	P.R.	Revenue from Federal Sources	Revenue from State Sources	Revenue from Local Sources	Revenue from Property Taxes		Accounts Receivable	Taxes Receivable	Account Titles	Amount	Debit Cash
7/1	Tax Distribution								100,000			100,000
7/2	Gen State Aid			50,000								50,000
7/4	Note Receivable							5,000				5,000
	Interest on Note				100							100
7/6	Tuition				3,000							3,000
	Jon Jones											
				50,000	3,100			5,000	100,000		=	158,000

APPENDIX H

Federal Withholding Tax Tables

The information in this Appendix is a portion of the Federal Withholding Tax Tables and is provided to readers who may not be familiar with such tables. This Appendix does provide information referred to in Chapter 21 and needed to complete some of that chapter's activities.

 **Department of the Treasury
Internal Revenue Service**

Publication 15
Cat. No. 10000W

Circular E, Employer's Tax Guide

(Rev. January 1995)

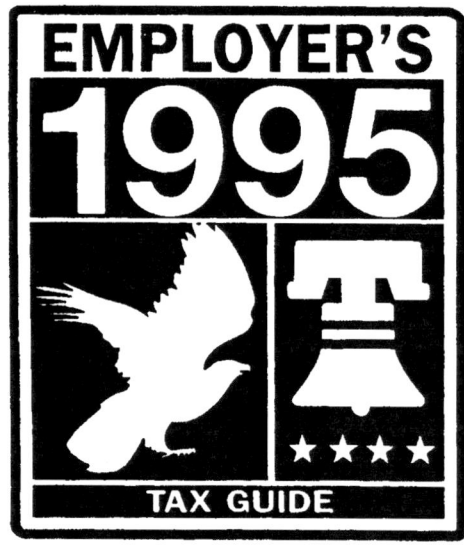

Table of Contents	Page
Calendar	2
Reminders	3
General Information	4

Section

1. **Are You an Employer?** ... 4
2. **Employer Identification Number (EIN)** ... 5
3. **Who Are Employees?** ... 5
4. **Employee's Social Security Number (SSN)** ... 5
5. **Taxable Wages** ... 5
   - Partially Exempt Employment ... 6
   - Supplemental Unemployment Compensation ... 6
   - Nonqualified Deferred Compensation ... 6
   - Employee Stock Options ... 6
   - Travel and Business Expenses ... 6
   - Moving Expenses ... 6
   - Payments to Nonresident Aliens ... 6
   - Employee's Portion of Taxes Paid by Employer ... 6
   - Fringe Benefits ... 6
   - Sick Pay ... 7
6. **Taxable Tips** ... 7
   - Allocated Tips ... 7
7. **Supplemental Wages** ... 7
   - Tips Treated as Supplemental Wages ... 8
   - Vacation Pay ... 8
   - Backpay Under a Statute ... 8
8. **Payroll Period** ... 8
9. **Withholding From Employees' Wages** ... 8
   - Form W-4 ... 8
   - Exemption From Income Tax Withholding ... 8
   - Withholding on Nonresident Aliens ... 8
   - Sending Certain Forms W-4 to the IRS ... 9
   - Filing Form W-4 on Magnetic Media ... 9
   - Invalid Forms W-4 ... 9
   - Amounts Exempt From Levy on Wages ... 9
10. **Figuring Withholding** ... 9
11. **Depositing Taxes** ... 9
    - Payments With Returns ... 9
    - Nonpayroll (Form 945) Tax Liabilities ... 9
    - Federal Tax Deposit (FTD) Coupon ... 9
    - How To Make Deposits ... 10
    - Depositing Without an EIN ... 10
    - Depositing Without Form 8109 ... 10
    - How To Claim Credit for Overpayments ... 10
    - Penalties ... 10
    - When To Deposit ... 11
    - Accuracy of Deposits (98% Rule) ... 12
    - Depositing Federal Unemployment (FUTA) Taxes ... 12
12. **Filing the Employer's Quarterly Federal Tax Return (Form 941)** ... 13
    - Seasonal Employers ... 13
    - Magnetic Tape Filing of Form 941 ... 13

Penalties 13
Trust Fund Recovery Penalty 13
Successor Employer 13
Reconciling Forms W-2, W-3, and 941 14

13. **Adjustments** 14
    Current Period Adjustments 14
    Prior Period Adjustments 15
    Filing a Claim (Form 843) 16

14. **Household Employees** 16

15. **Filing the Federal Unemployment (FUTA) Tax Return (Form 940 or 940-EZ)** 17
    Successor Employer 17
    Magnetic Tape Filing of Form 940 17

16. **Advance Payment of the Earned Income Credit** . 17
    Form W-5 17
    Change of Status 17
    Invalid Certificate 17
    How To Figure the Advance EIC Payment . . . 18
    Paying the Advance EIC to Employees 18
    Advance EIC Payments More Than Taxes Due . . 18
    Required Notice to Employees 19

17. **Example of How To Figure Employment Taxes** . 19

18. **Special Rules for Various Types of Services and Products** 24

19. **How to Use the Income Tax Withholding and Advance Earned Income Credit (EIC) Payment Tables** 30
    Percentage Method 30
    Amount of One Withholding Allowance Table . . 30
    Wage Bracket Method 30
    Alternative Methods of Income Tax Withholding . 30
    Advance Payment Methods for the EIC 30
    Whole-Dollar Withholding and Advance EIC . . 31

Tables:
Income Tax Withholding Tables:
  Percentage Method 32–33
  Wage Bracket Method 34–53
Advance EIC Payment Tables:
  Percentage Method 54–55
  Wage Bracket Method 56–59
Federal Tax Deposit (FTD) Coupon 60
Form 7018-A (order blank) 61
Index 63

17. Example of How To Figure Employment Taxes

Peter Cone owns a small furniture business that he runs with three part-time employees. In 1994, he paid one employee $600 a week, one employee $500 a week, and one employee $400 a week. He did not hire anyone else during the year, and the employees stayed with him the entire year.

It is Peter's practice to pay his employees on Monday. If Monday is a holiday, payday is Tuesday.

The sections that follow discuss how Peter figured his employment taxes for the year. They show how he figured his deposits and how he filled out Forms 940-EZ and 941. Only the fourth quarter Form 941 is illustrated.

Peter files Form 941 quarterly. On it, he reports:

- Income tax he withholds from his employees' wages; and
- Social security and Medicare taxes, both the part he withholds from his employees' wages and the part he pays as an employer.

Before filing Form 941 for the fourth quarter, Peter must deposit the taxes at various times during the quarter because his net tax liability each quarter regularly exceeds $500.

Each of Peter's employees has already filled out a Form W-4. Form W-4 tells him:

- How many withholding allowances the employee claims; and
- Whether to withhold at the "married" or at the "single" rate.

Using this information, Peter finds the correct amount to withhold in Circular E. He uses the wage bracket tables in the January 1994 Circular E to find the correct amount to withhold during the fourth quarter. The tables are for wages paid after December 1993.

In the fourth quarter of 1994, the first payday for Peter's employees is Monday, October 3. His income tax withholding for this payday is shown in the chart below:

Employee	Wages for the week	Withholding rate and allowances	Amount to be withheld
R. Apple	$600	married-3	$51.00
J. Jones	500	married-2	43.00
F. Plum	400	single-1	46.00
Total	$1,500		$140.00

Peter's liability for withheld income tax on this payday totals $140.00. If any of his employees had asked him (on Form W-4) to withhold an extra amount, he would have included it with the total.

Peter also withholds 6.2% of each employee's wages as social security tax and pays a 6.2% share himself, for a total of 12.4% in 1994. In addition, he withholds 1.45% of each employee's wages as Medicare tax and pays a 1.45% share himself, for a total of 2.9%. The total social security tax for this payday is $186.00 ($1,500 total wages times 12.4%), and the total Medicare tax is $43.50 ($1,500 total wages times 2.9%).

Social security tax applies to only the first $60,600 paid to each employee in 1994. The Medicare tax applies to all wages in 1994. If any of Peter's employees had already earned $60,600, or reached this limit on the October 4 payday, he would have included only the Medicare tax when figuring the tax. However, none of his employees will earn more than $60,600 in 1994.

None of the employees is eligible for advance earned income credit payments (discussed later).

On this payday, Peter's total liability for social security tax, Medicare tax, and withheld income tax is $369.50 ($186.00 plus $43.50 plus $140.00). The following chart shows his tax liability for the paydays in the fourth quarter:

Payday	Total wages paid	Income tax withheld	Social security (12.4%)	Medicare (2.9%)
Oct. 3	$1,500.00	$140.00	$186.00	$43.50
Oct. 11	1,500.00	140.00	186.00	43.50
Oct. 17	1,500.00	140.00	186.00	43.50
Oct. 24	1,500.00	140.00	186.00	43.50
Oct. 31	1,500.00	140.00	186.00	43.50
Nov. 7	1,500.00	140.00	186.00	43.50
Nov. 14	1,500.00	140.00	186.00	43.50
Nov. 21	1,500.00	140.00	186.00	43.50
Nov. 28	1,500.00	140.00	186.00	43.50
Dec. 5	1,500.00	140.00	186.00	43.50
Dec. 12	1,500.00	140.00	186.00	43.50
Dec. 19	1,500.00	140.00	186.00	43.50
Dec. 27	1,500.00	140.00	186.00	43.50
Total	$19,500.00	$1,820.00	$2,418.00	$565.50

Making Deposits

Peter's schedule for making deposits depends on whether he is a semiweekly or a monthly schedule depositor. The total employment taxes for his lookback period (July 1, 1992, to June 30, 1993) is less than $50,000. Therefore, he is a monthly depositor for all of 1994. The taxes accumulated for October ($1,847.50) must be deposited by November 15.

During November, Peter's payroll remains the same. The following chart shows how the social security, Medicare, and withheld income taxes he owes add up during November:

Payday	Total wages paid on the payday	Taxes owed for the payday	Taxes owed since last deposit requirement
Nov. 7	$1,500	$369.50	$369.50
Nov. 14	1,500	369.50	739.00
Nov. 21	1,500	369.50	1,108.50
Nov. 28	1,500	369.50	1,478.00

Because Peter is a monthly depositor for all of 1994, he must make a deposit of the taxes accumulated for November ($1,478.00) by December 15.

During December, Peter's payroll remains the same. The following chart shows how the social security, Medicare, and withheld income taxes he owes add up during December.

Payday	Total wages paid on the payday	Taxes owed for the payday	Taxes owed since last deposit requirement
Dec. 5	$1,500	$369.50	$369.50
Dec. 12	1,500	369.50	739.00
Dec. 19	1,500	369.50	1,108.50
Dec. 27	1,500	369.50	1,478.00

A $1,478.00 deposit by January 17, 1995, is required. (January 15 falls on Sunday and January 16 is a holiday).

SINGLE Persons—BIWEEKLY Payroll Period
(For Wages Paid in 1995)

If the wages are—		And the number of withholding allowances claimed is—									
At least	But less than	0	1	2	3	4	5	6	7	8	9
		The amount of income tax to be withheld is—									
$0	$105	0	0	0	0	0	0	0	0	0	0
105	110	1	0	0	0	0	0	0	0	0	0
110	115	2	0	0	0	0	0	0	0	0	0
115	120	3	0	0	0	0	0	0	0	0	0
120	125	3	0	0	0	0	0	0	0	0	0
125	130	4	0	0	0	0	0	0	0	0	0
130	135	5	0	0	0	0	0	0	0	0	0
135	140	6	0	0	0	0	0	0	0	0	0
140	145	6	0	0	0	0	0	0	0	0	0
145	150	7	0	0	0	0	0	0	0	0	0
150	155	8	0	0	0	0	0	0	0	0	0
155	160	9	0	0	0	0	0	0	0	0	0
160	165	9	0	0	0	0	0	0	0	0	0
165	170	10	0	0	0	0	0	0	0	0	0
170	175	11	0	0	0	0	0	0	0	0	0
175	180	12	0	0	0	0	0	0	0	0	0
180	185	12	0	0	0	0	0	0	0	0	0
185	190	13	0	0	0	0	0	0	0	0	0
190	195	14	0	0	0	0	0	0	0	0	0
195	200	15	0	0	0	0	0	0	0	0	0
200	205	15	1	0	0	0	0	0	0	0	0
205	210	16	2	0	0	0	0	0	0	0	0
210	215	17	2	0	0	0	0	0	0	0	0
215	220	18	3	0	0	0	0	0	0	0	0
220	225	18	4	0	0	0	0	0	0	0	0
225	230	19	5	0	0	0	0	0	0	0	0
230	235	20	5	0	0	0	0	0	0	0	0
235	240	21	6	0	0	0	0	0	0	0	0
240	245	21	7	0	0	0	0	0	0	0	0
245	250	22	8	0	0	0	0	0	0	0	0
250	260	23	9	0	0	0	0	0	0	0	0
260	270	25	10	0	0	0	0	0	0	0	0
270	280	26	12	0	0	0	0	0	0	0	0
280	290	28	13	0	0	0	0	0	0	0	0
290	300	29	15	0	0	0	0	0	0	0	0
300	310	31	16	2	0	0	0	0	0	0	0
310	320	32	18	3	0	0	0	0	0	0	0
320	330	34	19	5	0	0	0	0	0	0	0
330	340	35	21	6	0	0	0	0	0	0	0
340	350	37	22	8	0	0	0	0	0	0	0
350	360	38	24	9	0	0	0	0	0	0	0
360	370	40	25	11	0	0	0	0	0	0	0
370	380	41	27	12	0	0	0	0	0	0	0
380	390	43	28	14	0	0	0	0	0	0	0
390	400	44	30	15	1	0	0	0	0	0	0
400	410	46	31	17	2	0	0	0	0	0	0
410	420	47	33	18	4	0	0	0	0	0	0
420	430	49	34	20	5	0	0	0	0	0	0
430	440	50	36	21	7	0	0	0	0	0	0
440	450	52	37	23	8	0	0	0	0	0	0
450	460	53	39	24	10	0	0	0	0	0	0
460	470	55	40	26	11	0	0	0	0	0	0
470	480	56	42	27	13	0	0	0	0	0	0
480	490	58	43	29	14	0	0	0	0	0	0
490	500	59	45	30	16	2	0	0	0	0	0
500	520	62	47	33	18	4	0	0	0	0	0
520	540	65	50	36	21	7	0	0	0	0	0
540	560	68	53	39	24	10	0	0	0	0	0
560	580	71	56	42	27	13	0	0	0	0	0
580	600	74	59	45	30	16	1	0	0	0	0
600	620	77	62	48	33	19	4	0	0	0	0
620	640	80	65	51	36	22	7	0	0	0	0
640	660	83	68	54	39	25	10	0	0	0	0
660	680	86	71	57	42	28	13	0	0	0	0
680	700	89	74	60	45	31	16	2	0	0	0
700	720	92	77	63	48	34	19	5	0	0	0
720	740	95	80	66	51	37	22	8	0	0	0
740	760	98	83	69	54	40	25	11	0	0	0
760	780	101	86	72	57	43	28	14	0	0	0
780	800	104	89	75	60	46	31	17	3	0	0

SINGLE Persons—BIWEEKLY Payroll Period
(For Wages Paid in 1995)

If the wages are—		And the number of withholding allowances claimed is—										
At least	But less than	0	1	2	3	4	5	6	7	8	9	10
		The amount of income tax to be withheld is—										
$800	$820	107	92	78	63	49	34	20	6	0	0	0
820	840	110	95	81	66	52	37	23	9	0	0	0
840	860	113	98	84	69	55	40	26	12	0	0	0
860	880	116	101	87	72	58	43	29	15	0	0	0
880	900	119	104	90	75	61	46	32	18	3	0	0
900	920	122	107	93	78	64	49	35	21	6	0	0
920	940	125	110	96	81	67	52	38	24	9	0	0
940	960	128	113	99	84	70	55	41	27	12	0	0
960	980	133	116	102	87	73	58	44	30	15	1	0
980	1,000	138	119	105	90	76	61	47	33	18	4	0
1,000	1,020	144	122	108	93	79	64	50	36	21	7	0
1,020	1,040	150	125	111	96	82	67	53	39	24	10	0
1,040	1,060	155	128	114	99	85	70	56	42	27	13	0
1,060	1,080	161	134	117	102	88	73	59	45	30	16	1
1,080	1,100	166	140	120	105	91	76	62	48	33	19	4
1,100	1,120	172	145	123	108	94	79	65	51	36	22	7
1,120	1,140	178	151	126	111	97	82	68	54	39	25	10
1,140	1,160	183	156	129	114	100	85	71	57	42	28	13
1,160	1,180	189	162	135	117	103	88	74	60	45	31	16
1,180	1,200	194	168	141	120	106	91	77	63	48	34	19
1,200	1,220	200	173	146	123	109	94	80	66	51	37	22
1,220	1,240	206	179	152	126	112	97	83	69	54	40	25
1,240	1,260	211	184	157	130	115	100	86	72	57	43	28
1,260	1,280	217	190	163	136	118	103	89	75	60	46	31
1,280	1,300	222	196	169	142	121	106	92	78	63	49	34
1,300	1,320	228	201	174	147	124	109	95	81	66	52	37
1,320	1,340	234	207	180	153	127	112	98	84	69	55	40
1,340	1,360	239	212	185	158	132	115	101	87	72	58	43
1,360	1,380	245	218	191	164	137	118	104	90	75	61	46
1,380	1,400	250	224	197	170	143	121	107	93	78	64	49
1,400	1,420	256	229	202	175	148	124	110	96	81	67	52
1,420	1,440	262	235	208	181	154	127	113	99	84	70	55
1,440	1,460	267	240	213	186	160	133	116	102	87	73	58
1,460	1,480	273	246	219	192	165	138	119	105	90	76	61
1,480	1,500	278	252	225	198	171	144	122	108	93	79	64
1,500	1,520	284	257	230	203	176	149	125	111	96	82	67
1,520	1,540	290	263	236	209	182	155	128	114	99	85	70
1,540	1,560	295	268	241	214	188	161	134	117	102	88	73
1,560	1,580	301	274	247	220	193	166	139	120	105	91	76
1,580	1,600	306	280	253	226	199	172	145	123	108	94	79
1,600	1,620	312	285	258	231	204	177	151	126	111	97	82
1,620	1,640	318	291	264	237	210	183	156	129	114	100	85
1,640	1,660	323	296	269	242	216	189	162	135	117	103	88
1,660	1,680	329	302	275	248	221	194	167	140	120	106	91
1,680	1,700	334	308	281	254	227	200	173	146	123	109	94
1,700	1,720	340	313	286	259	232	205	179	152	126	112	97
1,720	1,740	346	319	292	265	238	211	184	157	130	115	100
1,740	1,760	351	324	297	270	244	217	190	163	136	118	103
1,760	1,780	357	330	303	276	249	222	195	168	141	121	106
1,780	1,800	362	336	309	282	255	228	201	174	147	124	109
1,800	1,820	368	341	314	287	260	233	207	180	153	127	112
1,820	1,840	374	347	320	293	266	239	212	185	158	131	115
1,840	1,860	379	352	325	298	272	245	218	191	164	137	118
1,860	1,880	385	358	331	304	277	250	223	196	169	143	121
1,880	1,900	390	364	337	310	283	256	229	202	175	148	124
1,900	1,920	396	369	342	315	288	261	235	208	181	154	127
1,920	1,940	402	375	348	321	294	267	240	213	186	159	132
1,940	1,960	407	380	353	326	300	273	246	219	192	165	138
1,960	1,980	413	386	359	332	305	278	251	224	197	171	144
1,980	2,000	418	392	365	338	311	284	257	230	203	176	149
2,000	2,020	424	397	370	343	316	289	263	236	209	182	155
2,020	2,040	431	403	376	349	322	295	268	241	214	187	160
2,040	2,060	437	408	381	354	328	301	274	247	220	193	166
2,060	2,080	443	414	387	360	333	306	279	252	225	199	172
2,080	2,100	449	420	393	366	339	312	285	258	231	204	177

$2,100 and over   Use Table 2(a) for a SINGLE person on page 32. Also see the instructions on page 30.

MARRIED Persons—BIWEEKLY Payroll Period
(For Wages Paid in 1995)

If the wages are—		And the number of withholding allowances claimed is—									
At least	But less than	0	1	2	3	4	5	6	7	8	9
		The amount of income tax to be withheld is—									
$0	$250	0	0	0	0	0	0	0	0	0	0
250	260	1	0	0	0	0	0	0	0	0	0
260	270	3	0	0	0	0	0	0	0	0	0
270	280	4	0	0	0	0	0	0	0	0	0
280	290	6	0	0	0	0	0	0	0	0	0
290	300	7	0	0	0	0	0	0	0	0	0
300	310	9	0	0	0	0	0	0	0	0	0
310	320	10	0	0	0	0	0	0	0	0	0
320	330	12	0	0	0	0	0	0	0	0	0
330	340	13	0	0	0	0	0	0	0	0	0
340	350	15	0	0	0	0	0	0	0	0	0
350	360	16	2	0	0	0	0	0	0	0	0
360	370	18	3	0	0	0	0	0	0	0	0
370	380	19	5	0	0	0	0	0	0	0	0
380	390	21	6	0	0	0	0	0	0	0	0
390	400	22	8	0	0	0	0	0	0	0	0
400	410	24	9	0	0	0	0	0	0	0	0
410	420	25	11	0	0	0	0	0	0	0	0
420	430	27	12	0	0	0	0	0	0	0	0
430	440	28	14	0	0	0	0	0	0	0	0
440	450	30	15	1	0	0	0	0	0	0	0
450	460	31	17	2	0	0	0	0	0	0	0
460	470	33	18	4	0	0	0	0	0	0	0
470	480	34	20	5	0	0	0	0	0	0	0
480	490	36	21	7	0	0	0	0	0	0	0
490	500	37	23	8	0	0	0	0	0	0	0
500	520	40	25	11	0	0	0	0	0	0	0
520	540	43	28	14	0	0	0	0	0	0	0
540	560	46	31	17	2	0	0	0	0	0	0
560	580	49	34	20	5	0	0	0	0	0	0
580	600	52	37	23	8	0	0	0	0	0	0
600	620	55	40	26	11	0	0	0	0	0	0
620	640	58	43	29	14	0	0	0	0	0	0
640	660	61	46	32	17	3	0	0	0	0	0
660	680	64	49	35	20	6	0	0	0	0	0
680	700	67	52	38	23	9	0	0	0	0	0
700	720	70	55	41	26	12	0	0	0	0	0
720	740	73	58	44	29	15	0	0	0	0	0
740	760	76	61	47	32	18	3	0	0	0	0
760	780	79	64	50	35	21	6	0	0	0	0
780	800	82	67	53	38	24	9	0	0	0	0
800	820	85	70	56	41	27	12	0	0	0	0
820	840	88	73	59	44	30	15	1	0	0	0
840	860	91	76	62	47	33	18	4	0	0	0
860	880	94	79	65	50	36	21	7	0	0	0
880	900	97	82	68	53	39	24	10	0	0	0
900	920	100	85	71	56	42	27	13	0	0	0
920	940	103	88	74	59	45	30	16	2	0	0
940	960	106	91	77	62	48	33	19	5	0	0
960	980	109	94	80	65	51	36	22	8	0	0
980	1,000	112	97	83	68	54	39	25	11	0	0
1,000	1,020	115	100	86	71	57	42	28	14	0	0
1,020	1,040	118	103	89	74	60	45	31	17	2	0
1,040	1,060	121	106	92	77	63	48	34	20	5	0
1,060	1,080	124	109	95	80	66	51	37	23	8	0
1,080	1,100	127	112	98	83	69	54	40	26	11	0
1,100	1,120	130	115	101	86	72	57	43	29	14	0
1,120	1,140	133	118	104	89	75	60	46	32	17	3
1,140	1,160	136	121	107	92	78	63	49	35	20	6
1,160	1,180	139	124	110	95	81	66	52	38	23	9
1,180	1,200	142	127	113	98	84	69	55	41	26	12
1,200	1,220	145	130	116	101	87	72	58	44	29	15
1,220	1,240	148	133	119	104	90	75	61	47	32	18
1,240	1,260	151	136	122	107	93	78	64	50	35	21
1,260	1,280	154	139	125	110	96	81	67	53	38	24
1,280	1,300	157	142	128	113	99	84	70	56	41	27
1,300	1,320	160	145	131	116	102	87	73	59	44	30
1,320	1,340	163	148	134	119	105	90	76	62	47	33
1,340	1,360	166	151	137	122	108	93	79	65	50	36
1,360	1,380	169	154	140	125	111	96	82	68	53	39

MARRIED Persons—BIWEEKLY Payroll Period
(For Wages Paid in 1995)

If the wages are—		And the number of withholding allowances claimed is—										
At least	But less than	0	1	2	3	4	5	6	7	8	9	10
		The amount of income tax to be withheld is—										
$1,380	$1,400	172	157	143	128	114	99	85	71	56	42	27
1,400	1,420	175	160	146	131	117	102	88	74	59	45	30
1,420	1,440	178	163	149	134	120	105	91	77	62	48	33
1,440	1,460	181	166	152	137	123	108	94	80	65	51	36
1,460	1,480	184	169	155	140	126	111	97	83	68	54	39
1,480	1,500	187	172	158	143	129	114	100	86	71	57	42
1,500	1,520	190	175	161	146	132	117	103	89	74	60	45
1,520	1,540	193	178	164	149	135	120	106	92	77	63	48
1,540	1,560	196	181	167	152	138	123	109	95	80	66	51
1,560	1,580	199	184	170	155	141	126	112	98	83	69	54
1,580	1,600	202	187	173	158	144	129	115	101	86	72	57
1,600	1,620	205	190	176	161	147	132	118	104	89	75	60
1,620	1,640	208	193	179	164	150	135	121	107	92	78	63
1,640	1,660	211	196	182	167	153	138	124	110	95	81	66
1,660	1,680	215	199	185	170	156	141	127	113	98	84	69
1,680	1,700	221	202	188	173	159	144	130	116	101	87	72
1,700	1,720	227	205	191	176	162	147	133	119	104	90	75
1,720	1,740	232	208	194	179	165	150	136	122	107	93	78
1,740	1,760	238	211	197	182	168	153	139	125	110	96	81
1,760	1,780	243	217	200	185	171	156	142	128	113	99	84
1,780	1,800	249	222	203	188	174	159	145	131	116	102	87
1,800	1,820	255	228	206	191	177	162	148	134	119	105	90
1,820	1,840	260	233	209	194	180	165	151	137	122	108	93
1,840	1,860	266	239	212	197	183	168	154	140	125	111	96
1,860	1,880	271	245	218	200	186	171	157	143	128	114	99
1,880	1,900	277	250	223	203	189	174	160	146	131	117	102
1,900	1,920	283	256	229	206	192	177	163	149	134	120	105
1,920	1,940	288	261	234	209	195	180	166	152	137	123	108
1,940	1,960	294	267	240	213	198	183	169	155	140	126	111
1,960	1,980	299	273	246	219	201	186	172	158	143	129	114
1,980	2,000	305	278	251	224	204	189	175	161	146	132	117
2,000	2,020	311	284	257	230	207	192	178	164	149	135	120
2,020	2,040	316	289	262	235	210	195	181	167	152	138	123
2,040	2,060	322	295	268	241	214	198	184	170	155	141	126
2,060	2,080	327	301	274	247	220	201	187	173	158	144	129
2,080	2,100	333	306	279	252	225	204	190	176	161	147	132
2,100	2,120	339	312	285	258	231	207	193	179	164	150	135
2,120	2,140	344	317	290	263	237	210	196	182	167	153	138
2,140	2,160	350	323	296	269	242	215	199	185	170	156	141
2,160	2,180	355	329	302	275	248	221	202	188	173	159	144
2,180	2,200	361	334	307	280	253	226	205	191	176	162	147
2,200	2,220	367	340	313	286	259	232	208	194	179	165	150
2,220	2,240	372	345	318	291	265	238	211	197	182	168	153
2,240	2,260	378	351	324	297	270	243	216	200	185	171	156
2,260	2,280	383	357	330	303	276	249	222	203	188	174	159
2,280	2,300	389	362	335	308	281	254	227	206	191	177	162
2,300	2,320	395	368	341	314	287	260	233	209	194	180	165
2,320	2,340	400	373	346	319	293	266	239	212	197	183	168
2,340	2,360	406	379	352	325	298	271	244	217	200	186	171
2,360	2,380	411	385	358	331	304	277	250	223	203	189	174
2,380	2,400	417	390	363	336	309	282	255	229	206	192	177
2,400	2,420	423	396	369	342	315	288	261	234	209	195	180
2,420	2,440	428	401	374	347	321	294	267	240	213	198	183
2,440	2,460	434	407	380	353	326	299	272	245	218	201	186
2,460	2,480	439	413	386	359	332	305	278	251	224	204	189
2,480	2,500	445	418	391	364	337	310	283	257	230	207	192
2,500	2,520	451	424	397	370	343	316	289	262	235	210	195
2,520	2,540	456	429	402	375	349	322	295	268	241	214	198
2,540	2,560	462	435	408	381	354	327	300	273	246	220	201
2,560	2,580	467	441	414	387	360	333	306	279	252	225	204
2,580	2,600	473	446	419	392	365	338	311	285	258	231	207
2,600	2,620	479	452	425	398	371	344	317	290	263	236	210
2,620	2,640	484	457	430	403	377	350	323	296	269	242	215
2,640	2,660	490	463	436	409	382	355	328	301	274	248	221
2,660	2,680	495	469	442	415	388	361	334	307	280	253	226

$2,680 and over   Use Table 2(b) for a **MARRIED person** on page 32. Also see the instructions on page 30.

APPENDIX I

Annual Financial Report 1993-94

The following is a sample Annual Financial Report for a school district in Illinois. This report corresponds to the budget in Appendix C and the Audit in Appendix E. The format is provided by the Illinois Sate Board of Education and is completed by each district's external auditor. This example of an Annual Financial Report is provided for readers who may not have access to such a document. This example is also provided to facilitate instruction in that all students and instructors can work from a uniform set of documents and financial data. This appendix relates directly to Appendix C, D and E.

Smith, Jones & Co., Ltd.
Certified Public Accountants
1 Main Street • Anytown, IL 66321
Telephone: 312/555-0000 • Fax: 312/555-9999

September 12, 1994

Board of Education
School District
111 Main Street
Anytown, IL 66321

Dear Board Members:

We have audited the basic financial statements of the   SCHOOL DISTRICT   as of and for the year ended June 30, 1994, as listed in the table of contents of this Annual Financial Report form. These financial statements are the responsibility of the school district's administration. Our responsibility is to express an opinion on these financial statements based on our audit.

Except as discussed in the following paragraph, we conducted our audit in accordance with generally accepted auditing standards; <u>Government Auditing Standards</u>, issued by the Comptroller General of the United States; and the provisions of Office of Management and Budget Circular A-128, "Audits of State and Local Governments." Those standards, and OMB Circular A-128, require that we plan and perform the audit to obtain reasonable assurance about whether the financial statements are free of material misstatement. An audit includes assessing the accounting principals used and significant estimates made by management, as well as evaluating the overall financial statement presentation. We believe that our audit provides a reasonable basis for our opinion.

Because the District does not maintain a detailed record of the historical cost of its fixed assets, we were unable to obtain sufficient evidence to form an opinion regarding the basis on which the general fixed assets are stated.

These financial statements are issued to comply with regulatory provisions prescribed by the Illinois State Board of Education, which is a comprehensive basis of accounting other than generally accepted accounting principles. They are intended to assure effective legislative and public oversight of school district financing and spending activities and accountable Illinois public school districts. Note 1 of these financial statements describes their basis of presentation.

The basic financial statements referred to above do not include the financial activities of the Hope Wall joint Agreement for Trainable Mentally Handicapped Program, which should be included in order to conform with generally accepted accounting principles. If the omitted component unit had been included, the assets and revenues of the special revenue fund type would have increased by $491,783 and $2,137,818, respectively. However, the excess of revenues over expenditures and fund balance of the special revenue fund type would have been unchanged.

APPENDIX I • 3

In our opinion, except for the effect of such adjustments, if any, as might have been disclosed with respect to the general fixed assets had historical records been available, and except for the effects on the financial statements of the omission described in the preceding paragraph, the aforementioned financial statements present fairly, in all material respects, the statements of position of the funds and account groups of the   SCHOOL DISTRICT   as of June 30, 1994 and the revenues and expenditures of its funds for the year then ended in conformity with the basis of accounting described in Note 1 to these financial statements.

Our audit was conducted for the purpose of forming an opinion on the basic financial statements taken as a whole. The accompanying supplementary schedules, listed in the table of contents of this Annual Financial Report form, are presented for purposes of additional analysis and are not a required part of the basic financial statements. The information has been subjected to the auditing procedures applied in our audit of the aforementioned financial statements and, in our opinion, are fairly stated in all material respects in relation to the basic financial statements taken as a whole.

/Signed/
Smith, Jones & Co., Ltd.

4 • APPENDIX I

Due at ESR on October 15th
Due at ISBE on November 15th

ILLINOIS STATE BOARD OF EDUCATION
Department of School Finance
Finance Section
100 North First Street
Springfield, Illinois 62777-0001

Illinois School District
ANNUAL FINANCIAL REPORT *

June 30, 1994

DISTRICT CODE (Leave blank)		REPORTING BASIS	*Certified Public Accountants* (See instruction on inside cover page before completing this form.)	
COUNTY			NAME OF AUDITING FIRM COMPLETING REPORT	
Kane		☐ Cash Basis	William F. Gurrie & Co., Ltd.	
DISTRICT NAME			NAME OF AUDIT SUPERVISOR	
West Aurora School District		☒ Modified Accrual	Andrew Mace	
DISTRICT NUMBER			STREET	
129			1010 Jorie Blvd., Suite 240	
STREET			CITY	ZIP CODE
80 South River Street P.O. Box 4430			Oak Brook	60521
CITY	ZIP CODE		ILLINOIS REGISTRATION NUMBER	TELEPHONE
Aurora	60506		60-2912	(708) 990-3131

REVIEWED BY: (Check one)**		COOK COUNTY ONLY		REVIEWED BY REGIONAL SUPERINTENDENT
☐ District Superintendent		☐ Township Treasurer		
☐ District Treasurer		In Cook County, the Township Treasurer and one appropriate		
☐ Chief School Business Official		school official must approve this report by signing in the space provided.		
NAME (Type or print)		NAME (Type or print)		TELEPHONE
TELEPHONE	DATE	TELEPHONE	DATE	DATE
SIGNATURE		SIGNATURE		SIGNATURE

* Based on the Illinois Program Accounting Manual for Local Education Agencies
** The Financial Data Questionnaire (page 2) must be completed by the appropriate school administrator as required by the School Code, Section 1A-8.
ISBE 50-35 (4/94)

APPENDIX I • 5

TABLE OF CONTENTS

Auditor's Opinion Letter	1
Notes to the Financial Statements	2
Audit Questionnaire	
Financial Data Questionnaire	
Basic Financial Statements	
Statement of Assets and Liabilities Arising from Cash Transactions/Statement of Position	3–6
Statements of Revenues Received/Revenues, Expenditures Disbursed/Expenditures, Other Financing Sources (Uses) and Changes in Fund Balances (All Funds)	7–8
Statements of Revenues Received/Revenues Budget vs. Actual (All Funds)	9–26
Statements of Expenditures Disbursed/Expenditures Budget vs. Actual (All Funds)	27–42
Supplementary Schedules	
Schedule of Ad Valorem Tax Receipts	43
Schedule of Tax Anticipation Warrants and Interest	44
Schedule of Tax Anticipation Notes and Interest	44
Schedule of Teachers' Orders and Interest	44
Schedule of Corporate Personal Property Replacement Tax Anticipation Notes	44
Schedule of of General State Aid Certificates	44
Schedule of Bonds Payable	45
Schedule of Restricted Local Tax Levies	46
Financial Data — Indirect Cost Rate Determination	47
Statistical Section	
Schedule of Capital Outlay and Depreciation	48
Operating Expenditures Per Pupil and Per Capita Tuition Charge 1993–1994	49–50

INSTRUCTIONS

1. <u>All schedules must be completed.</u>

2. Round all amounts to the nearest dollar.

3. Proper coding and reference to the Chart of Accounts (<u>Illinois Program Accounting Manual for Local Education Agencies</u>) eliminates the necessity for adding lines. Reports submitted with lines added and/or inconsistent rounding are unacceptable and will be sent back to the auditor preparing the report.

4. Any problems detected by the Office Audit Program should be resolved prior to submitting this report.

5. Forward the original and one copy to the Regional Superintendent by October 15, 1994, for his/her approval and certification.

6. The Regional Superintendent will forward the original to the Illinois State Board of Education by November 15, 1994.

ITEMIZATION TO ANNUAL FINANCIAL REPORT
JUNE 30, 1994

Page 5, Line 14 — Cash deficit and due to joint agreement

Page 15, Line 48 — Insurance settlement, sale of building

Page 19, Line 84 — Report card, alcohol drug intervention, staff development, object assessment, student app., alternative assessment, general administration library

Page 20, Line 84 — Miscellaneous state reimbursement

Page 25, Line 137 — Drug free schools

Page 29, Line 43 — Substance abuse

Page 31, Line 8 — Warehousing and health

Page 33, Line 11 — Paying agent fees

Page 38, Line 44 — Drug free schools expenditures

AUDIT QUESTIONNAIRE

All cash balances must be equal to or greater than "zero"a.

Circle Yes, No, or Not Applicable					Comments:
YES	NO	N/A	1.	Were all Student Activity Funds, Imprest Funds, Convenience Accounts, Trust and Agency Funds, and all other funds maintained by the district audited? If "No", give reason for not auditing.	
YES	NO	N/A	2.	Have all interfund loans been made, disclosed, and repaid in accordance with the provisions of Sections 10–22.33, 20–4 and 20–5 of the School Code? If "No", explain.	
YES	NO	N/A	3.	Has the district recognized all transactions on a strictly cash basis or strictly modified accrual basis? If "No", explain. (See Appendix F, Illinois Program Accounting Manual for Local Education Agencies, and Appendix L, Guide To Auditing and Reporting for Illinois Public Local Education Agencies.	
YES	NO	N/A	4.	Have all permanent transfers been made in accordance with the provisions of Sections 10–22.14, 10–22.44, 17–2.2a, 17–2A, 19–4, 20–5 and 20–8 of the School Code? If "No", explain.	
YES	NO	N/A	5.	Have bonds been executed in an appropriate amount on all custodians of funds in accordance with Sections 8–2, 10–20.19 and 19–6 of the School Code? If "No", explain.	
YES	NO	N/A	6.	Did your examination substantiate that the budget and the accounting records corresponded with the Illinois Program Accounting Manual for Local Education Agencies and were maintained in accordance with Sections 2–3.27 and 17–1 of the School Code? If "No", explain.	
YES	NO	N/A	7.	Were corporate personal property tax replacement monies deposited in accordance with the provisions of 30 ILCS 115/12 with respect to debt service (bonds issued prior to January 1, 1979) and retirement obligations? If "No", explain.	
YES	NO	N/A	8.	Did your examination substantiate that investments owned, deposits made and interest earned by the district were in the name of the district, were authorized by the Board of Education, were properly segregated (including segregated by fund) and invested in accordance with 30 ILCS 235/0.01 et seq., 30 ILCS 225/1 and Sections 8–7 and 10–20.19 of the School Code? If "No", explain.	
YES	NO	N/A	9.	Were tax anticipation warrants handled in accordance with 30 ILCS 305/2, 745 ILCS 10/9–107, School Code Section 17–16 and 50 ILCS 430/2 ? If "No", explain.	
YES	NO	(N/A)	10.	Were tax anticipation notes handled in accordance with 30 ILCS 305/2, and 50 ILCS 420/0.01 et seq.? If "No", explain.	
YES	NO	N/A	11.	Has the district refrained from issuing general obligation bonds in excess of the statutory limit per Section 19–1 of the School Code?	
YES	NO	(N/A)	12.	Were state aid anticipation certificates handled in accordance with 30 ILCS 305/2 and Section 18–18 of the School Code? If "No", explain.	
YES	NO	N/A	13.	Did your examination substantiate compliance with provisions of Section 10–20.21 of the School Code regarding competitive bids? If "No", explain.	
YES	NO	N/A	14.	Have all board members, administrators and other covered district employees filed an economic interest statement with the County Clerk in accordance with 5 ILCS 420/4A–101 et seq.? If "No", explain.	
YES	NO	N/A	15.	Did your review and testing of internal accounting controls substantiate that no material weaknesses or reportable conditions exist? If "No", explain.	
YES	NO	N/A	16.	Were restricted funds properly segregated in the accounting records and used only for restricted purposes in accordance with 745 ILCS 10/9–101 et seq. and Sections 17–2.2a, 17–2.2b, 17–2.2c, 17–2.4, and 17–2.11 of the School Code? If "No", explain.	

a   All interfund loans must be recorded and identified as such, even though unauthorized and/or illegal. Bank overdrafts must be shown as other current liabilities (Acc. 499). Use other current assets (Acc. 199) and other current liabilities (Acc. 499) to record illegal interfund loans. All investments must be allocated to the proper funds.

b   A "Yes" response indicates you have performed compliance audit procedures relating to all applicable statutes and have not noted any exceptions.

8 • APPENDIX I

FINANCIAL DATA QUESTIONNAIRE (the School Code, Section 1A-8)

INSTRUCTIONS: The Financial Data Questionnaire is designed to provide the informational needs required of the Illinois State Board of Education by the School Code, Section 1A-8. This questionnaire must be completed and signed by the appropriate school administrator responsible for this area.

		Comments:
(YES) NO	1. Did the district have all salaries paid within a period of 90 days or less from the due date?	
(YES) NO N/A	2. Did the district have all tuition payments due another school district for which there is no dispute regarding the validity or amount of the claim paid by January 1 of the year following the school year the payment was due?	
(YES) NO N/A	3. Did the district have all tuition payments due any joint agreement or cooperative educational program under a joint agreement paid within 120 days of the date specified in the joint board's articles of agreement?	
(YES) NO	4. Was the district free from defaulting on any debt instrument: notes, warrants, or bonds; or the interest on such instruments or in the rental due any authority for a period of 90 days?	
(YES) NO	5. Has the district refrained from contracting any loan not authorized by law?	
YES (NO)	6. Has the district refrained from issuing orders for wages as permitted in Sections 8-16, 32-7.2 and 34-76, the School Code?	
(YES) NO	7. Has the district refrained from issuing second year tax anticipation warrants when warrants in anticipation of the current year's taxes are still outstanding?	
(YES) NO	8. Has the district avoided adoption of budgets in which budgeted expenditures exceeded budgeted revenues and reserves for two consecutive years?	
(YES) NO	9. Is the district free from pending litigation which would adversely impact the attached financial statements?	

_____   Assistant Superintendent for Business   West Aurora School Dist. #129   Kane
Signed   *Title School Administrator*   *School District*   *County*

APPENDIX I • 9

Page 3

BASIC FINANCIAL STATEMENTS
STATEMENT OF ASSETS AND LIABILITIES ARISING FROM CASH TRANSACTIONS/STATEMENT OF POSITION June 30, 1994

ASSETS	ACCT. NO.	(1) EDUCATIONAL	(2) OPERATIONS AND MAINTENANCE	(3) BOND AND INTEREST	(4) TRANSPORTATION	(5) MUNICIPAL RETIREMENT/ SOCIAL SECURITY	(6) SITE & CONSTRUCTION/CAPITAL IMPROVEMENT	(7) WORKING CASH	(8) RENT	(9) FIRE PREVENTION AND SAFETY
CURRENT ASSETS (100)		(3350)	(3353)	(3356)	(3358)	(3361)	(3364)	(3366)	(3369)	(3465)
1. Cash (Accounts 101 through 105)		$ -	$ 541,302	$ 736,823	$ 281,194	$ 242,198	$ 91,716	$ 10,630	$ -	$ 983,188
Other Accrued Assets (GAAP)		(3351)	(3354)	(3357)	(3359)	(3362)	(3457)	(3367)	(3370)	(3466)
2. (Attach Itemization)	*	-	-	-	-	-	-	-	-	-
		(4)	(36)	(65)	(64)	(112)	(3458)	(2819)	(173)	(3467)
3. Taxes Receivable (GAAP)	110	9,295,730	1,580,383	1,601,847	530,977	456,680	-	-	-	-
		(5)	(37)		(85)	(113)	(133)			
4. Accounts Receivable (GAAP)	120	752,311	55,833		179,591	-	-			
			(40)		(88)			(2820)		
5. Loan to Educational Fund	151		-		-			3,670,000		
		(8)			(89)			(2821)		
6. Loan to Operations and Maintenance Fund	152	-			-			-		
		(9)	(41)					(2822)		
7. Loan to Transportation Fund	153	-	-					-		
		(3454)	(3455)		(3456)			(3459)		
8. Loan to Fire Prevention and Safety	154	-	-		-			-		
			(43)		(91)		(137)	(3448)		
9. Loan to Other Funds	155		-		38,878		-	-		
		(11)	(44)	(68)	(92)	(116)	(138)	(2824)	(177)	(3488)
10. Inventory	170	315,456	137,000		250,000		-	-	-	-
		(12)								
11. Investments	180	15,606,000	137,000	925,000	250,000	700,000	-	-	-	-
		(15)	(47)	(69)	(95)	(118)	(141)	(2826)	(179)	(3490)
Other Current Assets		-	-	-	-	-	-	-	-	-
12. (Attach Itemization)	199									
		(16)	(46)	(70)	(96)	(119)	(142)	(2827)	(180)	(3491)
13. TOTAL CURRENT ASSETS		$ 25,969,497	$ 2,314,518	$ 3,263,670	$ 1,280,640	$ 1,398,878	$ 91,716	$ 3,680,630	$ -	$ 983,188

* Line 2 should include amounts 130, 140, 162, 181, 192

10 • APPENDIX I

BASIC FINANCIAL STATEMENTS
STATEMENT OF ASSETS AND LIABILITIES ARISING FROM CASH TRANSACTIONS/STATEMENT OF POSITION June 30, 1994

ASSETS	ACCT. NO.	AGENCY FUND	ACCOUNT GROUPS GENERAL FIXED ASSETS	ACCOUNT GROUPS GENERAL LONG-TERM DEBT
CURRENT ASSETS (100)				
1. Cash (Accounts 101 through 105)		$ 351,842 (3374)		
Other Accrued Assets (GAAP)		- (3375)		
2. (Attach Itemization)	*			
3. Taxes Receivable (GAAP)	110			
4. Accounts Receivable (GAAP)	120			
5. Loan to Educational Fund	151			
Loan to Operations and				
6. Maintenance Fund	152			
7. Loan to Transportation Fund	153			
Loan to Fire Prevention				
8. and Safety Fund	154			
9. Loan to Other Funds	155			
10. Inventory	170	(2830)		
11. Investments	180	- (2831)		
Other Current Assets				
12. (Attach Itemization)	199	- (2832)		
13. TOTAL CURRENT ASSETS		$ 351,842 (2834)		
CAPITAL ASSETS (200)				
14. Land	201		$ 1,627,157 (212)	
15. Buildings	202		22,822,485 (213)	
Improvements Other than				
16. Buildings	203		466,798 (214)	
Equipment Other than				
17. Transportation	204		8,202,032 (215)	
18. Construction in Progress	205		- (2803)	
19. Transportation Equipment	206		1,968,856 (217)	
Amount Available in				
20. Debt Service Funds	304			1,703,558 (221)
Amount to be Provided				
21. for Payment of Bonds	305			5,641,442 (222)
Amount to be Provided for				
22. Payment Long-Term Debt Other	306			3,414,518 (3449)
23. TOTAL CAPITAL ASSETS			$ 35,067,328 (218)	$ 10,759,518 (223)

* Line 2 should include accounts 130, 140, 162, 181, 192

APPENDIX I • 11

BASIC FINANCIAL STATEMENTS
STATEMENT OF ASSETS AND LIABILITIES ARISING FROM CASH TRANSACTIONS/STATEMENT OF POSITION June 30, 1994

Page 5

LIABILITIES AND FUND BALANCE	ACCT. NO.	(1) EDUCATIONAL	(2) OPERATIONS AND MAINTENANCE	(3) BOND AND INTEREST	(4) TRANSPORTATION	(5) MUNICIPAL RETIREMENT/ SOCIAL SECURITY	(6) SITE & CONSTRUCTION/CAPITAL IMPROVEMENT	(7) WORKING CASH	(8) RENT	(9) FIRE PREVENTION AND SAFETY
CURRENT LIABILITIES (400)		(3352)	(3355)	(3428)	(3360)	(3363)	(3365)	(3368)		(3492)
1. Accrued Liabilities (GAAP)	*	$ 3,933,454	147,042		86,833	76,162			$ —	$ —
Corporate Personal Property Replacement Tax Anticipation		(2047) —	(2048) —	(2049) —	(2050) —	(2051) —			(2053) —	(3493) —
2. Notes Payable	406	—	—	—	—	—				(3494) —
3. Anticipation Warrants Payable	407	(18) 3,000,000	(50) —	(71) —	(98) —	(121) —				(3495) —
4. Anticipation Notes Payable	408	(19) —	(51) —	(72) —	(99) —	(122) —				
5. Teachers' Orders Payable	409	(20) —								(3496) —
State Aid Anticipation		(2373) —	(2375) —	(2442) —	(2413) —	(2415) —			(2444) —	(3497) —
6. Certificates Payable	410	—	—	—	—	—			—	
7. Loan from Educational Fund	431		(53) —		(101) —					(3498) —
Loan from Operations and Maintenance Fund	432	(22) —			(102) —					
8. Loan from Transportation Fund	433	(23) —	(54) —							(3499) —
9. Loan from Working Cash Fund	434	(24) 3,670,000	(55) —	(3450) —	(2686) —	(3451) —			(3452) —	(3500) —
10.		(25) —	(56) —		(103) —	(123) —	(145) —			
11. Payroll Deductions Payable Deferred Revenue	450	(27) —	(58) —	(73) —	(105) —	(124) —	(147) —	(2847) —	(183) —	(3501) —
12. (Modified Accrual) Due to Activity Fund	474	9,053,540	1,539,207	1,560,112	517,143	444,782				
13. Organizations Other Current Liabilities	480	(28) —	(59) —	(74) —	(106) —	(125) —	(148) —	(2848) —	(184) —	(3502) —
14. (Attach Itemization)	499	2,848,038	—	—	—	—				
LONG-TERM LIABILITIES (500)		(3460)	(3461)	(3462)	(3463)	(3464)	(3466)	(3467)	(3468)	(3503)
15. Bonds Payable	501	—	—	—	—	—	—	—	—	—
16. Other Long-Term Liabilities	599	(30) —	(61) —	(78) —	(108) —	(127) —	(150) —	(2849) —	(186) —	(3504) —
17. TOTAL LIABILITIES		$ 22,505,032	$ 1,686,249	$ 1,560,112	$ 603,976	$ 520,944	$ —	$ —	$ —	$ —
		(2374)	(2376)	(2443)	(2414)	(2416)	(2474)	(2850)	(2445)	(3505)
18. Reserved Fund Balance	703	(31) $ 3,464,465	(62) $ 628,269	(79) $ 1,703,558	(109) $ 676,664	(128) $ 877,934	(151) $ 91,716	(2851) $ 3,680,630	(187) $ —	(3506) $ 983,188
19. Unreserved Fund Balance Investments in General	704									
20. Fixed Assets	705									
21. TOTAL LIABILITIES AND FUND BALANCE		(32) $ 25,969,497	(63) $ 2,314,518	(80) $ 3,263,670	(110) $ 1,280,640	(129) $ 1,398,878	(152) $ 91,716	(2852) $ 3,680,630	(188) $ —	(3507) $ 983,188

* Line 1 should include accounts 402, 411-415, 420-441, 442, 461

12 • APPENDIX I

BASIC FINANCIAL STATEMENTS
STATEMENT OF ASSETS AND LIABILITIES ARISING FROM CASH TRANSACTIONS/STATEMENT OF POSITION June 30, 1994

LIABILITIES AND FUND BALANCE	ACCT. NO.	AGENCY FUND	ACCOUNT GROUPS — GENERAL FIXED ASSETS	ACCOUNT GROUPS — GENERAL LONG-TERM DEBT
CURRENT LIABILITIES (400)				
1. Accrued Liabilities (GAAP)	*			
Corporate Personal Property Replacement Tax Anticipation				
2. Notes Payable	406			
3. Anticipation Warrants Payable	407			
4. Anticipation Notes Payable	408			
5. Teachers' Orders Payable State Aid Anticipation	409			
6. Certificates Payable	410			
7. Loan from Educational Fund Loan from Operations and	431			
8. Maintenance Fund	432			
9. Loan from Transportation Fund	433			
10. Loan from Working Cash Fund	434			
11. Payroll Deductions Payable	450			
Deferred Revenue	474			
12. (Modified Accrual) Due to Activity Fund		$ (2853) 351,842		
13. Organizations	480	(2854)		
Other Current Liabilities	499	-		
14. (Attach Itemization)				
LONG-TERM LIABILITIES (500)				
15. Bonds Payable	501			$ (224) 7,345,000
				(2683)
16. Other Long-Term Liabilities	599			3,414,518 (226)
17. TOTAL LIABILITIES		$ (2855) 351,842		$ 10,759,518
18. Reserved Fund Balance	703	(3010) -		
19. Unreserved Fund Balance Investments in General	704	(3011) -		
20. Fixed Assets	705		$ (219) 35,087,328	
TOTAL LIABILITIES		$ (2856) 351,842	$ (220) 35,087,328	$ (227) 10,759,518
21. AND FUND BALANCE		351,842	35,087,328	10,759,518

* Line 1 should include amounts 402, 411-415, 420 441, 442, 461

APPENDIX I • 13

Page 7

BASIC FINANCIAL STATEMENTS
STATEMENT OF REVENUES RECEIVED/REVENUES, EXPENDITURES DISBURSED/EXPENDITURES, OTHER FINANCING SOURCES(USES) AND CHANGES IN FUND BALANCES
ALL FUNDS - FOR THE YEAR ENDED June 30, 1994

DESCRIPTION	ACCT. NO.	(1) EDUCATIONAL	(2) OPERATIONS AND MAINTENANCE	(3) BOND AND INTEREST	(4) TRANSPORTATION	(5) MUNICIPAL RETIREMENT/ SOCIAL SECURITY	(6) SITE & CONSTRUCTION/CAPITAL IMPROVEMENT	(7) WORKING CASH	(8) RENT	(9) FIRE PREVENTION AND SAFETY
RECEIPTS/REVENUES	Acct#	(2490)	(2503)	(2569)	(2530)	(2542)	(2594)	(3164)	(2577)	(3508)
1. Local Sources	1000	$ 20,504,996	$ 3,200,031	$ 3,074,395	$ 1,118,120	$ 1,074,532	$	$	$	$ 12,103
Flow-Through Receipts/Revenue		(3344)	(3345)		(3347)	(3348)				
2. from One LEA to Another LEA	2000	264,650	-		-	-				
		(2492)	(2505)	(2570)	(2532)	(2543)	(2595)		(2578)	(3509)
3. State Sources	3000	9,442,485	670,000	-	716,620	-	156,320		-	-
		(2493)	(2506)		(2533)	(2544)	(2596)			
4. Federal Sources	4000	1,980,772	-		-	-	-			
		(2494)	(2507)	(2571)	(2534)	(2545)	(2597)	(3165)	(2579)	(3510)
5. TOTAL RECEIPTS/REVENUES		$ 32,192,903	$ 3,870,031	$ 3,074,395	$ 1,834,740	$ 1,074,532	$ 156,320	$	$	$ 12,103
DISBURSEMENTS/EXPENDITURES	Fnct#	(2495)	(2508)		(2535)	(2546)	(2598)			(3511)
6. Instruction	1000	24,462,953				213,832				
		(2496)				(2547)				
7. Support Services	2000	7,591,623	3,314,737		1,897,825	659,548	364,604			88,715
		(2497)	(2509)		(2536)	(2548)				
8. Community Services	3000	100,109	-		-	1,920				
		(2498)	(2510)	(2572)	(2537)		(2599)		(2580)	(3512)
9. Nonprogrammed Charges	4000	862,661	635	-	-		-		-	-
		(2499)	(2511)	(2573)	(2538)	(2550)				(3513)
10. Debt Service	5000	77,994	-	3,136,334	-	-				-
		(2500)	(2512)	(2574)	(2539)	(2551)	(2600)		(2581)	(3514)
TOTAL DISBURSEMENTS/		$ 33,095,340	$ 3,315,372	$ 3,136,334	$ 1,897,825	$ 875,300	$ 364,604		$	$ 88,715
11. EXPENDITURES		(2501)	(2513)	(2575)	(2540)	(2552)	(2601)	(3166)	(2582)	(3515)
12. Excess of Receipts/Revenues Over (under) Disbursements/Expenditures		$ (902,437)	$ 554,659	$ (61,939)	$ (63,085)	$ 199,232	$ (208,284)	$	$	$ (76,612)
OTHER FINANCING SOURCES AND (USES)	Acct. No.									
Other Financing Sources	7000									
Transfer from Other Funds	7100									
Permanent Transfer from Working		(259)								
13. Cash Fund-Abolishment(Sec 20-8)	7110	-								
Permanent Transfer from Working		(260)	(371)	(3429)	(2701)	(3431)	(3422)		(3434)	(3516)
14. Cash Fund-Interest(Sec 20-5)	7120	-	-	-	-	-	-		-	-
Permanent Transfer from			(372)							
15. Educational Fund (Sec 17-2A)	7130	(2696)	(2697)	(2699)	(2702)	(2705)	(2708)	(2711)	(2715)	(3517)
Permanent Transfer of Interest	7140	-	-	-	-	-	300,000	-	-	-
16. (Section 10-22.44)										
Permanent Transfer from Site			(3100)	(3101)						
17. and Const. Fund (Sec 10-22.14)	7150		-	-						
Perm. Transfer of Excess Accum.			(3637)							
Fire Prev.&Safety Tax Proceeds	7160		-							
18. AInterest Earnings(Sec 17-2.11)				(3638)						
Perm. Transfer of Excess Accum										
Fire Prev &Safety Bond Proceeds	7170			-						
19. AInterestEarnings(Sec 10-22.14)										

14 • APPENDIX I

BASIC FINANCIAL STATEMENTS
STATEMENT OF REVENUES RECEIVED/REVENUES, EXPENDITURES DISBURSED/EXPENDITURES, OTHER FINANCING SOURCES(USES) AND CHANGES IN FUND BALANCES
ALL FUNDS – FOR THE YEAR ENDED June 30, 1994

DESCRIPTION	ACCT. NO.	(1) EDUCATIONAL	(2) OPERATIONS AND MAINTENANCE	(3) BOND AND INTEREST	(4) TRANSPORTATION	(5) MUNICIPAL RETIREMENT/ SOCIAL SECURITY	(6) SITE & CONSTRUC- TION/CAPITAL IMPROVEMENT	(7) WORKING CASH	(8) RENT	(9) FIRE PREVENTION AND SAFETY
Sale of Bonds	7200	$ (262)	$ (3017)	$ (3021)	$ (3022)	$ (3472)	$ (557)	$ (560)	$ (3475)	$ (3518)
20. Principal on Bonds Sold	7210	(283)	(3018)	(439)	(3023)		(558)	(561)		(3519)
21. Premium on Bonds Sold	7220	(264)	(3019)	(440)	(3024)		(559)	(562)		(3520)
22. Accrued Interest on Bonds Sold	7230									
Sale or Compensation for Fixed Assets	7300	(3469)	(3470)		(3471)	(3472)	(3473)	(3474)	(3475)	(3521)
23. Other Sources	7400	(3167)	(3173)	(3212)	(3190)	(3196)	(3234)	(3255)	(3218)	(3522)
24. (Attach Itemization)										
TOTAL OTHER FINANCING SOURCES		$ (3168)	$ (3174)	$ (3213)	$ (3191)	$ (3197)	$ (3235) 300,000	$ (3256)	$ (3219)	$ (3523)
25.	8000									
Other Financing Uses	8100									
Transfers to Other Funds Permanent Transfer of Working	8110							$ (2044)		
26. Cash Fund-Abolishment(Sec 20-8) Permanent Transfer of Working								(2045)		
27. Cash Fund-Interest(Sec 20-5) Permanent Transfer of	8120									
Educational Fund (Sec 17-2A)	8130	$ (2028)								
28. Permanent Transfer of Interest (Section 10-22.44)	8140	(2733) 300,000	$ (2745)	$ (2759)	$ (2779)	$ (3185)	$ (2797)		$ (2781)	$ (3641)
29. Permanent Transfer from Site and Const. Fund (Sec 10-22.14)	8150						(3108)			
30. Perm Transfer of Excess Accum Fire Prev &Safety Tax Proceeds										
31. &Interest Earnings(Sec 17-2.11)	8160									(3642)
Perm Transfer of Excess Accum FirePrev &Safety Bond Proceeds										
32. &Interest&Earnings(Sec 10-22.14)	8170									
Other Uses	8190	(3169)	(3175)	(3214)	(3192)	(3199)	(3236)	(3257)	(3220)	(3534)
33. (Attach Itemization)		(3170)	(3176)	(3215)	(3193)	(3199)	(3237)	(3257)	(3221)	(3525)
29. TOTAL OTHER FINANCING (USES)		$ (3171) 300,000	$ (3177)	$ (3216)	$ (3194)	$ (3200)	$ (3238)	$ (3258)	$ (3222)	$ (3526)
TOTAL OTHER FINANCING										
30. SOURCES (USES)		$ (3172) (300,000)	$ (3178)	$ (3217)	$ (3195)	$ (3201)	$ (3239) 300,000	$ (3259)	$ (3223)	$ (3527)
Excess of Receipts/Revenue and Other Fin. Sources Over (Under)										
31. Disb./Exp. & Other Fin. Uses		(1,202,437) (1356)	554,659 (1370)	(61,939) (1584)	(63,085) (1598)	199,232 (1612)	91,716 (1826)	(3260)	(1854)	(76,612) (3528)
32. FUND BALANCES – July 1, 1993		4,666,902 (2502)	73,610 (2514)	1,765,497 (2576)	739,749 (2541)	678,702 (2553)	1,059,800 (3281)	3,680,630		(3529)
Other Changes in Fund Balances							(1,059,800)			
33. Increases(Decreases)*		(1569)	(1583)	(1597)	(1611)	(1625)	(1639)	(3262)	(1667)	(3530)
34. FUND BALANCES – JUNE 30, 1994		$ 3,464,465	$ 628,269	$ 1,703,558	$ 676,664	$ 877,934	$ 91,716	$ 3,680,630		983,188

* Attach Itemization
** Any proceeds identified as restricted for Health/Life Safety purposes on the district's 1992-93 Annual Financial Report should be transferred to the new fund Fire Prevention & Safety Fund through other changes in fund balance line 38.

APPENDIX I • 15

Page 9

STATEMENT OF REVENUES RECEIVED/REVENUES, BUDGET TO ACTUAL, FOR THE YEAR ENDED JUNE 30, 1994

DESCRIPTION	ACCT NOS.	(1) EDUCATIONAL		(2) OPERATIONS AND MAINTENANCE		(3) BOND AND INTEREST		(4) TRANSPORTATION	
		BUDGET	ACTUAL	BUDGET	ACTUAL	BUDGET	ACTUAL	BUDGET	ACTUAL
REVENUE FROM LOCAL SOURCES	1000								
Ad Valorem Taxes Levied by Local Education Agency	1100								
1. General Levy	1110	$ 17,752,847	$ (231) 17,480,589	$ 2,791,000	$ (342) 2,840,579	$ 3,052,206	$ (423) 3,042,639	$ 899,300	$ (463) 953,704
2. Tort Immunity Levy	1120	$ —	$ (235) —	$ 100,000	$ (346) 97,099	$ —	$ (3015) —	$ —	$ (467) —
3. Facility Leasing Levy	1130	$ —	$ (2868) —	$ —	$ (3643) —				
4. Special Education Levy	1140	$ 240,553	$ 244,868	$ —	$ (354) —			$ —	$ (2872) —
5. Social Security/Medicare Only Levy	1150			$ —	$ (358) —	$ —	$ (431) —		
6. Area Vocational Construction Levy	1160	$ —	$ (239) —						
7. Summer School Levy	1170	$ —	$ (2956) —	$ —	$ (2960) —	$ —	$ (2964) —	$ —	$ (2968) —
8. Other Tax Levies (Attach Itemization)	1190	$ —	$ (240) —	$ —	$ (359) —	$ —	$ (432) —	$ —	$ (468) —
TOTAL AD VALOREM TAXES LEVIED BY LOCAL EDUCATION AGENCY	9.	$ 17,993,400	$ 17,725,457	$ 2,891,000	$ 2,937,678	$ 3,052,206	$ 3,042,639	$ 899,300	$ 953,704
PAYMENTS IN LIEU OF TAXES	1200								
10. Mobile Home Privilege Tax	1210	$ —	$ (241) (2055)	$ —	$ (360) (2056)	$ —	$ (433) (2057)	$ —	$ (469) (2058)
11. Payments from Local Housing Authorities	1220								
Corprate Personal Property *	1230	$ 600,000	$ (2621) 845,897	$ 75,000	$ (2630) 135,616	$ 127,607	$ (2638) —	$ 35,000	$ (2639) 44,242
12. Replacement Taxes									
13. Other Payments in lieu of Taxes	1290	$ —	$ (242) —	$ —	$ (361) —	$ —	$ (434) —	$ —	$ (470) —
14. TOTAL PAYMENTS IN LIEU OF TAXES		$ 600,000	$ (243) 845,897	$ 75,000	$ (362) 135,616	$ 127,607	$ (435) —	$ 35,000	$ (471) 44,242

* Corporate personal property replacement tax revenue must be first applied to the Bond & Interest Fund (Bonds issued prior to Jan. 1, 1979) and then the Municipal Retirement/Social Security Fund to replace tax revenue lost due to the abolition of the corporate personal property tax (Chapter 85, Section 616 of the Illinois Revised Statutes). This provision does not apply to taxes levied for medicare only purposes.

16 • APPENDIX I

STATEMENT OF REVENUES RECEIVED/REVENUES, BUDGET TO ACTUAL, FOR THE YEAR ENDED JUNE 30, 1994

Page 10

DESCRIPTION	ACCT NOS.	(5) MUNICIPAL RETIREM'T/S.S.		(6) SITE & CONST'N/CAP IMPRV		(7) WORKING CASH		(8) RENT		(9) FIRE PREVENTION & SAFETY	
		BUDGET	ACTUAL	BUDGET	ACTUAL	BUDGET	ACTUAL	BUDGET	ACTUAL	BUDGET	ACTUAL
REVENUE FROM LOCAL SOURCES	1000										
Ad Valorem Taxes Levied by Local Education Agency	1100	$	$ (524)	$	$ (3478)	$	$ (583)	$	$ (603)	$	$ (3531)
1. General Levy *	1110	917,100	995,152								
2. Tort Immunity Levy	1120										
3. Facility Leasing Levy	1130	$	$ (2876)								
4. Special Education Levy	1140	$									
5. Social Security/Medicare Only Levy	1150	$	$ (3265)								
6. Area Vocational Construction Levy	1160										
7. Summer School Levy	1170										
8. Other Tax Levies (Attach Itemization)	1190	$	$ (2972)	$	$ (3477)	$	$ (2976)	$	$ (2980)	$	$ (3532)
TOTAL AD VALOREM TAXES LEVIED		$	$ (525)	$	$ (3478)	$	$ (584)	$	$ (604)	$	$ (3533)
9. BY LOCAL EDUCATION AGENCY		917,100	995,152								
PAYMENTS IN LIEU OF TAXES	1200	$	$ (526)	$	$ (2693)	$		$	$ (605)	$	$ (3534)
10. Mobile Home Privilege Tax Payments from Local	1210	$	$ (2059)	$	$ (3479)	$	$ (2060)	$	$ (2061)	$	$ (3535)
11. Housing Authorities	1220	$		$		$		$		$	
12. Corprate Personal Property Replacement Taxes	1230	$ 72,900	$ (2847) 71,934	$	$ (3480)	$	$ (2654)	$	$ (2655)	$	$ (3536)
13. Other Payments in Lieu of Taxes	1290	$	$ (527)	$	$ (2694)	$	$ (586)	$	$ (606)	$	$ (3537)
14. TOTAL PAYMENTS IN LIEU OF TAXES		$ 72,900	$ (528) 71,934	$	$ (2695)	$	$ (587)	$	$ (607)	$	$ (3538)

* General levy should not include Social Security/Medicare.

APPENDIX I • 17

Page 1:

STATEMENT OF REVENUES RECEIVED/REVENUES, BUDGET TO ACTUAL, FOR THE YEAR ENDED JUNE 30, 1994

ACCT NOS.	DESCRIPTION	(1) EDUCATIONAL BUDGET	(1) EDUCATIONAL ACTUAL	(2) OPERATIONS AND MAINTENANCE BUDGET	(2) OPERATIONS AND MAINTENANCE ACTUAL	(3) BOND AND INTEREST BUDGET	(3) BOND AND INTEREST ACTUAL	(4) TRANSPORTATION BUDGET	(4) TRANSPORTATION ACTUAL
1300	Tuition		(244)						
1310	15. Regular Day School Tuition	$ 100,000	$ 3,050						
1320	16. Summer School Tuition	$ —	$ 9,705 (245)						
1330	17. Vocational Education Tuition	$ —	$ — (246)						
1340	18. Special Education Tuition	$ —	$ — (247)						
1350	19. Adult/Continuing Education Tuition	$ —	$ — (248)						
	20. TOTAL TUITION	$ 100,000	$ 12,755 (249)						
1400	Transportation Fees								
1410	Regular Day School Transportation Fees							$ —	$ — (472)
1411	Transportation Fees from Pupils or Parents							—	—
1412	21. Transportation Fees from Other LEA's							—	— (473)
1413	22. Transportation Fees from Private Sources							60,000	99,786
1415	23. Pupils - Cocurricular Activities							—	3,724 (475)
	24. Total Regular Day School Transportation Fees							60,000	103,510 (2003)
1420	25. Summer School Transportation Fees							$ —	$ 14,582 (476)
1430	Vocational Education Transportation Fees							$ —	$ — (477)
1431	26. Vocational Transportation Fees from Pupils or Parents							—	—
1432	27. Vocational Transportation Fees from Other LEAs							—	— (478)
1433	28. Vocational Transportation Fees from Other Sources							—	— (479)
	29. Total Vocational Education Transportation Fees							$ —	$ — (2004)
	30. Transportation Fees								

18 • APPENDIX I

STATEMENT OF REVENUES RECEIVED/REVENUES, BUDGET TO ACTUAL, FOR THE YEAR ENDED JUNE 30, 1994

Page 12

DESCRIPTION	ACCT NOS.	(5) MUNICIPAL RETIREM'T/S.S.		(6) SITE & CONST'N/CAP IMPRV		(7) WORKING CASH		(8) RENT		(9) FIRE PREVENTION & SAFETY	
		BUDGET	ACTUAL	BUDGET	ACTUAL	BUDGET	ACTUAL	BUDGET	ACTUAL	BUDGET	ACTUAL
Tuition	1300										
15. Regular Day School Tuition	1310										
16. Summer School Tuition	1320										
17. Vocational Education Tuition	1330										
18. Special Education Tuition	1340										
19. Adult/Continuing Education Tuition	1350										
20. TOTAL TUITION											
Transportation Fees	1400										
Regular Day School Transportation Fees	1410										
Transportation Fees from											
21. Pupils or Parents	1411										
Transportation Fees from											
22. Other LEA's	1412										
Transportation Fees from											
23. Private Sources	1413										
Transportation Fees from											
24. Pupils – Cocurricular Activities	1415										
Total Regular Day School											
25. Transportation Fees											
Summer School											
26. Transportation Fees	1420										
Vocational Education											
Transportation Fees	1430										
27. Fees from Pupils or Parents	1431										
Vocational Transportation											
28. Fees from Other LEAs	1432										
Vocational Transportation											
29. Fees from Other Sources	1433										
Total Vocational Education											
30. Transportation Fees											

Page 13

STATEMENT OF REVENUES RECEIVED/REVENUES, BUDGET TO ACTUAL, FOR THE YEAR ENDED JUNE 30, 1994

APPENDIX I • 19

ACCT. NOS.	DESCRIPTION	(1) EDUCATIONAL BUDGET	(1) EDUCATIONAL ACTUAL	(2) OPERATIONS AND MAINTENANCE BUDGET	(2) OPERATIONS AND MAINTENANCE ACTUAL	(3) BOND AND INTEREST BUDGET	(3) BOND AND INTEREST ACTUAL	(4) TRANSPORTATION BUDGET	(4) TRANSPORTATION ACTUAL
	Special Education Transportation Fees								
1440	Special Ed. Transportation							$ -	$ (480)
1441	Fees from Pupils or Parents								
	31. Special Ed. Transportation							$ -	$ (481)
1442	Fees from Other LEAs								-
	32. Special Ed. Transportation							$ -	$ (482)
1443	Fees from Other Sources								-
	33. Total Special Education							$ -	$ (2005)
	34. Transportation Fees								-
	Adult/Continuing Education								
1450	Transportation Fees							$ -	$ (483)
	35. TOTAL TRANSPORTATION							$ -	$ (484)
	FEES							60,000	118,092
	36. FEES								
1500	37. Earnings on Investments	$ 395,000	$ (250) 288,378	$ -	$ (363) -	$ 30,000	$ (436) 31,756	$ -	$ (485) 2,082
1600	38. Food Services	$ 777,800	$ (251) 873,212						
1700	39. Pupil Activities	$ 105,180	$ (252) 93,121	$ -	$ (364) -				
1800	40. Textbooks	$ 259,000	$ (253) 286,451						
	Other Revenue from								
1900	Local Sources								
1910	41. Rentals	$ -	$ (254) 420	$ 30,000	$ (365) 38,297				
1920	42. Contributions and Donations from Private Sources	$ -	$ (255) 2,801	$ -	$ (366) 4,866	$ -	$ (437) -	$ -	$ (486) -
1940	43. Services Provided Other LEA's	$ -	$ (257) -	$ -	$ (368) -				
1950	44. Refund of Prior Years' Disbursements/Expenditures	$ 20,500	$ (258) 4,275	$ -	$ (369) -	$ -	$ (438) -	$ -	$ (488) -
1990	Other								
1991	Payments from Other LEA's			$ -	$ (374) -				$ (489) -
1992	46. Sale of Vocational Projects	$ 55,000	$ (266) 62,445				$ (442) -		
1993	47. Local Fees	$ 21,000	$ (3376) 12,129						

20 • APPENDIX I

STATEMENT OF REVENUES RECEIVED/REVENUES, BUDGET TO ACTUAL, FOR THE YEAR ENDED JUNE 30, 1994

Page 14

DESCRIPTION	ACCT NOS.	(5) MUNICIPAL RETIREM'T/S.S. BUDGET	ACTUAL	(6) SITE & CONST'N/CAP IMPRV BUDGET	ACTUAL	(7) WORKING CASH BUDGET	ACTUAL	(8) RENT BUDGET	ACTUAL	(9) FIRE PREVENTION & SAFETY BUDGET	ACTUAL
Special Education Transportation Fees	1440										
31. Fees from Pupils or Parents	1441										
Special Ed. Transportation											
32. Fees from Other LEAs	1442										
Special Ed. Transportation											
33. Fees from Other Sources	1443										
Total Special Education											
34. Transportation Fees											
Adult/Continuing Education											
35. Transportation Fees	1450										
TOTAL TRANSPORTATION											
36. FEES		$	$ (529)	$	$ (554)	$	$ (588)	$	$ (608)	$	$ (3539)
37. Earnings on Investments	1500	10,000	7,446							5,000	12,103
38. Food Services	1600										
39. Pupil Activities	1700										
40. Textbooks	1800										
Other Revenue from Local Sources	1900										
41. Rentals	1910										
Contributions and Donations	1920	$	$ (530)	$	$ (555)	$	$ (589)	$	$ (609)	$	$ (3540)
42. from Private Sources											
43. Services Provided Other LEA's	1940										
Refund of Prior Years'	1950	$	$ (531)	$	$ (556)	$		$	$ (2714)	$	$ (3541)
44. Disbursements/Expenditures											
Other	1990										
Payments from Other											
45. LEA's	1991			$	$ (561)						
46. Sale of Vocational Projects	1992										
47. Local Fees	1993										

APPENDIX I • 21

Page 15

STATEMENT OF REVENUES RECEIVED/REVENUES, BUDGET TO ACTUAL, FOR THE YEAR ENDED JUNE 30, 1994

DESCRIPTION	ACCT NOS.	(1) EDUCATIONAL BUDGET	(1) EDUCATIONAL ACTUAL	(2) OPERATIONS AND MAINTENANCE BUDGET	(2) OPERATIONS AND MAINTENANCE ACTUAL	(3) BOND AND INTEREST BUDGET	(3) BOND AND INTEREST ACTUAL	(4) TRANSPORTATION BUDGET	(4) TRANSPORTATION ACTUAL
48. Other (Attach Itemization)	1999	$	$ (267) 297,655	$ 25,000	$ (376) 83,574	$	$ (444)	$ 2,000	$ (491)
49. TOTAL OTHER TOTAL OTHER REVENUE FROM		$ 76,000	$ (268) 372,229	$ 25,000	$ (377) 83,574	$	$ (445)	$ 2,000	$ (492)
50. LOCAL SOURCES *		$ 96,500	$ (269) 379,725	$ 55,000	$ (378) 126,737	$	$ (446)	$ 2,000	$ (493)
TOTAL REVENUE FROM LOCAL		$	$ (270)	$	$ (379)	$	$ (447)	$	$ (494)
51. SOURCES **		20,326,880	20,504,996	3,021,000	3,200,031	3,209,813	3,074,395	996,300	1,118,120
FLOW-THROUGH REVENUE FROM ONE LEA TO ANOTHER LEA	2000	$	$ (3266)	$	$ (3276)			$	$ (3283)
52. FLOW-THROUGH REVENUE FROM STATE SOURCES	2100	$ 140,000	$ 190,479	$	$ (3277)			$	$ (3284)
53. FLOW-THROUGH REVENUE FROM FEDERAL SOURCES	2200	$ 35,000	$ (3267) 74,171	$	$			$	$
54. TOTAL FLOW-THROUGH REVENUE FROM ONE LEA TO ANOTHER LEA		$ 175,000	$ (2878) 264,650	$	$ (2879)			$	$ (2880)
REVENUE FROM STATE SOURCES	3000	$	$	$	$ (381)	$	$ (448)	$	$ (496)
Unrestricted Grants-In-Aid	3100	$	$ (272)	$	$				
55. General State Aid	3110	$ 7,172,776	$ 7,191,262	$ 670,000	$ 670,000			$	$ (3033)
56. Supplementary State Aid	3120	$	$ (3027)	$	$ (3029)			$	$ (3031)
TOTAL UNRESTRICTED		$	$	$	$ (3030)	$	$ (3032)	$	$ (3034)
57. GRANTS-IN-AID		$ 7,172,776	$ 7,191,262	$ 670,000	$ 670,000				
Restricted Grants-In-Aid	3200	$	$ (3268)	$	$ (3278)			$	$ (497)
Transportation Aid	3210							140,000	287,559
58. Regular	3211	$	$ (3269)	$	$ (3279)				(498)
59. Special Education	3212							468,000	429,061
60. Vocational Education	3213	$	$ (3270)	$	$ (3280)				(499)
61. TOTAL TRANSPORTATION AID	3220 3249	$	$ (3271)	$	$ (3281)			608,000	(500) 716,620
Instructional Program Aid	3220								
62. Driver Education	3221	$ 52,268	$ (273) 53,788	$	$ (382)				
63. Technical Preparation Education	3222		$ (3644)						

* Total of Lines 41,42,43,44,45-50.
** Total of Lines 9,14,20,36,37,38,39,40,51.

22 • APPENDIX I

STATEMENT OF REVENUES RECEIVED/REVENUES, BUDGET TO ACTUAL, FOR THE YEAR ENDED JUNE 30, 1994

Page 16

	ACCT NOS.	(5) MUNICIPAL RETIREM'T/S.S. BUDGET	ACTUAL	(6) SITE & CONST'N/CAP IMPRV BUDGET	ACTUAL	(7) WORKING CASH BUDGET	ACTUAL	(8) RENT BUDGET	ACTUAL	(9) FIRE PREVENTION & SAFETY BUDGET	ACTUAL
DESCRIPTION											
48. Other (Attach Itemization)	1999	$ -	$ (533)	$ -	$ (563)	$ -	$ (2064)	$ -	$ (611)	$ -	$ (3542)
49. TOTAL OTHER		$ -	$ (534)	$ -	$ (564)	$ -	$ (2065)	$ -	$ (612)	$ -	$ (3543)
TOTAL OTHER REVENUE FROM											
50. LOCAL SOURCES *		$ -	$ (535)	$ -	$ (565)	$ -	$ (2066)	$ -	$ (613)	$ -	$ (3544)
51. TOTAL REVENUE FROM LOCAL SOURCES **		$ 1,000,000	$ 1,074,532	$ -	$ (566)	$ -	$ (598)	$ -	$ (614)	$ 5,000	$ 12,103
FLOW-THROUGH REVENUE FROM ONE LEA TO ANOTHER LEA	2000		$ (3290)								
52. FROM STATE SOURCES	2100	$ -	$ (3291)								
FLOW-THROUGH REVENUE											
53. FROM FEDERAL SOURCES	2200	$ -	$ (2881)								
TOTAL FLOW-THROUGH REVENUE											
54. FROM ONE LEA TO ANOTHER LEA		$ -									
REVENUE FROM STATE SOURCES	3000										
Unrestricted Grants-In-Aid	3100	$ -	$ (537)	$ -	$ (567)			$ -	$ (815)	$ -	$ (3546)
55. General State Aid	3110	$ -	$ (3035)	$ -	$ (3037)			$ -	$ (3039)	$ -	$ (3547)
56. Supplementary State Aid	3120										
TOTAL UNRESTRICTED											
57. GRANTS-IN-AID		$ -	$ (3036)	$ -	$ (3038)			$ -	$ (3040)	$ -	$ (3548)
Restricted Grants-In-Aid	3200										
Transportation Aid	3210										
58. Regular	3211										
59. Special Education	3212										
60. Vocational Education	3213										
61. TOTAL TRANSPORTATION AID	3220										
Instructional Program Aid	3249										
62. Driver Education	3221										
Technical Preparation											
63. Education	3222										

* Total of Lines 41, 42, 43, 44, 45-50.

** Total of Lines 9, 14, 20, 36, 37, 38, 39, 40, 51.

APPENDIX I • 23

Page 17

STATEMENT OF REVENUES RECEIVED/REVENUES, BUDGET TO ACTUAL, FOR THE YEAR ENDED JUNE 30, 1994

DESCRIPTION	ACCT. NOS.	(1) EDUCATIONAL BUDGET	(1) EDUCATIONAL ACTUAL	(2) OPERATIONS AND MAINTENANCE BUDGET	(2) OPERATIONS AND MAINTENANCE ACTUAL	(3) BOND AND INTEREST BUDGET	(3) BOND AND INTEREST ACTUAL	(4) TRANSPORTATION BUDGET	(4) TRANSPORTATION ACTUAL
64. Summer School	3223	$ -	$ (275) 8,897					$ -	$ (3103)
65. Bilingual Education Vocational Education- Regular	3224	186,133	(276) 201,854					-	(2063)
66. Part B (Formula Reimbursement) Vocational Education	3225	-	$ (277) -	$	$ (384)				
67. Grants and Contracts	3226	20,000	(278) 53,372		(385)				
68. Gifted Education	3227	53,984	(279) 88,430						
69. Adult Education- General	3228	-	(280) -		(386)				
70. Adult Education - Section 10-22.20	3229	-	(281) -		(387)				
71. Special Education Personnel	3231	749,155	(3272) 674,220		(3333)			-	(3285)
72. Spec Education Private Facility	3232	132,650	(3273) 186,624		(3334)			-	(3286)
73. Special Education Extraordinary	3233	171,933	(3274) 308,159		(3335)			-	(3287)
74. Special Education Orphanage	3234	85,000	(3377) 3,375		(3378)			-	(3379)
75. Reading Improvement Program	3240	162,260	(3043) 169,568					-	(3337)
76. Prekindergarten Program for At-Risk Students	3245	323,868	(3102) 349,026		(3436)			-	(3104)
77. TOTAL INSTRUCTIONAL PROGRAM AID *		$ 1,937,251	$ (3275) 2,097,313	$	$ (3282)			$ -	$ (3289)
School Lunch Aid	3250								
78. Lunch - Free	3251	25,350	(284) 28,204						
79. Breakfast - Free	3252	-	(285) 2,535						
80. TOTAL SCHOOL LUNCH AID		$ 25,350	$ (286) 30,739						

* Total of Lines 62,63,64,65,66,67,68,69,70,71,72,73,74,75,76.

24 • APPENDIX I

STATEMENT OF REVENUES RECEIVED/REVENUES, BUDGET TO ACTUAL, FOR THE YEAR ENDED JUNE 30, 1994

	ACCT NOS.	(5) MUNICIPAL RETIREM'T/S.S. BUDGET	(5) ACTUAL	(6) SITE & CONST'N/CAP IMPRV BUDGET	(6) ACTUAL	(7) WORKING CASH BUDGET	(7) ACTUAL	(8) RENT BUDGET	(8) ACTUAL	(9) FIRE PREVENTION & SAFETY BUDGET	(9) ACTUAL
64. Summer School	3223										
65. Bilingual Education Vocational Education- Regular	3224										
66. Part B (Formula Reimbursement) Vocational Education	3225										
67. Grants and Contracts	3226										
68. Gifted Education	3227			$	$ (568)						
69. Adult Education- General Adult Education -	3228				-						
70. Section 10-22.20	3229										
71. Special Education Personnel	3231										
72. Spec Education Private Facility	3232										
73. Special Education Extraordinary	3233										
74. Special Education Orphanage	3234										
75. Reading Improvement Program	3240	$ -	$ (3380)								
76. Prekindergarten Program for At-Risk Students	3245	-	(3332)								
77. TOTAL INSTRUCTIONAL * PROGRAM AID		$ -	$ (3292)	$ -	$ (3304)						
78. School Lunch Aid	3250										
78. Lunch - Free	3251										
79. Breakfast - Free	3252										
80. TOTAL SCHOOL LUNCH AID											

* Total of Lines 62,63,64,65,66,67,68,69,70,71,72,73,74,75,76.

Page 19
APPENDIX I • 25

STATEMENT OF REVENUES RECEIVED/REVENUES, BUDGET TO ACTUAL, FOR THE YEAR ENDED JUNE 30, 1994

	ACCT NOS.	(1) EDUCATIONAL		(2) OPERATIONS AND MAINTENANCE		(3) BOND AND INTEREST		(4) TRANSPORTATION	
DESCRIPTION		BUDGET	ACTUAL	BUDGET	ACTUAL	BUDGET	ACTUAL	BUDGET	ACTUAL
Capital Development Board	3260								
81. Bond Principal	3261						(449)		(501)
82. Bond Interest	3262						(450)		
TOTAL CAPITAL DEVELOPMENT BOARD		$	$	$	$	$	$ (451)	$	$ (502)
84. Other Grants-In-Aid (Attach Itemization)	3290	73,436	(287) 107,389		(390)				
85. TOTAL RESTRICTED GRANTS-IN-AID *		$ 2,036,037	$ (288) 2,235,441	$	$ (391)	$	$ (452)	$ 608,000	$ (502) 716,620
Payments Received in Lieu of Taxes	3300								
86. Orphans Tuition	3310		(289) 15,782						(503)
87. State Owned Housing	3320		(290)						
88. Tax Equivalent Grants	3330		(291)		(392)				(504)
89. State Impaction Aid	3340		(292)		(393)				
TOTAL PAYMENTS RECEIVED IN LIEU OF TAXES		$	$ (293) 15,782	$	$ (394)	$		$	$ (505)
91. TOTAL REVENUE FROM STATE SOURCES **		$ 9,208,813	$ (294) 9,442,485	$ 670,000	$ (395) 670,000	$	$ (453)	$ 608,000	$ (506) 716,620
REVENUE FROM FEDERAL SOURCES	4000								
Unrestricted Grants-In-Aid received Directly from Federal Government	4100		(295)		(396)				(507)
92. Public Law 81-874	4110	7,000	13,070						
Restricted Grants-In-Aid Received Directly from Federal Government	4300								
93. Emergency School Assistance Act	4320		(298)						(3105)
ESEA			(316)						
94. Title VII - Bilingual	4325	75,400	28,563						
EESA - Title VI, P.L. 98-377			(3044)						(3045)
95. Excellence in Education	4330								

* Total of Lines 61,77,80,83,84
** Total of Lines 57,85,90

26 • APPENDIX I

STATEMENT OF REVENUES RECEIVED/REVENUES, BUDGET TO ACTUAL, FOR THE YEAR ENDED JUNE 30, 1994

Page 20

DESCRIPTION	ACCT NOS.	(5) MUNICIPAL RETIREM'T/S.S. BUDGET	ACTUAL	(6) SITE& CONST'N/CAP IMPRV BUDGET	ACTUAL	(7) WORKING CASH BUDGET	ACTUAL	(8) RENT BUDGET	ACTUAL	(9) FIRE PREVENTION & SAFETY BUDGET	ACTUAL
Capital Development Board	3260										
81. Bond Principal	3261										
82. Bond Interest	3262										
TOTAL CAPITAL DEVELOPMENT BOARD		$	$ (2068)	$	$ (569)					$	$ (3549)
83. Other Grants-In-Aid	3290				156,320						
84. (Attach Itemization)			(2069)		(570)						(3550)
TOTAL RESTRICTED GRANTS-IN-AID *		$	$ —	$	$ 156,320					$	$ —
85. Payments Received in Lieu of Taxes	3300										
86. Orphans Tuition	3310										
87. State Owned Housing	3320										
88. Tax Equivalent Grants	3330	$	$ (538)								
89. State Impaction Aid	3340		(539)								
TOTAL PAYMENTS RECEIVED IN LIEU OF TAXES			(540)								
90. TOTAL REVENUE FROM STATE SOURCES **		$	$ (541)	$	$ (571)			$	$ (616)	$	$ (3551)
91. REVENUE FROM FEDERAL SOURCES					156,320						
Unrestricted Grants-In-Aid received Directly from Federal Government	4000 4100										
92. Public Law 81-874	4110	$	$ (542)								
Restricted Grants-In-Aid Received Directly from Federal Government	4300										
93. Emergency School Assistance Act	4320	$	$ (3106)								
ESEA	4325										
94. Title VII - Bilingual											
EESA - Title VI, P.L. 98-377		$	$ (3046)								
95. Excellence in Education	4330										

* Total of Lines 61,77,80,83,84
** Total of Lines 57,85,90

Page 21

STATEMENT OF REVENUES RECEIVED/REVENUES, BUDGET TO ACTUAL, FOR THE YEAR ENDED JUNE 30, 1994

	DESCRIPTION	ACCT NOS.	(1) EDUCATIONAL BUDGET	(1) EDUCATIONAL ACTUAL	(2) OPERATIONS AND MAINTENANCE BUDGET	(2) OPERATIONS AND MAINTENANCE ACTUAL	(3) BOND AND INTEREST BUDGET	(3) BOND AND INTEREST ACTUAL	(4) TRANSPORTATION BUDGET	(4) TRANSPORTATION ACTUAL
	Community Action	4340	$ --	$ (300)						
96.	Program - O.E.O		$ --	(301)						
97.	Head Start	4350	$ --	$ (302)						
98.	Public Law 81-815	4360	--	--						
	Construction									$ (508)
99.	Other	4390	$ --	$ (305)	$ --	$ (399)				--
	(Attach Itemization)		--	--						
	TOTAL RESTRICTED GRANTS-IN-AID		$ --	$ (306)	$ --	$ (400)			$ --	$ (510)
100.	RECEIVED DIRECTLY FROM FEDERAL GOVT	4400	75,400	28,563						
	Restricted Grants-In-Aid Received from Federal Gov't through State									
101.	Title III, Adult Basic Education - P.L. 102-73	4410	$ --	$ (307)	$ --	$ (401)				
	Carl D. Perkins Vocational and Applied Technology Educ. Act 1990, P.L. 101-392	4420								
102.	Vocational Act 1990, P.L. 101-392 Title IIA-State Leadership	4421	$ --	$ (3437)	$ --	$ (3440)				
103.	Vocational Act 1990, P.L. 101-392 Title IIB-Single Parents	4422	--	(3400)	--	(3407)				
104.	Vocational Act 1990, P.L. 101-392 Title IIB-Sex Equity	4423	--	(3401)	--	(3408)				
105.	Vocational Act 1990, P.L. 101-392 Title IIC-Secondary Voc. Educ. Prog.	4424	--	(3402)	--	(3409)				
106.	Vocational Act 1990, P.L. 101-392 Title IIIB-Consumer Homemaking	4425	--	(3404)	--	(3411)				
107.	Vocational Act 1990, P.L. 101-392 Title IIIE-Tech. Prep.	4426	--	(3405)	--	(3412)				
108.	Vocational Act 1990, P.L. 101-392 Title IIIF-Facilities and Equipment	4427	--	(3438)	--	(3441)				
109.	Vocational Act 1990, P.L. 101-392 Other (Attach Itemization)	4429	--	(3439)	--	(3442)				
110.	Total Carl D. Perkins Vocational & Applied Tech. Educ. Act 1990, P.L. 101-392		$ --	$ (3406)	$ --	$ (3413)				
111.	Transition Program for Refugee Children	4430	$ --	$ (2985)	$ --	$ (2986)			$ --	$ (2987)
112.	Emergency Immigrant Education Assistance	4435	$ --	$ (3067)	$ --	$ (3071)			$ --	$ (3073)

28 • APPENDIX I

STATEMENT OF REVENUES RECEIVED/REVENUES, BUDGET TO ACTUAL, FOR THE YEAR ENDED JUNE 30, 1994

Page 22

	DESCRIPTION	ACCT NOS.	(5) MUNICIPAL RETIREM'T/S.S. BUDGET	(5) ACTUAL	(6) SITE & CONST'N/CAP IMPRV BUDGET	(6) ACTUAL	(7) WORKING CASH BUDGET	(7) ACTUAL	(8) RENT BUDGET	(8) ACTUAL	(9) FIRE PREVENTION & SAFETY BUDGET	(9) ACTUAL
96.	Community Action Program - O.E.O	4340										
97.	Head Start	4350										
	Public Law 81-815				$	$ (572)						
98.	Construction	4360										
99.	Other (Attach Itemization)	4390	$	$ (543)	$	$ (573)					$	$ (3352)
	TOTAL RESTRICTED GRANTS-IN-AID		$	$ (544)	$	$ (574)					$	$ (3353)
100.	RECEIVED DIRECTLY FROM FEDERAL GOVT Restricted Grants-In-Aid Received from Federal Gov't through State	4400										
101.	Title III, Adult Basic Education - P.L. 102-73	4410										
	Carl D. Perkins Voc. and Applied Tech. Educ. Act 1990, P.L. 101-392 Vocational Act 1990, P.L. 101-392	4420	$	$ (3443)								
102.	Title IIA-State Leadership Vocational Act 1990, P.L. 101-392	4421		(3414)								
103.	Title IIB-Single Parents Vocational Act 1990, P.L. 101-392	4422		(3415)								
104.	Title IIB-Sex Equity Vocational Act 1990, P.L. 101-392	4423		(3416)								
105.	Title IIC-Sec. Voc. Educ. Prog. Vocational Act 1990, P.L. 101-392	4424		(3418)								
106.	Title IIIB-Consumer Homemaking Vocational Act 1990, P.L. 101-392	4425		(3419)								
107.	Title IIIE-Tech. Prep. Vocational Act 1990, P.L. 101-392	4426		(2444)								
108.	Title IIIF-Facilities and Eqpt. Vocational Act 1990, P.L. 101-392	4427		(3445)								
109.	Other (Attach Itemization) Total Carl D. Perkins Voc. & Applied Tech. Educ. Act 1990, P.L. 101-392	4429	$	$ (3420)								
110.	Transition Program for Refugee Children	4430	$	$ (2988)								
111.	Emergency Immigrant												
112.	Education Assistance	4435	$	$ (3075)								

APPENDIX I • 29

Page 23

STATEMENT OF REVENUES RECEIVED/REVENUES, BUDGET TO ACTUAL, FOR THE YEAR ENDED JUNE 30, 1994

	ACCT NOS.	(1) EDUCATIONAL		(2) OPERATIONS AND MAINTENANCE		(3) BOND AND INTEREST		(4) TRANSPORTATION	
DESCRIPTION		BUDGET	ACTUAL	BUDGET	ACTUAL	BUDGET	ACTUAL	BUDGET	ACTUAL
Education Consolidation and Imp. Act (ESEA) Chapter 1	4440		(312)		(406)				(511)
113. ESEA, Chapter 1, Educationally Deprived	4441	$ 682,706	797,491		(2721)				(2722)
114. ESEA, Chapter 1, Handicapped	4442	43,744	37,062		(2631)				(2640)
115. ESEA, Chapter 1, Migrant	4443	-	(2623)						
116. ESEA, Chapter 1, Neglected and Deliquent	4444	-	(2624)		(2632)				(2641)
117. ESEA - Chapter 1 Even Start	4445	135,006	123,411						
TOTAL ELEMENTARY AND SECONDARY		$ 861,456	957,964		(411)				(518)
118. EDUCATION ACT (ESEA) Chapter 1 Individuals with Disabilities Education Act (IDEA)	4450		(3645)(321)						
119. IDEA - Preschool	4451	-	(2626)		(2634)				(2643)
120. IDEA - Room & Board Reimbursement	4452	-	(2627)		(2635)				(2644)
121. IDEA - Discretionary Programs	4453	-	(2628)		(2636)				(2645)
122. IDEA - Flow-Through	4454	237,841	251,424		(2637)				(2646)
123. IDEA - Deaf Blind	4455	-	(3646)						
124. IDEA - Infant/Toddler	4456	-	(3068)		(3072)				(3074)
Total Individuals with Disabilities Education Act (IDEA)		$ 237,841	251,424		(410)				(515)
125.	4460		(320)						
School Lunch Program									
School Lunch -			(323)						
126. Regular Lunches	4461	$ 544,513	507,961						
127. School Lunch - Free and Reduced	4462	-	(324)(325)						
128. Special Milk	4463	-	(326)						
129. Breakfast	4464	5,500	21,206		(412)				
130. Non-Food Assistance	4465	-	(327)						

30 • APPENDIX I

STATEMENT OF REVENUES RECEIVED/REVENUES, BUDGET TO ACTUAL, FOR THE YEAR ENDED JUNE 30, 1994

Page 24

ACCT NOS.	DESCRIPTION	(5) MUNICIPAL RETIREM'T/S.S. BUDGET	(5) ACTUAL	(6) SITE & CONST'N/CAP IMPRV BUDGET	(6) ACTUAL	(7) WORKING CASH BUDGET	(7) ACTUAL	(8) RENT BUDGET	(8) ACTUAL	(9) FIRE PREVENTION & SAFETY BUDGET	(9) ACTUAL
4440	Education Consolidation and Imp. Act (ESEA) Chapter 1	$	$ (545)								
4441	ESEA, Chapter 1, Educationally Deprived	-	(2723)								
4442	ESEA, Chapter 1, Handicapped	-	(2648)								
4443	ESEA, Chapter 1, Migrant	-	(2649)								
4444	ESEA, Chapter 1, Neglected and Delinquent	-	-								
4445	ESEA - Chapter 1 Even Start	-	(3647)								
	TOTAL ELEMENTARY AND SECONDARY	$ -	$ (550)								
	EDUCATION ACT (ESEA) Chapter 1										
4450	Individuals with Disabilities Education Act (IDEA)	$ -	$ (2650)								
4451	IDEA - Preschool	-	(2851)								
4452	IDEA - Room & Board Reimbursement	-	(2652)								
4453	IDEA - Discretionary Programs	-	(2653)								
4454	IDEA - Flow-Through	-	(3648)								
4455	IDEA - Deaf Blind	-	(3076)								
4456	IDEA - Infant/Toddler	-	(549)								
	Total Individuals with Disabilities Education Act (IDEA)	$ -	$								
4460	School Lunch Program										
4461	School Lunch - Regular Lunches										
4462	School Lunch - Free and Reduced										
4463	Special Milk										
4464	Breakfast										
4465	Non-Food Assistance										

Page 25

APPENDIX I • 31

STATEMENT OF REVENUES RECEIVED/REVENUES, BUDGET TO ACTUAL, FOR THE YEAR ENDED JUNE 30, 1994

DESCRIPTION	ACCT NOS.	(1) EDUCATIONAL BUDGET	(1) EDUCATIONAL ACTUAL	(2) OPERATIONS AND MAINTENANCE BUDGET	(2) OPERATIONS AND MAINTENANCE ACTUAL	(3) BOND AND INTEREST BUDGET	(3) BOND AND INTEREST ACTUAL	(4) TRANSPORTATION BUDGET	(4) TRANSPORTATION ACTUAL
Payments in Lieu of 131. Commodities	4466	$ -	$ (328) (2989)						
Nutrition Education and 132. Training Act	4467								
TOTAL SCHOOL LUNCH PROGRAM		$ 550,013	$ (329) 529,167	$	$ (414)				
133. ESEA, Chapter 2	4470	$ 71,100	$ (2882) 66,114	$	$ (2883)			$	$ (2884)
134. Block Grant									
EESA, Title II Dwight D. Eisenhower 135. (Math/Science Education Act)	4475	$ 30,477	$ (3077) 31,083	$ -	$ (3078) -			$ -	$ (3079) -
Department of 136. Rehabilitation Services	4480	$ 23,840	$ (331) 44,221	$ -	$ (415) -				
137. Other (Attach Itemization)	4490	$ 67,549	$ (332) 51,474	$ -	$ (416) -			$ -	$ (517) -
TOTAL RESTRICTED GRANTS-IN-AID RECEIVED FROM FEDERAL GOV'T THROUGH THE STATE *		$ 1,842,276	$ (335) 1,931,447	$ -	$ (417) -			$ -	$ (518) -
Restricted Grants-In-Aid Received from 138. Federal Gov't- Intermediate Sources	4500								
Job Training Partnership Reform Act 139. (J.T.P.R.A.)	4530	$ -	$ (2990) 7,692	$ -	$ (2991) -			$ -	$ (2992) -
Other 140. (Attach Itemization)	4590	$ -	$ (2007) 7,692	$ -	$ (2009) -			$ -	$ (2012) -
TOTAL RESTRICTED GRANTS-IN-AID RECEIVED FROM 141. FEDERAL GOVT - INTERMEDIATE SOURCES		$ -	$ (334) -	$ -	$ (2010) -			$ -	$ (2013) -
TOTAL REVENUE FROM 142. FEDERAL SOURCES **		$ 1,924,676	$ (336) 1,980,772	$ -	$ (418) -			$ -	$ (519) -
143. TOTAL RECEIPTS/REVENUE (Total of Lines 51, 54, 91, 142)		$ 31,635,369	$ (337) 32,192,903	$ 3,691,000	$ (419) 3,870,031	$ 3,209,813	$ (454) 3,074,395	$ 1,604,300	$ (520) 1,834,740

* Total of Lines 101,110,111,112,118,125,133,134,135,136,137.
** Total of Lines 92,100,138,141.

32 • APPENDIX I

STATEMENT OF REVENUES RECEIVED/REVENUES, BUDGET TO ACTUAL, FOR THE YEAR ENDED JUNE 30, 1994

DESCRIPTION	ACCT NOS.	(5) MUNICIPAL RETIREM'T/S.S.		(6) SITE & CONST'N/CAP IMPRV		(7) WORKING CASH		(8) RENT		(9) FIRE PREVENTION & SAFETY	
		BUDGET	ACTUAL	BUDGET	ACTUAL	BUDGET	ACTUAL	BUDGET	ACTUAL	BUDGET	ACTUAL
Payments in Lieu of											
131. Commodities	4466										
Nutrition Education and											
132. Training Act	4467										
TOTAL SCHOOL LUNCH											
133. PROGRAM											
134. ESEA Chapter 2 Block Grant	4470	$ -	$ (2885)								
EESA, Title II – Dwight D.											
135. Eisenhower (Math & Science Educ Act)	4475	$ -	$ (3080)								
Department of											
136. Rehabilitation Services	4480										
137. Other (Attach Itemization)	4490	$ -	$ (551)	$ -	$ (578)						
TOTAL RESTRICTED GRANTS-IN-AID RECEIVED FROM FEDERAL GOV'T THROUGH THE STATE *		$ -	$ (2014)	$ -	$ (577)						
138.											
Restricted Grants-In-Aid from Fed. Gov't-Intermediate Sources	4500		$ (2993)								
Job Training Partnership Reform Act											
139. (J.T.P.R.A.)	4530	$ -	$ (2018)								
140. Other (Attach Itemization)	4590	$ -	$ (553)								
TOTAL RESTRICTED GRANTS-IN-AID FROM FEDERAL GOVT – INTERMEDIATE SOURCES											
141.											
TOTAL REVENUE FROM FEDERAL SOURCES **		$ -	$ (2001)		$ (578)						
142.											
TOTAL RECEIPTS/REVENUE		$ -	$ (2002)	$ -	(2019)	$ -	$ (599)	$ -	$ (617)	$ -	$ (3554)
143. (Total of Lines 51, 54, 91, 142)		1,000,000	1,074,532		156,320		-		-	5,000	(3555)
											12,103

* Total of Lines 101,110,111,112,118,125,133,134,135,136,137.
** Total of Lines 92,100,138,141.

APPENDIX I • 33

Page 27

STATEMENT OF EXPENDITURES DISBURSED/EXPENDITURES, BUDGET TO ACTUAL, FOR THE YEAR ENDED—June 30, 1994

DESCRIPTION	FUCT. NO.	(1) SALARIES	(2) EMPLOYEE BENEFITS	(3) PURCHASED SERVICES	(4) SUPPLIES AND MATERIALS	(5) CAPITAL OUTLAY	(6) OTHER OBJECTS	(7) TRANSFERS	(8) TUITION	(9) TOTAL	BUDGET
EDUCATION FUND (1)											
Instruction	1000										
1. Regular Programs	1100	$ (644) 17,129,590	$ (702) 874,780	$ (760) 133,650	$ (818) 319,915	$ (876) 161,867	$ (934) -		$ (1002) 10,882	$ (1032) 18,630,684	19,176,161
Special Education Programs		$ (3305) 2,495,774	$ (3307) 168,576	$ (3309) 160,879	$ (3311) 44,245	$ (3313) 2,289	$ (3315) -		$ (3317) 1,161,100	$ (3319) 4,032,863	3,448,425
2. (Total of Fuct No 1200-1220)	1200										
Educationally Deprived/		$ (2994) 487,334	$ (2995) 86,871	$ (2996) -	$ (2997) 16,716	$ (2998) 21,888	$ (2999) -		$ (3000) -	$ (3001) 612,809	539,550
3. Remedial Programs	1250										
4. Adult Education Programs	1300	$ (655) -		$ (711) -	$ (829) -	$ (887) -	$ (945) -		$ (1013) -	$ (1043) -	-
5. Vocational Programs	1400	$ (656) 380,950	$ (714) 10,630	$ (772) 1,639	$ (830) 18,035	$ (888) 9,040	$ (946) 527		$ (1014) 12,307	$ (1044) 433,128	429,993
6. Interscholastic Programs	1500	$ (657) 907	$ (715) 58	$ (773) 56,580	$ (831) 72,493	$ (889) 8,120	$ (947) -		$ (1015) -	$ (1045) 138,158	146,664
7. Summer School Programs	1600	$ (658) 48,208	$ (716) 358	$ (774) 14,582	$ (832) 2,643	$ (890) -	$ (948) -		$ (1016) -	$ (1046) 65,791	79,366
8. Gifted Programs	1650	$ (645) 5,410	$ (703) 1,699	$ (761) -	$ (819) 19,943	$ (877) -	$ (935) -		$ (1003) -	$ (1033) 27,052	16,030
9. Bilingual Programs	1800	$ (651) 458,905	$ (709) 37,798	$ (767) 5,150	$ (825) 20,615	$ (883) -	$ (941) -		$ (1009) -	$ (1039) 522,468	521,582
Truants' Alternative &		$ (3306) -	$ (3308) -	$ (3310) -	$ (3312) -	$ (3314) -	$ (3316) -		$ (3318) -	$ (3320) -	-
10. Optional Programs	1900										
11. TOTAL INSTRUCTION •		$ (659) 21,007,078	$ (717) 1,180,770	$ (775) 372,480	$ (833) 514,605	$ (891) 203,204	$ (949) 527		$ (1017) 1,184,289	$ (1047) 24,462,953	24,357,771
Support Services	2000										
Support Services – Pupils	2100										
12. Attendance and Social Work Services	2110	$ (660) 280,565	$ (718) 16,810	$ (776) -	$ (834) 3,635	$ (892) -	$ (950) -			$ (1048) 301,010	263,703
13. Guidance Services	2120	$ (661) 535,873	$ (719) 37,609	$ (777) 8,300	$ (835) 10,394	$ (893) -	$ (951) -			$ (1049) 592,176	632,526
14. Health Services	2130	$ (662) 179,071	$ (720) (5,621)	$ (778) 303	$ (836) 6,319	$ (894) -	$ (952) -			$ (1050) 180,072	198,025
15. Psychological Services	2140	$ (663) 192,032	$ (721) 10,558	$ (779) -	$ (837) 801	$ (895) -	$ (953) -			$ (1051) 203,391	188,301

34 • APPENDIX I

STATEMENT OF EXPENDITURES DISBURSED/EXPENDITURES, BUDGET TO ACTUAL, FOR THE YEAR ENDED—June 30, 1994

Page 28

DESCRIPTION (Fund 1 Continued)	FUCT. NO.	(1) SALARIES	(2) EMPLOYEE BENEFITS	(3) PURCHASED SERVICES	(4) SUPPLIES AND MATERIALS	(5) CAPITAL OUTLAY	(6) OTHER OBJECTS	(7) TRANSFERS	(8) TUITION	(9) TOTAL	BUDGET
Speech Pathology and Audiology Services	2150	$ (664) —	$ (722) —	$ (780) —	$ (838) 302	$ (896) —	$ (954) —			$ (1052) 302	800
16. Other Support Services—Pupils (Attach Itemization)	2190	(665) —	(723) —	(781) —	(839) —	(897) —	(955) —			(1053) —	—
17. TOTAL SUPPORT SERVICES—PUPILS		$ (666) 1,187,541	$ (724) 59,356	$ (782) 8,603	$ (840) 21,451	$ (898) —	$ (956) —			$ (1054) 1,276,951	1,283,355
18. SUPPORT SERVIVES—INSTRUCTIONAL STAFF	2200										
Improvement of Instruction Services	2210	$ (667) 233,077	$ (725) 20,437	$ (783) 163,544	$ (841) 107,419	$ (899) —	$ (957) —			$ (1055) 524,477	497,510
19. Educational Media Services	2220	(668) —	(726) —	(784) 3,777	(842) 41,612	(900) —	(958) —			(1056) 45,389	32,541
20. Assessment and Testing	2230	(669) —	(727) —	(785) —	(843) —	(901) —	(959) —			(1057) —	—
21. TOTAL SUPPORT SERVICES—INSTRUCTIONAL STAFF		$ (670) 233,077	$ (728) 20,437	$ (786) 167,321	$ (844) 149,031	$ (902) —	$ (960) —			$ (1058) 569,866	530,051
22. Support Services – General Administration	2300										
Board of Education Services	2310	$ (671) 84,734	$ (729) 1,499	$ (787) 33,981	$ (845) 94,423	$ (903) —	$ (961) —			$ (1059) 214,637	210,740
23. Executive Administration	2320	(672) 702,878	(730) 365,108	(788) 68,251	(846) 18,947	(904) —	(962) —			(1060) 1,155,184	1,059,380
24. Special Area Administrative Services	2330	(2657) 39,124	(2658) 2,093	(2659) 1,084	(2660) —	(2661) —	(2662) —			(2663) 42,301	24,299
25. TOTAL SUPPORT SERVICES – GENERAL ADMINISTRATION		$ (673) 826,736	$ (731) 368,700	$ (789) 103,316	$ (847) 113,370	$ (905) —	$ (963) —			$ (1061) 1,412,122	1,294,419
26. Support Services – School Administration	2400										
Office of the Principal Services	2410	$ (674) 1,652,216	$ (732) 137,461	$ (790) 39,315	$ (848) 65,499	$ (906) —	$ (964) —			$ (1062) 1,894,491	1,734,724
27. Other Support Services- School Administration (Attach Itemization)	2490	(675) —	(733) —	(791) —	(849) —	(907) —	(965) —			(1063) —	—
28. TOTAL SUPPORT SERVICES – SCHOOL ADMINISTRATION		$ (676) 1,652,216	$ (734) 137,461	$ (792) 39,315	$ (850) 65,499	$ (908) —	$ (966) —			$ (1064) 1,894,491	1,734,724

APPENDIX I • 35

Page 29

STATEMENT OF EXPENDITURES DISBURSED/EXPENDITURES, BUDGET TO ACTUAL, FOR THE YEAR ENDED—June 30, 1994

(Fund 1 Continued)

FUCT. NO.	DESCRIPTION	(1) SALARIES	(2) EMPLOYEE BENEFITS	(3) PURCHASED SERVICES	(4) SUPPLIES AND MATERIALS	(5) CAPITAL OUTLAY	(6) OTHER OBJECTS	(7) TRANSFERS	(8) TUITION	(9) TOTAL	BUDGET
2500	SUPPORT SERVICES - BUSINESS										
	Direction of Business	$ (677)	$ (735)	$ (793)	$ (851)	$ (909)	$ (967)			$ (1065)	$
2510	Support Services	-	-	-	3	-	-			3	20,000
		(678)	(738)	(794)	(852)	(910)	(968)			(1066)	
2520	Fiscal Services	153,204	10,215	-	-	-	-			163,419	169,025
		(679)	(737)	(795)	(853)	(911)	(969)			(1067)	
2540	Operation and Maintenance of Plant Services	175,677	6,746	236,450	2,306	518	-			421,697	498,413
		(680)	(738)	(796)	(854)	(912)	(970)			(1068)	
2550	Pupil Transportation Services	-	-	88,336	-	-	-			88,336	64,318
		(681)	(739)	(797)	(855)	(913)	(971)			(1069)	
2560	Food Service	116,705	3,514	1,404,732	1,340	-	-			1,526,291	1,406,800
		(682)	(740)	(798)	(856)	(914)	(972)			(1070)	
2570	Internal Services	-	1	32,208	(17,570)	127,079	-			141,718	294,237
		(684)	(742)	(800)	(858)	(916)	(974)			(1072)	
	TOTAL SUPPORT SERVICES-BUSINESS	$ 445,586	$ 20,476	$ 1,761,726	$ (13,921)	$ 127,597	$ -			$ 2,341,464	$ 2,452,793
2600	SUPPORT SERVICES - CENTRAL										
	Direction of Central	$ (685)	$ (743)	$ (801)	$ (859)	$ (917)	$ (975)			$ (1073)	$
2610	Support Services	-	-	-	-	-	-			-	-
	Planning, Research, Develop-	(686)	(744)	(802)	(860)	(918)	(976)			(1074)	
2620	ment and Evaluation Services	-	-	6,454	-	-	-			6,454	9,000
		(687)	(745)	(803)	(861)	(919)	(977)			(1075)	
2630	Information Services	-	-	-	1,266	-	-			1,266	10,000
		(688)	(746)	(804)	(862)	(920)	(978)			(1076)	
2640	Staff Services	-	-	3,221	-	-	-			3,221	5,000
		(690)	(748)	(806)	(864)	(922)	(980)			(1078)	
2660	Data Processing Services	-	-	-	39,986	26,818	-			66,804	42,500
		(692)	(750)	(808)	(866)	(924)	(982)			(1080)	
	TOTAL SUPPORT SERVICES-CENTRAL	$ -	$ -	$ 9,675	$ 41,252	$ 26,818	$ -			$ 77,745	$ 66,500
	OTHER SUPPORT SERVICES	(693)	(751)	(809)	(867)	(925)	(983)			(1081)	
2900	(Attach Itemization)	13,385	352	-	5,247	-	-			18,984	17,779
		(694)	(752)	(810)	(868)	(926)	(984)			(1082)	
	TOTAL SUPPORT SERVICES	$ 4,358,541	$ 606,782	$ 2,089,956	$ 381,929	$ 154,415	$ -			$ 7,591,623	$ 7,379,621
		(695)	(753)	(811)	(869)	(927)	(985)			(1083)	
3000	COMMUNITY SERVICES	84,854	35	1,539	13,681	-	-			100,109	103,560
4000	NONPROGRAMMED CHARGES										
4100	PAYMENTS TO OTHER GOVT. UNITS (IN-STATE)			(2888)			(2894)	(2900)	(2908)	(2912)	
				-			-	-	-	$ -	-
4110	Payments for Regular Programs										

APPENDIX I

STATEMENT OF EXPENDITURES DISBURSED/EXPENDITURES, BUDGET TO ACTUAL, FOR THE YEAR ENDED—June 30, 1994

Page 30

DESCRIPTION (Fund 1 Continued)	FUCT. NO.	(1) SALARIES	(2) EMPLOYEE BENEFITS	(3) PURCHASED SERVICES	(4) SUPPLIES AND MATERIALS	(5) CAPITAL OUTLAY	(6) OTHER OBJECTS	(7) TRANSFERS	(8) TUITION	(9) TOTAL	BUDGET
47. Payments for Special Education Programs	4120			$ (2889) —			$ (2895) (2896) —	$ (2901) (2902) —	$ (2907) 862,661 (2908) —	$ (2913) 862,661 (2914) —	$ 400,000 —
48. Payments for Adult/Continuing Education Programs	4130			(2891) —			(2897) —	(2903) —	(2909) —	(2915) —	—
49. Payments for Voc. Ed. Programs	4140			(2892) —			(2898) —	(2904) —	(2910) —	(2916) —	—
50. Payments for Community College Programs	4170			(2893) —			(2899) —	(2905) —	(2911) —	(2917) —	—
51. Other Payments to In-State Governmental Units (Attach Itemization)	4190										
52. TOTAL PAYMENTS TO OTHER GOVERNMENTAL UNITS (In-State)				$ (2728) —			$ (2020) —	$ (2021) —	$ (2024) 862,661	$ (2027) 862,661	$ 400,000
53. PAYMENT TO OTHER GOVERNMENT UNITS (Out-of-State)	4200			(2886) —			(2022) —	(2025) —	(2028) —	—	
54. TOTAL NONPROGRAMMED CHARGES				$ (2729) —			$ (986) —	$ (995) —	$ (1025) 862,661	$ (1044) 862,661	$ 400,000
DEBT SERVICES	5000										
DEBT SERVICES - INTEREST	5100										
55. Tax Anticipation Warrants	5110						$ (987) 77,994			$ (1085) 77,994	$ 77,500
56. Tax Anticipation Notes	5120						(988) —			(1086) —	—
57. Teachers' Orders	5130						(989) —			(1087) —	—
Corporate Personal Property							(2730) —			(2734) —	—
58. Replacement Tax Anticipation Notes	5150						(2731) —			(2735) —	—
State Aid Anticipation Certificates	5160										
59. Certificates							(990) —			(1088) —	—
60. Other (Attach Itemization)	5190										
61. TOTAL DEBT SERVICES							$ (992) 77,994			$ (1090) 77,994	$ 77,500
62. PROVISION FOR CONTINGENCIES	6000										$ 1,000,000
63. TOTAL DISBURSEMENTS/EXPENDITURES *		$ (696) 25,450,473	$ (754) 1,787,587	$ (812) 2,463,975	$ (870) 910,215	$ (928) 357,619	$ (993) 78,521	$ (996) —	$ (1026) 2,046,950	$ (1091) 33,095,340	$ 33,318,452
64. EXCESS (Deficiency) OF RECEIPTS/REVENUE OVER DISBURSEMENTS/EXPENDITURES										$ (1092) (902,437)	$ (1,683,083)

* Total of Lines 11,44,45,54,61,62

APPENDIX I • 37

Page 31

STATEMENT OF EXPENDITURES DISBURSED/EXPENDITURES, BUDGET TO ACTUAL, FOR THE YEAR ENDED—June 30, 1994

DESCRIPTION	FUCT. NO.	(1) SALARIES	(2) EMPLOYEE BENEFITS	(3) PURCHASED SERVICES	(4) SUPPLIES AND MATERIALS	(5) CAPITAL OUTLAY	(6) OTHER OBJECTS	(7) TRANSFERS	(8) TUITION	(9) TOTAL	BUDGET
OPERATIONS AND MAINTENANCE FUND (2)											
SUPPORT SERVICES	2000										
SUPPORT SERVICES - PUPILS	2100	$ (4013) -	$ (4014) -	$ (4015) -	$ (4016) -	$ (4017) -	$ (4018) -			$ (4019) -	-
OTHER SUPPORT SERVICES - PUPILS	2190										
1. (Attach Itemization)											
SUPPORT SERVICES-BUSINESS	2500										
Direction of Business		$ (1158) -	$ (1166) -	$ (1174) -	$ (1182) -	$ (1190) -	$ (1199) -			$ (1213) -	-
2. Support Services	2510										
Facilities Acquisition and		(1159) -	(1167) -	(1175) 7,416	(1183) -	(1191) 4,114	(1200) -			(1214) 11,530	12,600
3. Construction Services	2530										
Operation and Maintenance		(1160) 1,525,074	(1168) 115,248	(1176) 354,975	(1184) 1,289,060	(1192) 18,488	(1201) -			(1215) 3,302,845	3,233,299
4. of Plant Services	2540										
Public Transportation		(3421) -	(3422) -	(3423) -	(3424) -	(3425) -	(3426) -			(3427) -	-
5. Services	2550										
6. Food Services	2560					(1193) -				(1216) -	-
		$ (1162) 1,525,074	$ (1170) 115,248	$ (1178) 362,391	$ (1186) 1,289,060	$ (1195) 22,602	$ (1203) -			$ (1218) 3,314,375	3,245,899
7. TOTAL SUPPORT SERVICES-BUSINESS											
OTHER SUPPORTING SERVICES		$ (1163) -	$ (1171) -	$ (1179) 469	$ (1187) (107)	$ (1196) -	$ (1204) -			$ (1219) 362	-
8. (Attach Itemization)	2900										
		$ (1164) 1,525,074	$ (1172) 115,248	$ (1180) 362,860	$ (1188) 1,288,953	$ (1197) 22,602	$ (1205) -			$ (1220) 3,314,737	3,245,899
9. TOTAL SUPPORT SERVICES											
		$ (2736) -	$ (2737) -	$ (2738) -	$ (2739) -	$ (2740) -	$ (2741) -			$ (2744) -	-
10. COMMUNITY SERVICES	3000										
NONPROGRAMMED CHARGES	4000										
PAYMENTS TO OTHER GOVERN- MENTAL UNITS (In-State)	4100										

APPENDIX I

Page 32

STATEMENT OF EXPENDITURES DISBURSED/EXPENDITURES, BUDGET TO ACTUAL, FOR THE YEAR ENDED—June 30, 1994

DESCRIPTION	FUCT. NO.	(1) SALARIES	(2) EMPLOYEE BENEFITS	(3) PURCHASED SERVICES	(4) SUPPLIES AND MATERIALS	(5) CAPITAL OUTLAY	(6) OTHER OBJECTS	(7) TRANSFERS	(8) TUITION	(9) TOTAL	BUDGET
(Fund 2 Continued)											
11. Payments for Special Ed. Programs	4120						$ (2918) 635	$ (2921) -		$ (2925) 635	$ (2925) 42,870
12. Payments for Voc. Ed. Programs	4140						(2919) -	(2922) -		(2926) -	-
Other Payments to In-State							(2920) -	(2923) -		(2927) -	-
13. Government Units (Attach Itemization)	4190						$ (2030) 635	$ (2924) -		$ (2032) 635	$ 42,870
TOTAL PAYMENTS TO OTHER											
14. GOVERNMENTAL UNITS (In-State)						$ (2031) -	$ (3002) -		$ (2033) -	-
PAYMENT TO OTHER GOVERN-											
15. MENT UNITS (Out-of-State)	4200						$ (1206) 635	$ (2743) -		$ (1221) 635	$ 42,870
16. TOTAL NONPROGRAMMED CHARGES	5000										
DEBT SERVICES											
DEBT SERVICES - INTEREST	5100						$ (1207) -			$ (1222) -	-
17. Tax Anticipation Warrants	5110						(1208) -			(1223) -	-
18. Tax Anticipation Notes	5120						(2746) -			(2749) -	-
Corporate Personal Property Replacement Tax Anticipa-											
19. tion Notes	5150						(2747) -			(2750) -	-
20. Certificates	5160						(1209) -			(1224) -	-
21. Other (Attach Itemization)	5190						(1211) -			(1226) -	-
22. TOTAL DEBT SERVICES										$	$
23. PROVISION FOR CONTINGENCIES	6000						(1212) 635	(2748) -		(1227) 3,315,372	200,000
TOTAL ESTIMATED DISBURSEMENTS/ TOTAL EXPENDITURES *		$ (1165) 1,525,074	$ (1173) 115,248	$ (1181) 362,860	$ (1189) 1,288,953	$ (1198) 22,602					3,488,769
24. EXPENDITURES *										$ (1228) 554,659	$ 202,231
25. EXCESS (Deficiency) OF RECEIPTS/ REVENUE OVER DISBURSEMENTS/EXPENDITURES											

* Total of Lines 9,10,16,22,23

APPENDIX I • 39

Page 33

STATEMENT OF EXPENDITURES DISBURSED/EXPENDITURES, BUDGET TO ACTUAL, FOR THE YEAR ENDED—June 30, 1994

DESCRIPTION	FUCT. NO.	(1) SALARIES	(2) EMPLOYEE BENEFITS	(3) PURCHASED SERVICES	(4) SUPPLIES AND MATERIALS	(5) CAPITAL OUTLAY	(6) OTHER OBJECTS	(7) TRANSFERS	(8) TUITION	(9) TOTAL	BUDGET
BOND AND INTEREST FUND (3)											
Nonprogrammed Charges	4000										
PAYMENTS TO OTHER GOVERN—								(2753) $ -		(2755) $ -	-
1. MENTAL UNITS (In-State)	4100							(1258) -		(1262) $ -	-
2. TOTAL NONPROGRAMMED CHARGES											
DEBT SERVICES	5000										
DEBT SERVICES - INTEREST	5100						(1249) -			(1263) $ -	-
3. Tax Anticipation Warrants	5110						(1250) -			(1264) -	-
4. Tax Anticipation Notes	5120						(1251) 629,813			(1265) 629,813	659,812
5. Bonds	5140						(2751) -			(2757) -	-
6. Replacement Tax Anticipation Notes Corporate Personal Property	5150						(2752) -			(2754) -	-
State Aid Anticipation											
7. Certificates	5160						(1252) -			(1266) -	-
8. Other (Attach Itemization)	5190						(1253) 629,813			(1267) 629,813	-
TOTAL DEBT SERVICES -											
9. INTEREST							(1254) 2,500,000			(1268) 2,500,000	659,812
DEBT SERVICES - BOND PRINCIPAL	5200										
10. RETIRED				(1246) -			(1255) 6,521	(1259) -		(1269) 6,521	2,500,000
DEBT SERVICES - OTHER	5900										
11. (Attach Itemization)				(1247) -			(1256) 3,136,334	(1260) -		(1270) 3,136,334	-
TOTAL DEBT SERVICES											3,159,812
12. (Total of Lines 9,10,11)											
13. PROVISION FOR CONTINGENCIES	6000										50,000
TOTAL ESTIMATED DISBURSEMENTS/				(1248) -			(1257) 3,136,334	(1261) -		(1271) 3,136,334	3,209,812
14. EXPENDITURES *											
EXCESS (Deficiency) OF RECEIPTS/										(1272) (61,939)	1
15. REVENUE OVER DISBURSEMENTS/EXPENDITURES											

40 • APPENDIX I

STATEMENT OF EXPENDITURES DISBURSED/EXPENDITURES, BUDGET TO ACTUAL, FOR THE YEAR ENDED—June 30, 1994

Page 34

DESCRIPTION	FUCT. NO.	(1) SALARIES	(2) EMPLOYEE BENEFITS	(3) PURCHASED SERVICES	(4) SUPPLIES AND MATERIALS	(5) CAPITAL OUTLAY	(6) OTHER OBJECTS	(7) TRANSFERS	(8) TUITION	(9) TOTAL	BUDGET
TRANSPORTATION FUND (4)											
SUPPORT SERVICES	2000										
SUPPORT SERVICES – PUPILS	2100	$ (4020) —	$ (4021) —	$ (4022) —	$ (4023) —	$ (4024) —	$ (4025) —			$ (4026) —	$ —
OTHER SUPPORT SERVICES – PUPILS (Attach Itemization)	2190										
SUPPORT SERVICES – BUSINESS	2500										
Pupil Transportation Services	2550	(1274) 600,905	(1280) 69,687	(1286) 851,994	(1293) 207,826	(1299) 167,413	(1305) —			(1316) 1,897,825	1,902,178
OTHER SUPPORT SERVICES (Attach Itemization)	2900	(1277) —	(1283) —	(1289) —	(1296) —	(1302) —	(1308) —			(1319) —	—
4. TOTAL SUPPORT SERVICES		$ (1278) 600,905	$ (1284) 69,687	$ (1290) 851,994	$ (1297) 207,826	$ (1303) 167,413	$ (1309) —			$ (1320) 1,897,825	1,902,178
5. COMMUNITY SERVICES	3000	$ (2759) —	$ (2760) —	$ (2761) —	$ (2764) —	$ (2765) —	$ (2766) —			$ (2775) —	—
NONPROGRAMMED CHARGES	4000										
PAYMENTS TO OTHER GOVERNMENTAL UNITS (In-State)	4100										
6. Payments for Regular Programs	4110			$ (2928) —			$ (2934) —			$ (2946) —	—
7. Payments for Special Education Programs	4120			(2929) —			(2935) —			(2947) —	—
8. Payments for Adult/Continuing Education Programs	4130			(2930) —			(2936) —			(2948) —	—
9. Payments for Vocational Education Programs	4140			(2931) —			(2937) —			(2949) —	—
10. Payments for Community College Programs	4170			(2932) —			(2938) —			(2950) —	—
11. Other Payments to In-State Government Units (Attach Itemization)	4190			(2933) —			(2939) —			(2951) —	—
TOTAL PAYMENTS TO OTHER GOVERNMENTAL UNITS (In-State)				$ (2762) —			$ (2767) —	$ (2773) —		$ (2776) —	—
12. PAYMENTS TO OTHER GOVERNMENTAL UNITS (Out-of-State)	4200			$ (2763) —			$ (2768) —	—		$ (2778) —	—
13. MENTAL UNITS (Out-of-State)				(1291) —			(2769) —	(2016) —		(1321) —	—
14. TOTAL NONPROGRAMMED CHARGES											

Page 35

APPENDIX I • 41

STATEMENT OF EXPENDITURES DISBURSED/EXPENDITURES, BUDGET TO ACTUAL, FOR THE YEAR ENDED—June 30, 1994

(Fund 4 Continued)

DESCRIPTION	FUCT. NO.	(1) SALARIES	(2) EMPLOYEE BENEFITS	(3) PURCHASED SERVICES	(4) SUPPLIES AND MATERIALS	(5) CAPITAL OUTLAY	(6) OTHER OBJECTS	(7) TRANSFERS	(8) TUITION	(9) TOTAL	BUDGET
DEBT SERVICES	5000										
DEBT SERVICES – INTEREST	5100									$ (1322) $	—
15. Tax Anticipation Warrants	5110						$ (1310)			(1323)	—
16. Tax Anticipation Notes Corporate Personal Property	5120						(1311)			(2780)	—
17. Replacement Tax Anticipation Notes State Aid Anticipation	5150						(2770)			(2781)	—
18. Certificates	5160						(2771)			(1324)	—
19. Other (Attach Itemization) TOTAL DEBT SERVICES –	5190						(1312)			(1326) $	—
20. INTEREST							$ (1314)			—	—
21. PROVISION FOR CONTINGENCIES TOTAL DISBURSEMENTS/	6000	$ (1279) 600,905	$ (1285) 69,687	$ (1292) 851,994	$ (1298) 207,826	$ (1304) 167,413	$ (1315)	$ (2017)		$ (1327) $ 1,897,825	55,000 1,957,178
22. EXPENDITURES = EXCESS (Deficiency) OF RECEIPTS/										$ (1329) $ (63,085)	(352,878)
23. REVENUE OVER DISBURSEMENTS/EXPENDITURES											

* Total of Lines 4,5,14,20,21

42 • APPENDIX I

STATEMENT OF EXPENDITURES DISBURSED/EXPENDITURES, BUDGET TO ACTUAL, FOR THE YEAR ENDED-June 30, 1994

MUNICIPAL RETIREMENT/SOCIAL SECURITY FUND (5)

DESCRIPTION	FUCT. NO.	(1) SALARIES	(2) EMPLOYEE BENEFITS	(3) PURCHASED SERVICES	(4) SUPPLIES AND MATERIALS	(5) CAPITAL OUTLAY	(6) OTHER OBJECTS	(7) TRANSFERS	(8) TUITION	(9) TOTAL	BUDGET
Instruction	1000										
1. Regular Programs	1100		(3326) 101,238							(3329) $ 101,238	$ 94,744
Special Education Programs (Total of			(3327) 76,375							(3330) 76,375	87,601
2. Fuct. No. 1200-1220)	1200		(3003) 7,505							(3004) $ 7,505	$ 8,098
3. Remedial Programs Educationally Deprived/	1250		(1345) –							(1409) $ –	–
4. Adult Education Programs Vocational Education	1300										
5. Programs	1400		(1346) 1,233							(1410) $ 1,233	343
6. Interscholastic Programs	1500		(1347) 1,219							(1411) $ 1,219	1,140
7. Summer School Programs	1600		(1348) 5,559							(1412) $ 5,559	5,658
8. Gifted Programs	1650		(1335) 14							(1399) 14	18
9. Bilingual Programs	1800		(1341) 20,689							(1405) $ 20,689	22,827
10. Optional Programs Truants' Alternative &	1900		(3328) –							(3331) $ –	–
11. TOTAL INSTRUCTION			(1349) 213,832							(1413) $ 213,832	220,429
Support Services	2000										
Support Services – Pupils	2100										
12. Work Services Attendance and Social	2110		(1350) 2,432							(1414) $ 2,432	2,584
13. Guidance Services	2120		(1351) 4,239							(1415) 4,239	4,180
14. Health Services	2130		(1352) 23,106							(1416) 23,106	24,262
15. Psychological Services	2140		(1353) 1,445							(1417) 1,445	1,516
16. Audiology Services Speech Pathology and	2150		(1354) –							(1418) –	–
17. (Attach Itemization) Other Support Services -Pupils	2190		(1355) –							(1419) –	–
18. TOTAL SUPPORT SERVICES – PUPILS			(1356) 31,222							(1420) $ 31,222	32,542

Page 36

Page 37

STATEMENT OF EXPENDITURES DISBURSED/EXPENDITURES, BUDGET TO ACTUAL, FOR THE YEAR ENDED—June 30, 1994

DESCRIPTION (Fund 5 Continued)	FUCT. NO.	(1) SALARIES	(2) EMPLOYEE BENEFITS	(3) PURCHASED SERVICES	(4) SUPPLIES AND MATERIALS	(5) CAPITAL OUTLAY	(6) OTHER OBJECTS	(7) TRANSFERS	(8) TUITION	(9) TOTAL	BUDGET
SUPPORT SERVICES—											
INSTRUCTIONAL STAFF	2200										
19. Improvement of Instruction Services	2210		(1357) 4,316							$ (1421) 4,316	3,673
Educational Media			(1358)							(1422)	
20. Services	2220		—							—	—
21. Assessment and Testing	2230		(1359) —							(1423) —	—
TOTAL SUPPORT SERVICES —			(1360)							$ (1424)	
22. INSTRUCTIONAL STAFF			4,316							4,316	3,673
SUPPORT SERVICES - GENERAL ADMINISTRATION	2300										
23. Board of Education Services	2310		(1361) 92							$ (1425) 92	1,848
Executive Administrative			(1362)							(1426)	
24. Services	2320		60,654							60,654	60,108
Special Area			(2664)							(2665)	
25. Administrative Services	2330		6,115							6,115	6,329
TOTAL SUPPORT SERVICES —			(1363)							$ (1427)	
26. GENERAL ADMINISTRATION			66,861							66,861	68,285
SUPPORT SERVICES — SCHOOL ADMINISTRATION	2400										
Office of the Principal			(1364)							$ (1428)	
27. Services	2410		114,258							114,258	125,690
Other Support Services - School			(1365)							(1429)	
28. Administration (Attach Itemization)	2490		—							—	—
TOTAL SUPPORT SERVICES —			(1366)							$ (1430)	
29. SCHOOL ADMINISTRATION			114,258							114,258	125,690
SUPPORT SERVICES - BUSINESS	2500										
Direction of Business			(1367)							$ (1431)	
30. Support Services	2510		—							—	—
31. Fiscal Services	2520		(1368) 34,160							34,160	36,828

APPENDIX I • 43

44 • APPENDIX I

STATEMENT OF EXPENDITURES DISBURSED/EXPENDITURES, BUDGET TO ACTUAL, FOR THE YEAR ENDED—June 30, 1994

Page 3B

FUCT. NO.	DESCRIPTION	(1) SALARIES	(2) EMPLOYEE BENEFITS	(3) PURCHASED SERVICES	(4) SUPPLIES AND MATERIALS	(5) CAPITAL OUTLAY	(6) OTHER OBJECTS	(7) TRANSFERS	(8) TUITION	(9) TOTAL	BUDGET
	(Fund 5 Continued) Facilities Acquisition		(1369) $ —							(1433) $ —	$ —
32.	2530 and Construction Services		(1370) 272,760							(1434) 272,760	323,545
33.	2540 Operation and Maintenance of Plant Services		(1371) 124,748							(1435) 124,748	122,782
34.	2550 Pupil Transportation Services		(1372) 9,483							(1436) 9,483	12,178
35.	2560 Food Services		(1373) 3							(1437) 3	—
36.	2570 Internal Services										
37.	TOTAL SUPPORT SERVICES – BUSINESS		(1375) $ 441,154							(1439) $ 441,154	495,333
38.	2600 SUPPORT SERVICES – CENTRAL Direction of Central Support Services		(1376) $ —							(1440) $ —	—
39.	2610 Planning, Research, Development and Evaluation Services		(1377) —							(1441) —	—
40.	2620 Information Services		(1378) 29							(1442) 29	—
41.	2630 Staff Services		(1379) —							(1443) —	—
42.	2640 Data Processing Services		(1381) —							(1445) —	—
43.	2660 TOTAL SUPPORT SERVICES – CENTRAL		(1383) $ 29							(1447) $ 29	—
44.	2900 OTHER SUPPORT SERVICES (Attach Itemization)		(1384) $ 1,708							(1448) $ 1,708	1,844
45.	TOTAL SUPPORT SERVICES		(1385) $ 659,548							(1449) $ 659,548	727,367

APPENDIX I • 45

Page 39
(Fund 5 Continued)

STATEMENT OF EXPENDITURES DISBURSED/EXPENDITURES, BUDGET TO ACTUAL, FOR THE YEAR ENDED—June 30, 1994

DESCRIPTION	FUCT. NO.	(1) SALARIES	(2) EMPLOYEE BENEFITS	(3) PURCHASED SERVICES	(4) SUPPLIES AND MATERIALS	(5) CAPITAL OUTLAY	(6) OTHER OBJECTS	(7) TRANSFERS	(8) TUITION	(9) TOTAL	BUDGET
46. COMMUNITY SERVICES	3000		$ (1386) 1,920							$ (1450) 1,920	$ 2,204
Nonprogramed Charges	4000										
DEBT SERVICES	5000										
DEBT SERVICES – INTEREST	5100						$ (1388) –			$ (1451) –	–
47. Tax Anticipation Warrants	5110						(1389) –			(1452) –	–
48. Tax Anticipation Notes Corporate Personal Property	5120						(2782) –			(2784) –	–
49. Replacement Tax Anticipation Notes State Aid Anticipation	5150						(2783) –			(2785) –	–
50. Certificates	5160						(1390) –			(1453) –	–
Other	5190						(1391) –			(1454) –	–
51. (Attach Itemization) TOTAL DEBT SERVICES							–			$ –	$ –
52. INTEREST											
53. PROVISION FOR CONTINGENCIES TOTAL DISBURSEMENTS/	6000		$ (1387) 875,300				$ (1393) –			$ (1456) 875,300	$ 950,000
54. EXPENDITURES *										$ (1457) 199,232	50,000
55. EXCESS (Deficiency) OF RECEIPTS/ REVENUE OVER DISBURSEMENTS/EXPENDITURES											

46 • APPENDIX I

STATEMENT OF EXPENDITURES DISBURSED/EXPENDITURES, BUDGET TO ACTUAL, FOR THE YEAR ENDED—June 30, 1994

Page 40

DESCRIPTION	FUCT. NO.	(1) SALARIES	(2) EMPLOYEE BENEFITS	(3) PURCHASED SERVICES	(4) SUPPLIES AND MATERIALS	(5) CAPITAL OUTLAY	(6) OTHER OBJECTS	(7) TRANSFERS	(8) TUITION	(9) TOTAL	BUDGET
SITE AND CONSTRUCTION FUND (6)											
SUPPORT SERVICES	2000										
SUPPORT SERVICES - BUSINESS	2500										
Facilities Acquisition and		$ (1458)	$ (1464)	$ (1470)	$ (1476)	$ (1482)	$ (1488)			$ (1494)	
1. Construction Services	2530	-	-	-	355,604	9,000	-			364,604	285,170
TOTAL SUPPORT SERVICES -		$ (1460)	$ (1466)	$ (1472)	$ (1478)	$ (1484)	$ (1490)			$ (1496)	
2. BUSINESS		-	-	-	355,604	9,000	-			364,604	285,170
Other Support Services		$ (1461)	$ (1467)	$ (1473)	$ (1479)	$ (1485)	$ (1491)			$ (1497)	
3. (Attach Itemization)	2900	-	-	-	-	-	-			-	-
		$ (1462)	$ (1468)	$ (1474)	$ (1480)	$ (1486)	$ (1492)			$ (1498)	
4. TOTAL SUPPORT SERVICES		-	-	-	355,604	9,000	-			364,604	285,170
Nonprogramed Charges	4000										
Payments to other Govren-											
mental Units (In-State)	4100										
Payment for Special								$ (4035)		$ (4038)	
5. Education Programs	4120							-		-	-
Payment for Vocational								(4036)		(4039)	
6. Education Programs	4140							-		-	
Other Payments to In-State Gov't								(3655)		(3656)	
7. Units (Attach Itemization)	4190							-		-	-
TOTAL PAYMENTS TO OTHER								$ (4037)		$ (4040)	
8. GOVERNMENTAL UNITS (In-State)								-		-	-
Payments to other Govern-								(2037)		(2040)	
9. mental Units (Out-of-State)	4200							-		-	-
								$ (2038)		$ (2041)	
10. TOTAL NONPROGRAMMED CHARGES								-		-	-
11. Provision for Contingencies	6000										10,000
TOTAL DISBURSEMENTS/		$ (1463)	$ (1469)	$ (1475)	$ (1481)	$ (1487)	$ (1493)	$ (2070)		$ (1499)	
12. EXPENDITURES *		-	-	-	355,604	9,000	-	-		364,604	295,170
EXCESS (Deficiency) OF RECEIPTS/REVENUE										$ (1500)	
13. OVER DISBURSEMENTS/EXPENDITURES										(208,284)	(295,170)

* Total of Lines 4,10,11

WORKING CASH FUND (7) | Transactions related to the Working Cash Fund shall be reflected in the Basic Financial Statements, Page 7-8

Page 41

STATEMENT OF EXPENDITURES DISBURSED/EXPENDITURES, BUDGET TO ACTUAL, FOR THE YEAR ENDED—June 30, 1994

DESCRIPTION	FUCT. NO.	(1) SALARIES	(2) EMPLOYEE BENEFITS	(3) PURCHASED SERVICES	(4) SUPPLIES AND MATERIALS	(5) CAPITAL OUTLAY	(6) OTHER OBJECTS	(7) TRANSFERS	(8) TUITION	(9) TOTAL	BUDGET
RENT FUND (8)											
Debt Services	5000										
Corporate Personal Property							$ (3381)			$ (3383) $	—
1. Replacement Tax	5150						—			—	—
State Aid							$ (3382)			$ (3384) $	—
2. Anticipation Certificates	5160			$ (1507)			$ (1510)			$ (1513) $	—
				—			—			—	—
3. Debt Service - Other	5900			$ (1508)			$ (1511)			$ (1514) $	—
				—			—			—	—
4. TOTAL DEBT SERVICE				$ (1509)			$ (1512)			$ (1515) $	—
TOTAL DISBURSEMENTS/				—			—			—	—
5. EXPENDITURES											
EXCESS (Deficiency) OF RECEIPTS/										$ (1516) $	—
6. REVENUE OVER DISBURSEMENTS/EXPENDITURES										—	

APPENDIX I • 47

48 • APPENDIX I

Page 42

STATEMENT OF EXPENDITURES DISBURSED/EXPENDITURES, BUDGET TO ACTUAL, FOR THE YEAR ENDED June 30, 1994

FIRE PREVENTION AND SAFETY FUND (9)

DESCRIPTION	FUCT. NO.	(1) SALARIES	(2) EMPLOYEE BENEFITS	(3) PURCHASED SERVICES	(4) SUPPLIES AND MATERIALS	(5) CAPITAL OUTLAY	(6) OTHER OBJECTS	(7) TRANSFERS	(8) TUITION	(9) TOTAL	BUDGET
Support Services	2000										
Support Services - Business	2500	$ (3556)	$ (3563)	$ (3570)	$ (3577)	$ (3584)	$ (3591)			$ (3607)	
Facilities Acquisition and				5,208	14,519	79,404	–			88,715	1,145,000
1. Construction Services	2530	$ (3557)	$ (3564)	$ (3571)	$ (3578)	$ (3585)	$ (3592)			$ (3608)	
Operation & Maintenance of		–	–	–	–	–	–			–	–
2. Plant Services	2540	$ (3558)	$ (3565)	$ (3572)	$ (3579)	$ (3586)	$ (3593)			$ (3609)	
TOTAL SUPPORT SERVICES -		–	–	5,208	14,519	79,404	–			88,715	1,145,000
3. BUSINESS		$ (3559)	$ (3566)	$ (3573)	$ (3580)	$ (3587)	$ (3594)			$ (3610)	
OTHER SUPPORT SERVICES	2900	–	–	–	–	–	–			–	–
4. (ATTACH ITEMIZATION)		$ (3560)	$ (3567)	$ (3574)	$ (3581)	$ (3588)	$ (3595)			$ (3611)	
5. TOTAL SUPPORT SERVICES		–	–	5,208	14,519	79,404	–			88,715	1,145,000
NONPROGRAMMED CHARGES	4000							$ (3601)		$ (3612)	
Other Payments to In-State								–		–	–
6. Gov't Units (Attach Itemization)	4190							$ (3602)		$ (3613)	
TOTAL PAYMENTS TO OTHER								–		–	–
7. GOV'T UNITS (IN-STATE)											
DEBT SERVICES	5000										
DEBT SERVICES - INTEREST	5100						$ (3596)			$ (3614)	
							–			–	–
8. Tax Anticipation Warrants	5110						$ (3597)			$ (3615)	
							–			–	–
9. TOTAL DEBT SERVICES - INTEREST							$ (3598)			$ (3616)	
							–			–	–
PROVISION FOR CONTINGENCIES	6000						$ (3599)	$ (3603)		$ (3617)	
10. TOTAL DISBURSEMENT/							–	–		88,715	1,145,000
11. EXPENDITURES *											
OTHER FINANCING USES	8000										
EXCESS (Deficiency) OF RECEIPTS/REVENUE										$ (3620)	
12. OVER DISBURSEMENTS/EXPENDITURES										(76,612)	(1,140,000)

APPENDIX I • 49

Page 43

SCHEDULE OF AD VALOREM TAX RECEIPTS

	(A) TAXES RECEIVED 7-1-93 THRU 6-30-94 FROM 1993 LEVY AND PRIOR LEVIES	(B) Less: TAXES RECEIVED FROM 1992 LEVY AND PRIOR LEVIES	(C) TAXES RECEIVED FROM 1993 LEVY (Col.A - Col.B)	(D) ESTIMATED TAXES DUE FROM 1993 LEVY	(E) TOTAL ESTIMATED TAXES FROM 1993 LEVY (Col. C + Col. D)
	(1683)	(1699)	(1715)	(1731)	(1747)
1. Educational	$ 17,480,589	$ 8,129,179	$ 9,351,410	$ 9,109,507	$ 18,460,917
	(1684)	(1700)	(1716)	(1732)	(1748)
2. Operations and Maintenance	2,840,579	1,278,360	1,562,219	1,521,807	3,084,026
	(1685)	(1701)	(1717)	(1733)	(1749)
3. Bond and Interest	3,042,639	1,407,971	1,634,668	1,592,383	3,227,051
	(1686)	(1702)	(1718)	(1734)	(1750)
4. Transportation	953,704	411,847	541,857	527,840	1,069,697
	(1687)	(1703)	(1719)	(1735)	(1751)
5. Municipal Retirement	995,152	756,214	238,938	231,383	470,321
	(1688)	(1704)	(1720)	(1736)	(1752)
6. Working Cash	—	—	—	—	—
	(1689)	(1705)	(1721)	(1737)	(1753)
7. Rent	—	—	—	—	—
	(1690)	(1706)	(1722)	(1738)	(1754)
8. Capital Improvements	—	—	—	—	—
	(1691)	(1707)	(1723)	(1739)	(1755)
9. Tort Immunity	97,099	46,552	50,547	49,238	99,785
	(1692)	(1708)	(1724)	(1740)	(1756)
*10. Fire Prevention, Safety, Environmental/Energy Conservation	—	—	—	—	—
	(1693)	(1709)	(1725)	(1741)	(1757)
11. Special Education	244,868	110,078	134,790	131,304	266,094
	(1695)	(1711)	(1727)	(1743)	(1759)
*12. Area Vocational Construction	—	—	—	—	—
	(3385)	(3386)	(3387)	(3388)	(3389)
13. Social Security/Medicare Only	—	(227,099)	227,099	222,599	449,698
	(4041)	(4043)	(4045)	(4047)	(4049)
14. Summer School	—	—	—	—	—
	(4042)	(4044)	(4046)	(4048)	(4050)
15. Other (Attatch Itemization)	—	—	—	—	—
	(1696)	(1712)	(1728)	(1744)	(1760)
16. Textbooks (Cook County School Dist. #299 Only)	—	—	—	—	—
	(1697)	(1713)	(1729)	(1745)	(1761)
17. Playground (Cook County School Dist. #299 Only)	—	—	—	—	—
	(1698)	(1714)	(1730)	(1746)	(1762)
18. Totals	$ 25,654,630	$ 11,913,102	$ 13,741,528	$ 13,386,061	$ 27,127,589

* If bonds are issued for Fire Prevention, Safety, Environmental and Energy Conservation purposes or Area Vocational Construction purposes, the taxes received to retire the bonds and interest on same must be recorded in the Bond & Interest Fund, Line 3 of this schedule.

APPENDIX I

SCHEDULE OF TAX ANTICIPATION WARRANTS AND INTEREST

	(A) DATE OF FIRST ISSUE Fiscal Year 1994	(B) OUTSTANDING 7-1-93	(C) ISSUED 7-1-93 THROUGH 6-30-94	(D) RETIRED 7-1-93 THROUGH 6-30-94	(E) OUTSTANDING* 6-30-94	(F) ACCRUED INTEREST 7-1-93	(G) INTEREST 7-1-93 THROUGH 6-30-94	(H) INTEREST PAID 7-1-93 THROUGH 6-30-94	(I) ACCRUED INTEREST 6-30-94
1. Educational Fund	4-5-94	$ (1764) 4,500,000	$ (1778) 4,500,000	$ (1792) 6,000,000	$ (1806) 3,000,000	$ (1820)	$ (1834)	$ (1848) 77,994	$ (1862)
2. Operations and Maintenance Fund		(1765)	(1779)	(1793)	(1807)	(1821)	(1835)	(1849)	(1863)
3. Municipal Retirement/Social Security Fund		(1766)	(1780)	(1794)	(1808)	(1822)	(1836)	(1850)	(1864)
4. Transportation Fund		(1767)	(1781)	(1795)	(1809)	(1823)	(1837)	(1851)	(1865)
5. Bond and Interest Fund – Construction		(1768)	(1782)	(1796)	(1810)	(1824)	(1838)	(1852)	(1866)
6. Bond and Interest Fund – Working Cash		(1769)	(1783)	(1797)	(1811)	(1825)	(1839)	(1853)	(1867)
7. Bond and Interest Fund – Refunding Bonds		(1770)	(1784)	(1798)	(1812)	(1826)	(1840)	(1854)	(1868)
8. Other – Attach Itemization		(1771)	(1785)	(1799)	(1813)	(1827)	(1841)	(1855)	(1869)
		(3621)	(3623)	(3625)	(3627)	(3629)	(3631)	(3633)	(3635)
9. Fire Prevention and Safety		(1772)	(1786)	(1800)	(1814)	(1828)	(1842)	(1856)	(1870)
10. Totals		$ 4,500,000	$ 4,500,000	$ 6,000,000	$ 3,000,000	$	$	$ 77,994	$

SCHEDULE OF TAX ANTICIPATION NOTES AND INTEREST

11. Educational Fund	N/A	$ (1773)	$ (1787)	$ (1801)	$ (1815)	$ (1829)	$ (1843)	$ (1857)	$ (1871)
12. Operations and Maintenance Fund		(1774)	(1788)	(1802)	(1816)	(1830)	(1844)	(1858)	(1872)
13. Other – Attach Itemization		(1775)	(1789)	(1803)	(1817)	(1831)	(1845)	(1859)	(1873)
		(3622)	(3624)	(3626)	(3628)	(3630)	(3632)	(3634)	(3636)
14. Fire Prevention and Safety		(1776)	(1790)	(1804)	(1818)	(1832)	(1846)	(1860)	(1874)
15. Totals		$	$	$	$	$	$	$	$

SCHEDULE OF TEACHERS' ORDERS AND INTEREST

16. Education fund	N/A	$ (1777)	$ (1791)	$ (1805)	$ (1819)	$ (1833)	$ (1847)	$ (1861)	$ (1875)

SCHEDULE OF CORPORATE PERSONAL PROPERTY REPLACEMENT TAX ANTICIPATION NOTES

17. All Funds	N/A	$ (2666)	$ (2668)	$ (2670)	$ (2672)	$ (2674)	$ (2676)	$ (2678)	$ (2680)

SCHEDULE OF GENERAL STATE AID ANTICIPATION CERTIFICATES

18. All Funds	N/A	$ (2667)	$ (2669)	$ (2671)	$ (2673)	$ (2675)	$ (2677)	$ (2679)	$ (2681)

APPENDIX I • 51

Page 45

SCHEDULE OF BONDS PAYABLE

	(A)	(B)	(C)	(D)	(E)	(F)	(G)	TOTAL
1. Year of Bond Issue	1974	1984	1987	1991	1992			
1a. Amount of Original Issue	13,000,000	2,320,000	5,000,000	2,500,000	2,100,000			
1b. Type of Bond Issue*	#6	#4	#4	#4	#4			(1878)
2. Bonds Outstanding 7-1-93 **	$ 1,575,000	570,000	3,100,000	2,500,000	2,100,000	$	$	$ 9,845,000
ADD:								
3. Bonds Issued 7-1-93 Through 6-30-94								(1879) —
LESS:								(1880)
4. Bonds Retired 7-1-93 Through 6-30-94	1,575,000	350,000	575,000					2,500,000
	$	$	$	$	$	$	$	(1881)
5. Bonds Outstanding 6-30-94	$ —	220,000	2,525,000	2,500,000	2,100,000	$ —	$ —	7,345,000
6. Amount to be Provided to Retire Bonds	—	220,000	2,525,000	2,500,000	2,100,000	—	—	(1885) 7,345,000

* Each type of bond issue must be identified separately with the amount:

1. Working cash Fund Bonds
2. Funding Bonds
3. Refunding Bonds
4. Fire Prevention, Safety, Environmental & Energy Bonds
5. Tort Judgement Bonds
6. Building Bonds

** This total must agree with Page 44 Line 5, 1992-1993 Annual Financial Report based on the Illinois Program Accounting Manual for Local Education Agencies.

If more than one type of an individual bond issue, indicate % of original issue that relates to each type.

SCHEDULE OF RESTRICTED LOCAL TAX LEVIES
ANALYSIS OF CHANGES IN CASH BASIS FUND BALANCE

Page 46

	ACCOUNT NUMBER	(A) TORT IMMUNITY	(B) SPECIAL EDUCATION	(C) AREA VOCATIONAL CONSTRUCTION
1. Cash Basis Fund Balance, July 1, 1993 [a]		$ (1887) —	$ (1910) —	$ (1923)
2. Ad Valorem Taxes Received by Local Education Agency	1,2,4, or 5-1100	(1888) 97,099	(1911) 244,868	(1924) —
3. Earnings on Investments [b]	1,2,4,5, or 6-1500	(1889)	(1912)	(1925)
4. Sale of Bonds	6-7200	(3338)	(2046)	(1926)
5. Other Receipts from Local Sources (Attach Itemization)		(1890)	(1913)	(1927)
6. Public Law 81-874	1,2,4, or 5-4110	(1891)	(1915)	(1928)
7. Total Receipts (Total of Lines 2,3,4,5 and 6)		$ (1892) 97,099	$ (1916) 244,868	$ (1929) —
8. Total Amount Available (Total of Lines 1 and 7)		$ (1893) 97,099	$ (1917) 244,868	$ (1930) —
9. Special Education	1 or 5-1200		(2952) (1918) 244,868	$ (1931) —
10. Facilities Acquisition and Construction Services	2 or 6-2530 [c]			
11. Tort Immunity		$ (1894) 97,099		
12. Other (attach itemization)			(1919)	(1932)
13. Nonprogrammed Charges	1,2,4, or 6-4000		(1920)	(1933)
14. Total Disbursements (Total of Lines 9,10,11,12 and 13) [d]		$ (1896) 97,099	$ (1921) 244,868	$ (1934) —
15. Cash Basis Fund Balance, June 30, 1994 (Line 8 - 14)		$ (1897) —	$ (1922) —	$ (1935) —

a   Must agree with line 15, page 45, 1992-1993 Illinois School District Annual Financial Report. If different, please explain.

b   The local education agency shall invest, within two working days, all monies not needed immediately for district operation (Chapter 102, Section 34 of the Illinois Revised Statutes). Also, interest earned from the investment of tort immunity tax proceeds and/or bond issuances shall comply with the provisions of Chapter 122, Section 10-22.44 and/or Section 10-22.14 of the Illinois Revised Statutes.

c   Tort Immunity expenditures should be reported on this line regardless of the fund/function used.

APPENDIX I • 53

THIS PAGE MUST BE COMPLETED

The source document for this computation is the Illinois State Board of Education Form 50-35, Illinois School District Annual Financial Report, 1993-1994

ESTIMATED FINANCIAL DATA TO ASSIST INDIRECT COST RATE DETERMINATION

```
CODE _____
COUNTY _____
DISTRICT NAME _____
DISTRICT NUMBER _____
STREET _____
CITY _____ ZIP CODE _____
```

INSTRUCTIONS FOR COMPLETING FINANCIAL DATA INDIRECT COST RATE DETERMINATION

Indirect cost rates are computed from information provided within the body of the Annual Financial report. However, it is necessary that certain expenditure accounts be further subdivided to identify Federal program activities

Enter the disbursements/expenditures included within each function account that were charged to and reimbursed from any Federal grant program. Also include all amounts paid to or for other employees within each function account that work with Federal grant programs in the same capacity as those charged to and reimbursed from Federal grant programs. For example, if a district received funding from ESEA, Chapter 1, for a program director, the salaries of all other Federal grant program directors included in that function account must be included. Also include any benefits and/or purchased services paid on or to persons whose salaries are classified as direct costs in the function accounts that are listed.
DO NOT LEAVE ANY SPACES BLANK. Enter a zero on all lines where no costs are charged.
Section 1 Restricted Programs*

This section is applicable to Federal programs which restrict expenditures to those which "supplement but do not supplant" State or local effort. Some examples of restricted programs are ESEA, Chapters 1 and 2, Individuals with Disabilities Education Act (IDEA).

A. Support Services — Direct Costs (1—2000) and (5—2000)

   1. Direction of Business Support Services (1—2510) and (5—2510) -------------- $ —0— (2793)
      Enter the cost included within the Functions (1—2510) and (5—2510) Accounts, Direction of Business Support Services, charged directly to and reimbursed from Federal grant programs.

   2. Fiscal Services (1—2520) and (5—2520) ------------------------------ $ —0— (2794)
      Enter the cost included within the Functions (1—2520) and (5—2520) Accounts, Fiscal Services, charged directly to and reimbursed from Federal grant programs.

   3. Internal Services (1—2570) and (5—2570) --------------------------- $ —0— (2795)
      Enter the cost included within the Functions (1—2570) and (5—2570) Accounts, Internal Services, charged directly to and reimbursed from Federal grant programs.

   4. Staff Services (1—2640) and (5—2640) ----------------------------- $ —0— (2797)
      Enter the cost included within the Functions (1—2640) and (5—2640) Accounts, Staff Services, charged directly to and reimbursed from Federal grant programs.

   5. Data Processing Services (1—2660) and (5—2660) -------------------- $ —0— (2799)
      Enter the cost included within the Functions (1—2660) and (5—2660) Accounts, Data Processing Services, charged directly to and reimbursed from Federal grant programs.

Section 2 Unrestricted Programs*

This section is applicable to Federal programs whose funds may be used either to supplement, and/or supplant local funds.

B. Support Services — Direct Costs (1,2, and 5—2000)

   7. Operation and Maintenance of Plant Services (1,2, and 5—2540) -------------- $ —0— (2801)
      Enter the cost included within the Functions (1—2540), (2—2540), and (5—2540) Accounts, Operations and Maintenance of Plant Services, charged directly to and reimbursed from Federal grant programs.

* ALL CAPITAL OUTLAY MUST BE EXCLUDED

STATISTICAL INFORMATION *
SCHEDULE OF CAPITAL OUTLAY AND DEPRECIATION

THIS SCHEDULE MUST BE COMPLETED

	(A) COST 7-1-93	(B) Add: 1993-1994 ADDITIONS	(C) Less: 1993-1994 DELETIONS	(D) COST 6-30-94	LIFE IN YEARS	(E) ACCUMULATED DEPRECIATION 7-1-93	(F) Add: DEPRECIATION ALLOWABLE 1993-1994	(G) Less: DEPRECIATION DELETIONS 1993-1994	(H) ACCUMULATED DEPRECIATION 6-30-94	(I) BALANCE UNDEPRECIATED 6-30-94
1. Land	$ (1947) 1,627,157	$ (1953) ---	$ (1959) ---	$ (1965) 1,627,157		$ (1971) -0-	$ (1977) -0-	$ (1983) -0-	$ (1989) -0-	$ (1995) 1,627,157
2. Buildings	(1948) 22,813,485	(1954) 9,000	(1960) ---	(1966) 22,822,485	50	(1972) 11,026,276	(1978) 456,450	(1984)	(1990) 11,482,726	(1996) 11,339,759
3. Improvements Other than Building	(1949) 466,798	(1955) ---	(1961) ---	(1967) 466,798	20	(1973) 397,188	(1979) 23,340	(1985)	(1991) 420,528	(1997) 46,270
4. Equipment Other than Transportation	(1950) 7,642,924	(1956) 559,108	(1962) ---	(1968) 8,202,032	10 **	(1974) 5,918,802	(1980) 820,200	(1986)	(1992) 6,739,002	(1998) 1,463,030
	(3390)	(3391)	(3392)	(3393)						(3398)
5. Construction in Progress	---	---	---	---						---
6. Transportation Equipment	(1951) 1,898,843	(1957) 167,413	(1963) 97,400	(1969) 1,968,856	5 **	(1975) 1,540,816	(1981) 393,770	(1987)	(1993) 1,934,586	(1999) 34,270
7. Totals	(1952) $ 34,449,207	(1958) $ 735,521	(1964) $ 97,400	(1970) $ 35,087,328		(1976) $ 18,883,082	(1982) $ 1,693,760	(1988) $ ---	(1994) $ 20,576,842	(2000) $ 14,510,486

* Valuation of Transportation Equipment must be shown at historical cost. Valuation of other equipment, buildings, and land improvements should be shown on a Historical Cost Basis or an acceptable approximation of cost as described in Appendix B of the Illinois Program Accounting Manual. Column A and Column E must agree with Columns D and H, 1992-1993 Annual Financial Report.

** Some items costing $500 or more may be depreciated over a life of approximately (3) years. For additional information regarding those items, refer to current instructions for completing pupil transportation reimbursement forms.

ESTIMATED STATISTICAL INFORMATION, OPERATING EXPENDITURES PER PUPIL
AND PER CAPITA TUITION CHARGE COMPUTATIONS (1993-1994)

A. Total Expenditures

	FUND	PAGE	LINE	COLUMN			
1.	ED	30	63	9	Total Expenditures	$ 33,095,340	
2.	O&M	32	24	9	Total Expenditures	3,315,372	
3.	B&I	33	14	9	Total Expenditures	3,136,334	
4.	TR	35	22	9	Total Expenditures	1,897,825	
5.	MR/SS	39	54	9	Total Expenditures	875,300	
6.	RENT	41	5	9	Total Expenditures	-	
7.	Total (Lines 1 - 6)						$ 42,320,171

B. Less Receipts/Revenues or Disbursements/Expenditures Not Applicable to Operating Expense of Regular Program

	FUND	PAGE	LINE	COLUMN			
8.	TR	11	22	4	Reg. Trans. Fees from Other LEA's	$ -	
9.	TR	11	26	4	Summer School Transportation Fees	14,582	
10.	TR	11	28	4	Voc. Educ. Trans. Fees from other LEAs	-	
11.	TR	13	32	4	Spec. Educ. Trans. Fees from other LEAs	-	
12.	TR	13	35	4	Adult/Continuing Educ. Trans. Fees	-	
13.	O&M	17	69-70	2	State Adult Education	-	
14.	ED-O&M-TR, MR/SS	17-18	76	1,2,4,5	Prekindergarten Program (At-Risk)	349,026	
15.	ED	21	97	1	Head Start	-	
16.	O&M	21	101	2	Title III, Adult Basic Education	-	
17.	ED	27	4	1,2,3,4,6	Adult Education	-	
18.	ED	27	7	1,2,3,4,6	Summer School	65,791	
19.	ED	29	45	1,2,3,4,6	Community Services	100,109	
20.	ED	30	54	3,6	Nonprogrammed Charges	-	
21.	ED	30	63	5	Capital Outlay	357,619	
22.	ED	30	63	7	Transfers	-	
23.	ED	30	63	8	Tuition	2,046,950	
24.	O&M	31	10	1,2,3,4,6	Community Services	-	
25.	O&M	32	16	9	Nonprogrammed Charges	635	
26.	O&M	32	24	5	Capital Outlay	22,602	
27.	B&I	33	10	6	Bond Principal Retired	2,500,000	
28.	B&I	33	14	7	Transfers	-	
29.	TR	34	5	1,2,3,4,6	Community Services	-	
30.	TR	34	14	9	Nonprogrammed Charges	-	
31.	TR	35	22	5	Capital Outlay	167,413	
32.	MR/SS	36	4	2	Adult Education	-	
33.	MR/SS	36	7	2	Summer School	5,559	
34.	MR/SS	39	46	2	Community Services	1,920	
35.	Total Deductions (Lines 8 - 34)						$ 5,632,206
36.	Operating Expenses Regular K-12 (Line 7 minus Line 35)						36,687,965
37.	Average Daily Attendance (see below)					7,578	
38.	Operating Expense per Pupil (Line 36 divided by Line 37)						$ 4,841

C. Less Offsetting Receipts/Revenue

	FUND	PAGE	LINE	COLUMN			
39.	TR	11	21	4	Reg. Trans. Fees from Pupils or Parents	$ -	
40.	TR	11	23	4	Reg. Trans. Fees from Private Sources	99,786	
41.	TR	11	24	4	Reg. Trans. Fees -co-curricular	3,724	
42.	TR	11	27	4	Voc. Trans. Fees from Pupils or Parents	-	
43.	TR	11	29	4	Voc. Trans. Fees from Other Sources	-	
44.	TR	13	31	4	Spec. Educ. Trans. Fees from Pupils or Parents	-	
45.	TR	13	33	4	Spec. Educ. Trans. Fees from Other Sources	-	
46.	ED	13	38	1	Food Services	873,212	
47.	ED-O&M	13	39	1,2	Pupil Activities	93,121	
48.	ED	13	40	1	Textbooks	286,451	
49.	ED-O&M	13	41	1,2	Rentals	38,717	
50.	ED-O&M-TR	13	43	1,2,4	Services Provided Other LEA's	-	
51.	ED	13	47	1	Local Fees	12,129	
52.	ED-O&M-TR-MR/SS	15-16	54	1,2,4,5	Flow-Through Revenue From One LEA To Another LEA	264,650	
53.	ED-OM-TR	15	61	1,2,4	State Trans-Aid	716,620	
54.	ED-O&M	15	62	1,2	Driver Education	53,788	

(Continued on adjacent page)

1993-1994
ESTIMATED STATISTICAL INFORMATION, OPERATING EXPENDITURES PER PUPIL AND PER CAPITA TUITION CHARGE COMPUTATIONS
(Continued from page 49)

C. Less Offsetting Receipts/Revenue: (continued)

	FUND	PAGE	LINE	COLUMN			
55.	ED-TR	17	65	1,4	Bilingual Education	$	201,854
56.	ED-O&M	17	66	1,2	Vocational Education Reg. Part B Formula		-
57.	ED-O&M	17	67	1,2	Vocational Education Grants/Contracts		53,372
58.	ED	17	68	1	Gifted Education		88,430
59.	ED,O&M-TR	17	71-74	1,2,4	Special Education		1,172,378
60.	ED,TR,MR/SS	17-18	75	1,4,5	Reading Improvement Program		169,568
61.	ED	17	80	1	School Lunch Aid		30,739
62.	B&I	19	82	3	Capital Development Board-Interest		-
63.	ED-O&M-TR-MR/SS	19-20	84	1,2,4,5	Other Grants-In-Aid		107,389
64.	ED-O&M-TR-MR/SS	21-22	100	1,2,4,5	Restricted Grants-In-Aid from Fed. Gov.		28,563
65.	ED-O&M-MR/SS	21-22	110	1,2,5	Vocational & Applied Tech. Educ. Act 1990		-
66.	ED-O&M-TR-MR/SS	21-22	111	1,2,4,5	Transition Program for Refugee Children		-
67.	ED-O&M-TR-MR/SS	21-22	112	1,2,4,5	Emergency Immigrant Education Assistance		-
68.	ED-O&M-TR-MR/SS	23-24	118	1,2,4,5	ESEA, Chapter 1		957,964
69.	ED-O&M-TR-MR/SS	23-24	125	1,2,4,5	Individuals With Disabilities Educ. Act (IDEA)		251,424
70.	ED	25	133	1	School Lunch Program		529,167
71.	ED-O&M-TR-MR/SS	25-26	134	1,2,4,5	ESEA, Chapter 2 - Block grant		66,114
72.	ED-O&M-TR	25-26	135	1,2,4,5	ESEA, Title II (Math/Science Educ. Act)		31,083
73.	ED-O&M-TR	25	136	1,2,4	Department of Rehabilitation Services		44,221
74.	ED-O&M-TR-MR/SS	25-26	137	1,2,4,5	Other Grants-In-Aid		51,474
75.	ED-O&M-TR-MR/SS	25-26	139	1,2,4,5	Federal Revenue Received Through Intermediate Sources		7,692

76. Total Deductions for Tuition Computation (Line 39 - 75) $ 6,233,630

77. Transfer/tuition payments reported on Lines (14,15,18,19,20,22-25,28,29,30) from flow-through/mini-grants receipts/revenue shown on Lines (13 and 16) and Lines (39-75).   -

78. Net Operating Expense for Tuition Computation (Line 36 minus 76, plus 77)   30,454,335

79. Add Total Depreciation Allowance (Page 48, Col. F)   1,693,760

80. Total Allowance for Tuition Computation (Line 78 plus Line 79)   32,148,095

81. Average Daily Attendance (See below)   7,578

82. Per Capita Tuition Charge (Line 80 divided by Line 81)   4,242

COMPUTATION FOR AVERAGE DAILY ATTENDANCE
The source document for this computation is the General State Aid Entitlement for 1994-1995 (ISBE 50-11) Line 24   7,578

GLOSSARY

This glossary is a collection of accounting terminology that reaches beyond the scope of this book. While the significant words, principles and concepts used in this book are defined here, there are also accounting terms defined herein that are not part of this text. This is intentional so that this book can serve not only as a teaching tool, but that it can also be a reference tool, useful as further study is pursued.

The following terms and basic definitions are given to assist the reader and students in their development of not only a basic understanding of accounting principles and concepts but to help develop the vocabulary (jargon) of accounting and accountants. This should help facilitate improved communication between school administrators and those who create (internally or externally) financial and managerial accounting information.

While the list of terms is defined here is comprehensive, it is not all inclusive of terms used in this work.

The sources of the definitions given in this Glossary come from the following:

- Finkler, Steven A. (1992). *Finance and Accounting for Nonfinancial Managers*, Englewood Cliffs, N.J.: Prentice Hall.
- Fowler, William J., Jr.
- Illinois State Board of Education (1993). Chart of Accounts, Springfield, IL.
- Larson, Kermit D. (1989). Financial Accounting, Homewood, IL: Irwin.
- Securities Training Corporation (1988). Terminology of the Securities Industry, New York, NY: Author.
- Tidwell, SB. (1985). Financial and Managerial Accounting for Elementary and Secondary School Systems, 3rd Ed., Reston, VA: ASBO International.

A

Abatement: A complete or partial cancellation of a levy imposed by a government unit. Abatement usually applies to tax levies, special assessments and service charges.

Abatement of Expenditures: Return or cancellation of a part or all of a charge previously made, usually resulting from goods or materials of a quality other than specified for which allowances or refunds are made or which result in a resale of the materials originally purchased. The term can be applied to a loss or damage to property and applies to both current expenditures and capital outlay expenditures. Abatements result in reduction of expenditure accounts only when they occur during the same fiscal period as the expenditure, thereafter they become sources of revenue to the fund.

Abatement of Revenue: Return or cancellation of a part or all of any specific revenue previously recorded, usually resulting from a tax refund.

Account: A record of transactions affecting a specific item. An account must provide a space for its title, a space for recording increases in the amount of the item, a space for recording decreases in the amount of the item, a space for recording the year, month and date of each transaction, and a space for a posting reference.

Account Number: See *Coding*.

Accounting: A system for providing financial information. It is generally broken down into two principle divisions: financial accounting and managerial accounting.

Accounting Entity: Each school district is perceived and treated as if it is a separate entity that is distinct from other school districts, and as such, the financial records and reports of each school district should not include either the transactions or assets of another school district.

Accounting Period: A period of time at the end of which and for which financial statements are prepared. See also *Fiscal Period*.

Accounting Procedure: The arrangement of all processes which discover, record and summarize financial information to produce financial statements and reports and to provide internal control.

Accounting System: The total structure of records and procedures which discover, record, classify and report information of the financial position, operations, changes in fund equities, and changes in financial position of school district or any of its funds, account groups, and organizational components.

Accounts Payable: Liabilities or amounts owed on open account to private persons, firms, or corporations for goods and/or services received by a school district (but not including amounts due to other funds of the same school district or to other governmental units).

Accounts Receivable: Amounts claimed on open account from a private persons, firms, or corporations for goods and/or services received by a school district (but not including amounts due to other funds of the same school district or to other governmental units).

Accrual Basis: The basis of accounting under which revenues are recorded when earned and expenditures are recorded as soon as they result in liabilities for benefits received, notwithstanding that the receipt of the revenue or the payment of the expenditure or in part in another accounting period. See also *Accrue and Levy.*

Accrue: To record revenues when earned and to record expenditures as soon as they result in liabilities for benefits received, notwithstanding that receipt of cash or the payment of the expenditure may take place, in whole or in part, in another accounting period. See also *Accrual Basis, Accrued Assets, Accrued Expenses, Accrued Liabilities* and *Accrued Revenues.*

Accrued Asset: An asset arising from revenues earned but not yet collected or due, such as accrued interest receivable.

Accrued Expense: An expenses incurred during the current accounting period but which is not payable until a subsequent accounting period. See also *Accrual Basis and Accrue.*

Accrued Income: See *Accrued Revenue.*

Accrued Interest on Investments Purchased: Interest accrued on investments between the last interest payment date and the date of purchase. The account is carried as an asset until the first interest date after the purchase. At that time, an entry is made debiting cash and crediting the accrued interest on investment purchased account for the amount of interest purchased and an interest earnings account for the balance.

Accrued Interest Payable: A liability account which represents the amount of interest accrued at the balance sheet date but which is not due until a later date.

Accrued Liability: An amount owed but not yet due.

Accrued Revenue: Revenue earned during the current accounting period but which is not collected until the following accounting period.

Accrued Taxes Payable: A liability for taxes which has accrued since the last payment date but which is not yet due. Normally, this liability will be found in the enterprise fund.

Accrued Wages Payable: A liability for wages earned by employees between the last payment date and the balance sheet date but which is not yet due.

Accumulated Depreciation: See *Allowance for Depreciation.*

Activity: A specific or distinguishable line of work performed by one or more organizational components of a school system for the purpose of accomplishing a function for which the school district is responsible.

Activity Classification: A grouping of expenditures on the basis of specific lines of work performed by organizational units.

Actual Cash Value: The value of an investment or other asset at a particular point in time when it is sold or calculated as if the asset were sold.

Actual Revenue: Revenue received during the current accounting period.

Actuarial Basis: A basis used in computing the amount to be paid or collected periodically to a fund so that the total plus compounded earnings thereon will equal the required collections or payments of the fund. The factors taken into account in arriving at the amount include the length of time over which each collection or payment is to be made and the rate of return compounded on such amounts over its life. A trust fund for a public employee retirement system is an example of a fund set up on an actuarial basis.

Ad Valorem: In proportion to value. A basis for levy of taxes upon property.

Adjusting Entry: An entry that is prepared to correct the asset or liability account and to correct the related revenue or expenditure account.

Administration: The performance of executive duties, supervision, direction, correlation or coordination of a function.

Advance from the General Fund: An account in an enterprise or internal service fund which represents the fund's liability to the general fund, possibly for general obligation bonds which have been issued by a school district but whose proceeds have been used to finance facilities and operations of the enterprise fund or internal service fund.

Advance From ----- Fund: A liability account used to represent a long term liability owed by one fund to another fund in the same school district.

Advance To ----- Fund: An asset account which represents a long term claim by a fund from another fund of the same school district.

Agency Fund: A fund consisting of resources received and held by a school district as an agent for others; for example, taxes collected and held by a school district for another school district. Note: Sometimes resources held by one fund of a school district for other funds of the unit are handled through an agency fund. An example is taxes held by an agency fund for distribution among other funds.

Allocate: To divide a lump-sum appropriation into parts which are designated for expenditure by specific organization units and/or for specific purposes, activities or objectives.

Allocation: A part of a lump-sum appropriation which is designated for expenditure by specific organization unit and/or specific purposes, activities or objects.

Allot: To divide an appropriation into amounts which may be encumbered or expended during an allotment period.

Allotment: A part of an appropriation which may be encumbered or expended during the allotment period.

Allotment Ledger: A subsidiary ledger which contains an account for the unallotted appropriation for each purpose and showing the amount allotted periodically throughout the fiscal period, the balance available for additional allotment and other related information.

Allotment Period: A period of time less than one fiscal year in length during which the allotment is effective. Bimonthly and quarterly allotment periods are common.

Allowance: A deduction from revenue and assets due to some modifying circumstances. For example, time, usage and damage.

Allowance for Depreciation: The account in which is accumulated the periodic cost of the related asset which has been charged as depreciation expense. It is a control-asset account. Frequently referred to as accumulated depreciation.

Allowance for Depreciation—Building: The accumulation of periodic credits made to record the expiration in the service life of buildings which is attributable to wear and tear through use and lapse of time, obsolescence, inadequacy or other physical or functional cause. The account is shown in the balance sheets of enterprise and internal service funds as a deduction from buildings in order to arrive at a book value of buildings. Buildings carried in the accounts of agency or trust funds may or may not be depreciated depending on the conditions prevailing in each case. Frequently referred to as accumulated depreciation on buildings.

Allowance for Depreciation—Equipment: This account serves the same purpose for equipment as the allowance for depreciation—building serves for buildings.

Allowance for Uncollectable Accounts: See *Estimated Uncollectable Accounts Receivable.*

Allowance for Uncollectable Taxes: An account in which is recorded the amount of taxes estimated to be uncollectable. The balance of this account is shown as a deduction from taxes receivable account to which it relates in the balance sheet.

Amortization: (1) Gradual reduction, redemption or liquidation of the balance of an account according to a specified schedule of times and amounts. (2) Provision for payment of a debt by use of the *Debt Service Fund.*

Amount Available in Debt Service Funds—Serial Bonds: An

account in the general long-term debt group of accounts which designates the amount of assets available in the debt service fund for the retirement of general obligation serial bonds.

Amount Available in Debt Service Funds—Term Bonds: An account which provides the same information for general obligation term bonds as the amount available in debt service funds – serial bonds does for general obligation *Serial Bonds*.

Annual Budget: A budget applicable for a single, twelve-month, fiscal year.

Annual Financial Report (AFR): See *Consolidated Annual Financial Report (CAFR)*.

Annuities Payable: A liability account which records the amount of annuities due and payable to retired employees in a public employee retirement system.

Annuity: A series of equal money payments at equal intervals during a designated period of time. In school accounting the most frequent annuities are accumulations of debt service funds for term bonds and payments to retired employees under public employee retirement systems.

Annuity, Amount Of: The total amount of money accumulated or paid during an annuity period from an annuity and compound interest at a designated rate.

Annuity Period: The designated length of time during which an amount of annuity is accumulated or paid.

Apportionment: See *Allotment*.

Appraisal: (1) The act of appraising. See *Appraise*. (2) The estimated value resulting from such action.

Appraise: To make an estimate of value, particularly of the value of property.

Note: If the property is valued for the purposes of taxation, the less inclusive term assess is substituted for the above term.

Appropriation: An authorization granted by a legislative body, or the school board, to make expenditures and to incur obligations for special purposes. Note: An appropriation is usually limited in purpose, amount, and as to the time when it may be expended.

Appropriation Account: A budgetary account set up to record specific authorization to spend. The account is credited with original and any supplemental appropriations and is charged with reductions due to budgetary restrictions.

Appropriation Bill, Ordinance, or Resolution: A bill, ordinance, or resolution which gives appropriations legal effect. It is a method by which authority is granted by the school board to administrative officers to make expenditures for specific periods of time. It is frequently referred to as enactment of the expenditure side of the budget by the school board.

Appropriation, Bond Interest Expense: An expenditure authorized to account for interest due on a bond during the accounting period.

Appropriation Expenditure: An expenditure authorized by the appropriation act.

Note: Since all expenditures from a budgetary fund or governmental type fund must be authorized by the appropriation act, the term expenditures by itself is widely and properly used.

Appropriation Ledger: A subsidiary ledger containing an account for each appropriation. Each account usually shows the amount originally appropriated by the budget, budget increases or decreases during the year. On the same page, expenditure accounts and encumbrance accounts are used for budgetary control to determine the amount of the appropriation free for further commitment, encumbrances or expenditures. If allotments are made and a separate ledger is maintained for them, the appropriations ledger usually shows the amount originally appropriated, budget increases or decreases in the appropriation, the amounts allotted and the unallotted balance of the appropriation.

Appropriation, Principal of Bond Debt: An expenditure authorized to account for principal repayment on a bond during the accounting period.

Arbitrage: Buying and selling the same stock, bonds, etc., at the same time in different markets to profit from different prices. A technique employed to take advantage of price differences in separate markets. This is accomplished by purchasing in one market for immediate sale in another at a better price. With regard to municipalities, the proceeds from the sale of tax-free bonds may not be invested in taxable securities merely for the interest value which would be generated. However, the IRS generally allows such advantages to accrue to the municipality under several special conditions, including the requirement that 85% of the proceeds of the bond issue be used for the purpose for which they were issued within three years from issue date.

Assess: To value property officially for purposes of taxation. Note: The term is also sometimes used to denote the levy of taxes, but such usage is not correct because it fails to distinguish between the valuation process and the tax levy process.

Assessed Valuation: A valuation set upon real estate or other property by a government as a basis for levying taxes.

Assessment: (1) The process of making the official valuation of property for purposes of taxation. (2) The valuation placed upon property as a result of this process.

Assessment Roll: In the case of real property, the official list containing the legal description of each parcel of property and its assessed valuation. The name and address of the last known owner is usually also shown. In the case of personal property, the assessment roll is the official list containing the name and address of the owner, a description of the personal property and its assessed valuation.

Asset: Property and property right of a school district which has monetary value. Note: Conventionally, debit balances subject to final disposition, such as deferred charges and prepaid expenses, are classified as assets on the balance sheet.

Asset Account: An account that is used to record transactions affecting assets.

Audit: The examination of documents, records, reports, systems of internal control, accounting and financial procedures, and other evidence for one or more of the following purposes: (1) to ascertain whether the statements prepared from accounts present fairly the financial position, the results of operations, the changes in fund equity, and the changes in financial position of each of the funds and account groups of the school district in accordance with generally accepted accounting principles applicable to school district and on a basis consistent with that of the preceding year; (2) to determine the propriety, legality and mathematical accuracy of a school district's financial transactions; (3) to ascertain whether transactions have been properly recorded; and (4) to ascertain the stewardship of public officials who handle and are responsible for the financial resources of a school district.

Audit Program: A detailed outline of work to be done and the procedure to be followed during an audit, whether it is an internal audit conducted by members of the school district's internal auditing staff, by outside, independent accountants, or by auditors at the local, state, or federal level.

Audit Report: The report prepared by an auditor covering the audit or examination. As a rule, the report should include: (1) a statement of the scope of the examination; (2) explanatory comments (if any) concerning exceptions by the auditor as to application of generally accepted auditing standards; (3) opinion; (4) explanatory comments (if any) concerning verification procedures; (5) financial statements including footnotes which are an integral part of the financial statements, and schedules; and (6) sometimes statistical tables, supplementary comments and recommendations. The auditor's signature follows items (3) or (4).

Audited Voucher: A voucher which has been examined verified, and approved for payment.

Auditor's Opinion: A letter signed by an auditor which states that the financial statements have been examined in accordance with generally accepted auditing standards (with exceptions, if any) and which expresses an opinion on the fairness of presentation of the financial position, the results of operations, the changes in fund equity, and the changes in financial position of all of the funds and account groups of the school district that have been examined.

Authority: A governmental unit or public agency created to perform a single function or a restricted group of related activities. Usually such units are financed from service charges, fees and tolls but in some instances they have taxing powers. An authority may be completely independent of other governmental units or in some cases it may be partially dependent upon other governments for its creation, its financing or the exercise of certain powers.

B

Balance Sheet: A statement which discloses the assets, liabilities, and equities of a fund of a school district at a specified date. It is properly classified to exhibit the financial position of the fund or account group at that date. Note: If a single balance sheet is prepared for several funds, it must be in columnar or sectional form to exhibit the accounts of each fund and account group individually.

Balance Sheet Account: An account that is used to record transactions affecting the assets, liabilities and fund equities of a school district. See *Balance Sheet*.

Basis of Accounting: The time at which revenues, expenses, expenditures, transfers and related assets and liabilities are recognized in the accounts and are reported in the financial statements of the fund or account group.

Benchmarking: The process of testing a system against its design and purposes using actual data.

Betterment: An addition made to, or change made in, a fixed asset which is expected to prolong its life or increase its efficiency over and above that arising from maintenance and the cost of which is therefore added to the book value of the asset. Note: The term is sometimes applied to sidewalks, sewers and streets but these should preferably be designated as improvements.

Bond: A written promise to pay a specified sum of money called the face value or principal amount at a specified date or dates in the future, called maturity date(s), together with periodic interest at a specified rate. Note: The differences between a promissory note and a bond is that the latter runs for a longer period of time and requires greater legal formality.

Bond Anticipation Note: A short term interest bearing note issued by a school district in anticipation of bonds to be issued at a later date. These promissory notes are retired from the proceeds of the bond issue to which they are related.

Bond Authorized and Unissued: A bond which has been legally authorized but not issued and which can be sold without further authorization.

Bond Discount: The excess of the face value of a bond over the price for which it was acquired or sold. Note: The price does not include accrued interest at the date of acquisition or sale.

Bond Equivalent Yield: The annual rate of interest paid or earned on bonds purchased at a premium or discount. Interest paid or earned as stated on the face of the instrument plus or minus the amount of the premium or discount amortized for that period of time.

Bond Interest Expense: The cost of using borrowed money; a stated percentage of the principal amount of the debt charged for a specified period of time.

Bond Issue: The term used to describe the process used to sell (market) a school district's bonds.

Bond Issued: A bond that is sold.

Bond, Maturity Value: The value of the bond when it comes due for repayment. Generally this value is also the face value of the bond.

Bond Ordinance or Resolution: An ordinance or resolution authorizing a bond issue.

Bond Payable: The face value of a bond that is outstanding, issued and unpaid.

Bond Premium: The excess of the price at which the bond is sold or acquired over its face value.

Bond Proceeds Receivable: An account used to designate the amount receivable upon sale of bonds.

Bonded Debt: That portion of the indebtedness of a school district represented by outstanding bonds.

Book of Original Entry: The records in which the various transactions are formally recorded for the first time, such as the cash receipts journal, check register, voucher register, or general journal.

Book Value: (1) The amount shown on the books of the account. (2) The original cost of an asset less the accumulated depreciation to a date specified, if applicable.

Budget: A plan of financial operation embodying an estimate or proposed expenditures for a given period and the proposed means of financing them. Used without any modifier, the term usually indicates a financial plan for a single fiscal year.

Budgetary Account: Frequently referred to as a managerial account, a budgetary account is an account which makes it possible for a budgetary type fund (governmental type fund) to show how estimated revenue and revenue realized to date compare and how expenditures and encumbrances compare with appropriations during the fiscal period. Budgetary accounts are estimated revenues, appropriations, encumbrances, reserve for encumbrances, and budgeted fund balance accounts as distinguished from proprietary accounts. See also proprietary accounts.

Budgetary Control: The financial control or financial management of a school district or enterprise in accordance with an approved budget for the purpose of keeping expenditures within the limitations of available appropriations and available revenues.

Budgeted Fund Balance: A temporary account in which the excess of estimated revenue over appropriations is recorded instead of commingling it with the fund equity or fund balance, unappropriated, account when the budget is recorded in the accounts. Changes in the budget can be recorded during the accounting period in this account as long as it has a credit balance. Once a debit balance appears in this account, fund equity, unappropriated, is being absorbed. It is a management information account used during the fiscal period.

Buildings: A fixed asset account which reflects the acquisition value of permanent structures used to house persons and property owned by the school district. If buildings are purchased or constructed, this account includes the purchase or contract price of all permanent buildings and fixtures attached to and forming a permanent part of such buildings. If buildings are acquired by gift, the account reflects their appraised value at the date received.

C

Callable Bond: A type of bond which permits the issuer to pay the obligation before the stated maturity date by giving notice of redemption in a manner specified in the bond contract.

Capital: Residual interest in the assets of a school district that remains after deducting liabilities.

Capital Assets: See *Fixed Assets.*

Capital Budget: A plan of proposed capital outlays and the means of financing them for the current fiscal period. It is usually a part of the current budget. If a capital program is in operation, it will be the first year thereof. A capital program is sometimes referred to as a capital budget. See also *Capital Program.*

Capital Expenditures: See *Capital Outlays.*

Capital Improvement Program: See *Capital Program.*

Capital Outlays: Expenditures which result in the acquisition of or addition to fixed assets such as land, buildings and equipment.

Capital Program: A plan for capital expenditures to be incurred each year over a fixed period of years to meet capital needs arising from the long term work program or otherwise. It sets forth each project or other contemplated expenditure in which the school system is to have a part and specifies the full resources estimated to be available to finance the projected expenditures.

Capital Projects Fund: A fund created to account for all resources used for the acquisition of designated fixed assets by a school district except those financed by internal services funds, enterprise funds and certain trust funds. See also *Bond Fund.*

Capital Resources: Resources of a fixed or permanent nature, such as land and buildings, which cannot ordinarily be used to meet current expenditures.

Cash: Currency, coin, checks, postal and express money orders and bankers' drafts on hand or on deposit with an official or agent designated as custodian of cash and bank deposits.

Cash Basis: The basis of accounting under which revenues are recorded only when actually received, and only cash disbursements are recorded as expenditures.

Cash Discount: An allowance received or given if payment is completed within a stated period of time. Note: This term is not to be confused with trade discount.

Cash Receipts Journal: Any book of original entry of cash receipt transaction.

Character: A basis for classifying expenditures according to the periods they are presumed to benefit. See also *Character Classification*.

Cash in Bank: All funds on deposit with a bank or savings and loan institution normally in non-interest bearing accounts. Interest bearing accounts are recorded in investments.

Character Classification: A grouping of expenditures on the basis of the time periods they are presumed to benefit. The three groupings are: (1) expenses, presumed to benefit the current fiscal period; (2) provisions for retirement of debt, presumed to benefit prior fiscal periods primarily but also present and future periods; and (3) capital outlays, presumed to benefit the current and future capital periods.

Check: A bill of exchange drawn on a bank and payable on demand; a written order on a bank to pay on demand a specified sum of money to a named person, to his order, or to bearer, out of money on deposit to the credit of the maker. Note: A check differs from a warrant in that the latter is not necessarily payable on demand and may not be negotiable. It differs from a voucher in that the latter is not an order to pay.

Claim: A bill representing a demand for payment properly made out on required form, and filed with the board, itemizing items or services for which the claim is made and showing where, when and by whom performed.

Classification: A systematic arrangement of items into classes or related groups for analytical or control purposes.

Closing Account: An account that is used to record a closing entry.

Coding: A system of numbering or otherwise designating accounts, entries, invoices, vouchers, etc., in such a manner that the symbol used reveals quickly certain required information.

Combination Bond: A bond issued by a school district which is payable from the revenues of the school district but which is also backed by the full faith and credit of a related governmental unit.

Combined Balance Sheet: A single balance sheet which displays the individual balance sheets of each class of funds and account groups of a school district in separate, adjacent columns. Note: There are no inter-fund eliminations or consolidations in a combined balance sheet for a school district.

Combined Financial Report: A financial report that combines individual fund and account group statements.

Commercial-Type Funds: See *Enterprise funds.*

Compound Entry: An entry that is composed of more than one debit or more than one credit.

Consolidated Annual Financial Report (CAFR): The CAFR of a school district should contain an introductory section, financial section [including (a) an auditor's report, (b) general purpose financial statements, (c) combining and individual fund and account group statements and schedules] and statistical tables.

Construction Contracts Payable: Amounts due by a school district on contracts for construction of buildings, structures and other improvements.

Construction Work in Process: The cost of construction work undertaken but not yet completed.

Contingent Liability: An item which may become a liability as a result of conditions undetermined at a given date, such as guarantees pending, lawsuits, judgments under appeal, unsettled disputed claims, unfilled purchase orders and uncompleted contracts. Note: All contingent liabilities should be shown on the face of the balance sheet or in a footnote.

Contract Payable—retained Percentage: A liability on account of construction contracts which have been completed but on which part of the liability has not been paid pending final inspection or the lapse of a specified period of time, or both. The unpaid amount is usually stated as a percentage of the contract price.

Contracts Payable: Amounts due on contracts for assets, goods and services received by a school district.

Contribution from the General Fund: An equity amount in an enterprise fund or internal service fund which shows the amount of permanent fund capital contributed to the enterprise or internal service fund by the school district from general school revenues and resources.

Contribution From ------- Fund: This account is identical to *contribution from the general fund* except that the specific fund of origin is specified.

Control Account: An account in the general ledger in which are recorded the aggregate of debit and credit postings to a number of identical or related accounts called subsidiary ledger accounts. For example, the taxes receivable account is a control account supported by the aggregate of individual balances in individual property taxpayers' accounts. See also *General Ledger* and *Subsidiary Account.*

Corporate Balance Sheet: A balance sheet for a corporation showing liabilities and owner (or shareholder) equity placed to the right of assets.

Corporate Income Statement: A statement that shows whether or not the business achieved or failed to achieve one of its primary objectives -- earning a "profit" or net income.

Cost: The amount of money exchanged for property or services. Note: Costs may be incurred even before money is paid; that is, as soon as liability is incurred. Again, the cost of some property or service may in turn become a part of the cost of another property or service. For example, the cost of part or all of the materials purchased at a certain time will be reflected in the cost of articles made from such materials or in the cost of those services in the rendering of which the materials were used.

Cost Accounting: That method of accounting which provides for assembling and recording of all the elements of cost incurred to accomplish a purpose, to carry out an activity or operation, or to complete a unit of work or a specific job.

Cost Basis Accounting: That method of accounting which provides for the assembling and recording of all the elements of cost incurred to accomplish a purpose, to carry on an activity or operation, or to complete a unit of work or a specific job.

Cost Ledger: A subsidiary record where each project, job, production center, process, operation, product or service is given in a separate account to which all items entering into its cost are posted in required detail. Such accounts should be so arranged and kept that the results shown in them may be reconciled with and verified by a control account or accounts in the general ledger.

Cost of Goods Sold: A determination made at the end of an accounting period reflecting the (1) cost of merchandise on hand at the beginning of the period, (2) the cost of merchandise purchased during the period, and (3) the cost of unsold goods that remain at the end of the period.

Cost Records: All ledgers, supporting records, schedules, reports, invoices, vouchers and other documents reflecting the cost of projects, jobs, production centers, processes, operations, products or services, or the cost of any component.

Coupon Bond: A bearer bond, or a bond registered as to principal only, carrying coupons is evidence of future interest payments.

Credit (adjective): The right side of a "T" account.

Credit (noun): An amount entered on the right side of a "T" account.

Credit (verb): The act of entering an amount on the right side of a 'T" account.

Credit Account: An account that has a credit balance.

Credit Balance: An account where the sum of the credits exceeds the sum of the debits for that account.

Credit Entry: An entry that is made on the right side of a "T" account.

Current: A term applied to budgeting and accounting which designates the operation of the present fiscal period as opposed to past or future periods.

Current Asset: An asset which is available or can be made readily available to meet the cost of operations or to pay current liabilities. Some examples are cash, temporary investments and taxes receivable which will be collected within about a year from the balance sheet date.

Current Budget: The annual budget prepared for and effective during the present year; or, in the case of some state governments, the budget for the present biennium.

Current Expenses: See *Expenses.*

Current Fund: See *General Fund.*

Current Funds: Funds, the resources of which are expended for operating purposes during the current fiscal period. In its usual application in plural form, it refers to general, special revenue, debt service, internal service funds and enterprise funds of a school system. In the singular form, the current fund is synonymous with the General Fund.

Current Liability: Debt or obligation of the school district which is payable within a relatively short period of time, usually restricted to those coming due within a year or within an operating period.

Current Revenue: Revenues of a school system which are available to meet expenditures of the current fiscal period. See *Revenue.*

Current Taxes: (1) Taxes levied and becoming due during the current fiscal period, from the time the amount of the tax levy is first established to the date on which a penalty for nonpayment is attached. (2) Taxes levied in the preceding fiscal period but becoming due in the current fiscal period, from the time they become due to the date on which a penalty for nonpayment is attached.

Current Year Tax Levy: Taxes levied for the current fiscal period.

Customer Deposits: The liability of an enterprise fund for deposits made by customers as a prerequisite to receiving goods and/or services provided by the enterprise.

D

Debenture: An unsecured bond that depends upon the general credit of the issuing school district.

Debit (adjective): The left side of a "T" account.

Debit (noun): An amount entered on the left side of a "T" account.

Debit (verb): The act of entering an amount on the left side of a "T" account.

Debit Account: An account that has a debit balance.

Debit Balance: An account where the sum of the debits exceeds the sum of the credits for that account.

Debit Entry: An entry that is made on the left side of a "T" account.

Debt: An obligation resulting from borrowing of money or from the purchase of goods or services. Debts of school systems include bonds, time warrants, tax anticipation notes payable, accounts payable, vouchers payable, interest payable, and salaries payable.

Debt Limit: The maximum amount of gross or net debt which is legally permitted.

Debt Service Fund: A fund established to finance and account for the accumulation of financial resources over a long period of time which are to be used for the payment of interest and principal on all general obligation debt, serial and term, other than that payable exclusively from revenue debt issued for and serviced by school system. Formerly called Sinking Fund.

Debt Service Fund Requirements: The amounts of revenue which must be provided for a Debt Service Fund so that all principal and interest payments can be made in full on schedule.

Deferred Assets: See *Deferred Charges* and *Prepaid Expenses.*

Deferred Charge: An expenditures which is not chargeable to the current fiscal period in which made but is carried on the asset side of the balance sheet pending amortization or other disposition. An example is discount on bonds issued.

Deferred Credit: Credit balance or item which will be spread over the following accounting periods either as additions to revenues or as reductions to expenses. Examples are taxes collected in advance or premiums paid on bonds issued.

Deferred Income: See *Deferred Credits.*

Deferred Revenue: See *Deferred Credits.*

Deficit: (1) The excess of liabilities of a fund over its assets [frequently referred to as a fund deficit], (2) The excess of expenditures over revenues during an accounting period [frequently referred to as an operating deficit]; or, in the case of enterprise and internal service funds, the excess of expense over income during an accounting period.

Delinquent Taxes: Taxes remaining unpaid on and after the date on which a penalty for non-payment is attached. Even though the penalty may be subsequently waived and a portion of the taxes may be abated or cancelled, the unpaid balances continue to be delinquent taxes until abated, cancelled, paid or converted into tax liens.

Deposit: Money or securities placed with a bank or other institution or person, either as a deposit subject to withdrawal by check or as a special deposit made for a particular purpose.

Depreciation: (1) Expiration in the service life of fixed assets, other than wasting assets, attributable to wear and tear, deterioration, action of the physical elements, inadequacy and obsolescence. (2) The portion of the cost of a fixed asset other than a wasting asset which is charged as an expense during a particular fiscal period.

Direct Debt: The debt which a school district has incurred in its own name or assumed through the annexation of territory or through consolidation with another school district.

Depreciation Accounting: Loss in value or service life of fixed assets because of wear and tear through use, elapse time, inadequacy, or obsolescence.

Disbursements: Payments in cash.

Discount: An amount granted by a creditor reducing the amount invested in accounts receivable.

Double Entry: A system of bookkeeping which requires for every entry made to the debit side of an account or accounts and entry must be made for a corresponding amount or amounts to the credit side of another account or accounts.

Due From ------- Fund: An asset account used to indicate amounts collectible by a particular fund from another fund in the same school district for goods sold or services rendered. This account includes only short-term obligations on open account and not long-term loans. See *Advance -------- Fund*.

Due From -------- Government: Amounts claimed by the reporting school district from a governmental unit. These amounts may represent grants-in-aid, shared taxes, taxes collected by another unit, loans, and charges for services rendered by the reporting unit for another governmental unit.

Due To Fiscal Agent: Amounts due to fiscal agents, such as commercial banks, for paying a school district's maturing interest and principal payments on indebtedness.

Due To ------- Fund: A liability account used to indicate amounts owed by a particular fund to another fund in the same school district for money borrowed temporarily, goods sold or services rendered. These amounts include only short-term obligations on open account and not long-term loans.

Due To ------- Government: Amounts owed by a fund of the reporting school district to a named governmental unit. Earnings: See income and revenue.

E

Effective Interest Rate: The rate of earning on a bond investment based on the actual price paid for the bond, the coupon rate, the maturity date, and the length of time between interest dates, in contrast with the nominal interest rate.

Encumbrance Accounts: Purchase orders, contracts, and salary or other commitments which are chargeable to an appropriation and for which a part of the appropriation is reserved. They cease to be encumbrances when paid or when actual liability is set up.

Encumbrances: Obligations or commitments in the form of purchase orders, contracts issued or salary commitments which are chargeable to an appropriation and for which a part of the appropriation is reserved. They cease to be encumbrances when paid or when the title to goods or services is received and the actual liability is created. Frequently referred to as commitments.

Endowment Fund: A trust fund whose principal must be maintained inviolate but whose income may be expended. An endowment fund is accounted for as a non-expendable trust fund, the income from which is accounted for as an expendable trust fund.

Enterprise Debt: Debt which is to be retired primarily from the earnings of publicly owned and operated enterprises. See also *Revenue Bonds.*

Enterprise Fund: A proprietary type fund established to finance and account for the acquisition, operation, and maintenance of school district facilities and services which may be predominantly self-supporting by users charges. Examples of enterprise funds are those for food services, bookstores and athletic programs.

Entry: (1) The record of a financial transaction in its appropriate books of account. (2) The act of recording a financial transaction in the books of account.

Equipment: Physical property of a school district having a long period of usefulness, other than buildings and land.

Equity in General Fixed Assets: A classification of accounts in the general fixed assets group of accounts which indicate the sources from which general fixed assets were acquired. Carrying a credit balance, it is more descriptive of the nature of the accounts than "investment" in general fixed assets.

Estimated Revenue Account: If the account is kept on an accrual basis, this term designates the amount of revenue estimated to accrue during a given period, regardless of whether or not it is all to be collected during the period. If the account is kept on a cash basis, the term designates the amount of revenue estimated to be collected during a given period.

Estimated Revenue: For revenue accounts kept on the accrual basis, this term designates the amount of revenue estimated to accrue during a given period regardless of whether or not it is all to be collected during the period.

Estimated Uncollected Accounts Receivable: A contra-asset account. It is estimated to be the amount of accounts receivable that is not expected to be collected. It is subtracted from accounts receivable on the balance sheet to arrive at the book value of accounts receivable.

Estimated Uncollectable Taxes (Current or Delinquent): A contra-asset account, it is the amount that is not expected to be collected. It is subtracted from taxes receivable (current or delinquent) to arrive at the book value of these accounts. Note: Generally the longer a tax becomes delinquent, the less likely are its chances for being collected.

Exhibit: (1) A balance sheet or other principal financial statement. (2) Any formal financial statement that accompanies or is a part of a financial or audit report.

Expendable Trust Fund: A fiduciary fund, a trust fund whose resources, both principal and earnings, may be expended.

Expenditure Account: A charge incurred, whether paid or unpaid, which is presumed to benefit the current fiscal year.

Expenditures: The cost of goods delivered or services rendered, whether paid or unpaid, including expenses, provision for debt retirement not reported as a liability of the fund from which retired, and capital outlays. Note: Encumbrances are not expenditures. Expenditure accounts are used only in formal budgetary or governmental type funds.

Expenses: Charges incurred, whether paid or unpaid, for operation, maintenance, interest, and other charges which are presumed to benefit the current fiscal period. In budgetary funds, expenditure accounts are used to record expenses but, in proprietary type funds and certain trust funds, only expense accounts are used.

F

Face Value: As applied to securities, this term designates the amount stated on the security document.

Fidelity Bond: A written promise to idemnify against losses from theft, defalcation, or misappropriation of money or property by school officers and employees. See also *Surety Bond*.

Fiduciary Fund Type: A fund used to account for all transactions of a school district when the school district acts as an agent or trustee for another entity. Trust funds and agency funds are examples of fiduciary funds.

Financial Accounting: The recording and reporting of activities and events affecting the money of an administrative unit and its program.

Specifically, it is concerned (1) with determining what accounting records are to be maintained, how they will be maintained, and the procedures, methods, and forms to be used; (2) with recording, classifying, and summarizing activities or events; (3) with analyzing and interpreting recorded data; and (4) with preparing reports and statements which reflect conditions as of a given date, the results of operations for a specific period, and the evaluation of status and results of operation in terms of established objectives.

Financial and Compliance Audit: An audit that determines whether or not the financial statements of an audited school district present fairly the financial position and the results of financial operations in accordance with generally accepted accounting principles and whether or not the school district has complied with the laws and regulations that may have a material effect upon the financial statements.

Fiscal Agent: The person or entity charged with handling the financial transactions or services of a school district.

Fiscal Period: Any period of time at the end of which a school district determines the financial position, results of operations, changes in fund equities, and changes in financial position of each fund and account group. It may be monthly, quarterly, semiannually or annually.

Fixed Assets: Assets of a long-term character which are intended to continue to be held or used, such as land, buildings, machinery, furniture, and equipment. Note: The term does not indicate the immobility of an asset, which is a distinctive characteristic of a fixture.

Fixture: An attachment to buildings which are not intended to be removed and which cannot be removed without damage to the latter. Note: Those fixtures with a useful life presumed to be as long as that of the building itself are considered a part of such a building; all others are classed as equipment.

Function: A classification of a group of related activities aimed at accomplishing a major service, purpose or program for which a school district is responsible. For example, instruction is a function. See also *Activity, Character.*

Function Dimension: The classification of activities or actions which are performed to accomplish the objectives of the school district.

Functional Classification: A grouping of expenditures on the basis of the principal purposes for which they are made. Examples are supporting services and community services. See also *Activity, Character.*

Fund: A fiscal and accounting entity with a self-balancing set of accounts recording cash and other financial resources, together with all related liabilities and residual equities or balances, and changes therein, which are segregated for the purpose of carrying on specific activities or attaining certain objectives in accordance with special regulations, restrictions, or limitation. See also *General Fixed Assets Group of Accounts* and *General Long-Term Debt Group of Accounts.*

Fund Accounts: All accounts necessary to set forth the financial position, the financial operations, the changes in residual equities or balances, and the changes in financial position of a fund.

Fund Balance: The excess of the assets of a fund over its liabilities except in the case of funds subject to budgetary accounting where, prior to the end of a fiscal period, it represents the excess of the fund's assets and estimated revenues for the period over its liabilities and appropriations.

Fund Balance Sheet: A balance sheet for a single fund. See *Fund* and *Balance Sheet.*

Fund Equity Account: An account used to record the financial transactions determining the excess of a fund's assets less liabilities.

Fund Group: A group of funds which are similar in purpose and character. For example, several special revenue funds constitute a fund group.

Funded Debt: Same as *Bonded Debt*, which is the preferred term.

Funded Deficit: A fund deficit eliminated through the sale of bonds issued for that purpose.

Fund Equity: The excess of a fund's total assets over total liabilities; synonymous with the term fund balance.

G

General Fixed Assets: Those fixed assets of a school district which are not accounted for in an enterprise, internal services fund, or trust fund.

General Fixed Assets Group of Accounts: A self-balancing group of accounts set up to account for the general fixed assets of a school district. See *General Fixed Assets* and *Self-Balancing Group of Accounts*.

General Fund: A fund used to account for all transactions of a school district which are not accounted for in another fund. Note: The general fund is used to account for the ordinary operations or the basic educational programs of a school district which are financed from taxes and other general revenues. Identified as one of the formal budgetary funds or as a governmental type fund.

General Journal: A book of original entry for all entries of financial transactions that are not recorded in special journals such as a cash receipts journal, a voucher register, a cash payments journal or a check register.

General Ledger: A book, file, or other device which contains the accounts needed to reflect, in summary and in detail, the financial position, the results of financial operations, the changes in equities of a fund or account group used by a school district. Note: In double entry bookkeeping, the debits and credits in the general ledger are equal, and therefore the debit balances equal the credit balances. See also *Control Account, Subsidiary Account and Subsidiary Ledger*.

General Long-Term Debt: Long-term debt legally payable from general revenues and backed by the full faith and credit of a school district. See *Long-Term Debt*.

General Long-Term Debt Group of Accounts: The account group in which all unmatured general long-term liabilities of a school district are recorded but does not include long-term liabilities of proprietary funds and trust funds.

General Obligation Bond: A bond for whose payment the full faith and credit of the issuing body is pledged. More commonly, but not necessarily, general obligation bonds are considered to be those payable from taxes and other general revenues.

General Revenue: The revenues of a school district other than those derived from and retained in an enterprise. Note: If a portion of the net income in an enterprise fund is contributed to another non-enterprise fund, such as the general fund, the amounts transferred constitute general revenue of the school district.

Governmental Accounting: The composite activity of analyzing, recording summarizing, reporting, and interpreting the financial transactions of governmental units and agencies.

H

Historical Cost: The price at which an asset was originally obtained. If the asset was purchased, the cost would be the purchase price; if the asset was donated, the cost would be the value, if any, of the asset at the time of donation.

Horizontal Ratio: The ratio or ratios that can be created to compare a revenue or expenditure item in one fund with the same revenue or expenditure item in another or all funds (or some combination of funds). For example, salaries expended in one fund compared to all salaries in all funds.

I

Imprest System: A system for handling minor disbursements whereby a fixed amount of money, designated as petty cash, is set aside for this purpose. See also *Petty Cash.*

Improvements: Buildings, other structures, and other attachments or annexations to land which are intended to remain so attached or annexed, such as sidewalks, trees, drives, tunnels, drains, and sewers. Note: Sidewalks, curbing, sewers, and streets are sometimes referred to as betterments, but the term improvements is preferred.

Income: A term used in accounting for an enterprise fund or internal service fund to represent the excess of revenues earned over the expenses incurred in carrying on the fund's operations. It should not be used without an appropriate modifier, such as Operating, Gross, or Net. See also *Operating Income.* Note: The term Income should not be used in lieu of *Revenue* in non-enterprise funds.

Indebtedness: The amount of debt of the school district including principal and interest due on bonds issued.

Interest and Penalties Receivable on Taxes: The uncollected portion of interest and penalties receivable on taxes.

Interest Payable: The amount of interest that is due on outstanding obligations during a period of time. The amount may span more than one accounting period.

Interest Receivable on Investments: The amount of interest receivable on investments.

Inter-fund Account: An account in which transactions between funds are recorded.

Inter-fund Loan: Authorized loan made by one fund to another.

Inter-fund Loan Payable: The amount of an inter-fund loan that is due to be repaid during an accounting period.

Intergovernmental Revenue: Revenue received from other governments in the form of grants, shared revenues, or payments in lieu of taxes.

Interim Balance Sheet: A balance sheet that is prepared at the end of an accounting period other than the end of a fiscal year.

Interim Borrowing: (1) Short-term loan to be repaid from general revenues during the course of a fiscal year. (2) Short-term loan in anticipation of tax collections or bond issuance. See *Bond Anticipation Notes.*

Interim Statement: A financial statement prepared before the end of the current fiscal year and covering only financial transactions during the current year to date. See also *Statement.*

Internal Audit: An appraisal activity within a school district which: (1) determines the adequacy of the system of internal control; (2) verifies and safeguards assets; (3) determines the reliability of the accounting and reporting system; (4) ascertains compliance with established policies and procedures; and (5) appraises performance of activities and work programs.

Internal Control: A plan of organization under which employees' duties are so arranged and records and procedures are so designed as to make it possible to provide effective safeguards and accounting control over assets, liabilities, revenues, income, expenses and expenditures. Under such a system, the work of employees is subdivided so that no single employee performs a complete cycle of operations. Procedures to be followed which require proper authorization by designated officials for all actions to be taken.

Internal Services Fund: A proprietary type of fund established to finance and account for services and commodities furnished by a designated department or agency of the school district to other departments and agencies within a single school district. Amounts expended by the fund are restored to it either from operating earnings or by transfers from other funds, so that the original fund capital is kept intact. Formerly called a working capital fund.

Inventory: A detailed list showing quantities, descriptions, and values of property and frequently also shows units of measure and unit prices.

Investments: Securities and real estate held for the production of income in the form of interest, dividends, rentals, or lease income. The term does not include fixed assets used in operation of the school district.

Investments in General Fixed Assets: A widely used classification of accounts used to show the sources from which general fixed assets were acquired in the general fixed assets group of accounts. It has become an ambiguous title because the word "investment" usually implies that it is an asset account which normally carries a debit balance. As this type of account carries a credit balance, the term "equity" in general fixed assets is more descriptive of its nature.

J

Journal: Any book of original entry of a financial transaction. See also *Register*.

Journal Entry: See *Entry*.

Journal Voucher: A business paper provided for the recording of certain transactions or information in place of or supplementary to the journals or registers. The journal voucher usually contains an entry or entries, explanations, references to documentary evidence supporting the entry or entries, and the signature or initials of one or more officials who are designated to authorize the transaction.

Journalize: The act of making an entry in the general journal.

Judgment: An amount to be paid or collected by a school district as the result of a court decision, including a condemnation award in payment for private property taken for public use.

L

Land: A fixed asset account which reflects the cost or other valuation basis of land owned by a school district. If land is purchased, this account shows the purchase price and costs such as legal fees, filling and excavation costs, and the like which are incurred to put the land in condition for its intended use. If land is acquired by gift, the account reflects its appraised value at date received.

Ledger: A group of accounts in which are recorded the financial transaction of a fund of a school district.

Levy: To impose taxes, special assessments, or service charges for the support of school operations. The total amount of taxes, special assessments, or services charges imposed by a governmental unit.

Liability: Debt or other legal obligation arising out of transactions in the past which must be paid, renewed, or refunded at some future date. Note: The term does not include encumbrances.

Liability Accounts: An account used to designate a liability. Encumbrances are not liabilities; they become liabilities when the services or materials for which the encumbrance was established have been rendered or received.

Loan Fund: An agency fund whose principal and/or interest is loaned to individuals in accordance with the legal requirements.

Loans Receivable: Amounts which have been loaned to persons or organizations, including notes taken as security for such loans; where permitted by statutory authority. The account is usually carried only in the trust and agency fund's balance sheet.

Long-Term Budget: A budget prepared for a period longer than a fiscal year, or in the case of some state governments, a budget prepared for a period longer than a biennium. If the long-term budget is restricted to capital expenditures, it is called a Capital Program or a Capital Improvement Program.

Long-Term Debt: Debt with a maturity of more than one year after the date of issuance.

Long-Term Liability: A liability that is the responsibility of the school district and that spans a time period greater than the end of the fiscal year.

Long-Term Loan: A loan which extends for more than 5 years from the date the loan was obtained and is not received by serial or term bonds.

Long-Term Note Payable: The amount of outstanding debt obligation that is due to be paid during an accounting period.

M

Maintenance Expenditure: Repairs to fixed assets that do not clearly increase the value and/or useful life of the asset.

Managerial Accounting: Accounting process that is primarily concerned with internal reporting and relates to planning, controlling and evaluating financial performance of the school district.

Matured Bonds: Bonds which have reached or passed their maturity date.

Matured Bonds Payable: Bonds which have reached or passed their maturity date but which remain unpaid.

Matured Interest Payable: Interest on bonds which has reached the maturity date but which remains unpaid.

Maturity Date: The date at which a bond or other debt instrument is due to be repaid to the lender.

Maturity Value: The value of a bond or other debt instrument at the maturity date. Usually this will be the face value of the bond.

Modified Accrual Basis: The basis of accounting under which revenues are recorded when earned and expenditures are recorded when they result in a liability for the school district, but which also always for some transactions to be made on a cash basis.

Mortgage Bond: A bond secured by a mortgage against specified properties of a school district, usually its enterprises. If primarily payable from enterprise revenues, they are also classed as revenue bonds. See also *Revenue Bonds*.

Municipal Bonds: A bond issued by a state or local governmental unit.

N

Net Revenue Available for Debt Service: Gross operating revenues of an enterprise fund less operating and maintenance expenses but exclusive of bond interest. "Net revenue" as thus defined is used to compute "coverage" on revenue bond issues.

Nominal Interest Rate: The contractual interest rate shown on the face and in the body of a bond and representing the amount of interest to be paid, in contrast to the effective interest rate. See also *Coupon Rate*.

Non-expendable Trust Fund: A trust fund, the principal and sometimes also the earnings of which may not be expended. See also *Endowment Fund*.

Note: A written, short-term promise of the issues to repay a specified principal amount on a date certain, together with interest at a stated rate, or according to a formula for determining that rate, payable from a defined source of anticipated revenue.

Notes Payable: In general, an unconditional written promise signed by the maker to pay a certain sum in money on demand or at a fixed or determinable time either to the bearer or to the order of a person designated therein.

Notes Receivable: A note held by the school district which contains an unconditional written promise, signed by the maker, to pay a certain sum in money on demand or at a fixed or determinable future time either to the bearer or to the order of a person designated therein. The note may be held by the reporting school district as designated payee or by endorsement.

O

Object: The commodity or service obtained from a specific expenditure.

Object Classification: A category of goods or services purchased.

Object Dimension: The classification of services or commodities obtained as a result of a specific expenditure by the school district.

Operating Budget: A budget which applies to all revenue and expenditures other than capital outlay expenditures. See *Budget*.

Operating Expenses: (1) As used in the accounts of a school district's enterprise funds and internal services funds, the term means those costs which are necessary to the maintenance of the enterprise, the rendering of services, the sale of products, the production and disposition of commodities produced, and the collection of enterprise revenues. (2) The term is also sometimes used to describe expenses for general fund purposes.

Operating Income: Income of an enterprise fund which is derived from the sale of its goods and/or services. For example, income from the sale of lunches or from the sale of books is operating income. See also *Operating Revenues*.

Operating Revenue: Revenue derived from the operation of an enterprise fund and/or internal service fund of a business character.

Operating Statement: A statement summarizing the financial operations, i.e., the revenue and expenses or expenditures of a school fund for an accounting period as contrasted with a balance sheet which shows the financial position of the fund at a given moment.

Outstanding Bond: The amount of outstanding debt obligation of the school district for which a bond was sold.

Overhead Expenses: Those elements of cost necessary to the production of an article or the performance of a service which are of such a nature that the amount applicable to the product or service cannot be determined accurately or readily. Usually they relate to those expenses which do not become an integral part of the finished product or service, such as rent, heat, light, supplies, management and supervision.

P

Performance Audit: See *Program Compliance Audit.*

Performance Budget: A budget wherein expenditures are based primarily upon measurable performance of activities and work programs. A performance budget may also incorporate other bases of expenditure classification, such as character and object, but these are given a subordinate status to activity performance.

Perpetual Inventory: A system whereby the inventory of units of property at any date may be obtained directly from the records without resorting to an actual physical count. A record is provided for each item or group of items to be inventoried and is so divided as to provide a running record of goods ordered, received, and withdrawn, and the balance on hand, in units and in cost.

Petty Cash: A sum of money set aside for the purpose of paying small obligations for which the issuance of a formal voucher and check would be too expensive and time-consuming. Sometimes called a petty cash fund, with the term "fund" here being used in the commercial sense of earmarked liquid assets. See also *Imprest System.*

Post: The act of transferring to an account in a ledger the detailed or summarized data contained in the cash receipts book, check register, journal voucher, or similar books or documents of original entry.

Post Closing Trial Balance: A balance sheet statement that is prepared after closing entries are made to the revenue, expenditure and fund equity accounts.

Post to Ledger: The act of making an entry to the general ledger. Usually this act will occur when recording an entry from the general journal to the general ledger.

Posting: The act of transferring to an account in a ledger the data, either detailed or summarized, contained in a book of original entry.

Posting Reference: The notation made to the location of the account. Usually, the posting reference is the account code number.

Premium: See *Bond Premium.*

Prepaid Expenses: Expenses entered in the accounts for benefits not yet received. Prepaid expenses differ from deferred charges in that they are spread over a shorter period of time than deferred charges and are regularly recurring costs of operations. Examples of prepaid expenses are prepaid rent expense, prepaid interest expense, and premiums on unexpired insurance. An example of a deferred charge is unamortized discounts on bonds payable.

Prepaid Tax Revenue: The deposit of money with a school district or governmental unit on condition that the amount of deposited is to be applied against the tax liability of a designated taxpayer after the taxes have been levied and such liability has been established. See also *Taxes Collected in Advance.*

Principal of Bond Debt: The amount printed on the face of the instrument; the amount to be paid at the maturity date of the bond, exclusive of interest, premiums or discounts.

Pro-forma: For form's sake; an indication of form; an example. The term is used in conjunction with a noun to denote merely a sample form, document, statement, certificate, or presentation, either wholly or partially hypothetical, actual facts, estimates, or proposals.

Program: A plan of activities and procedures designed to accomplish a predetermined objective or set of allied objectives.

Program Budget: A budget where expenditures are based primarily on programs of work and secondarily on character and object. A program budget is a transitional type of budget between the traditional character and object budget, on the one hand, and the performance budget on the other. See also *Performance Budget,* and *Traditional Budget.*

Program Compliance Audit: An audit that determines the extent to which the desired results or benefits established by the legislature or other authorizing body are being achieved, the effectiveness of the school district and whether or not the school district has complied with significant laws and regulations applicable to the program.

Program Dimension: The classification of transactions relating to a group of interdependent, closely-related services and/or activities contributing to a common objective of the school district or program.

Project/Reporting Dimension: The grouping of transactions relating to a particular project that is used to prepare required reports for the school district or project.

Proprietary Account: An account which shows actual financial position and operations, such as actual assets, liabilities, fund balances, including reserves of fund equity, revenues, and expenditures, as distinguished from a budgetary account.

Proprietary Fund: A group of accounts which show actual financial conditions and operations such as actual assets, liabilities, reserves, surplus, revenues and expenditures, as distinguished from budgetary accounts.

Purchase Order: A document which authorizes the delivery of specified merchandise to the school district or the rendering of the making of a charge for them.

R

Rate: The percent at which services, commodities or financial obligations are obtained.

Ratio: An expression of a mathematical relationship between one quantity and another.

Ratio Analysis: The process of comparing a ratio to its past performance, current or conditions or to other similar ratios.

Redeemed Bond: A bond that is called for repayment at a specific price prior to the maturity date of the bond.

Refund (noun): An amount paid back or credit allowed because of an overcollection or return of an object sold.

Refund (verb): To pay back or to allow credit for an amount as a result of an overcollection or because of the return of an object sold. To provide for payment of a loan through cash or credit secured by a new loan.

Refunding Bond: Bond issued to retire bonds already outstanding. The refunding bond may be sold for cash and outstanding bonds redeemed in cash, or the refunding bond may be exchanged with holders of outstanding bonds.

Register: A record for the consecutive entry of a certain class of events, documents, or transactions with a proper notation of all the required particulars. Note: The form of register for accounting purposes varies from one-column to multi-columnar sheets of special design where on the entries are distributed, summarized, and aggregated for convenient posting to the accounts.

Registered Bond: A bond that is issued in the name of the owner and are recorded in the owner's name on the records of the issuer.

Reimbursement: Cash or other assets received as a repayment of the cost of work or services performed or of other expenditures made for or on behalf of another school unit or department or for an individual, firm, or corporation.

Replacement Cost: The current cost of an asset that would need to be replaced, usually via insurance, due to loss.

Requisition: A written demand or request, usually from one department to the purchasing officer or to another department, for specified articles or services.

Required Earnings: Synonymous or equivalent in meaning to estimated revenue from earnings such as interest income; a budgetary accounting term which indicates the amount of earnings estimated to be earned by the board of education at the time of adopting or revising the budget.

Required Taxation: Synonymous or equivalent in meaning to estimated revenue from tax levies; a budgetary accounting term which indicates the amount of taxes levied by adoption or revising the budget.

Reserve: An account which records a portion of the fund balance which must be segregated for some future use and which is, therefore, not available for further appropriation. A reserve for inventories equal in amount to the inventory of supplies on the balance sheet of a general fund is an example of such a reserve.

Reserve for Advance To ------ Fund: A reserve which represents the segregation of a portion of a fund balance to indicate that assets equal to the amount of the reserve are tied up in a long-term loan to another fund and are, not available for appropriation.

Reserve for Debt Retirement: An account which indicates the amount of the unappropriated debt service fund equity that has been set aside to be used for retirement of outstanding debt at its maturity date; an appropriation of the debt service fund's equity.

Reserve for Employees' Contributions: A reserve in a trust fund for a public employee retirement system which represents the amount of accumulated contributions made by employee members plus interest earnings credited in accordance with applicable legal provisions.

Reserve for Employer Contributions: A reserve in a trust fund for a public employee retirement system which represents the amount of accumulated contributions paid by the school district as employer plus interest earnings credited in accordance with applicable legal provisions.

Reserve for Encumbrances: A reserve representing the segregation or the appropriation of a portion of a fund balance to provide for unliquidated encumbrances. See also *Reserve*.

Reserve for Undistributed Interest Earnings: An unallocated reserve in a trust fund for a public employee retirement system which represents interest earnings of the system that have not been distributed to other reserves such as reserve for employees' contributions and the reserve for employer contributions.

Reserved-Fund Balance Account: A reserve representing that portion of a fund balance segregated to indicate that assets equal to the amount of the reserve are tied up and are, therefore, not available for appropriation. It is recommended that a separate reserve be established for each special purpose. One example of a special purpose would be restricted federal programs.

Restricted Asset: Money or other resources, the use of which is restricted by legal or contractual requirements. The most common example of restricted assets in school accounting are those arising out of revenue bond indentures in enterprise funds. Also called Restricted Funds, but this terminology is not preferred.

Retained Earnings: The accumulated earnings of an enterprise or internal services fund which have been retained in the fund and which are not reserved for any specific purpose.

Retired Bond: A bond that has been fully repaid.

Retirement Fund: A trust fund out of which retirement annuities and/or other benefits are paid to authorized and designated public employees. A retirement fund is accounted for as a trust fund.

Revenue: This term designates additions to assets which (1) do not increase any liability; (2) do not represent the recovery of an expenditure; (3) do not represent the cancellation of certain liabilities without a corresponding increase in other liabilities or a decrease in assets; and (4) do not represent contributions of fund capital in enterprise and internal services funds.

Revenue Account: An amount set aside to account for money received for some specified purpose.

Revenue Bond: A bond whose principal and interest are payable exclusively from earnings. In addition to a pledge of revenues, such bonds sometimes contain a mortgage on the enterprise's property and are then known as mortgage revenue bonds.

Revenue Bonds Payable: A liability account which represents the face value of revenue bonds issued and outstanding.

Revenue Source: The identification of the specific source from which revenues were derived or to which they are attributable.

Revenue Subsidiary Ledger: A general ledger account that is used to reduce the size of the general ledger by summarizing individual revenue accounts and that provides budgetary accounting control over each individual source of revenue.

Revenue Type: The identification of transactions that are described and coded as to the specific sources from which they are derived or to which they are attributable.

Revenues Collected in Advance: A liability account which represents revenues collected before they become due.

S

School Business Administration: The area of educational administration that deals with the financial and ancillary operations of a school district.

School Business Manager: The person charged with management of specific areas of school business administration.

School Business Official: A person involved with or working in a specific area of school business.

School Business Specialist: A person who works exclusively in and is determined to be an expert in a specific area of school business.

Securities: Bonds, notes, mortgages, or other forms of negotiable or non-negotiable instruments. See also *Investments*.

Self-balancing Group of Accounts: An independent self-balancing group of accounts which is set up to account for either the fixed assets or the long-term debts of a governmental unit which are not accounted for in its individual funds or account groups. See *General Fixed Assets Group of Accounts* and *General Long-term Debt Group of Accounts*.

Self-supporting or Self-liquidating Debt: Debt obligations whose principal and interest are payable solely from the earnings of the enterprise fund or internal services fund for the construction or improvement of which they were originally issued. See also *Revenue Bonds*.

Separation of Duties: The concept of determining responsibilities for people working in various employee classifications.

Serial Bonds: Issues redeemable by installments, each of which is to be paid in full, ordinarily out of revenues of the fiscal year in which it matures or revenues of the preceding year.

Shared Revenue: Revenue which is levied by one governmental unit but shared, usually in proportion to the amount collected, with another unit of government or class of governments.

Short-Term Debt: Debt with a maturity of one year or less after the date of issuance. Short-term debt usually includes bond anticipation notes payable, tax anticipation notes payable and warrants payable.

Sinking Fund Bond: A bond issued under an agreement which requires the school district to set aside periodically out of its revenues, a sum which, with compound earnings, will be sufficient to redeem the bond at its stated date of maturity. Sinking fund bonds are usually also term bonds. In lieu of establishing a sinking fund, today's terminology refers to the fund as a debt service fund.

Sound Value—actual Cash Value: An appraisal term; sound value or actual cash value is based on the cost of reproduction new, less the accrued depreciation to date.

Special Revenue Fund: A fund that is created to be used to account for financial transactions for designated educational purposes from special sources of revenue and that are not part of the school district's foundation education program.

Standard Cost: The predetermined cost of performing an operation or producing a product when labor, materials, and equipment are utilized efficiently under reasonable and normal conditions. Note: Normal conditions exist when there is an absence of special or extraordinary factors affecting the quality or quantity of the work performed, or the time or method of performing it.

Statement of Changes in Assets and Liabilities: A financial statement that is prepared at the close of an accounting period to identify the result of transactions occurring during the period that affected assets and liabilities.

Statement of Changes in Financial Position: A financial statement that identifies the amount of financial resources provided from all sources and how those resources were used during the accounting period.

Statements: (1) Used in a general sense, all of those formal written presentations which set forth financial information. (2) In technical accounting usage, those presentations of financial data which show the financial position and the results of financial operations of a fund, a group of accounts, or an entire school district for a particular accounting period. See also *Exhibit*.

Statute: A written law enacted by a duly organized and constituted legislative body.

Stores: Goods on hand in store rooms subject to requisition and use.

Straight-line Depreciation: The cost of an asset, less salvage value, is spread in equal periodic amounts over its estimated useful life.

Sub-activity: A specific line of work performed in carrying out a school activity. For example, cleaning buildings and replacing defective lamps would be sub-activities under the activity of operation and maintenance of plant.

Subsidiary Account: One of a group of related accounts which support in detail the debit or credit summaries recorded in a control account in the general ledger. An example is the individual property taxpayers' accounts for taxes receivable, the total of which agrees with the balance of the controlling account, taxes receivable, in the general ledger. See also *Control Account* and *Subsidiary Ledger.*

Subsidiary Control Account for Revenue: An account that appears in the general ledger used to summarize, or control, total estimated revenue or to summarize, or control, actual revenue and which provides budgetary accounting control over each individual source of revenue.

Subsidiary Expenditure Ledger: A controlling account in the general ledger that summarizes and compares expenditures and encumbrances (commitments) with appropriations at any time during the fiscal period.

Subsidiary Ledger: A group of subsidiary accounts the sum of the balances of which is equal to the balance of the related control account in the general ledger. See also *Control Account* and *Subsidiary Account.*

Subvention: That which aids; especially a grant, as of money; subsidy; giving of help or relief in danger, distress or difficulty.

Summarizing and Closing Accounts: See *Closing Account.*

Surety Bond: A written promise to pay damages or to indemnify against losses caused by the party or parties named in the document, through nonperformance or through defalcation. An example is a surety bond given by a contractor or by an official handling cash or securities.

T

T-account: A convenient method of displaying the increases or decreases to an account in the form of a "T" where the left side is the debit side and the right side is the credit side of the account.

Tax Anticipation Note Payable: A note (sometimes called a warrant) issued in anticipation of collection of taxes, usually retirable only from tax collections, and frequently only from the proceeds of the tax levy whose collection it anticipates.

Tax Certificate: A certificate issued by a governmental unit as evidence of the conditional transfer of title to tax-delinquent property from the original owner to the holder of the certificate. If the owner does not pay the amount of the tax arrearage and other charges required by the law during the specified period of redemption, the holder can foreclose to obtain title. Also called tax sale certificate and tax lien certificate in some jurisdictions.

Tax Rate Limit: The maximum rate at which a school district may levy a tax. The limit may apply to taxes raised for a particular purpose, or to taxes imposed for all purposes, and may apply to a single school district, or a class of school districts, or to all school districts operating in a particular area. Overall tax rate limits usually restrict levies for all purposes and of all governments, state and local, having jurisdiction in a given area.

Tax Roll: The official list showing the amount of taxes levied against each taxpayer or each parcel of property. Frequently, the tax roll and the assessment roll are combined, but even in these cases the two can be distinguished.

Taxes: Compulsory charges levied by a governmental unit for the purpose of financing services performed for the common benefit. Note: The term does not include specific charges made against particular persons or property for current or permanent benefits such as special assessments. Neither does the term include charges for services rendered only to those paying such charges as, for example, water service charges.

Taxes Collected in Advance: A liability for taxes collected before the tax levy has been made, before the taxes are payable, or before the amount of taxpayer liability has been established.

Taxes Levied for Other Units: Taxes levied by the reporting school districts as an agent for other school districts resulting in the need for a taxes receivable account and liability accounts to indicate the amount due to each of the other school districts. When collected, cash will be paid to these districts.

Taxes Receivable – Current: The uncollected portion of taxes which a school district has levied and which has become due but on which no penalty for non-payment is attached.

Taxes Receivable—Delinquent: Taxes remaining uncollected on and after the date on which a penalty for non-payment is attached. Even though the penalty may be subsequently waived and a portion of the taxes may be abated or cancelled, the unpaid balances continue to be delinquent taxes until paid, abated, cancelled by order of the board of education, or converted into tax liens.

Term Bond: A type of bond where the entire principal comes due or matures on one date.

Time Warrant: A negotiable obligation of a school district having a term shorter than bonds and frequently tendered to individuals and firms in exchange for contractual services, capital acquisitions, or equipment purchases.

Time Warrant Payable: The amount of time warrants outstanding and unpaid.

Total Accrued Depreciation: An appraisal phrase; the total accrued depreciation recognizes observed condition with proper consideration of usage, age, maintenance, and care, and with such regard for functional and economic factors as are determined relevant.

Trade Discount: An allowance, usually varying in percent with the volume of transactions, made to those engaged in certain businesses and allowable without respect to the time when the account is paid. Note: These discounts are commonly considered as a reduction of the sales or purchase price and not as an earning. The term is not to be confused with cash discount.

Traditional Budget: A term sometimes applied to the budget of a school district wherein expenditures are based entirely or primarily on objects of expenditure. See also *Program Budget* and *Performance Budget.*

Transaction: An event affecting an account.

Trial Balance: A list of the balances of the accounts in a ledger kept by double entry, with the debit and credit balances shown in separate columns. If the totals of the debit and credit columns are equal or their net balance agrees with a control account, the ledger from which the figures are taken is said to be in balance.

Trust Fund: A fund consisting of resources received and held by a school district as a trustee for another entity. See also *Agency Fund.*

U

Unamortized Discount on Bonds Payable: That portion of the excess of the face value of bonds over the amount received from their sale which remains to be written off periodically over the life of the bonds.

Unamortized Discounts on Investment: That portion of the excess of the face value of securities over the amount paid for them which has not been written off.

Unamortized Premiums on Bonds Payable: An account in an enterprise fund which represents that portion of the excess of bonds proceeds over face value, and which remains to be amortized over the remaining outstanding life of such bonds.

Unamortized Premium on Investments: That portion of the excess of the amount paid for securities over their face value which has not yet been amortized.

Unappropriated Budget Balance: Where the fund balance at the close of the preceding year is not included in the annual budget, this term designates that portion of the current fiscal year's estimated revenues which has not been appropriated. Also referred to as budgeted fund balance.

Unappropriated Debt Service Fund Equity: The portion of debt service fund equity that is not designated for a specific purpose.

Unappropriated Fund Equity Account: An account that contains amounts of the fund equity that is not designated for a specific purpose.

Unencumbered Appropriation: That portion of an appropriation not yet expended or encumbered.

Unreserved Fund Balance Accounts: The excess of the assets of a fund over its liabilities and reserves.

V

Vertical Ratio: The ratio or ratios that can be created to compare a revenue or expenditure item in one fund with other revenue or expenditure items (partial or total) in the same fund.

Voucher: A document which authorizes the payment of money and usually indicates the accounts to be charged.

W

Warrant: An order drawn by the school district to the school district treasurer ordering him/her to pay a specified amount to a payee named on the warrant. Once signed by the treasurer, the warrant becomes a check payable by a bank named on the warrant by the treasurer.

Warrants Payable: Warrants issued by the school district but not yet signed by the treasurer.